500 Lines or Less

500 Lines or Less
Experienced programmers solve interesting problems

Edited by Michael DiBernardo

500 Lines or Less

Edited by Michael DiBernardo

The full text of this book is available online at http://www.aosabook.org/.
All royalties from its sale will be donated to Amnesty International.

Product and company names mentioned herein may be the trademarks of their respective owners.

While every precaution has been taken in the preparation of this book, the editors and authors assume no responsibility for errors or omissions, or for damages resulting from the use of the information contained herein.

Front cover photo ©Kellar Wilson
Copyediting, cover design, and publishing support by Amy Brown: http://amyrbrown.ca

Revision Date: June 28, 2016

ISBN: 978-1-329-87127-4

Contents

Introduction
Michael DiBernardo

This is the fourth volume in the *Architecture of Open Source Applications* series, and the first to not feature the words "open source applications" anywhere in the title.

The first three volumes in the series were about big problems that big programs have to solve. For an engineer who is early in their career, it may be a challenge to understand and build upon programs that are much bigger than a few thousand lines of code, so, while big problems can be interesting to read about, they can also be challenging to learn from.

500 Lines or Less focuses on the design decisions that programmers make in the small when they are building something new. The programs you will read about in this book were all written from scratch for this purpose (although several of them were inspired by larger projects that the authors had worked on previously).

Before reading each chapter, we encourage you to first think about how you might solve the problem. What design considerations or constraints do you think the author is going to consider important? What abstractions do you expect to see? How do you think the problem is going to be decomposed? Then, when reading the chapter, try to identify what surprised you. It is our hope that you will learn more by doing this than by simply reading through each chapter from beginning to end.

Writing a useful program in fewer than 500 lines of source code—without resorting to cheap tricks—is a challenging exercise in itself; writing one to be read for pedagogical purposes when neatly rendered in a printed book is even tougher. As such, the editors have occasionally taken liberties with some of the source formatting when porting it into the book. The original source for each chapter can be found in the code subdirectory of its project folder.

We hope that the experiences of the authors in this book will help you grow out of your comfort zone in your own programming practice.

— Michael DiBernardo

Contributors

Michael DiBernardo (editorial): Michael DiBernardo is an engineer and director of delivery at Wave, and a past PyCon Canada chair. He writes at mikedebo.ca.

Amy Brown (editorial): Amy Brown is a freelance editor based in Toronto. She specializes in science and academic editing, and working with self-publishing authors. She co-edited the *Architecture of Open Source Applications* books with Greg Wilson.

Dethe Elza (Blockcode): Dethe is a geek dad, aesthetic programmer, mentor, and creator of the Waterbear visual programming tool. He co-hosts the Vancouver Maker Education Salons and wants to fill the world with robotic origami rabbits.

Malini Das (CI): Malini is a software engineer who is passionate about developing quickly (but safely!), and solving cross-functional problems. She has worked at Mozilla as a tools engineer and is currently honing her skills at Twitch.

Dustin J. Mitchell (Cluster): Dustin is an open source software developer and release engineer at Mozilla. He has worked on projects as varied as a host configuration system in Puppet, a Flask-based web framework, unit tests for firewall configurations, and a continuous integration framework in Twisted Python.

Daniel Rocco (Contingent): Daniel loves Python, coffee, craft, stout, object and system design, bourbon, teaching, trees, and Latin guitar. Thrilled that he gets to write Python for a living, he is always on the lookout for opportunities to learn from others in the community, and to contribute by sharing knowledge. He is a frequent speaker at PyAtl on introductory topics, testing, design, and shiny things; he loves seeing the spark of delight in people's eyes when someone shares a surprising or beautiful idea. Daniel lives in Atlanta with a microbiologist and four aspiring rocketeers.

Brandon Rhodes (Contingent): Brandon Rhodes started using Python in the late 1990s, and for 17 years has maintained the PyEphem library for amateur astronomers. He works at Dropbox, has taught Python programming courses for corporate clients, consulted on projects like the New England Wildflower Society's "Go Botany" Django site, and will be the chair of the PyCon conference in 2016 and 2017. Brandon believes that well-written code is a form of literature, that beautifully formatted code is a work of graphic design, and that correct code is one of the most transparent forms of thought.

A. Jesse Jiryu Davis (Crawler): Jesse is a staff engineer at MongoDB in New York. He wrote Motor, the async MongoDB Python driver, and he is the lead developer of the MongoDB C Driver and a member of the PyMongo team. He contributes to asyncio and Tornado. He writes at emptysqua.re.

Guido van Rossum (Crawler): Guido is the creator of Python, one of the major programming languages on and off the web. The Python community refers to him as the BDFL (Benevolent Dictator For Life), a title straight from a Monty Python skit.

Dann Toliver (Dagoba): Dann enjoys building things, like programming languages, databases, distributed systems, communities of smart friendly humans, and pony castles with his two-year-old.

Taavi Burns (DBDB): As the newest bass (and sometimes tenor) in Countermeasure, Taavi strives to break the mould…sometimes just by ignoring its existence. This is certainly true through the diversity of workplaces in his career: IBM (doing C and Perl), FreshBooks (all the things), Points.com (doing Python), and now at PagerDuty (doing Scala). Aside from that—when not gliding along on his Brompton folding bike—you might find him playing Minecraft with his son or engaging in parkour (or rock climbing, or other adventures) with his wife. He knits continental.

Leo Zovic: Leo (better known online as inaimathi) is a recovering graphic designer who has professionally written Scheme, Common Lisp, Erlang, Javascript, Haskell, Clojure, Go, Python,

PHP and C. He currently blogs about programming, plays board games and works at a Ruby-based startup in Toronto, Ontario.

Dr. Christian Muise (Flow shop): Dr. Muise is a Research Fellow with the Model-based Embedded and Robotic Systems group at MIT's Computer Science and Artificial Intelligence Laboratory. He is interested in a variety of topics including AI, data-driven projects, mapping, graph theory, and data visualization, as well as Celtic music, carving, soccer, and coffee.

Yoav Rubin (CircleDB): Yoav is a Senior Software Engineer at Microsoft, and prior to that was a Research Staff Member and a Master Inventor at IBM Research. He works now in the domain of data security in the cloud, and in the past his work focused on developing cloud- or web-based development environments. Yoav holds an MSc in Medical Research in the field of Neuroscience and BSc in Information Systems Engineering.

Cate Huston (Image filters): Cate is a developer and entrepreneur focused on mobile. She's lived and worked in the UK, Australia, Canada, China and the United States, as an engineer at Google, an Extreme Blue intern at IBM, and a ski instructor. Cate speaks internationally on mobile development, and her writing has been published on sites as varied as Lifehacker, The Daily Beast, The Eloquent Woman and Model View Culture. She co-curates Technically Speaking, blogs at Accidentally in Code and is @catehstn on Twitter.

Allison Kaptur (Interpreter): Allison is an engineer at Dropbox, where she helps maintain one of the largest networks of Python clients in the world. Before Dropbox, she was a facilitator at the Recurse Center, a writers' retreat for programmers in New York. She's spoken at PyCon North America about Python internals, and loves weird bugs.

Erick Dransch (Modeller): Erick is a software developer and 2D and 3D computer graphics enthusiast. He has worked on video games, 3D special effects software, and computer-aided design tools. If it involves simulating reality, chances are he'd like to learn more about it. You can find him online at erickdransch.com.

Carl Friedrich Bolz (Object model): Carl is a researcher at King's College London and is broadly interested in the implementation and optimization of all kinds of dynamic languages. He is one of the core authors of PyPy/RPython and has worked on implementations of Prolog, Racket, Smalltalk, PHP and Ruby.

Marina Samuel (OCR): Marina is an engineer at Mozilla and a current MSc student in Applied Computing (Artifical Intelligence) at the University of Toronto. She hopes to one day build robots that will take over the planet.

Dessy Daskalov (Pedometer): Dessy is an engineer by trade, an entrepreneur by passion, and a developer at heart. She's currently the CTO and co-founder of Nudge Rewards. When she's not busy building product with her team, she can be found teaching others to code, attending or hosting a Toronto tech event, and online at dessydaskalov.com and @dess_e.

Eunsuk Kang (Same-origin policy): Eunsuk is a PhD candidate and a member of the Software Design Group at MIT. He received his SM (Master of Science) in Computer Science from MIT (2010), and a Bachelor of Software Engineering from the University of Waterloo (2007). His research projects have focused on developing tools and techniques for software modeling and verification, with applications to security and safety-critical systems.

Santiago Perez (Same-origin policy): Santiago is a PhD student in the Software Design Group at MIT. He received his SM in Computer Science from MIT (2015), and an undergraduate degree from ITBA (2011). He used to work at Google, developing frameworks and tools to make engineers more productive (2012). He currently spends most of his time thinking about design and version control.

Daniel Jackson (Same-origin policy): Daniel is a professor in the Department of Electrical Engineering and Computer Science at MIT, and leads the Software Design Group in the Computer

Science and Artificial Intelligence Laboratory. He received an MA from Oxford University (1984) in Physics, and his SM (1988) and PhD (1992) in Computer Science from MIT. He was a software engineer for Logica UK Ltd. (1984-1986), Assistant Professor of Computer Science at Carnegie Mellon University (1992-1997), and has been at MIT since 1997. He has broad interests in software engineering, especially in development methods, design and specification, formal methods, and safety-critical systems.

Jessica B. Hamrick (Sampler): Jess is a PhD student at UC Berkeley where she studies human cognition by combining probabilistic models from machine learning with behavioral experiments from cognitive science. In her spare time, Jess is a core contributor to IPython and Jupyter. She also holds a BS and MEng in Computer Science from MIT.

Audrey Tang (Spreadsheet): A self-educated programmer and translator, Audrey works with Apple as an independent contractor on cloud service localization and natural language technologies. Audrey has previously designed and led the first working Perl 6 implementation, and served in computer language design committees for Haskell, Perl 5, and Perl 6. Currently Audrey is a full-time g0v contributor and leads Taiwan's first e-Rulemaking project.

Leah Hanson (Static analysis): Leah Hanson is a proud alum of Hacker School and loves helping people learn about Julia. She blogs at blog.leahhanson.us and tweets at @astrieanna.

Ned Batchelder (Template engine): Ned is a software engineer with a long career, currently working at edX to build open source software to educate the world. He's the maintainer of coverage.py, an organizer of Boston Python, and has spoken at many PyCons. He blogs at nedbatchelder.com. He once had dinner at the White House.

Greg Wilson (Web server): Greg is the founder of Software Carpentry, a crash course in computing skills for scientists and engineers. He has worked for 30 years in both industry and academia, and is the author or editor of several books on computing, including the 2008 Jolt Award winner *Beautiful Code* and the first two volumes of *The Architecture of Open Source Applications*. Greg received a PhD in Computer Science from the University of Edinburgh in 1993.

Acknowledgments

The *Architecture of Open Source Applications* series would not exist without the hard work of Amy Brown and Greg Wilson. This particular book would not have been possible without the incredible efforts of our army of technical reviewers:

Amber Yust	Gregory Eric Sanderson	Matthias Bussonnier
Andrew Gwozdziewycz	James O'Beirne	Max Mautner
Andrew Kuchling	Jan de Baat	Meggin Kearney
Andrew Svetlov	Jana Beck	Mike Aquino
Andy Shen	Jessica McKellar	Natalie Black
Anton Beloglazov	Jo Van Eyck	Nick Presta
Ben Trofatter	Joel Crocker	Nikhil Almeida
Borys Pierov	Johan Thelin	Nolan Prescott
Carise Fernandez	Johannes Fürmann	Paul Martin
Charles Stanhope	John Morrissey	Piotr Banaszkiewicz
Chris AtLee	Joseph Kaptur	Preston Holmes
Chris Seaton	Josh Crompton	Pulkit Sethi
Cyryl Płotnicki-Chudyk	Joshua T. Corbin	Rail Aliiev
Dan Langer	Kevin Huang	Ronen Narkis
Dan Shapiro	Maggie Zhou	Rose Ames
David Pokorny	Marc Towler	Sina Jahan
Eric Bouwers	Marcin Milewski	Stefan Turalski
Frederic De Groef	Marco Lancini	William Lachance
Graham Lee	Mark Reid	

Chris Seaton, John Morrissey, and Natalie Black deserve extended thanks for going above and beyond in their technical reviewing. The quantity and depth of their reviews was instrumental in moving the book forward at several sticking points.

We are very grateful to PagerDuty for their financial support.

Contributing

If you'd like to report errors or translate the content into other languages, please open an issue at `github.com/aosabook/500lines/` or contact us at `aosa@aosabook.org`.

## chapter 1

Blockcode: A visual programming toolkit
Dethe Elza

In block-based programming languages, you write programs by dragging and connecting blocks that represent parts of the program. Block-based languages differ from conventional programming languages, in which you type words and symbols.

Learning a programming language can be difficult because they are extremely sensitive to even the slightest of typos. Most programming languages are case-sensitive, have obscure syntax, and will refuse to run if you get so much as a semicolon in the wrong place—or worse, leave one out. Further, most programming languages in use today are based on English and their syntax cannot be localized.

In contrast, a well-done block language can eliminate syntax errors completely. You can still create a program which does the wrong thing, but you cannot create one with the wrong syntax: the blocks just won't fit that way. Block languages are more discoverable: you can see all the constructs and libraries of the language right in the list of blocks. Further, blocks can be localized into any human language without changing the meaning of the programming language.

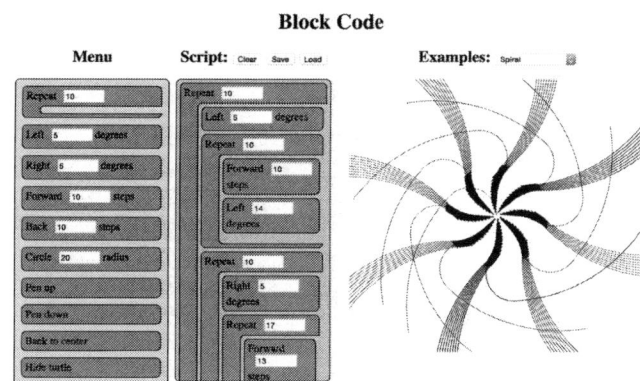

Figure 1.1: The Blockcode IDE in use

Block-based languages have a long history, with some of the prominent ones being Lego Mindstorms[1], Alice3D[2], StarLogo[3], and especially Scratch[4]. There are several tools for block-based

---

[1] http://www.lego.com/en-us/mindstorms/
[2] http://www.alice.org/index.php
[3] http://education.mit.edu/projects/starlogo-tng
[4] http://scratch.mit.edu/

programming on the web as well: Blockly[5], AppInventor[6], Tynker[7], and many more[8].

The code in this chapter is loosely based on the open-source project Waterbear[9], which is not a language but a tool for wrapping existing languages with a block-based syntax. Advantages of such a wrapper include the ones noted above: eliminating syntax errors, visual display of available components, ease of localization. Additionally, visual code can sometimes be easier to read and debug, and blocks can be used by pre-typing children. (We could even go further and put icons on the blocks, either in conjunction with the text names or instead of them, to allow pre-literate children to write programs, but we don't go that far in this example.)

The choice of turtle graphics for this language goes back to the Logo language, which was created specifically to teach programming to children. Several of the block-based languages above include turtle graphics, and it is a small enough domain to be able to capture in a tightly constrained project such as this.

If you would like to get a feel for what a block-based-language is like, you can experiment with the program that is built in this chapter from author's GitHub repository[10].

1.1 Goals and Structure

I want to accomplish a couple of things with this code. First and foremost, I want to implement a block language for turtle graphics, with which you can write code to create images through simple dragging-and-dropping of blocks, using as simple a structure of HTML, CSS, and JavaScript as possible. Second, but still important, I want to show how the blocks themselves can serve as a framework for other languages besides our mini turtle language.

To do this, we encapsulate everything that is specific to the turtle language into one file (turtle.js) that we can easily swap with another file. Nothing else should be specific to the turtle language; the rest should just be about handling the blocks (blocks.js and menu.js) or be generally useful web utilities (util.js, drag.js, file.js). That is the goal, although to maintain the small size of the project, some of those utilities are less general-purpose and more specific to their use with the blocks.

One thing that struck me when writing a block language was that the language is its own IDE. You can't just code up blocks in your favourite text editor; the IDE has to be designed and developed in parallel with the block language. This has some pros and cons. On the plus side, everyone will use a consistent environment and there is no room for religious wars about what editor to use. On the downside, it can be a huge distraction from building the block language itself.

The Nature of Scripts

A Blockcode script, like a script in any language (whether block- or text-based), is a sequence of operations to be followed. In the case of Blockcode the script consists of HTML elements which are iterated over, and which are each associated with a particular JavaScript function which will be run when that block's turn comes. Some blocks can contain (and are responsible for running) other blocks, and some blocks can contain numeric arguments which are passed to the functions.

---

[5] https://developers.google.com/blockly/
[6] http://appinventor.mit.edu/explore/
[7] http://www.tynker.com/
[8] http://en.wikipedia.org/wiki/Visual_programming_language
[9] http://waterbearlang.com/
[10] https://dethe.github.io/500lines/blockcode/

In most (text-based) languages, a script goes through several stages: a lexer converts the text into recognized tokens, a parser organizes the tokens into an abstract syntax tree, then depending on the language the program may be compiled into machine code or fed into an interpreter. That's a simplification; there can be more steps. For Blockcode, the layout of the blocks in the script area already represents our abstract syntax tree, so we don't have to go through the lexing and parsing stages. We use the Visitor pattern to iterate over those blocks and call predefined JavaScript functions associated with each block to run the program.

There is nothing stopping us from adding additional stages to be more like a traditional language. Instead of simply calling associated JavaScript functions, we could replace `turtle.js` with a block language that emits byte codes for a different virtual machine, or even C++ code for a compiler. Block languages exist (as part of the Waterbear project) for generating Java robotics code, for programming Arduino, and for scripting Minecraft running on Raspberry Pi.

Web Applications

In order to make the tool available to the widest possible audience, it is web-native. It's written in HTML, CSS, and JavaScript, so it should work in most browsers and platforms.

Modern web browsers are powerful platforms, with a rich set of tools for building great apps. If something about the implementation became too complex, I took that as a sign that I wasn't doing it "the web way" and, where possible, tried to re-think how to better use the browser tools.

An important difference between web applications and traditional desktop or server applications is the lack of a `main()` or other entry point. There is no explicit run loop because that is already built into the browser and implicit on every web page. All our code will be parsed and executed on load, at which point we can register for events we are interested in for interacting with the user. After the first run, all further interaction with our code will be through callbacks we set up and register, whether we register those for events (like mouse movement), timeouts (fired with the periodicity we specify), or frame handlers (called for each screen redraw, generally 60 frames per second). The browser does not expose full-featured threads either (only shared-nothing web workers).

1.2   Stepping Through the Code

I've tried to follow some conventions and best practices throughout this project. Each JavaScript file is wrapped in a function to avoid leaking variables into the global environment. If it needs to expose variables to other files it will define a single global per file, based on the filename, with the exposed functions in it. This will be near the end of the file, followed by any event handlers set by that file, so you can always glance at the end of a file to see what events it handles and what functions it exposes.

The code style is procedural, not object-oriented or functional. We could do the same things in any of these paradigms, but that would require more setup code and wrappers to impose on what exists already for the DOM. Recent work on Custom Elements[11] make it easier to work with the DOM in an OO way, and there has been a lot of great writing on Functional JavaScript[12], but either would require a bit of shoe-horning, so it felt simpler to keep it procedural.

There are eight source files in this project, but `index.html` and `blocks.css` are basic structure and style for the app and won't be discussed. Two of the JavaScript files won't be discussed in any detail either: `util.js` contains some helpers and serves as a bridge between different browser

---

[11]http://webcomponents.org/
[12]https://leanpub.com/javascript-allonge/read

implementations—similar to a library like jQuery but in less than 50 lines of code. file.js is a similar utility used for loading and saving files and serializing scripts.

These are the remaining files:

- block.js is the abstract representation of a block-based language.
- drag.js implements the key interaction of the language: allowing the user to drag blocks from a list of available blocks (the "menu") to assemble them into a program (the "script").
- menu.js has some helper code and is also responsible for actually running the user's program.
- turtle.js defines the specifics of our block language (turtle graphics) and initializes its specific blocks. This is the file that would be replaced in order to create a different block language.

blocks.js

Each block consists of a few HTML elements, styled with CSS, with some JavaScript event handlers for dragging-and-dropping and modifying the input argument. The blocks.js file helps to create and manage these groupings of elements as single objects. When a type of block is added to the block menu, it is associated with a JavaScript function to implement the language, so each block in the script has to be able to find its associated function and call it when the script runs.

Figure 1.2: An example block

Blocks have two optional bits of structure. They can have a single numeric parameter (with a default value), and they can be a container for other blocks. These are hard limits to work with, but would be relaxed in a larger system. In Waterbear there are also expression blocks which can be passed in as parameters; multiple parameters of a variety of types are supported. Here in the land of tight constraints we'll see what we can do with just one type of parameter.

```
<!-- The HTML structure of a block -->
<div class="block" draggable="true" data-name="Right">
    Right
    <input type="number" value="5">
    degrees
</div>
```

It's important to note that there is no real distinction between blocks in the menu and blocks in the script. Dragging treats them slightly differently based on where they are being dragged from, and when we run a script it only looks at the blocks in the script area, but they are fundamentally the same structures, which means we can clone the blocks when dragging from the menu into the script.

The createBlock(name, value, contents) function returns a block as a DOM element populated with all internal elements, ready to insert into the document. This can be used to create blocks for the menu, or for restoring script blocks saved in files or localStorage. While it is flexible this way, it is built specifically for the Blockcode "language" and makes assumptions about it, so if there is a value it assumes the value represents a numeric argument and creates an input of type "number". Since this is a limitation of the Blockcode, this is fine, but if we were to extend the blocks to support other types of arguments, or more than one argument, the code would have to change.

```
function createBlock(name, value, contents){
    var item = elem('div',
        {'class': 'block', draggable: true, 'data-name': name},
        [name]
    );
    if (value !== undefined && value !== null){
        item.appendChild(elem('input', {type: 'number', value: value}));
    }
    if (Array.isArray(contents)){
        item.appendChild(
            elem('div', {'class': 'container'}, contents.map(function(block){
                return createBlock.apply(null, block);
            })));
    }else if (typeof contents === 'string'){
        // Add units (degrees, etc.) specifier
        item.appendChild(document.createTextNode(' ' + contents));
    }
    return item;
}
```

We have some utilities for handling blocks as DOM elements:

- blockContents(block) retrieves the child blocks of a container block. It always returns a list if called on a container block, and always returns null on a simple block
- blockValue(block) returns the numerical value of the input on a block if the block has an input field of type number, or null if there is no input element for the block
- blockScript(block) will return a structure suitable for serializing with JSON, to save blocks in a form they can easily be restored from
- runBlocks(blocks) is a handler that runs each block in an array of blocks

```
function blockContents(block){
    var container = block.querySelector('.container');
    return container ? [].slice.call(container.children) : null;
}

function blockValue(block){
    var input = block.querySelector('input');
    return input ? Number(input.value) : null;
}

function blockUnits(block){
    if (block.children.length > 1 &&
        block.lastChild.nodeType === Node.TEXT_NODE &&
        block.lastChild.textContent){
        return block.lastChild.textContent.slice(1);
    }
}

function blockScript(block){
    var script = [block.dataset.name];
    var value = blockValue(block);
    if (value !== null){
```

```
            script.push(blockValue(block));
        }
        var contents = blockContents(block);
        var units = blockUnits(block);
        if (contents){script.push(contents.map(blockScript));}
        if (units){script.push(units);}
        return script.filter(function(notNull){ return notNull !== null; });
    }

    function runBlocks(blocks){
        blocks.forEach(function(block){ trigger('run', block); });
    }
```

drag.js

The purpose of drag.js is to turn static blocks of HTML into a dynamic programming language by implementing interactions between the menu section of the view and the script section. The user builds their program by dragging blocks from the menu into the script, and the system runs the blocks in the script area.

We're using HTML5 drag-and-drop; the specific JavaScript event handlers it requires are defined here. (For more information on using HTML5 drag-and-drop, see Eric Bidleman's article[13].) While it is nice to have built-in support for drag-and-drop, it does have some oddities and some pretty major limitations, like not being implemented in any mobile browser at the time of this writing.

We define some variables at the top of the file. When we're dragging, we'll need to reference these from different stages of the dragging callback dance.

```
var dragTarget = null; // Block we're dragging
var dragType = null; // Are we dragging from the menu or from the script?
var scriptBlocks = []; // Blocks in the script, sorted by position
```

Depending on where the drag starts and ends, drop will have different effects:

- If dragging from script to menu, delete dragTarget (remove block from script).
- If dragging from script to script, move dragTarget (move an existing script block).
- If dragging from menu to script, copy dragTarget (insert new block in script).
- If dragging from menu to menu, do nothing.

During the dragStart(evt) handler we start tracking whether the block is being copied from the menu or moved from (or within) the script. We also grab a list of all the blocks in the script which are not being dragged, to use later. The evt.dataTransfer.setData call is used for dragging between the browser and other applications (or the desktop), which we're not using, but have to call anyway to work around a bug.

```
    function dragStart(evt){
        if (!matches(evt.target, '.block')) return;
        if (matches(evt.target, '.menu .block')){
            dragType = 'menu';
        }else{
            dragType = 'script';
```

---
[13]http://www.html5rocks.com/en/tutorials/dnd/basics/

```
    }
    evt.target.classList.add('dragging');
    dragTarget = evt.target;
    scriptBlocks = [].slice.call(
        document.querySelectorAll('.script .block:not(.dragging)'));
    // For dragging to take place in Firefox, we have to set this, even if
    // we don't use it
    evt.dataTransfer.setData('text/html', evt.target.outerHTML);
    if (matches(evt.target, '.menu .block')){
        evt.dataTransfer.effectAllowed = 'copy';
    }else{
        evt.dataTransfer.effectAllowed = 'move';
    }
}
```

While we are dragging, the dragenter, dragover, and dragout events give us opportunities to add visual cues by highlighting valid drop targets, etc. Of these, we only make use of dragover.

```
function dragOver(evt){
    if (!matches(evt.target, '.menu, .menu *, .script, .script *, .content')) {
        return;
    }
    // Necessary. Allows us to drop.
    if (evt.preventDefault) { evt.preventDefault(); }
    if (dragType === 'menu'){
        // See the section on the DataTransfer object.
        evt.dataTransfer.dropEffect = 'copy';
    }else{
        evt.dataTransfer.dropEffect = 'move';
    }
    return false;
}
```

When we release the mouse, we get a drop event. This is where the magic happens. We have to check where we dragged from (set back in dragStart) and where we have dragged to. Then we either copy the block, move the block, or delete the block as needed. We fire off some custom events using trigger() (defined in util.js) for our own use in the block logic, so we can refresh the script when it changes.

```
function drop(evt){
    if (!matches(evt.target, '.menu, .menu *, .script, .script *')) return;
    var dropTarget = closest(
        evt.target, '.script .container, .script .block, .menu, .script');
    var dropType = 'script';
    if (matches(dropTarget, '.menu')){ dropType = 'menu'; }
    // stops the browser from redirecting.
    if (evt.stopPropagation) { evt.stopPropagation(); }
    if (dragType === 'script' && dropType === 'menu'){
        trigger('blockRemoved', dragTarget.parentElement, dragTarget);
        dragTarget.parentElement.removeChild(dragTarget);
    }else if (dragType ==='script' && dropType === 'script'){
```

```
        if (matches(dropTarget, '.block')){
            dropTarget.parentElement.insertBefore(
                dragTarget, dropTarget.nextSibling);
        }else{
            dropTarget.insertBefore(dragTarget, dropTarget.firstChildElement);
        }
        trigger('blockMoved', dropTarget, dragTarget);
    }else if (dragType === 'menu' && dropType === 'script'){
        var newNode = dragTarget.cloneNode(true);
        newNode.classList.remove('dragging');
        if (matches(dropTarget, '.block')){
            dropTarget.parentElement.insertBefore(
                newNode, dropTarget.nextSibling);
        }else{
            dropTarget.insertBefore(newNode, dropTarget.firstChildElement);
        }
        trigger('blockAdded', dropTarget, newNode);
    }
}
```

The dragEnd(evt) is called when we mouse up, but after we handle the drop event. This is where we can clean up, remove classes from elements, and reset things for the next drag.

```
function _findAndRemoveClass(klass){
    var elem = document.querySelector('.' + klass);
    if (elem){ elem.classList.remove(klass); }
}

function dragEnd(evt){
    _findAndRemoveClass('dragging');
    _findAndRemoveClass('over');
    _findAndRemoveClass('next');
}
```

menu.js

The file menu.js is where blocks are associated with the functions that are called when they run, and contains the code for actually running the script as the user builds it up. Every time the script is modified, it is re-run automatically.

"Menu" in this context is not a drop-down (or pop-up) menu, like in most applications, but is the list of blocks you can choose for your script. This file sets that up, and starts the menu off with a looping block that is generally useful (and thus not part of the turtle language itself). This is kind of an odds-and-ends file, for things that may not fit anywhere else.

Having a single file to gather random functions in is useful, especially when an architecture is under development. My theory of keeping a clean house is to have designated places for clutter, and that applies to building a program architecture too. One file or module becomes the catch-all for things that don't have a clear place to fit in yet. As this file grows it is important to watch for emerging patterns: several related functions can be spun off into a separate module (or joined together into a more general function). You don't want the catch-all to grow indefinitely, but only to be a temporary holding place until you figure out the right way to organize the code.

We keep around references to menu and script because we use them a lot; no point hunting through the DOM for them over and over. We'll also use scriptRegistry, where we store the scripts of blocks in the menu. We use a very simple name-to-script mapping which does not support either multiple menu blocks with the same name or renaming blocks. A more complex scripting environment would need something more robust.

We use scriptDirty to keep track of whether the script has been modified since the last time it was run, so we don't keep trying to run it constantly.

```
var menu = document.querySelector('.menu');
var script = document.querySelector('.script');
var scriptRegistry = {};
var scriptDirty = false;
```

When we want to notify the system to run the script during the next frame handler, we call runSoon() which sets the scriptDirty flag to true. The system calls run() on every frame, but returns immediately unless scriptDirty is set. When scriptDirty is set, it runs all the script blocks, and also triggers events to let the specific language handle any tasks it needs before and after the script is run. This decouples the blocks-as-toolkit from the turtle language to make the blocks re-usable (or the language pluggable, depending how you look at it).

As part of running the script, we iterate over each block, calling runEach(evt) on it, which sets a class on the block, then finds and executes its associated function. If we slow things down, you should be able to watch the code execute as each block highlights to show when it is running.

The requestAnimationFrame method below is provided by the browser for animation. It takes a function which will be called for the next frame to be rendered by the browser (at 60 frames per second) after the call is made. How many frames we actually get depends on how fast we can get work done in that call.

```
function runSoon(){ scriptDirty = true; }

function run(){
    if (scriptDirty){
        scriptDirty = false;
        Block.trigger('beforeRun', script);
        var blocks = [].slice.call(
            document.querySelectorAll('.script > .block'));
        Block.run(blocks);
        Block.trigger('afterRun', script);
    }else{
        Block.trigger('everyFrame', script);
    }
    requestAnimationFrame(run);
}
requestAnimationFrame(run);

function runEach(evt){
    var elem = evt.target;
    if (!matches(elem, '.script .block')) return;
    if (elem.dataset.name === 'Define block') return;
    elem.classList.add('running');
    scriptRegistry[elem.dataset.name](elem);
```

```
        elem.classList.remove('running');
    }
```

We add blocks to the menu using menuItem(name, fn, value, contents) which takes a normal block, associates it with a function, and puts in the menu column.

```
function menuItem(name, fn, value, units){
    var item = Block.create(name, value, units);
    scriptRegistry[name] = fn;
    menu.appendChild(item);
    return item;
}
```

We define repeat(block) here, outside of the turtle language, because it is generally useful in different languages. If we had blocks for conditionals and reading and writing variables they could also go here, or into a separate trans-language module, but right now we only have one of these general-purpose blocks defined.

```
function repeat(block){
    var count = Block.value(block);
    var children = Block.contents(block);
    for (var i = 0; i < count; i++){
        Block.run(children);
    }
}
menuItem('Repeat', repeat, 10, []);
```

turtle.js

turtle.js is the implementation of the turtle block language. It exposes no functions to the rest of the code, so nothing else can depend on it. This way we can swap out the one file to create a new block language and know nothing in the core will break.

Turtle programming is a style of graphics programming, first popularized by Logo, where you have an imaginary turtle carrying a pen walking on the screen. You can tell the turtle to pick up the pen (stop drawing, but still move), put the pen down (leaving a line everywhere it goes), move forward a number of steps, or turn a number of degrees. Just those commands, combined with looping, can create amazingly intricate images.

In this version of turtle graphics we have a few extra blocks. Technically we don't need both turn right and turn left because you can have one and get the other with negative numbers. Likewise move back can be done with move forward and negative numbers. In this case it felt more balanced to have both.

The image above was formed by putting two loops inside another loop and adding a move forward and turn right to each loop, then playing with the parameters interactively until I liked the image that resulted.

```
var PIXEL_RATIO = window.devicePixelRatio || 1;
var canvasPlaceholder = document.querySelector('.canvas-placeholder');
var canvas = document.querySelector('.canvas');
var script = document.querySelector('.script');
var ctx = canvas.getContext('2d');
```

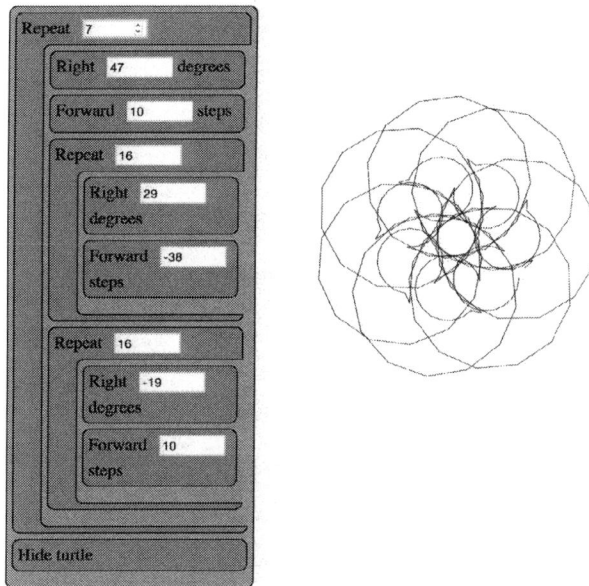

Figure 1.3: Example of Turtle code running

```
var cos = Math.cos, sin = Math.sin, sqrt = Math.sqrt, PI = Math.PI;
var DEGREE = PI / 180;
var WIDTH, HEIGHT, position, direction, visible, pen, color;
```

The reset() function clears all the state variables to their defaults. If we were to support multiple turtles, these variables would be encapsulated in an object. We also have a utility, deg2rad(deg), because we work in degrees in the UI, but we draw in radians. Finally, drawTurtle() draws the turtle itself. The default turtle is simply a triangle, but you could override this to draw a more aesthetically-pleasing turtle.

Note that drawTurtle uses the same primitive operations that we define to implement the turtle drawing. Sometimes you don't want to reuse code at different abstraction layers, but when the meaning is clear it can be a big win for code size and performance.

```
function reset(){
    recenter();
    direction = deg2rad(90); // facing "up"
    visible = true;
    pen = true; // when pen is true we draw, otherwise we move without drawing
    color = 'black';
}

function deg2rad(degrees){ return DEGREE * degrees; }

function drawTurtle(){
    var userPen = pen; // save pen state
    if (visible){
        penUp(); _moveForward(5); penDown();
        _turn(-150); _moveForward(12);
```

```
        _turn(-120); _moveForward(12);
        _turn(-120); _moveForward(12);
        _turn(30);
        penUp(); _moveForward(-5);
        if (userPen){
            penDown(); // restore pen state
        }
    }
}
```

We have a special block to draw a circle with a given radius at the current mouse position. We special-case drawCircle because, while you can certainly draw a circle by repeating MOVE 1 RIGHT 1 360 times, controlling the size of the circle is very difficult that way.

```
function drawCircle(radius){
    // Math for this is from http://www.mathopenref.com/polygonradius.html
    var userPen = pen; // save pen state
    if (visible){
        penUp(); _moveForward(-radius); penDown();
        _turn(-90);
        var steps = Math.min(Math.max(6, Math.floor(radius / 2)), 360);
        var theta = 360 / steps;
        var side = radius * 2 * Math.sin(Math.PI / steps);
        _moveForward(side / 2);
        for (var i = 1; i < steps; i++){
            _turn(theta); _moveForward(side);
        }
        _turn(theta); _moveForward(side / 2);
        _turn(90);
        penUp(); _moveForward(radius); penDown();
        if (userPen){
            penDown(); // restore pen state
        }
    }
}
```

Our main primitive is moveForward, which has to handle some elementary trigonometry and check whether the pen is up or down.

```
function _moveForward(distance){
    var start = position;
    position = {
        x: cos(direction) * distance * PIXEL_RATIO + start.x,
        y: -sin(direction) * distance * PIXEL_RATIO + start.y
    };
    if (pen){
        ctx.lineStyle = color;
        ctx.beginPath();
        ctx.moveTo(start.x, start.y);
        ctx.lineTo(position.x, position.y);
        ctx.stroke();
    }
```

```
    }
```

Most of the rest of the turtle commands can be easily defined in terms of what we've built above.

```
function penUp(){ pen = false; }
function penDown(){ pen = true; }
function hideTurtle(){ visible = false; }
function showTurtle(){ visible = true; }
function forward(block){ _moveForward(Block.value(block)); }
function back(block){ _moveForward(-Block.value(block)); }
function circle(block){ drawCircle(Block.value(block)); }
function _turn(degrees){ direction += deg2rad(degrees); }
function left(block){ _turn(Block.value(block)); }
function right(block){ _turn(-Block.value(block)); }
function recenter(){ position = {x: WIDTH/2, y: HEIGHT/2}; }
```

When we want a fresh slate, the clear function restores everything back to where we started.

```
function clear(){
    ctx.save();
    ctx.fillStyle = 'white';
    ctx.fillRect(0,0,WIDTH,HEIGHT);
    ctx.restore();
    reset();
    ctx.moveTo(position.x, position.y);
}
```

When this script first loads and runs, we use our reset and clear to initialize everything and draw the turtle.

```
onResize();
clear();
drawTurtle();
```

Now we can use the functions above, with the Menu.item function from menu.js, to make blocks for the user to build scripts from. These are dragged into place to make the user's programs.

```
Menu.item('Left', left, 5, 'degrees');
Menu.item('Right', right, 5, 'degrees');
Menu.item('Forward', forward, 10, 'steps');
Menu.item('Back', back, 10, 'steps');
Menu.item('Circle', circle, 20, 'radius');
Menu.item('Pen up', penUp);
Menu.item('Pen down', penDown);
Menu.item('Back to center', recenter);
Menu.item('Hide turtle', hideTurtle);
Menu.item('Show turtle', showTurtle);
```

1.3   Lessons Learned

Why Not Use MVC?

Model-View-Controller (MVC) was a good design choice for Smalltalk programs in the '80s and it can work in some variation or other for web apps, but it isn't the right tool for every problem. All the state (the "model" in MVC) is captured by the block elements in a block language anyway, so replicating it into Javascript has little benefit unless there is some other need for the model (if we were editing shared, distributed code, for instance).

An early version of Waterbear went to great lengths to keep the model in JavaScript and sync it with the DOM, until I noticed that more than half the code and 90% of the bugs were due to keeping the model in sync with the DOM. Eliminating the duplication allowed the code to be simpler and more robust, and with all the state on the DOM elements, many bugs could be found simply by looking at the DOM in the developer tools. So in this case there is little benefit to building further separation of MVC than we already have in HTML/CSS/JavaScript.

Toy Changes Can Lead to Real Changes

Building a small, tightly scoped version of the larger system I work on has been an interesting exercise. Sometimes in a large system there are things you are hesitant to change because they affect too many other things. In a tiny, toy version you can experiment freely and learn things which you can then take back to the larger system. For me, the larger system is Waterbear and this project has had a huge impact on the way Waterbear is structured.

Small Experiments Make Failure OK

Some of the experiments I was able to do with this stripped-down block language were:

- using HTML5 drag-and-drop,
- running blocks directly by iterating through the DOM calling associated functions,
- separating the code that runs cleanly from the HTML DOM,
- simplified hit testing while dragging,
- building our own tiny vector and sprite libraries (for the game blocks), and
- "live coding" where the results are shown whenever you change the block script.

The thing about experiments is that they do not have to succeed. We tend to gloss over failures and dead ends in our work, where failures are punished instead of treated as important vehicles for learning, but failures are essential if you are going to push forward. While I did get the HTML5 drag-and-drop working, the fact that it isn't supported at all on any mobile browser means it is a non-starter for Waterbear. Separating the code out and running code by iterating through the blocks worked so well that I've already begun bringing those ideas to Waterbear, with excellent improvements in testing and debugging. The simplified hit testing, with some modifications, is also coming back to Waterbear, as are the tiny vector and sprite libraries. Live coding hasn't made it to Waterbear yet, but once the current round of changes stabilizes I may introduce it.

What Are We Trying to Build, Really?

Building a small version of a bigger system puts a sharp focus on what the important parts really are. Are there bits left in for historical reasons that serve no purpose (or worse, distract from the purpose)? Are there features no-one uses but you have to pay to maintain? Could the user interface be streamlined? All these are great questions to ask while making a tiny version. Drastic changes, like re-organizing the layout, can be made without worrying about the ramifications cascading through a more complex system, and can even guide refactoring the complex system.

A Program is a Process, Not a Thing

There are things I wasn't able to experiment with in the scope of this project that I may use the blockcode codebase to test out in the future. It would be interesting to create "function" blocks which create new blocks out of existing blocks. Implementing undo/redo would be simpler in a constrained environment. Making blocks accept multiple arguments without radically expanding the complexity would be useful. And finding various ways to share block scripts online would bring the webbiness of the tool full circle.

## chapter 2

A Continuous Integration System
Malini Das

2.1   What is a Continuous Integration System?

When developing software, we want to be able to verify that our new features or bug fixes are safe and work as expected. We do this by running tests against our code. Sometimes, developers will run tests locally to verify that their changes are safe, but developers may not have the time to test their code on every system their software runs in. Further, as more and more tests are added the amount of time required to run them, even only locally, becomes less viable. Because of this, continuous integration systems have been created.

Continuous Integration (CI) systems are dedicated systems used to test new code. Upon a commit to the code repository, it is the responsibility of the continuous integration system to verify that this commit will not break any tests. To do this, the system must be able to fetch the new changes, run the tests and report its results. Like any other system, it should also be failure resistant. This means if any part of the system fails, it should be able to recover and continue from that point.

This test system should also handle load well, so that we can get test results in a reasonable amount of time in the event that commits are being made faster than the tests can be run. We can achieve this by distributing and parallelizing the testing effort. This project will demonstrate a small, bare-bones distributed continuous integration system that is designed for extensibility.

2.2   Project Limitations and Notes

This project uses Git as the repository for the code that needs to be tested. Only standard source code management calls will be used, so if you are unfamiliar with Git but are familiar with other version control systems (VCS) like svn or Mercurial, you can still follow along.

Due to the limitations of code length and unittest, I simplified test discovery. We will *only* run tests that are in a directory named `tests` within the repository.

Continuous integration systems monitor a master repository which is usually hosted on a web server, and not local to the CI's file systems. For the cases of our example, we will use a local repository instead of a remote repository.

Continuous integration systems need not run on a fixed, regular schedule. You can also have them run every few commits, or per-commit. For our example case, the CI system will run periodically. This means if it is set up to check for changes in five-second periods, it will run tests against the most recent commit made after the five-second period. It won't test every commit made within that period of time, only the most recent one.

This CI system is designed to check periodically for changes in a repository. In real-world CI systems, you can also have the repository observer get notified by a hosted repository. Github, for example, provides "post-commit hooks" which send out notifications to a URL. Following this model, the repository observer would be called by the web server hosted at that URL to respond to that notification. Since this is complex to model locally, we're using an observer model, where the repository observer will check for changes instead of being notified.

CI systems also have a reporter aspect, where the test runner reports its results to a component that makes them available for people to see, perhaps on a webpage. For simplicity, this project gathers the test results and stores them as files in the file system local to the dispatcher process.

Note that the architecture this CI system uses is just one possibility among many. This approach has been chosen to simplify our case study into three main components.

2.3   Introduction

The basic structure of a continuous integration system consists of three components: an observer, a test job dispatcher, and a test runner. The observer watches the repository. When it notices that a commit has been made, it notifies the job dispatcher. The job dispatcher then finds a test runner and gives it the commit number to test.

There are many ways to architect a CI system. We could have the observer, dispatcher and runner be the same process on a single machine. This approach is very limited since there is no load handling, so if more changes are added to the repository than the CI system can handle, a large backlog will accrue. This approach is also not fault-tolerant at all; if the computer it is running on fails or there is a power outage, there are no fallback systems, so no tests will run. The ideal system would be one that can handle as many test jobs as requested, and will do its best to compensate when machines go down.

To build a CI system that is fault-tolerant and load-bearing, in this project, each of these components is its own process. This will let each process be independent of the others, and let us run multiple instances of each process. This is useful when you have more than one test job that needs to be run at the same time. We can then spawn multiple test runners in parallel, allowing us to run as many jobs as needed, and prevent us from accumulating a backlog of queued tests.

In this project, not only do these components run as separate processes, but they also communicate via sockets, which will let us run each process on a separate, networked machine. A unique host/port address is assigned to each component, and each process can communicate with the others by posting messages at the assigned addresses.

This design will let us handle hardware failures on the fly by enabling a distributed architecture. We can have the observer run on one machine, the test job dispatcher on another, and the test runners on another, and they can all communicate with each other over a network. If any of these machines go down, we can schedule a new machine to go up on the network, so the system becomes fail-safe.

This project does not include auto-recovery code, as that is dependent on your distributed system's architecture, but in the real world, CI systems are run in a distributed environment like this so they can have failover redundancy (i.e., we can fall back to a standby machine if one of the machines a process was running on becomes defunct).

For the purposes of this project, each of these processes will be locally and manually started distinct local ports.

Files in this Project

This project contains Python files for each of these components: the repository observer (repo_observer.py), the test job dispatcher (dispatcher.py), and the test runner (test_runner.py). Each of these three processes communicate with each other using sockets, and since the code used to transmit information is shared by all of them, there is a helpers.py file that contains it, so each process imports the communicate function from here instead of having it duplicated in the file.

There are also bash script files used by these processes. These script files are used to execute bash and git commands in an easier way than constantly using Python's operating system-level modules like os and subprocess.

Lastly, there is a tests directory, which contains two example tests the CI system will run. One test will pass, and the other will fail.

Initial Setup

While this CI system is ready to work in a distributed system, let us start by running everything locally on one computer so we can get a grasp on how the CI system works without adding the risk of running into network-related issues. If you wish to run this in a distributed environment, you can run each component on its own machine.

Continuous integration systems run tests by detecting changes in a code repository, so to start, we will need to set up the repository our CI system will monitor.

Let's call this test_repo:

```
$ mkdir test_repo
$ cd test_repo
$ git init
```

This will be our master repository. This is where developers check in their code, so our CI should pull this repository and check for commits, then run tests. The thing that checks for new commits is the repository observer.

The repository observer works by checking commits, so we need at least one commit in the master repository. Let's commit our example tests so we have some tests to run.

Copy the tests folder from this code base to test_repo and commit it:

```
$ cp -r /this/directory/tests /path/to/test_repo/
$ cd /path/to/test\_repo
$ git add tests/
$ git commit -m "add tests"
```

Now you have a commit in the master repository.

The repo observer component will need its own clone of the code, so it can detect when a new commit is made. Let's create a clone of our master repository, and call it test_repo_clone_obs:

```
$ git clone /path/to/test_repo test_repo_clone_obs
```

The test runner will also need its own clone of the code, so it can checkout the repository at a given commit and run the tests. Let's create another clone of our master repository, and call it test_repo_clone_runner:

```
$ git clone /path/to/test_repo test_repo_clone_runner
```

2.4   The Components

The Repository Observer (`repo_observer.py`)

The repository observer monitors a repository and notifies the dispatcher when a new commit is seen. In order to work with all version control systems (since not all VCSs have built-in notification systems), this repository observer is written to periodically check the repository for new commits instead of relying on the VCS to notify it that changes have been made.

The observer will poll the repository periodically, and when a change is seen, it will tell the dispatcher the newest commit ID to run tests against. The observer checks for new commits by finding the current commit ID in its repository, then updates the repository, and lastly, it finds the latest commit ID and compares them. For the purposes of this example, the observer will only dispatch tests against the latest commit. This means that if two commits are made between a periodic check, the observer will only run tests against the latest commit. Usually, a CI system will detect all commits since the last tested commit, and will dispatch test runners for each new commit, but I have modified this assumption for simplicity.

The observer must know which repository to observe. We previously created a clone of our repository at /path/to/test_repo_clone_obs. The observer will use this clone to detect changes. To allow the repository observer to use this clone, we pass it the path when we invoke the `repo_observer.py` file. The repository observer will use this clone to pull from the main repository.

We must also give the observer the dispatcher's address, so the observer may send it messages. When you start the repository observer, you can pass in the dispatcher's server address using the `--dispatcher-server` command line argument. If you do not pass it in, it will assume the default address of `localhost:8888`.

```
def poll():
    parser = argparse.ArgumentParser()
    parser.add_argument("--dispatcher-server",
                        help="dispatcher host:port, " \
                        "by default it uses localhost:8888",
                        default="localhost:8888",
                        action="store")
    parser.add_argument("repo", metavar="REPO", type=str,
                        help="path to the repository this will observe")
    args = parser.parse_args()
    dispatcher_host, dispatcher_port = args.dispatcher_server.split(":")
```

Once the repository observer file is invoked, it starts the `poll()` function. This function parses the command line arguments, and then kicks off an infinite while loop. The while loop is used to periodically check the repository for changes. The first thing it does is call the `update_repo.sh` Bash script [1].

```
    while True:
        try:
            # call the bash script that will update the repo and check
```

---

[1] Bash is used because we need to check file existence, create files, and use Git, and a shell script is the most direct and easy way to achieve this. Alternatively, there are cross-platform Python packages you can use; for example, Python's os built-in module can be used for accessing the file system, and GitPython can be used for Git access, but they perform actions in a more roundabout way.

```
          # for changes. If there's a change, it will drop a .commit_id file
          # with the latest commit in the current working directory
          subprocess.check_output(["./update_repo.sh", args.repo])
      except subprocess.CalledProcessError as e:
          raise Exception("Could not update and check repository. " +
                          "Reason: %s" % e.output)
```

The update_repo.sh file is used to identify any new commits and let the repository observer know. It does this by noting what commit ID we are currently aware of, then pulls the repository, and checks the latest commit ID. If they match, no changes are made, so the repository observer doesn't need to do anything, but if there is a difference in the commit ID, then we know a new commit has been made. In this case, update_repo.sh will create a file called .commit_id with the latest commit ID stored in it.

A step-by-step breakdown of update_repo.sh is as follows. First, the script sources the run_or_fail.sh file, which provides the run_or_fail helper method used by all our shell scripts. This method is used to run the given command, or fail with the given error message.

```
#!/bin/bash

source run_or_fail.sh
```

Next, the script tries to remove a file named .commit_id. Since updaterepo.sh is called infinitely by the repo_observer.py file, if we previously had a new commit, then .commit_id was created, but holds a commit we already tested. Therefore, we want to remove that file, and create a new one only if a new commit is found.

```
bash rm -f .commit_id
```

After it removes the file (if it existed), it verifies that the repository we are observing exists, and then resets it to the most recent commit, in case anything caused it to get out of sync.

```
run_or_fail "Repository folder not found!" pushd $1 1> /dev/null
run_or_fail "Could not reset git" git reset --hard HEAD
```

It then calls git log and parses the output, looking for the most recent commit ID.

```
COMMIT=$(run_or_fail "Could not call 'git log' on repository" git log -n1)
if [ $? != 0 ]; then
  echo "Could not call 'git log' on repository"
  exit 1
fi
COMMIT_ID=`echo $COMMIT | awk '{ print $2 }'`
```

Then it pulls the repository, getting any recent changes, then gets the most recent commit ID.

```
run_or_fail "Could not pull from repository" git pull
COMMIT=$(run_or_fail "Could not call 'git log' on repository" git log -n1)
if [ $? != 0 ]; then
  echo "Could not call 'git log' on repository"
  exit 1
fi
NEW_COMMIT_ID=`echo $COMMIT | awk '{ print $2 }'`
```

Lastly, if the commit ID doesn't match the previous ID, then we know we have new commits to check, so the script stores the latest commit ID in a .commit_id file.

```
# if the id changed, then write it to a file
if [ $NEW_COMMIT_ID != $COMMIT_ID ]; then
  popd 1> /dev/null
  echo $NEW_COMMIT_ID > .commit_id
fi
```

When update_repo.sh finishes running in repo_observer.py, the repository observer checks for the existence of the .commit_id file. If the file does exist, then we know we have a new commit, and we need to notify the dispatcher so it can kick off the tests. The repository observer will check the dispatcher server's status by connecting to it and sending a 'status' request, to make sure there are no problems with it, and to make sure it is ready for instruction.

```
if os.path.isfile(".commit_id"):
    try:
        response = helpers.communicate(dispatcher_host,
                                       int(dispatcher_port),
                                       "status")
    except socket.error as e:
        raise Exception("Could not communicate with dispatcher server: %s" % e)
```

If it responds with "OK", then the repository observer opens the .commit_id file, reads the latest commit ID and sends that ID to the dispatcher, using a dispatch:<commit ID> request. It will then sleep for five seconds and repeat the process. We'll also try again in five seconds if anything went wrong along the way.

```
    if response == "OK":
        commit = ""
        with open(".commit_id", "r") as f:
            commit = f.readline()
        response = helpers.communicate(dispatcher_host,
                                       int(dispatcher_port),
                                       "dispatch:%s" % commit)
        if response != "OK":
            raise Exception("Could not dispatch the test: %s" %
            response)
        print "dispatched!"
    else:
        raise Exception("Could not dispatch the test: %s" %
        response)
time.sleep(5)
```

The repository observer will repeat this process forever, until you kill the process via a KeyboardInterrupt (Ctrl+c), or by sending it a kill signal.

The Dispatcher (dispatcher.py)

The dispatcher is a separate service used to delegate testing tasks. It listens on a port for requests from test runners and from the repository observer. It allows test runners to register themselves, and when given a commit ID from the repository observer, it will dispatch a test runner against the new commit. It also gracefully handles any problems with the test runners and will redistribute the commit ID to a new test runner if anything goes wrong.

When dispatch.py is executed, the serve function is called. First it parses the arguments that allow you to specify the dispatcher's host and port:

```
def serve():
    parser = argparse.ArgumentParser()
    parser.add_argument("--host",
                        help="dispatcher's host, by default it uses localhost",
                        default="localhost",
                        action="store")
    parser.add_argument("--port",
                        help="dispatcher's port, by default it uses 8888",
                        default=8888,
                        action="store")
    args = parser.parse_args()
```

This starts the dispatcher server, and two other threads. One thread runs the runner_checker function, and other runs the redistribute function.

```
    server = ThreadingTCPServer((args.host, int(args.port)), DispatcherHandler)
    print 'serving on %s:%s' % (args.host, int(args.port))

    ...

    runner_heartbeat = threading.Thread(target=runner_checker, args=(server,))
    redistributor = threading.Thread(target=redistribute, args=(server,))
    try:
        runner_heartbeat.start()
        redistributor.start()
        # Activate the server; this will keep running until you
        # interrupt the program with Ctrl+C or Cmd+C
        server.serve_forever()
    except (KeyboardInterrupt, Exception):
        # if any exception occurs, kill the thread
        server.dead = True
        runner_heartbeat.join()
        redistributor.join()
```

The runner_checker function periodically pings each registered test runner to make sure they are still responsive. If they become unresponsive, then that runner will be removed from the pool and its commit ID will be dispatched to the next available runner. The function will log the commit ID in the pending_commits variable.

```
    def runner_checker(server):
        def manage_commit_lists(runner):
            for commit, assigned_runner in server.dispatched_commits.iteritems():
                if assigned_runner == runner:
                    del server.dispatched_commits[commit]
                    server.pending_commits.append(commit)
```

```
                break
        server.runners.remove(runner)
    while not server.dead:
        time.sleep(1)
        for runner in server.runners:
            s = socket.socket(socket.AF_INET, socket.SOCK_STREAM)
            try:
                response = helpers.communicate(runner["host"],
                                               int(runner["port"]),
                                               "ping")
                if response != "pong":
                    print "removing runner %s" % runner
                    manage_commit_lists(runner)
            except socket.error as e:
                manage_commit_lists(runner)
```

The redistribute function is used to dispatch the commit IDs logged in pending_commits. When redistribute runs, it checks if there are any commit IDs in pending_commits. If so, it calls the dispatch_tests function with the commit ID.

```
def redistribute(server):
    while not server.dead:
        for commit in server.pending_commits:
            print "running redistribute"
            print server.pending_commits
            dispatch_tests(server, commit)
            time.sleep(5)
```

The dispatch_tests function is used to find an available test runner from the pool of registered runners. If one is available, it will send a runtest message to it with the commit ID. If none are currently available, it will wait two seconds and repeat this process. Once dispatched, it logs which commit ID is being tested by which test runner in the dispatched_commits variable. If the commit ID is in the pending_commits variable, dispatch_tests will remove it since it has already been successfully re-dispatched.

```
def dispatch_tests(server, commit_id):
    # NOTE: usually we don't run this forever
    while True:
        print "trying to dispatch to runners"
        for runner in server.runners:
            response = helpers.communicate(runner["host"],
                                           int(runner["port"]),
                                           "runtest:%s" % commit_id)
            if response == "OK":
                print "adding id %s" % commit_id
                server.dispatched_commits[commit_id] = runner
                if commit_id in server.pending_commits:
                    server.pending_commits.remove(commit_id)
                return
        time.sleep(2)
```

The dispatcher server uses the SocketServer module, which is a very simple server that is part of the standard library. There are four basic server types in the SocketServer module: TCP, UDP, UnixStreamServer and UnixDatagramServer. We will be using a TCP-based socket server so we can ensure continuous, ordered streams of data between servers, as UDP does not ensure this.

The default TCPServer provided by SocketServer can only handle one request at a time, so it cannot handle the case where the dispatcher is talking to one connection, say from a test runner, and then a new connection comes in, say from the repository observer. If this happens, the repository observer would have to wait for the first connection to complete and disconnect before it would be serviced. This is not ideal for our case, since the dispatcher server must be able to directly and swiftly communicate with all test runners and the repository observer.

In order for the dispatcher server to handle simultaneous connections, it uses the ThreadingTCPServer custom class, which adds threading ability to the default SocketServer. This means that any time the dispatcher receives a connection request, it spins off a new process just for that connection. This allows the dispatcher to handle multiple requests at the same time.

```
class ThreadingTCPServer(SocketServer.ThreadingMixIn, SocketServer.TCPServer):
    runners = [] # Keeps track of test runner pool
    dead = False # Indicate to other threads that we are no longer running
    dispatched_commits = {} # Keeps track of commits we dispatched
    pending_commits = [] # Keeps track of commits we have yet to dispatch
```

The dispatcher server works by defining handlers for each request. This is defined by the DispatcherHandler class, which inherits from SocketServer's BaseRequestHandler. This base class just needs us to define the handle function, which will be invoked whenever a connection is requested. The handle function defined in DispatcherHandler is our custom handler, and it will be called on each connection. It looks at the incoming connection request (self.request holds the request information), and parses out what command is being requested of it.

```
class DispatcherHandler(SocketServer.BaseRequestHandler):
    """
    The RequestHandler class for our dispatcher.
    This will dispatch test runners against the incoming commit
    and handle their requests and test results
    """
    command_re = re.compile(r"(\w+)(:.+)*")
    BUF_SIZE = 1024
    def handle(self):
        self.data = self.request.recv(self.BUF_SIZE).strip()
        command_groups = self.command_re.match(self.data)
        if not command_groups:
            self.request.sendall("Invalid command")
            return
        command = command_groups.group(1)
```

It handles four commands: status, register, dispatch, and results. status is used to check if the dispatcher server is up and running.

```
        if command == "status":
            print "in status"
            self.request.sendall("OK")
```

In order for the dispatcher to do anything useful, it needs to have at least one test runner registered. When register is called on a host:port pair, it stores the runner's information in a list (the runners object attached to the ThreadingTCPServer object) so it can communicate with the runner later, when it needs to give it a commit ID to run tests against.

```
elif command == "register":
    # Add this test runner to our pool
    print "register"
    address = command_groups.group(2)
    host, port = re.findall(r":(\w*)", address)
    runner = {"host": host, "port":port}
    self.server.runners.append(runner)
    self.request.sendall("OK")
```

dispatch is used by the repository observer to dispatch a test runner against a commit. The format of this command is dispatch:<commit ID>. The dispatcher parses out the commit ID from this message and sends it to the test runner.

```
elif command == "dispatch":
    print "going to dispatch"
    commit_id = command_groups.group(2)[1:]
    if not self.server.runners:
        self.request.sendall("No runners are registered")
    else:
        # The coordinator can trust us to dispatch the test
        self.request.sendall("OK")
        dispatch_tests(self.server, commit_id)
```

results is used by a test runner to report the results of a finished test run. The format of this command is results:<commit ID>:<length of results data in bytes>:<results>. The <commit ID> is used to identify which commit ID the tests were run against. The <length of results data in bytes> is used to figure out how big a buffer is needed for the results data. Lastly, <results> holds the actual result output.

```
elif command == "results":
    print "got test results"
    results = command_groups.group(2)[1:]
    results = results.split(":")
    commit_id = results[0]
    length_msg = int(results[1])
    # 3 is the number of ":" in the sent command
    remaining_buffer = self.BUF_SIZE - \
        (len(command) + len(commit_id) + len(results[1]) + 3)
    if length_msg > remaining_buffer:
        self.data += self.request.recv(length_msg - remaining_buffer).strip()
    del self.server.dispatched_commits[commit_id]
    if not os.path.exists("test_results"):
        os.makedirs("test_results")
    with open("test_results/%s" % commit_id, "w") as f:
        data = self.data.split(":")[3:]
        data = "\n".join(data)
        f.write(data)
    self.request.sendall("OK")
```

The Test Runner (`test_runner.py`)

The test runner is responsible for running tests against a given commit ID and reporting the results. It communicates only with the dispatcher server, which is responsible for giving it the commit IDs to run against, and which will receive the test results.

When the `test_runner.py` file is invoked, it calls the `serve` function which starts the test runner server, and also starts a thread to run the `dispatcher_checker` function. Since this startup process is very similar to the ones described in `repo_observer.py` and `dispatcher.py`, we omit the description here.

The `dispatcher_checker` function pings the dispatcher server every five seconds to make sure it is still up and running. This is important for resource management. If the dispatcher goes down, then the test runner will shut down since it won't be able to do any meaningful work if there is no dispatcher to give it work or to report to.

```
def dispatcher_checker(server):
    while not server.dead:
        time.sleep(5)
        if (time.time() - server.last_communication) > 10:
            try:
                response = helpers.communicate(
                                server.dispatcher_server["host"],
                                int(server.dispatcher_server["port"]),
                                "status")
                if response != "OK":
                    print "Dispatcher is no longer functional"
                    server.shutdown()
                    return
            except socket.error as e:
                print "Can't communicate with dispatcher: %s" % e
                server.shutdown()
                return
```

The test runner is a ThreadingTCPServer, like the dispatcher server. It requires threading because not only will the dispatcher be giving it a commit ID to run, but the dispatcher will be pinging the runner periodically to verify that it is still up while it is running tests.

```
class ThreadingTCPServer(SocketServer.ThreadingMixIn, SocketServer.TCPServer):
    dispatcher_server = None # Holds the dispatcher server host/port information
    last_communication = None # Keeps track of last communication from dispatcher
    busy = False # Status flag
    dead = False # Status flag
```

The communication flow starts with the dispatcher requesting that the runner accept a commit ID to run. If the test runner is ready to run the job, it responds with an acknowledgement to the dispatcher server, which then closes the connection. In order for the test runner server to both run tests and accept more requests from the dispatcher, it starts the requested test job on a new thread.

This means that when the dispatcher server makes a request (a ping, in this case) and expects a response, it will be done on a separate thread, while the test runner is busy running tests on its own thread. This allows the test runner server to handle multiple tasks simultaneously. Instead of this threaded design, it is possible to have the dispatcher server hold onto a connection with each test runner, but this would increase the dispatcher server's memory needs, and is vulnerable to network problems, like accidentally dropped connections.

The test runner server responds to two messages from the dispatcher. The first is `ping`, which is used by the dispatcher server to verify that the runner is still active.

```
class TestHandler(SocketServer.BaseRequestHandler):
    ...

    def handle(self):
        ....
        if command == "ping":
            print "pinged"
            self.server.last_communication = time.time()
            self.request.sendall("pong")
```

The second is `runtest`, which accepts messages of the form `runtest:<commit ID>`, and is used to kick off tests on the given commit. When runtest is called, the test runner will check to see if it is already running a test, and if so, it will return a BUSY response to the dispatcher. If it is available, it will respond to the server with an OK message, set its status as busy and run its `run_tests` function.

```
        elif command == "runtest":
            print "got runtest command: am I busy? %s" % self.server.busy
            if self.server.busy:
                self.request.sendall("BUSY")
            else:
                self.request.sendall("OK")
                print "running"
                commit_id = command_groups.group(2)[1:]
                self.server.busy = True
                self.run_tests(commit_id,
                                self.server.repo_folder)
                self.server.busy = False
```

This function calls the shell script `test_runner_script.sh`, which updates the repository to the given commit ID. Once the script returns, if it was successful at updating the repository we run the tests using unittest and gather the results in a file. When the tests have finished running, the test runner reads in the results file and sends it in a results message to the dispatcher.

```
    def run_tests(self, commit_id, repo_folder):
        # update repo
        output = subprocess.check_output(["./test_runner_script.sh",
                                          repo_folder, commit_id])
        print output
        # run the tests
        test_folder = os.path.join(repo_folder, "tests")
        suite = unittest.TestLoader().discover(test_folder)
        result_file = open("results", "w")
        unittest.TextTestRunner(result_file).run(suite)
        result_file.close()
        result_file = open("results", "r")
        # give the dispatcher the results
```

```
            output = result_file.read()
        helpers.communicate(self.server.dispatcher_server["host"],
                            int(self.server.dispatcher_server["port"]),
                            "results:%s:%s:%s" % (commit_id, len(output), output))
```

Here's `test_runner_script.sh`:

```
#!/bin/bash
REPO=$1
COMMIT=$2
source run_or_fail.sh
run_or_fail "Repository folder not found" pushd "$REPO" 1> /dev/null
run_or_fail "Could not clean repository" git clean -d -f -x
run_or_fail "Could not call git pull" git pull
run_or_fail "Could not update to given commit hash" git reset --hard "$COMMIT"
```

In order to run `test_runner.py`, you must point it to a clone of the repository to run tests against. In this case, you can use the previously created /path/to/test_repo `test_repo_clone_runner` clone as the argument. By default, `test_runner.py` will start its own server on localhost using a port in the range 8900-9000, and will try to connect to the dispatcher server at `localhost:8888`. You may pass it optional arguments to change these values. The `--host` and `--port` arguments are used to designate a specific address to run the test runner server on, and the `--dispatcher-server` argument specifies the address of the dispatcher.

Control Flow Diagram

Figure 2.1 is an overview diagram of this system. This diagram assumes that all three files (`repo_observer.py`, `dispatcher.py` and `test_runner.py`) are already running, and describes the actions each process takes when a new commit is made.

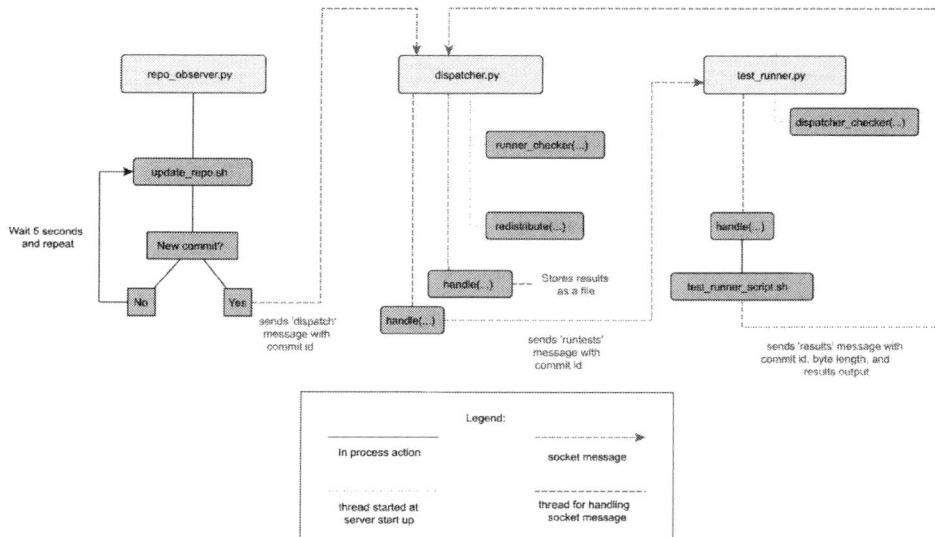

Figure 2.1: Control Flow

Running the Code

We can run this simple CI system locally, using three different terminal shells for each process. We start the dispatcher first, running on port 8888:

```
$ python dispatcher.py
```

In a new shell, we start the test runner (so it can register itself with the dispatcher):

```
$ python test_runner.py <path/to/test_repo_clone_runner>
```

The test runner will assign itself its own port, in the range 8900-9000. You may run as many test runners as you like.

Lastly, in another new shell, let's start the repo observer:

```
$ python repo_observer.py --dispatcher-server=localhost:8888 <path/to/repo_clone_obs>
```

Now that everything is set up, let's trigger some tests! To do that, we'll need to make a new commit. Go to your master repository and make an arbitrary change:

```
$ cd /path/to/test_repo
$ touch new_file
$ git add new_file
$ git commit -m"new file" new_file
```

Then repo_observer.py will realize that there's a new commit and notify the dispatcher. You can see the output in their respective shells, so you can monitor them. Once the dispatcher receives the test results, it stores them in a test_results/ folder in this code base, using the commit ID as the filename.

2.5   Error Handling

This CI system includes some simple error handling.

If you kill the test_runner.py process, dispatcher.py will figure out that the runner is no longer available and will remove it from the pool.

You can also kill the test runner, to simulate a machine crash or network failure. If you do so, the dispatcher will realize the runner went down and will give another test runner the job if one is available in the pool, or will wait for a new test runner to register itself in the pool.

If you kill the dispatcher, the repository observer will figure out it went down and will throw an exception. The test runners will also notice, and shut down.

2.6   Conclusion

By separating concerns into their own processes, we were able to build the fundamentals of a distributed continuous integration system. With processes communicating with each other via socket requests, we are able to distribute the system across multiple machines, helping to make our system more reliable and scalable.

Since the CI system is quite simple now, you can extend it yourself to be far more functional. Here are a few suggestions for improvements:

Per-Commit Test Runs

The current system will periodically check to see if new commits are run and will run the most recent commit. This should be improved to test each commit. To do this, you can modify the periodic checker to dispatch test runs for each commit in the log between the last-tested and the latest commit.

Smarter Test Runners

If the test runner detects that the dispatcher is unresponsive, it stops running. This happens even when the test runner is in the middle of running tests! It would be better if the test runner waited for a period of time (or indefinitely, if you do not care about resource management) for the dispatcher to come back online. In this case, if the dispatcher goes down while the test runner is actively running a test, instead of shutting down it will complete the test and wait for the dispatcher to come back online, and will report the results to it. This will ensure that we don't waste any effort the test runner makes, and that we will only run tests once per commit.

Real Reporting

In a real CI system, you would have the test results report to a reporter service which would gather the results, post them somewhere for people to review, and notify a list of interested parties when a failure or other notable event occurs. You can extend our simple CI system by creating a new process to get the reported results, instead of the dispatcher gathering the results. This new process could be a web server (or can connect to a web server) which could post the results online, and may use a mail server to alert subscribers to any test failures.

Test Runner Manager

Right now, you have to manually launch the `test_runner.py` file to start a test runner. Instead, you could create a test runner manager process which would assess the current load of test requests from the dispatcher and scale the number of active test runners accordingly. This process will receive the runtest messages and will start a test runner process for each request, and will kill unused processes when the load decreases.

Using these suggestions, you can make this simple CI system more robust and fault-tolerant, and you can integrate it with other systems, like a web-based test reporter.

If you wish to see the level of flexibility continuous integration systems can achieve, I recommend looking into Jenkins[2], a very robust, open-source CI system written in Java. It provides you with a basic CI system which you can extend using plugins. You may also access its source code through GitHub[3]. Another recommended project is Travis CI[4], which is written in Ruby and whose source code is also available through GitHub[5].

This has been an exercise in understanding how CI systems work, and how to build one yourself. You should now have a more solid understanding of what is needed to make a reliable distributed system, and you can now use this knowledge to develop more complex solutions.

---

[2] http://jenkins-ci.org/
[3] https://github.com/jenkinsci/jenkins/
[4] https://travis-ci.org/
[5] https://github.com/travis-ci/travis-ci

## chapter 3

Clustering by Consensus

Dustin J. Mitchell

3.1 Introduction

In this chapter, we'll explore implementation of a network protocol designed to support reliable distributed computation. Network protocols can be difficult to implement correctly, so we'll look at some techniques for minimizing bugs and for catching and fixing the remaining few. Building reliable software, too, requires some special development and debugging techniques.

3.2 Motivating Example

The focus of this chapter is on the protocol implementation, but as a motivating example let's consider a simple bank account management service. In this service, each account has a current balance and is identified with an account number. Users access the accounts by requesting operations like "deposit", "transfer", or "get-balance". The "transfer" operation operates on two accounts at once – the source and destination accounts – and must be rejected if the source account's balance is too low.

If the service is hosted on a single server, this is easy to implement: use a lock to make sure that transfer operations don't run in parallel, and verify the source account's balance in that method. However, a bank cannot rely on a single server for its critical account balances. Instead, the service is *distributed* over multiple servers, with each running a separate instance of exactly the same code. Users can then contact any server to perform an operation.

In a naive implementation of distributed processing, each server would keep a local copy of every account's balance. It would handle any operations it received, and send updates for account balances to other servers. But this approach introduces a serious failure mode: if two servers process operations for the same account at the same time, which new account balance is correct? Even if the servers share operations with one another instead of balances, two simultaneous transfers out of an account might overdraw the account.

Fundamentally, these failures occur when servers use their local state to perform operations, without first ensuring that the local state matches the state on other servers. For example, imagine that server A receives a transfer operation from Account 101 to Account 202, when server B has already processed another transfer of Account 101's full balance to Account 202, but not yet informed server A. The local state on server A is different from that on server B, so server A incorrectly allows the transfer to complete, even though the result is an overdraft on Account 101.

3.3 Distributed State Machines

The technique for avoiding such problems is called a "distributed state machine". The idea is that each server executes exactly the same deterministic state machine on exactly the same inputs. By the nature of state machines, then, each server will see exactly the same outputs. Operations such as "transfer" or "get-balance", together with their parameters (account numbers and amounts) represent the inputs to the state machine.

The state machine for this application is simple:

```
def execute_operation(state, operation):
    if operation.name == 'deposit':
        if not verify_signature(operation.deposit_signature):
            return state, False
        state.accounts[operation.destination_account] += operation.amount
        return state, True
    elif operation.name == 'transfer':
        if state.accounts[operation.source_account] < operation.amount:
            return state, False
        state.accounts[operation.source_account] -= operation.amount
        state.accounts[operation.destination_account] += operation.amount
        return state, True
    elif operation.name == 'get-balance':
        return state, state.accounts[operation.account]
```

Note that executing the "get-balance" operation does not modify the state, but is still implemented as a state transition. This guarantees that the returned balance is the latest information in the cluster of servers, and is not based on the (possibly stale) local state on a single server.

This may look different than the typical state machine you'd learn about in a computer science course. Rather than a finite set of named states with labeled transitions, this machine's state is the collection of account balances, so there are infinite possible states. Still, the usual rules of deterministic state machines apply: starting with the same state and processing the same operations will always produce the same output.

So, the distributed state machine technique ensures that the same operations occur on each host. But the problem remains of ensuring that every server agrees on the inputs to the state machine. This is a problem of *consensus*, and we'll address it with a derivative of the Paxos algorithm.

3.4 Consensus by Paxos

Paxos was described by Leslie Lamport in a fanciful paper, first submitted in 1990 and eventually published in 1998, entitled "The Part-Time Parliament"[1]. Lamport's paper has a great deal more detail than we will get into here, and is a fun read. The references at the end of the chapter describe some extensions of the algorithm that we have adapted in this implementation.

The simplest form of Paxos provides a way for a set of servers to agree on one value, for all time. Multi-Paxos builds on this foundation by agreeing on a numbered sequence of facts, one at a time. To implement a distributed state machine, we use Multi-Paxos to agree on each state-machine input, and execute them in sequence.

---

[1]L. Lamport, "The Part-Time Parliament," ACM Transactions on Computer Systems, 16(2):133–169, May 1998.

Simple Paxos

So let's start with "Simple Paxos", also known as the Synod protocol, which provides a way to agree on a single value that can never change. The name Paxos comes from the mythical island in "The Part-Time Parliament", where lawmakers vote on legislation through a process Lamport dubbed the Synod protocol.

The algorithm is a building block for more complex algorithms, as we'll see below. The single value we'll agree on in this example is the first transaction processed by our hypothetical bank. While the bank will process transactions every day, the first transaction will only occur once and never change, so we can use Simple Paxos to agree on its details.

The protocol operates in a series of ballots, each led by a single member of the cluster, called the proposer. Each ballot has a unique ballot number based on an integer and the proposer's identity. The proposer's goal is to get a majority of cluster members, acting as acceptors, to accept its value, but only if another value has not already been decided.

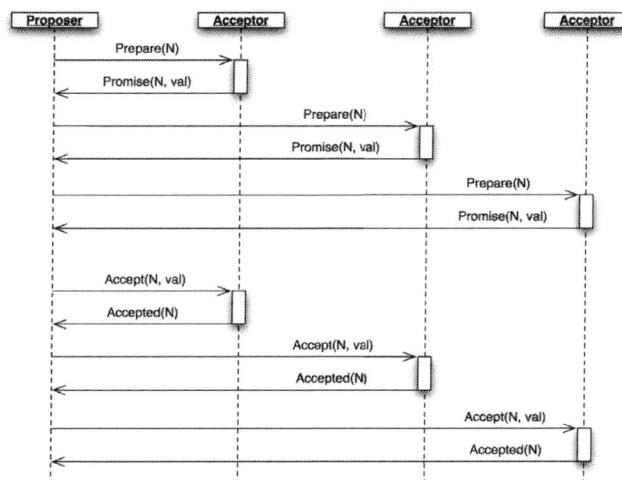

Figure 3.1: A Ballot

A ballot begins with the proposer sending a Prepare message with the ballot number N to the acceptors and waiting to hear from a majority (Figure 3.1.)

The Prepare message is a request for the accepted value (if any) with the highest ballot number less than N. Acceptors respond with a Promise containing any value they have already accepted, and promising not to accept any ballot numbered less than N in the future. If the acceptor has already made a promise for a larger ballot number, it includes that number in the Promise, indicating that the proposer has been pre-empted. In this case, the ballot is over, but the proposer is free to try again in another ballot (and with a larger ballot number).

When the proposer has heard back from a majority of the acceptors, it sends an Accept message, including the ballot number and value, to all acceptors. If the proposer did not receive any existing value from any acceptor, then it sends its own desired value. Otherwise, it sends the value from the highest-numbered promise.

Unless it would violate a promise, each acceptor records the value from the Accept message as accepted and replies with an Accepted message. The ballot is complete and the value decided when the proposer has heard its ballot number from a majority of acceptors.

Returning to the example, initially no other value has been accepted, so the acceptors all send back a `Promise` with no value, and the proposer sends an `Accept` containing its value, say:

```
operation(name='deposit', amount=100.00, destination_account='Mike DiBernardo')
```

If another proposer later initiates a ballot with a lower ballot number and a different operation (say, a transfer to acount `'Dustin J. Mitchell'`), the acceptors will simply not accept it. If that ballot has a larger ballot number, then the `Promise` from the acceptors will inform the proposer about Michael's $100.00 deposit operation, and the proposer will send that value in the `Accept` message instead of the transfer to Dustin. The new ballot will be accepted, but in favor of the same value as the first ballot.

In fact, the protocol will never allow two different values to be decided, even if the ballots overlap, messages are delayed, or a minority of acceptors fail.

When multiple proposers make a ballot at the same time, it is easy for neither ballot to be accepted. Both proposers then re-propose, and hopefully one wins, but the deadlock can continue indefinitely if the timing works out just right.

Consider the following sequence of events:

- Proposer A performs the `Prepare`/`Promise` phase for ballot number 1.
- Before Proposer A manages to get its proposal accepted, Proposer B performs a `Prepare`/`Promise` phase for ballot number 2.
- When Proposer A finally sends its `Accept` with ballot number 1, the acceptors reject it because they have already promised ballot number 2.
- Proposer A reacts by immediately sending a `Prepare` with a higher ballot number (3), before Proposer B can send its `Accept` message.
- Proposer B's subsequent `Accept` is rejected, and the process repeats.

With unlucky timing – more common over long-distance connections where the time between sending a message and getting a response is long – this deadlock can continue for many rounds.

Multi-Paxos

Reaching consensus on a single static value is not particularly useful on its own. Clustered systems such as the bank account service want to agree on a particular state (account balances) that changes over time. We use Paxos to agree on each operation, treated as a state machine transition.

Multi-Paxos is, in effect, a sequence of simple Paxos instances (slots), each numbered sequentially. Each state transition is given a "slot number", and each member of the cluster executes transitions in strict numeric order. To change the cluster's state (to process a transfer operation, for example), we try to achieve consensus on that operation in the next slot. In concrete terms, this means adding a slot number to each message, with all of the protocol state tracked on a per-slot basis.

Running Paxos for every slot, with its minimum of two round trips, would be too slow. Multi-Paxos optimizes by using the same set of ballot numbers for all slots, and performing the `Prepare`/`Promise` phase for all slots at once.

Paxos Made Pretty Hard

Implementing Multi-Paxos in practical software is notoriously difficult, spawning a number of papers mocking Lamport's "Paxos Made Simple" with titles like "Paxos Made Practical".

First, the multiple-proposers problem described above can become problematic in a busy environment, as each cluster member attempts to get its state machine operation decided in each slot. The fix is to elect a "leader" which is responsible for submitting ballots for each slot. All other cluster nodes then send new operations to the leader for execution. Thus, in normal operation with only one leader, ballot conflicts do not occur.

The `Prepare`/`Promise` phase can function as a kind of leader election: whichever cluster member owns the most recently promised ballot number is considered the leader. The leader is then free to execute the `Accept`/`Accepted` phase directly without repeating the first phase. As we'll see below, leader elections are actually quite complex.

Although simple Paxos guarantees that the cluster will not reach conflicting decisions, it cannot guarantee that any decision will be made. For example, if the initial `Prepare` message is lost and doesn't reach the acceptors, then the proposer will wait for a `Promise` message that will never arrive. Fixing this requires carefully orchestrated re-transmissions: enough to eventually make progress, but not so many that the cluster buries itself in a packet storm.

Another problem is the dissemination of decisions. A simple broadcast of a `Decision` message can take care of this for the normal case. If the message is lost, though, a node can remain permanently ignorant of the decision and unable to apply state machine transitions for later slots. So an implementation needs some mechanism for sharing information about decided proposals.

Our use of a distributed state machine presents another interesting challenge: start-up. When a new node starts, it needs to catch up on the existing state of the cluster. Although it can do so by catching up on decisions for all slots since the first, in a mature cluster this may involve millions of slots. Furthermore, we need some way to initialize a new cluster.

But enough talk of theory and algorithms – let's have a look at the code.

3.5   Introducing Cluster

The *Cluster* library in this chapter implements a simple form of Multi-Paxos. It is designed as a library to provide a consensus service to a larger application.

Users of this library will depend on its correctness, so it's important to structure the code so that we can see – and test – its correspondence to the specification. Complex protocols can exhibit complex failures, so we will build support for reproducing and debugging rare failures.

The implementation in this chapter is proof-of-concept code: enough to demonstrate that the core concept is practical, but without all of the mundane equipment required for use in production. The code is structured so that such equipment can be added later with minimal changes to the core implementation.

Let's get started.

Types and Constants

Cluster's protocol uses fifteen different message types, each defined as a Python `namedtuple`[2].

```
Accepted = namedtuple('Accepted', ['slot', 'ballot_num'])
Accept = namedtuple('Accept', ['slot', 'ballot_num', 'proposal'])
Decision = namedtuple('Decision', ['slot', 'proposal'])
Invoked = namedtuple('Invoked', ['client_id', 'output'])
```

---

[2]https://docs.python.org/3/library/collections.html

```
Invoke = namedtuple('Invoke', ['caller', 'client_id', 'input_value'])
Join = namedtuple('Join', [])
Active = namedtuple('Active', [])
Prepare = namedtuple('Prepare', ['ballot_num'])
Promise = namedtuple('Promise', ['ballot_num', 'accepted_proposals'])
Propose = namedtuple('Propose', ['slot', 'proposal'])
Welcome = namedtuple('Welcome', ['state', 'slot', 'decisions'])
Decided = namedtuple('Decided', ['slot'])
Preempted = namedtuple('Preempted', ['slot', 'preempted_by'])
Adopted = namedtuple('Adopted', ['ballot_num', 'accepted_proposals'])
Accepting = namedtuple('Accepting', ['leader'])
```

Using named tuples to describe each message type keeps the code clean and helps avoid some simple errors. The named tuple constructor will raise an exception if it is not given exactly the right attributes, making typos obvious. The tuples format themselves nicely in log messages, and as an added bonus don't use as much memory as a dictionary.

Creating a message reads naturally:

```
msg = Accepted(slot=10, ballot_num=30)
```

And the fields of that message are accessible with a minimum of extra typing:

```
got_ballot_num = msg.ballot_num
```

We'll see what these messages mean in the sections that follow. The code also introduces a few constants, most of which define timeouts for various messages:

```
JOIN_RETRANSMIT = 0.7
CATCHUP_INTERVAL = 0.6
ACCEPT_RETRANSMIT = 1.0
PREPARE_RETRANSMIT = 1.0
INVOKE_RETRANSMIT = 0.5
LEADER_TIMEOUT = 1.0
NULL_BALLOT = Ballot(-1, -1)  # sorts before all real ballots
NOOP_PROPOSAL = Proposal(None, None, None)  # no-op to fill otherwise empty slots
```

Finally, Cluster uses two data types named to correspond to the protocol description:

```
Proposal = namedtuple('Proposal', ['caller', 'client_id', 'input'])
Ballot = namedtuple('Ballot', ['n', 'leader'])
```

Component Model

Humans are limited by what we can hold in our active memory. We can't reason about the entire Cluster implementation at once – it's just too much, so it's easy to miss details. For similar reasons, large monolithic codebases are hard to test: test cases must manipulate many moving pieces and are brittle, failing on almost any change to the code.

To encourage testability and keep the code readable, we break Cluster down into a handful of classes corresponding to the roles described in the protocol. Each is a subclass of Role.

```
class Role(object):

    def __init__(self, node):
        self.node = node
        self.node.register(self)
        self.running = True
        self.logger = node.logger.getChild(type(self).__name__)

    def set_timer(self, seconds, callback):
        return self.node.network.set_timer(self.node.address, seconds,
                                           lambda: self.running and callback())

    def stop(self):
        self.running = False
        self.node.unregister(self)
```

The roles that a cluster node has are glued together by the Node class, which represents a single node on the network. Roles are added to and removed from the node as execution proceeds. Messages that arrive on the node are relayed to all active roles, calling a method named after the message type with a do_ prefix. These do_ methods receive the message's attributes as keyword arguments for easy access. The Node class also provides a send method as a convenience, using functools.partial to supply some arguments to the same methods of the Network class.

```
class Node(object):
    unique_ids = itertools.count()

    def __init__(self, network, address):
        self.network = network
        self.address = address or 'N%d' % self.unique_ids.next()
        self.logger = SimTimeLogger(
            logging.getLogger(self.address), {'network': self.network})
        self.logger.info('starting')
        self.roles = []
        self.send = functools.partial(self.network.send, self)

    def register(self, roles):
        self.roles.append(roles)

    def unregister(self, roles):
        self.roles.remove(roles)

    def receive(self, sender, message):
        handler_name = 'do_%s' % type(message).__name__

        for comp in self.roles[:]:
            if not hasattr(comp, handler_name):
                continue
            comp.logger.debug("received %s from %s", message, sender)
            fn = getattr(comp, handler_name)
            fn(sender=sender, **message._asdict())
```

Application Interface

The application creates and starts a Member object on each cluster member, providing an application-specific state machine and a list of peers. The member object adds a bootstrap role to the node if it is joining an existing cluster, or seed if it is creating a new cluster. It then runs the protocol (via Network.run) in a separate thread.

The application interacts with the cluster through the invoke method, which kicks off a proposal for a state transition. Once that proposal is decided and the state machine runs, invoke returns the machine's output. The method uses a simple synchronized Queue to wait for the result from the protocol thread.

```
class Member(object):

    def __init__(self, state_machine, network, peers, seed=None,
                 seed_cls=Seed, bootstrap_cls=Bootstrap):
        self.network = network
        self.node = network.new_node()
        if seed is not None:
            self.startup_role = seed_cls(self.node, initial_state=seed, peers=peers,
                                         execute_fn=state_machine)
        else:
            self.startup_role = bootstrap_cls(self.node,
                                              execute_fn=state_machine, peers=peers)
        self.requester = None

    def start(self):
        self.startup_role.start()
        self.thread = threading.Thread(target=self.network.run)
        self.thread.start()

    def invoke(self, input_value, request_cls=Requester):
        assert self.requester is None
        q = Queue.Queue()
        self.requester = request_cls(self.node, input_value, q.put)
        self.requester.start()
        output = q.get()
        self.requester = None
        return output
```

Role Classes

Let's look at each of the role classes in the library one by one.

Acceptor

The Acceptor implements the acceptor role in the protocol, so it must store the ballot number representing its most recent promise, along with the set of accepted proposals for each slot. It then responds to Prepare and Accept messages according to the protocol. The result is a short class that is easy to compare to the protocol.

For acceptors, Multi-Paxos looks a lot like Simple Paxos, with the addition of slot numbers to the messages.

```
class Acceptor(Role):

    def __init__(self, node):
        super(Acceptor, self).__init__(node)
        self.ballot_num = NULL_BALLOT
        self.accepted_proposals = {}  # {slot: (ballot_num, proposal)}

    def do_Prepare(self, sender, ballot_num):
        if ballot_num > self.ballot_num:
            self.ballot_num = ballot_num
            # we've heard from a scout, so it might be the next leader
            self.node.send([self.node.address], Accepting(leader=sender))

        self.node.send([sender], Promise(
            ballot_num=self.ballot_num,
            accepted_proposals=self.accepted_proposals
        ))

    def do_Accept(self, sender, ballot_num, slot, proposal):
        if ballot_num >= self.ballot_num:
            self.ballot_num = ballot_num
            acc = self.accepted_proposals
            if slot not in acc or acc[slot][0] < ballot_num:
                acc[slot] = (ballot_num, proposal)

        self.node.send([sender], Accepted(
            slot=slot, ballot_num=self.ballot_num))
```

Replica

The Replica class is the most complicated role class, as it has a few closely related responsibilities:

- Making new proposals;
- Invoking the local state machine when proposals are decided;
- Tracking the current leader; and
- Adding newly started nodes to the cluster.

The replica creates new proposals in response to Invoke messages from clients, selecting what it believes to be an unused slot and sending a Propose message to the current leader (Figure 3.2.) Furthermore, if the consensus for the selected slot is for a different proposal, the replica must re-propose with a new slot.

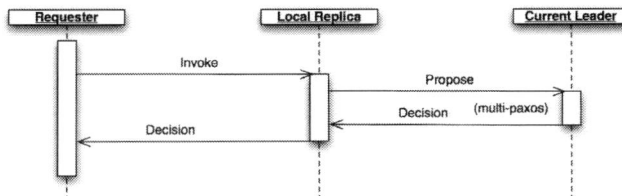

Figure 3.2: Replica Role Control Flow

`Decision` messages represent slots on which the cluster has come to consensus. Here, replicas store the new decision, then run the state machine until it reaches an undecided slot. Replicas distinguish *decided* slots, on which the cluster has agreed, from *committed* slots, which the local state machine has processed. When slots are decided out of order, the committed proposals may lag behind, waiting for the next slot to be decided. When a slot is committed, each replica sends an `Invoked` message back to the requester with the result of the operation.

In some circumstances, it's possible for a slot to have no active proposals and no decision. The state machine is required to execute slots one by one, so the cluster must reach a consensus on something to fill the slot. To protect against this possibility, replicas make a "no-op" proposal whenever they catch up on a slot. If such a proposal is eventually decided, then the state machine does nothing for that slot.

Likewise, it's possible for the same proposal to be decided twice. The replica skips invoking the state machine for any such duplicate proposals, performing no transition for that slot.

Replicas need to know which node is the active leader in order to send `Propose` messages to it. There is a surprising amount of subtlety required to get this right, as we'll see later. Each replica tracks the active leader using three sources of information.

When the leader role becomes active, it sends an `Adopted` message to the replica on the same node (Figure 3.3.)

Figure 3.3: Adopted

When the acceptor role sends a `Promise` to a new leader, it sends an `Accepting` message to its local replica (Figure 3.4.)

Figure 3.4: Accepting

The active leader sends `Active` messages as a heartbeat (Figure 3.5.) If no such message arrives before the LEADER_TIMEOUT expires, the replica assumes the leader is dead and moves on to the next leader. In this case, it's important that all replicas choose the *same* new leader, which we accomplish by sorting the members and selecting the next one in the list.

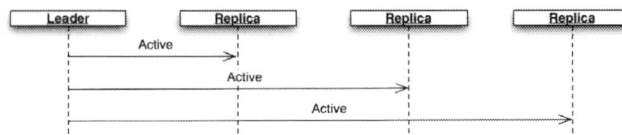

Figure 3.5: Active

Finally, when a node joins the network, the bootstrap role sends a `Join` message (Figure 3.6.) The replica responds with a `Welcome` message containing its most recent state, allowing the new node to come up to speed quickly.

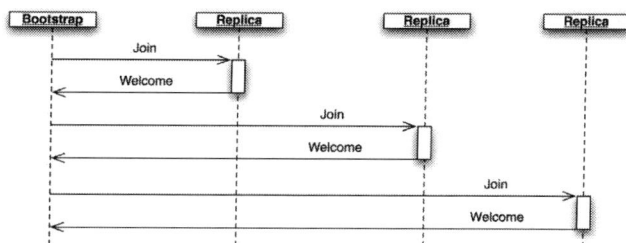

Figure 3.6: Bootstrap

```
class Replica(Role):

    def __init__(self, node, execute_fn, state, slot, decisions, peers):
        super(Replica, self).__init__(node)
        self.execute_fn = execute_fn
        self.state = state
        self.slot = slot
        self.decisions = decisions
        self.peers = peers
        self.proposals = {}
        # next slot num for a proposal (may lead slot)
        self.next_slot = slot
        self.latest_leader = None
        self.latest_leader_timeout = None

    # making proposals

    def do_Invoke(self, sender, caller, client_id, input_value):
        proposal = Proposal(caller, client_id, input_value)
        slot = next((s for s, p in self.proposals.iteritems() if p == proposal), None)
        # propose, or re-propose if this proposal already has a slot
        self.propose(proposal, slot)

    def propose(self, proposal, slot=None):
        """Send (or resend, if slot is specified) a proposal to the leader"""
        if not slot:
            slot, self.next_slot = self.next_slot, self.next_slot + 1
        self.proposals[slot] = proposal
        # find a leader we think is working - either the latest we know of, or
        # ourselves (which may trigger a scout to make us the leader)
        leader = self.latest_leader or self.node.address
        self.logger.info(
            "proposing %s at slot %d to leader %s" % (proposal, slot, leader))
        self.node.send([leader], Propose(slot=slot, proposal=proposal))

    # handling decided proposals

    def do_Decision(self, sender, slot, proposal):
        assert not self.decisions.get(self.slot, None), \
                "next slot to commit is already decided"
```

```
        if slot in self.decisions:
            assert self.decisions[slot] == proposal, \
                "slot %d already decided with %r!" % (slot, self.decisions[slot])
            return
        self.decisions[slot] = proposal
        self.next_slot = max(self.next_slot, slot + 1)

        # re-propose our proposal in a new slot if it lost its slot and wasn't a no-op
        our_proposal = self.proposals.get(slot)
        if (our_proposal is not None and
            our_proposal != proposal and our_proposal.caller):
            self.propose(our_proposal)

        # execute any pending, decided proposals
        while True:
            commit_proposal = self.decisions.get(self.slot)
            if not commit_proposal:
                break  # not decided yet
            commit_slot, self.slot = self.slot, self.slot + 1

            self.commit(commit_slot, commit_proposal)

    def commit(self, slot, proposal):
        """Actually commit a proposal that is decided and in sequence"""
        decided_proposals = [p for s, p in self.decisions.iteritems() if s < slot]
        if proposal in decided_proposals:
            self.logger.info(
                "not committing duplicate proposal %r, slot %d", proposal, slot)
            return  # duplicate

        self.logger.info("committing %r at slot %d" % (proposal, slot))
        if proposal.caller is not None:
            # perform a client operation
            self.state, output = self.execute_fn(self.state, proposal.input)
            self.node.send([proposal.caller],
                Invoked(client_id=proposal.client_id, output=output))

    # tracking the leader

    def do_Adopted(self, sender, ballot_num, accepted_proposals):
        self.latest_leader = self.node.address
        self.leader_alive()

    def do_Accepting(self, sender, leader):
        self.latest_leader = leader
        self.leader_alive()

    def do_Active(self, sender):
        if sender != self.latest_leader:
            return
        self.leader_alive()
```

```
def leader_alive(self):
    if self.latest_leader_timeout:
        self.latest_leader_timeout.cancel()

    def reset_leader():
        idx = self.peers.index(self.latest_leader)
        self.latest_leader = self.peers[(idx + 1) % len(self.peers)]
        self.logger.debug("leader timed out; tring the next one, %s",
            self.latest_leader)
    self.latest_leader_timeout = self.set_timer(LEADER_TIMEOUT, reset_leader)

# adding new cluster members

def do_Join(self, sender):
    if sender in self.peers:
        self.node.send([sender], Welcome(
            state=self.state, slot=self.slot, decisions=self.decisions))
```

Leader, Scout, and Commander

The leader's primary task is to take Propose messages requesting new ballots and produce decisions. A leader is "active" when it has successfully carried out the Prepare/Promise portion of the protocol. An active leader can immediately send an Accept message in response to a Propose.

In keeping with the class-per-role model, the leader delegates to the scout and commander roles to carry out each portion of the protocol.

```
class Leader(Role):

    def __init__(self, node, peers, commander_cls=Commander, scout_cls=Scout):
        super(Leader, self).__init__(node)
        self.ballot_num = Ballot(0, node.address)
        self.active = False
        self.proposals = {}
        self.commander_cls = commander_cls
        self.scout_cls = scout_cls
        self.scouting = False
        self.peers = peers

    def start(self):
        # reminder others we're active before LEADER_TIMEOUT expires
        def active():
            if self.active:
                self.node.send(self.peers, Active())
            self.set_timer(LEADER_TIMEOUT / 2.0, active)
        active()

    def spawn_scout(self):
        assert not self.scouting
        self.scouting = True
        self.scout_cls(self.node, self.ballot_num, self.peers).start()
```

```python
def do_Adopted(self, sender, ballot_num, accepted_proposals):
    self.scouting = False
    self.proposals.update(accepted_proposals)
    # note that we don't re-spawn commanders here; if there are undecided
    # proposals, the replicas will re-propose
    self.logger.info("leader becoming active")
    self.active = True

def spawn_commander(self, ballot_num, slot):
    proposal = self.proposals[slot]
    self.commander_cls(self.node, ballot_num, slot, proposal, self.peers).start()

def do_Preempted(self, sender, slot, preempted_by):
    if not slot:  # from the scout
        self.scouting = False
    self.logger.info("leader preempted by %s", preempted_by.leader)
    self.active = False
    self.ballot_num = Ballot((preempted_by or self.ballot_num).n + 1,
                             self.ballot_num.leader)

def do_Propose(self, sender, slot, proposal):
    if slot not in self.proposals:
        if self.active:
            self.proposals[slot] = proposal
            self.logger.info("spawning commander for slot %d" % (slot,))
            self.spawn_commander(self.ballot_num, slot)
        else:
            if not self.scouting:
                self.logger.info("got PROPOSE when not active - scouting")
                self.spawn_scout()
            else:
                self.logger.info("got PROPOSE while scouting; ignored")
    else:
        self.logger.info("got PROPOSE for a slot already being proposed")
```

The leader creates a scout role when it wants to become active, in response to receiving a Propose when it is inactive (Figure 3.7.) The scout sends (and re-sends, if necessary) a Prepare message, and collects Promise responses until it has heard from a majority of its peers or until it has been preempted. It communicates back to the leader with Adopted or Preempted, respectively.

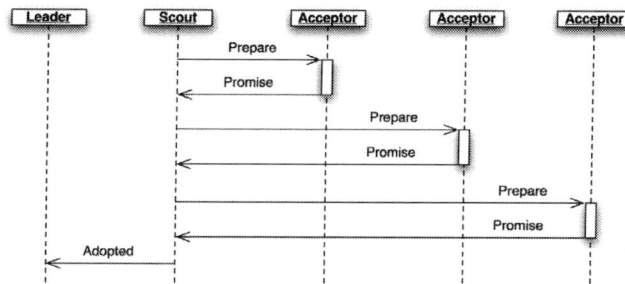

Figure 3.7: Scout

```
class Scout(Role):

    def __init__(self, node, ballot_num, peers):
        super(Scout, self).__init__(node)
        self.ballot_num = ballot_num
        self.accepted_proposals = {}
        self.acceptors = set([])
        self.peers = peers
        self.quorum = len(peers) / 2 + 1
        self.retransmit_timer = None

    def start(self):
        self.logger.info("scout starting")
        self.send_prepare()

    def send_prepare(self):
        self.node.send(self.peers, Prepare(ballot_num=self.ballot_num))
        self.retransmit_timer = self.set_timer(PREPARE_RETRANSMIT, self.send_prepare)

    def update_accepted(self, accepted_proposals):
        acc = self.accepted_proposals
        for slot, (ballot_num, proposal) in accepted_proposals.iteritems():
            if slot not in acc or acc[slot][0] < ballot_num:
                acc[slot] = (ballot_num, proposal)

    def do_Promise(self, sender, ballot_num, accepted_proposals):
        if ballot_num == self.ballot_num:
            self.logger.info("got matching promise; need %d" % self.quorum)
            self.update_accepted(accepted_proposals)
            self.acceptors.add(sender)
            if len(self.acceptors) >= self.quorum:
                # strip the ballot numbers from self.accepted_proposals, now that it
                # represents a majority
                accepted_proposals = \
                    dict((s, p) for s, (b, p) in self.accepted_proposals.iteritems())
                # We're adopted; note that this does *not* mean that no other
                # leader is active.  # Any such conflicts will be handled by the
                # commanders.
                self.node.send([self.node.address],
```

Dustin J. Mitchell   47

```
                    Adopted(ballot_num=ballot_num,
                            accepted_proposals=accepted_proposals))
            self.stop()
    else:
        # this acceptor has promised another leader a higher ballot number,
        # so we've lost
        self.node.send([self.node.address],
            Preempted(slot=None, preempted_by=ballot_num))
        self.stop()
```

The leader creates a commander role for each slot where it has an active proposal (Figure 3.8.) Like a scout, a commander sends and re-sends Accept messages and waits for a majority of acceptors to reply with Accepted, or for news of its preemption. When a proposal is accepted, the commander broadcasts a Decision message to all nodes. It responds to the leader with Decided or Preempted.

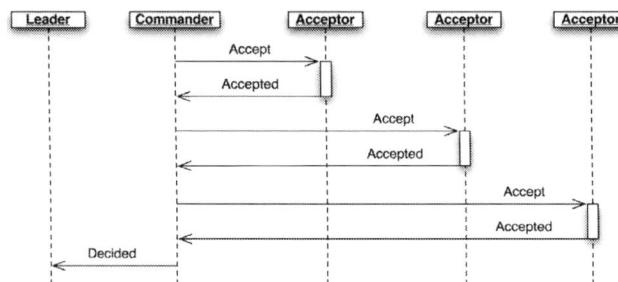

Figure 3.8: Commander

```
class Commander(Role):

    def __init__(self, node, ballot_num, slot, proposal, peers):
        super(Commander, self).__init__(node)
        self.ballot_num = ballot_num
        self.slot = slot
        self.proposal = proposal
        self.acceptors = set([])
        self.peers = peers
        self.quorum = len(peers) / 2 + 1

    def start(self):
        self.node.send(set(self.peers) - self.acceptors, Accept(
            slot=self.slot, ballot_num=self.ballot_num, proposal=self.proposal))
        self.set_timer(ACCEPT_RETRANSMIT, self.start)

    def finished(self, ballot_num, preempted):
        if preempted:
            self.node.send([self.node.address],
                            Preempted(slot=self.slot, preempted_by=ballot_num))
        else:
            self.node.send([self.node.address],
                            Decided(slot=self.slot))
        self.stop()
```

```
def do_Accepted(self, sender, slot, ballot_num):
    if slot != self.slot:
        return
    if ballot_num == self.ballot_num:
        self.acceptors.add(sender)
        if len(self.acceptors) < self.quorum:
            return
        self.node.send(self.peers, Decision(
                        slot=self.slot, proposal=self.proposal))
        self.finished(ballot_num, False)
    else:
        self.finished(ballot_num, True)
```

As an aside, a surprisingly subtle bug appeared here during development. At the time, the network simulator introduced packet loss even on messages within a node. When *all* Decision messages were lost, the protocol could not proceed. The replica continued to re-transmit Propose messages, but the leader ignored them as it already had a proposal for that slot. The replica's catch-up process could not find the result, as no replica had heard of the decision. The solution was to ensure that local messages are always delivered, as is the case for real network stacks.

Bootstrap

When a node joins the cluster, it must determine the current cluster state before it can participate. The bootstrap role handles this by sending Join messages to each peer in turn until it receives a Welcome. Bootstrap's communication diagram is shown above in Section 3.5.

An early version of the implementation started each node with a full set of roles (replica, leader, and acceptor), each of which began in a "startup" phase, waiting for information from the Welcome message. This spread the initialization logic around every role, requiring separate testing of each one. The final design has the bootstrap role adding each of the other roles to the node once startup is complete, passing the initial state to their constructors.

```
class Bootstrap(Role):

    def __init__(self, node, peers, execute_fn,
                    replica_cls=Replica, acceptor_cls=Acceptor, leader_cls=Leader,
                    commander_cls=Commander, scout_cls=Scout):
        super(Bootstrap, self).__init__(node)
        self.execute_fn = execute_fn
        self.peers = peers
        self.peers_cycle = itertools.cycle(peers)
        self.replica_cls = replica_cls
        self.acceptor_cls = acceptor_cls
        self.leader_cls = leader_cls
        self.commander_cls = commander_cls
        self.scout_cls = scout_cls

    def start(self):
        self.join()
```

```
def join(self):
    self.node.send([next(self.peers_cycle)], Join())
    self.set_timer(JOIN_RETRANSMIT, self.join)

def do_Welcome(self, sender, state, slot, decisions):
    self.acceptor_cls(self.node)
    self.replica_cls(self.node, execute_fn=self.execute_fn, peers=self.peers,
                     state=state, slot=slot, decisions=decisions)
    self.leader_cls(self.node, peers=self.peers, commander_cls=self.commander_cls,
                    scout_cls=self.scout_cls).start()
    self.stop()
```

Seed

In normal operation, when a node joins the cluster, it expects to find the cluster already running, with at least one node willing to respond to a Join message. But how does the cluster get started? One option is for the bootstrap role to determine, after attempting to contact every other node, that it is the first in the cluster. But this has two problems. First, for a large cluster it means a long wait while each Join times out. More importantly, in the event of a network partition, a new node might be unable to contact any others and start a new cluster.

Network partitions are the most challenging failure case for clustered applications. In a network partition, all cluster members remain alive, but communication fails between some members. For example, if the network link joining a cluster with nodes in Berlin and Taipei fails, the network is partitioned. If both parts of a cluster continue to operate during a partition, then re-joining the parts after the network link is restored can be challenging. In the Multi-Paxos case, the healed network would be hosting two clusters with different decisions for the same slot numbers.

To avoid this outcome, creating a new cluster is a user-specified operation. Exactly one node in the cluster runs the seed role, with the others running bootstrap as usual. The seed waits until it has received Join messages from a majority of its peers, then sends a Welcome with an initial state for the state machine and an empty set of decisions. The seed role then stops itself and starts a bootstrap role to join the newly-seeded cluster.

Seed emulates the Join/Welcome part of the bootstrap/replica interaction, so its communication diagram is the same as for the replica role.

```
class Seed(Role):

    def __init__(self, node, initial_state, execute_fn, peers,
                 bootstrap_cls=Bootstrap):
        super(Seed, self).__init__(node)
        self.initial_state = initial_state
        self.execute_fn = execute_fn
        self.peers = peers
        self.bootstrap_cls = bootstrap_cls
        self.seen_peers = set([])
        self.exit_timer = None

    def do_Join(self, sender):
        self.seen_peers.add(sender)
        if len(self.seen_peers) <= len(self.peers) / 2:
            return
```

```
        # cluster is ready - welcome everyone
        self.node.send(list(self.seen_peers), Welcome(
            state=self.initial_state, slot=1, decisions={}))

        # stick around for long enough that we don't hear any new JOINs from
        # the newly formed cluster
        if self.exit_timer:
            self.exit_timer.cancel()
        self.exit_timer = self.set_timer(JOIN_RETRANSMIT * 2, self.finish)

    def finish(self):
        # bootstrap this node into the cluster we just seeded
        bs = self.bootstrap_cls(self.node,
                                peers=self.peers, execute_fn=self.execute_fn)
        bs.start()
        self.stop()
```

Requester

The requester role manages a request to the distributed state machine. The role class simply sends Invoke messages to the local replica until it receives a corresponding Invoked. See the "Replica" section, above, for this role's communication diagram.

```
class Requester(Role):

    client_ids = itertools.count(start=100000)

    def __init__(self, node, n, callback):
        super(Requester, self).__init__(node)
        self.client_id = self.client_ids.next()
        self.n = n
        self.output = None
        self.callback = callback

    def start(self):
        self.node.send([self.node.address],
                       Invoke(caller=self.node.address,
                              client_id=self.client_id, input_value=self.n))
        self.invoke_timer = self.set_timer(INVOKE_RETRANSMIT, self.start)

    def do_Invoked(self, sender, client_id, output):
        if client_id != self.client_id:
            return
        self.logger.debug("received output %r" % (output,))
        self.invoke_timer.cancel()
        self.callback(output)
        self.stop()
```

Summary

To recap, cluster's roles are:

- Acceptor – make promises and accept proposals
- Replica – manage the distributed state machine: submitting proposals, committing decisions, and responding to requesters
- Leader – lead rounds of the Multi-Paxos algorithm
- Scout – perform the Prepare/Promise portion of the Multi-Paxos algorithm for a leader
- Commander – perform the Accept/Accepted portion of the Multi-Paxos algorithm for a leader
- Bootstrap – introduce a new node to an existing cluster
- Seed – create a new cluster
- Requester – request a distributed state machine operation

There is just one more piece of equipment required to make Cluster go: the network through which all of the nodes communicate.

3.6 Network

Any network protocol needs the ability to send and receive messages and a means of calling functions at a time in the future.

The Network class provides a simple simulated network with these capabilities and also simulates packet loss and message propagation delays.

Timers are handled using Python's heapq module, allowing efficient selection of the next event. Setting a timer involves pushing a Timer object onto the heap. Since removing items from a heap is inefficient, cancelled timers are left in place but marked as cancelled.

Message transmission uses the timer functionality to schedule a later delivery of the message at each node, using a random simulated delay. We again use functools.partial to set up a future call to the destination node's receive method with appropriate arguments.

Running the simulation just involves popping timers from the heap and executing them if they have not been cancelled and if the destination node is still active.

```
class Timer(object):

    def __init__(self, expires, address, callback):
        self.expires = expires
        self.address = address
        self.callback = callback
        self.cancelled = False

    def __cmp__(self, other):
        return cmp(self.expires, other.expires)

    def cancel(self):
        self.cancelled = True


class Network(object):
    PROP_DELAY = 0.03
    PROP_JITTER = 0.02
```

```
    DROP_PROB = 0.05

    def __init__(self, seed):
        self.nodes = {}
        self.rnd = random.Random(seed)
        self.timers = []
        self.now = 1000.0

    def new_node(self, address=None):
        node = Node(self, address=address)
        self.nodes[node.address] = node
        return node

    def run(self):
        while self.timers:
            next_timer = self.timers[0]
            if next_timer.expires > self.now:
                self.now = next_timer.expires
            heapq.heappop(self.timers)
            if next_timer.cancelled:
                continue
            if not next_timer.address or next_timer.address in self.nodes:
                next_timer.callback()

    def stop(self):
        self.timers = []

    def set_timer(self, address, seconds, callback):
        timer = Timer(self.now + seconds, address, callback)
        heapq.heappush(self.timers, timer)
        return timer

    def send(self, sender, destinations, message):
        sender.logger.debug("sending %s to %s", message, destinations)
        # avoid aliasing by making a closure containing distinct deep copy of
        # message for each dest
        def sendto(dest, message):
            if dest == sender.address:
                # reliably deliver local messages with no delay
                self.set_timer(sender.address, 0,
                               lambda: sender.receive(sender.address, message))
            elif self.rnd.uniform(0, 1.0) > self.DROP_PROB:
                delay = self.PROP_DELAY + self.rnd.uniform(-self.PROP_JITTER,
                                                           self.PROP_JITTER)
                self.set_timer(dest, delay,
                               functools.partial(self.nodes[dest].receive,
                                                 sender.address, message))
        for dest in (d for d in destinations if d in self.nodes):
            sendto(dest, copy.deepcopy(message))
```

While it's not included in this implementation, the component model allows us to swap in a real-world network implementation, communicating between actual servers on a real network, with no changes to the other components. Testing and debugging can take place using the simulated network, with production use of the library operating over real network hardware.

3.7   Debugging Support

When developing a complex system such as this, the bugs quickly transition from trivial, like a simple NameError, to obscure failures that only manifest after several minutes of (simulated) proocol operation. Chasing down bugs like this involves working backward from the point where the error became obvious. Interactive debuggers are useless here, as they can only step forward in time.

The most important debugging feature in Cluster is a *deterministic* simulator. Unlike a real network, it will behave exactly the same way on every run, given the same seed for the random number generator. This means that we can add additional debugging checks or output to the code and re-run the simulation to see the same failure in more detail.

Of course, much of that detail is in the messages exchanged by the nodes in the cluster, so those are automatically logged in their entirety. That logging includes the role class sending or receiving the message, as well as the simulated timestamp injected via the SimTimeLogger class.

```
class SimTimeLogger(logging.LoggerAdapter):

    def process(self, msg, kwargs):
        return "T=%.3f %s" % (self.extra['network'].now, msg), kwargs

    def getChild(self, name):
        return self.__class__(self.logger.getChild(name),
                              {'network': self.extra['network']})
```

A resilient protocol such as this one can often run for a long time after a bug has been triggered. For example, during development, a data aliasing error caused all replicas to share the same decisions dictionary. This meant that once a decision was handled on one node, all other nodes saw it as already decided. Even with this serious bug, the cluster produced correct results for several transactions before deadlocking.

Assertions are an important tool to catch this sort of error early. Assertions should include any invariants from the algorithm design, but when the code doesn't behave as we expect, asserting our expectations is a great way to see where things go astray.

```
assert not self.decisions.get(self.slot, None), \
       "next slot to commit is already decided"
if slot in self.decisions:
    assert self.decisions[slot] == proposal, \
        "slot %d already decided with %r!" % (slot, self.decisions[slot])
```

Identifying the right assumptions we make while reading code is a part of the art of debugging. In this code from Replica.do_Decision, the problem was that the Decision for the next slot to commit was being ignored because it was already in self.decisions. The underlying assumption being violated was that the next slot to be committed was not yet decided. Asserting this at the beginning of do_Decision identified the flaw and led quickly to the fix. Similarly, other bugs led to cases where different proposals were decided in the same slot – a serious error.

Many other assertions were added during development of the protocol, but in the interests of space, only a few remain.

3.8 Testing

Some time in the last ten years, coding without tests finally became as crazy as driving without a seatbelt. Code without tests is probably incorrect, and modifying code is risky without a way to see if its behavior has changed.

Testing is most effective when the code is organized for testability. There are a few active schools of thought in this area, but the approach we've taken is to divide the code into small, minimally connected units that can be tested in isolation. This agrees nicely with the role model, where each role has a specific purpose and can operate in isolation from the others, resulting in a compact, self-sufficient class.

Cluster is written to maximize that isolation: all communication between roles takes place via messages, with the exception of creating new roles. For the most part, then, roles can be tested by sending messages to them and observing their responses.

Unit Testing

The unit tests for Cluster are simple and short:

```
class Tests(utils.ComponentTestCase):
    def test_propose_active(self):
        """A PROPOSE received while active spawns a commander."""
        self.activate_leader()
        self.node.fake_message(Propose(slot=10, proposal=PROPOSAL1))
        self.assertCommanderStarted(Ballot(0, 'F999'), 10, PROPOSAL1)
```

This method tests a single behavior (commander spawning) of a single unit (the Leader class). It follows the well-known "arrange, act, assert" pattern: set up an active leader, send it a message, and check the result.

Dependency Injection

We use a technique called "dependency injection" to handle creation of new roles. Each role class which adds other roles to the network takes a list of class objects as constructor arguments, defaulting to the actual classes. For example, the constructor for Leader looks like this:

```
class Leader(Role):
    def __init__(self, node, peers, commander_cls=Commander, scout_cls=Scout):
        super(Leader, self).__init__(node)
        self.ballot_num = Ballot(0, node.address)
        self.active = False
        self.proposals = {}
        self.commander_cls = commander_cls
        self.scout_cls = scout_cls
        self.scouting = False
        self.peers = peers
```

The spawn_scout method (and similarly, spawn_commander) creates the new role object with self.scout_cls:

```
class Leader(Role):
    def spawn_scout(self):
        assert not self.scouting
        self.scouting = True
        self.scout_cls(self.node, self.ballot_num, self.peers).start()
```

The magic of this technique is that, in testing, Leader can be given fake classes and thus tested separately from Scout and Commander.

Interface Correctness

One pitfall of a focus on small units is that it does not test the interfaces between units. For example, unit tests for the acceptor role verify the format of the accepted attribute of the Promise message, and the unit tests for the scout role supply well-formatted values for the attribute. Neither test checks that those formats match.

One approach to fixing this issue is to make the interfaces self-enforcing. In Cluster, the use of named tuples and keyword arguments avoids any disagreement over messages' attributes. Because the only interaction between role classes is via messages, this covers a large part of the interface.

For specific issues such as the format of accepted_proposals, both the real and test data can be verified using the same function, in this case verifyPromiseAccepted. The tests for the acceptor use this method to verify each returned Promise, and the tests for the scout use it to verify every fake Promise.

Integration Testing

The final bulwark against interface problems and design errors is integration testing. An integration test assembles multiple units together and tests their combined effect. In our case, that means building a network of several nodes, injecting some requests into it, and verifying the results. If there are any interface issues not discovered in unit testing, they should cause the integration tests to fail quickly.

Because the protocol is intended to handle node failure gracefully, we test a few failure scenarios as well, including the untimely failure of the active leader.

Integration tests are harder to write than unit tests, because they are less well-isolated. For Cluster, this is clearest in testing the failed leader, as any node could be the active leader. Even with a deterministic network, a change in one message alters the random number generator's state and thus unpredictably changes later events. Rather than hard-coding the expected leader, the test code must dig into the internal state of each leader to find one that believes itself to be active.

Fuzz Testing

It's very difficult to test resilient code: it is likely to be resilient to its own bugs, so integration tests may not detect even very serious bugs. It is also hard to imagine and construct tests for every possible failure mode.

A common approach to this sort of problem is "fuzz testing": running the code repeatedly with randomly changing inputs until something breaks. When something *does* break, all of the debugging support becomes critical: if the failure can't be reproduced, and the logging information isn't sufficient to find the bug, then you can't fix it!

I performed some manual fuzz testing of cluster during development, but a full fuzz-testing infrastructure is beyond the scope of this project.

3.9   Power Struggles

A cluster with many active leaders is a very noisy place, with scouts sending ever-increasing ballot numbers to acceptors, and no ballots being decided. A cluster with no active leader is quiet, but equally nonfunctional. Balancing the implementation so that a cluster almost always agrees on exactly one leader is remarkably difficult.

It's easy enough to avoid fighting leaders: when preempted, a leader just accepts its new inactive status. However, this easily leads to a case where there are no active leaders, so an inactive leader will try to become active every time it gets a `Propose` message.

If the whole cluster doesn't agree on which member is the active leader, there's trouble: different replicas send `Propose` messages to different leaders, leading to battling scouts. So it's important that leader elections be decided quickly, and that all cluster members find out about the result as quickly as possible.

Cluster handles this by detecting a leader change as quickly as possible: when an acceptor sends a `Promise`, chances are good that the promised member will be the next leader. Failures are detected with a heartbeat protocol.

3.10   Further Extensions

Of course, there are plenty of ways we could extend and improve this implementation.

Catching Up

In "pure" Multi-Paxos, nodes which fail to receive messages can be many slots behind the rest of the cluster. As long as the state of the distributed state machine is never accessed except via state machine transitions, this design is functional. To read from the state, the client requests a state-machine transition that does not actually alter the state, but which returns the desired value. This transition is executed cluster-wide, ensuring that it returns the same value everywhere, based on the state at the slot in which it is proposed.

Even in the optimal case, this is slow, requiring several round trips just to read a value. If a distributed object store made such a request for every object access, its performance would be dismal. But when the node receiving the request is lagging behind, the request delay is much greater as that node must catch up to the rest of the cluster before making a successful proposal.

A simple solution is to implement a gossip-style protocol, where each replica periodically contacts other replicas to share the highest slot it knows about and to request information on unknown slots. Then even when a `Decision` message was lost, the replica would quickly find out about the decision from one of its peers.

Consistent Memory Usage

A cluster-management library provides reliability in the presence of unreliable components. It shouldn't add unreliability of its own. Unfortunately, Cluster will not run for long without failing due to ever-growing memory use and message size.

In the protocol definition, acceptors and replicas form the "memory" of the protocol, so they need to remember everything. These classes never know when they will receive a request for an old slot, perhaps from a lagging replica or leader. To maintain correctness, then, they keep a list of every decision, ever, since the cluster was started. Worse, these decisions are transmitted between replicas in `Welcome` messages, making these messages enormous in a long-lived cluster.

One technique to address this issue is to periodically "checkpoint" each node's state, keeping information about some limited number of decisions on hand. Nodes which are so out of date that they have not committed all slots up to the checkpoint must "reset" themselves by leaving and re-joining the cluster.

Persistent Storage

While it's OK for a minority of cluster members to fail, it's not OK for an acceptor to "forget" any of the values it has accepted or promises it has made.

Unfortunately, this is exactly what happens when a cluster member fails and restarts: the newly initialized Acceptor instance has no record of the promises its predecessor made. The problem is that the newly-started instance takes the place of the old.

There are two ways to solve this issue. The simpler solution involves writing acceptor state to disk and re-reading that state on startup. The more complex solution is to remove failed cluster members from the cluster, and require that new members be added to the cluster. This kind of dynamic adjustment of the cluster membership is called a "view change".

View Changes

Operations engineers need to be able to resize clusters to meet load and availability requirements. A simple test project might begin with a minimal cluster of three nodes, where any one can fail without impact. When that project goes "live", though, the additional load will require a larger cluster.

Cluster, as written, cannot change the set of peers in a cluster without restarting the entire cluster. Ideally, the cluster would be able to maintain a consensus about its membership, just as it does about state machine transitions. This means that the set of cluster members (the *view*) can be changed by special view-change proposals. But the Paxos algorithm depends on universal agreement about the members in the cluster, so we must define the view for each slot.

Lamport addresses this challenge in the final paragraph of "Paxos Made Simple":

> We can allow a leader to get α commands ahead by letting the set of servers that execute instance $i + \alpha$ of the consensus algorithm be specified by the state after execution of the ith state machine command. (Lamport, 2001)

The idea is that each instance of Paxos (slot) uses the view from α slots earlier. This allows the cluster to work on, at most, α slots at any one time, so a very small value of α limits concurrency, while a very large value of α makes view changes slow to take effect.

In early drafts of this implementation (dutifully preserved in the git history!), I implemented support for view changes (using α in place of 3). This seemingly simple change introduced a great deal of complexity:

- tracking the view for each of the last α committed slots and correctly sharing this with new nodes,
- ignoring proposals for which no slot is available,
- detecting failed nodes,
- properly serializing multiple competing view changes, and
- communicating view information between the leader and replica.

The result was far too large for this book!

3.11 References

In addition to the original Paxos paper and Lamport's follow-up "Paxos Made Simple"[3], our implementation added extensions that were informed by several other resources. The role names were taken from "Paxos Made Moderately Complex"[4]. "Paxos Made Live"[5] was helpful regarding snapshots in particular, and "Paxos Made Practical"[6] described view changes (although not of the type described here.) Liskov's "From Viewstamped Replication to Byzantine Fault Tolerance"[7] provided yet another perspective on view changes. Finally, a Stack Overflow discussion[8] was helpful in learning how members are added and removed from the system.

---

[3]L. Lamport, "Paxos Made Simple," ACM SIGACT News (Distributed Computing Column) 32, 4 (Whole Number 121, December 2001) 51-58.

[4]R. Van Renesse and D. Altinbuken, "Paxos Made Moderately Complex," ACM Comp. Survey 47, 3, Article 42 (Feb. 2015)

[5]T. Chandra, R. Griesemer, and J. Redstone, "Paxos Made Live - An Engineering Perspective," Proceedings of the twenty-sixth annual ACM symposium on Principles of distributed computing (PODC '07). ACM, New York, NY, USA, 398-407.

[6]http://www.scs.stanford.edu/~dm/home/papers/paxos.pdf

[7]B. Liskov, "From Viewstamped Replication to Byzantine Fault Tolerance," In *Replication*, Springer-Verlag, Berlin, Heidelberg 121-149 (2010)

[8]http://stackoverflow.com/questions/21353312/in-part-time-parliament-why-does-using-the-membership-from-decree-n-3-work-to

## chapter 4

Contingent: A Fully Dynamic Build System
Brandon Rhodes and Daniel Rocco

4.1   Introduction

Build systems have long been a standard tool within computer programming.

The standard make build system, for which its author won the ACM Software System Award, was first developed in 1976. It not only lets you declare that an output file depends upon one (or more) inputs, but lets you do this recursively. A program, for example, might depend upon an object file which itself depends upon the corresponding source code:

```
prog: main.o
        cc -o prog main.o

main.o: main.c
        cc -C -o main.o main.c
```

Should make discover, upon its next invocation, that the main.c source code file now has a more recent modify time than main.o, then it will not only rebuild the main.o object file but will also rebuild prog itself.

Build systems are a common semester project assigned to undergraduate computer science students — not only because build systems are used in nearly all software projects, but because their construction involves fundamental data structures and algorithms involving directed graphs (which this chapter will later discuss in more detail).

With decades of use and practice behind build systems, one might expect them to have become completely general-purpose and ready for even the most extravagant demands. But, in fact, one kind of common interaction between build artifacts — the problem of dynamic cross-referencing — is handled so poorly by most build systems that in this chapter we are inspired to not only rehearse the classic solution and data structures used to solve the make problem, but to extend that solution dramatically, to a far more demanding domain.

The problem, again, is cross-referencing. Where do cross-references tend to emerge? In text documents, documentation, and printed books!

4.2   The Problem: Building Document Systems

Systems to rebuild formatted documents from source always seem to do too much work, or too little.

They do too much work when they respond to a minor edit by making you wait for unrelated chapters to be re-parsed and re-formatted. But they can also rebuild too little, leaving you with an inconsistent final product.

Consider Sphinx[1], the document builder that is used for both the official Python language documentation and many other projects in the Python community. A Sphinx project's `index.rst` will usually include a table of contents:

```
Table of Contents
=================

.. toctree::

   install.rst
   tutorial.rst
   api.rst
```

This list of chapter filenames tells Sphinx to include a link to each of the three named chapters when it builds the `index.html` output file. It will also include links to any sections within each chapter. Stripped of its markup, the text that results from the above title and `toctree` command might be:

```
Table of Contents

• Installation

• Newcomers Tutorial
    • Hello, World
    • Adding Logging

• API Reference
    • Handy Functions
    • Obscure Classes
```

This table of contents, as you can see, is a mash-up of information from four different files. While its basic order and structure come from `index.rst`, the actual titles of each chapter and section are pulled from the three chapter source files themselves.

If you later reconsider the tutorial's chapter title — after all, the word "newcomer" sounds so quaint, as if your users are settlers who have just arrived in pioneer Wyoming — then you would edit the first line of `tutorial.rst` and write something better:

```
-Newcomers Tutorial
+Beginners Tutorial
 ==================

 Welcome to the tutorial!
 This text will take you through the basics of...
```

---
[1]http://sphinx-doc.org/

When you are ready to rebuild, Sphinx will do exactly the right thing! It will rebuild both the tutorial chapter itself, and the index. (Piping the output into `cat` makes Sphinx announce each rebuilt file on a separate line, instead of using bare carriage returns to repeatedly overwrite a single line with these progress updates.)

```
$ make html | cat
writing output... [ 50%] index
writing output... [100%] tutorial
```

Because Sphinx chose to rebuild both documents, not only will `tutorial.html` now feature its new title up at the top, but the output `index.html` will display the updated chapter title in the table of contents. Sphinx has rebuilt everything so that the output is consistent.

What if your edit to `tutorial.rst` is more minor?

```
Beginners Tutorial
==================


-Welcome to the tutorial!
+Welcome to our project tutorial!
This text will take you through the basics of...
```

In this case there is no need to rebuild `index.html` because this minor edit to the interior of a paragraph does not change any of the information in the table of contents. But it turns out that Sphinx is not quite as clever as it might have at first appeared! It will go ahead and perform the redundant work of rebuilding `index.html` even though the resulting contents will be exactly the same.

```
writing output... [ 50%] index
writing output... [100%] tutorial
```

You can run `diff` on the "before" and "after" versions of `index.html` to confirm that your small edit has had no effect on the front page — yet Sphinx made you wait while it was rebuilt anyway.

You might not even notice the extra rebuild effort for small documents that are easy to compile. But the delay to your workflow can become significant when you are making frequent tweaks and edits to documents that are long, complex, or that involve the generation of multimedia like plots or animations. While Sphinx is at least making an effort not to rebuild every chapter when you make a single change — it has not, for example, rebuilt `install.html` or `api.html` in response to your `tutorial.rst` edit — it is doing more than is necessary.

But it turns out that Sphinx does something even worse: it sometimes does too little, leaving you with inconsistent output that could be noticed by users.

To see one of its simplest failures, first add a cross reference to the top of your API documentation:

```
API Reference
=============

+Before reading this, try reading our :doc:'tutorial'!
+
The sections below list every function
and every single class and method offered...
```

With its usual caution as regards the table of contents, Sphinx will dutifully rebuild both this API reference document as well as the `index.html` home page of your project:

```
writing output... [ 50%] api
writing output... [100%] index
```

In the `api.html` output file you can confirm that Sphinx has included the attractive human-readable title of the tutorial chapter into the cross reference's anchor tag:

```
<p>Before reading this, try reading our
<a class="reference internal" href="tutorial.html">
  <em>Beginners Tutorial</em>
</a>!</p>
```

What if you now make another edit to the title at the top of the `tutorial.rst` file? You will have invalidated *three* output files:

1. The title at the top of `tutorial.html` is now out of date, so the file needs to be rebuilt.
2. The table of contents in `index.html` still has the old title, so that document needs to be rebuilt.
3. The embedded cross reference in the first paragraph of `api.html` still has the old chapter title, and also needs to be rebuilt.

What does Sphinx do?

```
writing output... [ 50%] index
writing output... [100%] tutorial
```

Whoops.

Only two files were rebuilt, not three. Sphinx has failed to correctly rebuild your documentation.

If you now push your HTML to the web, users will see the old title in the cross reference at the top of `api.html` but then a different title — the new one — once the link has carried them to `tutorial.html` itself. This can happen for many kinds of cross reference that Sphinx supports: chapter titles, section titles, paragraphs, classes, methods, and functions.

4.3   Build Systems and Consistency

The problem outlined above is not specific to Sphinx. Not only does it haunt other document systems, like LaTeX, but it can even plague projects that are simply trying to direct compilation steps with the venerable make utility, if their assets happen to cross-reference in interesting ways.

As the problem is ancient and universal, its solution is of equally long lineage:

```
$ rm -r _build/
$ make html
```

If you remove all of the output, you are guaranteed a complete rebuild! Some projects even alias `rm -r` to a target named `clean` so that only a quick `make clean` is necessary to wipe the slate.

By eliminating every copy of every intermediate or output asset, a hefty `rm -r` is able to force the build to start over again with nothing cached — with no memory of its earlier state that could possibly lead to a stale product.

But could we develop a better approach?

What if your build system were a persistent process that noticed every chapter title, every section title, and every cross-referenced phrase as it passed from the source code of one document into the text of another? Its decisions about whether to rebuild other documents after a change to a single source file could be precise, instead of mere guesses, and correct, instead of leaving the output in an inconsistent state.

The result would be a system like the old static make tool, but which learned the dependencies between files as they were built — that added and removed dependencies dynamically as cross references were added, updated, and deleted.

In the sections that follow we will construct such a tool, named Contingent, in Python. Contingent guarantees correctness in the presence of dynamic dependencies while performing the fewest possible rebuild steps. While it can be applied to any problem domain, we will run it against a small version of the problem outlined above.

4.4   Linking Tasks to Make a Graph

Any build system needs a way to link inputs and outputs. The three markup texts in our discussion above, for example, each produce a corresponding HTML output file. The most natural way to express these relationships is as a collection of boxes and arrows — or, in mathematical terminology, *nodes* and *edges* — to form a *graph* (Figure 4.1).

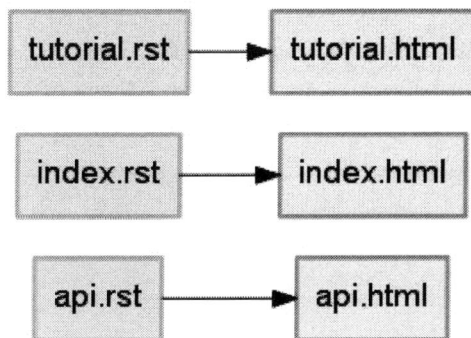

Figure 4.1: Three files generated by parsing three input texts.

Each language in which a programmer might tackle writing a build system will offer various data structures with which such a graph of nodes and edges might be represented.

How could we represent such a graph in Python?

The Python language gives priority to four generic data structures by giving them direct support in the language syntax. You can create new instances of these big-four data structures by simply typing their literal representation into your source code, and their four type objects are available as built-in symbols that can be used without being imported.

The **tuple** is a read-only sequence used to hold heterogeneous data — each slot in a tuple typically means something different. Here, a tuple holds together a hostname and port number, and would lose its meaning if the elements were re-ordered:

```
('dropbox.com', 443)
```

The **list** is a mutable sequence used to hold homogenous data — each item usually has the same structure and meaning as its peers. Lists can be used either to preserve data's original input order, or can be rearranged or sorted to establish a new and more useful order.

```
['C', 'Awk', 'TCL', 'Python', 'JavaScript']
```

The **set** does not preserve order. Sets remember only whether a given value has been added, not how many times, and are therefore the go-to data structure for removing duplicates from a data stream. For example, the following two sets will each have three elements:

```
{3, 4, 5}
{3, 4, 5, 4, 4, 3, 5, 4, 5, 3, 4, 5}
```

The **dict** is an associative data structure for storing values accessible by a key. Dicts let the programmer chose the key by which each value is indexed, instead of using automatic integer indexing as the tuple and list do. The lookup is backed by a hash table, which means that dict key lookup runs at the same speed whether the dict has a dozen or a million keys.

```
{'ssh': 22, 'telnet': 23, 'domain': 53, 'http': 80}
```

A key to Python's flexibility is that these four data structures are composable. The programmer can arbitrarily nest them inside each other to produce more complex data stores whose rules and syntax remain the simple ones of the underlying tuples, lists, sets, and dicts.

Given that each of our graph edges needs to know at least its origin node and its destination node, the simplest possible representation would be a tuple. The top edge in Figure 4.1 might look like:

```
('tutorial.rst', 'tutorial.html')
```

How can we store several edges? While our initial impulse might be to simply throw all of our edge tuples into a list, that would have disadvantages. A list is careful to maintain order, but it is not meaningful to talk about an absolute order for the edges in a graph. And a list would be perfectly happy to hold several copies of exactly the same edge, even though we only want it to be possible to draw a single arrow between `tutorial.rst` and `tutorial.html`. The correct choice is thus the set, which would have us represent Figure 4.1 as:

```
{('tutorial.rst', 'tutorial.html'),
 ('index.rst', 'index.html'),
 ('api.rst', 'api.html')}
```

This would allow quick iteration across all of our edges, fast insert and delete operations for a single edge, and a quick way to check whether a particular edge was present.

Unfortunately, those are not the only operations we need.

A build system like Contingent needs to understand the relationship between a given node and all the nodes connected to it. For example, when `api.rst` changes, Contingent needs to know which assets, if any, are affected by that change in order to minimize the work performed while also ensuring a complete build. To answer this question — "what nodes are downstream from `api.rst`?" — we need to examine the *outgoing* edges from `api.rst`.

But building the dependency graph requires that Contingent be concerned with a node's *inputs* as well. What inputs were used, for example, when the build system assembled the output document `tutorial.html`? It is by watching the input to each node that Contingent can know that `api.html` depends on `api.rst` but that `tutorial.html` does not. As sources change and rebuilds occur, Contingent rebuilds the incoming edges of each changed node to remove potentially stale edges and re-learn which resources a task uses this time around.

Our set-of-tuples does not make answering either of these questions easy. If we needed to know the relationship between api.html and the rest of the graph, we would need to traverse the entire set looking for edges that start or end at the api.html node.

An associative data structure like Python's dict would make these chores easier by allowing direct lookup of all the edges from a particular node:

```
{'tutorial.rst': {('tutorial.rst', 'tutorial.html')},
 'tutorial.html': {('tutorial.rst', 'tutorial.html')},
 'index.rst': {('index.rst', 'index.html')},
 'index.html': {('index.rst', 'index.html')},
 'api.rst': {('api.rst', 'api.html')},
 'api.html': {('api.rst', 'api.html')}}
```

Looking up the edges of a particular node would now be blazingly fast, at the cost of having to store every edge twice: once in a set of incoming edges, and once in a set of outgoing edges. But the edges in each set would have to be examined manually to see which are incoming and which are outgoing. It is also slightly redundant to keep naming the node over and over again in its set of edges.

The solution to both of these objections is to place incoming and outgoing edges in their own separate data structures, which will also absolve us of having to mention the node over and over again for every one of the edges in which it is involved.

```
incoming = {
    'tutorial.html': {'tutorial.rst'},
    'index.html': {'index.rst'},
    'api.html': {'api.rst'},
    }

outgoing = {
    'tutorial.rst': {'tutorial.html'},
    'index.rst': {'index.html'},
    'api.rst': {'api.html'},
    }
```

Notice that outgoing represents, directly in Python syntax, exactly what we drew in Figure 4.1 earlier: the source documents on the left will be transformed by the build system into the output documents on the right. For this simple example each source points to only one output — all the output sets have only one element — but we will see examples shortly where a single input node has multiple downstream consequences.

Every edge in this dictionary-of-sets data structure does get represented twice, once as an outgoing edge from one node (tutorial.rst → tutorial.html) and again as an incoming edge to the other (tutorial.html ← tutorial.rst). These two representations capture precisely the same relationship, just from the opposite perspectives of the two nodes at either end of the edge. But in return for this redundancy, the data structure supports the fast lookup that Contingent needs.

4.5   The Proper Use of Classes

You may have been surprised by the absence of classes in the above discussion of Python data structures. After all, classes are a frequent mechanism for structuring applications and a hardly less-frequent subject of heated debate among their adherents and detractors. Classes were once thought important enough that entire educational curricula were designed around them, and the majority of popular programming languages include dedicated syntax for defining and using them.

But it turns out that classes are often orthogonal to the question of data structure design. Rather than offering us an entirely alternative data modeling paradigm, classes simply repeat data structures that we have already seen:

- A class instance is *implemented* as a dict.
- A class instance is *used* like a mutable tuple.

The class offers key lookup through a prettier syntax, where you get to say `graph.incoming` instead of `graph["incoming"]`. But, in practice, class instances are almost never used as generic key-value stores. Instead, they are used to organize related but heterogeneous data by attribute name, with implementation details encapsulated behind a consistent and memorable interface.

So instead of putting a hostname and a port number together in a tuple and having to remember which came first and which came second, you create an `Address` class whose instances each have a `host` and a `port` attribute. You can then pass `Address` objects around where otherwise you would have had anonymous tuples. Code becomes easier to read and easier to write. But using a class instance does not really change any of the questions we faced above when doing data design; it just provides a prettier and less anonymous container.

The true value of classes, then, is not that they change the science of data design. The value of classes is that they let you *hide* your data design from the rest of a program!

Successful application design hinges upon our ability to exploit the powerful built-in data structures Python offers us while minimizing the volume of details we are required to keep in our heads at any one time. Classes provide the mechanism for resolving this apparent quandary: used effectively, a class provides a facade around some small subset of the system's overall design. When working within one subset — a Graph, for example — we can forget the implementation details of other subsets as long as we can remember their interfaces. In this way, programmers often find themselves navigating among several levels of abstraction in the course of writing a system, now working with the specific data model and implementation details for a particular subsystem, now connecting higher-level concepts through their interfaces.

For example, from the outside, code can simply ask for a new Graph instance:

```
>>> from contingent import graphlib
>>> g = graphlib.Graph()
```

without needing to understand the details of how Graph works. Code that is simply using the graph sees only interface verbs — the method calls — when manipulating a graph, as when an edge is added or some other operation performed:

```
>>> g.add_edge('index.rst', 'index.html')
>>> g.add_edge('tutorial.rst', 'tutorial.html')
>>> g.add_edge('api.rst', 'api.html')
```

Careful readers will have noticed that we added edges to our graph without explicitly creating "node" and "edge" objects, and that the nodes themselves in these early examples are simply strings. Coming from other languages and traditions, one might have expected to see user-defined classes and interfaces for everything in the system:

```
Graph g = new ConcreteGraph();
Node indexRstNode = new StringNode("index.rst");
```

```
Node indexHtmlNode = new StringNode("index.html");
Edge indexEdge = new DirectedEdge(indexRstNode, indexHtmlNode);
g.addEdge(indexEdge);
```

The Python language and community explicitly and intentionally emphasize using simple, generic data structures to solve problems, instead of creating custom classes for every minute detail of the problem we want to tackle. This is one facet of the notion of "Pythonic" solutions: Pythonic solutions try to minimize syntactic overhead and leverage Python's powerful built-in tools and extensive standard library.

With these considerations in mind, let's return to the Graph class, examining its design and implementation to see the interplay between data structures and class interfaces. When a new Graph instance is constructed, a pair of dictionaries has already been built to store edges using the logic we outlined in the previous section:

```
class Graph:
    """A directed graph of the relationships among build tasks."""

    def __init__(self):
        self._inputs_of = defaultdict(set)
        self._consequences_of = defaultdict(set)
```

The leading underscore in front of the attribute names _inputs_of and _consequences_of is a common convention in the Python community to signal that an attribute is private. This convention is one way the community suggests that programmers pass messages and warnings through space and time to each other. Recognizing the need to signal differences between public and internal object attributes, the community adopted the single leading underscore as a concise and fairly consistent indicator to other programmers, including our future selves, that the attribute is best treated as part of the invisible internal machinery of the class.

Why are we using a defaultdict instead of a standard dict? A common problem when composing dicts with other data structures is handling missing keys. With a normal dict, retrieving a key that does not exist raises a KeyError:

```
>>> consequences_of = {}
>>> consequences_of['index.rst'].add('index.html')
Traceback (most recent call last):
  ...
KeyError: 'index.rst'
```

Using a normal dict requires special checks throughout the code to handle this specific case, for example when adding a new edge:

```
# Special case to handle "we have not seen this task yet":

if input_task not in self._consequences_of:
    self._consequences_of[input_task] = set()

self._consequences_of[input_task].add(consequence_task)
```

This need is so common that Python includes a special utility, the defaultdict, which lets you provide a function that returns a value for absent keys. When we ask about an edge that the Graph hasn't yet seen, we will get back an empty set instead of an exception:

```
>>> from collections import defaultdict
>>> consequences_of = defaultdict(set)
>>> consequences_of['api.rst']
set()
```

Structuring our implementation this way means that each key's first use can look identical to second and subsequent times that a particular key is used:

```
>>> consequences_of['index.rst'].add('index.html')
>>> 'index.html' in consequences_of['index.rst']
True
```

Given these techniques, let's examine the implementation of add_edge, which we earlier used to build the graph for Figure 4.1.

```
def add_edge(self, input_task, consequence_task):
    """Add an edge: 'consequence_task' uses the output of 'input_task'."""
    self._consequences_of[input_task].add(consequence_task)
    self._inputs_of[consequence_task].add(input_task)
```

This method hides the fact that two, not one, storage steps are required for each new edge so that we know about it in both directions. And notice how add_edge() does not know or care whether either node has been seen before. Because the inputs and consequences data structures are each a defaultdict(set), the add_edge() method remains blissfully ignorant as to the novelty of a node — the defaultdict takes care of the difference by creating a new set object on the fly. As we saw above, add_edge() would be three times longer had we not used defaultdict. More importantly, it would be more difficult to understand and reason about the resulting code. This implementation demonstrates a Pythonic approach to problems: simple, direct, and concise.

Callers should also be given a simple way to visit every edge without having to learn how to traverse our data structure:

```
def edges(self):
    """Return all edges as ''(input_task, consequence_task)'' tuples."""
    return [(a, b) for a in self.sorted(self._consequences_of)
                   for b in self.sorted(self._consequences_of[a])]
```

The Graph.sorted() method makes an attempt to sort the nodes in a natural sort order (such as alphabetical) that can provide a stable output order for the user.

By using this traversal method we can see that, following our three "add" method calls earlier, g now represents the same graph that we saw in Figure 4.1.

```
>>> from pprint import pprint
>>> pprint(g.edges())
[('api.rst', 'api.html'),
 ('index.rst', 'index.html'),
 ('tutorial.rst', 'tutorial.html')]
```

Since we now have a real live Python object, and not just a figure, we can ask it interesting questions! For example, when Contingent is building a blog from source files, it will need to know things like "What depends on api.rst?" when the content of api.rst changes:

```
>>> g.immediate_consequences_of('api.rst')
['api.html']
```

This Graph is telling Contingent that, when api.rst changes, api.html is now stale and must
be rebuilt.

How about index.html?

```
>>> g.immediate_consequences_of('index.html')
[]
```

An empty list has been returned, signalling that index.html is at the right edge of the graph and
so nothing further needs to be rebuilt if it changes. This query can be expressed very simply thanks
to the work that has already gone in to laying out our data:

```
def immediate_consequences_of(self, task):
    """Return the tasks that use 'task' as an input."""
    return self.sorted(self._consequences_of[task])
```

```
>>> from contingent.rendering import as_graphviz
>>> open('figure1.dot', 'w').write(as_graphviz(g)) and None
```

Figure 4.1 ignored one of the most important relationships that we discovered in the opening
section of our chapter: the way that document titles appear in the table of contents. Let's fill in this
detail. We will create a node for each title string that needs to be generated by parsing an input file
and then passed to one of our other routines:

```
>>> g.add_edge('api.rst', 'api-title')
>>> g.add_edge('api-title', 'index.html')
>>> g.add_edge('tutorial.rst', 'tutorial-title')
>>> g.add_edge('tutorial-title', 'index.html')
```

The result is a graph (Figure 4.2) that could properly handle rebuilding the table of contents that
we discussed in the opening of this chapter.

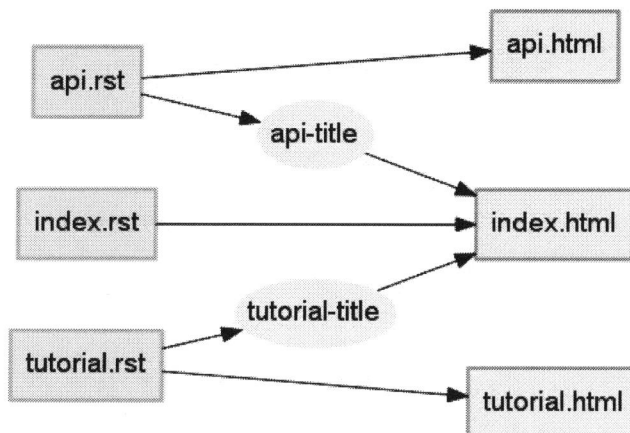

Figure 4.2: Being prepared to rebuild 'index.html' whenever any title that it mentions gets changed.

This manual walk-through illustrates what we will eventually have Contingent do for us: the
graph g captures the inputs and consequences for the various artifacts in our project's documentation.

4.6   Learning Connections

We now have a way for Contingent to keep track of tasks and the relationships between them. If we look more closely at Figure 4.2, however, we see that it is actually a little hand-wavy and vague: *how* is api.html produced from api.rst? How do we know that index.html needs the title from the tutorial? And how is this dependency resolved?

Our intuitive notion of these ideas served when we were constructing consequences graphs by hand, but unfortunately computers are not terribly intuitive, so we will need to be more precise about what we want.

What are the steps required to produce output from sources? How are these steps defined and executed? And how can Contingent know the connections between them?

In Contingent, build tasks are modeled as functions plus arguments. The functions define actions that a particular project understands how to perform. The arguments provide the specifics: *which* source document should be read, *which* blog title is needed. As they are running, these functions may in turn invoke *other* task functions, passing whatever arguments they need answers for.

To see how this works, we will actually now implement the documentation builder described at the beginning of the chapter. In order to prevent ourselves from wallowing around in a bog of details, for this illustration we will work with simplified input and output document formats. Our input documents will consist of a title on the first line, with the remainder of the text forming the body. Cross references will simply be source file names enclosed in backticks, which on output are replaced with the title from the corresponding document in the output.

Here is the content of our example index.txt, api.txt, and tutorial.txt, illustrating titles, document bodies, and cross-references from our little document format:

```
>>> index = """
... Table of Contents
... -----------------
... * 'tutorial.txt'
... * 'api.txt'
... """

>>> tutorial = """
... Beginners Tutorial
... ------------------
... Welcome to the tutorial!
... We hope you enjoy it.
... """

>>> api = """
... API Reference
... -------------
... You might want to read
... the 'tutorial.txt' first.
... """
```

Now that we have some source material to work with, what functions would a Contingent-based blog builder need?

In the simple examples above, the HTML output files proceed directly from the source, but in a realistic system, turning source into markup involves several steps: reading the raw text from disk, parsing the text to a convenient internal representation, processing any directives the author may have specified, resolving cross-references or other external dependencies (such as include files), and applying one or more view transformations to convert the internal representation to its output form.

Contingent manages tasks by grouping them into a `Project`, a sort of build system busybody that injects itself into the middle of the build process, noting every time one task talks to another to construct a graph of the relationships between all the tasks.

```
>>> from contingent.projectlib import Project, Task
>>> project = Project()
>>> task = project.task
```

A build system for the example given at the beginning of the chapter might involve a few tasks. Our `read()` task will pretend to read the files from disk. Since we really defined the source text in variables, all it needs to do is convert from a filename to the corresponding text.

```
>>> filesystem = {'index.txt': index,
...                'tutorial.txt': tutorial,
...                'api.txt': api}
...
>>> @task
... def read(filename):
...     return filesystem[filename]
```

The `parse()` task interprets the raw text of the file contents according to the specification of our document format. Our format is very simple: the title of the document appears on the first line, and the rest of the content is considered the document's body.

```
>>> @task
... def parse(filename):
...     lines = read(filename).strip().splitlines()
...     title = lines[0]
...     body = '\n'.join(lines[2:])
...     return title, body
```

Because the format is so simple, the parser is a little silly, but it illustrates the interpretive responsibilities that parsers are required to carry out. (Parsing in general is a very interesting subject and many books have been written either partially or completely about it.) In a system like Sphinx, the parser must understand the many markup tokens, directives, and commands defined by the system, transforming the input text into something the rest of the system can work with.

Notice the connection point between `parse()` and `read()` — the first task in parsing is to pass the filename it has been given to `read()`, which finds and returns the contents of that file.

The `title_of()` task, given a source file name, returns the document's title:

```
>>> @task
... def title_of(filename):
...     title, body = parse(filename)
...     return title
```

This task nicely illustrates the separation of responsibilities between the parts of a document processing system. The `title_of()` function works directly from an in-memory representation of a document — in this case, a tuple — instead of taking it upon itself to re-parse the entire document again just to find the title. The `parse()` function alone produces the in-memory representation, in accordance with the contract of the system specification, and the rest of the blog builder processing functions like `title_of()` simply use its output as their authority.

If you are coming from an orthodox object-oriented tradition, this function-oriented design may look a little weird. In an OO solution, `parse()` would return some sort of Document object that has `title_of()` as a method or property. In fact, Sphinx works exactly this way: its Parser subsystem produces a "Docutils document tree" object for the other parts of the system to use.

Contingent is not opinionated with regard to these differing design paradigms and supports either approach equally well. For this chapter we are keeping things simple.

The final task, `render()`, turns the in-memory representation of a document into an output form. It is, in effect, the inverse of `parse()`. Whereas `parse()` takes an input document conforming to a specification and converts it to an in-memory representation, `render()` takes an in-memory representation and produces an output document conforming to some specification.

```
>>> import re
>>>
>>> LINK = '<a href="{}">{}</a>'
>>> PAGE = '<h1>{}</h1>\n<p>\n{}\n<p>'
>>>
>>> def make_link(match):
...     filename = match.group(1)
...     return LINK.format(filename, title_of(filename))
...
>>> @task
... def render(filename):
...     title, body = parse(filename)
...     body = re.sub(r'`([^`]+)`', make_link, body)
...     return PAGE.format(title, body)
```

Here is an example run that will invoke every stage of the above logic — rendering `tutorial.txt` to produce its output:

```
>>> print(render('tutorial.txt'))
<h1>Beginners Tutorial</h1>
<p>
Welcome to the tutorial!
We hope you enjoy it.
<p>
```

Figure 4.3 illustrates the task graph that transitively connects all the tasks required to produce the output, from reading the input file, to parsing and transforming the document, and rendering it:

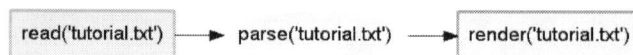

Figure 4.3: A task graph.

It turns out that Figure 4.3 was not hand-drawn for this chapter, but has been generated directly from Contingent! Building this graph is possible for the Project object because it maintains its own call stack, similar to the stack of live execution frames that Python maintains to remember which function to continue running when the current one returns.

Every time a new task is invoked, Contingent can assume that it has been called — and that its output will be used — by the task currently at the top of the stack. Maintaining the stack will require that several extra steps surround the invocation of a task T:

1. Push T onto the stack.
2. Execute T, letting it call any other tasks it needs.
3. Pop T off the stack.
4. Return its result.

To intercept task calls, the `Project` leverages a key Python feature: *function decorators*. A decorator is allowed to process or transform a function at the moment that it is being defined. The `Project.task` decorator uses this opportunity to package every task inside another function, a *wrapper*, which allows a clean separation of responsibilities between the wrapper — which will worry about graph and stack management on behalf of the Project — and our task functions that focus on document processing. Here is what the `task` decorator boilerplate looks like:

```
from functools import wraps

def task(function):
    @wraps(function)
    def wrapper(*args):
        # wrapper body, that will call function()
    return wrapper
```

This is an entirely typical Python decorator declaration. It can then be applied to a function by naming it after an @ character atop the def that creates the function:

```
@task
def title_of(filename):
    title, body = parse(filename)
    return title
```

When this definition is complete, the name `title_of` will refer to the wrapped version of the function. The wrapper can access the original version of the function via the name `function`, calling it at the appropriate time. The body of the Contingent wrapper runs something like this:

```
def task(function):
    @wraps(function)
    def wrapper(*args):
        task = Task(wrapper, args)
        if self.task_stack:
            self._graph.add_edge(task, self.task_stack[-1])
        self._graph.clear_inputs_of(task)
        self._task_stack.append(task)
        try:
            value = function(*args)
        finally:
            self._task_stack.pop()

        return value
    return wrapper
```

This wrapper performs several crucial maintenance steps:

1. Packages the task — a function plus its arguments — into a small object for convenience. The wrapper here names the wrapped version of the task function.
2. If this task has been invoked by a current task that is already underway, add an edge capturing the fact that this task is an input to the already-running task.
3. Forget whatever we might have learned last time about the task, since it might make new decisions this time — if the source text of the API guide no longer mentions the Tutorial, for example, then its render() will no longer ask for the title_of() the Tutorial document.
4. Push this task onto the top of the task stack in case it decides, in its turn, to invoke further tasks in the course of doing its work.
5. Invoke the task inside of a try...finally block that ensures we correctly remove the finished task from the stack, even if it dies by raising an exception.
6. Return the task's return value, so that callers of this wrapper will not be able to tell that they have not simply invoked the plain task function itself.

Steps 4 and 5 maintain the task stack itself, which is then used by step 2 to perform the consequences tracking that is our whole reason for building a task stack in the first place.

Since each task gets surrounded by its own copy of the wrapper function, the mere invocation and execution of the normal stack of tasks will produce a graph of relationships as an invisible side effect. That is why we were careful to use the wrapper around each processing step that we defined:

```
@task
def read(filename):
    # body of read

@task
def parse(filename):
    # body of parse

@task
def title_of(filename):
    # body of title_of

@task
def render(filename):
    # body of render
```

Thanks to these wrappers, when we called parse('tutorial.txt') the decorator learned the connection between parse and read. We can ask about the relationship by building another Task tuple and asking what the consequences would be if its output value changed:

```
>>> task = Task(read, ('tutorial.txt',))
>>> print(task)
read('tutorial.txt')
>>> project._graph.immediate_consequences_of(task)
[parse('tutorial.txt')]
```

The consequence of re-reading the tutorial.txt file and finding that its contents have changed is that we need to re-execute the parse() routine for that document. What happens if we render the entire set of documents? Will Contingent be able to learn the entire build process?

```
>>> for filename in 'index.txt', 'tutorial.txt', 'api.txt':
...     print(render(filename))
...     print('=' * 30)
...
<h1>Table of Contents</h1>
<p>
* <a href="tutorial.txt">Beginners Tutorial</a>
* <a href="api.txt">API Reference</a>
<p>
==============================
<h1>Beginners Tutorial</h1>
<p>
Welcome to the tutorial!
We hope you enjoy it.
<p>
==============================
<h1>API Reference</h1>
<p>
You might want to read
the <a href="tutorial.txt">Beginners Tutorial</a> first.
<p>
==============================
```

It worked! From the output, we can see that our transform substituted the document titles for the directives in our source documents, indicating that Contingent was able to discover the connections between the various tasks needed to build our documents.

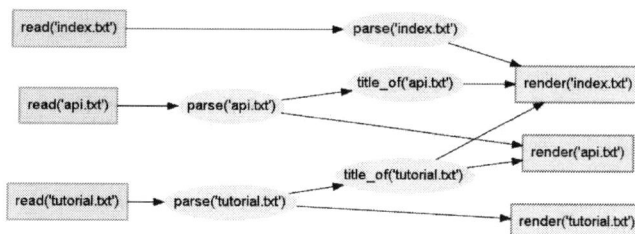

Figure 4.4: The complete set of relationships between our input files and our HTML outputs.

By watching one task invoke another through the `task` wrapper machinery, `Project` has automatically learned the graph of inputs and consequences. Since it has a complete consequences graph at its disposal, Contingent knows all the things to rebuild if the inputs to any tasks change.

4.7   Chasing Consequences

Once the initial build has run to completion, Contingent needs to monitor the input files for changes. When the user finishes a new edit and runs "Save", both the `read()` method and its consequences need to be invoked.

This will require us to walk the graph in the opposite order from the one in which it was created. It was built, you will recall, by calling `render()` for the API Reference and having that call `parse()` which finally invoked the `read()` task. Now we go in the other direction: we know that `read()` will now return new content, and we need to figure out what consequences lie downstream.

The process of compiling consequences is a recursive one, as each consequence can itself have further tasks that depended on it. We could perform this recursion manually through repeated calls to the graph. (Note that we are here taking advantage of the fact that the Python prompt saves the last value displayed under the name _ for use in the subsequent expression.)

```
>>> task = Task(read, ('api.txt',))
>>> project._graph.immediate_consequences_of(task)
[parse('api.txt')]
>>> t1, = _
>>> project._graph.immediate_consequences_of(t1)
[render('api.txt'), title_of('api.txt')]
>>> t2, t3 = _
>>> project._graph.immediate_consequences_of(t2)
[]
>>> project._graph.immediate_consequences_of(t3)
[render('index.txt')]
>>> t4, = _
>>> project._graph.immediate_consequences_of(t4)
[]
```

This recursive task of looking repeatedly for immediate consequences and only stopping when we arrive at tasks with no further consequences is a basic enough graph operation that it is supported directly by a method on the Graph class:

```
>>> # Secretly adjust pprint to a narrower-than-usual width:
>>> _pprint = pprint
>>> pprint = lambda x: _pprint(x, width=40)
>>> pprint(project._graph.recursive_consequences_of([task]))
[parse('api.txt'),
 render('api.txt'),
 title_of('api.txt'),
 render('index.txt')]
```

In fact, recursive_consequences_of() tries to be a bit clever. If a particular task appears repeatedly as a downstream consequence of several other tasks, then it is careful to only mention it once in the output list, and to move it close to the end so that it appears only after the tasks that are its inputs. This intelligence is powered by the classic depth-first implementation of a topological sort, an algorithm which winds up being fairly easy to write in Python through a hidden recursive helper function. Check out the graphlib.py source code for the details.

If, upon detecting a change, we are careful to re-run every task in the recursive consequences, then Contingent will be able to avoid rebuilding too little. Our second challenge, however, was to avoid rebuilding too much. Refer again to Figure 4.4. We want to avoid rebuilding all three documents every time that tutorial.txt is changed, since most edits will probably not affect its title but only its body. How can this be accomplished?

The solution is to make graph recomputation dependent on caching. When stepping forward through the recursive consequences of a change, we will only invoke tasks whose inputs are different than last time.

This optimization will involve a final data structure. We will give the Project a _todo set with which to remember every task for which at least one input value has changed, and which therefore requires re-execution. Because only tasks in `_todo` are out-of-date, the build process can skip running any tasks unless they appear there.

Again, Python's convenient and unified design makes these features very easy to code. Because task objects are hashable, `_todo` can simply be a set that remembers task items by identity — guaranteeing that a task never appears twice — and the `_cache` of return values from previous runs can be a dict with tasks as keys.

More precisely, the rebuild step must keep looping as long as `_todo` is non-empty. During each loop, it should:

- Call `recursive_consequences_of()` and pass in every task listed in `_todo`. The return value will be a list of not only the `_todo` tasks themselves, but also every task downstream of them — every task, in other words, that could possibly need re-execution if the outputs come out different this time.
- For each task in the list, check whether it is listed in `_todo`. If not, then we can skip running it, because none of the tasks that we have re-invoked upstream of it has produced a new return value that would require the task's recomputation.
- But for any task that is indeed listed in `_todo` by the time we reach it, we need to ask it to re-run and re-compute its return value. If the task wrapper function detects that this return value does not match the old cached value, then its downstream tasks will be automatically added to `_todo` before we reach them in the list of recursive consequences.

By the time we reach the end of the list, every task that could possibly need to be re-run should in fact have been re-run. But just in case, we will check `_todo` and try again if it is not yet empty. Even for very rapidly changing dependency trees, this should quickly settle out. Only a cycle — where, for example, task *A* needs the output of task *B* which itself needs the output of task *A* — could keep the builder in an infinite loop, and only if their return values never stabilize. Fortunately, real-world build tasks are typically without cycles.

Let us trace the behavior of this system through an example.

Suppose you edit `tutorial.txt` and change both the title and the body content. We can simulate this by modifying the value in our `filesystem` dict:

```
>>> filesystem['tutorial.txt'] = """
... The Coder Tutorial
... ------------------
... This is a new and improved
... introductory paragraph.
... """
```

Now that the contents have changed, we can ask the Project to re-run the `read()` task by using its `cache_off()` context manager that temporarily disables its willingness to return its old cached result for a given task and argument:

```
>>> with project.cache_off():
...     text = read('tutorial.txt')
```

The new tutorial text has now been read into the cache. How many downstream tasks will need to be re-executed?

To help us answer this question, the `Project` class supports a simple tracing facility that will tell us which tasks are executed in the course of a rebuild. Since the above change to `tutorial.txt` affects both its body and its title, everything downstream will need to be re-computed:

```
>>> project.start_tracing()
>>> project.rebuild()
>>> print(project.stop_tracing())
calling parse('tutorial.txt')
calling render('tutorial.txt')
calling title_of('tutorial.txt')
calling render('api.txt')
calling render('index.txt')
```

Looking back at Figure 4.4, you can see that, as expected, this is every task that is an immediate or downstream consequence of read('tutorial.txt').

But what if we edit it again, but this time leave the title the same?

```
>>> filesystem['tutorial.txt'] = """
... The Coder Tutorial
... ------------------
... Welcome to the coder tutorial!
... It should be read top to bottom.
... """
>>> with project.cache_off():
...     text = read('tutorial.txt')
```

This small, limited change should have no effect on the other documents.

```
>>> project.start_tracing()
>>> project.rebuild()
>>> print(project.stop_tracing())
calling parse('tutorial.txt')
calling render('tutorial.txt')
calling title_of('tutorial.txt')
```

Success! Only one document got rebuilt. The fact that title_of(), given a new input document, nevertheless returned the same value, means that all further downstream tasks were insulated from the change and did not get re-invoked.

4.8   Conclusion

There exist languages and programming methodologies under which Contingent would be a suffocating forest of tiny classes, with verbose names given to every concept in the problem domain.

When programming Contingent in Python, however, we skipped the creation of a dozen possible classes like TaskArgument and CachedResult and ConsequenceList. We instead drew upon Python's strong tradition of solving generic problems with generic data structures, resulting in code that repeatedly uses a small set of ideas from the core data structures tuple, list, set, and dict.

But does this not cause a problem?

Generic data structures are also, by their nature, anonymous. Our project._cache is a set. So is every collection of upstream and downstream nodes inside the Graph. Are we in danger of seeing generic set error messages and not knowing whether to look in the project or the graph implementation for the error?

In fact, we are not in danger!

Thanks to the careful discipline of encapsulation — of only allowing Graph code to touch the graph's sets, and Project code to touch the project's set — there will never be ambiguity if a set operation returns an error during a later phase of the project. The name of the innermost executing method at the moment of the error will necessarily direct us to exactly the class, and set, involved in the mistake. There is no need to create a subclass of set for every possible application of the data type, so long as we put that conventional underscore in front of data structure attributes and then are careful not to touch them from code outside of the class.

Contingent demonstrates how crucial the Facade pattern, from the epochal *Design Patterns* book, is for a well-designed Python program. Not every data structure and fragment of data in a Python program gets to be its own class. Instead, classes are used sparingly, at conceptual pivots in the code where a big idea — like the idea of a dependency graph — can be wrapped up into a Facade that hides the details of the simple generic data structures that lie beneath it.

Code outside of the Facade names the big concepts that it needs and the operations that it wants to perform. Inside of the Facade, the programmer manipulates the small and convenient moving parts of the Python programming language to make the operations happen.

## chapter 5

A Web Crawler With asyncio Coroutines
A. Jesse Jiryu Davis and Guido van Rossum

5.1   Introduction

Classical computer science emphasizes efficient algorithms that complete computations as quickly as possible. But many networked programs spend their time not computing, but holding open many connections that are slow, or have infrequent events. These programs present a very different challenge: to wait for a huge number of network events efficiently. A contemporary approach to this problem is asynchronous I/O, or "async".

This chapter presents a simple web crawler. The crawler is an archetypal async application because it waits for many responses, but does little computation. The more pages it can fetch at once, the sooner it completes. If it devotes a thread to each in-flight request, then as the number of concurrent requests rises it will run out of memory or other thread-related resource before it runs out of sockets. It avoids the need for threads by using asynchronous I/O.

We present the example in three stages. First, we show an async event loop and sketch a crawler that uses the event loop with callbacks: it is very efficient, but extending it to more complex problems would lead to unmanageable spaghetti code. Second, therefore, we show that Python coroutines are both efficient and extensible. We implement simple coroutines in Python using generator functions. In the third stage, we use the full-featured coroutines from Python's standard "asyncio" library[1], and coordinate them using an async queue.

5.2   The Task

A web crawler finds and downloads all pages on a website, perhaps to archive or index them. Beginning with a root URL, it fetches each page, parses it for links to unseen pages, and adds these to a queue. It stops when it fetches a page with no unseen links and the queue is empty.

We can hasten this process by downloading many pages concurrently. As the crawler finds new links, it launches simultaneous fetch operations for the new pages on separate sockets. It parses responses as they arrive, adding new links to the queue. There may come some point of diminishing returns where too much concurrency degrades performance, so we cap the number of concurrent requests, and leave the remaining links in the queue until some in-flight requests complete.

---

[1]Guido introduced the standard asyncio library, called "Tulip" then, at PyCon 2013.

5.3 The Traditional Approach

How do we make the crawler concurrent? Traditionally we would create a thread pool. Each thread would be in charge of downloading one page at a time over a socket. For example, to download a page from xkcd.com:

```
def fetch(url):
    sock = socket.socket()
    sock.connect(('xkcd.com', 80))
    request = 'GET {} HTTP/1.0\r\nHost: xkcd.com\r\n\r\n'.format(url)
    sock.send(request.encode('ascii'))
    response = b''
    chunk = sock.recv(4096)
    while chunk:
        response += chunk
        chunk = sock.recv(4096)

    # Page is now downloaded.
    links = parse_links(response)
    q.add(links)
```

By default, socket operations are *blocking*: when the thread calls a method like connect or recv, it pauses until the operation completes.[2] Consequently to download many pages at once, we need many threads. A sophisticated application amortizes the cost of thread-creation by keeping idle threads in a thread pool, then checking them out to reuse them for subsequent tasks; it does the same with sockets in a connection pool.

And yet, threads are expensive, and operating systems enforce a variety of hard caps on the number of threads a process, user, or machine may have. On Jesse's system, a Python thread costs around 50k of memory, and starting tens of thousands of threads causes failures. If we scale up to tens of thousands of simultaneous operations on concurrent sockets, we run out of threads before we run out of sockets. Per-thread overhead or system limits on threads are the bottleneck.

In his influential article "The C10K problem"[3], Dan Kegel outlines the limitations of multithreading for I/O concurrency. He begins,

> It's time for web servers to handle ten thousand clients simultaneously, don't you think?
> After all, the web is a big place now.

Kegel coined the term "C10K" in 1999. Ten thousand connections sounds dainty now, but the problem has changed only in size, not in kind. Back then, using a thread per connection for C10K was impractical. Now the cap is orders of magnitude higher. Indeed, our toy web crawler would work just fine with threads. Yet for very large scale applications, with hundreds of thousands of connections, the cap remains: there is a limit beyond which most systems can still create sockets, but have run out of threads. How can we overcome this?

---

[2]Even calls to send can block, if the recipient is slow to acknowledge outstanding messages and the system's buffer of outgoing data is full.

[3]http://www.kegel.com/c10k.html

5.4 Async

Asynchronous I/O frameworks do concurrent operations on a single thread using *non-blocking* sockets. In our async crawler, we set the socket non-blocking before we begin to connect to the server:

```
sock = socket.socket()
sock.setblocking(False)
try:
    sock.connect(('xkcd.com', 80))
except BlockingIOError:
    pass
```

Irritatingly, a non-blocking socket throws an exception from `connect`, even when it is working normally. This exception replicates the irritating behavior of the underlying C function, which sets `errno` to `EINPROGRESS` to tell you it has begun.

Now our crawler needs a way to know when the connection is established, so it can send the HTTP request. We could simply keep trying in a tight loop:

```
request = 'GET {} HTTP/1.0\r\nHost: xkcd.com\r\n\r\n'.format(url)
encoded = request.encode('ascii')

while True:
    try:
        sock.send(encoded)
        break  # Done.
    except OSError as e:
        pass

print('sent')
```

This method not only wastes electricity, but it cannot efficiently await events on *multiple* sockets. In ancient times, BSD Unix's solution to this problem was `select`, a C function that waits for an event to occur on a non-blocking socket or a small array of them. Nowadays the demand for Internet applications with huge numbers of connections has led to replacements like `poll`, then kqueue on BSD and epoll on Linux. These APIs are similar to `select`, but perform well with very large numbers of connections.

Python 3.4's `DefaultSelector` uses the best `select`-like function available on your system. To register for notifications about network I/O, we create a non-blocking socket and register it with the default selector:

```
from selectors import DefaultSelector, EVENT_WRITE

selector = DefaultSelector()

sock = socket.socket()
sock.setblocking(False)
try:
    sock.connect(('xkcd.com', 80))
except BlockingIOError:
    pass
```

```
def connected():
    selector.unregister(sock.fileno())
    print('connected!')

selector.register(sock.fileno(), EVENT_WRITE, connected)
```

We disregard the spurious error and call `selector.register`, passing in the socket's file descriptor and a constant that expresses what event we are waiting for. To be notified when the connection is established, we pass `EVENT_WRITE`: that is, we want to know when the socket is "writable". We also pass a Python function, `connected`, to run when that event occurs. Such a function is known as a *callback*.

We process I/O notifications as the selector receives them, in a loop:

```
def loop():
    while True:
        events = selector.select()
        for event_key, event_mask in events:
            callback = event_key.data
            callback()
```

The `connected` callback is stored as `event_key.data`, which we retrieve and execute once the non-blocking socket is connected.

Unlike in our fast-spinning loop above, the call to `select` here pauses, awaiting the next I/O events. Then the loop runs callbacks that are waiting for these events. Operations that have not completed remain pending until some future tick of the event loop.

What have we demonstrated already? We showed how to begin an operation and execute a callback when the operation is ready. An async *framework* builds on the two features we have shown—non-blocking sockets and the event loop—to run concurrent operations on a single thread.

We have achieved "concurrency" here, but not what is traditionally called "parallelism". That is, we built a tiny system that does overlapping I/O. It is capable of beginning new operations while others are in flight. It does not actually utilize multiple cores to execute computation in parallel. But then, this system is designed for I/O-bound problems, not CPU-bound ones.[4]

So our event loop is efficient at concurrent I/O because it does not devote thread resources to each connection. But before we proceed, it is important to correct a common misapprehension that async is *faster* than multithreading. Often it is not—indeed, in Python, an event loop like ours is moderately slower than multithreading at serving a small number of very active connections. In a runtime without a global interpreter lock, threads would perform even better on such a workload. What asynchronous I/O is right for, is applications with many slow or sleepy connections with infrequent events.[5][6]

---

[4] Python's global interpreter lock prohibits running Python code in parallel in one process anyway. Parallelizing CPU-bound algorithms in Python requires multiple processes, or writing the parallel portions of the code in C. But that is a topic for another day.

[5] Jesse listed indications and contraindications for using async in "What Is Async, How Does It Work, And When Should I Use It?", available at pyvideo.org.

[6] Mike Bayer compared the throughput of asyncio and multithreading for different workloads in his "Asynchronous Python and Databases": http://techspot.zzzeek.org/2015/02/15/asynchronous-python-and-databases/

5.5   Programming With Callbacks

With the runty async framework we have built so far, how can we build a web crawler? Even a simple URL-fetcher is painful to write.

We begin with global sets of the URLs we have yet to fetch, and the URLs we have seen:

```
urls_todo = set(['/'])
seen_urls = set(['/'])
```

The seen_urls set includes urls_todo plus completed URLs. The two sets are initialized with the root URL "/".

Fetching a page will require a series of callbacks. The connected callback fires when a socket is connected, and sends a GET request to the server. But then it must await a response, so it registers another callback. If, when that callback fires, it cannot read the full response yet, it registers again, and so on.

Let us collect these callbacks into a Fetcher object. It needs a URL, a socket object, and a place to accumulate the response bytes:

```
class Fetcher:
    def __init__(self, url):
        self.response = b''  # Empty array of bytes.
        self.url = url
        self.sock = None
```

We begin by calling Fetcher.fetch:

```
# Method on Fetcher class.
def fetch(self):
    self.sock = socket.socket()
    self.sock.setblocking(False)
    try:
        self.sock.connect(('xkcd.com', 80))
    except BlockingIOError:
        pass

    # Register next callback.
    selector.register(self.sock.fileno(),
                      EVENT_WRITE,
                      self.connected)
```

The fetch method begins connecting a socket. But notice the method returns before the connection is established. It must return control to the event loop to wait for the connection. To understand why, imagine our whole application was structured so:

```
# Begin fetching http://xkcd.com/353/
fetcher = Fetcher('/353/')
fetcher.fetch()

while True:
    events = selector.select()
    for event_key, event_mask in events:
        callback = event_key.data
        callback(event_key, event_mask)
```

All event notifications are processed in the event loop when it calls `select`. Hence `fetch` must hand control to the event loop, so that the program knows when the socket has connected. Only then does the loop run the `connected` callback, which was registered at the end of `fetch` above.

Here is the implementation of connected:

```
# Method on Fetcher class.
def connected(self, key, mask):
    print('connected!')
    selector.unregister(key.fd)
    request = 'GET {} HTTP/1.0\r\nHost: xkcd.com\r\n\r\n'.format(self.url)
    self.sock.send(request.encode('ascii'))

    # Register the next callback.
    selector.register(key.fd,
                      EVENT_READ,
                      self.read_response)
```

The method sends a GET request. A real application would check the return value of send in case the whole message cannot be sent at once. But our request is small and our application unsophisticated. It blithely calls send, then waits for a response. Of course, it must register yet another callback and relinquish control to the event loop. The next and final callback, `read_response`, processes the server's reply:

```
# Method on Fetcher class.
def read_response(self, key, mask):
    global stopped

    chunk = self.sock.recv(4096)  # 4k chunk size.
    if chunk:
        self.response += chunk
    else:
        selector.unregister(key.fd)  # Done reading.
        links = self.parse_links()

        # Python set-logic:
        for link in links.difference(seen_urls):
            urls_todo.add(link)
            Fetcher(link).fetch()  # <- New Fetcher.

        seen_urls.update(links)
        urls_todo.remove(self.url)
        if not urls_todo:
            stopped = True
```

The callback is executed each time the selector sees that the socket is "readable", which could mean two things: the socket has data or it is closed.

The callback asks for up to four kilobytes of data from the socket. If less is ready, chunk contains whatever data is available. If there is more, chunk is four kilobytes long and the socket remains readable, so the event loop runs this callback again on the next tick. When the response is complete, the server has closed the socket and chunk is empty.

The parse_links method, not shown, returns a set of URLs. We start a new fetcher for each new URL, with no concurrency cap. Note a nice feature of async programming with callbacks: we need no mutex around changes to shared data, such as when we add links to seen_urls. There is no preemptive multitasking, so we cannot be interrupted at arbitrary points in our code.

We add a global stopped variable and use it to control the loop:

```
stopped = False

def loop():
    while not stopped:
        events = selector.select()
        for event_key, event_mask in events:
            callback = event_key.data
            callback()
```

Once all pages are downloaded the fetcher stops the global event loop and the program exits.

This example makes async's problem plain: spaghetti code. We need some way to express a series of computations and I/O operations, and schedule multiple such series of operations to run concurrently. But without threads, a series of operations cannot be collected into a single function: whenever a function begins an I/O operation, it explicitly saves whatever state will be needed in the future, then returns. You are responsible for thinking about and writing this state-saving code.

Let us explain what we mean by that. Consider how simply we fetched a URL on a thread with a conventional blocking socket:

```
# Blocking version.
def fetch(url):
    sock = socket.socket()
    sock.connect(('xkcd.com', 80))
    request = 'GET {} HTTP/1.0\r\nHost: xkcd.com\r\n\r\n'.format(url)
    sock.send(request.encode('ascii'))
    response = b''
    chunk = sock.recv(4096)
    while chunk:
        response += chunk
        chunk = sock.recv(4096)

    # Page is now downloaded.
    links = parse_links(response)
    q.add(links)
```

What state does this function remember between one socket operation and the next? It has the socket, a URL, and the accumulating response. A function that runs on a thread uses basic features of the programming language to store this temporary state in local variables, on its stack. The function also has a "continuation"—that is, the code it plans to execute after I/O completes. The runtime remembers the continuation by storing the thread's instruction pointer. You need not think about restoring these local variables and the continuation after I/O. It is built in to the language.

But with a callback-based async framework, these language features are no help. While waiting for I/O, a function must save its state explicitly, because the function returns and loses its stack frame before I/O completes. In lieu of local variables, our callback-based example stores sock and response as attributes of self, the Fetcher instance. In lieu of the instruction pointer, it stores its continuation by registering the callbacks connected and read_response. As the application's features grow, so does the complexity of the state we manually save across callbacks. Such onerous bookkeeping makes the coder prone to migraines.

Even worse, what happens if a callback throws an exception, before it schedules the next callback in the chain? Say we did a poor job on the parse_links method and it throws an exception parsing some HTML:

```
Traceback (most recent call last):
  File "loop-with-callbacks.py", line 111, in <module>
    loop()
  File "loop-with-callbacks.py", line 106, in loop
    callback(event_key, event_mask)
  File "loop-with-callbacks.py", line 51, in read_response
    links = self.parse_links()
  File "loop-with-callbacks.py", line 67, in parse_links
    raise Exception('parse error')
Exception: parse error
```

The stack trace shows only that the event loop was running a callback. We do not remember what led to the error. The chain is broken on both ends: we forgot where we were going and whence we came. This loss of context is called "stack ripping", and in many cases it confounds the investigator. Stack ripping also prevents us from installing an exception handler for a chain of callbacks, the way a "try / except" block wraps a function call and its tree of descendents.[7]

So, even apart from the long debate about the relative efficiencies of multithreading and async, there is this other debate regarding which is more error-prone: threads are susceptible to data races if you make a mistake synchronizing them, but callbacks are stubborn to debug due to stack ripping.

5.6   Coroutines

We entice you with a promise. It is possible to write asynchronous code that combines the efficiency of callbacks with the classic good looks of multithreaded programming. This combination is achieved with a pattern called "coroutines". Using Python 3.4's standard asyncio library, and a package called "aiohttp", fetching a URL in a coroutine is very direct[8]:

```
@asyncio.coroutine
def fetch(self, url):
    response = yield from self.session.get(url)
    body = yield from response.read()
```

It is also scalable. Compared to the 50k of memory per thread and the operating system's hard limits on threads, a Python coroutine takes barely 3k of memory on Jesse's system. Python can easily start hundreds of thousands of coroutines.

The concept of a coroutine, dating to the elder days of computer science, is simple: it is a subroutine that can be paused and resumed. Whereas threads are preemptively multitasked by

---

[7]For a complex solution to this problem, see http://www.tornadoweb.org/en/stable/stack_context.html

[8]The @asyncio.coroutine decorator is not magical. In fact, if it decorates a generator function and the PYTHONASYNCIODEBUG environment variable is not set, the decorator does practically nothing. It just sets an attribute, _is_coroutine, for the convenience of other parts of the framework. It is possible to use asyncio with bare generators not decorated with @asyncio.coroutine at all.

the operating system, coroutines multitask cooperatively: they choose when to pause, and which coroutine to run next.

There are many implementations of coroutines; even in Python there are several. The coroutines in the standard "asyncio" library in Python 3.4 are built upon generators, a Future class, and the "yield from" statement. Starting in Python 3.5, coroutines are a native feature of the language itself[9]; however, understanding coroutines as they were first implemented in Python 3.4, using pre-existing language facilities, is the foundation to tackle Python 3.5's native coroutines.

To explain Python 3.4's generator-based coroutines, we will engage in an exposition of generators and how they are used as coroutines in asyncio, and trust you will enjoy reading it as much as we enjoyed writing it. Once we have explained generator-based coroutines, we shall use them in our async web crawler.

5.7 How Python Generators Work

Before you grasp Python generators, you have to understand how regular Python functions work. Normally, when a Python function calls a subroutine, the subroutine retains control until it returns, or throws an exception. Then control returns to the caller:

```
>>> def foo():
...     bar()
...
>>> def bar():
...     pass
```

The standard Python interpreter is written in C. The C function that executes a Python function is called, mellifluously, PyEval_EvalFrameEx. It takes a Python stack frame object and evaluates Python bytecode in the context of the frame. Here is the bytecode for foo:

```
>>> import dis
>>> dis.dis(foo)
  2           0 LOAD_GLOBAL              0 (bar)
              3 CALL_FUNCTION            0 (0 positional, 0 keyword pair)
              6 POP_TOP
              7 LOAD_CONST               0 (None)
             10 RETURN_VALUE
```

The foo function loads bar onto its stack and calls it, then pops its return value from the stack, loads None onto the stack, and returns None.

When PyEval_EvalFrameEx encounters the CALL_FUNCTION bytecode, it creates a new Python stack frame and recurses: that is, it calls PyEval_EvalFrameEx recursively with the new frame, which is used to execute bar.

It is crucial to understand that Python stack frames are allocated in heap memory! The Python interpreter is a normal C program, so its stack frames are normal stack frames. But the *Python* stack frames it manipulates are on the heap. Among other surprises, this means a Python stack frame can outlive its function call. To see this interactively, save the current frame from within bar:

---

[9]Python 3.5's built-in coroutines are described in PEP 492[10], "Coroutines with async and await syntax."

```
>>> import inspect
>>> frame = None
>>> def foo():
...     bar()
...
>>> def bar():
...     global frame
...     frame = inspect.currentframe()
...
>>> foo()
>>> # The frame was executing the code for 'bar'.
>>> frame.f_code.co_name
'bar'
>>> # Its back pointer refers to the frame for 'foo'.
>>> caller_frame = frame.f_back
>>> caller_frame.f_code.co_name
'foo'
```

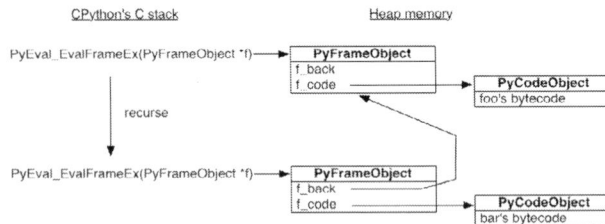

Figure 5.1: Function Calls

The stage is now set for Python generators, which use the same building blocks—code objects and stack frames—to marvelous effect.

This is a generator function:

```
>>> def gen_fn():
...     result = yield 1
...     print('result of yield: {}'.format(result))
...     result2 = yield 2
...     print('result of 2nd yield: {}'.format(result2))
...     return 'done'
...
```

When Python compiles gen_fn to bytecode, it sees the yield statement and knows that gen_fn is a generator function, not a regular one. It sets a flag to remember this fact:

```
>>> # The generator flag is bit position 5.
>>> generator_bit = 1 << 5
>>> bool(gen_fn.__code__.co_flags & generator_bit)
True
```

When you call a generator function, Python sees the generator flag, and it does not actually run the function. Instead, it creates a generator:

```
>>> gen = gen_fn()
>>> type(gen)
<class 'generator'>
```

A Python generator encapsulates a stack frame plus a reference to some code, the body of gen_fn:

```
>>> gen.gi_code.co_name
'gen_fn'
```

All generators from calls to gen_fn point to this same code. But each has its own stack frame. This stack frame is not on any actual stack, it sits in heap memory waiting to be used:

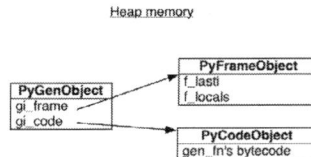

Figure 5.2: Generators

The frame has a "last instruction" pointer, the instruction it executed most recently. In the beginning, the last instruction pointer is -1, meaning the generator has not begun:

```
>>> gen.gi_frame.f_lasti
-1
```

When we call send, the generator reaches its first yield, and pauses. The return value of send is 1, since that is what gen passes to the yield expression:

```
>>> gen.send(None)
1
```

The generator's instruction pointer is now 3 bytecodes from the start, part way through the 56 bytes of compiled Python:

```
>>> gen.gi_frame.f_lasti
3
>>> len(gen.gi_code.co_code)
56
```

The generator can be resumed at any time, from any function, because its stack frame is not actually on the stack: it is on the heap. Its position in the call hierarchy is not fixed, and it need not obey the first-in, last-out order of execution that regular functions do. It is liberated, floating free like a cloud.

We can send the value "hello" into the generator and it becomes the result of the yield expression, and the generator continues until it yields 2:

```
>>> gen.send('hello')
result of yield: hello
2
```

Its stack frame now contains the local variable `result`:

```
>>> gen.gi_frame.f_locals
{'result': 'hello'}
```

Other generators created from gen_fn will have their own stack frames and local variables.

When we call send again, the generator continues from its second `yield`, and finishes by raising the special `StopIteration` exception:

```
>>> gen.send('goodbye')
result of 2nd yield: goodbye
Traceback (most recent call last):
  File "<input>", line 1, in <module>
StopIteration: done
```

The exception has a value, which is the return value of the generator: the string `"done"`.

5.8   Building Coroutines With Generators

So a generator can pause, and it can be resumed with a value, and it has a return value. Sounds like a good primitive upon which to build an async programming model, without spaghetti callbacks! We want to build a "coroutine": a routine that is cooperatively scheduled with other routines in the program. Our coroutines will be a simplified version of those in Python's standard "asyncio" library. As in asyncio, we will use generators, futures, and the "yield from" statement.

First we need a way to represent some future result that a coroutine is waiting for. A stripped-down version:

```
class Future:
    def __init__(self):
        self.result = None
        self._callbacks = []

    def add_done_callback(self, fn):
        self._callbacks.append(fn)

    def set_result(self, result):
        self.result = result
        for fn in self._callbacks:
            fn(self)
```

A future is initially "pending". It is "resolved" by a call to `set_result`.[11]

Let us adapt our fetcher to use futures and coroutines. We wrote `fetch` with a callback:

```
class Fetcher:
    def fetch(self):
        self.sock = socket.socket()
        self.sock.setblocking(False)
        try:
```

---

[11]This future has many deficiencies. For example, once this future is resolved, a coroutine that yields it should resume immediately instead of pausing, but with our code it does not. See asyncio's Future class for a complete implementation.

```
            self.sock.connect(('xkcd.com', 80))
        except BlockingIOError:
            pass
        selector.register(self.sock.fileno(),
                          EVENT_WRITE,
                          self.connected)

    def connected(self, key, mask):
        print('connected!')
        # And so on....
```

The fetch method begins connecting a socket, then registers the callback, connected, to be executed when the socket is ready. Now we can combine these two steps into one coroutine:

```
    def fetch(self):
        sock = socket.socket()
        sock.setblocking(False)
        try:
            sock.connect(('xkcd.com', 80))
        except BlockingIOError:
            pass

        f = Future()

        def on_connected():
            f.set_result(None)

        selector.register(sock.fileno(),
                          EVENT_WRITE,
                          on_connected)
        yield f
        selector.unregister(sock.fileno())
        print('connected!')
```

Now fetch is a generator function, rather than a regular one, because it contains a yield statement. We create a pending future, then yield it to pause fetch until the socket is ready. The inner function on_connected resolves the future.

But when the future resolves, what resumes the generator? We need a coroutine *driver*. Let us call it "task":

```
class Task:
    def __init__(self, coro):
        self.coro = coro
        f = Future()
        f.set_result(None)
        self.step(f)

    def step(self, future):
        try:
            next_future = self.coro.send(future.result)
        except StopIteration:
```

```
        return

    next_future.add_done_callback(self.step)

# Begin fetching http://xkcd.com/353/
fetcher = Fetcher('/353/')
Task(fetcher.fetch())

loop()
```

The task starts the `fetch` generator by sending None into it. Then `fetch` runs until it yields a future, which the task captures as `next_future`. When the socket is connected, the event loop runs the callback `on_connected`, which resolves the future, which calls `step`, which resumes `fetch`.

5.9   Factoring Coroutines With `yield from`

Once the socket is connected, we send the HTTP GET request and read the server response. These steps need no longer be scattered among callbacks; we gather them into the same generator function:

```
def fetch(self):
    # ... connection logic from above, then:
    sock.send(request.encode('ascii'))

    while True:
        f = Future()

        def on_readable():
            f.set_result(sock.recv(4096))

        selector.register(sock.fileno(),
                          EVENT_READ,
                          on_readable)
        chunk = yield f
        selector.unregister(sock.fileno())
        if chunk:
            self.response += chunk
        else:
            # Done reading.
            break
```

This code, which reads a whole message from a socket, seems generally useful. How can we factor it from `fetch` into a subroutine? Now Python 3's celebrated `yield from` takes the stage. It lets one generator *delegate* to another.

To see how, let us return to our simple generator example:

```
>>> def gen_fn():
...     result = yield 1
...     print('result of yield: {}'.format(result))
...     result2 = yield 2
...     print('result of 2nd yield: {}'.format(result2))
```

```
...        return 'done'
...
```

To call this generator from another generator, delegate to it with `yield from`:

```
>>> # Generator function:
>>> def caller_fn():
...        gen = gen_fn()
...        rv = yield from gen
...        print('return value of yield-from: {}'
...             .format(rv))
...
>>> # Make a generator from the
>>> # generator function.
>>> caller = caller_fn()
```

The caller generator acts as if it were gen, the generator it is delegating to:

```
>>> caller.send(None)
1
>>> caller.gi_frame.f_lasti
15
>>> caller.send('hello')
result of yield: hello
2
>>> caller.gi_frame.f_lasti  # Hasn't advanced.
15
>>> caller.send('goodbye')
result of 2nd yield: goodbye
return value of yield-from: done
Traceback (most recent call last):
  File "<input>", line 1, in <module>
StopIteration
```

While caller yields from gen, caller does not advance. Notice that its instruction pointer remains at 15, the site of its `yield from` statement, even while the inner generator gen advances from one `yield` statement to the next.[12] From our perspective outside caller, we cannot tell if the values it yields are from caller or from the generator it delegates to. And from inside gen, we cannot tell if values are sent in from caller or from outside it. The `yield from` statement is a frictionless channel, through which values flow in and out of gen until gen completes.

A coroutine can delegate work to a sub-coroutine with `yield from` and receive the result of the work. Notice, above, that caller printed "return value of yield-from: done". When gen completed, its return value became the value of the `yield from` statement in caller:

```
    rv = yield from gen
```

---

[12]In fact, this is exactly how "yield from" works in CPython. A function increments its instruction pointer before executing each statement. But after the outer generator executes "yield from", it subtracts 1 from its instruction pointer to keep itself pinned at the "yield from" statement. Then it yields to *its* caller. The cycle repeats until the inner generator throws StopIteration, at which point the outer generator finally allows itself to advance to the next instruction.

Earlier, when we criticized callback-based async programming, our most strident complaint was about "stack ripping": when a callback throws an exception, the stack trace is typically useless. It only shows that the event loop was running the callback, not *why*. How do coroutines fare?

```
>>> def gen_fn():
...     raise Exception('my error')
>>> caller = caller_fn()
>>> caller.send(None)
Traceback (most recent call last):
  File "<input>", line 1, in <module>
  File "<input>", line 3, in caller_fn
  File "<input>", line 2, in gen_fn
Exception: my error
```

This is much more useful! The stack trace shows caller_fn was delegating to gen_fn when it threw the error. Even more comforting, we can wrap the call to a sub-coroutine in an exception handler, the same is with normal subroutines:

```
>>> def gen_fn():
...     yield 1
...     raise Exception('uh oh')
...
>>> def caller_fn():
...     try:
...         yield from gen_fn()
...     except Exception as exc:
...         print('caught {}'.format(exc))
...
>>> caller = caller_fn()
>>> caller.send(None)
1
>>> caller.send('hello')
caught uh oh
```

So we factor logic with sub-coroutines just like with regular subroutines. Let us factor some useful sub-coroutines from our fetcher. We write a read coroutine to receive one chunk:

```
def read(sock):
    f = Future()

    def on_readable():
        f.set_result(sock.recv(4096))

    selector.register(sock.fileno(), EVENT_READ, on_readable)
    chunk = yield f   # Read one chunk.
    selector.unregister(sock.fileno())
    return chunk
```

We build on read with a read_all coroutine that receives a whole message:

```
def read_all(sock):
    response = []
```

```
# Read whole response.
chunk = yield from read(sock)
while chunk:
    response.append(chunk)
    chunk = yield from read(sock)

return b''.join(response)
```

If you squint the right way, the `yield from` statements disappear and these look like conventional functions doing blocking I/O. But in fact, `read` and `read_all` are coroutines. Yielding from `read` pauses `read_all` until the I/O completes. While `read_all` is paused, asyncio's event loop does other work and awaits other I/O events; `read_all` is resumed with the result of `read` on the next loop tick once its event is ready.

At the stack's root, `fetch` calls `read_all`:

```
class Fetcher:
    def fetch(self):
        # ... connection logic from above, then:
        sock.send(request.encode('ascii'))
        self.response = yield from read_all(sock)
```

Miraculously, the Task class needs no modification. It drives the outer `fetch` coroutine just the same as before:

```
Task(fetcher.fetch())
loop()
```

When `read` yields a future, the task receives it through the channel of `yield from` statements, precisely as if the future were yielded directly from `fetch`. When the loop resolves a future, the task sends its result into `fetch`, and the value is received by `read`, exactly as if the task were driving `read` directly:

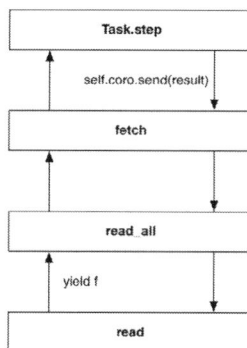

Figure 5.3: Yield From

To perfect our coroutine implementation, we polish out one mar: our code uses `yield` when it waits for a future, but `yield from` when it delegates to a sub-coroutine. It would be more refined if we used `yield from` whenever a coroutine pauses. Then a coroutine need not concern itself with what type of thing it awaits.

We take advantage of the deep correspondence in Python between generators and iterators. Advancing a generator is, to the caller, the same as advancing an iterator. So we make our Future class iterable by implementing a special method:

```
# Method on Future class.
def __iter__(self):
    # Tell Task to resume me here.
    yield self
    return self.result
```

The future's `__iter__` method is a coroutine that yields the future itself. Now when we replace code like this:

```
# f is a Future.
yield f
```

...with this:

```
# f is a Future.
yield from f
```

...the outcome is the same! The driving Task receives the future from its call to send, and when the future is resolved it sends the new result back into the coroutine.

What is the advantage of using `yield from` everywhere? Why is that better than waiting for futures with `yield` and delegating to sub-coroutines with `yield from`? It is better because now, a method can freely change its implementation without affecting the caller: it might be a normal method that returns a future that will *resolve* to a value, or it might be a coroutine that contains `yield from` statements and *returns* a value. In either case, the caller need only `yield from` the method in order to wait for the result.

Gentle reader, we have reached the end of our enjoyable exposition of coroutines in asyncio. We peered into the machinery of generators, and sketched an implementation of futures and tasks. We outlined how asyncio attains the best of both worlds: concurrent I/O that is more efficient than threads and more legible than callbacks. Of course, the real asyncio is much more sophisticated than our sketch. The real framework addresses zero-copy I/O, fair scheduling, exception handling, and an abundance of other features.

To an asyncio user, coding with coroutines is much simpler than you saw here. In the code above we implemented coroutines from first principles, so you saw callbacks, tasks, and futures. You even saw non-blocking sockets and the call to `select`. But when it comes time to build an application with asyncio, none of this appears in your code. As we promised, you can now sleekly fetch a URL:

```
@asyncio.coroutine
def fetch(self, url):
    response = yield from self.session.get(url)
    body = yield from response.read()
```

Satisfied with this exposition, we return to our original assignment: to write an async web crawler, using asyncio.

5.10 Coordinating Coroutines

We began by describing how we want our crawler to work. Now it is time to implement it with asyncio coroutines.

Our crawler will fetch the first page, parse its links, and add them to a queue. After this it fans out across the website, fetching pages concurrently. But to limit load on the client and server, we want some maximum number of workers to run, and no more. Whenever a worker finishes fetching a page, it should immediately pull the next link from the queue. We will pass through periods when there is not enough work to go around, so some workers must pause. But when a worker hits a page rich with new links, then the queue suddenly grows and any paused workers should wake and get cracking. Finally, our program must quit once its work is done.

Imagine if the workers were threads. How would we express the crawler's algorithm? We could use a synchronized queue[13] from the Python standard library. Each time an item is put in the queue, the queue increments its count of "tasks". Worker threads call task_done after completing work on an item. The main thread blocks on Queue.join until each item put in the queue is matched by a task_done call, then it exits.

Coroutines use the exact same pattern with an asyncio queue! First we import it[14]:

```
try:
    from asyncio import JoinableQueue as Queue
except ImportError:
    # In Python 3.5, asyncio.JoinableQueue is
    # merged into Queue.
    from asyncio import Queue
```

We collect the workers' shared state in a crawler class, and write the main logic in its crawl method. We start crawl on a coroutine and run asyncio's event loop until crawl finishes:

```
loop = asyncio.get_event_loop()

crawler = crawling.Crawler('http://xkcd.com',
                           max_redirect=10)

loop.run_until_complete(crawler.crawl())
```

The crawler begins with a root URL and max_redirect, the number of redirects it is willing to follow to fetch any one URL. It puts the pair (URL, max_redirect) in the queue. (For the reason why, stay tuned.)

```
class Crawler:
    def __init__(self, root_url, max_redirect):
        self.max_tasks = 10
        self.max_redirect = max_redirect
        self.q = Queue()
        self.seen_urls = set()

        # aiohttp's ClientSession does connection pooling and
        # HTTP keep-alives for us.
```

---

[13]https://docs.python.org/3/library/queue.html
[14]https://docs.python.org/3/library/asyncio-sync.html

```
    self.session = aiohttp.ClientSession(loop=loop)

    # Put (URL, max_redirect) in the queue.
    self.q.put((root_url, self.max_redirect))
```

The number of unfinished tasks in the queue is now one. Back in our main script, we launch the event loop and the `crawl` method:

```
loop.run_until_complete(crawler.crawl())
```

The `crawl` coroutine kicks off the workers. It is like a main thread: it blocks on `join` until all tasks are finished, while the workers run in the background.

```
    @asyncio.coroutine
    def crawl(self):
        """Run the crawler until all work is done."""
        workers = [asyncio.Task(self.work())
                   for _ in range(self.max_tasks)]

        # When all work is done, exit.
        yield from self.q.join()
        for w in workers:
            w.cancel()
```

If the workers were threads we might not wish to start them all at once. To avoid creating expensive threads until it is certain they are necessary, a thread pool typically grows on demand. But coroutines are cheap, so we simply start the maximum number allowed.

It is interesting to note how we shut down the crawler. When the `join` future resolves, the worker tasks are alive but suspended: they wait for more URLs but none come. So, the main coroutine cancels them before exiting. Otherwise, as the Python interpreter shuts down and calls all objects' destructors, living tasks cry out:

```
ERROR:asyncio:Task was destroyed but it is pending!
```

And how does `cancel` work? Generators have a feature we have not yet shown you. You can throw an exception into a generator from outside:

```
>>> gen = gen_fn()
>>> gen.send(None)  # Start the generator as usual.
1
>>> gen.throw(Exception('error'))
Traceback (most recent call last):
  File "<input>", line 3, in <module>
  File "<input>", line 2, in gen_fn
Exception: error
```

The generator is resumed by `throw`, but it is now raising an exception. If no code in the generator's call stack catches it, the exception bubbles back up to the top. So to cancel a task's coroutine:

```
    # Method of Task class.
    def cancel(self):
        self.coro.throw(CancelledError)
```

Wherever the generator is paused, at some `yield from` statement, it resumes and throws an exception. We handle cancellation in the task's `step` method:

```
# Method of Task class.
def step(self, future):
    try:
        next_future = self.coro.send(future.result)
    except CancelledError:
        self.cancelled = True
        return
    except StopIteration:
        return

    next_future.add_done_callback(self.step)
```

Now the task knows it is cancelled, so when it is destroyed it does not rage against the dying of the light.

Once `crawl` has canceled the workers, it exits. The event loop sees that the coroutine is complete (we shall see how later), and it too exits:

```
loop.run_until_complete(crawler.crawl())
```

The `crawl` method comprises all that our main coroutine must do. It is the worker coroutines that get URLs from the queue, fetch them, and parse them for new links. Each worker runs the `work` coroutine independently:

```
@asyncio.coroutine
def work(self):
    while True:
        url, max_redirect = yield from self.q.get()

        # Download page and add new links to self.q.
        yield from self.fetch(url, max_redirect)
        self.q.task_done()
```

Python sees that this code contains `yield from` statements, and compiles it into a generator function. So in `crawl`, when the main coroutine calls `self.work` ten times, it does not actually execute this method: it only creates ten generator objects with references to this code. It wraps each in a Task. The Task receives each future the generator yields, and drives the generator by calling `send` with each future's result when the future resolves. Because the generators have their own stack frames, they run independently, with separate local variables and instruction pointers.

The worker coordinates with its fellows via the queue. It waits for new URLs with:

```
url, max_redirect = yield from self.q.get()
```

The queue's `get` method is itself a coroutine: it pauses until someone puts an item in the queue, then resumes and returns the item.

Incidentally, this is where the worker will be paused at the end of the crawl, when the main coroutine cancels it. From the coroutine's perspective, its last trip around the loop ends when `yield from` raises a `CancelledError`.

When a worker fetches a page it parses the links and puts new ones in the queue, then calls task_done to decrement the counter. Eventually, a worker fetches a page whose URLs have all been fetched already, and there is also no work left in the queue. Thus this worker's call to task_done decrements the counter to zero. Then crawl, which is waiting for the queue's join method, is unpaused and finishes.

We promised to explain why the items in the queue are pairs, like:

```
# URL to fetch, and the number of redirects left.
('http://xkcd.com/353', 10)
```

New URLs have ten redirects remaining. Fetching this particular URL results in a redirect to a new location with a trailing slash. We decrement the number of redirects remaining, and put the next location in the queue:

```
# URL with a trailing slash. Nine redirects left.
('http://xkcd.com/353/', 9)
```

The aiohttp package we use would follow redirects by default and give us the final response. We tell it not to, however, and handle redirects in the crawler, so it can coalesce redirect paths that lead to the same destination: if we have already seen this URL, it is in self.seen_urls and we have already started on this path from a different entry point:

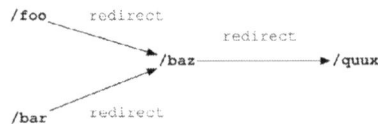

Figure 5.4: Redirects

The crawler fetches "foo" and sees it redirects to "baz", so it adds "baz" to the queue and to seen_urls. If the next page it fetches is "bar", which also redirects to "baz", the fetcher does not enqueue "baz" again. If the response is a page, rather than a redirect, fetch parses it for links and puts new ones in the queue.

```
@asyncio.coroutine
def fetch(self, url, max_redirect):
    # Handle redirects ourselves.
    response = yield from self.session.get(
        url, allow_redirects=False)

    try:
        if is_redirect(response):
            if max_redirect > 0:
                next_url = response.headers['location']
                if next_url in self.seen_urls:
                    # We have been down this path before.
                    return
```

```
            # Remember we have seen this URL.
            self.seen_urls.add(next_url)

            # Follow the redirect. One less redirect remains.
            self.q.put_nowait((next_url, max_redirect - 1))
        else:
            links = yield from self.parse_links(response)
            # Python set-logic:
            for link in links.difference(self.seen_urls):
                self.q.put_nowait((link, self.max_redirect))
            self.seen_urls.update(links)
    finally:
        # Return connection to pool.
        yield from response.release()
```

If this were multithreaded code, it would be lousy with race conditions. For example, the worker checks if a link is in seen_urls, and if not the worker puts it in the queue and adds it to seen_urls. If it were interrupted between the two operations, then another worker might parse the same link from a different page, also observe that it is not in seen_urls, and also add it to the queue. Now that same link is in the queue twice, leading (at best) to duplicated work and wrong statistics.

However, a coroutine is only vulnerable to interruption at yield from statements. This is a key difference that makes coroutine code far less prone to races than multithreaded code: multithreaded code must enter a critical section explicitly, by grabbing a lock, otherwise it is interruptible. A Python coroutine is uninterruptible by default, and only cedes control when it explicitly yields.

We no longer need a fetcher class like we had in the callback-based program. That class was a workaround for a deficiency of callbacks: they need some place to store state while waiting for I/O, since their local variables are not preserved across calls. But the fetch coroutine can store its state in local variables like a regular function does, so there is no more need for a class.

When fetch finishes processing the server response it returns to the caller, work. The work method calls task_done on the queue and then gets the next URL from the queue to be fetched.

When fetch puts new links in the queue it increments the count of unfinished tasks and keeps the main coroutine, which is waiting for q.join, paused. If, however, there are no unseen links and this was the last URL in the queue, then when work calls task_done the count of unfinished tasks falls to zero. That event unpauses join and the main coroutine completes.

The queue code that coordinates the workers and the main coroutine is like this[15]:

```
class Queue:
    def __init__(self):
        self._join_future = Future()
        self._unfinished_tasks = 0
        # ... other initialization ...

    def put_nowait(self, item):
        self._unfinished_tasks += 1
        # ... store the item ...
```

---

[15]The actual asyncio.Queue implementation uses an asyncio.Event in place of the Future shown here. The difference is an Event can be reset, whereas a Future cannot transition from resolved back to pending.

```
def task_done(self):
    self._unfinished_tasks -= 1
    if self._unfinished_tasks == 0:
        self._join_future.set_result(None)

@asyncio.coroutine
def join(self):
    if self._unfinished_tasks > 0:
        yield from self._join_future
```

The main coroutine, crawl, yields from join. So when the last worker decrements the count of unfinished tasks to zero, it signals crawl to resume, and finish.

The ride is almost over. Our program began with the call to crawl:

```
loop.run_until_complete(self.crawler.crawl())
```

How does the program end? Since crawl is a generator function, calling it returns a generator. To drive the generator, asyncio wraps it in a task:

```
class EventLoop:
    def run_until_complete(self, coro):
        """Run until the coroutine is done."""
        task = Task(coro)
        task.add_done_callback(stop_callback)
        try:
            self.run_forever()
        except StopError:
            pass

class StopError(BaseException):
    """Raised to stop the event loop."""

def stop_callback(future):
    raise StopError
```

When the task completes, it raises StopError, which the loop uses as a signal that it has arrived at normal completion.

But what's this? The task has methods called add_done_callback and result? You might think that a task resembles a future. Your instinct is correct. We must admit a detail about the Task class we hid from you: a task is a future.

```
class Task(Future):
    """A coroutine wrapped in a Future."""
```

Normally a future is resolved by someone else calling set_result on it. But a task resolves *itself* when its coroutine stops. Remember from our earlier exploration of Python generators that when a generator returns, it throws the special StopIteration exception:

```
# Method of class Task.
def step(self, future):
    try:
```

```
            next_future = self.coro.send(future.result)
        except CancelledError:
            self.cancelled = True
            return
        except StopIteration as exc:

            # Task resolves itself with coro's return
            # value.
            self.set_result(exc.value)
            return

        next_future.add_done_callback(self.step)
```

So when the event loop calls `task.add_done_callback(stop_callback)`, it prepares to be stopped by the task. Here is `run_until_complete` again:

```
# Method of event loop.
def run_until_complete(self, coro):
    task = Task(coro)
    task.add_done_callback(stop_callback)
    try:
        self.run_forever()
    except StopError:
        pass
```

When the task catches `StopIteration` and resolves itself, the callback raises `StopError` from within the loop. The loop stops and the call stack is unwound to `run_until_complete`. Our program is finished.

5.11   Conclusion

Increasingly often, modern programs are I/O-bound instead of CPU-bound. For such programs, Python threads are the worst of both worlds: the global interpreter lock prevents them from actually executing computations in parallel, and preemptive switching makes them prone to races. Async is often the right pattern. But as callback-based async code grows, it tends to become a dishevelled mess. Coroutines are a tidy alternative. They factor naturally into subroutines, with sane exception handling and stack traces.

If we squint so that the `yield from` statements blur, a coroutine looks like a thread doing traditional blocking I/O. We can even coordinate coroutines with classic patterns from multi-threaded programming. There is no need for reinvention. Thus, compared to callbacks, coroutines are an inviting idiom to the coder experienced with multithreading.

But when we open our eyes and focus on the `yield from` statements, we see they mark points when the coroutine cedes control and allows others to run. Unlike threads, coroutines display where our code can be interrupted and where it cannot. In his illuminating essay "Unyielding"[16], Glyph Lefkowitz writes, "Threads make local reasoning difficult, and local reasoning is perhaps the most important thing in software development." Explicitly yielding, however, makes it possible to "understand the behavior (and thereby, the correctness) of a routine by examining the routine itself rather than examining the entire system."

---

[16]https://glyph.twistedmatrix.com/2014/02/unyielding.html

This chapter was written during a renaissance in the history of Python and async. Generator-based coroutines, whose devising you have just learned, were released in the "asyncio" module with Python 3.4 in March 2014. In September 2015, Python 3.5 was released with coroutines built in to the language itself. These native coroutinesare declared with the new syntax "async def", and instead of "yield from", they use the new "await" keyword to delegate to a coroutine or wait for a Future.

Despite these advances, the core ideas remain. Python's new native coroutines will be syntactically distinct from generators but work very similarly; indeed, they will share an implementation within the Python interpreter. Task, Future, and the event loop will continue to play their roles in asyncio.

Now that you know how asyncio coroutines work, you can largely forget the details. The machinery is tucked behind a dapper interface. But your grasp of the fundamentals empowers you to code correctly and efficiently in modern async environments.

## chapter 6

Dagoba: an in-memory graph database
Dann Toliver

6.1   Prologue

> "When we try to pick out anything by itself we find that it is bound fast by a thousand invisible cords that cannot be broken, to everything in the universe." —John Muir

> "What went forth to the ends of the world to traverse not itself, God, the sun, Shakespeare, a commercial traveller, having itself traversed in reality itself becomes that self." — James Joyce

A long time ago, when the world was still young, all data walked happily in single file. If you wanted your data to jump over a fence, you just set the fence down in its path and each datum jumped it in turn. Punch cards in, punch cards out. Life was easy and programming was a breeze.

Then came the random access revolution, and data grazed freely across the hillside. Herding data became a serious concern: if you can access any piece of data at any time, how do you know which one to pick next? Techniques were developed for corralling the data by forming links between items[1], marshaling groups of units into formation through their linking assemblage. Questioning data meant picking a sheep and pulling along everything connected to it.

Later programmers departed from this tradition, imposing a set of rules on how data would be aggregated[2]. Rather than tying disparate data directly together they would cluster by content, decomposing data into bite-sized pieces, collected in pens and collared with name tags. Questions were posed declaratively, resulting in accumulating pieces of partially decomposed data (a state the relationalists refer to as "normal") into a frankencollection returned to the programmer.

For much of recorded history this relational model reigned supreme. Its dominance went unchallenged through two major language wars and countless skirmishes. It offered everything you could

---

[1] One of the very first database designs was the hierarchical model, which grouped items into tree-shaped hierarchies and is still used as the basis of IBM's IMS product, a high-speed transaction processing system. It's influence can also been seen in XML, file systems and geographic information storage. The network model, invented by Charles Bachmann and standardized by CODASYL, generalized the hierarchical model by allowing multiple parents, forming a DAG instead of a tree. These navigational database models came in to vogue in the 1960s and continued their dominance until performance gains made relational databases usable in the 1980s.

[2] Edgar F. Codd developed relational database theory while working at IBM, but Big Blue feared that a relational database would cannibalize the sales of IMS. While IBM eventually built a research prototype called System R, it was based around a new non-relational language called SEQUEL, instead of Codd's original Alpha language. The SEQUEL language was copied by Larry Ellison in his Oracle Database based on pre-launch conference papers, and the name changed to SQL to avoid trademark disputes.

ask for in a model, for the small price of inefficiency, clumsiness and lack of scalability. For eons that was a price programmers were willing to pay. Then the internet happened.

The distributed revolution changed everything, again. Data broke free of spacial constraints and roamed from machine to machine. CAP-wielding theorists busted the relational monopoly, opening the door to new herding techniques—some of which hark back to the earliest attempts to domesticate random-access data. We're going to look at one of these, a style known as the graph database.

6.2   Take One

Within this chapter we're going to build a graph database[3]. As we build it we're going to explore the problem space, generate multiple solutions for our design decisions, compare those solutions to understand the tradeoffs between them, and finally choose the right solution for our system. A higher-than-usual precedence is put on code compactness, but the process will otherwise mirror that used by software professionals since time immemorial. The purpose of this chapter is to teach this process. And to build a graph database[4].

Using a graph database will allow us to solve some interesting problems in an elegant fashion. Graphs are a very natural data structure for exploring connections between things. A graph in this sense is a set of vertices and a set of edges; in other words, it's a bunch of dots connected by lines. And a database? A "data base" is like a fort for data. You put data in it and get data back out of it.

So what kinds of problems can we solve with a graph database? Well, suppose that you enjoy tracking ancestral trees: parents, grandparents, cousins twice removed, that kind of thing. You'd like to develop a system that allows you to make natural and elegant queries like "Who are Thor's second cousins once removed?" or "What is Freyja's connection to the Valkyries?"

A reasonable schema for this data structure would be to have a table of entities and a table of relationships. A query for Thor's parents might look like

```
SELECT e.* FROM entities as e, relationships as r
WHERE r.out = "Thor" AND r.type = "parent" AND r.in = e.id
```

But how do we extend that to grandparents? We need to do a subquery, or use some other type of vendor-specific extension to SQL. And by the time we get to second cousins once removed we're going to have *a lot* of SQL.

What would we like to write? Something both concise and flexible; something that models our query in a natural way and extends to other queries like it. second_cousins('Thor') is concise, but it doesn't give us any flexibility. The SQL above is flexible, but lacks concision.

Something like Thor.parents.parents.parents.children.children.children strikes a reasonably good balance. The primitives give us flexibility to ask many similar questions, but the query is concise and natural. This particular phrasing gives us too many results, as it includes first cousins and siblings, but we're going for gestalt here.

What's the simplest thing we can build that gives us this kind of interface? We could make a list of vertices and a list of edges, just like the relational schema, and then build some helper functions. It might look something like this:

---

[3]This database started life as a library for managing Directed Acyclic Graphs, or DAGs. Its name "Dagoba" was originally intended to come with a silent 'h' at the end, an homage to the swampy fictional planet, but reading the back of a chocolate bar one day we discovered the sans-h version refers to a place for silently contemplating the connections between things, which seems even more fitting.

[4]The two purposes of this chapter are to teach this process, to build a graph database, and to have fun.

```
V = [ 1, 2, 3, 4, 5, 6, 7, 8, 9, 10, 11, 12, 13, 14, 15 ]
E = [ [1,2], [1,3], [2,4], [2,5], [3,6], [3,7], [4,8]
    , [4,9], [5,10], [5,11], [6,12], [6,13], [7,14], [7,15] ]

parents = function(vertices) {
  var accumulator = []
  for(var i=0; i < E.length; i++) {
    var edge = E[i]
    if(vertices.indexOf(edge[1]) !== -1)
      accumulator.push(edge[0])
  }
  return accumulator
}
```

The essence of the above function is to iterate over a list, evaluating some code for each item and building up an accumulator of results. That's not quite as clear as it could be, though, because the looping construct introduces some unnecessary complexity.

It'd be nice if there was a more specific looping construct designed for this purpose. As it happens, the reduce function does exactly that: given a list and a function, it evaluates the function for each element of the list, while threading the accumulator through each evaluation pass.

Written in this more functional style our queries are shorter and clearer:

```
parents  = (vertices) => E.reduce( (acc, [parent, child])
        => vertices.includes(child)  ? acc.concat(parent) : acc , [] )
children = (vertices) => E.reduce( (acc, [parent, child])
        => vertices.includes(parent) ? acc.concat(child)  : acc , [] )
```

Given a list of vertices we reduce over the edges, adding an edge's parent to the accumulator if the edge's child is in our input list. The children function is identical, but examines the edge's parent to determine whether to add the edge's child.

Those functions are valid JavaScript, but use a few features which browsers haven't implemented as of this writing. This translated version will work today:

```
parents  = function(x) { return E.reduce(
  function(acc, e) { return ~x.indexOf(e[1]) ? acc.concat(e[0]) : acc }, [] )}
children = function(x) { return E.reduce(
  function(acc, e) { return ~x.indexOf(e[0]) ? acc.concat(e[1]) : acc }, [] )}
```

Now we can say something like:

```
children(children(children(parents(parents(parents([8]))))))
```

It reads backwards and gets us lost in silly parens, but is otherwise pretty close to what we wanted. Take a minute to look at the code. Can you see any ways to improve it?

We're treating the edges as a global variable, which means we can only ever have one database at a time using these helper functions. That's pretty limiting.

We're also not using the vertices at all. What does that tell us? It implies that everything we need is in the edges array, which in this case is true: the vertex values are scalars, so they exist independently in the edges array. If we want to answer questions like "What is Freyja's connection to the Valkyries?" we'll need to add more data to the vertices, which means making them compound values, which means the edges array should reference vertices instead of copying their value.

The same holds true for our edges: they contain an "in" vertex and an "out" vertex[5], but no elegant way to incorporate additional information. We'll need that to answer questions like "How many stepparents did Loki have?" or "How many children did Odin have before Thor was born?"

You don't have to squint very hard to tell that the code for our two selectors looks very similar, which suggests there may be a deeper abstraction from which they spring.

Do you see any other issues?

6.3   Build a Better Graph

Let's solve a few of the problems we've discovered. Having our vertices and edges be global constructs limits us to one graph at a time, but we'd like to have more. To solve this we'll need some structure. Let's start with a namespace.

```
Dagoba = {}                              // the namespace
```

We'll use an object as our namespace. An object in JavaScript is mostly just an unordered set of key/value pairs. We only have four basic data structures to choose from in JavaScript, so we'll be using this one a lot. (A fun question to ask people at parties is "What are the four basic data structures in JavaScript?")

Now we need some graphs. We can build these using a classic OOP pattern, but JavaScript offers us prototypal inheritance, which means we can build up a prototype object—we'll call it Dagoba.G— and then instantiate copies of that using a factory function. An advantage of this approach is that we can return different types of objects from the factory, instead of binding the creation process to a single class constructor. So we get some extra flexibility for free.

```
Dagoba.G = {}                            // the prototype

Dagoba.graph = function(V, E) {          // the factory
  var graph = Object.create( Dagoba.G )

  graph.edges       = []                 // fresh copies so they're not shared
  graph.vertices    = []
  graph.vertexIndex = {}                 // a lookup optimization

  graph.autoid = 1                       // an auto-incrementing ID counter

  if(Array.isArray(V)) graph.addVertices(V) // arrays only, because you wouldn't
  if(Array.isArray(E)) graph.addEdges(E)    //   call this with singular V and E

  return graph
}
```

---

[5]Notice that we're modeling edges as a pair of vertices. Also notice that those pairs are ordered, because we're using arrays. That means we're modeling a *directed graph*, where every edge has a starting vertex and an ending vertex. Our "dots and lines" visual model becomes a "dots and arrows" model. This adds complexity to our model, because we have to keep track of the direction of edges, but it also allows us to ask more interesting questions, like "which vertices point to vertex 3?" or "which vertex has the most outgoing edges?" If we need to model an undirected graph we could add a reversed edge for each existing edge in our directed graph. It can be cumbersome to go the other direction: simulating a directed graph from an undirected one. Can you think of a way to do it?

We'll accept two optional arguments: a list of vertices and a list of edges. JavaScript is rather lax about parameters, so all named parameters are optional and default to undefined if not supplied[6]. We will often have the vertices and edges before building the graph and use the V and E parameters, but it's also common to not have those at creation time and to build the graph up programmatically[7].

Then we create a new object that has all of our prototype's strengths and none of its weaknesses. We build a brand new array (one of the other basic JS data structures) for our edges, another for the vertices, a new object called vertexIndex and an ID counter—more on those latter two later. (Think: Why can't we just put these in the prototype?)

Then we call addVertices and addEdges from inside our factory, so let's define those now.

```
Dagoba.G.addVertices = function(vs) { vs.forEach(this.addVertex.bind(this)) }
Dagoba.G.addEdges    = function(es) { es.forEach(this.addEdge  .bind(this)) }
```

Okay, that was too easy—we're just passing off the work to addVertex and addEdge. We should define those now too.

```
Dagoba.G.addVertex = function(vertex) {          // accepts a vertex-like object
  if(!vertex._id)
    vertex._id = this.autoid++
  else if(this.findVertexById(vertex._id))
    return Dagoba.error('A vertex with that ID already exists')

  this.vertices.push(vertex)
  this.vertexIndex[vertex._id] = vertex          // a fancy index thing
  vertex._out = []; vertex._in = []              // placeholders for edge pointers
  return vertex._id
}
```

If the vertex doesn't already have an _id property we assign it one using our autoid.[8] If the _id already exists on a vertex in our graph then we reject the new vertex. Wait, when would that happen? And what exactly is a vertex?

In a traditional object-oriented system we would expect to find a vertex class, which all vertices would be an instance of. We're going to take a different approach and consider as a vertex any object containing the three properties _id, _in and _out. Why is that? Ultimately, it comes down to giving Dagoba control over which data is shared with the host application.

If we create some Dagoba.Vertex instance inside the addVertex function, our internal data will never be shared with the host application. If we accept a Dagoba.Vertex instance as the argument to our addVertex function, the host application could retain a pointer to that vertex object and manipulate it at runtime, breaking our invariants.

So if we create a vertex instance object, we're forced to decide up front whether we will always copy the provided data into a new object—potentially doubling our space usage—or allow the host application unfettered access to the database objects. There's a tension here between performance and protection, and the right balance depends on your specific use case.

---

[6]It's also lax in the other direction: all functions are variadic, and all arguments are available by position via the arguments object, which is almost like an array but not quite. ("Variadic" is a fancy way of saying a function has indefinite arity. "A function has indefinite arity" is a fancy way of saying it takes a variable number of variables.)

[7]The Array.isArray checks here are to distinguish our two different use cases, but in general we won't be doing many of the validations one would expect of production code, in order to focus on the architecture instead of the trash bins.

[8]Why can't we just use this.vertices.length here?

Duck typing on the vertex's properties allows us to make that decision at run time, by either deep copying[9] the incoming data or using it directly as a vertex[10]. We don't always want to put the responsibility for balancing safety and performance in the hands of the user, but because these two sets of use cases diverge so widely the extra flexibility is important.

Now that we've got our new vertex we'll add it to our graph's list of vertices, add it to the vertexIndex for efficient lookup by _id, and add two additional properties to it: _out and _in, which will both become lists of edges[11].

```
Dagoba.G.addEdge = function(edge) {                    // accepts an edge-like object
  edge._in  = this.findVertexById(edge._in)
  edge._out = this.findVertexById(edge._out)

  if(!(edge._in && edge._out))
    return Dagoba.error("That edge's " + (edge._in ? 'out' : 'in')
                                      + " vertex wasn't found")

  edge._out._out.push(edge)                            // edge's out vertex's out edges
  edge._in._in.push(edge)                              // vice versa

  this.edges.push(edge)
}
```

First we find both vertices which the edge connects, then reject the edge if it's missing either vertex. We'll use a helper function to log an error on rejection. All errors flow through this helper function, so we can override its behavior on a per-application basis. We could later extend this to allow onError handlers to be registered, so the host application could link in its own callbacks without overwriting the helper. We might allow such handlers to be registered per-graph, per-application, or both, depending on the level of flexibility required.

```
Dagoba.error = function(msg) {
  console.log(msg)
  return false
}
```

Then we'll add our new edge to both vertices' edge lists: the edge's out vertex's list of out-side edges, and the in vertex's list of in-side edges.

And that's all the graph structure we need for now!

---

[9]Often when faced with space leaks due to deep copying the solution is to use a path-copying persistent data structure, which allows mutation-free changes for only $\log N$ extra space. But the problem remains: if the host application retains a pointer to the vertex data then it can mutate that data any time, regardless of what strictures we impose in our database. The only practical solution is deep copying vertices, which doubles our space usage. Dagoba's original use case involves vertices that are treated as immutable by the host application, which allows us to avoid this issue, but requires a certain amount of discipline on the part of the user.

[10]We could make this decision based on a Dagoba-level configuration parameter, a graph-specific configuration, or possibly some type of heuristic.

[11]We use the term *list* to refer to the abstract data structure requiring push and iterate operations. We use JavaScript's "array" concrete data structure to fulfill the API required by the list abstraction. Technically both "list of edges" and "array of edges" are correct, so which we use at a given moment depends on context: if we are relying on the specific details of JavaScript arrays, like the .length property, we will say "array of edges". Otherwise we say "list of edges", as an indication that any list implementation would suffice.

6.4   Enter the Query

There are really only two parts to this system: the part that holds the graph and the part that answers questions about the graph. The part that holds the graph is pretty simple, as we've seen. The query part is a little trickier.

We'll start just like before, with a prototype and a query factory.

```
Dagoba.Q = {}

Dagoba.query = function(graph) {                    // factory
  var query = Object.create( Dagoba.Q )

  query.   graph = graph                            // the graph itself
  query.   state = []                               // state for each step
  query. program = []                               // list of steps to take
  query.gremlins = []                               // gremlins for each step

  return query
}
```

Now's a good time to introduce some friends.

A *program* is a series of *steps*. Each step is like a pipe in a pipeline—a piece of data comes in one end, is transformed in some fashion, and goes out the other end. Our pipeline doesn't quite work like that, but it's a good first approximation.

Each step in our program can have *state*, and query.state is a list of per-step states that index correlates with the list of steps in query.program.

A *gremlin* is a creature that travels through the graph doing our bidding. A gremlin might be a surprising thing to find in a database, but they trace their heritage back to Tinkerpop's Blueprints[12], and the Gremlin and Pacer query languages[13]. They remember where they've been and allow us to find answers to interesting questions.

Remember that question we wanted to answer about Thor's second cousins once removed? We decided Thor.parents.parents.parents.children.children.children was a pretty good way of expressing that. Each parents or children instance is a step in our program. Each of those steps contains a reference to its *pipetype*, which is the function that performs that step's operation.

That query in our actual system might look like:

```
g.v('Thor').out().out().out().in().in().in()
```

Each of the steps is a function call, and so they can take *arguments*. The interpreter passes the step's arguments to the step's pipetype function, so in the query g.v('Thor').out(2, 3) the out pipetype function would receive [2, 3] as its first parameter.

We'll need a way to add steps to our query. Here's a helper function for that:

```
Dagoba.Q.add = function(pipetype, args) { // add a new step to the query
  var step = [pipetype, args]
  this.program.push(step)                           // step is a pair of pipetype and its args
  return this
}
```

[12]http://euranova.eu/upl_docs/publications/an-empirical-comparison-of-graph-databases.pdf
[13]http://edbt.org/Proceedings/2013-Genova/papers/workshops/a29-holzschuher.pdf

Each step is a composite entity, combining the pipetype function with the arguments to apply to that function. We could combine the two into a partially applied function at this stage, instead of using a tuple [14], but then we'd lose some introspective power that will prove helpful later.

We'll use a small set of query initializers that generate a new query from a graph. Here's one that starts most of our examples: the v method. It builds a new query, then uses our add helper to populate the initial query program. This makes use of the vertex pipetype, which we'll look at soon.

```
Dagoba.G.v = function() {                         // query initializer: g.v() -> query
  var query = Dagoba.query(this)
  query.add('vertex', [].slice.call(arguments)) // add a step to our program
  return query
}
```

Note that `[].slice.call(arguments)` is JS parlance for "please pass me an array of this function's arguments". You would be forgiven for supposing that arguments is already an array, since it behaves like one in many situations, but it is lacking much of the functionality we utilize in modern JavaScript arrays.

6.5 The Problem with Being Eager

Before we look at the pipetypes themselves we're going to take a diversion into the exciting world of execution strategy. There are two main schools of thought: the Call By Value clan, also known as eager beavers, are strict in their insistence that all arguments be evaluated before the function is applied. Their opposing faction, the Call By Needians, are content to procrastinate until the last possible moment before doing anything—they are, in a word, lazy.

JavaScript, being a strict language, will process each of our steps as they are called. We would then expect the evaluation of g.v('Thor').out().in() to first find the Thor vertex, then find all vertices connected to it by outgoing edges, and from each of those vertices finally return all vertices they are connected to by inbound edges.

In a non-strict language we would get the same result—the execution strategy doesn't make much difference here. But what if we added a few additional calls? Given how well-connected Thor is, our g.v('Thor').out().out().out().in().in().in() query may produce many results—in fact, because we're not limiting our vertex list to unique results, it may produce many more results than we have vertices in our total graph.

We're probably only interested in getting a few unique results out, so we'll change the query a bit: g.v('Thor').out().out().out().in().in().in().unique().take(10). Now our query produces at most 10 results. What happens if we evaluate this eagerly, though? We're still going to have to build up septillions of results before returning only the first 10.

All graph databases have to support a mechanism for doing as little work as possible, and most choose some form of non-strict evaluation to do so. Since we're building our own interpreter, the lazy evaluation of our program is possible, but we may have to contend with some consequences.

---

[14] A tuple is another abstract data structure—one that is more constrained than a list. In particular a tuple has a fixed size: in this case we're using a 2-tuple (also known as a "pair" in the technical jargon of data structure researchers). Using the term for the most constrained abstract data structure required is a nicety for future implementors.

6.6 Ramifications of Evaluation Strategy on our Mental Model

Up until now our mental model for evaluation has been very simple:

- request a set of vertices
- pass the returned set as input to a pipe
- repeat as necessary

We would like to retain that model for our users, because it's easier to reason about, but as we've seen we can no longer use that model for the implementation. Having users think in a model that differs from the actual implementation is a source of much pain. A leaky abstraction is a small-scale version of this; in the large it can lead to frustration, cognitive dissonance and ragequits.

Our case is nearly optimal for this deception, though: the answer to any query will be the same, regardless of execution model. The only difference is the performance. The tradeoff is between having all users learn a more complicated model prior to using the system, or forcing a subset of users to transfer from the simple model to the complicated model in order to better reason about query performance.

Some factors to consider when wrestling with this decision are:

- the relative cognitive difficulty of learning the simple model versus the more complex model;
- the additional cognitive load imposed by first using the simple model and then advancing to the complex one versus skipping the simple and learning only the complex;
- the subset of users required to make the transition, in terms of their proportional size, cognitive availability, available time, and so on.

In our case this tradeoff makes sense. For most uses queries will return results fast enough that users needn't be concerned with optimizing their query structure or learning the deeper model. Those who will are the users writing advanced queries over large datasets, and they are also likely the users most well-equipped to transition to a new model. Additionally, our hope is that there is only a small increase in difficulty imposed by using the simple model before learning the more complex one.

We'll go into more detail on this new model soon, but in the meantime here are some highlights to keep in mind during the next section:

- Each pipe returns one result at a time, not a set of results. Each pipe may be activated many times while evaluating a query.
- A read/write head controls which pipe is activated next. The head starts at the end of the pipeline, and its movement is directed by the result of the currently active pipe.
- That result might be one of the aforementioned gremlins. Each gremlin represents a potential query result, and they carry state with them through the pipes. Gremlins cause the head to move to the right.
- A pipe can return a result of 'pull', which signals the head that it needs input and moves it to the right.
- A result of 'done' tells the head that nothing prior needs to be activated again, and moves the head left.

6.7 Pipetypes

Pipetypes make up the core of our system. Once we understand how each one works, we'll have a better basis for understanding how they're invoked and sequenced together in the interpreter.

We'll start by making a place to put our pipetypes, and a way to add new ones.

```
Dagoba.Pipetypes = {}

Dagoba.addPipetype = function(name, fun) {              // adds a chainable method
  Dagoba.Pipetypes[name] = fun
  Dagoba.Q[name] = function() {
    return this.add(name, [].slice.apply(arguments)) }  // capture pipetype and args
}
```

The pipetype's function is added to the list of pipetypes, and then a new method is added to the query object. Every pipetype must have a corresponding query method. That method adds a new step to the query program, along with its arguments.

When we evaluate g.v('Thor').out('parent').in('parent') the v call returns a query object, the out call adds a new step and returns the query object, and the in call does the same. This is what enables our method-chaining API.

Note that adding a new pipetype with the same name replaces the existing one, which allows runtime modification of existing pipetypes. What's the cost of this decision? What are the alternatives?

```
Dagoba.getPipetype = function(name) {
  var pipetype = Dagoba.Pipetypes[name]              // a pipetype is a function

  if(!pipetype)
    Dagoba.error('Unrecognized pipetype: ' + name)

  return pipetype || Dagoba.fauxPipetype
}
```

If we can't find a pipetype, we generate an error and return the default pipetype, which acts like an empty conduit: if a message comes in one side, it gets passed out the other.

```
Dagoba.fauxPipetype = function(_, _, maybe_gremlin) {   // pass the result upstream
  return maybe_gremlin || 'pull'                        // or send a pull downstream
}
```

See those underscores? We use those to label params that won't be used in our function. Most other pipetypes will use all three parameters, and have all three parameter names. This allows us to distinguish at a glance which parameters a particular pipetype relies on.

This underscore technique is also important because it makes the comments line up nicely. No, seriously. If programs "must be written for people to read, and only incidentally for machines to execute"[15], then it immediately follows that our predominant concern should be making code pretty.

Vertex

Most pipetypes we meet will take a gremlin and produce more gremlins, but this particular pipetype generates gremlins from just a string. Given an vertex ID it returns a single new gremlin. Given a query it will find all matching vertices, and yield one new gremlin at a time until it has worked through them.

---

[15]https://mitpress.mit.edu/sicp/front/node3.html

```
Dagoba.addPipetype('vertex', function(graph, args, gremlin, state) {
  if(!state.vertices)
    state.vertices = graph.findVertices(args)        // state initialization

  if(!state.vertices.length)                         // all done
    return 'done'

  var vertex = state.vertices.pop()                  // OPT: requires vertex cloning
  return Dagoba.makeGremlin(vertex, gremlin.state)   // gremlins from as/back queries
})
```

We first check to see if we've already gathered matching vertices, otherwise we try to find some. If there are any vertices, we'll pop one off and return a new gremlin sitting on that vertex. Each gremlin can carry around its own state, like a journal of where it's been and what interesting things it has seen on its journey through the graph. If we receive a gremlin as input to this step we'll copy its journal for the exiting gremlin.

Note that we're directly mutating the state argument here, and not passing it back. An alternative would be to return an object instead of a gremlin or signal, and pass state back that way. That complicates our return value, and creates some additional garbage [16]. If JS allowed multiple return values it would make this option more elegant.

We would still need to find a way to deal with the mutations, though, as the call site maintains a reference to the original variable. What if we had some way to determine whether a particular reference is "unique"—that it is the only reference to that object?

If we know a reference is unique then we can get the benefits of immutability while avoiding expensive copy-on-write schemes or complicated persistent data structures. With only one reference we can't tell whether the object has been mutated or a new object has been returned with the changes we requested: "observed immutability" is maintained [17].

There are a couple of common ways of determining this: in a statically typed system we might make use of uniqueness types [18] to guarantee at compile time that each object has only one reference. If we had a reference counter [19]—even just a cheap two-bit sticky counter—we could know at runtime that an object only has one reference and use that knowledge to our advantage.

JavaScript doesn't have either of these facilities, but we can get almost the same effect if we're really, really disciplined. Which we will be. For now.

In-N-Out

Walking the graph is as easy as ordering a burger. These two lines set up the in and out pipetypes for us.

---

[16] Very short lived garbage though, which is the second best kind.

[17] Two references to the same mutable data structure act like a pair of walkie-talkies, allowing whoever holds them to communicate directly. Those walkie-talkies can be passed around from function to function, and cloned to create a whole lot of walkie-talkies. This completely subverts the natural communication channels your code already possesses. In a system with no concurrency you can sometimes get away with it, but introduce multithreading or asynchronous behavior and all that walkie-talkie squawking can become a real drag.

[18] Uniqueness types were dusted off in the Clean language, and have a non-linear relationship with linear types, which are themselves a subtype of substructural types.

[19] Most modern JS runtimes employ generational garbage collectors, and the language is intentionally kept at arm's length from the engine's memory management to curtail a source of programmatic non-determinism.

```
Dagoba.addPipetype('out', Dagoba.simpleTraversal('out'))
Dagoba.addPipetype('in',  Dagoba.simpleTraversal('in'))
```

The `simpleTraversal` function returns a pipetype handler that accepts a gremlin as its input, and spawns a new gremlin each time it's queried. Once those gremlins are gone, it sends back a 'pull' request to get a new gremlin from its predecessor.

```
Dagoba.simpleTraversal = function(dir) {
  var find_method = dir == 'out' ? 'findOutEdges' : 'findInEdges'
  var edge_list   = dir == 'out' ? '_in' : '_out'

  return function(graph, args, gremlin, state) {
    if(!gremlin && (!state.edges || !state.edges.length))      // query initialization
      return 'pull'

    if(!state.edges || !state.edges.length) {                  // state initialization
      state.gremlin = gremlin
      state.edges = graph[find_method](gremlin.vertex)         // get matching edges
                        .filter(Dagoba.filterEdges(args[0]))
    }

    if(!state.edges.length)                                    // nothing more to do
      return 'pull'

    var vertex = state.edges.pop()[edge_list]                  // use up an edge
    return Dagoba.gotoVertex(state.gremlin, vertex)
  }
}
```

The first couple of lines handle the differences between the in version and the out version. Then we're ready to return our pipetype function, which looks quite a bit like the vertex pipetype we just saw. That's a little surprising, since this one takes in a gremlin whereas the vertex pipetype creates gremlins *ex nihilo*.

Yet we can see the same beats being hit here, with the addition of a query initialization step. If there's no gremlin and we're out of available edges then we pull. If we have a gremlin but haven't yet set state then we find any edges going the appropriate direction and add them to our state. If there's a gremlin but its current vertex has no appropriate edges then we pull. And finally we pop off an edge and return a freshly cloned gremlin on the vertex to which it points.

Glancing at this code we see `!state.edges.length` repeated in each of the three clauses. It's tempting to refactor this to reduce the complexity of those conditionals. There are two issues keeping us from doing so.

One is relatively minor: the third `!state.edges.length` means something different from the first two, since `state.edges` has been changed between the second and third conditional. This actually encourages us to refactor, because having the same label mean two different things inside a single function usually isn't ideal.

The second is more serious. This isn't the only pipetype function we're writing, and we'll see these ideas of query initialization and/or state initialization repeated over and over. When writing code, there's always a balancing act between structured qualities and unstructured qualities. Too much structure and you pay a high cost in boilerplate and abstraction complexity. Too little structure and you'll have to keep all the plumbing minutia in your head.

```
```

In this case, with a dozen or so pipetypes, the right choice seems to be to style each of the pipetype functions as similarly as possible, and label the constituent pieces with comments. So we resist our impulse to refactor this particular pipetype, because doing so would reduce uniformity, but we also resist the urge to engineer a formal structural abstraction for query initialization, state initialization, and the like. If there were hundreds of pipetypes that latter choice would probably be the right one: the complexity cost of the abstraction is constant, while the benefit accrues linearly with the number of units. When handling that many moving pieces, anything you can do to enforce regularity among them is helpful.

Property

Let's pause for a moment to consider an example query based on the three pipetypes we've seen. We can ask for Thor's grandparents like this[20]:

```
g.v('Thor').out('parent').out('parent').run()
```

But what if we wanted their names? We could put a map on the end of that:

```
g.v('Thor').out('parent').out('parent').run()
 .map(function(vertex) {return vertex.name})
```

But this is a common enough operation that we'd prefer to write something more like:

```
g.v('Thor').out('parent').out('parent').property('name').run()
```

Plus this way the property pipe is an integral part of the query, instead of something appended after. This has some interesting benefits, as we'll soon see.

```
Dagoba.addPipetype('property', function(graph, args, gremlin, state) {
  if(!gremlin) return 'pull'                              // query initialization
  gremlin.result = gremlin.vertex[args[0]]
  return gremlin.result == null ? false : gremlin         // false for bad props
})
```

Our query initialization here is trivial: if there's no gremlin, we pull. If there is a gremlin, we'll set its result to the property's value. Then the gremlin can continue onward. If it makes it through the last pipe its result will be collected and returned from the query. Not all gremlins have a result property. Those that don't return their most recently visited vertex.

Note that if the property doesn't exist we return false instead of the gremlin, so property pipes also act as a type of filter. Can you think of a use for this? What are the tradeoffs in this design decision?

Unique

If we want to collect all Thor's grandparents' grandchildren—his cousins, his siblings, and himself—we could do a query like this: g.v('Thor').in().in().out().out().run(). That would give us many duplicates, however. In fact there would be at least four copies of Thor himself. (Can you think of a time when there might be more?)

To resolve this we introduce a new pipetype called 'unique'. Our new query produces output in one-to-one correspondence with the grandchildren:

---

[20]The run() at the end of the query invokes the interpreter and returns results.

```
g.v('Thor').in().in().out().out().unique().run()
```

The pipetype implementation:

```
Dagoba.addPipetype('unique', function(graph, args, gremlin, state) {
  if(!gremlin) return 'pull'                        // query initialization
  if(state[gremlin.vertex._id]) return 'pull'       // reject repeats
  state[gremlin.vertex._id] = true
  return gremlin
})
```

A unique pipe is purely a filter: it either passes the gremlin through unchanged or it tries to pull a new gremlin from the previous pipe.

We initialize by trying to collect a gremlin. If the gremlin's current vertex is in our cache, then we've seen it before so we try to collect a new one. Otherwise, we add the gremlin's current vertex to our cache and pass it along. Easy peasy.

Filter

We've seen two simplistic ways of filtering, but sometimes we need more elaborate constraints. What if we want to find all of Thor's siblings whose weight is greater than their height [21]? This query would give us our answer:

```
g.v('Thor').out().in().unique()
  .filter(function(asgardian) { return asgardian.weight > asgardian.height })
  .run()
```

If we want to know which of Thor's siblings survive Ragnarök we can pass filter an object:

```
g.v('Thor').out().in().unique().filter({survives: true}).run()
```

Here's how it works:

```
Dagoba.addPipetype('filter', function(graph, args, gremlin, state) {
  if(!gremlin) return 'pull'                              // query initialization

  if(typeof args[0] == 'object')                          // filter by object
    return Dagoba.objectFilter(gremlin.vertex, args[0])
        ? gremlin : 'pull'

  if(typeof args[0] != 'function') {
    Dagoba.error('Filter is not a function: ' + args[0])
    return gremlin                                        // keep things moving
  }

  if(!args[0](gremlin.vertex, gremlin)) return 'pull'      // gremlin fails filter
  return gremlin
})
```

---

[21] With weight in skippund and height in fathoms, naturally. Depending on the density of Asgardian flesh this may return many results, or none at all. (Or just Volstagg, if we're allowing Shakespeare by way of Jack Kirby into our pantheon.)

If the filter's first argument is not an object or function then we trigger an error, and pass the gremlin along. Pause for a minute, and consider the alternatives. Why would we decide to continue the query once an error is encountered?

There are two reasons this error might arise. The first involves a programmer typing in a query, either in a REPL or directly in code. When run, that query will produce results, and also generate a programmer-observable error. The programmer then corrects the error to further filter the set of results produced. Alternatively, the system could display only the error and produce no results, and fixing all errors would allow results to be displayed.

The second possibility is that the filter is being applied dynamically at run time. This is a much more important case, because the person invoking the query is not necessarily the author of the query code. Because this is on the web, our default rule is to always show results, and to never break things. It is usually preferable to soldier on in the face of trouble rather than succumb to our wounds and present the user with a grisly error message.

For those occasions when showing too few results is better than showing too many, Dagoba.error can be overridden to throw an error, thereby circumventing the natural control flow.

Take

We don't always want all the results at once. Sometimes we only need a handful of results; say we want a dozen of Thor's contemporaries, so we walk all the way back to the primeval cow Auðumbla:

```
g.v('Thor').out().out().out().out().in().in().in().in().unique().take(12).run()
```

Without the take pipe that query could take quite a while to run, but thanks to our lazy evaluation strategy the query with the take pipe is very efficient.

Sometimes we just want one at a time: we'll process the result, work with it, and then come back for another one. This pipetype allows us to do that as well.

```
q = g.v('Auðumbla').in().in().in().property('name').take(1)

q.run() // ['Odin']
q.run() // ['Vili']
q.run() // ['Vé']
q.run() // []
```

Our query can function in an asynchronous environment, allowing us to collect more results as needed. When we run out, an empty array is returned.

```
Dagoba.addPipetype('take', function(graph, args, gremlin, state) {
  state.taken = state.taken || 0                    // state initialization

  if(state.taken == args[0]) {
    state.taken = 0
    return 'done'                                   // all done
  }

  if(!gremlin) return 'pull'                         // query initialization
  state.taken++
  return gremlin
})
```

We initialize state.taken to zero if it doesn't already exist. JavaScript has implicit coercion, but coerces undefined into NaN, so we have to be explicit here [22].

Then when state.taken reaches args[0] we return 'done', sealing off the pipes before us. We also reset the state.taken counter, allowing us to repeat the query later.

We do those two steps before query initialization to handle the cases of take(0) and take() [23]. Then we increment our counter and return the gremlin.

As

These next four pipetypes work as a group to allow more advanced queries. This one just allows you to label the current vertex. We'll use that label with the next two pipetypes.

```
Dagoba.addPipetype('as', function(graph, args, gremlin, state) {
  if(!gremlin) return 'pull'                      // query initialization
  gremlin.state.as = gremlin.state.as || {}       // init the 'as' state
  gremlin.state.as[args[0]] = gremlin.vertex      // set label to vertex
  return gremlin
})
```

After initializing the query, we ensure the gremlin's local state has an as parameter. Then we set a property of that parameter to the gremlin's current vertex.

Merge

Once we've labeled vertices we can extract them using merge. If we want Thor's parents, grandparents and great-grandparents we can do something like this:

```
g.v('Thor').out().as('parent').out().as('grandparent').out().as('great-grandparent')
          .merge('parent', 'grandparent', 'great-grandparent').run()
```

Here's the merge pipetype:

```
Dagoba.addPipetype('merge', function(graph, args, gremlin, state) {
  if(!state.vertices && !gremlin) return 'pull'        // query initialization

  if(!state.vertices || !state.vertices.length) {      // state initialization
    var obj = (gremlin.state||{}).as || {}
    state.vertices = args.map(function(id) {return obj[id]}).filter(Boolean)
  }

  if(!state.vertices.length) return 'pull'             // done with this batch

  var vertex = state.vertices.pop()
  return Dagoba.makeGremlin(vertex, gremlin.state)
})
```

---

[22] Some would argue it's best to be explicit all the time. Others would argue that a good system for implicits makes for more concise, readable code, with less boilerplate and a smaller surface area for bugs. One thing we can all agree on is that making effective use of JavaScript's implicit coercion requires memorizing a lot of non-intuitive special cases, making it a minefield for the uninitiated.

[23] What would you expect each of those to return? What do they actually return?

We map over each argument, looking for it in the gremlin's list of labeled vertices. If we find it, we clone the gremlin to that vertex. Note that only gremlins that make it to this pipe are included in the merge—if Thor's mother's parents aren't in the graph, she won't be in the result set.

Except

We've already seen cases where we would like to say "Give me all Thor's siblings who are not Thor". We can do that with a filter:

```
g.v('Thor').out().in().unique()
            .filter(function(asgardian) {return asgardian._id != 'Thor'}).run()
```

It's more straightforward with as and except:

```
g.v('Thor').as('me').out().in().except('me').unique().run()
```

But there are also queries that would be difficult to try to filter. What if we wanted Thor's uncles and aunts? How would we filter out his parents? It's easy with as and except [24]:

```
g.v('Thor').out().as('parent').out().in().except('parent').unique().run()

Dagoba.addPipetype('except', function(graph, args, gremlin, state) {
  if(!gremlin) return 'pull'                              // query initialization
  if(gremlin.vertex == gremlin.state.as[args[0]]) return 'pull'
  return gremlin
})
```

Here we're checking whether the current vertex is equal to the one we stored previously. If it is, we skip it.

Back

Some of the questions we might ask involve checking further into the graph, only to return later to our point of origin if the answer is in the affirmative. Suppose we wanted to know which of Fjörgynn's daughters had children with one of Bestla's sons?

```
g.v('Fjörgynn').in().as('me')    // first gremlin's state.as is Frigg
 .in()                           // first gremlin's vertex is now Baldr
 .out().out()                    // clone that gremlin for each grandparent
 .filter({_id: 'Bestla'})        // keep only the gremlin on grandparent Bestla
 .back('me').unique().run()      // jump gremlin's vertex back to Frigg and exit
```

Here's the definition for back:

```
Dagoba.addPipetype('back', function(graph, args, gremlin, state) {
  if(!gremlin) return 'pull'                              // query initialization
  return Dagoba.gotoVertex(gremlin, gremlin.state.as[args[0]])
})
```

We're using the Dagoba.gotoVertex helper function to do all real work here. Let's take a look at that and some other helpers now.

---

[24]There are certain conditions under which this particular query might yield unexpected results. Can you think of any? How could you modify it to handle those cases?

6.8 Helpers

The pipetypes above rely on a few helpers to do their jobs. Let's take a quick look at those before diving in to the interpreter.

Gremlins

Gremlins are simple creatures: they have a current vertex, and some local state. So to make a new one we just need to make an object with those two things.

```
Dagoba.makeGremlin = function(vertex, state) {
  return {vertex: vertex, state: state || {} }
}
```

Any object that has a vertex property and a state property is a gremlin by this definition, so we could just inline the constructor, but wrapping it in a function allows us to add new properties to all gremlins in a single place.

We can also take an existing gremlin and send it to a new vertex, as we saw in the back pipetype and the simpleTraversal function.

```
Dagoba.gotoVertex = function(gremlin, vertex) {          // clone the gremlin
  return Dagoba.makeGremlin(vertex, gremlin.state)
}
```

Note that this function actually returns a brand new gremlin: a clone of the old one, sent to our desired destination. That means a gremlin can sit on a vertex while its clones are sent out to explore many other vertices. This is exactly what happens in simpleTraversal.

As an example of possible enhancements, we could add a bit of state to keep track of every vertex the gremlin visits, and add new pipetypes to take advantage of those paths.

Finding

The vertex pipetype uses the findVertices function to collect a set of initial vertices from which to begin our query.

```
Dagoba.G.findVertices = function(args) {                 // vertex finder helper
  if(typeof args[0] == 'object')
    return this.searchVertices(args[0])
  else if(args.length == 0)
    return this.vertices.slice()                         // OPT: slice is costly
  else
    return this.findVerticesByIds(args)
}
```

This function receives its arguments as a list. If the first one is an object it passes it to searchVertices, allowing queries like:

```
g.v({_id:'Thor'}).run()
g.v({species: 'Aesir'}).run()
```

Otherwise, if there are arguments it gets passed to `findVerticesByIds`, which handles queries like `g.v('Thor', 'Odin').run()`.

If there are no arguments at all, then our query looks like `g.v().run()`. This isn't something you'll want to do frequently with large graphs, especially since we're slicing the vertex list before returning it. We slice because some call sites manipulate the returned list directly by popping items off as they work through them. We could optimize this use case by cloning at the call site, or by avoiding those manipulations. (We could keep a counter in state instead of popping.)

```
Dagoba.G.findVerticesByIds = function(ids) {
  if(ids.length == 1) {
    var maybe_vertex = this.findVertexById(ids[0])        // maybe it's a vertex
    return maybe_vertex ? [maybe_vertex] : []             // or maybe it isn't
  }

  return ids.map( this.findVertexById.bind(this) ).filter(Boolean)
}

Dagoba.G.findVertexById = function(vertex_id) {
  return this.vertexIndex[vertex_id]
}
```

Note the use of `vertexIndex` here. Without that index we'd have to go through each vertex in our list one at a time to decide if it matched the ID—turning a constant time operation into a linear time one, and any $O(n)$ operations that directly rely on it into $O(n^2)$ operations.

```
Dagoba.G.searchVertices = function(filter) {          // match on filter's properties
  return this.vertices.filter(function(vertex) {
    return Dagoba.objectFilter(vertex, filter)
  })
}
```

The `searchVertices` function uses the `objectFilter` helper on every vertex in the graph. We'll look at `objectFilter` in the next section, but in the meantime, can you think of a way to search through the vertices lazily?

Filtering

We saw that `simpleTraversal` uses a filtering function on the edges it encounters. It's a simple function, but powerful enough for our purposes.

```
Dagoba.filterEdges = function(filter) {
  return function(edge) {
    if(!filter)                               // no filter: everything is valid
      return true

    if(typeof filter == 'string')             // string filter: label must match
      return edge._label == filter

    if(Array.isArray(filter))                 // array filter: must contain label
      return !!~filter.indexOf(edge._label)
```

```
    return Dagoba.objectFilter(edge, filter)     // object filter: check edge keys
  }
}
```

The first case is no filter at all: `g.v('Odin').in().run()` traverses all edges to Odin.

The second case filters on the edge's label: `g.v('Odin').in('parent').run()` traverses those edges with a label of 'parent'.

The third case accepts an array of labels: `g.v('Odin').in(['parent', 'spouse']).run()` traverses both parent and spouse edges.

And the fourth case uses the objectFilter function we saw before:

```
Dagoba.objectFilter = function(thing, filter) {
  for(var key in filter)
    if(thing[key] !== filter[key])
      return false

  return true
}
```

This allows us to query the edge using a filter object:

```
'g.v('Odin').in({_label: 'spouse', order: 2}).run()'     // finds Odin's second wife
```

6.9   The Interpreter's Nature

We've arrived at the top of the narrative mountain, ready to receive our prize: the interpreter. The code is actually fairly compact, but the model has a bit of subtlety.

We compared programs to pipelines earlier, and that's a good mental model for writing queries. As we saw, though, we need a different model for the actual implementation. That model is more like a Turing machine than a pipeline: there's a read/write head that sits over a particular step. It "reads" the step, changes its "state", and then moves either right or left.

Reading the step means evaluating the pipetype function. As we saw above, each of those functions accepts as input the entire graph, its own arguments, maybe a gremlin, and its own local state. As output it provides a gremlin, false, or a signal of 'pull' or 'done'. This output is what our quasi-Turing machine reads in order to change the machine's state.

That state comprises just two variables: one to record steps that are 'done', and another to record the `results` of the query. Those are updated, and then either the machine head moves or the query finishes and the result is returned.

We've now described all the state in our machine. We'll have a list of results that starts empty:

```
var results = []
```

An index of the last 'done' step that starts behind the first step:

```
var done = -1
```

We need a place to store the most recent step's output, which might be a gremlin—or it might be nothing—so we'll call it `maybe_gremlin`:

```
var maybe_gremlin = false
```

And finally we'll need a program counter to indicate the position of the read/write head.

```
var pc = this.program.length - 1
```

Except... wait a second. How are we going to get lazy [25]? The traditional way of building a lazy system out of an eager one is to store parameters to function calls as "thunks" instead of evaluating them. You can think of a thunk as an unevaluated expression. In JS, which has first-class functions and closures, we can create a thunk by wrapping a function and its arguments in a new anonymous function which takes no arguments:

```
function sum() {
  return [].slice.call(arguments).reduce(function(acc, n) { return acc + (n|0) }, 0)
}

function thunk_of_sum_1_2_3() { return sum(1, 2, 3) }

function thunker(fun, args) {
  return function() {return fun.apply(fun, args)}
}

function thunk_wrapper(fun) {
  return function() {
    return thunker.apply(null, [fun].concat([[].slice.call(arguments)]))
  }
}

sum(1, 2, 3)            // -> 6
thunk_of_sum_1_2_3()    // -> 6
thunker(sum, [1, 2, 3])() // -> 6

var sum2 = thunk_wrapper(sum)
var thunk = sum2(1, 2, 3)
thunk()                 // -> 6
```

None of the thunks are invoked until one is actually needed, which usually implies some type of output is required: in our case the result of a query. Each time the interpreter encounters a new function call, we wrap it in a thunk. Recall our original formulation of a query: `children(children(children(parents(parents(parents([8]))))))`. Each of those layers would be a thunk, wrapped up like an onion.

There are a couple of tradeoffs with this approach: one is that spatial performance becomes more difficult to reason about, because of the potentially vast thunk graphs that can be created. Another is that our program is now expressed as a single thunk, and we can't do much with it at that point.

This second point isn't usually an issue, because of the phase separation between when our compiler runs its optimizations and when all the thunking occurs at runtime. In our case we don't have that advantage: because we're using method chaining to implement a fluent interface [26] if we

---

[25] Technically we need to implement an interpreter with non-strict semantics, which means it will only evaluate when forced to do so. Lazy evaluation is a technique used for implementing non-strictness. It's a bit lazy of us to conflate the two, so we will only disambiguate when forced to do so.

[26] Method chaining lets us write `g.v('Thor').in().out().run()` instead of the six lines of non-fluent JS required to accomplish the same thing.

also use thunks to achieve laziness we would thunk each new method as it is called, which means by the time we get to run() we have only a thunk as our input, and no way to optimize our query.

Interestingly, our fluent interface hides another difference between our query language and regular programming languages. The query g.v('Thor').in().out().run() could be rewritten as run(out(in(v(g, 'Thor')))) if we weren't using method chaining. In JS we would first process g and 'Thor', then v, then in, out and run, working from the inside out. In a language with non-strict semantics we would work from the outside in, processing each consecutive nested layer of arguments only as needed.

So if we start evaluating our query at the end of the statement, with run, and work our way back to v('Thor'), calculating results only as needed, then we've effectively achieved non-strictness. The secret is in the linearity of our queries. Branches complicate the process graph and also introduce opportunities for duplicate calls, which require memoization to avoid wasted work. The simplicity of our query language means we can implement an equally simple interpreter based on our linear read/write head model.

In addition to allowing runtime optimizations, this style has many other benefits related to the ease of instrumentation: history, reversibility, stepwise debugging, query statistics. All these are easy to add dynamically because we control the interpreter and have left it as a virtual machine evaluator instead of reducing the program to a single thunk.

6.10   Interpreter, Unveiled

```
Dagoba.Q.run = function() {              // a machine for query processing

  var max = this.program.length - 1      // index of the last step in the program
  var maybe_gremlin = false              // a gremlin, a signal string, or false
  var results = []                       // results for this particular run
  var done = -1                          // behindwhich things have finished
  var pc = max                           // our program counter

  var step, state, pipetype

  while(done < max) {
    var ts = this.state
    step = this.program[pc]              // step is a pair of pipetype and args
    state = (ts[pc] = ts[pc] || {})      // this step's state must be an object
    pipetype = Dagoba.getPipetype(step[0]) // a pipetype is just a function
```

Here max is just a constant, and step, state, and pipetype cache information about the current step. We've entered the driver loop, and we won't stop until the last step is done.

```
    maybe_gremlin = pipetype(this.graph, step[1], maybe_gremlin, state)
```

Calling the step's pipetype function with its arguments.

```
    if(maybe_gremlin == 'pull') {        // 'pull' means the pipe wants more input
      maybe_gremlin = false
      if(pc-1 > done) {
        pc--                             // try the previous pipe
        continue
```

```
    } else {
        done = pc                          // previous pipe is done, so we are too
    }
}
```

To handle the 'pull' case we first set `maybe_gremlin` [27] to false. We're overloading our 'maybe' here by using it as a channel to pass the 'pull' and 'done' signals, but once one of those signals is sucked out we go back to thinking of this as a proper 'maybe'.

If the step before us isn't 'done' [28] we'll move the head backward and try again. Otherwise, we mark ourselves as 'done' and let the head naturally fall forward.

```
if(maybe_gremlin == 'done') {              // 'done' tells us the pipe is finished
    maybe_gremlin = false
    done = pc
}
```

Handling the 'done' case is even easier: set `maybe_gremlin` to false and mark this step as 'done'.

```
pc++                                       // move on to the next pipe

if(pc > max) {
    if(maybe_gremlin)
        results.push(maybe_gremlin)        // a gremlin popped out of the pipeline
    maybe_gremlin = false
    pc--                                   // take a step back
    }
}
```

We're done with the current step, and we've moved the head to the next one. If we're at the end of the program and `maybe_gremlin` contains a gremlin, we'll add it to the results, set `maybe_gremlin` to false and move the head back to the last step in the program.

This is also the initialization state, since `pc` starts as `max`. So we start here and work our way back, and end up here again at least once for each final result the query returns.

```
results = results.map(function(gremlin) { // return projected results, or vertices
    return gremlin.result != null
        ? gremlin.result : gremlin.vertex } )

return results
}
```

We're out of the driver loop now: the query has ended, the results are in, and we just need to process and return them. If any gremlin has its result set we'll return that, otherwise we'll return the gremlin's final vertex. Are there other things we might want to return? What are the tradeoffs here?

---

[27] We call it `maybe_gremlin` to remind ourselves that it could be a gremlin, or it could be something else. Also because originally it was either a gremlin or Nothing.

[28] Recall that done starts at -1, so the first step's predecessor is always done.

6.11 Query Transformers

Now we have a nice compact interpreter for our query programs, but we're still missing something. Every modern DBMS comes with a query optimizer as an essential part of the system. For non-relational databases, optimizing our query plan rarely yields the exponential speedups seen in their relational cousins [29], but it's still an important aspect of database design.

What's the simplest thing we could do that could reasonably be called a query optimizer? Well, we could write little functions for transforming our query programs before we run them. We'll pass a program in as input and get a different program back out as output.

```
Dagoba.T = []                              // transformers (more than meets the eye)

Dagoba.addTransformer = function(fun, priority) {
  if(typeof fun != 'function')
    return Dagoba.error('Invalid transformer function')

  for(var i = 0; i < Dagoba.T.length; i++)  // OPT: binary search
    if(priority > Dagoba.T[i].priority) break

  Dagoba.T.splice(i, 0, {priority: priority, fun: fun})
}
```

Now we can add query transformers to our system. A query transformer is a function that accepts a program and returns a program, plus a priority level. Higher priority transformers are placed closer to the front of the list. We're ensuring fun is a function, because we're going to evaluate it later [30].

We'll assume there won't be an enormous number of transformer additions, and walk the list linearly to add a new one. We'll leave a note in case this assumption turns out to be false—a binary search is much more time-optimal for long lists, but adds a little complexity and doesn't really speed up short lists.

To run these transformers we're going to inject a single line of code in to the top of our interpreter:

```
Dagoba.Q.run = function() {                    // our virtual machine for querying
  this.program = Dagoba.transform(this.program) // activate the transformers
```

We'll use that to call this function, which just passes our program through each transformer in turn:

```
Dagoba.transform = function(program) {
  return Dagoba.T.reduce(function(acc, transformer) {
    return transformer.fun(acc)
  }, program)
}
```

Up until this point, our engine has traded simplicity for performance, but one of the nice things about this strategy is that it leaves doors open for global optimizations that may have been unavailable if we had opted to optimize locally as we designed the system.

---

[29] Or, more pointedly, a poorly phrased query is less likely to yield exponential slowdowns. As an end-user of an RDBMS the aesthetics of query quality can often be quite opaque.

[30] Note that we're keeping the domain of the priority parameter open, so it can be an integer, a rational, a negative number, or even things like Infinity or NaN.

Optimizing a program can often increase complexity and reduce the elegance of the system, making it harder to reason about and maintain. Breaking abstraction barriers for performance gains is one of the more egregious forms of optimization, but even something seemingly innocuous like embedding performance-oriented code into business logic makes maintenance more difficult.

In light of that, this type of "orthogonal optimization" is particularly appealing. We can add optimizers in modules or even user code, instead of having them tightly coupled to the engine. We can test them in isolation, or in groups, and with the addition of generative testing we could even automate that process, ensuring that our available optimizers play nicely together.

We can also use this transformer system to add new functionality unrelated to optimization. Let's look at a case of that now.

6.12 Aliases

Making a query like g.v('Thor').out().in() is quite compact, but is this Thor's siblings or his mates? Neither interpretation is fully satisfying. It'd be nicer to say what mean: either g.v('Thor').parents().children() or g.v('Thor').children().parents().

We can use query transformers to make aliases with just a couple of extra helper functions:

```
Dagoba.addAlias = function(newname, oldname, defaults) {
  defaults = defaults || []                      // default arguments for the alias
  Dagoba.addTransformer(function(program) {
    return program.map(function(step) {
      if(step[0] != newname) return step
      return [oldname, Dagoba.extend(step[1], defaults)]
    })
  }, 100)                                         // 100 because aliases run early

  Dagoba.addPipetype(newname, function() {})
}
```

We're adding a new name for an existing step, so we'll need to create a query transformer that converts the new name to the old name whenever it's encountered. We'll also need to add the new name as a method on the main query object, so it can be pulled into the query program.

If we could capture missing method calls and route them to a handler function then we might be able to run this transformer with a lower priority, but there's currently no way to do that. Instead we will run it with a high priority of 100 so the aliased methods are added before they are invoked.

We call another helper to merge the incoming step's arguments with the alias's default arguments. If the incoming step is missing an argument then we'll use the alias's argument for that slot.

```
Dagoba.extend = function(list, defaults) {
  return Object.keys(defaults).reduce(function(acc, key) {
    if(typeof list[key] != 'undefined') return acc
    acc[key] = defaults[key]
    return acc
  }, list)
}
```

Now we can make those aliases we wanted:

```
Dagoba.addAlias('parents', 'out')
Dagoba.addAlias('children', 'in')
```

We can also start to specialize our data model a little more, by labeling each edge between a parent and child as a 'parent' edge. Then our aliases would look like this:

```
Dagoba.addAlias('parents', 'out', ['parent'])
Dagoba.addAlias('children', 'in', ['parent'])
```

Now we can add edges for spouses, step-parents, or even jilted ex-lovers. If we enhance our addAlias function we can introduce new aliases for grandparents, siblings, or even cousins:

```
Dagoba.addAlias('grandparents', [ ['out', 'parent'], ['out', 'parent']])
Dagoba.addAlias('siblings',     [ ['as', 'me'], ['out', 'parent']
                                , ['in', 'parent'], ['except', 'me']])
Dagoba.addAlias('cousins',      [ ['out', 'parent'], ['as', 'folks']
                                , ['out', 'parent'], ['in', 'parent']
                                , ['except', 'folks'], ['in', 'parent']
                                , ['unique']])
```

That cousins alias is kind of cumbersome. Maybe we could expand our addAlias function to allow ourselves to use other aliases in our aliases, and call it like this:

```
Dagoba.addAlias('cousins',      [ 'parents', ['as', 'folks']
                                , 'parents', 'children'
                                , ['except', 'folks'], 'children', 'unique'])
```

Now instead of

```
g.v('Forseti').parents().as('parents').parents().children()
                    .except('parents').children().unique()
```

we can just say g.v('Forseti').cousins().

We've introduced a bit of a pickle, though: while our addAlias function is resolving an alias it also has to resolve other aliases. What if parents called some other alias, and while we were resolving cousins we had to stop to resolve parents and then resolve its aliases and so on? What if one of parents aliases ultimately called cousins?

This brings us in to the realm of dependency resolution [31], a core component of modern package managers. There are a lot of fancy tricks for choosing ideal versions, tree shaking, general optimizations and the like, but the basic idea is fairly simple. We're going to make a graph of all the dependencies and their relationships, and then try to find a way to line up the vertices while making all the arrows go from left to right. If we can, then this particular sorting of the vertices is called a 'topological ordering', and we've proven that our dependency graph has no cycles: it is a Directed Acyclic Graph (DAG). If we fail to do so then our graph has at least one cycle.

On the other hand, we expect that our queries will generally be rather short (100 steps would be a very long query) and that we'll have a reasonably low number of transformers. Instead of fiddling around with DAGs and dependency management we could return 'true' from the transform function if anything changed, and then run it until it stops being productive. This requires each transformer to be idempotent, but that's a useful property for transformers to have. What are the pros and cons of these two pathways?

---

[31] You can learn more about dependency resolution in Chapter 4.

6.13 Performance

All production graph databases share a particular performance characteristic: graph traversal queries are constant time with respect to total graph size [32]. In a non-graph database, asking for the list of someone's friends can require time proportional to the number of entries, because in the naive worst-case you have to look at every entry. This means if a query over ten entries takes a millisecond, then a query over ten million entries will take almost two weeks. Your friend list would arrive faster if sent by Pony Express [33]!

To alleviate this dismal performance most databases index over oft-queried fields, which turns an $O(n)$ search into an $O(logn)$ search. This gives considerably better search performance, but at the cost of some write performance and a lot of space—indices can easily double the size of a database. Careful balancing of the space/time tradeoffs of indices is part of the perpetual tuning process for most databases.

Graph databases sidestep this issue by making direct connections between vertices and edges, so graph traversals are just pointer jumps; no need to scan through every item, no need for indices, no extra work at all. Now finding your friends has the same price regardless of the total number of people in the graph, with no additional space cost or write time cost. One downside to this approach is that the pointers work best when the whole graph is in memory on the same machine. Effectively sharding a graph database across multiple machines is still an active area of research [34].

We can see this at work in the microcosm of Dagoba if we replace the functions for finding edges. Here's a naive version that searches through all the edges in linear time. It's similar to our very first implementation, but uses all the structures we've since built.

```
Dagoba.G.findInEdges  = function(vertex) {
  return this.edges.filter(function(edge) {return edge._in._id  == vertex._id} )
}
Dagoba.G.findOutEdges = function(vertex) {
  return this.edges.filter(function(edge) {return edge._out._id == vertex._id} )
}
```

We can add an index for edges, which gets us most of the way there with small graphs but has all the classic indexing issues for large ones.

```
Dagoba.G.findInEdges  = function(vertex) { return this.inEdgeIndex [vertex._id] }
Dagoba.G.findOutEdges = function(vertex) { return this.outEdgeIndex[vertex._id] }
```

And here we have our old friends back again: pure, sweet index-free adjacency.

```
Dagoba.G.findInEdges  = function(vertex) { return vertex._in  }
Dagoba.G.findOutEdges = function(vertex) { return vertex._out }
```

Run these yourself to experience the graph database difference [37].

---

[32] The fancy term for this is "index-free adjacency".

[33] Though only in operation for 18 months due to the arrival of the transcontinental telegraph and the outbreak of the American Civil War, the Pony Express is still remembered today for delivering mail coast to coast in just ten days.

[34] Sharding a graph database requires partitioning the graph. Optimal graph partitioning is NP-hard[35], even for simple graphs like trees and grids, and good approximations also have exponential asymptotic complexity[36].

[37] In modern JavaScript engines filtering a list is quite fast—for small graphs the naive version can actually be faster than the index-free version due to the underlying data structures and the way the code is JIT compiled. Try it with different sizes of graphs to see how the two approaches scale.

6.14 Serialization

Having a graph in memory is great, but how do we get it there in the first place? We saw that our graph constructor can take a list of vertices and edges and create a graph for us, but once the graph has been built how do we get the vertices and edges back out?

Our natural inclination is to do something like JSON.stringify(graph), which produces the terribly helpful error "TypeError: Converting circular structure to JSON". During the graph construction process the vertices were linked to their edges, and the edges are all linked to their vertices, so now everything refers to everything else. So how can we extract our nice neat lists again? JSON replacer functions to the rescue.

The JSON.stringify function takes a value to stringify, but it also takes two additional parameters: a replacer function and a whitespace number [38]. The replacer allows you to customize how the stringification proceeds.

We need to treat the vertices and edges a bit differently, so we're going to manually merge the two sides into a single JSON string.

```
Dagoba.jsonify = function(graph) {
  return '{"V":' + JSON.stringify(graph.vertices, Dagoba.cleanVertex)
       + ',"E":' + JSON.stringify(graph.edges,    Dagoba.cleanEdge)
       + '}'
}
```

And these are the replacers for vertices and edges.

```
Dagoba.cleanVertex = function(key, value) {
  return (key == '_in' || key == '_out') ? undefined : value
}

Dagoba.cleanEdge = function(key, value) {
  return (key == '_in' || key == '_out') ? value._id : value
}
```

The only difference between them is what they do when a cycle is about to be formed: for vertices, we skip the edge list entirely. For edges, we replace each vertex with its ID. That gets rid of all the cycles we created while building the graph.

We're manually manipulating JSON in Dagoba.jsonify, which generally isn't recommended as the JSON format is rather persnickety. Even in a dose this small it's easy to miss something and hard to visually confirm correctness.

We could merge the two replacer functions into a single function, and use that new replacer function over the whole graph by doing JSON.stringify(graph, my_cool_replacer). This frees us from having to manually massage the JSON output, but the resulting code may be quite a bit messier. Try it yourself and see if you can come up with a well-factored solution that avoids hand-coded JSON. (Bonus points if it fits in a tweet.)

---

[38] Pro tip: Given a deep tree deep_tree, running JSON.stringify(deep_tree, 0, 2) in the JS console is a quick way to make it human readable.

6.15 Persistence

Persistence is usually one of the trickier parts of a database: disks are relatively safe but slow. Batching writes, making them atomic, journaling—these are difficult to make both fast and correct.

Fortunately, we're building an *in-memory* database, so we don't have to worry about any of that! We may, though, occasionally want to save a copy of the database locally for fast restart on page load. We can use the serializer we just built to do exactly that. First let's wrap it in a helper function:

```
Dagoba.G.toString = function() { return Dagoba.jsonify(this) }
```

In JavaScript an object's toString function is called whenever that object is coerced into a string. So if g is a graph, then g+" will be the graph's serialized JSON string.

The fromString function isn't part of the language specification, but it's handy to have around.

```
Dagoba.fromString = function(str) {           // another graph constructor
  var obj = JSON.parse(str)                    // this can throw
  return Dagoba.graph(obj.V, obj.E)
}
```

Now we'll use those in our persistence functions. The toString function is hiding—can you spot it?

```
Dagoba.persist = function(graph, name) {
  name = name || 'graph'
  localStorage.setItem('DAGOBA::'+name, graph)
}

Dagoba.depersist = function (name) {
  name = 'DAGOBA::' + (name || 'graph')
  var flatgraph = localStorage.getItem(name)
  return Dagoba.fromString(flatgraph)
}
```

We preface the name with a faux namespace to avoid polluting the localStorage properties of the domain, as it can get quite crowded in there. There's also usually a low storage limit, so for larger graphs we'd probably want to use a Blob of some sort.

There are also potential issues if multiple browser windows from the same domain are persisting and depersisting simultaneously. The localStorage space is shared between those windows, and they're potentially on different event loops, so there's the possibility of one carelessly overwriting the work of another. The spec says there should be a mutex required for read/write access to localStorage, but it's inconsistently implemented between different browsers, and even with it a simple implementation like ours could still encounter issues.

If we wanted our persistence implementation to be multi-window–concurrency aware, then we could make use of the storage events that are fired when localStorage is changed to update our local graph accordingly.

6.16 Updates

Our out pipetype copies the vertex's out-going edges and pops one off each time it needs one. Building that new data structure takes time and space, and pushes more work on to the memory manager. We could have instead used the vertex's out-going edge list directly, keeping track of our place with a counter variable. Can you think of a problem with that approach?

If someone deletes an edge we've visited while we're in the middle of a query, that would change the size of our edge list, and we'd then skip an edge because our counter would be off. To solve this we could lock the vertices involved in our query, but then we'd either lose our capacity to regularly update the graph, or the ability to have long-lived query objects responding to requests for more results on-demand. Even though we're in a single-threaded event loop, our queries can span multiple asynchronous re-entries, which means concurrency concerns like this are a very real problem.

So we'll pay the performance price to copy the edge list. There's still a problem, though, in that long-lived queries may not see a completely consistent chronology. We will traverse every edge belonging to a vertex at the moment we visit it, but we visit vertices at different clock times during our query. Suppose we save a query like var q = g.v('Odin').children().children().take(2) and then call q.run() to gather two of Odin's grandchildren. Some time later we need to pull another two grandchildren, so we call q.run() again. If Odin has had a new grandchild in the intervening time, we may or may not see it, depending on whether the parent vertex was visited the first time we ran the query.

One way to fix this non-determinism is to change the update handlers to add versioning to the data. We'll then change the driver loop to pass the graph's current version in to the query, so we're always seeing a consistent view of the world as it existed when the query was first initialized. Adding versioning to our database also opens the door to true transactions, and automated rollback/retries in an STM-like fashion.

6.17   Future Directions

We saw one way of gathering ancestors earlier:

```
g.v('Thor').out().as('parent')
          .out().as('grandparent')
          .out().as('great-grandparent')
          .merge(['parent', 'grandparent', 'great-grandparent'])
          .run()
```

This is pretty clumsy, and doesn't scale well—what if we wanted six layers of ancestors? Or to look through an arbitrary number of ancestors until we found what we wanted?

It'd be nice if we could say something like this instead:

```
g.v('Thor').out().all().times(3).run()
```

What we'd like to get out of this is something like the query above—maybe:

```
g.v('Thor').out().as('a')
          .out().as('b')
          .out().as('c')
          .merge(['a', 'b', 'c'])
          .run()'
```

after the query transformers have all run. We could run the times transformer first, to produce:

```
g.v('Thor').out().all().out().all().out().all().run()
```

Then run the `all` transformer and have it transform each `all` into a uniquely labeled `as`, and put a `merge` after the last `as`.

There are a few problems with this, though. For one, this `as`/`merge` technique only works if every pathway is present in the graph: if we're missing an entry for one of Thor's great-grandparents then we will skip valid entries. For another, what happens if we want to do this to just part of a query and not the whole thing? What if there are multiple `all`s?

To solve that first problem we're going to have to treat `all`s as something more than just as/merge. We need each parent gremlin to actually skip the intervening steps. We can think of this as a kind of teleportation—jumping from one part of the pipeline directly to another—or we can think of it as a certain kind of branching pipeline, but either way it complicates our model somewhat. Another approach would be to think of the gremlin as passing through the intervening pipes in a sort of suspended animation, until awoken by a special pipe. Scoping the suspending/unsuspending pipes may be tricky, however.

The next two problems are easier. To modify just part of a query we'll wrap that portion in special start/end steps, like `g.v('Thor').out().start().in().out().end().times(4).run()`. Actually, if the interpreter knows about these special pipetypes we don't need the end step, because the end of a sequence is always a special pipetype. We'll call these special pipetypes "adverbs", because they modify regular pipetypes like adverbs modify verbs.

To handle multiple `all`s we need to run all `all` transformers twice: once before `times`, to mark all `all`s uniquely, and again after `times` to re-mark all marked `all`s uniquely.

There's still the issue of searching through an unbounded number of ancestors—for example, how do we find out which of Ymir's descendants are scheduled to survive Ragnarök? We could make individual queries like `g.v('Ymir').in().filter({survives: true})` and `g.v('Ymir').in().in().in().in().filter({survives: true})`, and manually collect the results ourselves, but that's pretty awful.

We'd like to use an adverb like this:

```
g.v('Ymir').in().filter({survives: true}).every()
```

which would work like `all`+`times` but without enforcing a limit. We may want to impose a particular strategy on the traversal, though, like a stolid BFS or YOLO DFS, so `g.v('Ymir').in().filter({survives:  true}).bfs()` would be more flexible. Phrasing it this way allows us to state complicated queries like "check for Ragnarök survivors, skipping every other generation" in a straightforward fashion: `g.v('Ymir').in().filter({survives: true}).in().bfs()`.

6.18   Wrapping Up

So what have we learned? Graph databases are great for storing interconnected [39] data that you plan to query via graph traversals. Adding non-strict semantics allows for a fluent interface over queries you could never express in an eager system for performance reasons, and allows you to cross async boundaries. Time makes things complicated, and time from multiple perspectives (i.e., concurrency) makes things very complicated, so whenever we can avoid introducing a temporal dependency (e.g.,

---

[39] Not *too* interconnected, though—you'd like the number of edges to grow in direct proportion to the number of vertices. In other words, the average number of edges connected to a vertex shouldn't vary with the size of the graph. Most systems we'd consider putting in a graph database already have this property: if Loki had 100,000 additional grandchildren the degree of the Thor vertex wouldn't increase.

state, observable effects, etc.) we make reasoning about our system easier. Building in a simple, decoupled and painfully unoptimized style leaves the door open for global optimizations later on, and using a driver loop allows for orthogonal optimizations—each without introducing the brittleness and complexity that is the hallmark of most optimization techniques.

That last point can't be overstated: keep it simple. Eschew optimization in favor of simplicity. Work hard to achieve simplicity by finding the right model. Explore many possibilities. The chapters in this book provide ample evidence that highly non-trivial applications can have a small, tight kernel. Once you find that kernel for the application you are building, fight to keep complexity from polluting it. Build hooks for attaching additional functionality, and maintain your abstraction barriers at all costs. Using these techniques well is not easy, but they can give you leverage over otherwise intractable problems.

Acknowledgements

Many thanks are due to Amy Brown, Michael DiBernardo, Colin Lupton, Scott Rostrup, Michael Russo, Erin Toliver, and Leo Zovic for their invaluable contributions to this chapter.

## chapter 7

DBDB: Dog Bed Database
Taavi Burns

7.1   Introduction

DBDB (Dog Bed Database) is a Python library that implements a simple key/value database. It lets you associate a key with a value, and store that association on disk for later retrieval.

DBDB aims to preserve data in the face of computer crashes and error conditions. It also avoids holding all data in RAM at once so you can store more data than you have RAM.

7.2   Memory

I remember the first time I was really stuck on a bug. When I finished typing in my BASIC program and ran it, weird sparkly pixels showed up on the screen, and the program aborted early. When I went back to look at the code, the last few lines of the program were gone.

One of my mom's friends knew how to program, so we set up a call. Within a few minutes of speaking with her, I found the problem: the program was too big, and had encroached onto video memory. Clearing the screen truncated the program, and the sparkles were artifacts of Applesoft BASIC's behaviour of storing program state in RAM just beyond the end of the program.

From that moment onwards, I cared about memory allocation. I learned about pointers and how to allocate memory with malloc. I learned how my data structures were laid out in memory. And I learned to be very, very careful about how I changed them.

Some years later, while reading about a process-oriented language called Erlang, I learned that it didn't actually have to copy data to send messages between processes, because everything was immutable. I then discovered immutable data structures in Clojure, and it really began to sink in.

When I read about CouchDB in 2013, I just smiled and nodded, recognising the structures and mechanisms for managing complex data as it changes.

I learned that you can design systems built around immutable data.

Then I agreed to write a book chapter.

I thought that describing the core data storage concepts of CouchDB (as I understood them) would be fun.

While trying to write a binary tree algorithm that mutated the tree in place, I got frustrated with how complicated things were getting. The number of edge cases and trying to reason about how changes in one part of the tree affected others was making my head hurt. I had no idea how I was going to explain all of this.

Remembering lessons learned, I took a peek at a recursive algorithm for updating immutable binary trees and it turned out to be relatively straightforward.

I learned, once again, that it's easier to reason about things that don't change.

So starts the story.

7.3   Why Is it Interesting?

Most projects require a database of some kind. You really shouldn't write your own; there are many edge cases that will bite you, even if you're just writing JSON to disk:

- What happens if your filesystem runs out of space?
- What happens if your laptop battery dies while saving?
- What if your data size exceeds available memory? (Unlikely for most applications on modern desktop computers... but not unlikely for a mobile device or server-side web application.)

However, if you want to *understand* how a database handles all of these problems, writing one for yourself can be a good idea.

The techniques and concepts we discuss here should be applicable to any problem that needs to have rational, predictable behaviour when faced with failure.

Speaking of failure...

7.4   Characterizing Failure

Databases are often characterized by how closely they adhere to the ACID properties: atomicity, consistency, isolation, and durability.

Updates in DBDB are atomic and durable, two attributes which are described later in the chapter. DBDB provides no consistency guarantees as there are no constraints on the data stored. Isolation is likewise not implemented.

Application code can, of course, impose its own consistency guarantees, but proper isolation requires a transaction manager. We won't attempt that here; however, you can learn more about transaction management in the CircleDB chapter (Chapter 10).

We also have other system-maintenance problems to think about. Stale data is not reclaimed in this implementation, so repeated updates (even to the same key) will eventually consume all disk space. (You will shortly discover why this is the case.) PostgreSQL[1] calls this reclamation "vacuuming" (which makes old row space available for re-use), and CouchDB[2] calls it "compaction" (by rewriting the "live" parts of the data into a new file, and atomically moving it over the old one).

DBDB could be enhanced to add a compaction feature, but it is left as an exercise for the reader[3].

7.5   The Architecture of DBDB

DBDB separates the concerns of "put this on disk somewhere" (how data are laid out in a file; the physical layer) from the logical structure of the data (a binary tree in this example; the logical layer) from the contents of the key/value store (the association of key a to value foo; the public API).

---

[1]http://www.postgresql.org/
[2]http://couchdb.apache.org/
[3]Bonus feature: Can you guarantee that the compacted tree structure is balanced? This helps maintain performance over time.

Many databases separate the logical and physical aspects as it is is often useful to provide alternative implementations of each to get different performance characteristics, e.g. DB2's SMS (files in a filesystem) versus DMS (raw block device) tablespaces, or MySQL's alternative engine implementations[4].

7.6 Discovering the Design

Most of the chapters in this book describe how a program was built from inception to completion. However, that is not how most of us interact with the code we're working on. We most often discover code that was written by others, and figure out how to modify or extend it to do something different.

In this chapter, we'll assume that DBDB is a completed project, and walk through it to learn how it works. Let's explore the structure of the entire project first.

Organisational Units

Units are ordered here by distance from the end user; that is, the first module is the one that a user of this program would likely need to know the most about, while the last is something they should have very little interaction with.

- `tool.py` defines a command-line tool for exploring a database from a terminal window.
- `interface.py` defines a class (DBDB) which implements the Python dictionary API using the concrete `BinaryTree` implementation. This is how you'd use DBDB inside a Python program.
- `logical.py` defines the logical layer. It's an abstract interface to a key/value store.

    - `LogicalBase` provides the API for logical updates (like get, set, and commit) and defers to a concrete subclass to implement the updates themselves. It also manages storage locking and dereferencing internal nodes.
    - `ValueRef` is a Python object that refers to a binary blob stored in the database. The indirection lets us avoid loading the entire data store into memory all at once.

- `binary_tree.py` defines a concrete binary tree algorithm underneath the logical interface.

    - `BinaryTree` provides a concrete implementation of a binary tree, with methods for getting, inserting, and deleting key/value pairs. `BinaryTree` represents an immutable tree; updates are performed by returning a new tree which shares common structure with the old one.
    - `BinaryNode` implements a node in the binary tree.
    - `BinaryNodeRef` is a specialised `ValueRef` which knows how to serialise and deserialise a `BinaryNode`.

- `physical.py` defines the physical layer. The `Storage` class provides persistent, (mostly) append-only record storage.

These modules grew from attempting to give each class a single responsibility. In other words, each class should have only one reason to change.

---

[4]http://dev.mysql.com/doc/refman/5.7/en/storage-engines.html

Reading a Value

We'll start with the simplest case: reading a value from the database. Let's see what happens when we try to get the value associated with key foo in example.db:

```
$ python -m dbdb.tool example.db get foo
```

This runs the main() function from module dbdb.tool:

```python
# dbdb/tool.py
def main(argv):
    if not (4 <= len(argv) <= 5):
        usage()
        return BAD_ARGS
    dbname, verb, key, value = (argv[1:] + [None])[:4]
    if verb not in {'get', 'set', 'delete'}:
        usage()
        return BAD_VERB
    db = dbdb.connect(dbname)          # CONNECT
    try:
        if verb == 'get':
            sys.stdout.write(db[key])  # GET VALUE
        elif verb == 'set':
            db[key] = value
            db.commit()
        else:
            del db[key]
            db.commit()
    except KeyError:
        print("Key not found", file=sys.stderr)
        return BAD_KEY
    return OK
```

The connect() function opens the database file (possibly creating it, but never overwriting it) and returns an instance of DBDB:

```python
# dbdb/__init__.py
def connect(dbname):
    try:
        f = open(dbname, 'r+b')
    except IOError:
        fd = os.open(dbname, os.O_RDWR | os.O_CREAT)
        f = os.fdopen(fd, 'r+b')
    return DBDB(f)

# dbdb/interface.py
class DBDB(object):

    def __init__(self, f):
        self._storage = Storage(f)
        self._tree = BinaryTree(self._storage)
```

We see right away that DBDB has a reference to an instance of `Storage`, but it also shares that reference with `self._tree`. Why? Can't `self._tree` manage access to the storage by itself?

The question of which objects "own" a resource is often an important one in a design, because it gives us hints about what changes might be unsafe. Let's keep that question in mind as we move on.

Once we have a DBDB instance, getting the value at key is done via a dictionary lookup (`db[key]`), which causes the Python interpreter to call `DBDB.__getitem__()`.

```
# dbdb/interface.py
class DBDB(object):
# ...
    def __getitem__(self, key):
        self._assert_not_closed()
        return self._tree.get(key)

    def _assert_not_closed(self):
        if self._storage.closed:
            raise ValueError('Database closed.')
```

`__getitem__()` ensures that the database is still open by calling `_assert_not_closed`. Aha! Here we see at least one reason why DBDB needs direct access to our `Storage` instance: so it can enforce preconditions. (Do you agree with this design? Can you think of a different way that we could do this?)

DBDB then retrieves the value associated with key on the internal `_tree` by calling `_tree.get()`, which is provided by `LogicalBase`:

```
# dbdb/logical.py
class LogicalBase(object):
# ...
    def get(self, key):
        if not self._storage.locked:
            self._refresh_tree_ref()
        return self._get(self._follow(self._tree_ref), key)
```

`get()` checks if we have the storage locked. We're not 100% sure *why* there might be a lock here, but we can guess that it probably exists to allow writers to serialize access to the data. What happens if the storage isn't locked?

```
# dbdb/logical.py
class LogicalBase(object):
# ...
def _refresh_tree_ref(self):
        self._tree_ref = self.node_ref_class(
            address=self._storage.get_root_address())
```

`_refresh_tree_ref` resets the tree's "view" of the data with what is currently on disk, allowing us to perform a completely up-to-date read.

What if storage *is* locked when we attempt a read? This means that some other process is probably changing the data we want to read right now; our read is not likely to be up-to-date with the current state of the data. This is generally known as a "dirty read". This pattern allows many readers to access data without ever worrying about blocking, at the expense of being slightly out-of-date.

For now, let's take a look at how we actually retrieve the data:

```
# dbdb/binary_tree.py
class BinaryTree(LogicalBase):
# ...
    def _get(self, node, key):
        while node is not None:
            if key < node.key:
                node = self._follow(node.left_ref)
            elif node.key < key:
                node = self._follow(node.right_ref)
            else:
                return self._follow(node.value_ref)
        raise KeyError
```

This is a standard binary tree search, following refs to their nodes. We know from reading the BinaryTree documentation that Nodes and NodeRefs are value objects: they are immutable and their contents never change. Nodes are created with an associated key and value, and left and right children. Those associations also never change. The content of the whole BinaryTree only visibly changes when the root node is replaced. This means that we don't need to worry about the contents of our tree being changed while we are performing the search.

Once the associated value is found, it is written to stdout by main() without adding any extra newlines, to preserve the user's data exactly.

Inserting and Updating

Now we'll set key foo to value bar in example.db:

```
$ python -m dbdb.tool example.db set foo bar
```

Again, this runs the main() function from module dbdb.tool. Since we've seen this code before, we'll just highlight the important parts:

```
# dbdb/tool.py
def main(argv):
    ...
    db = dbdb.connect(dbname)          # CONNECT
    try:
        ...
        elif verb == 'set':
            db[key] = value            # SET VALUE
            db.commit()                # COMMIT
        ...
    except KeyError:
        ...
```

This time we set the value with db[key] = value which calls DBDB.__setitem__().

```
# dbdb/interface.py
class DBDB(object):
# ...
    def __setitem__(self, key, value):
        self._assert_not_closed()
        return self._tree.set(key, value)
```

__setitem__ ensures that the database is still open and then stores the association from key to value on the internal _tree by calling _tree.set().

_tree.set() is provided by LogicalBase:

```
# dbdb/logical.py
class LogicalBase(object):
# ...
    def set(self, key, value):
        if self._storage.lock():
            self._refresh_tree_ref()
        self._tree_ref = self._insert(
            self._follow(self._tree_ref), key, self.value_ref_class(value))
```

set() first checks the storage lock:

```
# dbdb/storage.py
class Storage(object):
    ...
    def lock(self):
        if not self.locked:
            portalocker.lock(self._f, portalocker.LOCK_EX)
            self.locked = True
            return True
        else:
            return False
```

There are two important things to note here:

- Our lock is provided by a 3rd-party file-locking library called portalocker[5].
- lock() returns False if the database was already locked, and True otherwise.

Returning to _tree.set(), we can now understand why it checked the return value of lock() in the first place: it lets us call _refresh_tree_ref for the most recent root node reference so we don't lose updates that another process may have made since we last refreshed the tree from disk. Then it replaces the root tree node with a new tree containing the inserted (or updated) key/value.

Inserting or updating the tree doesn't mutate any nodes, because _insert() returns a new tree. The new tree shares unchanged parts with the previous tree to save on memory and execution time. It's natural to implement this recursively:

```
# dbdb/binary_tree.py
class BinaryTree(LogicalBase):
# ...
    def _insert(self, node, key, value_ref):
        if node is None:
            new_node = BinaryNode(
                self.node_ref_class(), key, value_ref, self.node_ref_class(), 1)
        elif key < node.key:
            new_node = BinaryNode.from_node(
                node,
                left_ref=self._insert(
                    self._follow(node.left_ref), key, value_ref))
```

[5]https://pypi.python.org/pypi/portalocker

```
        elif node.key < key:
            new_node = BinaryNode.from_node(
                node,
                right_ref=self._insert(
                    self._follow(node.right_ref), key, value_ref))
        else:
            new_node = BinaryNode.from_node(node, value_ref=value_ref)
        return self.node_ref_class(referent=new_node)
```

Notice how we always return a new node (wrapped in a NodeRef). Instead of updating a node to point to a new subtree, we make a new node which shares the unchanged subtree. This is what makes this binary tree an immutable data structure.

You may have noticed something strange here: we haven't made any changes to anything on disk yet. All we've done is manipulate our view of the on-disk data by moving tree nodes around.

In order to actually write these changes to disk, we need an explicit call to commit(), which we saw as the second part of our set operation in tool.py at the beginning of this section.

Committing involves writing out all of the dirty state in memory, and then saving the disk address of the tree's new root node.

Starting from the API:

```
# dbdb/interface.py
class DBDB(object):
# ...
    def commit(self):
        self._assert_not_closed()
        self._tree.commit()
```

The implementation of _tree.commit() comes from LogicalBase:

```
# dbdb/logical.py
class LogicalBase(object)
# ...
    def commit(self):
        self._tree_ref.store(self._storage)
        self._storage.commit_root_address(self._tree_ref.address)
```

All NodeRefs know how to serialise themselves to disk by first asking their children to serialise via prepare_to_store():

```
# dbdb/logical.py
class ValueRef(object):
# ...
    def store(self, storage):
        if self._referent is not None and not self._address:
            self.prepare_to_store(storage)
            self._address = storage.write(self.referent_to_string(self._referent))
```

self._tree_ref in LogicalBase is actually a BinaryNodeRef (a subclass of ValueRef) in this case, so the concrete implementation of prepare_to_store() is:

```
# dbdb/binary_tree.py
class BinaryNodeRef(ValueRef):
    def prepare_to_store(self, storage):
        if self._referent:
            self._referent.store_refs(storage)
```

The BinaryNode in question, _referent, asks its refs to store themselves:

```
# dbdb/binary_tree.py
class BinaryNode(object):
# ...
    def store_refs(self, storage):
        self.value_ref.store(storage)
        self.left_ref.store(storage)
        self.right_ref.store(storage)
```

This recurses all the way down for any NodeRef which has unwritten changes (i.e., no _address).

Now we're back up the stack in ValueRef's store method again. The last step of store() is to serialise this node and save its storage address:

```
# dbdb/logical.py
class ValueRef(object):
# ...
    def store(self, storage):
        if self._referent is not None and not self._address:
            self.prepare_to_store(storage)
            self._address = storage.write(self.referent_to_string(self._referent))
```

At this point the NodeRef's _referent is guaranteed to have addresses available for all of its own refs, so we serialise it by creating a bytestring representing this node:

```
# dbdb/binary_tree.py
class BinaryNodeRef(ValueRef):
# ...
    @staticmethod
    def referent_to_string(referent):
        return pickle.dumps({
            'left': referent.left_ref.address,
            'key': referent.key,
            'value': referent.value_ref.address,
            'right': referent.right_ref.address,
            'length': referent.length,
        })
```

Updating the address in the store() method is technically a mutation of the ValueRef. Because it has no effect on the user-visible value, we can consider it to be immutable.

Once store() on the root _tree_ref is complete (in LogicalBase.commit()), we know that all of the data are written to disk. We can now commit the root address by calling:

```
# dbdb/physical.py
class Storage(object):
# ...
```

```
def commit_root_address(self, root_address):
    self.lock()
    self._f.flush()
    self._seek_superblock()
    self._write_integer(root_address)
    self._f.flush()
    self.unlock()
```

We ensure that the file handle is flushed (so that the OS knows we want all the data saved to stable storage like an SSD) and write out the address of the root node. We know this last write is atomic because we store the disk address on a sector boundary. It's the very first thing in the file, so this is true regardless of sector size, and single-sector disk writes are guaranteed to be atomic by the disk hardware.

Because the root node address has either the old or new value (never a bit of old and a bit of new), other processes can read from the database without getting a lock. An external process might see the old or the new tree, but never a mix of the two. In this way, commits are atomic.

Because we write the new data to disk and call the fsync syscall[6] before we write the root node address, uncommitted data are unreachable. Conversely, once the root node address has been updated, we know that all the data it references are also on disk. In this way, commits are also durable.

We're done!

How NodeRefs Save Memory

To avoid keeping the entire tree structure in memory at the same time, when a logical node is read in from disk the disk address of its left and right children (as well as its value) are loaded into memory. Accessing children and their values requires one extra function call to NodeRef.get() to dereference ("really get") the data.

All we need to construct a NodeRef is an address:

```
+---------+
| NodeRef |
| ------- |
| addr=3  |
| get()   |
+---------+
```

Calling get() on it will return the concrete node, along with that node's references as NodeRefs:

```
+---------+     +---------+       +---------+
| NodeRef |     | Node    |       | NodeRef |
| ------- |     | ------- | +-> | ------- |
| addr=3  |     | key=A   | |   | addr=1  |
| get() ------> | value=B | |   +---------+
+---------+     | left  ----+
                | right ----+   +---------+
                +---------+ |   | NodeRef |
                         +-> | ------- |
                            | addr=2  |
                            +---------+
```

---
[6]Calling fsync on a file descriptor asks the operating system and hard drive (or SSD) to write all buffered data immediately. Operating systems and drives don't usually write everything immediately in order to improve performance.

When changes to the tree are not committed, they exist in memory with references from the root down to the changed leaves. The changes aren't saved to disk yet, so the changed nodes contain concrete keys and values and no disk addresses. The process doing the writing can see uncommitted changes and can make more changes before issuing a commit, because `NodeRef.get()` will return the uncommitted value if it has one; there is no difference between committed and uncommitted data when accessed through the API. All the updates will appear atomically to other readers because changes aren't visible until the new root node address is written to disk. Concurrent updates are blocked by a lockfile on disk. The lock is acquired on first update, and released after commit.

Exercises for the Reader

DBDB allows many processes to read the same database at once without blocking; the tradeoff is that readers can sometimes retrieve stale data. What if we needed to be able to read some data consistently? A common use case is reading a value and then updating it based on that value. How would you write a method on DBDB to do this? What tradeoffs would you have to incur to provide this functionality?

The algorithm used to update the data store can be completely changed out by replacing the string `BinaryTree` in `interface.py`. Data stores tend to use more complex types of search trees such as B-trees, B+ trees, and others to improve the performance. While a balanced binary tree (and this one isn't) needs to do $O(log_2(n))$ random node reads to find a value, a B+ tree needs many fewer, for example $O(log_{32}(n))$ because each node splits 32 ways instead of just 2. This makes a huge different in practice, since looking through 4 billion entries would go from $log_2(2^{32}) = 32$ to $log_{32}(2^{32}) \approx 6.4$ lookups. Each lookup is a random access, which is incredibly expensive for hard disks with spinning platters. SSDs help with the latency, but the savings in I/O still stand.

By default, values are stored by `ValueRef` which expects bytes as values (to be passed directly to `Storage`). The binary tree nodes themselves are just a sublcass of `ValueRef`. Storing richer data via json or msgpack is a matter of writing your own and setting it as the `value_ref_class`. `BinaryNodeRef` is an example of using pickle[7] to serialise data.

Database compaction is another interesting exercise. Compacting can be done via an infix-of-median traversal of the tree writing things out as you go. It's probably best if the tree nodes all go together, since they're what's traversed to find any piece of data. Packing as many intermediate nodes as possible into a disk sector should improve read performance, at least right after compaction. There are some subtleties here (for example, memory usage) if you try to implement this yourself. And remember: always benchmark performance enhancements before and after! You'll often be surprised by the results.

Patterns and Principles

Test interfaces, not implementation. As part of developing DBDB, I wrote a number of tests that described how I wanted to be able to use it. The first tests ran against an in-memory version of the database, then I extended DBDB to persist to disk, and even later added the concept of NodeRefs. Most of the tests didn't have to change, which gave me confidence that things were still working.

Respect the Single Responsibility Principle. Classes should have at most one reason to change. That's not strictly the case with DBDB, but there are multiple avenues of extension with only localised changes required. Refactoring as I added features was a pleasure!

---

[7]https://docs.python.org/3.4/library/pickle.html

Summary

DBDB is a simple database that makes simple guarantees, and yet things still became complicated in a hurry. The most important thing I did to manage this complexity was to implement an ostensibly mutable object with an immutable data structure. I encourage you to consider this technique the next time you find yourself in the middle of a tricky problem that seems to have more edge cases than you can keep track of.

## chapter 8

An Event-Driven Web Framework
Leo Zovic

In 2013, I decided to write a web-based game prototyping tool[1] for card and board games called *House*. In these types of games, it is common for one player to wait for another player to make a move; however, when the other player finally does take action, we would like for the waiting player to be notified of the move quickly thereafter.

This is a problem that turns out to be more complicated than it first seems. In this chapter, we'll explore the issues with using HTTP to build this sort of interaction, and then we'll build a *web framework* in Common Lisp that allows us to solve similar problems in the future.

8.1   The Basics of HTTP Servers

At the simplest level, an HTTP exchange is a single request followed by a single response. A *client* sends a request, which includes a resource identifier, an HTTP version tag, some headers and some parameters. The *server* parses that request, figures out what to do about it, and sends a response which includes the same HTTP version tag, a response code, some headers and a response body. (For more on this, see Chapter 22.)

Notice that, in this description, the server responds to a request from a specific client. In our case, we want each player to be updated about *any* moves as soon as they happen, rather than only getting notifications when their own move is made. This means we need the server to *push* messages to clients without first receiving a request for the information.[2]

There are several standard approaches to enabling server push over HTTP.

Comet/Long Poll

The "long poll" technique has the client send the server a new request as soon as it receives a response. Instead of fulfilling that request right away, the server waits on a subsequent event to respond. This is a bit of a semantic distinction, since the client is still taking action on every update.

---

[1] https://github.com/Inaimathi/deal

[2] One solution to this problem is to force the clients to *poll* the server. That is, each client would periodically send the server a request asking if anything has changed. This can work for simple applications, but in this chapter we're going to focus on the solutions available to you when this model stops working.

Server-Sent Events (SSE)

Server-sent events require that the client initiates a connection and then keeps it open. The server periodically writes new data to the connection without closing it, and the client interprets incoming new messages as they arrive rather than waiting for the response connection to terminate. This is a bit more efficient than the Comet/long poll approach because each message doesn't have to incur the overhead of new HTTP headers.

WebSockets

WebSockets are a communication protocol built on top of HTTP. The server and client open up an HTTP conversation, then perform a handshake and protocol escalation. The end result is that they're still communicating over TCP/IP, but they're not using HTTP to do it at all. The advantage this has over SSEs is that you can customize the protocol for efficiency.

Long-Lived Connections

These three approaches are quite different from one another, but they all share an important characteristic: they all depend on long-lived connections. Long polling depends on the server keeping requests around until new data is available, SSEs keep an open stream between client and server to which data is periodically written, and WebSockets change the protocol a particular connection is using, but leave it open.

To see why this might cause problems for your average HTTP server, let's consider how the underlying implementation might work.

Traditional HTTP Server Architecture

A single HTTP server processes many requests concurrently. Historically, many HTTP servers have used a *thread-per-request* architecture. That is, for each incoming request, the server creates a thread to do the work necessary to respond.

Since each of these connections is intended to be short-lived, we don't need many threads executing in parallel to handle them all. This model also simplifies the *implementation* of the server by enabling the server programmer to write code as if there were only one connection being handled at any given time. It also gives us the freedom to clean up failed or "zombie" connections and their associated resources by killing the corresponding thread and letting the garbage collector do its job.

The key observation is that an HTTP server hosting a "traditional" web application that has N concurrent users might only need to handle a very small fraction of N requests *in parallel* to succeed. For the type of interactive application that we are trying to build, N users will almost certainly require the application to maintain at least N connections in parallel, at once.

The consequence of keeping long-lived connections around is that we'll need either:

- A platform where threads are "cheap" enough that we can use large numbers of them at once.
- A server architecture that can handle many connections with a single thread.

There are programming environments such as Racket[3], Erlang[4], and Haskell[5] that provide thread-like constructs that are "lightweight" enough to consider the first option. This approach requires

---

[3] http://racket-lang.org/
[4] http://www.erlang.org/
[5] http://hackage.haskell.org/package/base-4.7.0.1/docs/Control-Concurrent.html

the programmer to explicitly deal with synchronization issues, which are going to be much more prevalent in a system where connections are open for a long time and likely all competing for similar resources. Specifically, if we have some sort of central data shared by several users simultaneously, we will need to coordinate reads and writes of that data in some way.

If we don't have cheap threads at our disposal or we are unwilling to work with explicit synchronization, we must consider having a single thread handle many connections.[6] In this model, our single thread is going to be handling tiny "slices" of many requests all at once, switching between them as efficiently as it possibly can. This system architecture pattern is most commonly referred to as *event-driven* or *event-based*.[7]

Since we are only managing a single thread, we don't have to worry as much about protecting shared resources from simultaneous access. However, we do have a unique problem of our own in this model. Since our single thread is working on all in-flight requests at once, we must make sure that it **never blocks**. Blocking on any connection blocks the entire server from making progress on any other request. We have to be able to move on to another client if the current one can't be serviced further, and we need to be able to do so in a manner that doesn't throw out the work done so far.[8]

While it is uncommon for a programmer to explicitly tell a thread to stop working, many common operations carry a risk of blocking. Because threads are so prevalent, and reasoning about asynchronicity is a heavy burden on the programmer, many languages and their frameworks assume that blocking on I/O is a desirable property. This makes it very easy to block somewhere *by accident*. Luckily, Common Lisp does provide us with a minimal set of asynchronous I/O primitives which we can build on top of.

Architectural Decisions

Now that we've studied the background of this problem, we've arrived at the point where we need to make informed decisions about *what* we are building.

At the time I started thinking about this project, Common Lisp didn't have a complete green-thread implementation, and the standard portable threading library[9] doesn't qualify as "really REALLY cheap". The options amounted to either picking a different language, or building an event-driven web server for my purpose. I chose the latter.

In addition to the server architecture, we also need to choose which of the three server-push approaches to use. The use-case we are considering (an interactive multiplayer board game) requires frequent updates to each client, but relatively sparse requests *from* each client, which fits the SSE approach to pushing updates, so we'll go with this.

Now that we've motivated our architectural decision and decided on a mechanism for simulating bidirectional communication between clients and server, let's get started on building our web framework. We'll start by building a relatively "dumb" server first, and then we'll extend it into a

---

[6]We could consider a more general system that handles N concurrent users with M threads for some configurable value of M; in this model, the N connections are said to be *multiplexed* across the M threads. In this chapter, we are going to focus on writing a program where M is fixed at 1; however, the lessons learned here should be partially applicable to the more general model.

[7]This nomenclature is a bit confusing, and has its origin in early operating-systems research. It refers to how communication is done between multiple concurrent processes. In a thread-based system, communication is done through a synchronized resource such as shared memory. In an event-based system, processes generally communicate through a queue where they post items that describe what they have done or what they want done, which is maintained by our single thread of execution. Since these items generally describe desired or past actions, they are referred to as 'events'.

[8]See Chapter 5 for another take on this problem.

[9]http://common-lisp.net/project/bordeaux-threads/

web-application framework that lets us focus on *what* our heavily-interactive program needs to do, and not *how* it is doing it.

8.2   Building an Event-Driven Web Server

Most programs that use a single process to manage concurrent streams of work use a pattern called an *event loop*. Let's look at what an event loop for our web server might look like.

The Event Loop

Our event loop needs to:

- listen for incoming connections;
- handle all new handshakes or incoming data on existing connections;
- clean up dangling sockets that are unexpectedly killed (e.g. by an interrupt)

```
(defmethod start ((port integer))
  (let ((server (socket-listen
         usocket:*wildcard-host* port
         :reuse-address t
         :element-type 'octet))
    (conns (make-hash-table)))
    (unwind-protect
     (loop (loop for ready
          in (wait-for-input
             (cons server (alexandria:hash-table-keys conns))
             :ready-only t)
        do (process-ready ready conns)))
     (loop for c being the hash-keys of conns
    do (loop while (socket-close c)))
    (loop while (socket-close server)))))
```

If you haven't written a Common Lisp program before, this code block requires some explanation. What we have written here is a *method definition*. While Lisp is popularly known as a functional language, it also has its own system for object-oriented programming called "The Common Lisp Object System", which is usually abbreviated as "CLOS".[10]

CLOS and Generic Functions

In CLOS, instead of focusing on classes and methods, we write *generic functions*[11] that are implemented as collections of *methods*. In this model, methods don't *belong to* classes, they *specialize on* types.[12] The start method we just wrote is a unary method where the argument port is *specialized on* the type integer. This means that we could have several implementations of start where port varies in type, and the runtime will select which implementation to use depending on the type of port when start is called.

---

[10]Pronounced "kloss", "see-loss" or "see-lows", depending on who you talk to.

[11]http://www.gigamonkeys.com/book/object-reorientation-generic-functions.html

[12]The Julia programming language takes a similar approach to object-oriented programming; you can learn more about it in Chapter 20.

More generally, methods can specialize on more than one argument. When a method is called, the runtime:

- dispatches on the type of its arguments to figure out which method body should be run, and
- runs the appropriate function.

Processing Sockets

We'll see another generic function at work in process-ready, which was called earlier from our event loop. It processes a ready socket with one of two methods, depending on the type of socket we are handling.

The two types we're concerned with are the stream-usocket, which represents a client socket that will make a request and expect to be sent some data back, and the stream-server-usocket, which represents our local TCP listener that will have new client connections for us to deal with.

If a stream-server-socket is ready, that means there's a new client socket waiting to start a conversation. We call socket-accept to accept the connection, and then put the result in our connection table so that our event loop can begin processing it with the others.

```
(defmethod process-ready ((ready stream-server-usocket) (conns hash-table))
  (setf (gethash (socket-accept ready :element-type 'octet) conns) nil))
```

When a stream-usocket is ready, that means that it has some bytes ready for us to read. (It's also possible that the other party has terminated the connection.)

```
(defmethod process-ready ((ready stream-usocket) (conns hash-table))
  (let ((buf (or (gethash ready conns)
                 (setf (gethash ready conns)
                       (make-instance 'buffer :bi-stream (flex-stream ready))))))
    (if (eq :eof (buffer! buf))
    (ignore-errors
      (remhash ready conns)
      (socket-close ready))
    (let ((too-big?
            (> (total-buffered buf)
               +max-request-size+))
          (too-old?
            (> (- (get-universal-time) (started buf))
               +max-request-age+))
          (too-needy?
            (> (tries buf)
               +max-buffer-tries+)))
      (cond (too-big?
             (error! +413+ ready)
             (remhash ready conns))
            ((or too-old? too-needy?)
             (error! +400+ ready)
             (remhash ready conns))
            ((and (request buf) (zerop (expecting buf)))
             (remhash ready conns)
             (when (contents buf)
               (setf (parameters (request buf))
```

```
          (nconc (parse buf) (parameters (request buf))))))
      (handler-case
          (handle-request ready (request buf))
        (http-assertion-error () (error! +400+ ready))
        ((and (not warning)
          (not simple-error)) (e)
          (error! +500+ ready e))))
    (t
     (setf (contents buf) nil)))))))
```

This is more involved than the first case. We:

1. Get the buffer associated with this socket, or create it if it doesn't exist yet;
2. Read output into that buffer, which happens in the call to `buffer!`;
3. If that read got us an `:eof`, the other side hung up, so we discard the socket *and* its buffer;
4. Otherwise, we check if the buffer is one of `complete?`, `too-big?`, `too-old?` or `too-needy?`. If so, we remove it from the connections table and return the appropriate HTTP response.

This is the first time we're seeing I/O in our event loop. In our discussion in Section 8.1, we mentioned that we have to be very careful about I/O in an event-driven system, because we could accidentally block our single thread. So, what do we do here to ensure that this doesn't happen? We have to explore our implementation of `buffer!` to find out exactly how this works.

Processing Connections Without Blocking

The basis of our approach to processing connections without blocking is the library function `read-char-no-hang`[13], which immediately returns `nil` when called on a stream that has no available data. Where there is data to be read, we use a buffer to store intermediate input for this connection.

```
(defmethod buffer! ((buffer buffer))
  (handler-case
      (let ((stream (bi-stream buffer)))
        (incf (tries buffer))
        (loop for char = (read-char-no-hang stream) until (null char)
           do (push char (contents buffer))
           do (incf (total-buffered buffer))
           when (request buffer) do (decf (expecting buffer))
           when (line-terminated? (contents buffer))
           do (multiple-value-bind (parsed expecting) (parse buffer)
              (setf (request buffer) parsed
                    (expecting buffer) expecting)
              (return char))
           when (> (total-buffered buffer) +max-request-size+) return char
           finally (return char)))
    (error () :eof)))
```

When `buffer!` is called on a buffer, it:

- increments the `tries` count, so that we can evict "needy" buffers in `process-ready`;
- loops to read characters from the input stream, and

---

[13]http://clhs.lisp.se/Body/f_rd_c_1.htm

- returns the last character it read if it has read all of the available input.

It also tracks any \r\n\r\n sequences so that we can later detect complete requests. Finally, if any error results, it returns an :eof to signal that process-ready should discard this connection.

The buffer type is a CLOS *class*[14]. Classes in CLOS let us define a type with fields called slots. We don't see the behaviours associated with buffer on the class definition, because (as we've already learned), we do that using generic functions like buffer!.

defclass does allow us to specify getters/setters (readers/accessors), and slot initializers; :initform specifies a default value, while :initarg identifies a hook that the caller of make-instance can use to provide a default value.

```
(defclass buffer ()
  ((tries :accessor tries :initform 0)
   (contents :accessor contents :initform nil)
   (bi-stream :reader bi-stream :initarg :bi-stream)
   (total-buffered :accessor total-buffered :initform 0)
   (started :reader started :initform (get-universal-time))
   (request :accessor request :initform nil)
   (expecting :accessor expecting :initform 0)))
```

Our buffer class has seven slots:

- tries, which keeps count of how many times we've tried reading into this buffer
- contents, which contains what we've read so far
- bi-stream, which a hack around some of those Common Lisp-specific, non-blocking-I/O annoyances I mentioned earlier
- total-buffered, which is a count of chars we've read so far
- started, which is a timestamp that tells us when we created this buffer
- request, which will eventually contain the request we construct from buffered data
- expecting, which will signal how many more chars we're expecting (if any) after we buffer the request headers

Interpreting Requests

Now that we've seen how we incrementally assemble full requests from bits of data that are pooled into our buffers, what happens when we have a full request ready for handling? This happens in the method handle-request.

```
(defmethod handle-request ((socket usocket) (req request))
  (aif (lookup (resource req) *handlers*)
       (funcall it socket (parameters req))
       (error! +404+ socket)))
```

This method adds another layer of error handling so that if the request is old, big, or needy, we can send a 400 response to indicate that the client provided us with some bad or slow data. However, if any *other* error happens here, it's because the programer made a mistake defining a *handler*, which should be treated as a 500 error. This will inform the client that something went wrong on the server as a result of their legitimate request.

---

[14]http://www.gigamonkeys.com/book/object-reorientation-classes.html

If the request is well-formed, we do the tiny and obvious job of looking up the requested resource in the *handlers* table. If we find one, we funcall it, passing along the client socket as well as the parsed request parameters. If there's no matching handler in the *handlers* table, we instead send along a 404 error. The handler system will be part of our full-fledged *web framework*, which we'll discuss in a later section.

We still haven't seen how requests are parsed and interpreted from one of our buffers, though. Let's look at that next:

```
(defmethod parse ((buf buffer))
  (let ((str (coerce (reverse (contents buf)) 'string)))
    (if (request buf)
        (parse-params str)
        (parse str))))
```

This high-level method delegates to a specialization of parse that works with plain strings, or to parse-params that interprets the buffer contents as HTTP parameters. These are called depending on how much of the request we've already processed; the final parse happens when we already have a partial request saved in the buffer, at which point we're only looking to parse the request body.

```
(defmethod parse ((str string))
  (let ((lines (split "\\r?\\n" str)))
    (destructuring-bind (req-type path http-version) (split " " (pop lines))
      (declare (ignore req-type))
      (assert-http (string= http-version "HTTP/1.1"))
      (let* ((path-pieces (split "\\?" path))
             (resource (first path-pieces))
             (parameters (second path-pieces))
             (req (make-instance 'request :resource resource)))
    (loop
      for header = (pop lines)
      for (name value) = (split ": " header)
      until (null name)
      do (push (cons (->keyword name) value) (headers req)))
    (setf (parameters req) (parse-params parameters))
    req))))
```

```
(defmethod parse-params ((params null)) nil)
```

```
(defmethod parse-params ((params string))
  (loop for pair in (split "&" params)
     for (name val) = (split "=" pair)
     collect (cons (->keyword name) (or val ""))))
```

In the parse method specializing on string, we transform the content into usable pieces. We do so on strings instead of working directly with buffers because this makes it easier to test the actual parsing code in an environment like an interpreter or REPL.

The parsing process is:

1. Split on "\\r?\\n".
2. Split the first line of that on " " to get the request type (POST, GET, etc)/URI path/http-version.
3. Assert that we're dealing with an HTTP/1.1 request.

4. Split the URI path on "?", which gives us plain resource separate from any GET parameters.
5. Make a new `request` instance with the resource in place.
6. Populate that `request` instance with each split header line.
7. Set that `request`s parameters to the result of parsing our GET parameters.

As you might expect by now, `request` is an instance of a CLOS class:

```
(defclass request ()
  ((resource :accessor resource :initarg :resource)
   (headers :accessor headers :initarg :headers :initform nil)
   (parameters :accessor parameters :initarg :parameters :initform nil)))
```

We've now seen how our clients can send requests and have them interpreted and handled by our server. The last thing we have to implement as part of our core server interface is the capability to write responses back to the client.

Rendering Responses

Before we discuss rendering responses, we have to consider that there are two kinds of responses that we may be returning to our clients. The first is a "normal" HTTP response, complete with HTTP headers and body. We represent these kinds of responses with instances of the response class:

```
(defclass response ()
  ((content-type
    :accessor content-type :initform "text/html" :initarg :content-type)
   (charset
    :accessor charset :initform "utf-8")
   (response-code
    :accessor response-code :initform "200 OK" :initarg :response-code)
   (keep-alive?
    :accessor keep-alive? :initform nil :initarg :keep-alive?)
   (body
    :accessor body :initform nil :initarg :body)))
```

The second is an SSE message[15], which we will use to send an incremental update to our clients.

```
(defclass sse ()
  ((id :reader id :initarg :id :initform nil)
   (event :reader event :initarg :event :initform nil)
   (retry :reader retry :initarg :retry :initform nil)
   (data :reader data :initarg :data)))
```

We'll send an HTTP response whenever we receive a full HTTP request; however, how do we know when and where to send SSE messages without an originating client request?

A simple solution is to register *channels*[16], to which we'll subscribe sockets as necessary.

---

[15]http://www.w3.org/TR/eventsource/

[16]We're incidentally introducing some new syntax here. This is our way of declaring a mutable variable. It has the form (defparameter <name> <value> <optional docstring>).

```
(defparameter *channels* (make-hash-table))

(defmethod subscribe! ((channel symbol) (sock usocket))
  (push sock (gethash channel *channels*))
  nil)
```

We can then publish! notifications to said channels as soon as they become available.

```
(defmethod publish! ((channel symbol) (message string))
  (awhen (gethash channel *channels*)
    (setf (gethash channel *channels*)
          (loop with msg = (make-instance 'sse :data message)
          for sock in it
          when (ignore-errors
            (write! msg sock)
            (force-output (socket-stream sock))
            sock)
          collect it))))
```

In publish!, we call write! to actually write an sse to a socket. We'll also need a specialization of write! on responses to write full HTTP responses as well. Let's handle the HTTP case first.

```
(defmethod write! ((res response) (socket usocket))
  (handler-case
      (with-timeout (.2)
    (let ((stream (flex-stream socket)))
      (flet ((write-ln (&rest sequences)
          (mapc (lambda (seq) (write-sequence seq stream)) sequences)
          (crlf stream)))
        (write-ln "HTTP/1.1 " (response-code res))
        (write-ln
         "Content-Type: " (content-type res) "; charset=" (charset res))
        (write-ln "Cache-Control: no-cache, no-store, must-revalidate")
        (when (keep-alive? res)
          (write-ln "Connection: keep-alive")
          (write-ln "Expires: Thu, 01 Jan 1970 00:00:01 GMT"))
        (awhen (body res)
          (write-ln "Content-Length: " (write-to-string (length it)))
          (crlf stream)
          (write-ln it))
        (values))))
    (trivial-timeout:timeout-error ()
      (values))))
```

This version of write! takes a response and a usocket named sock, and writes content to a stream provided by sock. We locally define the function write-ln which takes some number of sequences, and writes them out to the stream followed by a crlf. This is for readability; we could instead have called write-sequence/crlf directly.

Note that we're doing the "Must not block" thing again. While writes are likely to be buffered and are at lower risk of blocking than reads, we still don't want our server to grind to a halt if something goes wrong here. If the write takes more than 0.2 seconds[17], we just move on (throwing out the current socket) rather than waiting any longer.

Writing an SSE out is conceptually similar to writing out a response:

```
(defmethod write! ((res sse) (socket usocket))
  (let ((stream (flex-stream socket)))
    (handler-case
    (with-timeout (.2)
      (format
        stream "~@[id: ~a~%~]~@[event: ~a~%~]~@[retry: ~a~%~]data: ~a~%~%"
        (id res) (event res) (retry res) (data res)))
    (trivial-timeout:timeout-error ()
      (values)))))
```

This is simpler than working with full HTTP responses since the SSE message standard doesn't specify CRLF line-endings, so we can get away with a single format call. The ~@[...~] blocks are *conditional directives*, which allow us to gracefully handle nil slots. For example, if (id res) is non-nil, we'll output id: <the id here>, otherwise we will ignore the directive entirely. The payload of our incremental update data is the only required slot of sse, so we can include it without worrying about it being nil. And again, we're not waiting around for *too* long. After 0.2 seconds, we'll time out and move on to the next thing if the write hasn't completed by then.

Error Responses

Our treatment of the request/response cycle so far hasn't covered what happens when something goes wrong. Specifically, we used the error! function in handle-request and process-ready without describing what it does.

```
(define-condition http-assertion-error (error)
  ((assertion :initarg :assertion :initform nil :reader assertion))
  (:report (lambda (condition stream)
        (format stream "Failed assertions '~s'"
            (assertion condition)))))
```

define-condition creates new error classes in Common Lisp. In this case, we are defining an HTTP assertion error, and stating that it will specifically need to know the actual assertion it's acting on, and a way to output itself to a stream. In other languages, you'd call this a method. Here, it's a function that happens to be the slot value of a class.

How do we represent errors to the client? Let's define the 4xx and 5xx-class HTTP errors that we'll be using often:

```
(defparameter +404+
  (make-instance
    'response :response-code "404 Not Found"
    :content-type "text/plain"
    :body "Resource not found..."))
```

---

[17]with-timeout has different implementations on different Lisps. In some environments, it may create another thread or process to monitor the one that invoked it. While we'd only be creating at most one of these at a time, it is a relatively heavyweight operation to be performing per-write. We might want to consider an alternative approach in those environments.

```
(defparameter +400+
  (make-instance
   'response :response-code "400 Bad Request"
   :content-type "text/plain"
   :body "Malformed, or slow HTTP request..."))

(defparameter +413+
  (make-instance
   'response :response-code "413 Request Entity Too Large"
   :content-type "text/plain"
   :body "Your request is too long..."))

(defparameter +500+
  (make-instance
   'response :response-code "500 Internal Server Error"
   :content-type "text/plain"
   :body "Something went wrong on our end..."))
```

Now we can see what error! does:

```
(defmethod error! ((err response) (sock usocket) &optional instance)
  (declare (ignorable instance))
  (ignore-errors
    (write! err sock)
    (socket-close sock)))
```

It takes an error response and a socket, writes the response to the socket and closes it (ignoring errors, in case the other end has already disconnected). The instance argument here is for logging/debugging purposes.

And with that, we have an event-driven web server that can respond to HTTP requests or send SSE messages, complete with error handling!

8.3   Extending the Server Into a Web Framework

We have now built a reasonably functional web server that will move requests, responses, and messages to and from clients. The actual work of any web application hosted by this server is done by delegating to handler functions, which were introduced in Section 8.2 but left underspecified.

The interface between our server and the hosted application is an important one, because it dictates how easily application programmers can work with our infrastructure. Ideally, our handler interface would map parameters from a request to a function that does the real work:

```
(define-handler (source :is-stream? nil) (room)
  (subscribe! (intern room :keyword) sock))

(define-handler (send-message) (room name message)
  (publish! (intern room :keyword)
        (encode-json-to-string
          `((:name . ,name) (:message . ,message)))))

(define-handler (index) ()
```

```
(with-html-output-to-string (s nil :prologue t :indent t)
  (:html
    (:head (:script
            :type "text/javascript"
            :src "/static/js/interface.js"))
    (:body (:div :id "messages")
      (:textarea :id "input")
      (:button :id "send" "Send")))))
```

One of the concerns I had in mind when writing House was that, like any application open to the greater internet, it would be processing requests from untrusted clients. It would be nice to be able to say specifically what *type* of data each request should contain by providing a small *schema* that describes the data. Our previous list of handlers would then look like this:

```
(defun len-between (min thing max)
  (>= max (length thing) min))

(define-handler (source :is-stream? nil)
    ((room :string (len-between 0 room 16)))
  (subscribe! (intern room :keyword) sock))

(define-handler (send-message)
    ((room :string (len-between 0 room 16))
     (name :string (len-between 1 name 64))
     (message :string (len-between 5 message 256)))
  (publish! (intern room :keyword)
      (encode-json-to-string
        `((:name . ,name) (:message . ,message)))))

(define-handler (index) ()
  (with-html-output-to-string (s nil :prologue t :indent t)
    (:html
      (:head (:script
              :type "text/javascript"
              :src "/static/js/interface.js"))
      (:body (:div :id "messages")
        (:textarea :id "input")
        (:button :id "send" "Send")))))
```

While we are still working with Lisp code, this interface is starting to look almost like a *declarative language*, in which we state *what* we want our handlers to validate without thinking too much about *how* they are going to do it. What we are doing is building a *domain-specific language* (DSL) for handler functions; that is, we are creating a specific convention and syntax that allows us to concisely express exactly what we want our handlers to validate. This approach of building a small language to solve the problem at hand is frequently used by Lisp programmers, and it is a useful technique that can be applied in other programming languages.

A DSL for Handlers

Now that we have a loose specification for how we want our handler DSL to look, how do we implement it? That is, what specifically do we expect to happen when we call define-handler?

Let's consider the definition for send-message from above:

```
(define-handler (send-message)
    ((room :string (len-between 0 room 16))
     (name :string (len-between 1 name 64))
     (message :string (len-between 5 message 256)))
  (publish! (intern room :keyword)
        (encode-json-to-string
           '((:name . ,name) (:message . ,message)))))
```

What we would like define-handler to do here is:

1. Bind the action (publish!   ...) to the URI /send-message in the handlers table.
2. When a request to this URI is made:

   - Ensure that the HTTP parameters room, name and message were included.
   - Validate that room is a string no longer than 16 characters, name is a string of between 1 and 64 characters (inclusive) and that message is a string of between 5 and 256 characters (also inclusive).

3. After the response has been returned, close the channel.

While we could write Lisp functions to do all of these things, and then manually assemble the pieces ourselves, a more common approach is to use a Lisp facility called macros to *generate* the Lisp code for us. This allows us to concisely express what we want our DSL to do, without having to maintain a lot of code to do it. You can think of a macro as an "executable template" that will be expanded into Lisp code at runtime.

Here's our define-handler macro[18]:

```
(defmacro define-handler
    ((name &key (is-stream? t) (content-type "text/html")) (&rest args)
     &body body)
  (if is-stream?
      '(bind-handler
      ,name (make-closing-handler
            (:content-type ,content-type)
            ,args ,@body))
      '(bind-handler
      ,name (make-stream-handler ,args ,@body))))
```

It delegates to three other macros (bind-handler, make-closing-handler, make-stream-handler) that we will define later. make-closing-handler will create a handler for a full HTTP request/response cycle; make-stream-handler will instead handle an SSE message. The predicate is-stream? distinguishes between these cases for us. The backtick and comma are macro-specific operators that we can use to "cut holes" in our code that will be filled out by values specified in our Lisp code when we actually use define-handler.

Notice how closely our macro conforms to our specification of what we wanted define-handler to do: If we were to write a series of Lisp functions to do all of these things, the intent of the code would be much more difficult to discern by inspection.

---

[18]I should note, the below code-block is VERY unconventional indentation for Common Lisp. Arglists are typically not broken up over multiple lines, and are usually kept on the same line as the macro/function name. I had to do it to stick to the line-width guidelines for this book, but would otherwise prefer to have longer lines that break naturally at places dictated by the content of the code.

Expanding a Handler

Let's step through the expansion for the `send-message` handler so that we better understand what is actually going on when Lisp "expands" our macro for us. We'll use the macro expansion feature from the SLIME[19] Emacs mode to do this. Calling `macro-expander` on `define-handler` will expand our macro by one "level", leaving our helper macros in their still-condensed form:

```
(BIND-HANDLER
 SEND-MESSAGE
 (MAKE-CLOSING-HANDLER
  (:CONTENT-TYPE "text/html")
  ((ROOM :STRING (LEN-BETWEEN 0 ROOM 16))
   (NAME :STRING (LEN-BETWEEN 1 NAME 64))
   (MESSAGE :STRING (LEN-BETWEEN 5 MESSAGE 256)))
  (PUBLISH! (INTERN ROOM :KEYWORD)
        (ENCODE-JSON-TO-STRING
          '((:NAME ,@NAME) (:MESSAGE ,@MESSAGE)))))))
```

Our macro has already saved us a bit of typing by substituting our `send-message` specific code into our handler template. `bind-handler` is another macro which maps a URI to a handler function on our handlers table; since it's now at the root of our expansion, let's see how it is defined before expanding this further.

```
(defmacro bind-handler (name handler)
  (assert (symbolp name) nil "'name' must be a symbol")
  (let ((uri (if (eq name 'root) "/" (format nil "/~(~a~)" name))))
    '(progn
       (when (gethash ,uri *handlers*)
       (warn ,(format nil "Redefining handler '~a'" uri)))
       (setf (gethash ,uri *handlers*) ,handler))))
```

The binding happens in the last line: `(setf (gethash ,uri *handlers*) ,handler)`, which is what hash-table assignments look like in Common Lisp (modulo the commas, which are part of our macro). Note that the `assert` is outside of the quoted area, which means that it'll be run as soon as the macro is *called* rather than when its result is evaluated.

When we further expand our expansion of the `send-message` `define-handler` above, we get:

```
(PROGN
  (WHEN (GETHASH "/send-message" *HANDLERS*)
    (WARN "Redefining handler '/send-message'"))
  (SETF (GETHASH "/send-message" *HANDLERS*)
    (MAKE-CLOSING-HANDLER
     (:CONTENT-TYPE "text/html")
     ((ROOM :STRING (LEN-BETWEEN 0 ROOM 16))
      (NAME :STRING (LEN-BETWEEN 1 NAME 64))
      (MESSAGE :STRING (LEN-BETWEEN 5 MESSAGE 256)))
     (PUBLISH! (INTERN ROOM :KEYWORD)
           (ENCODE-JSON-TO-STRING
             '((:NAME ,@NAME) (:MESSAGE ,@MESSAGE)))))))
```

---

[19]https://common-lisp.net/project/slime/

This is starting to look more like a custom implementation of what we would have written to marshal a request from a URI to a handler function, had we written it all ourselves. But we didn't have to!

We still have make-closing-handler left to go in our expansion. Here is its definition:

```
(defmacro make-closing-handler
    ((&key (content-type "text/html")) (&rest args) &body body)
  `(lambda (sock parameters)
     (declare (ignorable parameters))
     ,(arguments
        args
        `(let ((res (make-instance
                      'response
                      :content-type ,content-type
                      :body (progn ,@body))))
           (write! res sock)
           (socket-close sock)))))
```

So making a closing-handler involves making a lambda, which is just what you call anonymous functions in Common Lisp. We also set up an interior scope that makes a response out of the body argument we're passing in, performs a write! to the requesting socket, then closes it. The remaining question is, what is arguments?

```
(defun arguments (args body)
  (loop with res = body
      for arg in args
      do (match arg
      ((guard arg-sym (symbolp arg-sym))
       (setf res `(let ((,arg-sym ,(arg-exp arg-sym))) ,res)))
      ((list* arg-sym type restrictions)
       (setf res
         (let ((sym (or (type-expression
                          (arg-exp arg-sym)
                          type restrictions)
                        (arg-exp arg-sym))))
           `(let ((,arg-sym ,sym))
              ,@(awhen (type-assertion arg-sym type restrictions)
                  `((assert-http ,it)))
              ,res)))))
      finally (return res)))
```

Welcome to the hard part. arguments turns the validators we registered with our handler into a tree of parse attempts and assertions. type-expression, arg-exp, and type-assertion are used to implement and enforce a "type system" for the kinds of data we're expecting in our responses; we'll discuss them in Section 8.3. Using this together with make-closing-handler would implement the validation rules we wrote here:

```
(define-handler (send-message)
    ((room :string (>= 16 (length room)))
     (name :string (>= 64 (length name) 1))
     (message :string (>= 256 (length message) 5)))
```

```
(publish! (intern room :keyword)
     (encode-json-to-string
       '((:name . ,name) (:message . ,message)))))
```

...as an "unrolled" sequence of checks needed to validate the request:

```
(LAMBDA (SOCK #:COOKIE?1111 SESSION PARAMETERS)
  (DECLARE (IGNORABLE SESSION PARAMETERS))
  (LET ((ROOM (AIF (CDR (ASSOC :ROOM PARAMETERS))
            (URI-DECODE IT)
            (ERROR (MAKE-INSTANCE
                 'HTTP-ASSERTION-ERROR
                 :ASSERTION 'ROOM)))))
    (ASSERT-HTTP (>= 16 (LENGTH ROOM)))
    (LET ((NAME (AIF (CDR (ASSOC :NAME PARAMETERS))
              (URI-DECODE IT)
              (ERROR (MAKE-INSTANCE
                   'HTTP-ASSERTION-ERROR
                   :ASSERTION 'NAME)))))
      (ASSERT-HTTP (>= 64 (LENGTH NAME) 1))
      (LET ((MESSAGE (AIF (CDR (ASSOC :MESSAGE PARAMETERS))
                (URI-DECODE IT)
                (ERROR (MAKE-INSTANCE
                     'HTTP-ASSERTION-ERROR
                     :ASSERTION 'MESSAGE)))))
        (ASSERT-HTTP (>= 256 (LENGTH MESSAGE) 5))
        (LET ((RES (MAKE-INSTANCE
                'RESPONSE :CONTENT-TYPE "text/html"
                :COOKIE (UNLESS #:COOKIE?1111
                      (TOKEN SESSION))
                :BODY (PROGN
                    (PUBLISH!
                     (INTERN ROOM :KEYWORD)
                     (ENCODE-JSON-TO-STRING
                      '((:NAME ,@NAME)
                       (:MESSAGE ,@MESSAGE)))))))) )
          (WRITE! RES SOCK)
          (SOCKET-CLOSE SOCK))))))
```

This gets us the validation we need for full HTTP request/response cycles. What about our SSEs? make-stream-handler does the same basic thing as make-closing-handler, except that it writes an SSE rather than a RESPONSE, and it calls force-output instead of socket-close because we want to flush data over the connection without closing it:

```
(defmacro make-stream-handler ((&rest args) &body body)
  '(lambda (sock parameters)
     (declare (ignorable parameters))
     ,(arguments
       args
       '(let ((res (progn ,@body)))
       (write! (make-instance
           'response
```

```
            :keep-alive? t
            :content-type "text/event-stream")
          sock)
      (write!
        (make-instance 'sse :data (or res "Listening..."))
        sock)
      (force-output
        (socket-stream sock))))))

(defmacro assert-http (assertion)
  '(unless ,assertion
     (error (make-instance
         'http-assertion-error
         :assertion ',assertion))))
```

assert-http is a macro that creates the boilerplate code we need in error cases. It expands into a check of the given assertion, throws an http-assertion-error if it fails, and packs the original assertion along in that event.

```
(defmacro assert-http (assertion)
  '(unless ,assertion
     (error (make-instance
         'http-assertion-error
         :assertion ',assertion))))
```

HTTP "Types"

In the previous section, we briefly touched on three expressions that we're using to implement our HTTP type validation system: arg-exp, type-expression and type-assertion. Once you understand those, there will be no magic left in our framework. We'll start with the easy one first.

arg-exp

arg-exp takes a symbol and creates an aif expression that checks for the presence of a parameter.

```
(defun arg-exp (arg-sym)
  '(aif (cdr (assoc ,(->keyword arg-sym) parameters))
     (uri-decode it)
     (error (make-instance
         'http-assertion-error
         :assertion ',arg-sym))))
```

Evaluating arg-exp on a symbol looks like:

```
HOUSE> (arg-exp 'room)
(AIF (CDR (ASSOC :ROOM PARAMETERS))
     (URI-DECODE IT)
     (ERROR (MAKE-INSTANCE
         'HTTP-ASSERTION-ERROR
         :ASSERTION 'ROOM)))
HOUSE>
```

We've been using forms like `aif` and `awhen` without understanding how they work, so let's take some time to explore them now.

Recall that Lisp code is itself represented as a tree. That's what the parentheses are for; they show us how leaves and branches fit together. If we step back to what we were doing in the previous section, `make-closing-handler` calls a function called `arguments` to generate part of the Lisp tree it's constructing, which in turn calls some tree-manipulating helper functions, including `arg-exp`, to generate its return value.

That is, we've built a small system that takes a Lisp expression as input, and produces a different Lisp expression as output. Possibly the simplest way of conceptualizing this is as a simple Common–Lisp-to-Common–Lisp compiler that is specialized to the problem at hand.

A widely used classification of such compilers is as *anaphoric macros*. This term comes from the linguistic concept of an *anaphor*, which is the use of one word as a substitute for a group of words that preceded it. `aif` and `awhen` are anaphoric macros, and they're the only ones that I tend to often use. There are many more availabile in the anaphora package[20].

As far as I know, anaphoric macros were first defined by Paul Graham in an OnLisp chapter[21]. The use case he gives is a situation where you want to do some sort of expensive or semi-expensive check, then do something conditionally on the result. In the above context, we're using `aif` to do a check the result of an `alist` traversal.

```
(aif (cdr (assoc :room parameters))
     (uri-decode it)
     (error (make-instance
          'http-assertion-error
          :assertion 'room)))
```

This takes the `cdr` of looking up the symbol `:room` in the association list `parameters`. If that returns a non-nil value, `uri-decode` it, otherwise throw an error of the type `http-assertion-error`.

In other words, the above is equivalent to:

```
(let ((it (cdr (assoc :room parameters))))
  (if it
      (uri-decode it)
      (error (make-instance
           'http-assertion-error
           :assertion 'room))))
```

Strongly-typed functional languages like Haskell often use a Maybe type in this situation. In Common Lisp, we capture the symbol `it` in the expansion as the name for the result of the check.

Understanding this, we should be able to see that `arg-exp` is generating a specific, repetitive, piece of the code tree that we eventually want to evaluate. In this case, the piece that checks for the presence of the given parameter among the handlers' `parameters`. Now, let's move onto. . .

type-expression

```
(defgeneric type-expression (parameter type)
  (:documentation
    "A type-expression will tell the server
```

---

[20]http://www.cliki.net/Anaphora
[21]http://dunsmor.com/lisp/onlisp/onlisp_18.html

```
how to convert a parameter from a string to
a particular, necessary type."))
...
(defmethod type-expression (parameter type) nil)
```

This is a generic function that generates new tree structures (coincidentally Lisp code), rather than just a function. The only thing the above tells you is that by default, a `type-expression` is NIL. Which is to say, we don't have one. If we encounter a NIL, we use the raw output of `arg-exp`, but that doesn't tell us much about the most common case. To see that, let's take a look at a built-in (to `:house`) `define-http-type` expression.

```
(define-http-type (:integer)
    :type-expression `(parse-integer ,parameter :junk-allowed t)
    :type-assertion `(numberp ,parameter))
```

An `:integer` is something we're making from a parameter by using `parse-integer`. The `junk-allowed` parameter tells `parse-integer` that we're not confident the data we're giving it is actually parseable, so we need to make sure that the returned result is an integer. If it isn't, we get this behaviour:

```
HOUSE> (type-expression 'blah :integer)
(PARSE-INTEGER BLAH :JUNK-ALLOWED T)
HOUSE>
```

`define-http-handler`[22] is one of the exported symbols for our framework. This lets our application programmers define their own types to simplify parsing above the handful of "builtins" that we give them (`:string`, `:integer`, `:keyword`, `:json`, `:list-of-keyword` and `:list-of-integer`).

```
(defmacro define-http-type ((type) &key type-expression type-assertion)
  (with-gensyms (tp)
    `(let ((,tp ,type))
       ,@(when type-expression
          `((defmethod type-expression (parameter (type (eql ,tp)))
              ,type-expression)))
       ,@(when type-assertion
          `((defmethod type-assertion (parameter (type (eql ,tp)))
              ,type-assertion))))))
```

It works by creating `type-expression` and `type-assertion` method definitions for the type being defined. We could let users of our framework do this manually without much trouble; however, adding this extra level of indirection gives us, the framework programmers, the freedom to change *how* types are implemented without forcing our users to re-write their specifications. This isn't just an academic consideration; I've personally made radical changes to this part of the system when first building it, and was pleased to find that I had to make very few edits to the applications that depended on it.

Let's take a look at the expansion of that integer definition to see how it works in detail:

---

[22]This macro is difficult to read because it tries hard to make its output human-readable, by expanding NILs away using `,@` where possible.

```
(LET ((#:TP1288 :INTEGER))
  (DEFMETHOD TYPE-EXPRESSION (PARAMETER (TYPE (EQL #:TP1288)))
    '(PARSE-INTEGER ,PARAMETER :JUNK-ALLOWED T))
  (DEFMETHOD TYPE-ASSERTION (PARAMETER (TYPE (EQL #:TP1288)))
    '(NUMBERP ,PARAMETER)))
```

As we said, it doesn't reduce code size by much, but it does prevent us from needing to care what the specific parameters of those methods are, or even that they're methods at all.

type-assertion

Now that we can define types, let's look at how we use `type-assertion` to validate that a parse satisfies our requirements. It, too, takes the form of a complementary `defgeneric`/`defmethod` pair just like `type-expression`:

```
(defgeneric type-assertion (parameter type)
  (:documentation
   "A lookup assertion is run on a parameter
immediately after conversion. Use it to restrict
 the space of a particular parameter."))
...
(defmethod type-assertion (parameter type) nil)
```

Here's what this one outputs:

```
HOUSE> (type-assertion 'blah :integer)
(NUMBERP BLAH)
HOUSE>
```

There are cases where `type-assertion` won't need to do anything. For example, since HTTP parameters are given to us as strings, our `:string` type assertion has nothing to validate:

```
HOUSE> (type-assertion 'blah :string)
NIL
HOUSE>
```

All Together Now

We did it! We built a web framework on top of an event-driven webserver implementation. Our framework (and handler DSL) defines new applications by:

- Mapping URLs to handlers;
- Defining handlers to enforce the type safety and validation rules on requests;
- Optionally specifying new types for handlers as required.

Now we can describe our application like this:

```
(defun len-between (min thing max)
  (>= max (length thing) min))

(define-handler (source :is-stream? nil)
    ((room :string (len-between 0 room 16)))
```

```
      (subscribe! (intern room :keyword) sock))

(define-handler (send-message)
    ((room :string (len-between 0 room 16))
     (name :string (len-between 1 name 64))
     (message :string (len-between 5 message 256)))
  (publish! (intern room :keyword)
        (encode-json-to-string
          '((:name . ,name) (:message . ,message)))))

(define-handler (index) ()
  (with-html-output-to-string (s nil :prologue t :indent t)
    (:html
     (:head (:script
         :type "text/javascript"
         :src "/static/js/interface.js"))
     (:body (:div :id "messages")
       (:textarea :id "input")
       (:button :id "send" "Send")))))

(start 4242)
```

Once we write interface.js to provide the client-side interactivity, this will start an HTTP chat server on port 4242 and listen for incoming connections.

## chapter 9

A Flow Shop Scheduler
Dr. Christian Muise

9.1   A Flow Shop Scheduler

Flow shop scheduling is one of the most challenging and well-studied problems in operations research. Like many challenging optimization problems, finding the best solution is just not possible for problems of a practical size. In this chapter we consider the implementation of a flow shop scheduling solver that uses a technique called *local search*. Local search allows us to find a solution that is "pretty good" when finding the best solution isn't possible. The solver will try and find new solutions to the problem for a given amount of time, and finish by returning the best solution found.

The idea behind local search is to improve an existing solution heuristically by considering similar solutions that may be a little better. The solver uses a variety of strategies to (1) try and find similar solutions, and (2) choose one that is promising to explore next. The implementation is written in Python, and has no external requirements. By leveraging some of Python's lesser-known functionality, the solver dynamically changes its search strategy during the solving process based on which strategies work well.

First, we provide some background material on the flow shop scheduling problem and local search techniques. We then look in detail at the general solver code and the various heuristics and neighbourhood selection strategies that we use. Next we consider the dynamic strategy selection that the solver uses to tie everything together. Finally, we conclude with a summary of the project and some lessons learned through the implementation process.

9.2   Background

Flow Shop Scheduling

The flow shop scheduling problem is an optimization problem in which we must determine the processing time for various tasks in a job in order to schedule the tasks to minimize the total time it takes to complete the job. Take, for example, a car manufacturer with an assembly line where each part of the car is completed in sequence on different machines. Different orders may have custom requirements, making the task of painting the body, for example, vary from one car to the next. In our example, each car is a new *job* and each part for the car is called a *task*. Every job will have the same sequence of tasks to complete.

The objective in flow shop scheduling is to minimize the total time it takes to process all of the tasks from every job to completion. (Typically, this total time is referred to as the *makespan*.) This problem has many applications, but is most related to optimizing production facilities.

Every flow shop problem consists of n machines and m jobs. In our car example, there will be n stations to work on the car and m cars to make in total. Each job is made up of exactly n tasks, and we can assume that the i-th task of a job must use machine i and requires a predetermined amount of processing time: $p(j, i)$ is the processing time for the ith task of job j. Further, the order of the tasks for any given job should follow the order of the machines available; for a given job, task i must be completed prior to the start of task $i + 1$. In our car example, we wouldn't want to start painting the car before the frame was assembled. The final restriction is that no two tasks can be processed on a machine simultaneously.

Because the order of tasks within a job is predetermined, a solution to the flow shop scheduling problem can be represented as a permutation of the jobs. The order of jobs processed on a machine will be the same for every machine, and given a permutation, a task for machine i in job j is scheduled to be the latest of the following two possibilities:

1. The completion of the task for machine i in job $j - 1$ (i.e., the most recent task on the same machine), or
2. The completion of the task for machine $i - 1$ in job j (i.e., the most recent task on the same job)

Because we select the maximum of these two values, idle time for either machine i or job j will be created. It is this idle time that we ultimately want to minimize, as it will push the total makespan to be larger.

Due to the simple form of the problem, any permutation of jobs is a valid solution, and the optimal solution will correspond to *some* permutation. Thus, we search for improved solutions by changing the permutation of jobs and measuring the corresponding makespan. In what follows, we refer to a permutation of the jobs as a *candidate*.

Let's consider a simple example with two jobs and two machines. The first job has tasks **A** and **B**, which take 1 and 2 minutes to complete respectively. The second job has tasks **C** and **D**, which take 2 and 1 minutes to complete respectively. Recall that **A** must come before **B** and **C** must come before **D**. Because there are two jobs, we have just two permutations to consider. If we order job 2 before job 1, the makespan is 5 (Figure 9.1); on the other hand, if we order job 1 before job 2, the makespan is only 4 (Figure 9.2).

Figure 9.1: Flow Shop Example 1

Figure 9.2: Flow Shop Example 2

Notice that there is no budge room to push any of the tasks earlier. A guiding principle for a good permutation is to minimize the time in which any machine is left without a task to process.

Local Search

Local search is a strategy for solving optimization problems when the optimal solution is too hard to compute. Intuitively, it moves from one solution that seems pretty good to another solution that seems even better. Rather than considering every possible solution as a candidate to focus on next, we define what is known as a *neighbourhood*: the set of solutions considered to be similar to the current solution. Because any permutation of jobs is a valid solution, we can view any mechanism that shuffles the jobs around as a local search procedure (this is in fact what we do below).

To use local search formally, we must answer a few questions:

1. What solution should we start with?
2. Given a solution, what are the neighbouring solutions that we should consider?
3. Given the set of candidate neighbours, which one should we consider moving to next?

The following three sections address these questions in turn.

9.3   General Solver

In this section we provide the general framework for the flow shop scheduler. To begin, we have the necessary Python imports and the settings for the solver:

```
import sys, os, time, random

from functools import partial
from collections import namedtuple
from itertools import product

import neighbourhood as neigh
import heuristics as heur

##############
## Settings ##
##############
TIME_LIMIT = 300.0 # Time (in seconds) to run the solver
TIME_INCREMENT = 13.0 # Time (in seconds) in between heuristic measurements
DEBUG_SWITCH = False # Displays intermediate heuristic info when True
MAX_LNS_NEIGHBOURHOODS = 1000 # Maximum number of neighbours to explore in LNS
```

There are two settings that should be explained further. The TIME_INCREMENT setting will be used as part of the dynamic strategy selection, and the MAX_LNS_NEIGHBOURHOODS setting will be used as part of the neighbourhood selection strategy. Both are described in more detail below.

These settings could be exposed to the user as command line parameters, but at this stage we instead provide the input data as parameters to the program. The input problem—a problem from the Taillard benchmark set—is assumed to be in a standard format for flow shop scheduling. The following code is used as the __main__ method for the solver file, and calls the appropriate functions based on the number of parameters input to the program:

```
if __name__ == '__main__':

    if len(sys.argv) == 2:
        data = parse_problem(sys.argv[1], 0)
```

```
    elif len(sys.argv) == 3:
        data = parse_problem(sys.argv[1], int(sys.argv[2]))
    else:
        print "\nUsage: python flow.py <Taillard problem file> [<instance number>]\n"
        sys.exit(0)

    (perm, ms) = solve(data)
    print_solution(data, perm)
```

We will describe the parsing of Taillard problem files shortly. (The files are available online[1].)

The solve method expects the data variable to be a list of integers containing the activity durations for each job. The solve method starts by initializing a global set of strategies (to be described below). The key is that we use strat_* variables to maintain statistics on each of the strategies. This aids in selecting the strategy dynamically during the solving process.

```
def solve(data):
    """Solves an instance of the flow shop scheduling problem"""

    # We initialize the strategies here to avoid cyclic import issues
    initialize_strategies()
    global STRATEGIES

    # Record the following for each strategy:
    #   improvements: The amount a solution was improved by this strategy
    #   time_spent: The amount of time spent on the strategy
    #   weights: The weights that correspond to how good a strategy is
    #   usage: The number of times we use a strategy
    strat_improvements = {strategy: 0 for strategy in STRATEGIES}
    strat_time_spent = {strategy: 0 for strategy in STRATEGIES}
    strat_weights = {strategy: 1 for strategy in STRATEGIES}
    strat_usage = {strategy: 0 for strategy in STRATEGIES}
```

One appealing feature of the flow shop scheduling problem is that *every* permutation is a valid solution, and at least one will have the optimal makespan (though many will have horrible makespans). Thankfully, this allows us to forgo checking that we stay within the space of feasible solutions when going from one permutation to another—everything is feasible!

However, to start a local search in the space of permutations, we must have an initial permutation. To keep things simple, we seed our local search by shuffling the list of jobs randomly:

```
    # Start with a random permutation of the jobs
    perm = range(len(data))
    random.shuffle(perm)
```

Next, we initialize the variables that allow us to keep track of the best permutation found so far, as well as the timing information for providing output.

---

[1]http://mistic.heig-vd.ch/taillard/problemes.dir/ordonnancement.dir/ordonnancement.html

```
# Keep track of the best solution
best_make = makespan(data, perm)
best_perm = perm
res = best_make

# Maintain statistics and timing for the iterations
iteration = 0
time_limit = time.time() + TIME_LIMIT
time_last_switch = time.time()

time_delta = TIME_LIMIT / 10
checkpoint = time.time() + time_delta
percent_complete = 10

print "\nSolving..."
```

As this is a local search solver, we simply continue to try and improve solutions as long as the time limit has not been reached. We provide output indicating the progress of the solver and keep track of the number of iterations we have computed:

```
while time.time() < time_limit:

    if time.time() > checkpoint:
        print " %d %%" % percent_complete
        percent_complete += 10
        checkpoint += time_delta

    iteration += 1
```

Below we describe how the strategy is picked, but for now it is sufficient to know that the strategy provides a neighbourhood function and a heuristic function. The former gives us a set of *next candidates* to consider while the latter chooses the *best candidate* from the set. From these functions, we have a new permutation (perm) and a new makespan result (res):

```
# Heuristically choose the best strategy
strategy = pick_strategy(STRATEGIES, strat_weights)

old_val = res
old_time = time.time()

# Use the current strategy's heuristic to pick the next permutation from
# the set of candidates generated by the strategy's neighbourhood
candidates = strategy.neighbourhood(data, perm)
perm = strategy.heuristic(data, candidates)
res = makespan(data, perm)
```

The code for computing the makespan is quite simple: we can compute it from a permutation by evaluating when the final job completes. We will see below how compile_solution works, but for now it suffices to know that a 2D array is returned and the element at [-1][-1] corresponds to the start time of the final job in the schedule:

```
def makespan(data, perm):
    """Computes the makespan of the provided solution"""
    return compile_solution(data, perm)[-1][-1] + data[perm[-1]][-1]
```

To help select a strategy, we keep statistics on (1) how much the strategy has improved the solution, (2) how much time the strategy has spent computing information, and (3) how many times the strategy was used. We also update the variables for the best permutation if we stumble upon a better solution:

```
# Record the statistics on how the strategy did
strat_improvements[strategy] += res - old_val
strat_time_spent[strategy] += time.time() - old_time
strat_usage[strategy] += 1

if res < best_make:
    best_make = res
    best_perm = perm[:]
```

At regular intervals, the statistics for strategy use are updated. We removed the associated snippet for readability, and detail the code below. As a final step, once the while loop is complete (i.e., the time limit is reached) we output some statistics about the solving process and return the best permutation along with its makespan:

```
print " %d %%\n" % percent_complete
print "\nWent through %d iterations." % iteration

print "\n(usage) Strategy:"
results = sorted([(strat_weights[STRATEGIES[i]], i)
                  for i in range(len(STRATEGIES))], reverse=True)
for (w, i) in results:
    print "(%d) \t%s" % (strat_usage[STRATEGIES[i]], STRATEGIES[i].name)

return (best_perm, best_make)
```

Parsing Problems

As input to the parsing procedure, we provide the file name where the input can be found and the example number that should be used. (Each file contains a number of instances.)

```
def parse_problem(filename, k=1):
    """Parse the kth instance of a Taillard problem file

    The Taillard problem files are a standard benchmark set for the problem
    of flow shop scheduling.

    print "\nParsing..."
```

We start the parsing by reading in the file and identifying the line that separates each of the problem instances:

```
with open(filename, 'r') as f:
    # Identify the string that separates instances
    problem_line = ('/number of jobs, number of machines, initial seed, '
                    'upper bound and lower bound :/')

    # Strip spaces and newline characters from every line
    lines = map(str.strip, f.readlines())
```

To make locating the correct instance easier, we assume that lines will be separated by a '/' character. This allows us to split the file based on a common string that appears at the top of every instance, and adding a '/' character to the start of the first line allows the string processing below to work correctly regardless of the instance we choose. We also detect when a provided instance number is out of range given the collection of instances found in the file.

```
# We prep the first line for later
lines[0] = '/' + lines[0]

# We also know '/' does not appear in the files, so we can use it as
#   a separator to find the right lines for the kth problem instance
try:
    lines = '/'.join(lines).split(problem_line)[k].split('/')[2:]
except IndexError:
    max_instances = len('/'.join(lines).split(problem_line)) - 1
    print "\nError: Instance must be within 1 and %d\n" % max_instances
    sys.exit(0)
```

We parse the data directly, converting the processing time of each task to an integer and storing it in a list. Finally, we zip the data to invert the rows and columns so that the format respects what is expected by the solving code above. (Every item in data should correspond to a particular job.)

```
# Split every line based on spaces and convert each item to an int
data = [map(int, line.split()) for line in lines]

# We return the zipped data to rotate the rows and columns, making each
#   item in data the durations of tasks for a particular job
return zip(*data)
```

Compiling Solutions

A solution to the flow shop scheduling problem consists of precise timing for each task in every job. Because we represent a solution implicitly with a permutation of the jobs, we introduce the compile_solution function to convert a permutation to precise times. As input, the function takes in the data for the problem (giving us the duration of every task) and a permutation of jobs.

The function begins by initializing the data structure used to store the starting time for each task, and then including the tasks from the first job in the permutation.

```
def compile_solution(data, perm):
    """Compiles a scheduling on the machines given a permutation of jobs"""

    num_machines = len(data[0])
```

```
# Note that using [[]] * m would be incorrect, as it would simply
#  copy the same list m times (as opposed to creating m distinct lists).
machine_times = [[] for _ in range(num_machines)]

# Assign the initial job to the machines
machine_times[0].append(0)
for mach in range(1,num_machines):
    # Start the next task in the job when the previous finishes
    machine_times[mach].append(machine_times[mach-1][0] +
                               data[perm[0]][mach-1])
```

We then add all the tasks for the remaining jobs. The first task in a job will always start as soon as the first task in the previous job completes. For the remaining tasks, we schedule the job as early as possible: the maximum out of the completion time of the previous task in the same job and the completion time of the previous task on the same machine.

```
# Assign the remaining jobs
for i in range(1, len(perm)):

    # The first machine never contains any idle time
    job = perm[i]
    machine_times[0].append(machine_times[0][-1] + data[perm[i-1]][0])

    # For the remaining machines, the start time is the max of when the
    #  previous task in the job completed, or when the current machine
    #  completes the task for the previous job.
    for mach in range(1, num_machines):
        machine_times[mach].append(max(
            machine_times[mach-1][i] + data[perm[i]][mach-1],
            machine_times[mach][i-1] + data[perm[i-1]][mach]))

return machine_times
```

Printing Solutions

When the solving process is complete, the program outputs information about the solution in a compact form. Rather than providing the precise timing of every task for every job, we output the following pieces of information:

1. The permutation of jobs that yielded the best makespan
2. The computed makespan of the permutation
3. The start time, finish time, and idle time for every machine
4. The start time, finish time, and idle time for every job

The start time for a job or machine corresponds to the start of the first task in the job or on the machine. Similarly, the finish time for a job or machine corresponds to the end of the final task in the job or on the machine. The idle time is the amount of slack in between tasks for a particular job or machine. Ideally we would like to reduce the amount of idle time, as it means the overall process time will be reduced as well.

The code to compile the solution (i.e., to compute the start times for every task) has already been discussed, and outputting the permutation and makespan are trivial:

```
def print_solution(data, perm):
    """Prints statistics on the computed solution"""

    sol = compile_solution(data, perm)

    print "\nPermutation: %s\n" % str([i+1 for i in perm])

    print "Makespan: %d\n" % makespan(data, perm)
```

Next, we use the string formatting functionality in Python to print the table of start, end, and idle times for each of the machines and jobs. Note that the idle time for a job is the time from when the job started to its completion, minus the sum of the processing times for each task in the job. We compute the idle time for a machine in a similar fashion.

```
row_format ="{:>15}" * 4
print row_format.format('Machine', 'Start Time', 'Finish Time', 'Idle Time')
for mach in range(len(data[0])):
    finish_time = sol[mach][-1] + data[perm[-1]][mach]
    idle_time = (finish_time - sol[mach][0]) - sum([job[mach] for job in data])
    print row_format.format(mach+1, sol[mach][0], finish_time, idle_time)

results = []
for i in range(len(data)):
    finish_time = sol[-1][i] + data[perm[i]][-1]
    idle_time = (finish_time - sol[0][i]) - sum([time for time in data[perm[i]]])
    results.append((perm[i]+1, sol[0][i], finish_time, idle_time))

print "\n"
print row_format.format('Job', 'Start Time', 'Finish Time', 'Idle Time')
for r in sorted(results):
    print row_format.format(*r)

print "\n\nNote: Idle time does not include initial or final wait time.\n"
```

9.4 Neighbourhoods

The idea behind local search is to move *locally* from one solution to other solutions nearby. We refer to the *neighbourhood* of a given solution as the other solutions that are local to it. In this section, we detail four potential neighbourhoods, each of increasing complexity.

The first neighbourhood produces a given number of random permutations. This neighbourhood does not even consider the solution that we begin with, and so the term "neighbourhood" stretches the truth. However, including some randomness in the search is good practice, as it promotes exploration of the search space.

```
def neighbours_random(data, perm, num = 1):
    # Returns <num> random job permutations, including the current one
    candidates = [perm]
    for i in range(num):
        candidate = perm[:]
        random.shuffle(candidate)
```

```
            candidates.append(candidate)
        return candidates
```

For the next neighbourhood, we consider swapping any two jobs in the permutation. By using the `combinations` function from the `itertools` package, we can easily iterate through every pair of indices and create a new permutation that corresponds to swapping the jobs located at each index. In a sense, this neighbourhood creates permutations that are very similar to the one we began with.

```
def neighbours_swap(data, perm):
    # Returns the permutations corresponding to swapping every pair of jobs
    candidates = [perm]
    for (i,j) in combinations(range(len(perm)), 2):
        candidate = perm[:]
        candidate[i], candidate[j] = candidate[j], candidate[i]
        candidates.append(candidate)
    return candidates
```

The next neighbourhood we consider uses information specific to the problem at hand. We find the jobs with the most idle time and consider swapping them in every way possible. We take in a value `size` which is the number of jobs we consider: the `size` most idle jobs. The first step in the process is to compute the idle time for every job in the permutation:

```
def neighbours_idle(data, perm, size=4):
    # Returns the permutations of the <size> most idle jobs
    candidates = [perm]

    # Compute the idle time for each job
    sol = flow.compile_solution(data, perm)
    results = []

    for i in range(len(data)):
        finish_time = sol[-1][i] + data[perm[i]][-1]
        idle_time = (finish_time - sol[0][i]) - sum([t for t in data[perm[i]]])
        results.append((idle_time, i))
```

Next, we compute the list of `size` jobs that have the most idle time.

```
    # Take the <size> most idle jobs
    subset = [job_ind for (idle, job_ind) in reversed(sorted(results))][:size]
```

Finally, we construct the neighbourhood by considering every permutation of the most idle jobs that we have identified. To find the permutations, we make use of the `permutations` function from the `itertools` package.

```
    # Enumerate the permutations of the idle jobs
    for ordering in permutations(subset):
        candidate = perm[:]
        for i in range(len(ordering)):
            candidate[subset[i]] = perm[ordering[i]]
        candidates.append(candidate)

    return candidates
```

The final neighbourhood that we consider is commonly referred to as *Large Neighbourhood Search* (LNS). Intuitively, LNS works by considering small subsets of the current permutation in isolation—locating the best permutation of the subset of jobs gives us a single candidate for the LNS neighbourhood. By repeating this process for several (or all) subsets of a particular size, we can increase the number of candidates in the neighbourhood. We limit the number that are considered through the MAX_LNS_NEIGHBOURHOODS parameter, as the number of neighbours can grow quite quickly. The first step in the LNS computation is to compute the random list of job sets that we will consider swapping using the combinations function of the itertools package:

```
def neighbours_LNS(data, perm, size = 2):
    # Returns the Large Neighbourhood Search neighbours
    candidates = [perm]

    # Bound the number of neighbourhoods in case there are too many jobs
    neighbourhoods = list(combinations(range(len(perm)), size))
    random.shuffle(neighbourhoods)
```

Next, we iterate through the subsets to find the best permutation of jobs in each one. We have seen similar code above for iterating through all permutations of the most idle jobs. The key difference here is that we record only the best permutation for the subset, as the larger neighbourhood is constructed by choosing one permutation for each subset of the considered jobs.

```
    for subset in neighbourhoods[:flow.MAX_LNS_NEIGHBOURHOODS]:

        # Keep track of the best candidate for each neighbourhood
        best_make = flow.makespan(data, perm)
        best_perm = perm

        # Enumerate every permutation of the selected neighbourhood
        for ordering in permutations(subset):
            candidate = perm[:]
            for i in range(len(ordering)):
                candidate[subset[i]] = perm[ordering[i]]
            res = flow.makespan(data, candidate)
            if res < best_make:
                best_make = res
                best_perm = candidate

        # Record the best candidate as part of the larger neighbourhood
        candidates.append(best_perm)

    return candidates
```

If we were to set the size parameter to be equal to the number of jobs, then every permutation would be considered and the best one selected. In practice, however, we need to limit the size of the subset to around 3 or 4; anything larger would cause the neighbours_LNS function to take a prohibitive amount of time.

9.5   Heuristics

A heuristic returns a single candidate permutation from a set of provided candidates. The heuristic is also given access to the problem data in order to evaluate which candidate might be preferred.

The first heuristic that we consider is heur_random. This heuristic randomly selects a candidate from the list without evaluating which one might be preferred:

```
def heur_random(data, candidates):
    # Returns a random candidate choice
    return random.choice(candidates)
```

The next heuristic heur_hillclimbing uses the other extreme. Rather than randomly selecting a candidate, it selects the candidate that has the best makespan. Note that the list scores will contain tuples of the form (make,perm) where make is the makespan value for permutation perm. Sorting such a list places the tuple with the best makespan at the start of the list; from this tuple we return the permutation.

```
def heur_hillclimbing(data, candidates):
    # Returns the best candidate in the list
    scores = [(flow.makespan(data, perm), perm) for perm in candidates]
    return sorted(scores)[0][1]
```

The final heuristic, heur_random_hillclimbing, combines both the random and hillclimbing heuristics above. When performing local search, you may not always want to choose a random candidate, or even the best one. The heur_random_hillclimbing heuristic returns a "pretty good" solution by choosing the best candidate with probability 0.5, then the second best with probability 0.25, and so on. The while-loop essentially flips a coin at every iteration to see if it should continue increasing the index (with a limit on the size of the list). The final index chosen corresponds to the candidate that the heuristic selects.

```
def heur_random_hillclimbing(data, candidates):
    # Returns a candidate with probability proportional to its rank in sorted quality
    scores = [(flow.makespan(data, perm), perm) for perm in candidates]
    i = 0
    while (random.random() < 0.5) and (i < len(scores) - 1):
        i += 1
    return sorted(scores)[i][1]
```

Because makespan is the criteria that we are trying to optimize, hillclimbing will steer the local search process towards solutions with a better makespan. Introducing randomness allows us to explore the neighbourhood instead of going blindly towards the best-looking solution at every step.

9.6   Dynamic Strategy Selection

At the heart of the local search for a good permutation is the use of a particular heuristic and neighbourhood function to jump from one solution to another. How do we choose one set of options over another? In practice, it frequently pays off to switch strategies during the search. The dynamic strategy selection that we use will switch between combinations of heuristic and neighbourhood functions to try and shift dynamically to those strategies that work best. For us, a *strategy* is a particular configuration of heuristic and neighbourhood functions (including their parameter values.)

To begin, our code constructs the range of strategies that we want to consider during solving. In the strategy initialization, we use the `partial` function from the `functools` package to partially assign the parameters for each of the neighbourhoods. Additionally, we construct a list of the heuristic functions, and finally we use the product operator to add every combination of neighbourhood and heuristic function as a new strategy.

```
################
## Strategies ##
###################################################
## A strategy is a particular configuration
##   of neighbourhood generator (to compute
##   the next set of candidates) and heuristic
##   computation (to select the best candidate).
##

STRATEGIES = []

# Using a namedtuple is a little cleaner than using dictionaries.
#  E.g., strategy['name'] versus strategy.name
Strategy = namedtuple('Strategy', ['name', 'neighbourhood', 'heuristic'])

def initialize_strategies():

    global STRATEGIES

    # Define the neighbourhoods (and parameters) that we would like to use
    neighbourhoods = [
        ('Random Permutation', partial(neigh.neighbours_random, num=100)),
        ('Swapped Pairs', neigh.neighbours_swap),
        ('Large Neighbourhood Search (2)', partial(neigh.neighbours_LNS, size=2)),
        ('Large Neighbourhood Search (3)', partial(neigh.neighbours_LNS, size=3)),
        ('Idle Neighbourhood (3)', partial(neigh.neighbours_idle, size=3)),
        ('Idle Neighbourhood (4)', partial(neigh.neighbours_idle, size=4)),
        ('Idle Neighbourhood (5)', partial(neigh.neighbours_idle, size=5))
    ]

    # Define the heuristics that we would like to use
    heuristics = [
        ('Hill Climbing', heur.heur_hillclimbing),
        ('Random Selection', heur.heur_random),
        ('Biased Random Selection', heur.heur_random_hillclimbing)
    ]

    # Combine every neighbourhood and heuristic strategy
    for (n, h) in product(neighbourhoods, heuristics):
        STRATEGIES.append(Strategy("%s / %s" % (n[0], h[0]), n[1], h[1]))
```

Once the strategies are defined, we do not necessarily want to stick with a single option during search. Instead, we select randomly any one of the strategies, but *weight the selection* based on how well the strategy has performed. We describe the weighting below, but for the `pick_strategy` function, we need only a list of strategies and a corresponding list of relative weights (any number will do). To select a random strategy with the given weights, we pick a number uniformly between 0 and the sum of all weights. Subsequently, we find the lowest index i such that the sum of all of the weights for indices smaller than i is greater than the random number that we have chosen. This technique, sometimes referred to as *roulette wheel selection*, will randomly pick a strategy for us and give a greater chance to those strategies with higher weight.

```
def pick_strategy(strategies, weights):
    # Picks a random strategy based on its weight: roulette wheel selection
    #   Rather than selecting a strategy entirely at random, we bias the
    #   random selection towards strategies that have worked well in the
    #   past (according to the weight value).
    total = sum([weights[strategy] for strategy in strategies])
    pick = random.uniform(0, total)
    count = weights[strategies[0]]

    i = 0
    while pick > count:
        count += weights[strategies[i+1]]
        i += 1

    return strategies[i]
```

What remains is to describe how the weights are augmented during the search for a solution. This occurs in the main while loop of the solver at regularly timed intervals (defined with the `TIME_INCREMENT` variable):

```
        # At regular intervals, switch the weighting on the strategies available.
        #   This way, the search can dynamically shift towards strategies that have
        #   proven more effective recently.
        if time.time() > time_last_switch + TIME_INCREMENT:

            time_last_switch = time.time()
```

Recall that `strat_improvements` stores the sum of all improvements that a strategy has made while `strat_time_spent` stores the time that the strategy has been given during the last interval. We normalize the improvements made by the total time spent for each strategy to get a metric of how well each strategy has performed in the last interval. Because a strategy may not have had a chance to run at all, we choose a small amount of time as a default value.

```
            # Normalize the improvements made by the time it takes to make them
            results = sorted([
                (float(strat_improvements[s]) / max(0.001, strat_time_spent[s]), s)
                for s in STRATEGIES])
```

Now that we have a ranking of how well each strategy has performed, we add k to the weight of the best strategy (assuming we had k strategies), $k - 1$ to the next best strategy, etc. Each strategy will have its weight increased, and the worst strategy in the list will see an increase of only 1.

```
# Boost the weight for the successful strategies
for i in range(len(STRATEGIES)):
    strat_weights[results[i][1]] += len(STRATEGIES) - i
```

As an extra measure, we artificially bump up all of the strategies that were not used. This is done so that we do not forget about a strategy entirely. While one strategy may appear to perform badly in the beginning, later in the search it can prove quite useful.

```
# Additionally boost the unused strategies to avoid starvation
if results[i][0] == 0:
    strat_weights[results[i][1]] += len(STRATEGIES)
```

Finally, we output some information about the strategy ranking (if the DEBUG_SWITCH flag is set), and we reset the `strat_improvements` and `strat_time_spent` variables for the next interval.

```
if DEBUG_SWITCH:
    print "\nComputing another switch..."
    print "Best: %s (%d)" % (results[0][1].name, results[0][0])
    print "Worst: %s (%d)" % (results[-1][1].name, results[-1][0])
    print results
    print sorted([strat_weights[STRATEGIES[i]]
                  for i in range(len(STRATEGIES))])

strat_improvements = {strategy: 0 for strategy in STRATEGIES}
strat_time_spent = {strategy: 0 for strategy in STRATEGIES}
```

9.7 Discussion

In this chapter we have seen what can be accomplished with a relatively small amount of code to solve the complex optimization problem of flow shop scheduling. Finding the best solution to a large optimization problem such as the flow shop can be difficult. In a case like this, we can turn to approximation techniques such as local search to compute a solution that is *good enough*. With local search we can move from one solution to another, aiming to find one of good quality.

The general intuition behind local search can be applied to a wide range of problems. We focused on (1) generating a neighbourhood of related solutions to a problem from one candidate solution, and (2) establishing ways to evaluate and compare solutions. With these two components in hand, we can use the local search paradigm to find a valuable solution when the best option is simply too difficult to compute.

Rather than using any one strategy to solve the problem, we saw how a strategy can be chosen dynamically to shift during the solving process. This simple and powerful technique gives the program the ability to mix and match partial strategies for the problem at hand, and it also means that the developer does not have to hand-tailor the strategy.

## chapter 10

An Archaeology-Inspired Database
Yoav Rubin

10.1   Introduction

Software development is often viewed as a rigorous process, where the inputs are requirements and the output is the working product. However, software developers are people, with their own perspectives and biases which color the outcome of their work.

In this chapter, we will explore how a change in a common perspective affects the design and implementation of a well-studied type of software: a database.

Database systems are designed to store and query data. This is something that all information workers do; however, the systems themselves were designed by computer scientists. As a result, modern database systems are highly influenced by computer scientists' definition of what data is, and what can be done with it.

For example, most modern databases implement updates by overwriting old data in-place instead of appending the new data and keeping the old. This mechanism, nicknamed "place-oriented programming" by Rich Hickey[1], saves storage space but makes it impossible to retrieve the entire history of a particular record. This design decision reflects the computer scientist's perspective that "history" is less important than the price of its storage.

If you were to instead ask an archaeologist where the old data can be found, the answer would be "hopefully, it's just buried underneath".

(Disclaimer: My understanding of the views of a typical archaeologist is based on visiting a few museums, reading several Wikipedia articles, and watching the entire Indiana Jones series.)

Designing a Database Like an Archaeologist

If we were to ask our friendly archaeologist to design a database, we might expect the requirements to reflect what would be found at an excavation site:

- All data is found and catalogued at the site.
- Digging deeper will expose the state of things in times past.
- Artifacts found at the same layer are from the same period.
- Each artifact will consist of state that it accumulated in different periods.

For example, a wall may have Roman symbols on it on one layer, and in a lower layer there may be Greek symbols. Both these observations are recorded as part of the wall's state.

---

[1] http://www.infoq.com/presentations/Value-Values

This analogy is visualized in Figure 10.1:

- The entire circle is the excavation site.
- Each ring is a *layer* (here numbered from 0 to 4).
- Each slice is a labeled artifact ('A' through 'E').
- Each artifact has a 'symbol' attribute (where a blank means that no update was made).
- Solid arrows denote a change in symbol between layers
- Dotted arrows are arbitrary relationships of interest between artifacts (e.g., from 'E' to 'A').

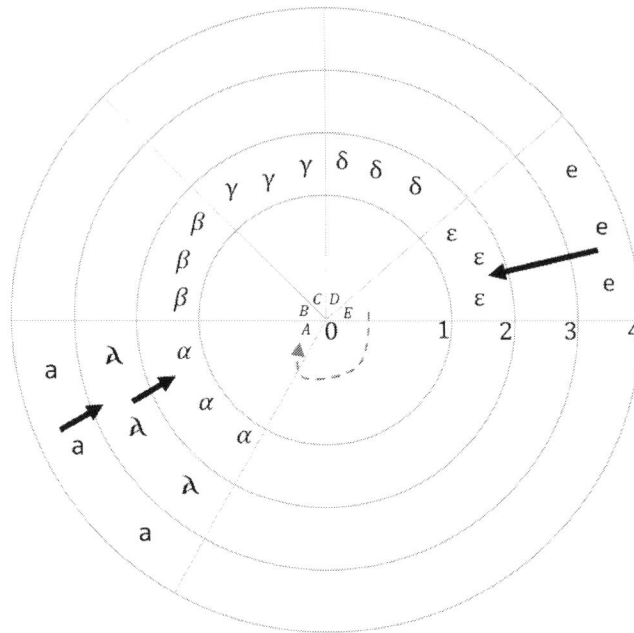

Figure 10.1: The Excavation Site

If we translate the archaeologist's language into terms a database designer would use:

- The excavation site is a *database*.
- Each artifact is an *entity* with a corresponding *ID*.
- Each entity has a set of *attributes*, which may change over time.
- Each attribute has a specific *value* at a specific time.

This may look very different from the kinds of databases you are used to working with. This design is sometimes referred to as "functional database", since it uses ideas from the domain of functional programming. The rest of the chapter describes how to implement such a database.

Since we are building a functional database, we will be using a functional programming language called Clojure.

Clojure has several qualities that make it a good implementation language for a functional database, such as out-of-the-box immutability, higher order functions, and metaprogramming facilities. But ultimately, the reason Clojure was chosen was its emphasis on clean, rigorous design, which few programming languages possess.

10.2   Laying the Foundation

Let's start by declaring the core constructs that make up our database.

```
(defrecord Database [layers top-id curr-time])
```

A database consists of:

1. Layers of entities, each with its own unique timestamp (the rings in Figure 1).
2. A top-id value which is the next available unique ID.
3. The time at which the database was last updated.

```
(defrecord Layer [storage VAET AVET VEAT EAVT])
```

Each layer consists of:

1. A data store for entities.
2. Indexes that are used to speed up queries to the database. (These indexes and the meaning of their names will be explained later.)

In our design, a single conceptual 'database' may consist of many Database instances, each of which represents a snapshot of the database at curr-time. A Layer may share the exact same entity with another Layer if the entity's state hasn't changed between the times that they represent.

Entities

Our database wouldn't be of any use without entities to store, so we define those next. As discussed before, an entity has an ID and a list of attributes; we create them using the make-entity function.

```
(defrecord Entity [id attrs])

(defn make-entity
    ([] (make-entity :db/no-id-yet))
    ([id] (Entity.  id {})))
```

Note that if no ID is given, the entity's ID is set to be :db/no-id-yet, which means that something else is responsible for giving it an ID. We'll see how that works later.

Attributes

Each attribute consists of its name, value, and the timestamps of its most recent update as well as the one before that. Each attribute also has two fields that describe its type and cardinality.

In the case that an attribute is used to represent a relationship to another entity, its type will be :db/ref and its value will be the ID of the related entity. This simple type system also acts as an extension point. Users are free to define their own types and leverage them to provide additional semantics for their data.

An attribute's cardinality specifies whether the attribute represents a single value or a set of values. We use this field to determine the set of operations that are permitted on this attribute.

Creating an attribute is done using the make-attr function.

```
(defrecord Attr [name value ts prev-ts])

(defn make-attr
    ([name value type ; these ones are required
        & {:keys [cardinality] :or {cardinality :db/single}} ]
      {:pre [(contains? #{:db/single :db/multiple} cardinality)]}
      (with-meta (Attr. name value -1 -1) {:type type :cardinality cardinality})))
```

There are a couple of interesting patterns used in this constructor function:

- We use Clojure's *Design by Contract* pattern to validate that the cardinality parameter is a permissible value.
- We use Clojure's destructuring mechanism to provide a default value of :db/single if one is not given.
- We use Clojure's metadata capabilities to distinguish between an attribute's data (name, value and timestamps) and its metadata (type and cardinality). In Clojure, metadata handling is done using the functions with-meta (to set) and meta (to read).

Attributes only have meaning if they are part of an entity. We make this connection with the add-attr function, which adds a given attribute to an entity's attribute map (called :attrs).

Note that instead of using the attribute's name directly, we first convert it into a keyword to adhere to Clojure's idiomatic usage of maps.

```
(defn add-attr [ent attr]
    (let [attr-id (keyword (:name attr))]
      (assoc-in ent [:attrs attr-id] attr)))
```

Storage

So far we have talked a lot about *what* we are going to store, without thinking about *where* we are going to store it. In this chapter, we resort to the simplest storage mechanism: storing the data in memory. This is certainly not reliable, but it simplifies development and debugging and allows us to focus on more interesting parts of the program.

We will access the storage via a simple *protocol*, which will make it possible to define additional storage providers for a database owner to select from.

```
(defprotocol Storage
    (get-entity [storage e-id] )
    (write-entity [storage entity])
    (drop-entity [storage entity]))
```

And here's our in-memory implementation of the protocol, which uses a map as the store:

```
(defrecord InMemory [] Storage
    (get-entity [storage e-id] (e-id storage))
    (write-entity [storage entity] (assoc storage (:id entity) entity))
    (drop-entity [storage entity] (dissoc storage (:id entity))))
```

Indexing the Data

Now that we've defined the basic elements of our database, we can start thinking about how we're going to query it. By virtue of how we've structured our data, any query is necessarily going to be interested in at least one of an entity's ID, and the name and value of some of its attributes. This triplet of (`entity-id`, `attribute-name`, `attribute-value`) is important enough to our query process that we give it an explicit name: a *datom*.

Datoms are important because they represent facts, and our database accumulates facts.

If you've used a database system before, you are probably already familiar with the concept of an *index*, which is a supporting data structure that consumes extra space in order to decrease the average query time. In our database, an index is a three-leveled structure which stores the components of a datom in a specific order. Each index derives its name from the order it stores the datom's components in.

For example, let's look at at the index sketched in Figure 10.2:

- The first level stores entity-IDs
- The second level stores the related attribute-names
- The third level stores the related value

This index is named EAVT, as the top level map holds Entity IDs, the second level holds Attribute names, and the leaves hold Values. The "T" comes from the fact that each layer in the database has its own indexes, hence the index itself is relevant for a specific Time.

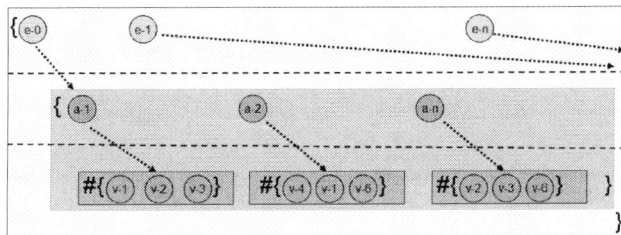

Figure 10.2: EAVT

Figure 10.3 shows an index that would be called AVET since:

- The first level map holds attribute-name.
- The second level map holds the values (of the attributes).
- The third level set holds the entity-IDs (of the entities whose attribute is at the first level).

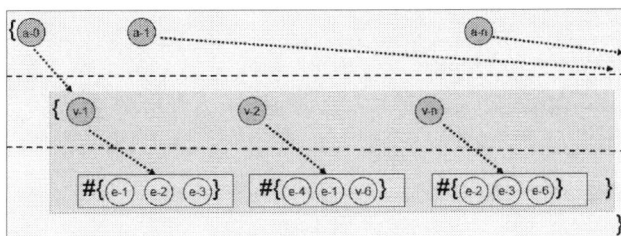

Figure 10.3: AVET

Our indexes are implemented as a map of maps, where the keys of the root map act as the first level, each such key points to a map whose keys act as the index's second-level and the values are the index's third level. Each element in the third level is a set, holding the leaves of the index.

EAVT index	AVET index
JC $\Rightarrow$ {lives-in $\Rightarrow$ {Rome}}	lives-in $\Rightarrow$ {Rome $\Rightarrow$ {JC, B}}, {Egypt $\Rightarrow$ {Cleo}}
B $\Rightarrow$ {lives-in $\Rightarrow$ {Rome}}	river $\Rightarrow$ {Rome $\Rightarrow$ {Tiber}}, {Egypt $\Rightarrow$ {Nile}}
Cleo $\Rightarrow$ {lives-in $\Rightarrow$ {Egypt}}	
Rome $\Rightarrow$ {river $\Rightarrow$ {Tiber}}	
Egypt $\Rightarrow$ {river $\Rightarrow$ {Nile}}	

VEAT index	VAET index
Rome $\Rightarrow$ {JC $\Rightarrow$ {lives-in}}, {B $\Rightarrow$ {lives-in}}	Rome $\Rightarrow$ {lives-in $\Rightarrow$ {JC, B}}
Egypt $\Rightarrow$ {Cleo $\Rightarrow$ {lives-in}}	Egypt $\Rightarrow$ {lives-in $\Rightarrow$ {Cleo}}
Tiber $\Rightarrow$ {Rome $\Rightarrow$ {river}}	Tiber $\Rightarrow$ {river $\Rightarrow$ {Rome}}
Nile $\Rightarrow$ {Egypt $\Rightarrow$ {river}}	Nile $\Rightarrow$ {river $\Rightarrow$ {Egypt}}

Table 10.1: Indexes

Each index stores the components of a datom as some permutation of its canonical 'EAV' ordering (entity_id, attribute-name, attribute-value). However, when we are working with datoms *outside* of the index, we expect them to be in canonical format. We thus provide each index with functions from-eav and to-eav to convert to and from these orderings.

In most database systems, indexes are an optional component; for example, in an RDBMS (Relational Database Management System) like PostgreSQL or MySQL, you will choose to add indexes only to certain columns in a table. We provide each index with a usage-pred function that determines for an attribute whether it should be included in this index or not.

```
(defn make-index [from-eav to-eav usage-pred]
    (with-meta {} {:from-eav from-eav :to-eav to-eav :usage-pred usage-pred}))

(defn from-eav [index] (:from-eav (meta index)))
(defn to-eav [index] (:to-eav (meta index)))
(defn usage-pred [index] (:usage-pred (meta index)))
```

In our database there are four indexes: EAVT (see Figure 10.2), AVET (see Figure 10.3), VEAT and VAET. We can access these as a vector of values returned from the indexes function.

```
(defn indexes[] [:VAET :AVET :VEAT :EAVT])
```

To demonstrate how all of this comes together, the result of indexing the following five entities is visualized in Table 10.1.

1. Julius Caesar (also known as JC) lives in Rome
2. Brutus (also known as B) lives in Rome
3. Cleopatra (also known as Cleo) lives in Egypt
4. Rome's river is the Tiber
5. Egypt's river is the Nile

Database

We now have all the components we need to construct our database. Initializing our database means:

- creating an initial empty layer with no data
- creating a set of empty indexes
- setting its `top-id` and `curr-time` to be 0

```
(defn ref? [attr] (= :db/ref (:type (meta attr))))

(defn always[& more] true)

(defn make-db []
   (atom
      (Database. [(Layer.
                  (fdb.storage.InMemory.) ; storage
                  (make-index #(vector %3 %2 %1) #(vector %3 %2 %1) #(ref? %));VAET
                  (make-index #(vector %2 %3 %1) #(vector %3 %1 %2) always);AVET
                  (make-index #(vector %3 %1 %2) #(vector %2 %3 %1) always);VEAT
                  (make-index #(vector %1 %2 %3) #(vector %1 %2 %3) always);EAVT
                  )] 0 0)))
```

There is one snag, though: all collections in Clojure are immutable. Since write operations are pretty critical in a database, we define our structure to be an *Atom*, which is a Clojure reference type that provides the capability of atomic writes.

You may be wondering why we use the `always` function for the AVET, VEAT and EAVT indexes, and the `ref?` predicate for the VAET index. This is because these indexes are used in different scenarios, which we'll see later when we explore queries in depth.

Basic Accessors

Before we can build complex querying facilities for our database, we need to provide a lower-level API that different parts of the system can use to retrieve the components we've built by their associated identifiers from any point in time. Consumers of the database can also use this API; however, it is more likely that they will be using the more fully-featured components built on top of it.

This lower-level API is composed of the following four accessor functions:

```
(defn entity-at
   ([db ent-id] (entity-at db (:curr-time db) ent-id))
   ([db ts ent-id] (get-entity (get-in db [:layers ts :storage]) ent-id)))

(defn attr-at
   ([db ent-id attr-name] (attr-at db ent-id attr-name (:curr-time db)))
   ([db ent-id attr-name ts] (get-in (entity-at db ts ent-id) [:attrs attr-name])))

(defn value-of-at
   ([db ent-id attr-name]  (:value (attr-at db ent-id attr-name)))
   ([db ent-id attr-name ts] (:value (attr-at db ent-id attr-name ts))))

(defn indx-at
   ([db kind] (indx-at db kind (:curr-time db)))
   ([db kind ts] (kind ((:layers db) ts))))
```

Since we treat our database just like any other value, each of these functions take a database as an argument. Each element is retrieved by its associated identifier, and optionally the timestamp of interest. This timestamp is used to find the corresponding layer that our lookup should be applied to.

Evolution

A first usage of the basic accessors is to provide a "read-into-the-past" API. This is possible as, in our database, an update operation is done by appending a new layer (as opposed to overwriting). Therefore we can use the prev-ts property to look at the attribute at that layer, and continue looking deeper into history to observe how the attribute's value evolved throughout time.

The function evolution-of does exactly that. It returns a sequence of pairs, each consisting of the timestamp and value of an attribute's update.

```
(defn evolution-of [db ent-id attr-name]
    (loop [res [] ts (:curr-time db)]
      (if (= -1 ts) (reverse res)
          (let [attr (attr-at db ent-id attr-name ts)]
            (recur (conj res {(:ts attr) (:value attr)})  (:prev-ts attr))))))
```

10.3   Data Behavior and Life Cycle

So far, our discussion has focused on the structure of our data: what the core components are and how they are aggregated together. It's time to explore the dynamics of our system: how data is changed over time through the add–update–remove *data lifecycle*.

As we've already discussed, data in an archaeologist's world never actually changes. Once it is created, it exists forever and can only be hidden from the world by data in a newer layer. The term "hidden" is crucial here. Older data does not "disappear"—it is buried, and can be revealed again by exposing an older layer. Conversely, updating data means obscuring the old by adding a new layer on top of it with something else. We can thus "delete" data by adding a layer of "nothing" on top of it.

This means that when we talk about data lifecycle, we are really talking about adding layers to our data over time.

The Bare Necessities

The data lifecycle consists of three basic operations:
- adding an entity with the add-entity function
- removing an entity with the remove-entity function
- updating an entity with the update-entity function

Remember that, even though these functions provide the illusion of mutability, all that we are really doing in each case is adding another layer to the data. Also, since we are using Clojure's persistent data structures, from the caller's perspective we pay the same price for these operations as for an "in-place" change (i.e., negligible performance overhead), while maintaining immutability for all other users of the data structure.

Adding an Entity

Adding an entity requires us to do three things:

- prepare the entity for addition (by giving it an ID and a timestamp)
- place the entity in storage
- update indexes as necessary

These steps are performed in the add-entity function.

```
(defn add-entity [db ent]
   (let [[fixed-ent next-top-id] (fix-new-entity db ent)
         layer-with-updated-storage (update-in
                             (last (:layers db)) [:storage] write-entity fixed-ent)
         add-fn (partial add-entity-to-index fixed-ent)
         new-layer (reduce add-fn layer-with-updated-storage (indexes))]
     (assoc db :layers (conj (:layers db) new-layer) :top-id next-top-id)))
```

Preparing an entity is done by calling the fix-new-entity function and its auxiliary functions
next-id, next-ts and update-creation-ts. These latter two helper functions are responsible for
finding the next timestamp of the database (done by next-ts), and updating the creation timestamp
of the given entity (done by update-creation-ts). Updating the creation timestamp of an entity
means going over the attributes of the entity and updating their :ts fields.

```
(defn- next-ts [db] (inc (:curr-time db)))

(defn- update-creation-ts [ent ts-val]
   (reduce #(assoc-in %1 [:attrs %2 :ts ] ts-val) ent (keys (:attrs ent))))

(defn- next-id [db ent]
   (let [top-id (:top-id db)
         ent-id (:id ent)
         increased-id (inc top-id)]
     (if (= ent-id :db/no-id-yet)
         [(keyword (str increased-id)) increased-id]
         [ent-id top-id])))

(defn- fix-new-entity [db ent]
   (let [[ent-id next-top-id] (next-id db ent)
         new-ts                (next-ts db)]
     [(update-creation-ts (assoc ent :id ent-id) new-ts) next-top-id]))
```

To add the entity to storage, we locate the most recent layer in the database and update the storage
in that layer with a new layer, the results of which are stored in layer-with-updated-storage.

Finally, we must update the indexes. This means, for each of the indexes (done by the combination
of reduce and the partial-ed add-entity-to-index at the add-entity function):

- Find the attributes that should be indexed (see the combination of filter with the index's
  usage-pred that operates on the attributes in add-entity-to-index)
- Build an index-path from the the entity's ID (see the combination of the partial-ed
  update-entry-in-index with from-eav at the update-attr-in-index function)
- Add that path to the index (see the update-entry-in-index function)

```
(defn- add-entity-to-index [ent layer ind-name]
   (let [ent-id (:id ent)
         index (ind-name layer)
         all-attrs  (vals (:attrs ent))
         relevant-attrs (filter #((usage-pred index) %) all-attrs)
         add-in-index-fn (fn [ind attr]
                              (update-attr-in-index ind ent-id (:name attr)
                                                               (:value attr)
                                                               :db/add))]
      (assoc layer ind-name  (reduce add-in-index-fn index relevant-attrs))))

(defn- update-attr-in-index [index ent-id attr-name target-val operation]
   (let [colled-target-val (collify target-val)
         update-entry-fn (fn [ind vl]
                             (update-entry-in-index
                               ind
                               ((from-eav index) ent-id attr-name vl)
                               operation))]
     (reduce update-entry-fn index colled-target-val)))

(defn- update-entry-in-index [index path operation]
   (let [update-path (butlast path)
         update-value (last path)
         to-be-updated-set (get-in index update-path #{})]
     (assoc-in index update-path (conj to-be-updated-set update-value))))
```

All of these components are added as a new layer to the given database. All that's left is to update the database's timestamp and top-id fields. That last step occurs on the last line of add-entity, which also returns the updated database.

We also provide an add-entities convenience function that adds multiple entities to the database in one call by iteratively applying add-entity.

```
(defn add-entities [db ents-seq] (reduce add-entity db ents-seq))
```

Removing an Entity

Removing an entity from our database means adding a layer in which it does not exist. To do this, we need to:

- Remove the entity itself
- Update any attributes of other entities that reference it
- Clear the entity from our indexes

This "construct-without" process is executed by the remove-entity function, which looks very similar to add-entity:

```
(defn remove-entity [db ent-id]
   (let [ent (entity-at db ent-id)
         layer (remove-back-refs db ent-id (last (:layers db)))
         no-ref-layer (update-in layer [:VAET] dissoc ent-id)
         no-ent-layer (assoc no-ref-layer :storage
                                     (drop-entity
```

```
                                        (:storage no-ref-layer) ent))
       new-layer (reduce (partial remove-entity-from-index ent)
                                   no-ent-layer (indexes))]
     (assoc db :layers (conj  (:layers db) new-layer))))
```

Reference removal is done by the remove-back-refs function:

```
(defn- remove-back-refs [db e-id layer]
   (let [reffing-datoms (reffing-to e-id layer)
         remove-fn (fn[d [e a]] (update-entity db e a e-id :db/remove))
         clean-db (reduce remove-fn db reffing-datoms)]
     (last (:layers clean-db))))
```

We begin by using reffing-datoms-to to find all entities that reference ours in the given layer; it returns a sequence of triplets that contain the ID of the referencing entity, as well as the attribute name and the ID of the removed entity.

```
(defn- reffing-to [e-id layer]
   (let [vaet (:VAET layer)]
        (for [[attr-name reffing-set] (e-id vaet)
              reffing reffing-set]
           [reffing attr-name])))
```

We then apply update-entity to each triplet to update the attributes that reference our removed entity. (We'll explore how update-entity works in the next section.)

The last step of remove-back-refs is to clear the reference itself from our indexes, and more specifically from the VAET index, since it is the only index that stores reference information.

Updating an Entity

At its essence, an update is the modification of an entity's attribute's value. The modification process itself depends on the cardinality of the attribute: an attribute with cardinality :db/multiple holds a set of values, so we must allow items to be added to or removed from this set, or the set to be replaced entirely. An attribute with cardinality :db/single holds a single value, and thus only allows replacement.

Since we also have indexes that provide lookups directly on attributes and their values, these will also have to be updated.

As with add-entity and remove-entity, we won't actually be modifying our entity in place, but will instead add a new layer which contains the updated entity.

```
(defn update-entity
   ([db ent-id attr-name new-val]
    (update-entity db ent-id attr-name new-val :db/reset-to))
   ([db ent-id attr-name new-val operation]
      (let [update-ts (next-ts db)
            layer (last (:layers db))
            attr (attr-at db ent-id attr-name)
            updated-attr (update-attr attr new-val update-ts operation)
            fully-updated-layer (update-layer layer ent-id
                                              attr updated-attr
                                              new-val operation)]
        (update-in db [:layers] conj fully-updated-layer))))
```

To update an attribute, we locate it with `attr-at` and then use `update-attr` to perform the actual update.

```
(defn- update-attr [attr new-val new-ts operation]
    {:pre [(if (single? attr)
             (contains? #{:db/reset-to :db/remove} operation)
             (contains? #{:db/reset-to :db/add :db/remove} operation))]}
    (-> attr
        (update-attr-modification-time new-ts)
        (update-attr-value new-val operation)))
```

We use two helper functions to perform the update. `update-attr-modification-time` updates timestamps to reflect the creation of the black arrows in Figure 1:

```
(defn- update-attr-modification-time
  [attr new-ts]
      (assoc attr :ts new-ts :prev-ts (:ts attr)))
```

`update-attr-value` actually updates the value:

```
(defn- update-attr-value [attr value operation]
    (cond
        (single? attr)     (assoc attr :value #{value})
        ; now we're talking about an attribute of multiple values
        (= :db/reset-to operation)
          (assoc attr :value value)
        (= :db/add operation)
          (assoc attr :value (CS/union (:value attr) value))
        (= :db/remove operation)
          (assoc attr :value (CS/difference (:value attr) value))))
```

All that remains is to remove the old value from the indexes and add the new one to them, and then construct the new layer with all of our updated components. Luckily, we can leverage the code we wrote for adding and removing entities to do this.

Transactions

Each of the operations in our low-level API acts on a single entity. However, nearly all databases have a way for users to do multiple operations as a single *transaction*. This means:

- The batch of operations is viewed as a single atomic operation, so all of the operations either succeed together or fail together.
- The database is in a valid state before and after the transaction.
- The batch update appears to be *isolated*; other queries should never see a database state in which only some of the operations have been applied.

We can fulfill these requirements through an interface that consumes a database and a set of operations to be performed, and produces a database whose state reflects the given changes. All of the changes submitted in the batch should be applied through the addition of a *single* layer. However, we have a problem: All of the functions we wrote in our low-level API add a new layer to the database. If we were to perform a batch with n operations, we would thus see n new layers added, when what we would really like is to have exactly one new layer.

The key here is that the layer we want is the *top* layer that would be produced by performing those updates in sequence. Therefore, the solution is to execute the user's operations one after another, each creating a new layer. When the last layer is created, we take only that top layer and place it on the initial database (leaving all the intermediate layers to pine for the fjords). Only after we've done all this will we update the database's timestamp.

All this is done in the transact-on-db function, which receives the initial value of the database and the batch of operations to perform, and returns its updated value.

```
(defn transact-on-db [initial-db ops]
    (loop [[op & rst-ops] ops transacted initial-db]
      (if op
          (recur rst-ops (apply (first op) transacted (rest op)))
          (let [initial-layer  (:layers initial-db)
                new-layer (last (:layers transacted))]
            (assoc initial-db :layers (conj initial-layer new-layer)
                              :curr-time (next-ts initial-db)
                              :top-id (:top-id transacted))))))
```

Note here that we used the term *value*, meaning that only the caller to this function is exposed to the updated state; all other users of the database are unaware of this change (as a database is a value, and therefore cannot change). In order to have a system where users can be exposed to state changes performed by others, users do not interact directly with the database, but rather refer to it using another level of indirection. This additional level is implemented using Clojure's Atom, a reference type. Here we leverage the main three key features of an Atom, which are:

1. It references a value.
2. It is possible to update the referencing of the Atom to another value by executing a transaction (using Clojure's Software Transaction Memory capabilities). The transaction accepts an Atom and a function. That function operates on the value of the Atom and returns a new value. After the execution of the transaction, the Atom references the value that was returned from the function.
3. Getting to the value that is referenced by the Atom is done by dereferencing it, which returns the state of that Atom at that time.

In between Clojure's Atom and the work done in transact-on-db, there's still a gap to be bridged; namely, to invoke the transaction with the right inputs.

To have the simplest and clearest APIs, we would like users to just provide the Atom and the list of operations, and have the database transform the user input into a proper transaction.

That transformation occurs in the following transaction call chain:

```
transact    _transact   swap!   transact-on-db
```

Users call transact with the Atom (i.e., the connection) and the operations to perform, which relays its input to _transact, adding to it the name of the function that updates the Atom (swap!).

```
(defmacro transact [db-conn & txs]  '(_transact ~db-conn swap! ~@txs))
```

_transact prepares the call to swap!. It does so by creating a list that begins with swap!, followed by the Atom, then the transact-on-db symbol and the batch of operations.

```
(defmacro _transact [db op & txs]
   (when txs
     (loop [[frst-tx# & rst-tx#] txs  res#  [op db 'transact-on-db]  accum-txs# []]
       (if frst-tx#
          (recur rst-tx# res#  (conj  accum-txs#  (vec frst-tx#)))
          (list* (conj res#  accum-txs#))))))
```

swap! invokes transact-on-db within a transaction (with the previously prepared arguments), and transact-on-db creates the new state of the database and returns it.

At this point we can see that with few minor tweaks, we can also provide a way to ask "what if" questions. This can be done by replacing swap! with a function that would not make any change to the system. This scenario is implemented with the what-if call chain:

what-if → _transact → _what-if → transact-on-db

The user calls what-if with the database value and the operations to perform. It then relays these inputs to _transact, adding to them a function that mimics swap!'s APIs, without its effect (callled _what-if).

```
(defmacro what-if [db & ops]  '(_transact ~db _what-if  ~@ops))
```

_transact prepares the call to _what-if. It does so by creating a list that begins with _what-if, followed by the database, then the transact-on-db symbol and the batch of operations. _what-if invokes transact-on-db, just like swap! does in the transaction scenario, but does not inflict any change on the system.

```
(defn- _what-if [db f txs]  (f db txs))
```

Note that we are not using functions, but macros. The reason for using macros here is that arguments to macros do not get evaluated as the call happens; this allows us to offer a cleaner API design where the user provides the operations structured in the same way that any function call is structured in Clojure.

The above process can be seen in the following examples. For Transaction, the user call:

```
(transact db-conn  (add-entity e1) (update-entity e2 atr2 val2 :db/add))
```

changes into:

```
(_transact db-conn swap! (add-entity e1) (update-entity e2 atr2 val2 :db/add))
```

which becomes:

```
(swap! db-conn transact-on-db [[add-entity e1][update-entity e2 atr2 val2 :db/add]])
```

For what-if, the user call:

```
(what-if my-db (add-entity e3) (remove-entity e4))
```

changes into:

```
(_transact my-db _what-if (add-entity e3) (remove-entity e4))
```

then:

```
(_what-if my-db transact-on-db [[add-entity e3] [remove-entity e4]])
```

and eventually:

```
(transact-on-db my-db  [[add-entity e3] [remove-entity e4]])
```

10.4 Insight Extraction as Libraries

At this point we have the core functionality of the database in place, and it is time to add its *raison d'être*: insights extraction. The architecture approach we used here is to allow adding these capabilities as libraries, as different usages of the database would need different such mechanisms.

Graph Traversal

A reference connection between entities is created when an entity's attribute's type is :db/ref, which means that the value of that attribute is an ID of another entity. When a referring entity is added to the database, the reference is indexed at the VAET index.

The information found in the VAET index can be leveraged to extract all the incoming links to an entity. This is done in the incoming-refs function, which collects all the leaves that are reachable from the entity at that index:

```
(defn incoming-refs [db ts ent-id & ref-names]
   (let [vaet (indx-at db :VAET ts)
         all-attr-map (vaet ent-id)
         filtered-map (if ref-names
                          (select-keys ref-names all-attr-map)
                          all-attr-map)]
      (reduce into #{} (vals filtered-map))))
```

We can also go through all of a given entity's attributes and collect all the values of attributes of type :db/ref, and by that extract all the outgoing references from that entity. This is done by the outgoing-refs function.

```
(defn outgoing-refs [db ts ent-id & ref-names]
   (let [val-filter-fn (if ref-names #(vals (select-keys ref-names %)) vals)]
   (if-not ent-id []
     (->> (entity-at db ts ent-id)
          (:attrs) (val-filter-fn) (filter ref?) (mapcat :value)))))
```

These two functions act as the basic building blocks for any graph traversal operation, as they are the ones that raise the level of abstraction from entities and attributes to nodes and links in a graph. Once we have the ability to look at our database as a graph, we can provide various graph traversing and querying APIs. We leave this as a solved exercise to the reader; one solution can be found in the chapter's source code (see graph.clj).

10.5 Querying the Database

The second library we present provides querying capabilities, which is the main concern of this section. A database is not very useful to its users without a powerful query mechanism. This feature is usually exposed to users through a *query language* that is used to declaratively specify the set of data of interest.

Our data model is based on accumulation of facts (i.e., datoms) over time. For this model, a natural place to look for the right query language is *logic programming*. A commonly used query language influenced by logic programming is *Datalog* which, in addition to being well-suited for our data model, has a very elegant adaptation to Clojure's syntax. Our query engine will implement a subset of the Datalog language from the Datomic database[2].

Query Language

Let's look at an example query in our proposed language. This query asks: "What are the names and birthdays of entities who like pizza, speak English, and who have a birthday this month?"

```
{   :find [?nm ?bd ]
    :where [
        [?e  :likes "pizza"]
        [?e  :name  ?nm]
        [?e  :speak "English"]
        [?e  :bday (bday-mo? ?bd)]]]}
```

Syntax

We use the syntax of Clojure's data literals directly to provide the basic syntax for our queries. This allows us to avoid having to write a specialized parser, while still providing a form that is familiar and easily readable to programmers familiar with Clojure.

A query is a map with two items:

- An item with :where as a key, and with a *rule* as a value. A rule is a vector of *clauses*, and a clause is a vector composed of three *predicates*, each of which operates on a different component of a datom. In the example above, [?e :likes "pizza"] is a clause. This :where item defines a rule that acts as a filter on datoms in our database (like a SQL WHERE clause.)
- An item with :find as a key, and with a vector as a value. The vector defines which components of the selected datom should be projected into the results (like a SQL SELECT clause.)

The description above omits a crucial requirement: how to make different clauses sync on a value (i.e., make a join operation between them), and how to structure the found values in the output (specified by the :find part).

We fulfill both of these requirements using *variables*, which are denoted with a leading ?. The only exception to this definition is the "don't care" variable _ (underscore).

A clause in a query is composed of three predicates; Table 10.2 defines what can act as a predicate in our query language.

Limitations of our Query Language

Engineering is all about managing tradeoffs, and designing our query engine is no different. In our case, the main tradeoff we must address is feature-richness versus complexity. Resolving this tradeoff requires us to look at common use-cases of the system, and from there deciding what limitations would be acceptable.

In our database, we decided to build a query engine with the following limitations:

- Users cannot define logical operations between the clauses; they are always 'ANDed' together. (This can be worked around by using unary or binary predicates.)

---

[2]http://docs.datomic.com/query.html

Name	Meaning	Example
Constant	Is the value of the datom item equal to the constant?	`:likes`
Variable	Bind the value of the datom item to the variable and return true.	`?e`
Don't-care	Always returns true.	`_`
Unary operator	Unary operation that takes a variable as its operand. Bind the datom's item's value to the variable (unless it's an _). Replace the variable with the value of the item in the datom. Return the application of the operation.	`(bday-mo? _)`
Binary operator	A binary operation that requires a variable as an operand. Bind the datom's item's value to the variable (unless it's an _). Replace the variable with the value of the item in the datom. Return the result of the operation.	`(&gt; ?age 20)`

Table 10.2: Predicates

- If there is more than one clause in a query, there must be one variable that is found in all of the clauses of that query. This variable acts as a joining variable. This limitation simplifies the query optimizer.
- A query is only executed on a single database.

While these design decisions result in a query language that is less rich than Datalog, we are still able to support many types of simple but useful queries.

Query Engine Design

While our query language allows the user to specify *what* they want to access, it hides the details of *how* this will be accomplished. The query engine is the database component responsible for yielding the data for a given query.

This involves four steps:

1. Transformation to internal representation: Transform the query from its textual form into a data structure that is consumed by the query planner.
2. Building a query plan: Determine an efficient *plan* for yielding the results of the given query. In our case, a query plan is a function to be invoked.
3. Executing the plan: Execute the plan and send its results to the next phase.
4. Unification and reporting: Extract only the results that need to be reported and format them as specified.

Phase 1: Transformation

In this phase, we transform the given query from a representation that is easy for the user to understand into a representation that can be consumed efficiently by the query planner.

The :find part of the query is transformed into a set of the given variable names:

```
(defmacro symbol-col-to-set [coll] (set (map str coll)))
```

The :where part of the query retains its nested vector structure. However, each of the terms in each of the clauses is replaced with a predicate according to Table 10.2.

```
(defmacro clause-term-expr [clause-term]
  (cond
   (variable? (str clause-term)) ;variable
    #(= % %)
```

Query Clause	Predicate Clause	Meta Clause
[?e :likes "pizza"]	[#(= % %) #(= % :likes) #(= % "pizza")]	["?e" nil nil]
[?e :name ?nm]	[#(= % %) #(= % :name) #(= % %)]	["?e" nil "?nm"]
[?e :speak "English"]	[#(= % %) #(= % :speak) #(= % "English")]	["?e" nil nil]
[?e :bday (bday-mo? ?bd)]	[#(= % %) #(= % :bday) #(bday-mo? %)]	["?e" nil "?bd"]

Table 10.3: Clauses

```
(not (coll? clause-term)) ;constant
  '#(= % ~clause-term)
(= 2 (count clause-term)) ;unary operator
  '#(~(first clause-term) %)
(variable? (str (second clause-term)));binary operator, 1st operand is variable
  '#(~(first clause-term) % ~(last clause-term))
(variable? (str (last clause-term)));binary operator, 2nd operand is variable
  '#(~(first clause-term) ~(second clause-term) %)))
```

For each clause, a vector with the variable names used in that clause is set as its metadata.

```
(defmacro clause-term-meta [clause-term]
  (cond
  (coll? clause-term) (first (filter #(variable? % false) (map str clause-term)))
  (variable? (str clause-term) false) (str clause-term)
  :no-variable-in-clause nil))
```

We use pred-clause to iterate over the terms in each clause:

```
(defmacro pred-clause [clause]
  (loop [[trm# & rst-trm#] clause exprs# [] metas# []]
    (if   trm#
        (recur rst-trm# (conj exprs# '(clause-term-expr ~ trm#))
                    (conj metas#'(clause-term-meta ~ trm#)))
        (with-meta exprs# {:db/variable metas#}))))
```

Iterating over the clauses themselves happens in q-clauses-to-pred-clauses:

```
(defmacro  q-clauses-to-pred-clauses [clauses]
    (loop [[frst# & rst#] clauses preds-vecs# []]
      (if-not frst#  preds-vecs#
        (recur rst# '(conj ~preds-vecs# (pred-clause ~frst#))))))
```

We are once again relying on the fact that macros do not eagerly evaluate their arguments. This allows us to define a simpler API where users provide variable names as symbols (e.g., ?name) instead of asking the user to understand the internals of the engine by providing variable names as strings (e.g., "?name"), or even worse, quoting the variable name (e.g., '?name).

At the end of this phase, our example yields the following set for the :find part:

#{"?nm" "?bd"}

and the following structure in Table 10.3 for the :where part. (Each cell in the *Predicate Clause* column holds the metadata found in its neighbor at the *Meta Clause* column.)

This structure acts as the query that is executed in a later phase, once the engine decides on the right plan of execution.

Joining variable operates on	Index to use
Entity IDs	AVET
Attribute names	VEAT
Attribute values	EAVT

Table 10.4: Index Selection

Phase 2: Making a Plan

In this phase, we inspect the query in order to construct a good plan to produce the result it describes.

In general, this will involve choosing the appropriate index (Table 10.4) and constructing a plan in the form of a function. We choose the index based on the *single* joining variable (that can operate on only a single kind of element).

The reasoning behind this mapping will become clearer in the next section, when we actually execute the plan produced. For now, just note that the key here is to select an index whose leaves hold the elements that the joining variable operates on.

Locating the index of the joining variable is done by index-of-joining-variable:

```
(defn index-of-joining-variable [query-clauses]
   (let [metas-seq  (map #(:db/variable (meta %)) query-clauses)
         collapsing-fn (fn [accV v] (map #(when (= %1 %2) %1)  accV v))
         collapsed (reduce collapsing-fn metas-seq)]
     (first (keep-indexed #(when (variable? %2 false) %1)  collapsed))))
```

We begin by extracting the metadata of each clause in the query. This extracted metadata is a 3-element vector; each element is either a variable name or nil. (Note that there is no more than one variable name in that vector.) Once the vector is extracted, we produce from it (by reducing it) a single value, which is either a variable name or nil. If a variable name is produced, then it appeared in all of the metadata vectors at the same index; i.e., this is the joining variable. We can thus choose to use the index relevant for this joining variable based on the mapping described above.

Once the index is chosen, we construct our plan, which is a function that closes over the query and the index name and executes the operations necessary to return the query results.

```
(defn build-query-plan [query]
   (let [term-ind (index-of-joining-variable query)
         ind-to-use (case term-ind 0 :AVET 1 :VEAT 2 :EAVT)]
     (partial single-index-query-plan query ind-to-use)))
```

In our example the chosen index is the AVET index, as the joining variable acts on the entity IDs.

Phase 3: Execution of the Plan

We saw in the previous phase that our query plan ends by calling single-index-query-plan. This function will:

1. Apply each predicate clause on an index (each predicate on its appropriate index level).
2. Perform an AND operation across the results.
3. Merge the results into a simpler data structure.

```
(defn single-index-query-plan [query indx db]
   (let [q-res (query-index (indx-at db indx) query)]
     (bind-variables-to-query q-res (indx-at db indx))))
```

Entity ID	Attribute Name	Attribute Value
1	:name	USA
	:likes	Pizza
	:speak	English
	:bday	July 4, 1776
2	:name	France
	:likes	Red wine
	:speak	French
	:bday	July 14, 1789
3	:name	Canada
	:likes	Snow
	:speak	English
	:bday	July 1, 1867

Table 10.5: Example entities

To better explain this process we'll demonstrate it using our exemplary query, assuming that our database holds the entities in Table 10.5.

Now it is time to go deeper into the rabbit hole and take a look at the query-index function, where our query finally begins to yield some results:

```
(defn query-index [index pred-clauses]
    (let [result-clauses (filter-index index pred-clauses)
          relevant-items (items-that-answer-all-conditions (map last result-clauses)
                                                           (count pred-clauses))
          cleaned-result-clauses (map (partial mask-path-leaf-with-items
                                               relevant-items)
                                      result-clauses)]
        (filter #(not-empty (last %)) cleaned-result-clauses)))
```

This function starts by applying the predicate clauses on the previously chosen index. Each application of a predicate clause on an index returns a *result clause*.

The main characteristics of a result are:

1. It is built of three items, each from a different level of the index, and each passed its respective predicate.
2. The order of items matches the index's levels structure. (Predicate clauses are always in EAV order.) The re-ordering is done when applying the index's from-eav on the predicate clause.
3. The metadata of the predicate clause is attached to it.

All of this is done in the function filter-index.

```
(defn filter-index [index predicate-clauses]
    (for [pred-clause predicate-clauses
          :let [[lvl1-prd lvl2-prd lvl3-prd] (apply (from-eav index) pred-clause)]
          [k1 l2map] index   ; keys and values of the first level
          :when (try (lvl1-prd k1) (catch Exception e false))
          [k2 l3-set] l2map   ; keys and values of the second level
          :when (try (lvl2-prd k2) (catch Exception e false))
          :let [res (set (filter lvl3-prd l3-set))] ]
      (with-meta [k1 k2 res] (meta pred-clause))))
```

Assuming the query was executed on July 4th, the results of executing it on the above data are seen in Table 10.6.

Result Clause	Result Meta
[:likes Pizza #{1}]	["?e" nil nil]
[:name USA #{1}]	["?e" nil "?nm"]
[:speak "English" #{1, 3}]	["?e" nil nil]
[:bday "July 4, 1776" #{1}]	["?e" nil "?bd"]
[:name France #{2}]	["?e" nil "?nm"]
[:bday "July 14, 1789" #{2}]	["?e" nil "?bd"]
[:name Canada #{3}]	["?e" nil "?nm"]
[:bday "July 1, 1867" {3}]	["?e" nil "?bd"]

Table 10.6: Query results

Result Clause	Result Meta
[:likes Pizza #{1}]	["?e" nil nil]
[:name USA #{1}]	["?e" nil "?nm"]
[:bday "July 4, 1776" #{1}]	["?e" nil "?bd"]
[:speak "English" #{1}]	["?e" nil nil]

Table 10.7: Filtered query results

Once we have produced all of the result clauses, we need to perform an AND operation between them. This is done by finding all of the elements that passed all the predicate clauses:

```
(defn items-that-answer-all-conditions [items-seq num-of-conditions]
   (->> items-seq ; take the items-seq
        (map vec) ; make each collection (actually a set) into a vector
        (reduce into []) ;reduce all the vectors into one vector
        (frequencies) ;count for each item in how many collections (sets) it was in
        (filter #(<= num-of-conditions (last %))) ;items that answered all conditions
        (map first) ; take from the duos the items themselves
        (set))) ; return it as set
```

In our example, the result of this step is a set that holds the value *1* (which is the entity ID of USA).

We now have to remove the items that didn't pass all of the conditions:

```
(defn mask-path-leaf-with-items [relevant-items path]
    (update-in path [2] CS/intersection relevant-items))
```

Finally, we remove all of the result clauses that are "empty" (i.e., their last item is empty). We do this in the last line of the query-index function. Our example leaves us with the items in Table 10.7.

We are now ready to report the results. The result clause structure is unwieldy for this purpose, so we will convert it into an an index-like structure (map of maps)—with a significant twist.

To understand the twist, we must first introduce the idea of a *binding pair*, which is a pair that matches a variable name to its value. The variable name is the one used at the predicate clauses, and the value is the value found in the result clauses.

The twist to the index structure is that now we hold a binding pair of the entity-id / attr-name / value in the location where we held an entity-id / attr-name / value in an index:

```
(defn bind-variables-to-query [q-res index]
   (let [seq-res-path (mapcat (partial combine-path-and-meta (from-eav index))
                              q-res)
         res-path (map #(->> %1 (partition 2)(apply (to-eav index))) seq-res-path)]
     (reduce #(assoc-in %1  (butlast %2) (last %2)) {} res-path)))
```

```
(defn combine-path-and-meta [from-eav-fn path]
    (let [expanded-path [(repeat (first path)) (repeat (second path)) (last path)]
          meta-of-path (apply from-eav-fn (map repeat (:db/variable (meta path))))
          combined-data-and-meta-path (interleave meta-of-path expanded-path)]
      (apply (partial map vector) combined-data-and-meta-path)))
```

At the end of phase 3 of our example execution, we have the following structure at hand:

```
{[1 "?e"]{
    {[:likes nil]    ["Pizza" nil]}
    {[:name nil]     ["USA" "?nm"]}
    {[:speaks nil]   ["English" nil]}
    {[:bday nil] ["July 4, 1776" "?bd"]}
}}
```

Phase 4: Unify and Report

At this point, we've produced a superset of the results that the user initially asked for. In this phase, we'll extract the values that the user wants. This process is called *unification*: it is here that we will unify the binding pairs structure with the vector of variable names that the user defined in the :find clause of the query.

```
(defn unify [binded-res-col needed-vars]
    (map (partial locate-vars-in-query-res needed-vars) binded-res-col))
```

Each unification step is handled by locate-vars-in-query-result, which iterates over a query result (structured as an index entry, but with binding pairs) to detect all the variables and values that the user asked for.

```
(defn locate-vars-in-query-res [vars-set q-res]
    (let [[e-pair av-map]  q-res
          e-res (resultify-bind-pair vars-set [] e-pair)]
      (map (partial resultify-av-pair vars-set e-res)  av-map)))

(defn resultify-bind-pair [vars-set accum pair]
    (let [[ var-name _] pair]
      (if (contains? vars-set var-name) (conj accum pair) accum)))

(defn resultify-av-pair [vars-set accum-res av-pair]
    (reduce (partial resultify-bind-pair vars-set) accum-res av-pair))
```

At the end of this phase, the results for our example are:

```
[("?nm" "USA") ("?bd" "July 4, 1776")]
```

Running the Show

We've finally built all of the components we need for our user-facing query mechanism, the q macro, which receives as arguments a database and a query.

```
(defmacro q
  [db query]
  `(let [pred-clauses#  (q-clauses-to-pred-clauses ~(:where query))
         needed-vars# (symbol-col-to-set  ~(:find query))
         query-plan# (build-query-plan pred-clauses#)
         query-internal-res# (query-plan# ~db)]
     (unify query-internal-res# needed-vars#)))
```

10.6 Summary

Our journey started with a conception of a different kind of database, and ended with one that:

- Supports ACI transactions (durability was lost when we decided to have the data stored in-memory).
- Supports "what if" interactions.
- Answers time-related questions.
- Handles simple datalog queries that are optimized with indexes.
- Provides APIs for graph queries.
- Introduces and implements the notion of evolutionary queries.

There are still many things that we could improve: We could add caching to several components to improve performance; support richer queries; and add real storage support to provide data durability, to name a few.

However, our final product can do a great many things, and was implemented in 488 lines of Clojure source code, 73 of which are blank lines and 55 of which are docstrings.

Finally, there's one thing that is still missing: a name. The only sensible option for an in-memory, index-optimized, query-supporting, library developer-friendly, time-aware functional database implemented in 360 lines of Clojure code is CircleDB.

## chapter 11

Making Your Own Image Filters
Cate Huston

11.1   A Brilliant Idea (That Wasn't All That Brilliant)

When I was traveling in China I often saw series of four paintings showing the same place in different seasons. Color—the cool whites of winter, pale hues of spring, lush greens of summer, and reds and yellows of fall—is what visually differentiates the seasons. Around 2011, I had what I thought was a brilliant idea: I wanted to be able to visualize a photo series as a series of colors. I thought it would show travel, and progression through the seasons.

But I didn't know how to calculate the dominant color from an image. I thought about scaling the image down to a 1x1 square and seeing what was left, but that seemed like cheating. I knew how I wanted to display the images, though: in a layout called the Sunflower layout[1]. It's the most efficient way to lay out circles.

I left this project for years, distracted by work, life, travel, talks. Eventually I returned to it, figured out how to calculate the dominant color, and finished my visualization[2]. That is when I discovered that this idea wasn't, in fact, brilliant. The progression wasn't as clear as I hoped, the dominant color extracted wasn't generally the most appealing shade, the creation took a long time (a couple of seconds per image), and it took hundreds of images to make something cool (Figure 11.1).

You might think this would be discouraging, but by the time I got to this point I had learned many things that hadn't come my way before — about color spaces and pixel manipulation — and I had started making those cool partially colored images, the kind you find on postcards of London with a red bus or phone booth and everything else in grayscale.

I used a framework called Processing[3] because I was familiar with it from developing programming curricula, and because I knew it made it easy to create visual applications. It's a tool originally designed for artists, so it abstracts away much of the boilerplate. It allowed me to play and experiment.

University, and later work, filled up my time with other people's ideas and priorities. Part of finishing this project was learning how to carve out time to make progress on my own ideas; I required about four hours of good mental time a week. A tool that allowed me to move faster was therefore really helpful, even necessary—although it came with its own set of problems, especially around writing tests.

I felt that thorough tests were especially important for validating how the project was working, and for making it easier to pick up and resume a project that was often on ice for weeks, even months

---

[1]http://www.catehuston.com/applets/Sunflower/index.html
[2]http://www.catehuston.com/blog/2013/09/02/visualising-a-photo-series/
[3]https://processing.org/

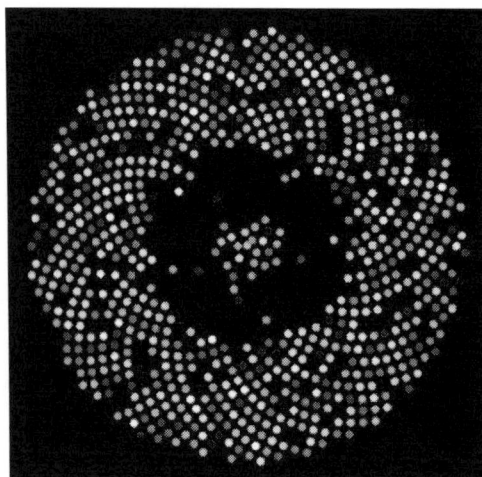

Figure 11.1: Sunflower layout

at a time. Tests (and blogposts!) formed the documentation for this project. I could leave failing tests to document what should happen that I hadn't figured out yet, and make changes with confidence that if I changed something that I had forgotten was critical, the tests would remind me.

This chapter will cover some details about Processing and talk you through color spaces, decomposing an image into pixels and manipulating them, and unit testing something that wasn't designed with testing in mind. But I hope it will also prompt you to make some progress on whatever idea you haven't made time for lately; even if your idea turns out to be as terrible as mine was, you may make something cool and learn something fascinating in the process.

11.2   The App

This chapter will show you how to create an image filter application that you can use to manipulate your digital images using filters that you create. We'll use Processing, a programming language and development environment built in Java. We'll cover setting up the application in Processing, some of the features of Processing, aspects of color representation, and how to create color filters (mimicking what was used in old-fashioned photography). We'll also create a special kind of filter that can only be done digitally: determining the dominant hue of an image and showing or hiding it, to create eerie partially colored images.

Finally, we'll add a thorough test suite, and cover how to handle some of the limitations of Processing when it comes to testability.

11.3   Background

Today we can take a photo, manipulate it, and share it with all our friends in a matter of seconds. However, a long long time ago (in digital terms), it was a process that took weeks.

In the old days, we would take the picture, then when we had used a whole roll of film, we would take it in to be developed (often at the pharmacy). We'd pick up the developed pictures some days later—and discover that there was something wrong with many of them. Hand not steady enough?

Random person or thing that we didn't notice at the time? Overexposed? Underexposed? Of course by then it was too late to remedy the problem.

The process that turned the film into pictures was one that most people didn't understand. Light was a problem, so you had to be careful with the film. There was a process, involving darkened rooms and chemicals, that they sometimes showed in films or on TV.

But probably even fewer people understand how we get from the point-and-click on our smartphone camera to an image on Instagram. There are actually many similarities.

Photographs, the Old Way

Photographs are created by the effect of light on a light-sensitive surface. Photographic film is covered in silver halide crystals. (Extra layers are used to create color photographs — for simplicity let's just stick to black-and-white photography here.)

When talking an old-fashioned photograph — with film — the light hits the film according to what you're pointing at, and the crystals at those points are changed in varying degrees, according to the amount of light. Then, the development process[4] converts the silver salts to metallic silver, creating the negative. The negative has the light and dark areas of the image inverted. Once the negatives have been developed, there is another series of steps to reverse the image and print it.

Photographs, the Digital Way

When taking pictures using our smartphones or digital cameras, there is no film. There is something called an *active-pixel sensor* which functions in a similar way. Where we used to have silver crystals, now we have pixels — tiny squares. (In fact, pixel is short for "picture element".) Digital images are made up of pixels, and the higher the resolution the more pixels there are. This is why low-resolution images are described as "pixelated" — you can start to see the squares. These pixels are stored in an array, with the number in each array "box" containing the color.

In Figure 11.2, we see a high-resolution picture of some blow-up animals taken at MoMA in NYC. Figure 11.3 is the same image blown up, but with just 24 x 32 pixels.

See how it's so blurry? We call that *pixelation*, which means the image is too big for the number of pixels it contains and the squares become visible. Here we can use it to get a better sense of an image being made up of squares of color.

What do these pixels look like? If we print out the colors of some of the pixels in the middle (10,10 to 10,14) using the handy `Integer.toHexString` in Java, we get hex colors:

```
FFE8B1
FFFAC4
FFFCC3
FFFCC2
FFF5B7
```

Hex colors are six characters long. The first two are the red value, the second two the green value, and the third two the blue value. Sometimes there are an extra two characters which are the alpha value. In this case FFFAC4 means:

---

[4]http://photography.tutsplus.com/tutorials/step-by-step-guide-to-developing-black-and-white-t-max-film-{}-photo-2580

Figure 11.2: Blow-up animals at MoMA NY

- red = FF (hex) = 255 (base 10)
- green = FA (hex) = 250 (base 10)
- blue = C4 (hex) = 196 (base 10)

11.4   Running the App

In Figure 11.4, we have a picture of our app running. It's very much developer-designed, I know, but we only have 500 lines of Java to work with so something had to suffer! You can see the list of commands on the right. Some things we can do:

- Adjust the RGB filters.
- Adjust the "hue tolerance".
- Set the dominant hue filters, to either show or hide the dominant hue.
- Apply our current setting (it is infeasible to run this every key press).
- Reset the image.
- Save the image we have made.

Processing makes it simple to create a little application and do image manipulation; it has a very visual focus. We'll work with the Java-based version, although Processing has now been ported to other languages.

Figure 11.3: Blow-up animals, blown up

For this tutorial, I use Processing in Eclipse by adding `core.jar` to my build path. If you want, you can use the Processing IDE, which removes the need for a lot of boilerplate Java code. If you later want to port it over to Processing.js and upload it online, you need to replace the file chooser with something else.

There are detailed instructions with screenshots in the project's repository[5]. If you are familiar with Eclipse and Java already you may not need them.

11.5 Processing Basics

Size and Color

We don't want our app to be a tiny grey window, so the two essential methods that we will start by overriding are `setup()`[6], and `draw()`[7]. The `setup()` method is only called when the app starts, and is where we do things like set the size of the app window. The `draw()` method is called for every animation, or after some action can be triggered by calling `redraw()`. (As covered in the Processing Documentation, `draw()` should not be called explicitly.)

---

[5]https://github.com/aosabook/500lines/blob/master/image-filters/SETUP.MD
[6]http://processing.org/reference/setup_.html
[7]http://processing.org/reference/draw_.html

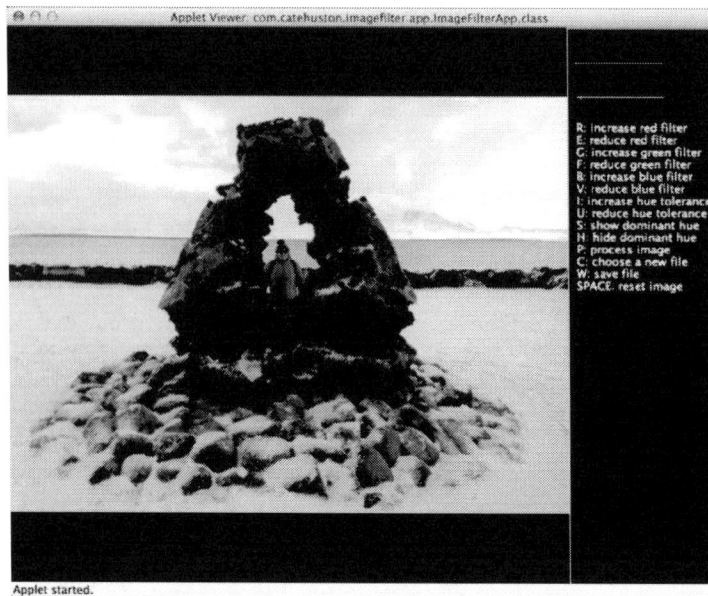

Figure 11.4: The App

Processing is designed to work nicely to create animated sketches, but in this case we don't want animation[8], we want to respond to key presses. To prevent animation (which would be a drag on performance) we will call noLoop()[9] from setup. This means that draw() will only be called immediately after setup(), and whenever we call redraw().

```
private static final int WIDTH = 360;
private static final int HEIGHT = 240;

public void setup() {
  noLoop();

  // Set up the view.
  size(WIDTH, HEIGHT);
  background(0);
}

public void draw() {
  background(0);
}
```

These don't really do much yet, but try running the app again, adjusting the constants in WIDTH and HEIGHT, to see different sizes.

background(0) specifies a black background. Try changing the number passed to background() and see what happens — it's the alpha value, and so if you only pass one number in, it is always greyscale. Alternatively, you can call background(int r, int g, int b).

---

[8]If we wanted to create an animated sketch we would not call noLoop() (or, if we wanted to start animating later, we would call loop()). The frequency of the animation is determined by frameRate().

[9]http://www.processing.org/reference/noLoop_.html

pixels[]	Array containing the color of every pixel in the image
width	Image width in pixels
height	Image height in pixels

Table 11.1: PImage fields

loadPixels	Loads the pixel data for the image into its 'pixels[]' array
updatePixels	Updates the image with the data in its 'pixels[]' array
resize	Changes the size of an image to a new width and height
get	Reads the color of any pixel or grabs a rectangle of pixels
set	Writes a color to any pixel or writes an image into another
save	Saves the image to a TIFF, TARGA, PNG, or JPEG file

Table 11.2: PImage methods

PImage

The PImage object[10] is the Processing object that represents an image. We're going to be using this a lot, so it's worth reading through the documentation. It has three fields (Table 11.1) as well as some methods that we will use (Table 11.2).

File Chooser

Processing handles most of the file choosing process; we just need to call `selectInput()`[11], and implement a callback (which must be public).

To people familiar with Java this might seem odd; a listener or a lambda expression might make more sense. However, as Processing was developed as a tool for artists, for the most part these things have been abstracted away by the language to keep it unintimidating. This is a choice the designers made: to prioritize simplicity and approachability over power and flexibility. If you use the stripped-down Processing editor, rather than Processing as a library in Eclipse, you don't even need to define class names.

Other language designers with different target audiences make different choices, as they should. For example, in Haskell, a purely functional language, purity of functional language paradigms is prioritised over everything else. This makes it a better tool for mathematical problems than for anything requiring IO.

```
// Called on key press.
private void chooseFile() {
  // Choose the file.
  selectInput("Select a file to process:", "fileSelected");
}

public void fileSelected(File file) {
  if (file == null) {
    println("User hit cancel.");
  } else {
    // save the image
    redraw(); // update the display
  }
}
```

---

[10]http://processing.org/reference/PImage.html
[11]http://www.processing.org/reference/selectInput_.html

Responding to Key Presses

Normally in Java, responding to key presses requires adding listeners and implementing anonymous functions. However, as with the file chooser, Processing handles a lot of this for us. We just need to implement keyPressed()[12].

```
public void keyPressed() {
  print("key pressed: " + key);
}
```

If you run the app again, every time you press a key it will output it to the console. Later, you'll want to do different things depending on what key was pressed, and to do this you just switch on the key value. (This exists in the PApplet superclass, and contains the last key pressed.)

11.6   Writing Tests

This app doesn't do a lot yet, but we can already see number of places where things can go wrong; for example, triggering the wrong action with key presses. As we add complexity, we add more potential problems, such as updating the image state incorrectly, or miscalculating pixel colors after applying a filter. I also just enjoy (some think weirdly) writing unit tests. Whilst some people seem to think of testing as a thing that delays checking code in, I see tests as my #1 debugging tool, and as an opportunity to deeply understand what is going on in my code.

I adore Processing, but it's designed to create visual applications, and in this area maybe unit testing isn't a huge concern. It's clear it isn't written for testability; in fact it's written in such a way that makes it untestable, as is. Part of this is because it hides complexity, and some of that hidden complexity is really useful in writing unit tests. The use of static and final methods make it much harder to use mocks (objects that record interaction and allow you to fake part of your system to verify another part is behaving correctly), which rely on the ability to subclass.

We might start a greenfield project with great intentions to do Test Driven Development (TDD) and achieve perfect test coverage, but in reality we are usually looking at a mass of code written by various and assorted people and trying to figure out what it is supposed to be doing, and how and why it is going wrong. Then maybe we don't write perfect tests, but writing tests at all will help us navigate the situation, document what is happening and move forward.

We create "seams" that allow us to break something up from its amorphous mass of tangled pieces and verify it in parts. To do this, we will sometimes create wrapper classes that can be mocked. These classes do nothing more than hold a collection of similar methods, or forward calls on to another object that cannot be mocked (due to final or static methods), and as such they are very dull to write, but key to creating seams and making the code testable.

I used JUnit for tests, as I was working in Java with Processing as a library. For mocking I used Mockito. You can download Mockito[13] and add the JAR to your buildpath in the same way you added core.jar. I created two helper classes that make it possible to mock and test the app (otherwise we can't test behavior involving PImage or PApplet methods).

IFAImage is a thin wrapper around PImage. PixelColorHelper is a wrapper around applet pixel color methods. These wrappers call the final, and static methods, but the caller methods are neither final nor static themselves — this allows them to be mocked. These are deliberately lightweight, and

---

[12]https://www.processing.org/reference/keyPressed_.html
[13]https://code.google.com/p/mockito/downloads/list

0	1	2	3
4	5	6	7
8	9	10	11
12	13	14	15

Table 11.3: Pixel indices for a 4x4 image

we could have gone further, but this was sufficient to address the major problem of testability when using Processing — static, and final methods. The goal was to make an app, after all — not a unit testing framework for Processing!

A class called `ImageState` forms the "model" of this application, removing as much logic from the class extending `PApplet` as possible, for better testability. It also makes for a cleaner design and separation of concerns: the App controls the interactions and the UI, not the image manipulation.

11.7   Do-It-Yourself Filters

RGB Filters

Before we start writing more complicated pixel processing, we can start with a short exercise that will get us comfortable doing pixel manipulation. We'll create standard (red, green, blue) color filters that will allow us to create the same effect as placing a colored plate over the lens of a camera, only letting through light with enough red (or green, or blue).

By applying different RGB filters to an image we can make it almost seem like the seasons are different depending which colors are filtered out and which are emphasized. (Remember the four-seasons paintings we imagined earlier?)

How do we do it?

- Set the filter. (You can combine red, green and blue filters as in the image earlier; I haven't in these examples so that the effect is clearer.)
- For each pixel in the image, check its RGB value.
- If the red is less than the red filter, set the red to zero.
- If the green is less than the green filter, set the green to zero.
- If the blue is less than the blue filter, set the blue to zero.
- Any pixel with insufficient of all of these colors will be black.

Although our image is 2-dimensional, the pixels live in a 1-dimensional array starting top-left and moving left to right, top to bottom[14]. The array indices for a 4x4 image are shown here:

```
public void applyColorFilter(PApplet applet, IFAImage img, int minRed,
        int minGreen, int minBlue, int colorRange) {
  img.loadPixels();
  int numberOfPixels = img.getPixels().length;
  for (int i = 0; i < numberOfPixels; i++) {
    int pixel = img.getPixel(i);
    float alpha = pixelColorHelper.alpha(applet, pixel);
    float red = pixelColorHelper.red(applet, pixel);
    float green = pixelColorHelper.green(applet, pixel);
    float blue = pixelColorHelper.blue(applet, pixel);
```

---

[14]https://processing.org/tutorials/pixels/

```
    red = (red >= minRed) ? red : 0;
    green = (green >= minGreen) ? green : 0;
    blue = (blue >= minBlue) ? blue : 0;

    image.setPixel(i, pixelColorHelper.color(applet, red, green, blue, alpha));
  }
}
```

Color

As our first example of an image filter showed, the concept and representation of colors in a program is very important to understanding how our filters work. To prepare ourselves for working on our next filter, let's explore the concept of color a bit more.

We were using a concept in the previous section called "color space", which is way of representing color digitally. Kids mixing paints learn that colors can be made from other colors; things work slightly differently in digital (less risk of being covered in paint!) but similar. Processing makes it really easy to work with whatever color space you want, but you need to know which one to pick, so it's important to understand how they work.

RGB colors

The color space that most programmers are familiar with is RGBA: red, green, blue and alpha; it's what we were using above. In hexadecimal (base 16), the first two digits are the amount of red, the second two blue, the third two green, and the final two (if they are there) are the alpha value. The values range from 00 in base 16 (0 in base 10) through to FF (255 in base 10). The alpha represents opacity, where 0 is transparent and 100% is opaque.

HSB or HSV colors

This color space is not quite as well known as RGB. The first number represents the hue, the second number the saturation (how intense the color is), and the third number the brightness. The HSB color space can be represented by a cone: The hue is the position around the cone, saturation the distance from the centre, and brightness the height (0 brightness is black).

Extracting the Dominant Hue from an Image

Now that we're comfortable with pixel manipulation, let's do something that we could only do digitally. Digitally, we can manipulate the image in a way that isn't so uniform.

When I look through my stream of pictures I can see themes emerging. The nighttime series I took at sunset from a boat on Hong Kong harbour, the grey of North Korea, the lush greens of Bali, the icy whites and pale blues of an Icelandic winter. Can we take a picture and pull out that main color that dominates the scene?

It makes sense to use the HSB color space for this — we are interested in the hue when figuring out what the main color is. It's possible to do this using RGB values, but more difficult (we would have to compare all three values) and it would be more sensitive to darkness. We can change to the HSB color space using colorMode[15].

---

[15]http://processing.org/reference/colorMode_.html

Having settled on this color space, it's simpler than it would have been using RGB. We need to find the hue of each pixel, and figure out which is most "popular". We probably don't want to be exact — we want to group very similar hues together, and we can handle this using two strategies.

Firstly we will round the decimals that come back to whole numbers, as this makes it simple to determine which "bucket" we put each pixel in. Secondly we can change the range of the hues. If we think back to the cone representation above, we might think of hues as having 360 degrees (like a circle). Processing uses 255 by default, which is the same as is typical for RGB (255 is FF in hexadecimal). The higher the range we use, the more distinct the hues in the picture will be. Using a smaller range will allow us to group together similar hues. Using a 360 degree range, it's unlikely that we will be able to tell the difference between a hue of 224 and a hue of 225, as the difference is very small. If we make the range one-third of that, 120, both these hues become 75 after rounding.

We can change the range of hues using colorMode. If we call colorMode(HSB, 120) we have just made our hue detection a bit less than half as exact as if we used the 255 range. We also know that our hues will fall into 120 "buckets", so we can simply go through our image, get the hue for a pixel, and add one to the corresponding count in an array. This will be $O(n)$, where n is the number of pixels, as it requires action on each one.

```
for(int px in pixels) {
  int hue = Math.round(hue(px));
  hues[hue]++;
}
```

At the end we can print this hue to the screen, or display it next to the picture.

Once we've extracted the "dominant" hue, we can choose to either show or hide it in the image. We can show the dominant hue with varying tolerance (ranges around it that we will accept). Pixels that don't fall into this range can be changed to grayscale by setting the value based on the brightness. Alternatively, we can hide the dominant hue by setting the color for pixels with that hue to greyscale, and leaving other pixels as they are.

Each image requires a double pass (looking at each pixel twice), so on images with a large number of pixels it can take a noticeable amount of time.

```
public HSBColor getDominantHue(PApplet applet, IFAImage image, int hueRange) {
  image.loadPixels();
  int numberOfPixels = image.getPixels().length;
  int[] hues = new int[hueRange];
  float[] saturations = new float[hueRange];
  float[] brightnesses = new float[hueRange];

  for (int i = 0; i < numberOfPixels; i++) {
    int pixel = image.getPixel(i);
    int hue = Math.round(pixelColorHelper.hue(applet, pixel));
    float saturation = pixelColorHelper.saturation(applet, pixel);
    float brightness = pixelColorHelper.brightness(applet, pixel);
    hues[hue]++;
    saturations[hue] += saturation;
    brightnesses[hue] += brightness;
  }

  // Find the most common hue.
  int hueCount = hues[0];
```

```
    int hue = 0;
    for (int i = 1; i < hues.length; i++) {
      if (hues[i] > hueCount) {
        hueCount = hues[i];
        hue = i;
      }
    }

    // Return the color to display.
    float s = saturations[hue] / hueCount;
    float b = brightnesses[hue] / hueCount;
    return new HSBColor(hue, s, b);
}


public void processImageForHue(PApplet applet, IFAImage image, int hueRange,
      int hueTolerance, boolean showHue) {
    applet.colorMode(PApplet.HSB, (hueRange - 1));
    image.loadPixels();
    int numberOfPixels = image.getPixels().length;
    HSBColor dominantHue = getDominantHue(applet, image, hueRange);
    // Manipulate photo, grayscale any pixel that isn't close to that hue.
    float lower = dominantHue.h - hueTolerance;
    float upper = dominantHue.h + hueTolerance;
    for (int i = 0; i < numberOfPixels; i++) {
      int pixel = image.getPixel(i);
      float hue = pixelColorHelper.hue(applet, pixel);
      if (hueInRange(hue, hueRange, lower, upper) == showHue) {
        float brightness = pixelColorHelper.brightness(applet, pixel);
        image.setPixel(i, pixelColorHelper.color(applet, brightness));
      }
    }
    image.updatePixels();
}
```

Combining Filters

With the UI as it is, the user can combine the red, green, and blue filters together. If they combine
the dominant hue filters with the red, green, and blue filters the results can sometimes be a little
unexpected, because of changing the color spaces.

Processing has some built-in methods[16] that support the manipulation of images; for example,
invert and blur.

To achieve effects like sharpening, blurring, or sepia we apply matrices. For every pixel of the
image, take the sum of products where each product is the color value of the current pixel or a
neighbor of it, with the corresponding value of the filter matrix[17]. There are some special matrices
of specific values that sharpen images.

---

[16]https://www.processing.org/reference/filter_.html
[17]http://lodev.org/cgtutor/filtering.html

11.8   Architecture

There are three main components to the app (Figure 11.5).

The App

The app consists of one file: `ImageFilterApp.java`. This extends PApplet (the Processing app superclass) and handles layout, user interaction, etc. This class is the hardest to test, so we want to keep it as small as possible.

Model

Model consists of three files: `HSBColor.java` is a simple container for HSB colors (consisting of hue, saturation, and brightness). `IFAImage` is a wrapper around PImage for testability. (PImage contains a number of final methods which cannot be mocked.) Finally, `ImageState.java` is the object which describes the state of the image — what level of filters should be applied, and which filters — and handles loading the image. (Note: The image needs to be reloaded whenever color filters are adjusted down, and whenever the dominant hue is recalculated. For clarity, we just reload each time the image is processed.)

Color

Color consists of two files: `ColorHelper.java` is where all the image processing and filtering takes place, and `PixelColorHelper.java` abstracts out final PApplet methods for pixel colors for testability.

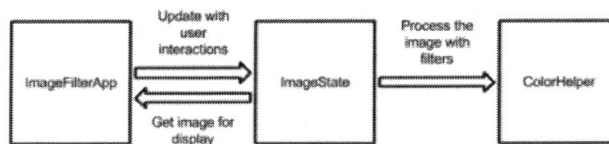

Figure 11.5: Architecture diagram

Wrapper Classes and Tests

Briefly mentioned above, there are two wrapper classes (`IFAImage` and `PixelColorHelper`) that wrap library methods for testability. This is because, in Java, the keyword "final" indicates a method that cannot be overridden or hidden by subclasses, which means they cannot be mocked.

`PixelColorHelper` wraps methods on the applet. This means we need to pass the applet in to each method call. (Alternatively, we could make it a field and set it on initialization.)

```
package com.catehuston.imagefilter.color;

import processing.core.PApplet;

public class PixelColorHelper {
```

```
public float alpha(PApplet applet, int pixel) {
  return applet.alpha(pixel);
}

public float blue(PApplet applet, int pixel) {
  return applet.blue(pixel);
}

public float brightness(PApplet applet, int pixel) {
  return applet.brightness(pixel);
}

public int color(PApplet applet, float greyscale) {
  return applet.color(greyscale);
}

public int color(PApplet applet, float red, float green, float blue,
        float alpha) {
  return applet.color(red, green, blue, alpha);
}

public float green(PApplet applet, int pixel) {
  return applet.green(pixel);
}

public float hue(PApplet applet, int pixel) {
  return applet.hue(pixel);
}

public float red(PApplet applet, int pixel) {
  return applet.red(pixel);
}

public float saturation(PApplet applet, int pixel) {
  return applet.saturation(pixel);
}
}
```

IFAImage is a wrapper around PImage, so in our app we don't initialize a PImage, but rather an IFAImage — although we do have to expose the PImage so that it can be rendered.

```
package com.catehuston.imagefilter.model;

import processing.core.PApplet;
import processing.core.PImage;

public class IFAImage {

  private PImage image;

  public IFAImage() {
    image = null;
```

```
    }

    public PImage image() {
      return image;
    }

    public void update(PApplet applet, String filepath) {
      image = null;
      image = applet.loadImage(filepath);
    }

    // Wrapped methods from PImage.
    public int getHeight() {
      return image.height;
    }

    public int getPixel(int px) {
      return image.pixels[px];
    }

    public int[] getPixels() {
      return image.pixels;
    }

    public int getWidth() {
      return image.width;
    }

    public void loadPixels() {
      image.loadPixels();
    }

    public void resize(int width, int height) {
      image.resize(width, height);
    }

    public void save(String filepath) {
      image.save(filepath);
    }

    public void setPixel(int px, int color) {
      image.pixels[px] = color;
    }

    public void updatePixels() {
      image.updatePixels();
    }
  }
}
```

Finally, we have our simple container class, HSBColor. Note that it is immutable (once created, it cannot be changed). Immutable objects are better for thread safety (something we have no need of here!) but are also easier to understand and reason about. In general, I tend to make simple model classes immutable unless I find a good reason for them not to be.

Some of you may know that there are already classes representing color in Processing[18] and in Java itself[19]. Without going too much into the details of these, both of them are more focused on RGB color, and the Java class in particular adds way more complexity than we need. We would probably be okay if we did want to use Java's awt.Color; however awt GUI components cannot be used in Processing[20], so for our purposes creating this simple container class to hold these bits of data we need is easiest.

```
package com.catehuston.imagefilter.model;

public class HSBColor {

  public final float h;
  public final float s;
  public final float b;

  public HSBColor(float h, float s, float b) {
    this.h = h;
    this.s = s;
    this.b = b;
  }
}
```

ColorHelper and Associated Tests

ColorHelper is where all the image manipulation lives. The methods in this class could be static if not for needing a PixelColorHelper. (Although we won't get into the debate about the merits of static methods here.)

```
package com.catehuston.imagefilter.color;

import processing.core.PApplet;

import com.catehuston.imagefilter.model.HSBColor;
import com.catehuston.imagefilter.model.IFAImage;

public class ColorHelper {

  private final PixelColorHelper pixelColorHelper;

  public ColorHelper(PixelColorHelper pixelColorHelper) {
    this.pixelColorHelper = pixelColorHelper;
  }

  public boolean hueInRange(float hue, int hueRange, float lower, float upper) {
    // Need to compensate for it being circular - can go around.
```

---

[18]https://www.processing.org/reference/color_datatype.html
[19]https://docs.oracle.com/javase/7/docs/api/java/awt/Color.html
[20]http://processing.org/reference/javadoc/core/processing/core/PApplet.html

```
    if (lower < 0) {
      lower += hueRange;
    }
    if (upper > hueRange) {
      upper -= hueRange;
    }
    if (lower < upper) {
      return hue < upper && hue > lower;
    } else {
      return hue < upper || hue > lower;
    }
  }

  public HSBColor getDominantHue(PApplet applet, IFAImage image, int hueRange) {
    image.loadPixels();
    int numberOfPixels = image.getPixels().length;
    int[] hues = new int[hueRange];
    float[] saturations = new float[hueRange];
    float[] brightnesses = new float[hueRange];

    for (int i = 0; i < numberOfPixels; i++) {
      int pixel = image.getPixel(i);
      int hue = Math.round(pixelColorHelper.hue(applet, pixel));
      float saturation = pixelColorHelper.saturation(applet, pixel);
      float brightness = pixelColorHelper.brightness(applet, pixel);
      hues[hue]++;
      saturations[hue] += saturation;
      brightnesses[hue] += brightness;
    }

    // Find the most common hue.
    int hueCount = hues[0];
    int hue = 0;
    for (int i = 1; i < hues.length; i++) {
      if (hues[i] > hueCount) {
        hueCount = hues[i];
        hue = i;
      }
    }

    // Return the color to display.
    float s = saturations[hue] / hueCount;
    float b = brightnesses[hue] / hueCount;
    return new HSBColor(hue, s, b);
  }

  public void processImageForHue(PApplet applet, IFAImage image, int hueRange,
      int hueTolerance, boolean showHue) {
    applet.colorMode(PApplet.HSB, (hueRange - 1));
    image.loadPixels();
    int numberOfPixels = image.getPixels().length;
```

```
    HSBColor dominantHue = getDominantHue(applet, image, hueRange);
    // Manipulate photo, grayscale any pixel that isn't close to that hue.
    float lower = dominantHue.h - hueTolerance;
    float upper = dominantHue.h + hueTolerance;
    for (int i = 0; i < numberOfPixels; i++) {
      int pixel = image.getPixel(i);
      float hue = pixelColorHelper.hue(applet, pixel);
      if (hueInRange(hue, hueRange, lower, upper) == showHue) {
        float brightness = pixelColorHelper.brightness(applet, pixel);
        image.setPixel(i, pixelColorHelper.color(applet, brightness));
      }
    }
    image.updatePixels();
  }

  public void applyColorFilter(PApplet applet, IFAImage image, int minRed,
      int minGreen, int minBlue, int colorRange) {
    applet.colorMode(PApplet.RGB, colorRange);
    image.loadPixels();
    int numberOfPixels = image.getPixels().length;
    for (int i = 0; i < numberOfPixels; i++) {
      int pixel = image.getPixel(i);
      float alpha = pixelColorHelper.alpha(applet, pixel);
      float red = pixelColorHelper.red(applet, pixel);
      float green = pixelColorHelper.green(applet, pixel);
      float blue = pixelColorHelper.blue(applet, pixel);

      red = (red >= minRed) ? red : 0;
      green = (green >= minGreen) ? green : 0;
      blue = (blue >= minBlue) ? blue : 0;

      image.setPixel(i, pixelColorHelper.color(applet, red, green, blue, alpha));
    }
  }
}
```

We don't want to test this with whole images, because we want images that we know the properties of and reason about. We approximate this by mocking the images and making them return an array of pixels — in this case, 5. This allows us to verify that the behavior is as expected. Earlier we covered the concept of mock objects, and here we see their use. We are using Mockito[21] as our mock object framework.

To create a mock we use the @Mock annotation on an instance variable, and it will be mocked at runtime by the MockitoJUnitRunner.

To stub (set the behavior of) a method, we use:

```
when(mock.methodCall()).thenReturn(value)
```

To verify a method was called, we use verify(mock.methodCall()).

[21]http://docs.mockito.googlecode.com/hg/org/mockito/Mockito.html

We'll show a few example test cases here; if you'd like to see the rest, visit the source folder for this project in the *500 Lines or Less* GitHub repository[22].

```
package com.catehuston.imagefilter.color;

/* ... Imports omitted ... */

@RunWith(MockitoJUnitRunner.class)
public class ColorHelperTest {

  @Mock PApplet applet;
  @Mock IFAImage image;
  @Mock PixelColorHelper pixelColorHelper;

  ColorHelper colorHelper;

  private static final int px1 = 1000;
  private static final int px2 = 1010;
  private static final int px3 = 1030;
  private static final int px4 = 1040;
  private static final int px5 = 1050;
  private static final int[] pixels = { px1, px2, px3, px4, px5 };

  @Before public void setUp() throws Exception {
    colorHelper = new ColorHelper(pixelColorHelper);
    when(image.getPixels()).thenReturn(pixels);
    setHsbValuesForPixel(0, px1, 30F, 5F, 10F);
    setHsbValuesForPixel(1, px2, 20F, 6F, 11F);
    setHsbValuesForPixel(2, px3, 30F, 7F, 12F);
    setHsbValuesForPixel(3, px4, 50F, 8F, 13F);
    setHsbValuesForPixel(4, px5, 30F, 9F, 14F);
  }

  private void setHsbValuesForPixel(int px, int color, float h, float s, float b) {
    when(image.getPixel(px)).thenReturn(color);
    when(pixelColorHelper.hue(applet, color)).thenReturn(h);
    when(pixelColorHelper.saturation(applet, color)).thenReturn(s);
    when(pixelColorHelper.brightness(applet, color)).thenReturn(b);
  }

  private void setRgbValuesForPixel(int px, int color, float r, float g, float b,
            float alpha) {
    when(image.getPixel(px)).thenReturn(color);
    when(pixelColorHelper.red(applet, color)).thenReturn(r);
    when(pixelColorHelper.green(applet, color)).thenReturn(g);
    when(pixelColorHelper.blue(applet, color)).thenReturn(b);
    when(pixelColorHelper.alpha(applet, color)).thenReturn(alpha);
  }

  @Test public void testHsbColorFromImage() {
```

---

[22]https://github.com/aosabook/500lines/tree/master/image-filters

```
    HSBColor color = colorHelper.getDominantHue(applet, image, 100);
    verify(image).loadPixels();

    assertEquals(30F, color.h, 0);
    assertEquals(7F, color.s, 0);
    assertEquals(12F, color.b, 0);
  }

  @Test public void testProcessImageNoHue() {
    when(pixelColorHelper.color(applet, 11F)).thenReturn(11);
    when(pixelColorHelper.color(applet, 13F)).thenReturn(13);
    colorHelper.processImageForHue(applet, image, 60, 2, false);
    verify(applet).colorMode(PApplet.HSB, 59);
    verify(image, times(2)).loadPixels();
    verify(image).setPixel(1, 11);
    verify(image).setPixel(3, 13);
  }

  @Test public void testApplyColorFilter() {
    setRgbValuesForPixel(0, px1, 10F, 12F, 14F, 60F);
    setRgbValuesForPixel(1, px2, 20F, 22F, 24F, 70F);
    setRgbValuesForPixel(2, px3, 30F, 32F, 34F, 80F);
    setRgbValuesForPixel(3, px4, 40F, 42F, 44F, 90F);
    setRgbValuesForPixel(4, px5, 50F, 52F, 54F, 100F);

    when(pixelColorHelper.color(applet, 0F, 0F, 0F, 60F)).thenReturn(5);
    when(pixelColorHelper.color(applet, 20F, 0F, 0F, 70F)).thenReturn(15);
    when(pixelColorHelper.color(applet, 30F, 32F, 0F, 80F)).thenReturn(25);
    when(pixelColorHelper.color(applet, 40F, 42F, 44F, 90F)).thenReturn(35);
    when(pixelColorHelper.color(applet, 50F, 52F, 54F, 100F)).thenReturn(45);

    colorHelper.applyColorFilter(applet, image, 15, 25, 35, 100);
    verify(applet).colorMode(PApplet.RGB, 100);
    verify(image).loadPixels();

    verify(image).setPixel(0, 5);
    verify(image).setPixel(1, 15);
    verify(image).setPixel(2, 25);
    verify(image).setPixel(3, 35);
    verify(image).setPixel(4, 45);
  }
}
```

Notice that:

- We use the MockitoJUnit runner.
- We mock PApplet, IFAImage (created for expressly this purpose), and ImageColorHelper.
- Test methods are annotated with @Test[23]. If you want to ignore a test (e.g., whilst debugging) you can add the annotation @Ignore.
- In setup(), we create the pixel array and have the mock image always return it.
- Helper methods make it easier to set expectations for recurring tasks (e.g., set*ForPixel()).

Image State and Associated Tests

ImageState holds the current "state" of the image — the image itself, and the settings and filters that will be applied. We'll omit the full implementation of ImageState here, but we'll show how it can be tested. You can visit the source repository for this project to see the full details.

```
package com.catehuston.imagefilter.model;

import processing.core.PApplet;
import com.catehuston.imagefilter.color.ColorHelper;

public class ImageState {

  enum ColorMode {
    COLOR_FILTER,
    SHOW_DOMINANT_HUE,
    HIDE_DOMINANT_HUE
  }

  private final ColorHelper colorHelper;
  private IFAImage image;
  private String filepath;

  public static final int INITIAL_HUE_TOLERANCE = 5;

  ColorMode colorModeState = ColorMode.COLOR_FILTER;
  int blueFilter = 0;
  int greenFilter = 0;
  int hueTolerance = 0;
  int redFilter = 0;

  public ImageState(ColorHelper colorHelper) {
    this.colorHelper = colorHelper;
    image = new IFAImage();
    hueTolerance = INITIAL_HUE_TOLERANCE;
  }
  /* ... getters & setters */
  public void updateImage(PApplet applet, int hueRange, int rgbColorRange,
          int imageMax) { ... }
```

---

[23]Method names in tests need not start with test as of JUnit 4, but habits are hard to break.

```java
  public void processKeyPress(char key, int inc, int rgbColorRange,
          int hueIncrement, int hueRange) { ... }

  public void setUpImage(PApplet applet, int imageMax) { ... }

  public void resetImage(PApplet applet, int imageMax) { ... }

  // For testing purposes only.
  protected void set(IFAImage image, ColorMode colorModeState,
          int redFilter, int greenFilter, int blueFilter, int hueTolerance) { ... }
}
```

Here we can test that the appropriate actions happen for the given state; that fields are incremented and decremented appropriately.

```java
package com.catehuston.imagefilter.model;

/* ... Imports omitted ... */

@RunWith(MockitoJUnitRunner.class)
public class ImageStateTest {

  @Mock PApplet applet;
  @Mock ColorHelper colorHelper;
  @Mock IFAImage image;

  private ImageState imageState;

  @Before public void setUp() throws Exception {
    imageState = new ImageState(colorHelper);
  }

  private void assertState(ColorMode colorMode, int redFilter,
      int greenFilter, int blueFilter, int hueTolerance) {
    assertEquals(colorMode, imageState.getColorMode());
    assertEquals(redFilter, imageState.redFilter());
    assertEquals(greenFilter, imageState.greenFilter());
    assertEquals(blueFilter, imageState.blueFilter());
    assertEquals(hueTolerance, imageState.hueTolerance());
  }

  @Test public void testUpdateImageDominantHueHidden() {
    imageState.setFilepath("filepath");
    imageState.set(image, ColorMode.HIDE_DOMINANT_HUE, 5, 10, 15, 10);

    imageState.updateImage(applet, 100, 100, 500);

    verify(image).update(applet, "filepath");
    verify(colorHelper).processImageForHue(applet, image, 100, 10, false);
    verify(colorHelper).applyColorFilter(applet, image, 5, 10, 15, 100);
    verify(image).updatePixels();
  }
```

```
@Test public void testUpdateDominantHueShowing() {
  imageState.setFilepath("filepath");
  imageState.set(image, ColorMode.SHOW_DOMINANT_HUE, 5, 10, 15, 10);

  imageState.updateImage(applet, 100, 100, 500);

  verify(image).update(applet, "filepath");
  verify(colorHelper).processImageForHue(applet, image, 100, 10, true);
  verify(colorHelper).applyColorFilter(applet, image, 5, 10, 15, 100);
  verify(image).updatePixels();
}

@Test public void testUpdateRGBOnly() {
  imageState.setFilepath("filepath");
  imageState.set(image, ColorMode.COLOR_FILTER, 5, 10, 15, 10);

  imageState.updateImage(applet, 100, 100, 500);

  verify(image).update(applet, "filepath");
  verify(colorHelper, never()).processImageForHue(any(PApplet.class),
            any(IFAImage.class), anyInt(), anyInt(), anyBoolean());
  verify(colorHelper).applyColorFilter(applet, image, 5, 10, 15, 100);
  verify(image).updatePixels();
}

@Test public void testKeyPress() {
  imageState.processKeyPress('r', 5, 100, 2, 200);
  assertState(ColorMode.COLOR_FILTER, 5, 0, 0, 5);

  imageState.processKeyPress('e', 5, 100, 2, 200);
  assertState(ColorMode.COLOR_FILTER, 0, 0, 0, 5);

  imageState.processKeyPress('g', 5, 100, 2, 200);
  assertState(ColorMode.COLOR_FILTER, 0, 5, 0, 5);

  imageState.processKeyPress('f', 5, 100, 2, 200);
  assertState(ColorMode.COLOR_FILTER, 0, 0, 0, 5);

  imageState.processKeyPress('b', 5, 100, 2, 200);
  assertState(ColorMode.COLOR_FILTER, 0, 0, 5, 5);

  imageState.processKeyPress('v', 5, 100, 2, 200);
  assertState(ColorMode.COLOR_FILTER, 0, 0, 0, 5);

  imageState.processKeyPress('h', 5, 100, 2, 200);
  assertState(ColorMode.HIDE_DOMINANT_HUE, 0, 0, 0, 5);

  imageState.processKeyPress('i', 5, 100, 2, 200);
  assertState(ColorMode.HIDE_DOMINANT_HUE, 0, 0, 0, 7);
```

```java
      imageState.processKeyPress('u', 5, 100, 2, 200);
      assertState(ColorMode.HIDE_DOMINANT_HUE, 0, 0, 0, 5);

      imageState.processKeyPress('h', 5, 100, 2, 200);
      assertState(ColorMode.COLOR_FILTER, 0, 0, 0, 5);

      imageState.processKeyPress('s', 5, 100, 2, 200);
      assertState(ColorMode.SHOW_DOMINANT_HUE, 0, 0, 0, 5);

      imageState.processKeyPress('s', 5, 100, 2, 200);
      assertState(ColorMode.COLOR_FILTER, 0, 0, 0, 5);

      // Random key should do nothing.
      imageState.processKeyPress('z', 5, 100, 2, 200);
      assertState(ColorMode.COLOR_FILTER, 0, 0, 0, 5);
   }

   @Test public void testSave() {
      imageState.set(image, ColorMode.SHOW_DOMINANT_HUE, 5, 10, 15, 10);
      imageState.setFilepath("filepath");
      imageState.processKeyPress('w', 5, 100, 2, 200);

      verify(image).save("filepath-new.png");
   }

   @Test public void testSetupImageLandscape() {
      imageState.set(image, ColorMode.SHOW_DOMINANT_HUE, 5, 10, 15, 10);
      when(image.getWidth()).thenReturn(20);
      when(image.getHeight()).thenReturn(8);
      imageState.setUpImage(applet, 10);
      verify(image).update(applet, null);
      verify(image).resize(10, 4);
   }

   @Test public void testSetupImagePortrait() {
      imageState.set(image, ColorMode.SHOW_DOMINANT_HUE, 5, 10, 15, 10);
      when(image.getWidth()).thenReturn(8);
      when(image.getHeight()).thenReturn(20);
      imageState.setUpImage(applet, 10);
      verify(image).update(applet, null);
      verify(image).resize(4, 10);
   }

   @Test public void testResetImage() {
      imageState.set(image, ColorMode.SHOW_DOMINANT_HUE, 5, 10, 15, 10);
      imageState.resetImage(applet, 10);
      assertState(ColorMode.COLOR_FILTER, 0, 0, 0, 5);
   }
}
```

Notice that:
- We exposed a protected initialization method set for testing that helps us quickly get the system under test into a specific state.
- We mock PApplet, ColorHelper, and IFAImage (created expressly for this purpose).
- This time we use a helper (assertState()) to simplify asserting the state of the image.

Measuring test coverage

I use EclEmma[24] to measure test coverage within Eclipse. Overall for the app we have 81% test coverage, with none of ImageFilterApp covered, 94.8% for ImageState, and 100% for ColorHelper.

ImageFilterApp

This is where everything is tied together, but we want as little as possible here. The App is hard to unit test (much of it is layout), but because we've pushed so much of the app's functionality into our own tested classes, we're able to assure ourselves that the important parts are working as intended.

We set the size of the app, and do the layout. (These things are verified by running the app and making sure it looks okay — no matter how good the test coverage, this step should not be skipped!)

```
package com.catehuston.imagefilter.app;

import java.io.File;

import processing.core.PApplet;

import com.catehuston.imagefilter.color.ColorHelper;
import com.catehuston.imagefilter.color.PixelColorHelper;
import com.catehuston.imagefilter.model.ImageState;

@SuppressWarnings("serial")
public class ImageFilterApp extends PApplet {

    static final String INSTRUCTIONS = "...";

    static final int FILTER_HEIGHT = 2;
    static final int FILTER_INCREMENT = 5;
    static final int HUE_INCREMENT = 2;
    static final int HUE_RANGE = 100;
    static final int IMAGE_MAX = 640;
    static final int RGB_COLOR_RANGE = 100;
    static final int SIDE_BAR_PADDING = 10;
    static final int SIDE_BAR_WIDTH = RGB_COLOR_RANGE + 2 * SIDE_BAR_PADDING + 50;

    private ImageState imageState;

    boolean redrawImage = true;

    @Override
```

---

[24]http://www.eclemma.org/installation.html\#marketplace

```
public void setup() {
  noLoop();
  imageState = new ImageState(new ColorHelper(new PixelColorHelper()));

  // Set up the view.
  size(IMAGE_MAX + SIDE_BAR_WIDTH, IMAGE_MAX);
  background(0);

  chooseFile();
}

@Override
public void draw() {
  // Draw image.
  if (imageState.image().image() != null && redrawImage) {
    background(0);
    drawImage();
  }

  colorMode(RGB, RGB_COLOR_RANGE);
  fill(0);
  rect(IMAGE_MAX, 0, SIDE_BAR_WIDTH, IMAGE_MAX);
  stroke(RGB_COLOR_RANGE);
  line(IMAGE_MAX, 0, IMAGE_MAX, IMAGE_MAX);

  // Draw red line
  int x = IMAGE_MAX + SIDE_BAR_PADDING;
  int y = 2 * SIDE_BAR_PADDING;
  stroke(RGB_COLOR_RANGE, 0, 0);
  line(x, y, x + RGB_COLOR_RANGE, y);
  line(x + imageState.redFilter(), y - FILTER_HEIGHT,
      x + imageState.redFilter(), y + FILTER_HEIGHT);

  // Draw green line
  y += 2 * SIDE_BAR_PADDING;
  stroke(0, RGB_COLOR_RANGE, 0);
  line(x, y, x + RGB_COLOR_RANGE, y);
  line(x + imageState.greenFilter(), y - FILTER_HEIGHT,
      x + imageState.greenFilter(), y + FILTER_HEIGHT);

  // Draw blue line
  y += 2 * SIDE_BAR_PADDING;
  stroke(0, 0, RGB_COLOR_RANGE);
  line(x, y, x + RGB_COLOR_RANGE, y);
  line(x + imageState.blueFilter(), y - FILTER_HEIGHT,
      x + imageState.blueFilter(), y + FILTER_HEIGHT);

  // Draw white line.
  y += 2 * SIDE_BAR_PADDING;
  stroke(HUE_RANGE);
  line(x, y, x + 100, y);
```

```
    line(x + imageState.hueTolerance(), y - FILTER_HEIGHT,
        x + imageState.hueTolerance(), y + FILTER_HEIGHT);

    y += 4 * SIDE_BAR_PADDING;
    fill(RGB_COLOR_RANGE);
    text(INSTRUCTIONS, x, y);
    updatePixels();
}

// Callback for selectInput(), has to be public to be found.
public void fileSelected(File file) {
  if (file == null) {
    println("User hit cancel.");
  } else {
    imageState.setFilepath(file.getAbsolutePath());
    imageState.setUpImage(this, IMAGE_MAX);
    redrawImage = true;
    redraw();
  }
}

private void drawImage() {
  imageMode(CENTER);
  imageState.updateImage(this, HUE_RANGE, RGB_COLOR_RANGE, IMAGE_MAX);
  image(imageState.image().image(), IMAGE_MAX/2, IMAGE_MAX/2,
            imageState.image().getWidth(), imageState.image().getHeight());
  redrawImage = false;
}

@Override
public void keyPressed() {
  switch(key) {
  case 'c':
    chooseFile();
    break;
  case 'p':
    redrawImage = true;
    break;
  case ' ':
    imageState.resetImage(this, IMAGE_MAX);
    redrawImage = true;
    break;
  }
  imageState.processKeyPress(key, FILTER_INCREMENT, RGB_COLOR_RANGE,
            HUE_INCREMENT, HUE_RANGE);
  redraw();
}

private void chooseFile() {
  // Choose the file.
  selectInput("Select a file to process:", "fileSelected");
```

```
    }
}
```

Notice that:

- Our implementation extends `PApplet`.
- Most work is done in `ImageState`.
- `fileSelected()` is the callback for `selectInput()`.
- `static final` constants are defined up at the top.

11.9   The Value of Prototyping

In real world programming, we spend a lot of time on productionisation work. Making things look just so. Maintaining 99.9% uptime. We spend more time on corner cases than refining algorithms.

These constraints and requirements are important for our users. However there's also space for freeing ourselves from them to play and explore.

Eventually, I decided to port this to a native mobile app. Processing has an Android library, but as many mobile developers do, I opted to go iOS first. I had years of iOS experience, although I'd done little with CoreGraphics, but I don't think even if I had had this idea initially, I would have been able to build it straight away on iOS. The platform forced me to operate in the RGB color space, and made it hard to extract the pixels from the image (hello, C). Memory and waiting was a major risk.

There were exhilarating moments, when it worked for the first time. When it first ran on my device... without crashing. When I optimized memory usage by 66% and cut seconds off the runtime. And there were large periods of time locked away in a dark room, cursing intermittently.

Because I had my prototype, I could explain to my business partner and our designer what I was thinking and what the app would do. It meant I deeply understood how it would work, and it was just a question of making it work nicely on this other platform. I knew what I was aiming for, so at the end of a long day shut away fighting with it and feeling like I had little to show for it I kept going... and hit an exhilarating moment and milestone the following morning.

So, how do you find the dominant color in an image? There's an app for that: Show & Hide[25].

---

[25]http://showandhide.com

## chapter 12

A Python Interpreter Written in Python

Allison Kaptur

12.1   Introduction

Byterun is a Python interpreter implemented in Python. Through my work on Byterun, I was surprised and delighted to discover that the fundamental structure of the Python interpreter fits easily into the 500-line size restriction. This chapter will walk through the structure of the interpreter and give you enough context to explore it further. The goal is not to explain everything there is to know about interpreters—like so many interesting areas of programming and computer science, you could devote years to developing a deep understanding of the topic.

Byterun was written by Ned Batchelder and myself, building on the work of Paul Swartz. Its structure is similar to the primary implementation of Python, CPython, so understanding Byterun will help you understand interpreters in general and the CPython interpreter in particular. (If you don't know which Python you're using, it's probably CPython.) Despite its short length, Byterun is capable of running most simple Python programs[1].

A Python Interpreter

Before we begin, let's narrow down what we mean by "a Python interpreter". The word "interpreter" can be used in a variety of different ways when discussing Python. Sometimes interpreter refers to the Python REPL, the interactive prompt you get by typing `python` at the command line. Sometimes people use "the Python interpreter" more or less interchangeably with "Python" to talk about executing Python code from start to finish. In this chapter, "interpreter" has a more narrow meaning: it's the last step in the process of executing a Python program.

Before the interpreter takes over, Python performs three other steps: lexing, parsing, and compiling. Together, these steps transform the programmer's source code from lines of text into structured *code objects* containing instructions that the interpreter can understand. The interpreter's job is to take these code objects and follow the instructions.

You may be surprised to hear that compiling is a step in executing Python code at all. Python is often called an "interpreted" language like Ruby or Perl, as opposed to a "compiled" language like C or Rust. However, this terminology isn't as precise as it may seem. Most interpreted languages, including Python, do involve a compilation step. The reason Python is called "interpreted" is that the compilation step does relatively less work (and the interpreter does relatively more) than in a

---

[1]This chapter is based on bytecode produced by Python 3.5 or earlier, as there were some changes to the bytecode specification in Python 3.6.

compiled language. As we'll see later in the chapter, the Python compiler has much less information about the behavior of a program than a C compiler does.

A Python Python Interpreter

Byterun is a Python interpreter written in Python. This may strike you as odd, but it's no more odd than writing a C compiler in C. (Indeed, the widely used C compiler gcc is written in C.) You could write a Python interpreter in almost any language.

Writing a Python interpreter in Python has both advantages and disadvantages. The biggest disadvantage is speed: executing code via Byterun is much slower than executing it in CPython, where the interpreter is written in C and carefully optimized. However, Byterun was designed originally as a learning exercise, so speed is not important to us. The biggest advantage to using Python is that we can more easily implement *just* the interpreter, and not the rest of the Python run-time, particularly the object system. For example, Byterun can fall back to "real" Python when it needs to create a class. Another advantage is that Byterun is easy to understand, partly because it's written in a high-level language (Python!) that many people find easy to read. (We also exclude interpreter optimizations in Byterun—once again favoring clarity and simplicity over speed.)

12.2   Building an Interpreter

Before we start to look at the code of Byterun, we need some higher-level context on the structure of the interpreter. How does the Python interpreter work?

The Python interpreter is a *virtual machine*, meaning that it is software that emulates a physical computer. This particular virtual machine is a stack machine: it manipulates several stacks to perform its operations (as contrasted with a register machine, which writes to and reads from particular memory locations).

The Python interpreter is a *bytecode interpreter*: its input is instruction sets called *bytecode*. When you write Python, the lexer, parser, and compiler generate code objects for the interpreter to operate on. Each code object contains a set of instructions to be executed—that's the bytecode—plus other information that the interpreter will need. Bytecode is an *intermediate representation* of Python code: it expresses the source code that you wrote in a way the interpreter can understand. It's analogous to the way that assembly language serves as an intermediate representation between C code and a piece of hardware.

A Tiny Interpreter

To make this concrete, let's start with a very minimal interpreter. This interpreter can only add numbers, and it understands just three instructions. All code it can execute consists of these three instructions in different combinations. The three instructions are these:

- LOAD_VALUE
- ADD_TWO_VALUES
- PRINT_ANSWER

Since we're not concerned with the lexer, parser, and compiler in this chapter, it doesn't matter how the instruction sets are produced. You can imagine writing 7 + 5 and having a compiler emit a combination of these three instructions. Or, if you have the right compiler, you can write Lisp syntax that's turned into the same combination of instructions. The interpreter doesn't care. All that matters is that our interpreter is given a well-formed arrangement of the instructions.

Suppose that

```
7 + 5
```

produces this instruction set:

```
what_to_execute = {
    "instructions": [("LOAD_VALUE", 0),  # the first number
                     ("LOAD_VALUE", 1),  # the second number
                     ("ADD_TWO_VALUES", None),
                     ("PRINT_ANSWER", None)],
    "numbers": [7, 5] }
```

The Python interpreter is a *stack machine*, so it must manipulate stacks to add two numbers (Figure 12.1.) The interpreter will begin by executing the first instruction, LOAD_VALUE, and pushing the first number onto the stack. Next it will push the second number onto the stack. For the third instruction, ADD_TWO_VALUES, it will pop both numbers off, add them together, and push the result onto the stack. Finally, it will pop the answer back off the stack and print it.

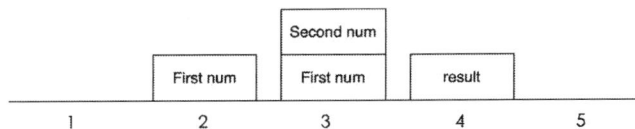

Figure 12.1: A stack machine

The LOAD_VALUE instruction tells the interpreter to push a number on to the stack, but the instruction alone doesn't specify which number. Each instruction needs an extra piece of information, telling the interpreter where to find the number to load. So our instruction set has two pieces: the instructions themselves, plus a list of constants the instructions will need. (In Python, what we're calling "instructions" is the bytecode, and the "what to execute" object below is the *code object*.)

Why not just put the numbers directly in the instructions? Imagine if we were adding strings together instead of numbers. We wouldn't want to have the strings stuffed in with the instructions, since they could be arbitrarily large. This design also means we can have just one copy of each object that we need, so for example to add 7 + 7, "numbers" could be just [7].

You may be wondering why instructions other than ADD_TWO_VALUES were needed at all. Indeed, for the simple case of adding two numbers, the example is a little contrived. However, this instruction is a building block for more complex programs. For example, with just the instructions we've defined so far, we can already add together three values—or any number of values—given the right set of these instructions. The stack provides a clean way to keep track of the state of the interpreter, and it will support more complexity as we go along.

Now let's start to write the interpreter itself. The interpreter object has a stack, which we'll represent with a list. The object also has a method describing how to execute each instruction. For example, for LOAD_VALUE, the interpreter will push the value onto the stack.

```
class Interpreter:
    def __init__(self):
        self.stack = []
```

```
def LOAD_VALUE(self, number):
    self.stack.append(number)

def PRINT_ANSWER(self):
    answer = self.stack.pop()
    print(answer)

def ADD_TWO_VALUES(self):
    first_num = self.stack.pop()
    second_num = self.stack.pop()
    total = first_num + second_num
    self.stack.append(total)
```

These three functions implement the three instructions our interpreter understands. The interpreter needs one more piece: a way to tie everything together and actually execute it. This method, run_code, takes the what_to_execute dictionary defined above as an argument. It loops over each instruction, processes the arguments to that instruction if there are any, and then calls the corresponding method on the interpreter object.

```
def run_code(self, what_to_execute):
    instructions = what_to_execute["instructions"]
    numbers = what_to_execute["numbers"]
    for each_step in instructions:
        instruction, argument = each_step
        if instruction == "LOAD_VALUE":
            number = numbers[argument]
            self.LOAD_VALUE(number)
        elif instruction == "ADD_TWO_VALUES":
            self.ADD_TWO_VALUES()
        elif instruction == "PRINT_ANSWER":
            self.PRINT_ANSWER()
```

To test it out, we can create an instance of the object and then call the run_code method with the instruction set for adding 7 + 5 defined above.

```
interpreter = Interpreter()
interpreter.run_code(what_to_execute)
```

Sure enough, it prints the answer: 12.

Although this interpreter is quite limited, this process is almost exactly how the real Python interpreter adds numbers. There are a couple of things to note even in this small example.

First of all, some instructions need arguments. In real Python bytecode, about half of instructions have arguments. The arguments are packed in with the instructions, much like in our example. Notice that the arguments to the *instructions* are different than the arguments to the methods that are called.

Second, notice that the instruction for ADD_TWO_VALUES did not require any arguments. Instead, the values to be added together were popped off the interpreter's stack. This is the defining feature of a stack-based interpreter.

Remember that given valid instruction sets, without any changes to our interpreter, we can add more than two numbers at a time. Consider the instruction set below. What do you expect to happen? If you had a friendly compiler, what code could you write to generate this instruction set?

```
what_to_execute = {
    "instructions": [("LOAD_VALUE", 0),
                     ("LOAD_VALUE", 1),
                     ("ADD_TWO_VALUES", None),
                     ("LOAD_VALUE", 2),
                     ("ADD_TWO_VALUES", None),
                     ("PRINT_ANSWER", None)],
    "numbers": [7, 5, 8] }
```

At this point, we can begin to see how this structure is extensible: we can add methods on the interpreter object that describe many more operations (as long as we have a compiler to hand us well-formed instruction sets).

Variables

Next let's add variables to our interpreter. Variables require an instruction for storing the value of a variable, STORE_NAME; an instruction for retrieving it, LOAD_NAME; and a mapping from variable names to values. For now, we'll ignore namespaces and scoping, so we can store the variable mapping on the interpreter object itself. Finally, we'll have to make sure that what_to_execute has a list of the variable names, in addition to its list of constants.

```
>>> def s():
...     a = 1
...     b = 2
...     print(a + b)
# a friendly compiler transforms 's' into:
    what_to_execute = {
        "instructions": [("LOAD_VALUE", 0),
                         ("STORE_NAME", 0),
                         ("LOAD_VALUE", 1),
                         ("STORE_NAME", 1),
                         ("LOAD_NAME", 0),
                         ("LOAD_NAME", 1),
                         ("ADD_TWO_VALUES", None),
                         ("PRINT_ANSWER", None)],
        "numbers": [1, 2],
        "names":   ["a", "b"] }
```

Our new implementation is below. To keep track of what names are bound to what values, we'll add an environment dictionary to the __init__ method. We'll also add STORE_NAME and LOAD_NAME. These methods first look up the variable name in question and then use the dictionary to store or retrieve its value.

The arguments to an instruction can now mean two different things: They can either be an index into the "numbers" list, or they can be an index into the "names" list. The interpreter knows which it should be by checking what instruction it's executing. We'll break out this logic—and the mapping of instructions to what their arguments mean—into a separate method.

```
class Interpreter:
    def __init__(self):
        self.stack = []
        self.environment = {}

    def STORE_NAME(self, name):
        val = self.stack.pop()
        self.environment[name] = val

    def LOAD_NAME(self, name):
        val = self.environment[name]
        self.stack.append(val)

    def parse_argument(self, instruction, argument, what_to_execute):
        """ Understand what the argument to each instruction means."""
        numbers = ["LOAD_VALUE"]
        names = ["LOAD_NAME", "STORE_NAME"]

        if instruction in numbers:
            argument = what_to_execute["numbers"][argument]
        elif instruction in names:
            argument = what_to_execute["names"][argument]

        return argument

    def run_code(self, what_to_execute):
        instructions = what_to_execute["instructions"]
        for each_step in instructions:
            instruction, argument = each_step
            argument = self.parse_argument(instruction, argument, what_to_execute)

            if instruction == "LOAD_VALUE":
                self.LOAD_VALUE(argument)
            elif instruction == "ADD_TWO_VALUES":
                self.ADD_TWO_VALUES()
            elif instruction == "PRINT_ANSWER":
                self.PRINT_ANSWER()
            elif instruction == "STORE_NAME":
                self.STORE_NAME(argument)
            elif instruction == "LOAD_NAME":
                self.LOAD_NAME(argument)
```

Even with just five instructions, the run_code method is starting to get tedious. If we kept this structure, we'd need one branch of the if statement for each instruction. Here, we can make use of Python's dynamic method lookup. We'll always define a method called FOO to execute the instruction called FOO, so we can use Python's getattr function to look up the method on the fly instead of using the big if statement. The run_code method then looks like this:

```
def execute(self, what_to_execute):
    instructions = what_to_execute["instructions"]
    for each_step in instructions:
        instruction, argument = each_step
        argument = self.parse_argument(instruction, argument, what_to_execute)
        bytecode_method = getattr(self, instruction)
        if argument is None:
            bytecode_method()
        else:
            bytecode_method(argument)
```

12.3   Real Python Bytecode

At this point, we'll abandon our toy instruction sets and switch to real Python bytecode. The structure of bytecode is similar to our toy interpreter's verbose instruction sets, except that it uses one byte instead of a long name to identify each instruction. To understand this structure, we'll walk through the bytecode of a short function. Consider the example below:

```
>>> def cond():
...     x = 3
...     if x < 5:
...         return 'yes'
...     else:
...         return 'no'
...
```

Python exposes a boatload of its internals at run time, and we can access them right from the REPL. For the function object cond, cond.__code__ is the code object associated it, and cond.__code__.co_code is the bytecode. There's almost never a good reason to use these attributes directly when you're writing Python code, but they do allow us to get up to all sorts of mischief—and to look at the internals in order to understand them.

```
>>> cond.__code__.co_code  # the bytecode as raw bytes
b'd\x01\x00}\x00\x00|\x00\x00d\x02\x00k\x00\x00r\x16\x00d\x03\x00Sd\x04\x00Sd\x00
   \x00S'
>>> list(cond.__code__.co_code)  # the bytecode as numbers
[100, 1, 0, 125, 0, 0, 124, 0, 0, 100, 2, 0, 107, 0, 0, 114, 22, 0, 100, 3, 0, 83,
 100, 4, 0, 83, 100, 0, 0, 83]
```

When we just print the bytecode, it looks unintelligible—all we can tell is that it's a series of bytes. Luckily, there's a powerful tool we can use to understand it: the dis module in the Python standard library.

dis is a bytecode disassembler. A disassembler takes low-level code that is written for machines, like assembly code or bytecode, and prints it in a human-readable way. When we run dis.dis, it outputs an explanation of the bytecode it has passed.

```
>>> dis.dis(cond)
  2           0 LOAD_CONST               1 (3)
              3 STORE_FAST               0 (x)

  3           6 LOAD_FAST                0 (x)
              9 LOAD_CONST               2 (5)
             12 COMPARE_OP               0 (<)
             15 POP_JUMP_IF_FALSE       22

  4          18 LOAD_CONST               3 ('yes')
             21 RETURN_VALUE

  6     >>   22 LOAD_CONST               4 ('no')
             25 RETURN_VALUE
             26 LOAD_CONST               0 (None)
             29 RETURN_VALUE
```

What does all this mean? Let's look at the first instruction LOAD_CONST as an example. The number in the first column (2) shows the line number in our Python source code. The second column is an index into the bytecode, telling us that the LOAD_CONST instruction appears at position zero. The third column is the instruction itself, mapped to its human-readable name. The fourth column, when present, is the argument to that instruction. The fifth column, when present, is a hint about what the argument means.

Consider the first few bytes of this bytecode: [100, 1, 0, 125, 0, 0]. These six bytes represent two instructions with their arguments. We can use dis.opname, a mapping from bytes to intelligible strings, to find out what instructions 100 and 125 map to:

```
>>> dis.opname[100]
'LOAD_CONST'
>>> dis.opname[125]
'STORE_FAST'
```

The second and third bytes—1, 0—are arguments to LOAD_CONST, while the fifth and sixth bytes—0, 0—are arguments to STORE_FAST. Just like in our toy example, LOAD_CONST needs to know where to find its constant to load, and STORE_FAST needs to find the name to store. (Python's LOAD_CONST is the same as our toy interpreter's LOAD_VALUE, and LOAD_FAST is the same as LOAD_NAME.) So these six bytes represent the first line of code, x = 3. (Why use two bytes for each argument? If Python used just one byte to locate constants and names instead of two, you could only have 256 names/constants associated with a single code object. Using two bytes, you can have up to 256 squared, or 65,536.)

Conditionals and Loops

So far, the interpreter has executed code simply by stepping through the instructions one by one. This is a problem; often, we want to execute certain instructions many times, or skip them under certain conditions. To allow us to write loops and if statements in our code, the interpreter must be able to jump around in the instruction set. In a sense, Python handles loops and conditionals with GOTO statements in the bytecode! Look at the disassembly of the function cond again:

```
>>> dis.dis(cond)
  2           0 LOAD_CONST               1 (3)
              3 STORE_FAST               0 (x)

  3           6 LOAD_FAST                0 (x)
              9 LOAD_CONST               2 (5)
             12 COMPARE_OP               0 (<)
             15 POP_JUMP_IF_FALSE       22

  4          18 LOAD_CONST               3 ('yes')
             21 RETURN_VALUE

  6     >>   22 LOAD_CONST               4 ('no')
             25 RETURN_VALUE
             26 LOAD_CONST               0 (None)
             29 RETURN_VALUE
```

The conditional if x < 5 on line 3 of the code is compiled into four instructions: LOAD_FAST, LOAD_CONST, COMPARE_OP, and POP_JUMP_IF_FALSE. x < 5 generates code to load x, load 5, and compare the two values. The instruction POP_JUMP_IF_FALSE is responsible for implementing the if. This instruction will pop the top value off the interpreter's stack. If the value is true, then nothing happens. (The value can be "truthy"—it doesn't have to be the literal True object.) If the value is false, then the interpreter will jump to another instruction.

The instruction to land on is called the jump target, and it's provided as the argument to the POP_JUMP instruction. Here, the jump target is 22. The instruction at index 22 is LOAD_CONST on line 6. (dis marks jump targets with >>.) If the result of x < 5 is False, then the interpreter will jump straight to line 6 (return "no"), skipping line 4 (return "yes"). Thus, the interpreter uses jump instructions to selectively skip over parts of the instruction set.

Python loops also rely on jumping. In the bytecode below, notice that the line while x < 5 generates almost identical bytecode to if x < 10. In both cases, the comparison is calculated and then POP_JUMP_IF_FALSE controls which instruction is executed next. At the end of line 4—the end of the loop's body—the instruction JUMP_ABSOLUTE always sends the interpreter back to instruction 9 at the top of the loop. When x < 5 becomes false, then POP_JUMP_IF_FALSE jumps the interpreter past the end of the loop, to instruction 34.

```
>>> def loop():
...         x = 1
...     while x < 5:
...             x = x + 1
...     return x
...
>>> dis.dis(loop)
  2           0 LOAD_CONST               1 (1)
              3 STORE_FAST               0 (x)

  3           6 SETUP_LOOP              26 (to 35)
        >>    9 LOAD_FAST                0 (x)
             12 LOAD_CONST               2 (5)
             15 COMPARE_OP               0 (<)
             18 POP_JUMP_IF_FALSE       34
```

```
4          21 LOAD_FAST            0 (x)
           24 LOAD_CONST           1 (1)
           27 BINARY_ADD
           28 STORE_FAST           0 (x)
           31 JUMP_ABSOLUTE        9
     >>    34 POP_BLOCK

5    >>    35 LOAD_FAST            0 (x)
           38 RETURN_VALUE
```

Explore Bytecode

I encourage you to try running dis.dis on functions you write. Some questions to explore:

- What's the difference between a for loop and a while loop to the Python interpreter?
- How can you write different functions that generate identical bytecode?
- How does elif work? What about list comprehensions?

12.4   Frames

So far, we've learned that the Python virtual machine is a stack machine. It steps and jumps through instructions, pushing and popping values on and off a stack. There are still some gaps in our mental model, though. In the examples above, the last instruction is RETURN_VALUE, which corresponds to the return statement in the code. But where does the instruction return to?

To answer this question, we must add a layer of complexity: the frame. A frame is a collection of information and context for a chunk of code. Frames are created and destroyed on the fly as your Python code executes. There's one frame corresponding to each *call* of a function—so while each frame has one code object associated with it, a code object can have many frames. If you had a function that called itself recursively ten times, you'd have eleven frames—one for each level of recursion and one for the module you started from. In general, there's a frame for each scope in a Python program. For example, each module, each function call, and each class definition has a frame.

Frames live on the *call stack*, a completely different stack from the one we've been discussing so far. (The call stack is the stack you're most familiar with already—you've seen it printed out in the tracebacks of exceptions. Each line in a traceback starting with "File 'program.py', line 10" corresponds to one frame on the call stack.) The stack we've been examining—the one the interpreter is manipulating while it executes bytecode—we'll call the *data stack*. There's also a third stack, called the *block stack*. Blocks are used for certain kinds of control flow, particularly looping and exception handling. Each frame on the call stack has its own data stack and block stack.

Let's make this concrete with an example. Suppose the Python interpreter is currently executing the line marked 3 below. The interpreter is in the middle of a call to foo, which is in turn calling bar. The diagram shows a schematic of the call stack of frames, the block stacks, and the data stacks. (This code is written like a REPL session, so we've first defined the needed functions.) At the moment we're interested in, the interpreter is executing foo(), at the bottom, which then reaches in to the body of foo and then up into bar.

```
>>> def bar(y):
...     z = y + 3      # <--- (3) ... and the interpreter is here.
...     return z
...
>>> def foo():
...     a = 1
...     b = 2
...     return a + bar(b) # <--- (2) ... which is returning a call to bar ...
...
>>> foo()                # <--- (1) We're in the middle of a call to foo ...
3
```

	bar Frame (newest)	Block stack: []
Call		Data stack: [2, 3]
	foo Frame	Block stack: []
Stack		Data stack: [1]
	main (module) Frame (oldest)	Block stack: []
		Data stack: []

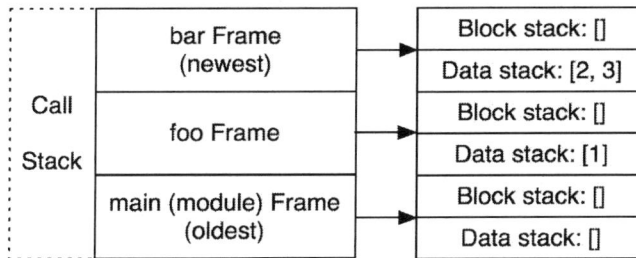

Figure 12.2: The call stack

At this point, the interpreter is in the middle of the function call to bar. There are three frames on the call stack: one for the module level, one for the function foo, and one for bar (Figure 12.2.) Once bar returns, the frame associated with it is popped off the call stack and discarded.

The bytecode instruction RETURN_VALUE tells the interpreter to pass a value between frames. First it will pop the top value off the data stack of the top frame on the call stack. Then it pops the entire frame off the call stack and throws it away. Finally, the value is pushed onto the data stack on the next frame down.

When Ned Batchelder and I were working on Byterun, for a long time we had a significant error in our implementation. Instead of having one data stack on each frame, we had just one data stack on the entire virtual machine. We had dozens of tests made up of little snippets of Python code which we ran through Byterun and through the real Python interpreter to make sure the same thing happened in both interpreters. Nearly all of these tests were passing. The only thing we couldn't get working was generators. Finally, reading the CPython code more carefully, we realized the mistake[2]. Moving a data stack onto each frame fixed the problem.

Looking back on this bug, I was amazed at how little of Python relied on each frame having a different data stack. Nearly all operations in the Python interpreter carefully clean up the data stack, so the fact that the frames were sharing the same stack didn't matter. In the example above, when bar finishes executing, it'll leave its data stack empty. Even if foo shared the same stack, the values would be lower down. However, with generators, a key feature is the ability to pause a frame, return to some other frame, and then return to the generator frame later and have it be in exactly the same state that you left it.

---

[2]My thanks to Michael Arntzenius for his insight on this bug.

12.5   Byterun

We now have enough context about the Python interpreter to begin examining Byterun.

There are four kinds of objects in Byterun:

- A VirtualMachine class, which manages the highest-level structure, particularly the call stack of frames, and contains a mapping of instructions to operations. This is a more complex version of the Intepreter object above.
- A Frame class. Every Frame instance has one code object and manages a few other necessary bits of state, particularly the global and local namespaces, a reference to the calling frame, and the last bytecode instruction executed.
- A Function class, which will be used in place of real Python functions. Recall that calling a function creates a new frame in the interpreter. We implement Function so that we control the creation of new Frames.
- A Block class, which just wraps the three attributes of blocks. (The details of blocks aren't central to the Python interpreter, so we won't spend much time on them, but they're included here so that Byterun can run real Python code.)

The VirtualMachine Class

Only one instance of VirtualMachine will be created each time the program is run, because we only have one Python interpreter. VirtualMachine stores the call stack, the exception state, and return values while they're being passed between frames. The entry point for executing code is the method run_code, which takes a compiled code object as an argument. It starts by setting up and running a frame. This frame may create other frames; the call stack will grow and shrink as the program executes. When the first frame eventually returns, execution is finished.

```
class VirtualMachineError(Exception):
    pass

class VirtualMachine(object):
    def __init__(self):
        self.frames = []    # The call stack of frames.
        self.frame = None   # The current frame.
        self.return_value = None
        self.last_exception = None

    def run_code(self, code, global_names=None, local_names=None):
        """ An entry point to execute code using the virtual machine."""
        frame = self.make_frame(code, global_names=global_names,
                                local_names=local_names)
        self.run_frame(frame)
```

The Frame Class

Next we'll write the Frame object. The frame is a collection of attributes with no methods. As mentioned above, the attributes include the code object created by the compiler; the local, global, and builtin namespaces; a reference to the previous frame; a data stack; a block stack; and the last instruction executed. (We have to do a little extra work to get to the builtin namespace because

Python treats this namespace differently in different modules; this detail is not important to the virtual machine.)

```python
class Frame(object):
    def __init__(self, code_obj, global_names, local_names, prev_frame):
        self.code_obj = code_obj
        self.global_names = global_names
        self.local_names = local_names
        self.prev_frame = prev_frame
        self.stack = []
        if prev_frame:
            self.builtin_names = prev_frame.builtin_names
        else:
            self.builtin_names = local_names['__builtins__']
            if hasattr(self.builtin_names, '__dict__'):
                self.builtin_names = self.builtin_names.__dict__

        self.last_instruction = 0
        self.block_stack = []
```

Next, we'll add frame manipulation to the virtual machine. There are three helper functions for frames: one to create new frames (which is responsible for sorting out the namespaces for the new frame) and one each to push and pop frames on and off the frame stack. A fourth function, run_frame, does the main work of executing a frame. We'll come back to this soon.

```python
class VirtualMachine(object):
    [... snip ...]

    # Frame manipulation
    def make_frame(self, code, callargs={}, global_names=None, local_names=None):
        if global_names is not None and local_names is not None:
            local_names = global_names
        elif self.frames:
            global_names = self.frame.global_names
            local_names = {}
        else:
            global_names = local_names = {
                '__builtins__': __builtins__,
                '__name__': '__main__',
                '__doc__': None,
                '__package__': None,
            }
        local_names.update(callargs)
        frame = Frame(code, global_names, local_names, self.frame)
        return frame

    def push_frame(self, frame):
        self.frames.append(frame)
        self.frame = frame

    def pop_frame(self):
```

```
        self.frames.pop()
        if self.frames:
            self.frame = self.frames[-1]
        else:
            self.frame = None

    def run_frame(self):
        pass
        # we'll come back to this shortly
```

The Function Class

The implementation of the Function object is somewhat twisty, and most of the details aren't critical to understanding the interpreter. The important thing to notice is that calling a function—invoking the __call__ method—creates a new Frame object and starts running it.

```
class Function(object):
    """
    Create a realistic function object, defining the things the interpreter expects.
    """
    __slots__ = [
        'func_code', 'func_name', 'func_defaults', 'func_globals',
        'func_locals', 'func_dict', 'func_closure',
        '__name__', '__dict__', '__doc__',
        '_vm', '_func',
    ]

    def __init__(self, name, code, globs, defaults, closure, vm):
        """You don't need to follow this closely to understand the interpreter."""
        self._vm = vm
        self.func_code = code
        self.func_name = self.__name__ = name or code.co_name
        self.func_defaults = tuple(defaults)
        self.func_globals = globs
        self.func_locals = self._vm.frame.f_locals
        self.__dict__ = {}
        self.func_closure = closure
        self.__doc__ = code.co_consts[0] if code.co_consts else None

        # Sometimes, we need a real Python function.  This is for that.
        kw = {
            'argdefs': self.func_defaults,
        }
        if closure:
            kw['closure'] = tuple(make_cell(0) for _ in closure)
        self._func = types.FunctionType(code, globs, **kw)

    def __call__(self, *args, **kwargs):
        """When calling a Function, make a new frame and run it."""
        callargs = inspect.getcallargs(self._func, *args, **kwargs)
        # Use callargs to provide a mapping of arguments: values to pass into the new
```

```
        # frame.
        frame = self._vm.make_frame(
            self.func_code, callargs, self.func_globals, {}
        )
        return self._vm.run_frame(frame)

def make_cell(value):
    """Create a real Python closure and grab a cell."""
    # Thanks to Alex Gaynor for help with this bit of twistiness.
    fn = (lambda x: lambda: x)(value)
    return fn.__closure__[0]
```

Next, back on the `VirtualMachine` object, we'll add some helper methods for data stack manipulation. The bytecodes that manipulate the stack always operate on the current frame's data stack. This will make our implementations of POP_TOP, LOAD_FAST, and all the other instructions that touch the stack more readable.

```
class VirtualMachine(object):
    [... snip ...]

    # Data stack manipulation
    def top(self):
        return self.frame.stack[-1]

    def pop(self):
        return self.frame.stack.pop()

    def push(self, *vals):
        self.frame.stack.extend(vals)

    def popn(self, n):
        """Pop a number of values from the value stack.
        A list of 'n' values is returned, the deepest value first.
        """
        if n:
            ret = self.frame.stack[-n:]
            self.frame.stack[-n:] = []
            return ret
        else:
            return []
```

Before we get to running a frame, we need two more methods.

The first, `parse_byte_and_args`, takes a bytecode, checks if it has arguments, and parses the arguments if so. This method also updates the frame's attribute `last_instruction`, a reference to the last instruction executed. A single instruction is one byte long if it doesn't have an argument, and three bytes if it does have an argument; the last two bytes are the argument. The meaning of the argument to each instruction depends on which instruction it is. For example, as mentioned above, for POP_JUMP_IF_FALSE, the argument to the instruction is the jump target. For BUILD_LIST, it is the number of elements in the list. For LOAD_CONST, it's an index into the list of constants.

Some instructions use simple numbers as their arguments. For others, the virtual machine has to do a little work to discover what the arguments mean. The `dis` module in the standard library exposes a cheatsheet explaining what arguments have what meaning, which makes our code more compact. For example, the list dis.hasname tells us that the arguments to LOAD_NAME, IMPORT_NAME, LOAD_GLOBAL, and nine other instructions have the same meaning: for these instructions, the argument represents an index into the list of names on the code object.

```
class VirtualMachine(object):
    [... snip ...]

    def parse_byte_and_args(self):
        f = self.frame
        opoffset = f.last_instruction
        byteCode = f.code_obj.co_code[opoffset]
        f.last_instruction += 1
        byte_name = dis.opname[byteCode]
        if byteCode >= dis.HAVE_ARGUMENT:
            # index into the bytecode
            arg = f.code_obj.co_code[f.last_instruction:f.last_instruction+2]
            f.last_instruction += 2    # advance the instruction pointer
            arg_val = arg[0] + (arg[1] * 256)
            if byteCode in dis.hasconst:    # Look up a constant
                arg = f.code_obj.co_consts[arg_val]
            elif byteCode in dis.hasname:   # Look up a name
                arg = f.code_obj.co_names[arg_val]
            elif byteCode in dis.haslocal:  # Look up a local name
                arg = f.code_obj.co_varnames[arg_val]
            elif byteCode in dis.hasjrel:   # Calculate a relative jump
                arg = f.last_instruction + arg_val
            else:
                arg = arg_val
            argument = [arg]
        else:
            argument = []

        return byte_name, argument
```

The next method is dispatch, which looks up the operations for a given instruction and executes them. In the CPython interpreter, this dispatch is done with a giant switch statement that spans 1,500 lines! Luckily, since we're writing Python, we can be more compact. We'll define a method for each byte name and then use getattr to look it up. Like in the toy interpreter above, if our instruction is named FOO_BAR, the corresponding method would be named byte_FOO_BAR. For the moment, we'll leave the content of these methods as a black box. Each bytecode method will return either None or a string, called why, which is an extra piece of state the interpreter needs in some cases. These return values of the individual instruction methods are used only as internal indicators of interpreter state—don't confuse these with return values from executing frames.

```
class VirtualMachine(object):
    [... snip ...]

    def dispatch(self, byte_name, argument):
        """ Dispatch by bytename to the corresponding methods.
        Exceptions are caught and set on the virtual machine."""
```

```python
        # When later unwinding the block stack,
        # we need to keep track of why we are doing it.
        why = None
        try:
            bytecode_fn = getattr(self, 'byte_%s' % byte_name, None)
            if bytecode_fn is None:
                if byte_name.startswith('UNARY_'):
                    self.unaryOperator(byte_name[6:])
                elif byte_name.startswith('BINARY_'):
                    self.binaryOperator(byte_name[7:])
                else:
                    raise VirtualMachineError(
                        "unsupported bytecode type: %s" % byte_name
                    )
            else:
                why = bytecode_fn(*argument)
        except:
            # deal with exceptions encountered while executing the op.
            self.last_exception = sys.exc_info()[:2] + (None,)
            why = 'exception'

        return why

    def run_frame(self, frame):
        """Run a frame until it returns (somehow).
        Exceptions are raised, the return value is returned.
        """
        self.push_frame(frame)
        while True:
            byte_name, arguments = self.parse_byte_and_args()

            why = self.dispatch(byte_name, arguments)

            # Deal with any block management we need to do
            while why and frame.block_stack:
                why = self.manage_block_stack(why)

            if why:
                break

        self.pop_frame()

        if why == 'exception':
            exc, val, tb = self.last_exception
            e = exc(val)
            e.__traceback__ = tb
            raise e

        return self.return_value
```

The `Block` Class

Before we implement the methods for each bytecode instruction, we'll briefly discuss blocks. A block is used for certain kinds of flow control, specifically exception handling and looping. The block is reponsible for making sure that the data stack is in the appropriate state when the operation is finished. For example, in a loop, a special iterator object remains on the stack while the loop is running, but is popped off when it is finished. The interpreter must keep track of whether the loop is continuing or is finished.

To keep track of this extra piece of information, the interpreter sets a flag to indicate its state. We implement this flag as a variable called why, which can be None or one of the strings "continue", "break", "exception", or "return". This indicates what kind of manipulation of the block stack and data stack should happen. To return to the iterator example, if the top of the block stack is a loop block and the why code is continue, the iterator object should remain on the data stack, but if the why code is break, it should be popped off.

The precise details of block manipulation are rather fiddly, and we won't spend more time on this, but interested readers are encouraged to take a careful look.

```python
Block = collections.namedtuple("Block", "type, handler, stack_height")

class VirtualMachine(object):
    [... snip ...]

    # Block stack manipulation
    def push_block(self, b_type, handler=None):
        stack_height = len(self.frame.stack)
        self.frame.block_stack.append(Block(b_type, handler, stack_height))

    def pop_block(self):
        return self.frame.block_stack.pop()

    def unwind_block(self, block):
        """Unwind the values on the data stack corresponding to a given block."""
        if block.type == 'except-handler':
            # The exception itself is on the stack as type, value, and traceback.
            offset = 3
        else:
            offset = 0

        while len(self.frame.stack) > block.level + offset:
            self.pop()

        if block.type == 'except-handler':
            traceback, value, exctype = self.popn(3)
            self.last_exception = exctype, value, traceback

    def manage_block_stack(self, why):
        """ """
        frame = self.frame
        block = frame.block_stack[-1]
        if block.type == 'loop' and why == 'continue':
            self.jump(self.return_value)
```

```
                why = None
                return why

            self.pop_block()
            self.unwind_block(block)

            if block.type == 'loop' and why == 'break':
                why = None
                self.jump(block.handler)
                return why

            if (block.type in ['setup-except', 'finally'] and why == 'exception'):
                self.push_block('except-handler')
                exctype, value, tb = self.last_exception
                self.push(tb, value, exctype)
                self.push(tb, value, exctype) # yes, twice
                why = None
                self.jump(block.handler)
                return why

            elif block.type == 'finally':
                if why in ('return', 'continue'):
                    self.push(self.return_value)

                self.push(why)

                why = None
                self.jump(block.handler)
                return why
        return why
```

12.6   The Instructions

All that's left is to implement the dozens of methods for instructions. The actual instructions are the
least interesting part of the interpreter, so we show only a handful here, but the full implementation
is available on GitHub[3]. (Enough instructions are included here to execute all the code samples that
we disassembled above.)

```
class VirtualMachine(object):
    [... snip ...]

    ## Stack manipulation

    def byte_LOAD_CONST(self, const):
        self.push(const)

    def byte_POP_TOP(self):
        self.pop()
```

---

[3]https://github.com/nedbat/byterun

```
## Names
def byte_LOAD_NAME(self, name):
    frame = self.frame
    if name in frame.f_locals:
        val = frame.f_locals[name]
    elif name in frame.f_globals:
        val = frame.f_globals[name]
    elif name in frame.f_builtins:
        val = frame.f_builtins[name]
    else:
        raise NameError("name '%s' is not defined" % name)
    self.push(val)

def byte_STORE_NAME(self, name):
    self.frame.f_locals[name] = self.pop()

def byte_LOAD_FAST(self, name):
    if name in self.frame.f_locals:
        val = self.frame.f_locals[name]
    else:
        raise UnboundLocalError(
            "local variable '%s' referenced before assignment" % name
        )
    self.push(val)

def byte_STORE_FAST(self, name):
    self.frame.f_locals[name] = self.pop()

def byte_LOAD_GLOBAL(self, name):
    f = self.frame
    if name in f.f_globals:
        val = f.f_globals[name]
    elif name in f.f_builtins:
        val = f.f_builtins[name]
    else:
        raise NameError("global name '%s' is not defined" % name)
    self.push(val)

## Operators

BINARY_OPERATORS = {
    'POWER':    pow,
    'MULTIPLY': operator.mul,
    'FLOOR_DIVIDE': operator.floordiv,
    'TRUE_DIVIDE':  operator.truediv,
    'MODULO':   operator.mod,
    'ADD':      operator.add,
    'SUBTRACT': operator.sub,
    'SUBSCR':   operator.getitem,
    'LSHIFT':   operator.lshift,
```

```python
    'RSHIFT':   operator.rshift,
    'AND':      operator.and_,
    'XOR':      operator.xor,
    'OR':       operator.or_,
}

def binaryOperator(self, op):
    x, y = self.popn(2)
    self.push(self.BINARY_OPERATORS[op](x, y))

COMPARE_OPERATORS = [
    operator.lt,
    operator.le,
    operator.eq,
    operator.ne,
    operator.gt,
    operator.ge,
    lambda x, y: x in y,
    lambda x, y: x not in y,
    lambda x, y: x is y,
    lambda x, y: x is not y,
    lambda x, y: issubclass(x, Exception) and issubclass(x, y),
]

def byte_COMPARE_OP(self, opnum):
    x, y = self.popn(2)
    self.push(self.COMPARE_OPERATORS[opnum](x, y))

## Attributes and indexing

def byte_LOAD_ATTR(self, attr):
    obj = self.pop()
    val = getattr(obj, attr)
    self.push(val)

def byte_STORE_ATTR(self, name):
    val, obj = self.popn(2)
    setattr(obj, name, val)

## Building

def byte_BUILD_LIST(self, count):
    elts = self.popn(count)
    self.push(elts)

def byte_BUILD_MAP(self, size):
    self.push({})

def byte_STORE_MAP(self):
    the_map, val, key = self.popn(3)
    the_map[key] = val
```

```
            self.push(the_map)

    def byte_LIST_APPEND(self, count):
        val = self.pop()
        the_list = self.frame.stack[-count] # peek
        the_list.append(val)

    ## Jumps

    def byte_JUMP_FORWARD(self, jump):
        self.jump(jump)

    def byte_JUMP_ABSOLUTE(self, jump):
        self.jump(jump)

    def byte_POP_JUMP_IF_TRUE(self, jump):
        val = self.pop()
        if val:
            self.jump(jump)

    def byte_POP_JUMP_IF_FALSE(self, jump):
        val = self.pop()
        if not val:
            self.jump(jump)

    ## Blocks

    def byte_SETUP_LOOP(self, dest):
        self.push_block('loop', dest)

    def byte_GET_ITER(self):
        self.push(iter(self.pop()))

    def byte_FOR_ITER(self, jump):
        iterobj = self.top()
        try:
            v = next(iterobj)
            self.push(v)
        except StopIteration:
            self.pop()
            self.jump(jump)

    def byte_BREAK_LOOP(self):
        return 'break'

    def byte_POP_BLOCK(self):
        self.pop_block()

    ## Functions

    def byte_MAKE_FUNCTION(self, argc):
```

```
        name = self.pop()
        code = self.pop()
        defaults = self.popn(argc)
        globs = self.frame.f_globals
        fn = Function(name, code, globs, defaults, None, self)
        self.push(fn)

    def byte_CALL_FUNCTION(self, arg):
        lenKw, lenPos = divmod(arg, 256) # KWargs not supported here
        posargs = self.popn(lenPos)

        func = self.pop()
        frame = self.frame
        retval = func(*posargs)
        self.push(retval)

    def byte_RETURN_VALUE(self):
        self.return_value = self.pop()
        return "return"
```

12.7   Dynamic Typing: What the Compiler Doesn't Know

One thing you've probably heard is that Python is a "dynamic" language—particularly that it's "dynamically typed". The work we've done to this point sheds some light on this description.

One of the things "dynamic" means in this context is that a lot of work is done at run time. We saw earlier that the Python compiler doesn't have much information about what the code actually does. For example, consider the short function mod below. mod takes two arguments and returns the first modulo the second. In the bytecode, we see that the variables a and b are loaded, then the bytecode BINARY_MODULO performs the modulo operation itself.

```
>>> def mod(a, b):
...     return a % b
>>> dis.dis(mod)
  2           0 LOAD_FAST             0 (a)
              3 LOAD_FAST             1 (b)
              6 BINARY_MODULO
              7 RETURN_VALUE
>>> mod(19, 5)
4
```

Calculating 19 % 5 yields 4—no surprise there. What happens if we call it with different arguments?

```
>>> mod("by%sde", "teco")
'bytecode'
```

What just happened? You've probably seen this syntax before, but in a different context:

```
>>> print("by%sde" % "teco")
bytecode
```

Using the symbol % to format a string for printing means invoking the instruction BINARY_MODULO. This instruction mods together the top two values on the stack when the instruction executes—regardless of whether they're strings, intcgcrs, or instances of a class you defined yourself. The bytecode was generated when the function was compiled (effectively, when it was defined) and the same bytecode is used with different types of arguments.

The Python compiler knows relatively little about the effect the bytecode will have. It's up to the interpreter to determine the type of the object that BINARY_MODULO is operating on and do the right thing for that type. This is why Python is described as *dynamically typed*: you don't know the types of the arguments to this function until you actually run it. By contrast, in a language that's statically typed, the programmer tells the compiler up front what type the arguments will be (or the compiler figures them out for itself).

The compiler's ignorance is one of the challenges to optimizing Python or analyzing it statically—just looking at the bytecode, without actually running the code, you don't know what each instruction will do! In fact, you could define a class that implements the __mod__ method, and Python would invoke that method if you use % on your objects. So BINARY_MODULO could run any code at all!

Just looking at the following code, the first calculation of a % b seems wasteful.

```
def mod(a,b):
    a % b
    return a %b
```

Unfortunately, a static analysis of this code—the kind of you can do without running it—can't be certain that the first a % b really does nothing. Calling __mod__ with % might write to a file, or interact with another part of your program, or do literally anything else that's possible in Python. It's hard to optimize a function when you don't know what it does! In Russell Power and Alex Rubinsteyn's great paper "How fast can we make interpreted Python?", they note, "In the general absence of type information, each instruction must be treated as INVOKE_ARBITRARY_METHOD."

12.8   Conclusion

Byterun is a compact Python interpreter that's easier to understand than CPython. Byterun replicates CPython's primary structural details: a stack-based interpreter operating on instruction sets called bytecode. It steps or jumps through these instructions, pushing to and popping from a stack of data. The interpreter creates, destroys, and jumps between frames as it calls into and returns from functions and generators. Byterun shares the real interpreter's limitations, too: because Python uses dynamic typing, the interpreter must work hard at run time to determine the correct behavior of a program.

I encourage you to disassemble your own programs and to run them using Byterun. You'll quickly run into instructions that this shorter version of Byterun doesn't implement. The full implementation can be found at https://github.com/nedbat/byterun—or, by carefully reading the real CPython interpreter's ceval.c, you can implement it yourself!

12.9   Acknowledgements

Thanks to Ned Batchelder for originating this project and guiding my contributions, Michael Arntzenius for his help debugging the code and editing the prose, Leta Montopoli for her edits, and the entire Recurse Center community for their support and interest. Any errors are my own.

## chapter 13

A 3D Modeller

Erick Dransch

13.1   Introduction

Humans are innately creative. We continuously design and build novel, useful, and interesting things. In modern times, we write software to assist in the design and creation process. Computer-aided design (CAD) software allows creators to design buildings, bridges, video game art, film monsters, 3D printable objects, and many other things before building a physical version of the design.

At their core, CAD tools are a method of abstracting the 3-dimensional design into something that can be viewed and edited on a 2-dimensional screen. To fulfill that definition, CAD tools must offer three basic pieces of functionality. Firstly, they must have a data structure to represent the object that's being designed: this is the computer's understanding of the 3-dimensional world that the user is building. Secondly, the CAD tool must offer some way to display the design on the user's screen. The user is designing a physical object with 3 dimensions, but the computer screen has only 2 dimensions. The CAD tool must model how we perceive objects, and draw them to the screen in a way that the user can understand all 3 dimensions of the object. Thirdly, the CAD tool must offer a way to interact with the object being designed. The user must be able to add to and modify the design in order to produce the desired result. Additionally, all tools would need a way to save and load designs from disk so that users can collaborate, share, and save their work.

A domain-specific CAD tool offers many additional features for the specific requirements of the domain. For example, an architecture CAD tool would offer physics simulations to test climate stresses on the building, a 3D printing tool would have features that check whether the object is actually valid to print, an electrical CAD tool would simulate the physics of electricity running through copper, and a film special effects suite would include features to accurately simulate pyrokinetics.

However, all CAD tools must include at least the three features discussed above: a data structure to represent the design, the ability to display it to the screen, and a method to interact with the design.

With that in mind, let's explore how we can represent a 3D design, display it to the screen, and interact with it, in 500 lines of Python.

13.2   Rendering as a Guide

The driving force behind many of the design decisions in a 3D modeller is the rendering process. We want to be able to store and render complex objects in our design, but we want to keep the complexity of the rendering code low. Let us examine the rendering process, and explore the data structure for the design that allows us to store and draw arbitarily complex objects with simple rendering logic.

Managing Interfaces and the Main Loop

Before we begin rendering, there are a few things we need to set up. First, we need to create a window to display our design in. Secondly, we want to communicate with graphics drivers to render to the screen. We would rather not communicate directly with graphics drivers, so we use a cross-platform abstraction layer called OpenGL, and a library called GLUT (the OpenGL Utility Toolkit) to manage our window.

A Note About OpenGL

OpenGL is a graphical application programming interface for cross-platform development. It's the standard API for developing graphics applications across platforms. OpenGL has two major variants: Legacy OpenGL and Modern OpenGL.

Rendering in OpenGL is based on polygons defined by vertices and normals. For example, to render one side of a cube, we specify the 4 vertices and the normal of the side.

Legacy OpenGL provides a "fixed function pipeline". By setting global variables, the programmer can enable and disable automated implementations of features such as lighting, coloring, face culling, etc. OpenGL then automatically renders the scene with the enabled functionality. This functionality is deprecated.

Modern OpenGL, on the other hand, features a programmable rendering pipeline where the programmer writes small programs called "shaders" that run on dedicated graphics hardware (GPUs). The programmable pipeline of Modern OpenGL has replaced Legacy OpenGL.

In this project, despite the fact that it is deprecated, we use Legacy OpenGL. The fixed functionality provided by Legacy OpenGL is very useful for keeping code size small. It reduces the amount of linear algebra knowledge required, and it simplifies the code we will write.

About GLUT

GLUT, which is bundled with OpenGL, allows us to create operating system windows and to register user interface callbacks. This basic functionality is sufficient for our purposes. If we wanted a more full-featured library for window management and user interaction, we would consider using a full windowing toolkit like GTK or Qt.

The Viewer

To manage the setting up of GLUT and OpenGL, and to drive the rest of the modeller, we create a class called Viewer. We use a single Viewer instance, which manages window creation and rendering, and contains the main loop for our program. In the initialization process for Viewer, we create the GUI window and initialize OpenGL.

The function init_interface creates the window that the modeller will be rendered into and specifies the function to be called when the design needs to rendered. The init_opengl function sets up the OpenGL state needed for the project. It sets the matrices, enables backface culling, registers a light to illuminate the scene, and tells OpenGL that we would like objects to be colored. The init_scene function creates the Scene objects and places some initial nodes to get the user started.

We will see more about the Scene data structure shortly. Finally, `init_interaction` registers callbacks for user interaction, as we'll discuss later.

After initializing `Viewer`, we call `glutMainLoop` to transfer program execution to GLUT. This function never returns. The callbacks we have registered on GLUT events will be called when those events occur.

```python
class Viewer(object):
    def __init__(self):
        """ Initialize the viewer. """
        self.init_interface()
        self.init_opengl()
        self.init_scene()
        self.init_interaction()
        init_primitives()

    def init_interface(self):
        """ initialize the window and register the render function """
        glutInit()
        glutInitWindowSize(640, 480)
        glutCreateWindow("3D Modeller")
        glutInitDisplayMode(GLUT_SINGLE | GLUT_RGB)
        glutDisplayFunc(self.render)

    def init_opengl(self):
        """ initialize the opengl settings to render the scene """
        self.inverseModelView = numpy.identity(4)
        self.modelView = numpy.identity(4)

        glEnable(GL_CULL_FACE)
        glCullFace(GL_BACK)
        glEnable(GL_DEPTH_TEST)
        glDepthFunc(GL_LESS)

        glEnable(GL_LIGHT0)
        glLightfv(GL_LIGHT0, GL_POSITION, GLfloat_4(0, 0, 1, 0))
        glLightfv(GL_LIGHT0, GL_SPOT_DIRECTION, GLfloat_3(0, 0, -1))

        glColorMaterial(GL_FRONT_AND_BACK, GL_AMBIENT_AND_DIFFUSE)
        glEnable(GL_COLOR_MATERIAL)
        glClearColor(0.4, 0.4, 0.4, 0.0)

    def init_scene(self):
        """ initialize the scene object and initial scene """
        self.scene = Scene()
        self.create_sample_scene()

    def create_sample_scene(self):
        cube_node = Cube()
        cube_node.translate(2, 0, 2)
        cube_node.color_index = 2
        self.scene.add_node(cube_node)
```

```
        sphere_node = Sphere()
        sphere_node.translate(-2, 0, 2)
        sphere_node.color_index = 3
        self.scene.add_node(sphere_node)

        hierarchical_node = SnowFigure()
        hierarchical_node.translate(-2, 0, -2)
        self.scene.add_node(hierarchical_node)

    def init_interaction(self):
        """ init user interaction and callbacks """
        self.interaction = Interaction()
        self.interaction.register_callback('pick', self.pick)
        self.interaction.register_callback('move', self.move)
        self.interaction.register_callback('place', self.place)
        self.interaction.register_callback('rotate_color', self.rotate_color)
        self.interaction.register_callback('scale', self.scale)

    def main_loop(self):
        glutMainLoop()

if __name__ == "__main__":
    viewer = Viewer()
    viewer.main_loop()
```

Before we dive into the render function, we should discuss a little bit of linear algebra.

Coordinate Space

For our purposes, a Coordinate Space is an origin point and a set of 3 basis vectors, usually the x, y, and z axes.

Point

Any point in 3 dimensions can be represented as an offset in the x, y, and z directions from the origin point. The representation of a point is relative to the coordinate space that the point is in. The same point has different representations in different coordinate spaces. Any point in 3 dimensions can be represented in any 3-dimensional coordinate space.

Vector

A vector is an x, y, and z value representing the difference between two points in the x, y, and z axes, respectively.

Transformation Matrix

In computer graphics, it is convenient to use multiple different coordinate spaces for different types of points. Transformation matrices convert points from one coordinate space to another coordinate space. To convert a vector v from one coordinate space to another, we multiply by a transformation matrix M: $v' = Mv$. Some common transformation matrices are translations, scaling, and rotations.

Model, World, View, and Projection Coordinate Spaces

To draw an item to the screen, we need to convert between a few different coordinate spaces.

The right hand side of Figure 13.1[1], including all of the transformations from Eye Space to Viewport Space will all be handled for us by OpenGL.

Conversion from eye space to homogeneous clip space is handled by `gluPerspective`, and conversion to normalized device space and viewport space is handled by `glViewport`. These two matrices are multiplied together and stored as the GL_PROJECTION matrix. We don't need to know the terminology or the details of how these matrices work for this project.

We do, however, need to manage the left hand side of the diagram ourselves. We define a matrix which converts points in the model (also called a mesh) from the model spaces into the world space, called the model matrix. We alse define the view matrix, which converts from the world space into the eye space. In this project, we combine these two matrices to obtain the ModelView matrix.

To learn more about the full graphics rendering pipeline, and the coordinate spaces involved, refer to chapter 2 of *Real Time Rendering*[2], or another introductory computer graphics book.

Rendering with the Viewer

The render function begins by setting up any of the OpenGL state that needs to be done at render time. It initializes the projection matrix via `init_view` and uses data from the interaction member to initialize the ModelView matrix with the transformation matrix that converts from the scene space to world space. We will see more about the Interaction class below. It clears the screen with `glClear` and it tells the scene to render itself, and then renders the unit grid.

We disable OpenGL's lighting before rendering the grid. With lighting disabled, OpenGL renders items with solid colors, rather than simulating a light source. This way, the grid has visual differentiation from the scene. Finally, `glFlush` signals to the graphics driver that we are ready for the buffer to be flushed and displayed to the screen.

```
# class Viewer
def render(self):
    """ The render pass for the scene """
    self.init_view()

    glEnable(GL_LIGHTING)
    glClear(GL_COLOR_BUFFER_BIT | GL_DEPTH_BUFFER_BIT)

    # Load the modelview matrix from the current state of the trackball
    glMatrixMode(GL_MODELVIEW)
    glPushMatrix()
    glLoadIdentity()
    loc = self.interaction.translation
    glTranslated(loc[0], loc[1], loc[2])
```

[1]Thanks to Dr. Anton Gerdelan for the image. His OpenGL tutorial book is available at http://antongerdelan.net/opengl/.
[2]http://www.realtimerendering.com/

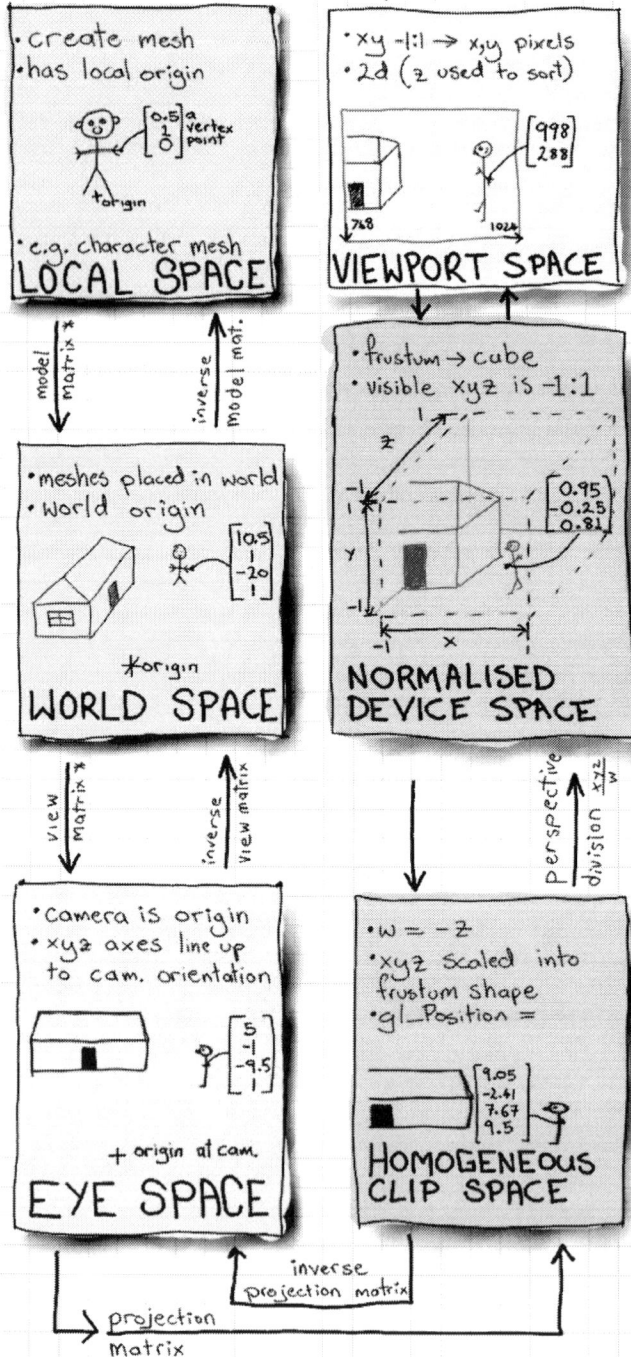

Figure 13.1: Transformation Pipeline

```
    glMultMatrixf(self.interaction.trackball.matrix)

    # store the inverse of the current modelview.
    currentModelView = numpy.array(glGetFloatv(GL_MODELVIEW_MATRIX))
    self.modelView = numpy.transpose(currentModelView)
    self.inverseModelView = inv(numpy.transpose(currentModelView))

    # render the scene. This will call the render function for each object
    # in the scene
    self.scene.render()

    # draw the grid
    glDisable(GL_LIGHTING)
    glCallList(G_OBJ_PLANE)
    glPopMatrix()

    # flush the buffers so that the scene can be drawn
    glFlush()

def init_view(self):
    """ initialize the projection matrix """
    xSize, ySize = glutGet(GLUT_WINDOW_WIDTH), glutGet(GLUT_WINDOW_HEIGHT)
    aspect_ratio = float(xSize) / float(ySize)

    # load the projection matrix. Always the same
    glMatrixMode(GL_PROJECTION)
    glLoadIdentity()

    glViewport(0, 0, xSize, ySize)
    gluPerspective(70, aspect_ratio, 0.1, 1000.0)
    glTranslated(0, 0, -15)
```

What to Render: The Scene

Now that we've initialized the rendering pipeline to handle drawing in the world coordinate space, what are we going to render? Recall that our goal is to have a design consisting of 3D models. We need a data structure to contain the design, and we need use this data structure to render the design. Notice above that we call `self.scene.render()` from the viewer's render loop. What is the scene?

The Scene class is the interface to the data structure we use to represent the design. It abstracts away details of the data structure and provides the necessary interface functions required to interact with the design, including functions to render, add items, and manipulate items. There is one Scene object, owned by the viewer. The Scene instance keeps a list of all of the items in the scene, called node_list. It also keeps track of the selected item. The render function on the scene simply calls render on each of the members of node_list.

```
class Scene(object):

    # the default depth from the camera to place an object at
    PLACE_DEPTH = 15.0
```

```
def __init__(self):
    # The scene keeps a list of nodes that are displayed
    self.node_list = list()
    # Keep track of the currently selected node.
    # Actions may depend on whether or not something is selected
    self.selected_node = None

def add_node(self, node):
    """ Add a new node to the scene """
    self.node_list.append(node)

def render(self):
    """ Render the scene. """
    for node in self.node_list:
        node.render()
```

Nodes

In the Scene's render function, we call render on each of the items in the Scene's node_list. But what are the elements of that list? We call them *nodes*. Conceptually, a node is anything that can be placed in the scene. In object-oriented software, we write Node as an abstract base class. Any classes that represent objects to be placed in the Scene will inherit from Node. This base class allows us to reason about the scene abstractly. The rest of the code base doesn't need to know about the details of the objects it displays; it only needs to know that they are of the class Node.

Each type of Node defines its own behavior for rendering itself and for any other interactions. The Node keeps track of important data about itself: translation matrix, scale matrix, color, etc. Multiplying the node's translation matrix by its scaling matrix gives the transformation matrix from the node's model coordinate space to the world coordinate space. The node also stores an axis-aligned bounding box (AABB). We'll see more about AABBs when we discuss selection below.

The simplest concrete implementation of Node is a *primitive*. A primitive is a single solid shape that can be added the scene. In this project, the primitives are Cube and Sphere.

```
class Node(object):
    """ Base class for scene elements """
    def __init__(self):
        self.color_index = random.randint(color.MIN_COLOR, color.MAX_COLOR)
        self.aabb = AABB([0.0, 0.0, 0.0], [0.5, 0.5, 0.5])
        self.translation_matrix = numpy.identity(4)
        self.scaling_matrix = numpy.identity(4)
        self.selected = False

    def render(self):
        """ renders the item to the screen """
        glPushMatrix()
        glMultMatrixf(numpy.transpose(self.translation_matrix))
        glMultMatrixf(self.scaling_matrix)
        cur_color = color.COLORS[self.color_index]
        glColor3f(cur_color[0], cur_color[1], cur_color[2])
        if self.selected:  # emit light if the node is selected
            glMaterialfv(GL_FRONT, GL_EMISSION, [0.3, 0.3, 0.3])
```

```
            self.render_self()

            if self.selected:
                glMaterialfv(GL_FRONT, GL_EMISSION, [0.0, 0.0, 0.0])
            glPopMatrix()

    def render_self(self):
        raise NotImplementedError(
            "The Abstract Node Class doesn't define 'render_self'")

class Primitive(Node):
    def __init__(self):
        super(Primitive, self).__init__()
        self.call_list = None

    def render_self(self):
        glCallList(self.call_list)


class Sphere(Primitive):
    """ Sphere primitive """
    def __init__(self):
        super(Sphere, self).__init__()
        self.call_list = G_OBJ_SPHERE


class Cube(Primitive):
    """ Cube primitive """
    def __init__(self):
        super(Cube, self).__init__()
        self.call_list = G_OBJ_CUBE
```

Rendering nodes is based on the transformation matrices that each node stores. The transformation matrix for a node is the combination of its scaling matrix and its translation matrix. Regardless of the type of node, the first step to rendering is to set the OpenGL ModelView matrix to the transformation matrix to convert from the model coordinate space to the view coordinate space. Once the OpenGL matrices are up to date, we call render_self to tell the node to make the necessary OpenGL calls to draw itself. Finally, we undo any changes we made to the OpenGL state for this specific node. We use the glPushMatrix and glPopMatrix functions in OpenGL to save and restore the state of the ModelView matrix before and after we render the node. Notice that the node stores its color, location, and scale, and applies these to the OpenGL state before rendering.

If the node is currently selected, we make it emit light. This way, the user has a visual indication of which node they have selected.

To render primitives, we use the call lists feature from OpenGL. An OpenGL call list is a series of OpenGL calls that are defined once and bundled together under a single name. The calls can be dispatched with glCallList(LIST_NAME). Each primitive (Sphere and Cube) defines the call list required to render it (not shown).

For example, the call list for a cube draws the 6 faces of the cube, with the center at the origin and the edges exactly 1 unit long.

```
# Pseudocode Cube definition
# Left face
((-0.5, -0.5, -0.5), (-0.5, -0.5, 0.5), ( 0.5, 0.5, 0.5), (-0.5, 0.5, -0.5)),
# Back face
((-0.5, -0.5, -0.5), (-0.5, 0.5, -0.5), (0.5, 0.5, -0.5), (0.5, -0.5, -0.5)),
# Right face
((0.5, -0.5, -0.5), (0.5, 0.5, -0.5), (0.5, 0.5, 0.5), (0.5, -0.5, 0.5)),
# Front face
((-0.5, -0.5, 0.5), (0.5, -0.5, 0.5), (0.5, 0.5, 0.5), (-0.5, 0.5, 0.5)),
# Bottom face
((-0.5, -0.5, 0.5), (-0.5, -0.5, -0.5), (0.5, -0.5, -0.5), (0.5, -0.5, 0.5)),
# Top face
((-0.5, 0.5, -0.5), (-0.5, 0.5, 0.5), (0.5, 0.5, 0.5), (0.5, 0.5, -0.5))
```

Using only primitives would be quite limiting for modelling applications. 3D models are generally made up of multiple primitives (or triangular meshes, which are outside the scope of this project). Fortunately, our design of the Node class facilitates Scene nodes that are made up of multiple primitives. In fact, we can support arbitrary groupings of nodes with no added complexity.

As motivation, let us consider a very basic figure: a typical snowman, or snow figure, made up of three spheres. Even though the figure is comprised of three separate primitives, we would like to be able to treat it as a single object.

We create a class called HierarchicalNode, a Node that contains other nodes. It manages a list of "children". The render_self function for hierarchical nodes simply calls render_self on each of the child nodes. With the HierarchicalNode class, it is very easy to add figures to the scene. Now, defining the snow figure is as simple as specifying the shapes that comprise it, and their relative positions and sizes.

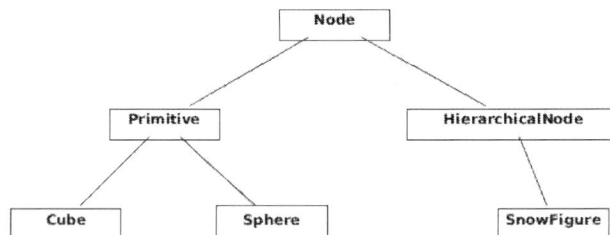

Figure 13.2: Hierarchy of 'Node' subclasses

```
class HierarchicalNode(Node):
    def __init__(self):
        super(HierarchicalNode, self).__init__()
        self.child_nodes = []

    def render_self(self):
        for child in self.child_nodes:
            child.render()
```

```
class SnowFigure(HierarchicalNode):
    def __init__(self):
        super(SnowFigure, self).__init__()
        self.child_nodes = [Sphere(), Sphere(), Sphere()]
        self.child_nodes[0].translate(0, -0.6, 0) # scale 1.0
        self.child_nodes[1].translate(0, 0.1, 0)
        self.child_nodes[1].scaling_matrix = numpy.dot(
            self.scaling_matrix, scaling([0.8, 0.8, 0.8]))
        self.child_nodes[2].translate(0, 0.75, 0)
        self.child_nodes[2].scaling_matrix = numpy.dot(
            self.scaling_matrix, scaling([0.7, 0.7, 0.7]))
        for child_node in self.child_nodes:
            child_node.color_index = color.MIN_COLOR
        self.aabb = AABB([0.0, 0.0, 0.0], [0.5, 1.1, 0.5])
```

You might observe that the Node objects form a tree data structure. The render function, through hierarchical nodes, does a depth-first traversal through the tree. As it traverses, it keeps a stack of ModelView matrices, used for conversion into the world space. At each step, it pushes the current ModelView matrix onto the stack, and when it completes rendering of all child nodes, it pops the matrix off the stack, leaving the parent node's ModelView matrix at the top of the stack.

By making the Node class extensible in this way, we can add new types of shapes to the scene without changing any of the other code for scene manipulation and rendering. Using the node concept to abstract away the fact that one Scene object may have many children is known as the Composite design pattern.

User Interaction

Now that our modeller is capable of storing and displaying the scene, we need a way to interact with it. There are two types of interactions that we need to facilitate. First, we need the capability of changing the viewing perspective of the scene. We want to be able to move the eye, or camera, around the scene. Second, we need to be able to add new nodes and to modify nodes in the scene.

To enable user interaction, we need to know when the user presses keys or moves the mouse. Luckily, the operating system already knows when these events happen. GLUT allows us to register a function to be called whenever a certain event occurs. We write functions to interpret key presses and mouse movement, and tell GLUT to call those functions when the corresponding keys are pressed. Once we know which keys the user is pressing, we need to interpret the input and apply the intended actions to the scene.

The logic for listening to operating system events and interpreting their meaning is found in the Interaction class. The Viewer class we wrote earlier owns the single instance of Interaction. We will use the GLUT callback mechanism to register functions to be called when a mouse button is pressed (glutMouseFunc), when the mouse is moved (glutMotionFunc), when a keyboard button is pressed (glutKeyboardFunc), and when the arrow keys are pressed (glutSpecialFunc). We'll see the functions that handle input events shortly.

```
class Interaction(object):
    def __init__(self):
        """ Handles user interaction """
        # currently pressed mouse button
        self.pressed = None
```

```
    # the current location of the camera
    self.translation = [0, 0, 0, 0]
    # the trackball to calculate rotation
    self.trackball = trackball.Trackball(theta = -25, distance=15)
    # the current mouse location
    self.mouse_loc = None
    # Unsophisticated callback mechanism
    self.callbacks = defaultdict(list)

    self.register()

def register(self):
    """ register callbacks with glut """
    glutMouseFunc(self.handle_mouse_button)
    glutMotionFunc(self.handle_mouse_move)
    glutKeyboardFunc(self.handle_keystroke)
    glutSpecialFunc(self.handle_keystroke)
```

Operating System Callbacks

In order to meaningfully interpret user input, we need to combine knowledge of the mouse position, mouse buttons, and keyboard. Because interpreting user input into meaningful actions requires many lines of code, we encapsulate it in a separate class, away from the main code path. The Interaction class hides unrelated complexity from the rest of the codebase and translates operating system events into application-level events.

```
# class Interaction
def translate(self, x, y, z):
    """ translate the camera """
    self.translation[0] += x
    self.translation[1] += y
    self.translation[2] += z

def handle_mouse_button(self, button, mode, x, y):
    """ Called when the mouse button is pressed or released """
    xSize, ySize = glutGet(GLUT_WINDOW_WIDTH), glutGet(GLUT_WINDOW_HEIGHT)
    y = ySize - y  # invert the y coordinate because OpenGL is inverted
    self.mouse_loc = (x, y)

    if mode == GLUT_DOWN:
        self.pressed = button
        if button == GLUT_RIGHT_BUTTON:
            pass
        elif button == GLUT_LEFT_BUTTON:   # pick
            self.trigger('pick', x, y)
        elif button == 3:  # scroll up
            self.translate(0, 0, 1.0)
        elif button == 4:  # scroll up
            self.translate(0, 0, -1.0)
    else:  # mouse button release
        self.pressed = None
```

```
    glutPostRedisplay()

def handle_mouse_move(self, x, screen_y):
    """ Called when the mouse is moved """
    xSize, ySize = glutGet(GLUT_WINDOW_WIDTH), glutGet(GLUT_WINDOW_HEIGHT)
    y = ySize - screen_y  # invert the y coordinate because OpenGL is inverted
    if self.pressed is not None:
        dx = x - self.mouse_loc[0]
        dy = y - self.mouse_loc[1]
        if self.pressed == GLUT_RIGHT_BUTTON and self.trackball is not None:
            # ignore the updated camera loc because we want to always
            # rotate around the origin
            self.trackball.drag_to(self.mouse_loc[0], self.mouse_loc[1], dx, dy)
        elif self.pressed == GLUT_LEFT_BUTTON:
            self.trigger('move', x, y)
        elif self.pressed == GLUT_MIDDLE_BUTTON:
            self.translate(dx/60.0, dy/60.0, 0)
        else:
            pass
        glutPostRedisplay()
    self.mouse_loc = (x, y)

def handle_keystroke(self, key, x, screen_y):
    """ Called on keyboard input from the user """
    xSize, ySize = glutGet(GLUT_WINDOW_WIDTH), glutGet(GLUT_WINDOW_HEIGHT)
    y = ySize - screen_y
    if key == 's':
        self.trigger('place', 'sphere', x, y)
    elif key == 'c':
        self.trigger('place', 'cube', x, y)
    elif key == GLUT_KEY_UP:
        self.trigger('scale', up=True)
    elif key == GLUT_KEY_DOWN:
        self.trigger('scale', up=False)
    elif key == GLUT_KEY_LEFT:
        self.trigger('rotate_color', forward=True)
    elif key == GLUT_KEY_RIGHT:
        self.trigger('rotate_color', forward=False)
    glutPostRedisplay()
```

Internal Callbacks

In the code snippet above, you will notice that when the Interaction instance interprets a user action, it calls self.trigger with a string describing the action type. The trigger function on the Interaction class is part of a simple callback system that we will use for handling application-level events. Recall that the init_interaction function on the Viewer class registers callbacks on the Interaction instance by calling register_callback.

```
# class Interaction
def register_callback(self, name, func):
    self.callbacks[name].append(func)
```

Callback	Arguments	Purpose
pick	x:number, y:number	Selects the node at the mouse pointer location
place	shape:string, x:number, y:number	Places a shape of the specified type at the mouse pointer location.
rotate_color	forward:boolean	Rotates the color of the currently selected node.
scale	up:boolean	Scales the currently selected node up or down.

Table 13.1: Interaction callbacks and arguments

When user interface code needs to trigger an event on the scene, the Interaction class calls all of the saved callbacks it has for that specific event:

```
# class Interaction
def trigger(self, name, *args, **kwargs):
    for func in self.callbacks[name]:
        func(*args, **kwargs)
```

This application-level callback system abstracts away the need for the rest of the system to know about operating system input. Each application-level callback represents a meaningful request within the application. The Interaction class acts as a translator between operating system events and application-level events. This means that if we decided to port the modeller to another toolkit in addition to GLUT, we would only need to replace the Interaction class with a class that converts the input from the new toolkit into the same set of meaningful application-level callbacks. We use callbacks and arguments in Table 13.1.

This simple callback system provides all of the functionality we need for this project. In a production 3D modeller, however, user interface objects are often created and destroyed dynamically. In that case, we would need a more sophisticated event listening system, where objects can both register and un-register callbacks for events.

Interfacing with the Scene

With our callback mechanism, we can receive meaningful information about user input events from the Interaction class. We are ready to apply these actions to the Scene.

Moving the Scene

In this project, we accomplish camera motion by transforming the scene. In other words, the camera is at a fixed location and user input moves the scene instead of moving the camera. The camera is placed at [0, 0, -15] and faces the world space origin. (Alternatively, we could change the perspective matrix to move the camera instead of the scene. This design decision has very little impact on the rest of the project.) Revisiting the render function in the Viewer, we see that the Interaction state is used to transform the OpenGL matrix state before rendering the Scene. There are two types of interaction with the scene: rotation and translation.

Rotating the Scene with a Trackball

We accomplish rotation of the scene by using a *trackball* algorithm. The trackball is an intuitive interface for manipulating the scene in three dimensions. Conceptually, a trackball interface functions as if the scene was inside a transparent globe. Placing a hand on the surface of the globe and pushing it rotates the globe. Similarly, clicking the right mouse button and moving it on the screen rotates the scene. You can find out more about the theory of the trackball at the OpenGL Wiki[3]. In this project, we use a trackball implementation provided as part of Glumpy[4].

We interact with the trackball using the `drag_to` function, with the current location of the mouse as the starting location and the change in mouse location as parameters.

```
self.trackball.drag_to(self.mouse_loc[0], self.mouse_loc[1], dx, dy)
```

The resulting rotation matrix is `trackball.matrix` in the viewer when the scene is rendered.

Aside: Quaternions

Rotations are traditionally represented in one of two ways. The first is a rotation value around each axis; you could store this as a 3-tuple of floating point numbers. The other common representation for rotations is a quaternion, an element composed of a vector with x, y, and z coordinates, and a w rotation. Using quaternions has numerous benefits over per-axis rotation; in particular, they are more numerically stable. Using quaternions avoids problems like gimbal lock. The downside of quaternions is that they are less intuitive to work with and harder to understand. If you are brave and would like to learn more about quaternions, you can refer to this explanation[5].

The trackball implementation avoids gimbal lock by using quaternions internally to store the rotation of the scene. Luckily, we do not need to work with quaternions directly, because the matrix member on the trackball converts the rotation to a matrix.

Translating the Scene

Translating the scene (i.e., sliding it) is much simpler than rotating it. Scene translations are provided with the mouse wheel and the left mouse button. The left mouse button translates the scene in the x and y coordinates. Scrolling the mouse wheel translates the scene in the z coordinate (towards or away from the camera). The `Interaction` class stores the current scene translation and modifies it with the `translate` function. The viewer retrieves the `Interaction` camera location during rendering to use in a `glTranslated` call.

Selecting Scene Objects

Now that the user can move and rotate the entire scene to get the perspective they want, the next step is to allow the user to modify and manipulate the objects that make up the scene.

In order for the user to manipulate objects in the scene, they need to be able to select items.

To select an item, we use the current projection matrix to generate a ray that represents the mouse click, as if the mouse pointer shoots a ray into the scene. The selected node is the closest node to the camera with which the ray intersects. Thus the problem of picking reduced to the problem of finding intersections between a ray and nodes in the scene. So the question is: How do we tell if the ray hits a node?

Calculating exactly whether a ray intersects with a node is a challenging problem in terms of both complexity of code and of performance. We would need to write a ray-object intersection check for each type of primitive. For scene nodes with complex mesh geometries with many faces,

---

[3]http://www.opengl.org/wiki/Object_Mouse_Trackball
[4]https://code.google.com/p/glumpy/source/browse/glumpy/trackball.py
[5]http://3dgep.com/?p=1815

calculating exact ray-object intersection would require testing the ray against each face and would be computationally expensive.

For the purposes of keeping the code compact and performance reasonable, we use a simple, fast approximation for the ray-object intersection test. In our implementation, each node stores an axis-aligned bounding box (AABB), which is an approximation of the space it occupies. To test whether a ray intersects with a node, we test whether the ray intersects with the node's AABB. This implementation means that all nodes share the same code for intersection tests, and it means that the performance cost is constant and small for all node types.

```
# class Viewer
def get_ray(self, x, y):
    """
    Generate a ray beginning at the near plane, in the direction that
    the x, y coordinates are facing

    Consumes: x, y coordinates of mouse on screen
    Return: start, direction of the ray
    """
    self.init_view()

    glMatrixMode(GL_MODELVIEW)
    glLoadIdentity()

    # get two points on the line.
    start = numpy.array(gluUnProject(x, y, 0.001))
    end = numpy.array(gluUnProject(x, y, 0.999))

    # convert those points into a ray
    direction = end - start
    direction = direction / norm(direction)

    return (start, direction)

def pick(self, x, y):
    """ Execute pick of an object. Selects an object in the scene. """
    start, direction = self.get_ray(x, y)
    self.scene.pick(start, direction, self.modelView)
```

To determine which node was clicked on, we traverse the scene to test whether the ray hits any nodes. We deselect the currently selected node and then choose the node with the intersection closest to the ray origin.

```
# class Scene
def pick(self, start, direction, mat):
    """
    Execute selection.

    start, direction describe a Ray.
    mat is the inverse of the current modelview matrix for the scene.
    """
    if self.selected_node is not None:
```

```
        self.selected_node.select(False)
        self.selected_node = None

    # Keep track of the closest hit.
    mindist = sys.maxint
    closest_node = None
    for node in self.node_list:
        hit, distance = node.pick(start, direction, mat)
        if hit and distance < mindist:
            mindist, closest_node = distance, node

    # If we hit something, keep track of it.
    if closest_node is not None:
        closest_node.select()
        closest_node.depth = mindist
        closest_node.selected_loc = start + direction * mindist
        self.selected_node = closest_node
```

Within the Node class, the `pick` function tests whether the ray intersects with the axis-aligned bounding box of the Node. If a node is selected, the `select` function toggles the selected state of the node. Notice that the AABB's `ray_hit` function accepts the transformation matrix between the box's coordinate space and the ray's coordinate space as the third parameter. Each node applies its own transformation to the matrix before making the `ray_hit` function call.

```
# class Node
def pick(self, start, direction, mat):
    """
    Return whether or not the ray hits the object

    Consume:
    start, direction form the ray to check
    mat is the modelview matrix to transform the ray by
    """

    # transform the modelview matrix by the current translation
    newmat = numpy.dot(
        numpy.dot(mat, self.translation_matrix),
        numpy.linalg.inv(self.scaling_matrix)
    )
    results = self.aabb.ray_hit(start, direction, newmat)
    return results

def select(self, select=None):
    """ Toggles or sets selected state """
    if select is not None:
        self.selected = select
    else:
        self.selected = not self.selected
```

The ray-AABB selection approach is very simple to understand and implement. However, the results are wrong in certain situations.

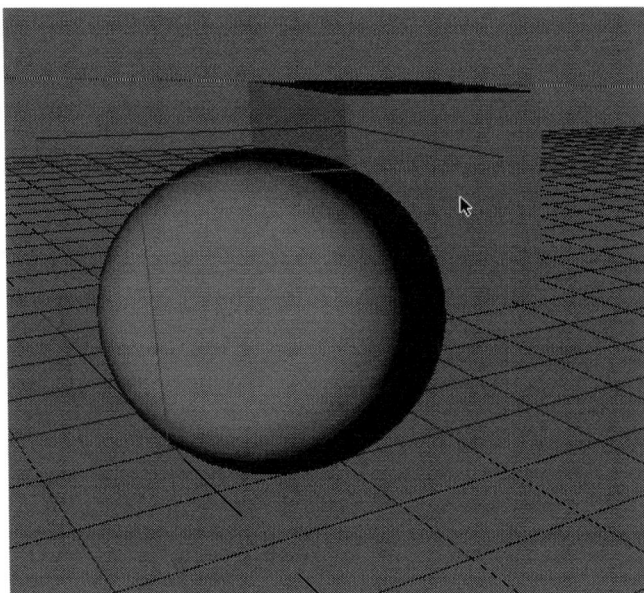

Figure 13.3: AABB Error

For example, in the case of the Sphere primitive, the sphere itself only touches the AABB in the centre of each of the AABB's faces. However if the user clicks on the corner of the Sphere's AABB, the collision will be detected with the Sphere, even if the user intended to click past the Sphere onto something behind it (Figure 13.3).

This trade-off between complexity, performance, and accuracy is common in computer graphics and in many areas of software engineering.

Modifying Scene Objects

Next, we would like to allow the user to manipulate the selected nodes. They might want to move, resize, or change the color of the selected node. When the user inputs a command to manipulate a node, the Interaction class converts the input into the action that the user intended, and calls the corresponding callback.

When the Viewer receives a callback for one of these events, it calls the appropriate function on the Scene, which in turn applies the transformation to the currently selected Node.

```
# class Viewer
def move(self, x, y):
    """ Execute a move command on the scene. """
    start, direction = self.get_ray(x, y)
    self.scene.move_selected(start, direction, self.inverseModelView)

def rotate_color(self, forward):
    """
    Rotate the color of the selected Node.
    Boolean 'forward' indicates direction of rotation.
    """
    self.scene.rotate_selected_color(forward)
```

```
def scale(self, up):
    """ Scale the selected Node. Boolean up indicates scaling larger."""
    self.scene.scale_selected(up)
```

Changing Color

Manipulating color is accomplished with a list of possible colors. The user can cycle through the list with the arrow keys. The scene dispatches the color change command to the currently selected node.

```
# class Scene
def rotate_selected_color(self, forwards):
    """ Rotate the color of the currently selected node """
    if self.selected_node is None: return
    self.selected_node.rotate_color(forwards)
```

Each node stores its current color. The `rotate_color` function simply modifies the current color of the node. The color is passed to OpenGL with `glColor` when the node is rendered.

```
# class Node
def rotate_color(self, forwards):
    self.color_index += 1 if forwards else -1
    if self.color_index > color.MAX_COLOR:
        self.color_index = color.MIN_COLOR
    if self.color_index < color.MIN_COLOR:
        self.color_index = color.MAX_COLOR
```

Scaling Nodes

As with color, the scene dispatches any scaling modifications to the selected node, if there is one.

```
# class Scene
def scale_selected(self, up):
    """ Scale the current selection """
    if self.selected_node is None: return
    self.selected_node.scale(up)
```

Each node stores a current matrix that stores its scale. A matrix that scales by parameters x, y and z in those respective directions is:

$$\begin{bmatrix} x & 0 & 0 & 0 \\ 0 & y & 0 & 0 \\ 0 & 0 & z & 0 \\ 0 & 0 & 0 & 1 \end{bmatrix}$$

When the user modifies the scale of a node, the resulting scaling matrix is multiplied into the current scaling matrix for the node.

```
# class Node
def scale(self, up):
    s =  1.1 if up else 0.9
    self.scaling_matrix = numpy.dot(self.scaling_matrix, scaling([s, s, s]))
    self.aabb.scale(s)
```

The function scaling returns such a matrix, given a list of the x, y, and z scaling factors.

```
def scaling(scale):
    s = numpy.identity(4)
    s[0, 0] = scale[0]
    s[1, 1] = scale[1]
    s[2, 2] = scale[2]
    s[3, 3] = 1
    return s
```

Moving Nodes

In order to translate a node, we use the same ray calculation we used for picking. We pass the ray that represents the current mouse location in to the scene's move function. The new location of the node should be on the ray. In order to determine where on the ray to place the node, we need to know the node's distance from the camera. Since we stored the node's location and distance from the camera when it was selected (in the pick function), we can use that data here. We find the point that is the same distance from the camera along the target ray and we calculate the vector difference between the new and old locations. We then translate the node by the resulting vector.

```
# class Scene
def move_selected(self, start, direction, inv_modelview):
    """

    Move the selected node, if there is one.

    Consume:
    start, direction describes the Ray to move to
    mat is the modelview matrix for the scene
    """

    if self.selected_node is None: return

    # Find the current depth and location of the selected node
    node = self.selected_node
    depth = node.depth
    oldloc = node.selected_loc

    # The new location of the node is the same depth along the new ray
    newloc = (start + direction * depth)

    # transform the translation with the modelview matrix
    translation = newloc - oldloc
    pre_tran = numpy.array([translation[0], translation[1], translation[2], 0])
    translation = inv_modelview.dot(pre_tran)

    # translate the node and track its location
    node.translate(translation[0], translation[1], translation[2])
    node.selected_loc = newloc
```

Notice that the new and old locations are defined in the camera coordinate space. We need our translation to be defined in the world coordinate space. Thus, we convert the camera space translation into a world space translation by multiplying by the inverse of the modelview matrix.

As with scale, each node stores a matrix which represents its translation. A translation matrix looks like:

$$\begin{bmatrix} 1 & 0 & 0 & x \\ 0 & 1 & 0 & y \\ 0 & 0 & 1 & z \\ 0 & 0 & 0 & 1 \end{bmatrix}$$

When the node is translated, we construct a new translation matrix for the current translation, and multiply it into the node's translation matrix for use during rendering.

```
# class Node
def translate(self, x, y, z):
    self.translation_matrix = numpy.dot(
        self.translation_matrix,
        translation([x, y, z]))
```

The `translation` function returns a translation matrix given a list representing the x, y, and z translation distances.

```
def translation(displacement):
    t = numpy.identity(4)
    t[0, 3] = displacement[0]
    t[1, 3] = displacement[1]
    t[2, 3] = displacement[2]
    return t
```

Placing Nodes

Node placement uses techniques from both picking and translation. We use the same ray calculation for the current mouse location to determine where to place the node.

```
# class Viewer
def place(self, shape, x, y):
    """ Execute a placement of a new primitive into the scene. """
    start, direction = self.get_ray(x, y)
    self.scene.place(shape, start, direction, self.inverseModelView)
```

To place a new node, we first create the new instance of the corresponding type of node and add it to the scene. We want to place the node underneath the user's cursor, so we find a point on the ray, at a fixed distance from the camera. Again, the ray is represented in camera space, so we convert the resulting translation vector into the world coordinate space by multiplying it by the inverse modelview matrix. Finally, we translate the new node by the calculated vector.

```
# class Scene
def place(self, shape, start, direction, inv_modelview):
    """
    Place a new node.

    Consume:
    shape the shape to add
    start, direction describes the Ray to move to
    inv_modelview is the inverse modelview matrix for the scene
    """
    new_node = None
    if shape == 'sphere': new_node = Sphere()
    elif shape == 'cube': new_node = Cube()
    elif shape == 'figure': new_node = SnowFigure()

    self.add_node(new_node)

    # place the node at the cursor in camera-space
    translation = (start + direction * self.PLACE_DEPTH)

    # convert the translation to world-space
    pre_tran = numpy.array([translation[0], translation[1], translation[2], 1])
    translation = inv_modelview.dot(pre_tran)

    new_node.translate(translation[0], translation[1], translation[2])
```

13.3 Summary

Congratulations! We've successfully implemented a tiny 3D modeller!

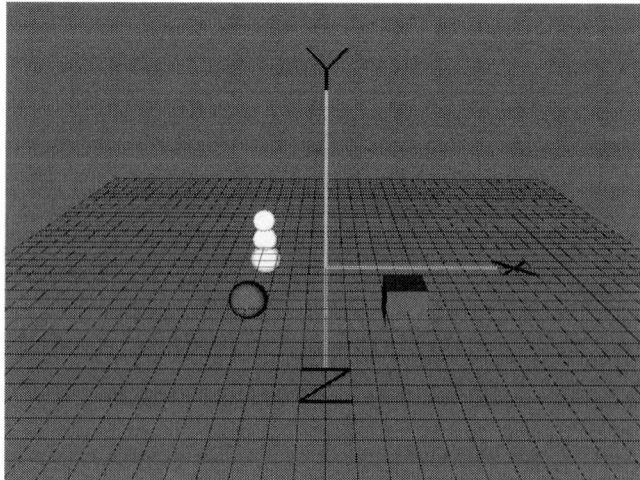

Figure 13.4: Sample Scene

We saw how to develop an extensible data structure to represent the objects in the scene. We noticed that using the Composite design pattern and a tree-based data structure makes it easy to traverse the scene for rendering and allows us to add new types of nodes with no added complexity. We leveraged this data structure to render the design to the screen, and manipulated OpenGL matrices in the traversal of the scene graph. We built a very simple callback system for application-level events, and used it to encapsulate handling of operating system events. We discussed possible implementations for ray-object collision detection, and the trade-offs between correctness, complexity, and performance. Finally, we implemented methods for manipulating the contents of the scene.

You can expect to find these same basic building blocks in production 3D software. The scene graph structure and relative coordinate spaces are found in many types of 3D graphics applications, from CAD tools to game engines. One major simplification in this project is in the user interface. A production 3D modeller would be expected to have a complete user interface, which would necessitate a much more sophisticated events system instead of our simple callback system.

We could do further experimentation to add new features to this project. Try one of these:

- Add a Node type to support triangle meshes for arbitrary shapes.
- Add an undo stack, to allow undo/redo of modeller actions.
- Save/load the design using a 3D file format like DXF.
- Integrate a rendering engine: export the design for use in a photorealistic renderer.
- Improve collision detection with accurate ray-object intersection.

13.4   Further Exploration

For further insight into real-world 3D modelling software, a few open source projects are interesting.

Blender[6] is an open source full-featured 3D animation suite. It provides a full 3D pipeline for building special effects in video, or for game creation. The modeller is a small part of this project, and it is a good example of integrating a modeller into a large software suite.

OpenSCAD[7] is an open source 3D modelling tool. It is not interactive; rather, it reads a script file that specifies how to generate the scene. This gives the designer "full control over the modelling process".

For more information about algorithms and techniques in computer graphics, Graphics Gems[8] is a great resource.

---

[6]http://www.blender.org/
[7]http://www.openscad.org/
[8]http://tog.acm.org/resources/GraphicsGems/

## chapter 14

A Simple Object Model
Carl Friedrich Bolz

14.1 Introduction

Object-oriented programming is one of the major programming paradigms in use today, with a lot of languages providing some form of object-orientation. While on the surface the mechanisms that different object-oriented programming languages provide to the programmer are very similar, the details can vary a lot. Commonalities of most languages are the presence of objects and some kind of inheritance mechanism. Classes, however, are a feature that not every language supports directly. For example, in prototype-based languages like Self or JavaScript, the concept of class does not exist and objects instead inherit directly from each other.

Understanding the differences between different object models can be interesting. They often reveal the family resemblance between different languages. It can be useful to put the model of a new language into the context of the models of other languages, both to quickly understand the new model, and to get a better feeling for the programming language design space.

This chapter explores the implementation of a series of very simple object models. It starts out with simple instances and classes, and the ability to call methods on instances. This is the "classical" object-oriented approach that was established in early OO languages such as Simula 67 and Smalltalk. This model is then extended step by step, the next two steps exploring different language design choices, and the last step improving the efficiency of the object model. The final model is not that of a real language, but an idealized, simplified version of Python's object model.

The object models presented in this chapter will be implemented in Python. The code works on both Python 2.7 and 3.4. To understand the behaviour and the design choices better, the chapter will also present tests for the object model. The tests can be run with either py.test or nose.

The choice of Python as an implementation language is quite unrealistic. A "real" VM is typically implemented in a low-level language like C/C++ and needs a lot of attention to engineering detail to make it efficient. However, the simpler implementation language makes it easier to focus on actual behaviour differences instead of getting bogged down by implementation details.

14.2 Method-Based Model

The object model we will start out with is an extremely simplified version of that of Smalltalk. Smalltalk was an object-oriented programming language designed by Alan Kay's group at Xerox PARC in the 1970s. It popularized object-oriented programming, and is the source of many features found in today's programming languages. One of the core tenets of Smalltalk's language design was "everything is an object". Smalltalk's most immediate successor in use today is Ruby, which uses a more C-like syntax but retains most of Smalltalk's object model.

The object model in this section will have classes and instances of them, the ability to read and write attributes into objects, the ability to call methods on objects, and the ability for a class to be a subclass of another class. Right from the beginning, classes will be completely ordinary objects that can themselves have attributes and methods.

A note on terminology: In this chapter I will use the word "instance" to mean -"an object that is not a class".

A good approach to start with is to write a test to specify what the to-be-implemented behaviour should be. All tests presented in this chapter will consist of two parts. First, a bit of regular Python code defining and using a few classes, and making use of increasingly advanced features of the Python object model. Second, the corresponding test using the object model we will implement in this chapter, instead of normal Python classes.

The mapping between using normal Python classes and using our object model will be done manually in the tests. For example, instead of writing obj.attribute in Python, in the object model we would use a method obj.read_attr("attribute"). This mapping would, in a real language implementation, be done by the interpreter of the language, or a compiler.

A further simplification in this chapter is that we make no sharp distinction between the code that implements the object model and the code that is used to write the methods used in the objects. In a real system, the two would often be implemented in different programming languages.

Let us start with a simple test for reading and writing object fields.

```python
def test_read_write_field():
    # Python code
    class A(object):
        pass
    obj = A()
    obj.a = 1
    assert obj.a == 1

    obj.b = 5
    assert obj.a == 1
    assert obj.b == 5

    obj.a = 2
    assert obj.a == 2
    assert obj.b == 5

    # Object model code
    A = Class(name="A", base_class=OBJECT, fields={}, metaclass=TYPE)
    obj = Instance(A)
    obj.write_attr("a", 1)
    assert obj.read_attr("a") == 1

    obj.write_attr("b", 5)
    assert obj.read_attr("a") == 1
    assert obj.read_attr("b") == 5

    obj.write_attr("a", 2)
```

```
    assert obj.read_attr("a") == 2
    assert obj.read_attr("b") == 5
```

The test uses three things that we have to implement. The classes Class and Instance represent
classes and instances of our object model, respectively. There are two special instances of class:
OBJECT and TYPE. OBJECT corresponds to object in Python and is the ultimate base class of the
inheritance hierarchy. TYPE corresponds to type in Python and is the type of all classes.

To do anything with instances of Class and Instance, they implement a shared interface by
inheriting from a shared base class Base that exposes a number of methods:

```
class Base(object):
    """ The base class that all of the object model classes inherit from. """

    def __init__(self, cls, fields):
        """ Every object has a class. """
        self.cls = cls
        self._fields = fields

    def read_attr(self, fieldname):
        """ read field 'fieldname' out of the object """
        return self._read_dict(fieldname)

    def write_attr(self, fieldname, value):
        """ write field 'fieldname' into the object """
        self._write_dict(fieldname, value)

    def isinstance(self, cls):
        """ return True if the object is an instance of class cls """
        return self.cls.issubclass(cls)

    def callmethod(self, methname, *args):
        """ call method 'methname' with arguments 'args' on object """
        meth = self.cls._read_from_class(methname)
        return meth(self, *args)

    def _read_dict(self, fieldname):
        """ read an field 'fieldname' out of the object's dict """
        return self._fields.get(fieldname, MISSING)

    def _write_dict(self, fieldname, value):
        """ write a field 'fieldname' into the object's dict """
        self._fields[fieldname] = value

MISSING = object()
```

The Base class implements storing the class of an object, and a dictionary containing the field
values of the object. Now we need to implement Class and Instance. The constructor of Instance
takes the class to be instantiated and initializes the fields dict as an empty dictionary. Otherwise
Instance is just a very thin subclass around Base that does not add any extra functionality.

The constructor of Class takes the name of the class, the base class, the dictionary of the class
and the metaclass. For classes, the fields are passed into the constructor by the user of the object

model. The class constructor also takes a base class, which the tests so far don't need but which we will make use of in the next section.

```
class Instance(Base):
    """Instance of a user-defined class. """

    def __init__(self, cls):
        assert isinstance(cls, Class)
        Base.__init__(self, cls, {})


class Class(Base):
    """ A User-defined class. """

    def __init__(self, name, base_class, fields, metaclass):
        Base.__init__(self, metaclass, fields)
        self.name = name
        self.base_class = base_class
```

Since classes are also a kind of object, they (indirectly) inherit from Base. Thus, the class needs to be an instance of another class: its metaclass.

Now our first test almost passes. The only missing bit is the definition of the base classes TYPE and OBJECT, which are both instances of Class. For these we will make a major departure from the Smalltalk model, which has a fairly complex metaclass system. Instead we will use the model introduced in ObjVlisp[1], which Python adopted.

In the ObjVlisp model, OBJECT and TYPE are intertwined. OBJECT is the base class of all classes, meaning it has no base class. TYPE is a subclass of OBJECT. By default, every class is an instance of TYPE. In particular, both TYPE and OBJECT are instances of TYPE. However, the programmer can also subclass TYPE to make a new metaclass:

```
# set up the base hierarchy as in Python (the ObjVLisp model)
# the ultimate base class is OBJECT
OBJECT = Class(name="object", base_class=None, fields={}, metaclass=None)
# TYPE is a subclass of OBJECT
TYPE = Class(name="type", base_class=OBJECT, fields={}, metaclass=None)
# TYPE is an instance of itself
TYPE.cls = TYPE
# OBJECT is an instance of TYPE
OBJECT.cls = TYPE
```

To define new metaclasses, it is enough to subclass TYPE. However, in the rest of this chapter we won't do that; we'll simply always use TYPE as the metaclass of every class.

Now the first test passes. The second test checks that reading and writing attributes works on classes as well. It's easy to write, and passes immediately.

---

[1] P. Cointe, "Metaclasses are first class: The ObjVlisp Model," SIGPLAN Not, vol. 22, no. 12, pp. 156–162, 1987.

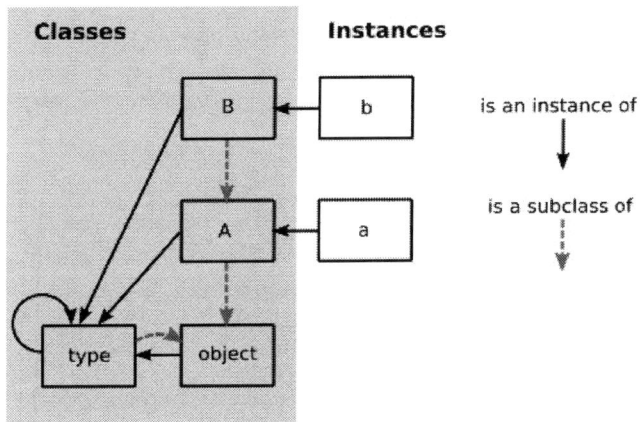

Figure 14.1: Inheritance

```
def test_read_write_field_class():
    # classes are objects too
    # Python code
    class A(object):
        pass
    A.a = 1
    assert A.a == 1
    A.a = 6
    assert A.a == 6

    # Object model code
    A = Class(name="A", base_class=OBJECT, fields={"a": 1}, metaclass=TYPE)
    assert A.read_attr("a") == 1
    A.write_attr("a", 5)
    assert A.read_attr("a") == 5
```

isinstance Checking

So far we haven't taken advantage of the fact that objects have classes. The next test implements the isinstance machinery:

```
def test_isinstance():
    # Python code
    class A(object):
        pass
    class B(A):
        pass
    b = B()
    assert isinstance(b, B)
    assert isinstance(b, A)
    assert isinstance(b, object)
    assert not isinstance(b, type)

    # Object model code
```

```
A = Class(name="A", base_class=OBJECT, fields={}, metaclass=TYPE)
B = Class(name="B", base_class=A, fields={}, metaclass=TYPE)
b = Instance(B)
assert b.isinstance(B)
assert b.isinstance(A)
assert b.isinstance(OBJECT)
assert not b.isinstance(TYPE)
```

To check whether an object `obj` is an instance of a certain class `cls`, it is enough to check whether `cls` is a superclass of the class of `obj`, or the class itself. To check whether a class is a superclass of another class, the chain of superclasses of that class is walked. If and only if the other class is found in that chain, it is a superclass. The chain of superclasses of a class, including the class itself, is called the "method resolution order" of that class. It can easily be computed recursively:

```
class Class(Base):
    ...

    def method_resolution_order(self):
        """ compute the method resolution order of the class """
        if self.base_class is None:
            return [self]
        else:
            return [self] + self.base_class.method_resolution_order()

    def issubclass(self, cls):
        """ is self a subclass of cls? """
        return cls in self.method_resolution_order()
```

With that code, the test passes.

Calling Methods

The remaining missing feature for this first version of the object model is the ability to call methods on objects. In this chapter we will implement a simple single inheritance model.

```
def test_callmethod_simple():
    # Python code
    class A(object):
        def f(self):
            return self.x + 1
    obj = A()
    obj.x = 1
    assert obj.f() == 2

    class B(A):
        pass
    obj = B()
    obj.x = 1
    assert obj.f() == 2 # works on subclass too

    # Object model code
```

```
    def f_A(self):
        return self.read_attr("x") + 1
    A = Class(name="A", base_class=OBJECT, fields={"f": f_A}, metaclass=TYPE)
    obj = Instance(A)
    obj.write_attr("x", 1)
    assert obj.callmethod("f") == 2

    B = Class(name="B", base_class=A, fields={}, metaclass=TYPE)
    obj = Instance(B)
    obj.write_attr("x", 2)
    assert obj.callmethod("f") == 3
```

To find the correct implementation of a method that is sent to an object, we walk the method resolution order of the class of the object. The first method found in the dictionary of one of the classes in the method resolution order is called:

```
class Class(Base):
    ...

    def _read_from_class(self, methname):
        for cls in self.method_resolution_order():
            if methname in cls._fields:
                return cls._fields[methname]
        return MISSING
```

Together with the code for `callmethod` in the Base implementation, this passes the test.

To make sure that methods with arguments work as well, and that overriding of methods is implemented correctly, we can use the following slightly more complex test, which already passes:

```
def test_callmethod_subclassing_and_arguments():
    # Python code
    class A(object):
        def g(self, arg):
            return self.x + arg
    obj = A()
    obj.x = 1
    assert obj.g(4) == 5

    class B(A):
        def g(self, arg):
            return self.x + arg * 2
    obj = B()
    obj.x = 4
    assert obj.g(4) == 12

    # Object model code
    def g_A(self, arg):
        return self.read_attr("x") + arg
    A = Class(name="A", base_class=OBJECT, fields={"g": g_A}, metaclass=TYPE)
    obj = Instance(A)
    obj.write_attr("x", 1)
```

```
assert obj.callmethod("g", 4) == 5

def g_B(self, arg):
    return self.read_attr("x") + arg * 2
B = Class(name="B", base_class=A, fields={"g": g_B}, metaclass=TYPE)
obj = Instance(B)
obj.write_attr("x", 4)
assert obj.callmethod("g", 4) == 12
```

14.3   Attribute-Based Model

Now that the simplest version of our object model is working, we can think of ways to change it.
This section will introduce the distinction between a method-based model and an attribute-based
model. This is one of the core differences between Smalltalk, Ruby, and JavaScript on the one hand
and Python and Lua on the other hand.

The method-based model has the method-calling as the primitive of program execution:

```
result = obj.f(arg1, arg2)
```

The attribute-based model splits up method calling into two steps: looking up an attribute and
calling the result:

```
method = obj.f
result = method(arg1, arg2)
```

This difference can be shown in the following test:

```
def test_bound_method():
    # Python code
    class A(object):
        def f(self, a):
            return self.x + a + 1
    obj = A()
    obj.x = 2
    m = obj.f
    assert m(4) == 7

    class B(A):
        pass
    obj = B()
    obj.x = 1
    m = obj.f
    assert m(10) == 12 # works on subclass too

    # Object model code
    def f_A(self, a):
        return self.read_attr("x") + a + 1
    A = Class(name="A", base_class=OBJECT, fields={"f": f_A}, metaclass=TYPE)
    obj = Instance(A)
    obj.write_attr("x", 2)
```

```
m = obj.read_attr("f")
assert m(4) == 7

B = Class(name="B", base_class=A, fields={}, metaclass=TYPE)
obj = Instance(B)
obj.write_attr("x", 1)
m = obj.read_attr("f")
assert m(10) == 12
```

While the setup is the same as the corresponding test for method calls, the way that the methods are called is different. First, the attribute with the name of the method is looked up on the object. The result of that lookup operation is a *bound method*, an object that encapsulates both the object as well as the function found in the class. Next, that bound method is called with a call operation[2].

To implement this behaviour, we need to change the `Base.read_attr` implementation. If the attribute is not found in the dictionary, it is looked for in the class. If it is found in the class, and the attribute is a callable, it needs to be turned into a bound method. To emulate a bound method we simply use a closure. In addition to changing `Base.read_attr` we can also change `Base.callmethod` to use the new approach to calling methods to make sure all the tests still pass.

```
class Base(object):
    ...
    def read_attr(self, fieldname):
        """ read field 'fieldname' out of the object """
        result = self._read_dict(fieldname)
        if result is not MISSING:
            return result
        result = self.cls._read_from_class(fieldname)
        if _is_bindable(result):
            return _make_boundmethod(result, self)
        if result is not MISSING:
            return result
        raise AttributeError(fieldname)

    def callmethod(self, methname, *args):
        """ call method 'methname' with arguments 'args' on object """
        meth = self.read_attr(methname)
        return meth(*args)

def _is_bindable(meth):
    return callable(meth)

def _make_boundmethod(meth, self):
    def bound(*args):
        return meth(self, *args)
    return bound
```

The rest of the code does not need to be changed at all.

---

[2]It seems that the attribute-based model is conceptually more complex, because it needs both method lookup and call. In practice, calling something is defined by looking up and calling a special attribute `__call__`, so conceptual simplicity is regained. This won't be implemented in this chapter, however.)

14.4 Meta-Object Protocols

In addition to "normal" methods that are called directly by the program, many dynamic languages support *special methods*. These are methods that aren't meant to be called directly but will be called by the object system. In Python those special methods usually have names that start and end with two underscores; e.g., __init__. Special methods can be used to override primitive operations and provide custom behaviour for them instead. Thus, they are hooks that tell the object model machinery exactly how to do certain things. Python's object model has dozens of special methods[3].

Meta-object protocols were introduced by Smalltalk, but were used even more by the object systems for Common Lisp, such as CLOS. That is also where the name *meta-object protocol*, for collections of special methods, was coined[4].

In this chapter we will add three such meta-hooks to our object model. They are used to fine-tune what exactly happens when reading and writing attributes. The special methods we will add first are __getattr__ and __setattr__, which closely follow the behaviour of Python's namesakes.

Customizing Reading and Writing and Attribute

The method __getattr__ is called by the object model when the attribute that is being looked up is not found by normal means; i.e., neither on the instance nor on the class. It gets the name of the attribute being looked up as an argument. An equivalent of the __getattr__ special method was part of early Smalltalk[5] systems under the name doesNotUnderstand:.

The case of __setattr__ is a bit different. Since setting an attribute always creates it, __setattr__ is always called when setting an attribute. To make sure that a __setattr__ method always exists, the OBJECT class has a definition of __setattr__. This base implementation simply does what setting an attribute did so far, which is write the attribute into the object's dictionary. This also makes it possible for a user-defined __setattr__ to delegate to the base OBJECT.__setattr__ in some cases.

A test for these two special methods is the following:

```
def test_getattr():
    # Python code
    class A(object):
        def __getattr__(self, name):
            if name == "fahrenheit":
                return self.celsius * 9. / 5. + 32
            raise AttributeError(name)

        def __setattr__(self, name, value):
            if name == "fahrenheit":
                self.celsius = (value - 32) * 5. / 9.
            else:
                # call the base implementation
                object.__setattr__(self, name, value)
    obj = A()
    obj.celsius = 30
```

---

[3] https://docs.python.org/2/reference/datamodel.html\#special-method-names
[4] G. Kiczales, J. des Rivieres, and D. G. Bobrow, The Art of the Metaobject Protocol. Cambridge, Mass: The MIT Press, 1991.
[5] A. Goldberg, Smalltalk-80: The Language and its Implementation. Addison-Wesley, 1983, page 61.

```
    assert obj.fahrenheit == 86 # test __getattr__
    obj.celsius = 40
    assert obj.fahrenheit == 104

    obj.fahrenheit = 86 # test __setattr__
    assert obj.celsius == 30
    assert obj.fahrenheit == 86

    # Object model code
    def __getattr__(self, name):
        if name == "fahrenheit":
            return self.read_attr("celsius") * 9. / 5. + 32
        raise AttributeError(name)
    def __setattr__(self, name, value):
        if name == "fahrenheit":
            self.write_attr("celsius", (value - 32) * 5. / 9.)
        else:
            # call the base implementation
            OBJECT.read_attr("__setattr__")(self, name, value)

    A = Class(name="A", base_class=OBJECT,
            fields={"__getattr__": __getattr__, "__setattr__": __setattr__},
            metaclass=TYPE)
    obj = Instance(A)
    obj.write_attr("celsius", 30)
    assert obj.read_attr("fahrenheit") == 86 # test __getattr__
    obj.write_attr("celsius", 40)
    assert obj.read_attr("fahrenheit") == 104
    obj.write_attr("fahrenheit", 86) # test __setattr__
    assert obj.read_attr("celsius") == 30
    assert obj.read_attr("fahrenheit") == 86
```

To pass these tests, the Base.read_attr and Base.write_attr methods need to be changed:

```
class Base(object):
    ...

    def read_attr(self, fieldname):
        """ read field 'fieldname' out of the object """
        result = self._read_dict(fieldname)
        if result is not MISSING:
            return result
        result = self.cls._read_from_class(fieldname)
        if _is_bindable(result):
            return _make_boundmethod(result, self)
        if result is not MISSING:
            return result
        meth = self.cls._read_from_class("__getattr__")
        if meth is not MISSING:
            return meth(self, fieldname)
        raise AttributeError(fieldname)
```

```
def write_attr(self, fieldname, value):
    """ write field 'fieldname' into the object """
    meth = self.cls._read_from_class("__setattr__")
    return meth(self, fieldname, value)
```

The procedure for reading an attribute is changed to call the __getattr__ method with the fieldname as an argument, if the method exists, instead of raising an error. Note that __getattr__ (and indeed all special methods in Python) is looked up on the class only, instead of recursively calling self.read_attr("__getattr__"). That is because the latter would lead to an infinite recursion of read_attr if __getattr__ were not defined on the object.

Writing of attributes is fully deferred to the __setattr__ method. To make this work, OBJECT needs to have a __setattr__ method that calls the default behaviour, as follows:

```
def OBJECT__setattr__(self, fieldname, value):
    self._write_dict(fieldname, value)
OBJECT = Class("object", None, {"__setattr__": OBJECT__setattr__}, None)
```

The behaviour of OBJECT__setattr__ is like the previous behaviour of write_attr. With these modifications, the new test passes.

Descriptor Protocol

The above test to provide automatic conversion between different temperature scales worked but was annoying to write, as the attribute name needed to be checked explicitly in the __getattr__ and __setattr__ methods. To get around this, the *descriptor protocol* was introduced in Python.

While __getattr__ and __setattr__ are called on the object the attribute is being read from, the descriptor protocol calls a special method on the *result* of getting an attribute from an object. It can be seen as the generalization of binding a method to an object – and indeed, binding a method to an object is done using the descriptor protocol. In addition to bound methods, the most important use case for the descriptor protocol in Python is the implementation of staticmethod, classmethod and property.

In this subsection we will introduce the subset of the descriptor protocol which deals with binding objects. This is done using the special method __get__, and is best explained with an example test:

```
def test_get():
    # Python code
    class FahrenheitGetter(object):
        def __get__(self, inst, cls):
            return inst.celsius * 9. / 5. + 32

    class A(object):
        fahrenheit = FahrenheitGetter()
    obj = A()
    obj.celsius = 30
    assert obj.fahrenheit == 86

    # Object model code
    class FahrenheitGetter(object):
        def __get__(self, inst, cls):
            return inst.read_attr("celsius") * 9. / 5. + 32
```

```
A = Class(name="A", base_class=OBJECT,
          fields={"fahrenheit": FahrenheitGetter()},
          metaclass=TYPE)
obj = Instance(A)
obj.write_attr("celsius", 30)
assert obj.read_attr("fahrenheit") == 86
```

The __get__ method is called on the FahrenheitGetter instance after that has been looked up in the class of obj. The arguments to __get__ are the instance where the lookup was done[6].

Implementing this behaviour is easy. We simply need to change _is_bindable and _make_boundmethod:

```
def _is_bindable(meth):
    return hasattr(meth, "__get__")


def _make_boundmethod(meth, self):
    return meth.__get__(self, None)
```

This makes the test pass. The previous tests about bound methods also still pass, as Python's functions have a __get__ method that returns a bound method object.

In practice, the descriptor protocol is quite a lot more complex. It also supports __set__ to override what setting an attribute means on a per-attribute basis. Also, the current implementation is cutting a few corners. Note that _make_boundmethod calls the method __get__ on the implementation level, instead of using meth.read_attr("__get__"). This is necessary since our object model borrows functions and thus methods from Python, instead of having a representation for them that uses the object model. A more complete object model would have to solve this problem.

14.5   Instance Optimization

While the first three variants of the object model were concerned with behavioural variation, in this last section we will look at an optimization without any behavioural impact. This optimization is called *maps* and was pioneered in the VM for the Self programming language[7]. It is still one of the most important object model optimizations: it's used in PyPy and all modern JavaScript VMs, such as V8 (where the optimization is called *hidden classes*).

The optimization starts from the following observation: In the object model as implemented so far all instances use a full dictionary to store their attributes. A dictionary is implemented using a hash map, which takes a lot of memory. In addition, the dictionaries of instances of the same class typically have the same keys as well. For example, given a class Point, the keys of all its instances' dictionaries are likely "x" and "y".

The maps optimization exploits this fact. It effectively splits up the dictionary of every instance into two parts. A part storing the keys (the map) that can be shared between all instances with the same set of attribute names. The instance then only stores a reference to the shared map and the values of the attributes in a list (which is a lot more compact in memory than a dictionary). The map stores a mapping from attribute names to indexes into that list.

A simple test of that behaviour looks like this:

---

[6] In Python the second argument is the class where the attribute was found, though we will ignore that here.
[7] C. Chambers, D. Ungar, and E. Lee, "An efficient implementation of SELF, a dynamically-typed object-oriented language based on prototypes," in OOPSLA, 1989, vol. 24.

```
def test_maps():
    # white box test inspecting the implementation
    Point = Class(name="Point", base_class=OBJECT, fields={}, metaclass=TYPE)
    p1 = Instance(Point)
    p1.write_attr("x", 1)
    p1.write_attr("y", 2)
    assert p1.storage == [1, 2]
    assert p1.map.attrs == {"x": 0, "y": 1}

    p2 = Instance(Point)
    p2.write_attr("x", 5)
    p2.write_attr("y", 6)
    assert p1.map is p2.map
    assert p2.storage == [5, 6]

    p1.write_attr("x", -1)
    p1.write_attr("y", -2)
    assert p1.map is p2.map
    assert p1.storage == [-1, -2]

    p3 = Instance(Point)
    p3.write_attr("x", 100)
    p3.write_attr("z", -343)
    assert p3.map is not p1.map
    assert p3.map.attrs == {"x": 0, "z": 1}
```

Note that this is a different flavour of test than the ones we've written before. All previous tests just tested the behaviour of the classes via the exposed interfaces. This test instead checks the implementation details of the Instance class by reading internal attributes and comparing them to predefined values. Therefore this test can be called a *white-box* test.

The attrs attribute of the map of p1 describes the layout of the instance as having two attributes "x" and "y" which are stored at position 0 and 1 of the storage of p1. Making a second instance p2 and adding to it the same attributes in the same order will make it end up with the same map. If, on the other hand, a different attribute is added, the map can of course not be shared.

The Map class looks like this:

```
class Map(object):
    def __init__(self, attrs):
        self.attrs = attrs
        self.next_maps = {}

    def get_index(self, fieldname):
        return self.attrs.get(fieldname, -1)

    def next_map(self, fieldname):
        assert fieldname not in self.attrs
        if fieldname in self.next_maps:
            return self.next_maps[fieldname]
        attrs = self.attrs.copy()
        attrs[fieldname] = len(attrs)
        result = self.next_maps[fieldname] = Map(attrs)
```

```
        return result

EMPTY_MAP = Map({})
```

Maps have two methods, get_index and next_map. The former is used to find the index of an attribute name in the object's storage. The latter is used when a new attribute is added to an object. In that case the object needs to use a different map, which next_map computes. The method uses the next_maps dictionary to cache already created maps. That way, objects that have the same layout also end up using the same Map object.

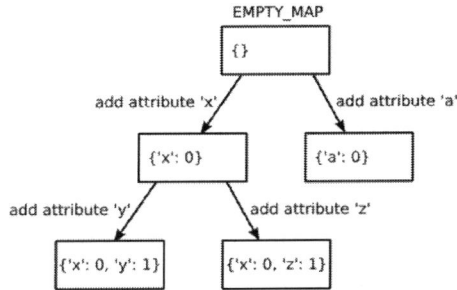

Figure 14.2: Map transitions

The Instance implementation that uses maps looks like this:

```
class Instance(Base):
    """Instance of a user-defined class. """

    def __init__(self, cls):
        assert isinstance(cls, Class)
        Base.__init__(self, cls, None)
        self.map = EMPTY_MAP
        self.storage = []

    def _read_dict(self, fieldname):
        index = self.map.get_index(fieldname)
        if index == -1:
            return MISSING
        return self.storage[index]

    def _write_dict(self, fieldname, value):
        index = self.map.get_index(fieldname)
        if index != -1:
            self.storage[index] = value
        else:
            new_map = self.map.next_map(fieldname)
            self.storage.append(value)
            self.map = new_map
```

The class now passes None as the fields dictionary to Base, as Instance will store the content of the dictionary in another way. Therefore it needs to override the _read_dict and _write_dict methods. In a real implementation, we would refactor the Base class so that it is no longer responsible for storing the fields dictionary, but for now having instances store None there is good enough.

A newly created instance starts out using the EMPTY_MAP, which has no attributes, and empty storage. To implement _read_dict, the instance's map is asked for the index of the attribute name. Then the corresponding entry of the storage list is returned.

Writing into the fields dictionary has two cases. On the one hand the value of an existing attribute can be changed. This is done by simply changing the storage at the corresponding index. On the other hand, if the attribute does not exist yet, a *map transition* (Figure 14.2) is needed using the next_map method. The value of the new attribute is appended to the storage list.

What does this optimization achieve? It optimizes use of memory in the common case where there are many instances with the same layout. It is not a universal optimization: code that creates instances with wildly different sets of attributes will have a larger memory footprint than if we just use dictionaries.

This is a common problem when optimizing dynamic languages. It is often not possible to find optimizations that are faster or use less memory in all cases. In practice, the optimizations chosen apply to how the language is *typically* used, while potentially making behaviour worse for programs that use extremely dynamic features.

Another interesting aspect of maps is that, while here they only optimize for memory use, in actual VMs that use a just-in-time (JIT) compiler they also improve the performance of the program. To achieve that, the JIT uses the maps to compile attribute lookups to a lookup in the objects' storage at a fixed offset, getting rid of all dictionary lookups completely[8].

14.6   Potential Extensions

It is easy to extend our object model and experiment with various language design choices. Here are some possibilities:

- The easiest thing to do is to add further special methods. Some easy and interesting ones to add are __init__, __getattribute__, __set__.
- The model can be very easily extended to support multiple inheritance. To do this, every class would get a list of base classes. Then the Class.method_resolution_order method would need to be changed to support looking up methods. A simple method resolution order could be computed using a depth-first search with removal of duplicates. A more complicated but better one is the C3 algorithm[9], which adds better handling in the base of diamond-shaped multiple inheritance hierarchies and rejects insensible inheritance patterns.
- A more radical change is to switch to a prototype model, which involves the removal of the distinction between classes and instances.

14.7   Conclusions

Some of the core aspects of the design of an object-oriented programming language are the details of its object model. Writing small object model prototypes is an easy and fun way to understand the inner workings of existing languages better and to get insights into the design space of object-oriented

---

[8] How that works is beyond the scope of this chapter. I tried to give a reasonably readable account of it in a paper I wrote a few years ago. It uses an object model that is basically a variant of the one in this chapter: C. F. Bolz, A. Cuni, M. Fijałkowski, M. Leuschel, S. Pedroni, and A. Rigo, "Runtime feedback in a meta-tracing JIT for efficient dynamic languages," in Proceedings of the 6th Workshop on Implementation, Compilation, Optimization of Object-Oriented Languages, Programs and Systems, New York, NY, USA, 2011, pp. 9:1–9:8.
[9] https://www.python.org/download/releases/2.3/mro/

languages. Playing with object models is a good way to experiment with different language design ideas without having to worry about the more boring parts of language implementation, such as parsing and executing code.

Such object models can also be useful in practice, not just as vehicles for experimentation. They can be embedded in and used from other languages. Examples of this approach are common: the GObject object model, written in C, that's used in GLib and other Gnome libraries; or the various class system implementations in JavaScript.

## chapter 15

Optical Character Recognition (OCR)
Marina Samuel

15.1   Introduction

What if your computer could wash your dishes, do your laundry, cook you dinner, and clean your home? I think I can safely say that most people would be happy to get a helping hand! But what would it take for a computer to be able to perform these tasks in the same way that humans can?

The famous computer scientist Alan Turing proposed the Turing Test as a way to identify whether a machine could have intelligence indistinguishable from that of a human being. The test involves a human posing questions to two hidden entities, one human, and the other a machine, and trying to identify which is which. If the interrogator is unable to identify the machine, then the machine is considered to have human-level intelligence.

While there is a lot of controversy surrounding whether the Turing Test is a valid assessment of intelligence, and whether we can build such intelligent machines, there is no doubt that machines with some degree of intelligence already exist. There is currently software that helps robots navigate an office and perform small tasks, or help those suffering with Alzheimer's. More common examples of Artificial Intelligence (A.I.) are the way that Google estimates what you're looking for when you search for some keywords, or the way that Facebook decides what to put in your news feed.

One well known application of A.I. is Optical Character Recognition (OCR). An OCR system is a piece of software that can take images of handwritten characters as input and interpret them into machine readable text. While you may not think twice when depositing a handwritten cheque into a bank machine , there is some interesting work going on in the background. This chapter will examine a working example of a simple OCR system that recognizes numerical digits using an Artificial Neural Network (ANN). But first, let's establish a bit more context.

15.2   What is Artificial Intelligence?

While Turing's definition of intelligence sounds reasonable, at the end of the day what constitutes intelligence is fundamentally a philosophical debate. Computer scientists have, however, categorized certain types of systems and algorithms into branches of AI. Each branch is used to solve certain sets of problems. These branches include the following examples, as well as many others[1]:

---

[1] http://www-formal.stanford.edu/jmc/whatisai/node2.html

- Logical and probabilistic deduction and inference based on some predefined knowledge of a world. e.g. Fuzzy inference[2] can help a thermostat decide when to turn on the air conditioning when it detects that the temperature is hot and the atmosphere is humid
- Heuristic search. e.g. Searching can be used to find the best possible next move in a game of chess by searching all possible moves and choosing the one that most improves your position
- Machine learning (ML) with feedback models. e.g. Pattern-recognition problems like OCR.

In general, ML involves using large data sets to train a system to identify patterns. The training data sets may be labelled, meaning the system's expected outputs are specified for given inputs, or unlabelled meaning expected outputs are not specified. Algorithms that train systems with unlabelled data are called *unsupervised* algorithms and those that train with labelled data are called *supervised*. Many ML algorithms and techniques exist for creating OCR systems, of which ANNs are one approach.

15.3   Artificial Neural Networks

What Are ANNs?

An ANN is a structure consisting of interconnected nodes that communicate with one another. The structure and its functionality are inspired by neural networks found in a biological brain. Hebbian Theory[3] explains how these networks can learn to identify patterns by physically altering their structure and link strengths. Similarly, a typical ANN (shown in Figure 15.1) has connections between nodes that have a weight which is updated as the network learns. The nodes labelled "+1" are called *biases*. The leftmost blue column of nodes are *input nodes*, the middle column contains *hidden nodes*, and the rightmost column contains *output nodes*. There may be many columns of hidden nodes, known as *hidden layers*.

The values inside all of the circular nodes in Figure 15.1 represent the output of the node. If we call the output of the nth node from the top in layer L as a $n(L)$ and the connection between the ith node in layer L and the jth node in layer $L+1$ as $w_j^{(L)}i$, then the output of node $a_2^{(2)}$ is:

$$a_2^{(2)} = f(w_{21}^{(1)} x_1 + w_{22}^{(1)} x_2 + b_2^{(1)})$$

where $f(.)$ is known as the *activation function* and b is the *bias*. An activation function is the decision-maker for what type of output a node has. A bias is an additional node with a fixed output of 1 that may be added to an ANN to improve its accuracy. We'll see more details on both of these in Section 15.4.

This type of network topology is called a *feedforward* neural network because there are no cycles in the network. ANNs with nodes whose outputs feed into their inputs are called recurrent neural networks. There are many algorithms that can be applied to train feedforward ANNs; one commonly used algorithm is called *backpropagation*. The OCR system we will implement in this chapter will use backpropagation.

How Do We Use ANNs?

Like most other ML approaches, the first step for using backpropagation is to decide how to transform or reduce our problem into one that can be solved by an ANN. In other words, how can we manipulate

---

[2]http://www.cs.princeton.edu/courses/archive/fall07/cos436/HIDDEN/Knapp/fuzzy004.htm
[3]http://www.nbb.cornell.edu/neurobio/linster/BioNB420/hebb.pdf

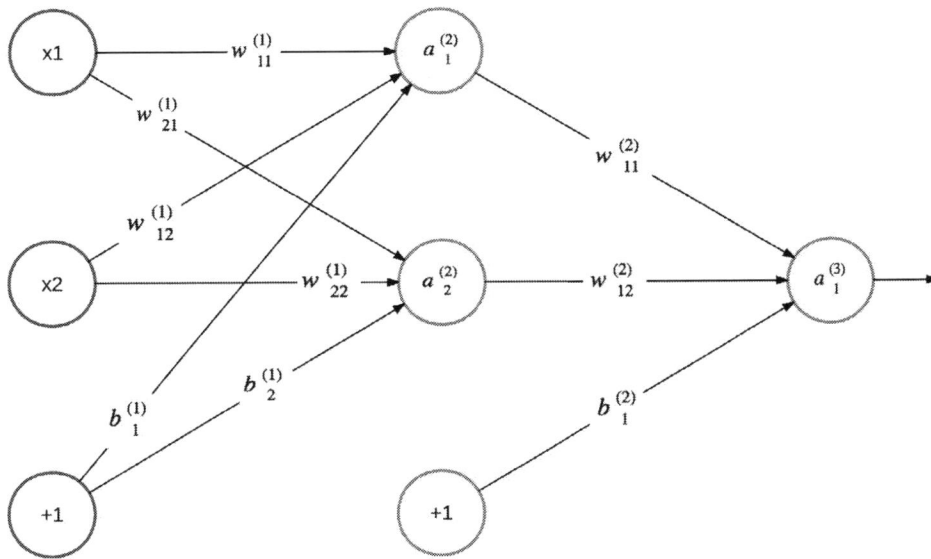

Figure 15.1: An Artificial Neural Network

our input data so we can feed it into the ANN? For the case of our OCR system, we can use the positions of the pixels for a given digit as input. It is worth noting that, often times, choosing the input data format is not this simple. If we were analyzing large images to identify shapes in them, for instance, we may need to pre-process the image to identify contours within it. These contours would be the input.

Once we've decided on our input data format, what's next? Since backpropagation is a supervised algorithm, it will need to be trained with labelled data, as mentioned in Section 15.2. Thus, when passing the pixel positions as training input, we must also pass the associated digit. This means that we must find or gather a large data set of drawn digits and associated values.

The next step is to partition the data set into a training set and validation set. The training data is used to run the backpropagation algorithm to set the weights of the ANN. The validation data is used to make predictions using the trained network and compute its accuracy. If we were comparing the performance of backpropagation vs. another algorithm on our data, we would split the data[4] into 50% for training, 25% for comparing performance of the 2 algorithms (validation set) and the final 25% for testing accuracy of the chosen algorithm (test set). Since we're not comparing algorithms, we can group one of the 25% sets as part of the training set and use 75% of the data to train the network and 25% for validating that it was trained well.

The purpose of identifying the accuracy of the ANN is two-fold. First, it is to avoid the problem of *overfitting*. Overfitting occurs when the network has a much higher accuracy on predicting the training set than the validation set. Overfitting tells us that the chosen training data does not generalize well enough and needs to be refined. Secondly, testing the accuracy of several different numbers of hidden layers and hidden nodes helps in designing the most optimal ANN size. An optimal ANN size will have enough hidden nodes and layers to make accurate predictions but also as few nodes/connections as possible to reduce computational overhead that may slow down training and

---

[4]http://www-group.slac.stanford.edu/sluo/Lectures/stat_lecture_files/sluo2006lec7.pdf

predictions. Once the optimal size has been decided and the network has been trained, it's ready to make predictions!

15.4   Design Decisions in a Simple OCR System

In the last few paragraphs we've gone over some of the basics of feedforward ANNs and how to use them. Now it's time to talk about how we can build an OCR system.

First off, we must decide what we want our system to be able to do. To keep things simple, let's allow users to draw a single digit and be able to train the OCR system with that drawn digit or to request that the system predict what the drawn digit is. While an OCR system could run locally on a single machine, having a client-server setup gives much more flexibility. It makes crowd-sourced training of an ANN possible and allows powerful servers to handle intensive computations.

Our OCR system will consist of 5 main components, divided into 5 files. There will be:

- a client (ocr.js)
- a server (server.py)
- a simple user interface (ocr.html)
- an ANN trained via backpropagation (ocr.py)
- an ANN design script (neural_network_design.py)

The user interface will be simple: a canvas to draw digits on and buttons to either train the ANN or request a prediction. The client will gather the drawn digit, translate it into an array, and pass it to the server to be processed either as a training sample or as a prediction request. The server will simply route the training or prediction request by making API calls to the ANN module. The ANN module will train the network with an existing data set on its first initialization. It will then save the ANN weights to a file and re-load them on subsequent startups. This module is where the core of training and prediction logic happens. Finally, the design script is for experimenting with different hidden node counts and deciding what works best. Together, these pieces give us a very simplistic, but functional OCR system.

Now that we've thought about how the system will work at a high level, it's time to put the concepts into code!

A Simple Interface (ocr.html)

As mentioned earlier, the first step is to gather data for training the network. We could upload a sequence of hand-written digits to the server, but that would be awkward. Instead, we could have users actually handwrite the digits on the page using an HTML canvas. We could then give them a couple of options to either train or test the network, where training the network also involves specifying what digit was drawn. This way it is possible to easily outsource the data collection by pointing people to a website to receive their input. Here's some HTML to get us started.

```
<html>
<head>
    <script src="ocr.js"></script>
    <link rel="stylesheet" type="text/css" href="ocr.css">
</head>
<body onload="ocrDemo.onLoadFunction()">
    <div id="main-container" style="text-align: center;">
        <h1>OCR Demo</h1>
```

```
        <canvas id="canvas" width="200" height="200"></canvas>
        <form name="input">
            <p>Digit: <input id="digit" type="text"> </p>
            <input type="button" value="Train" onclick="ocrDemo.train()">
            <input type="button" value="Test" onclick="ocrDemo.test()">
            <input type="button" value="Reset" onclick="ocrDemo.resetCanvas();"/>
        </form>
    </div>
</body>
</html>
```

An OCR Client (ocr.js)

Since a single pixel on an HTML canvas might be hard to see, we can represent a single pixel for the ANN input as a square of 10x10 real pixels. Thus the real canvas is 200x200 pixels and it is represented by a 20x20 canvas from the perspective of the ANN. The variables below will help us keep track of these measurements.

```
var ocrDemo = {
    CANVAS_WIDTH: 200,
    TRANSLATED_WIDTH: 20,
    PIXEL_WIDTH: 10, // TRANSLATED_WIDTH = CANVAS_WIDTH / PIXEL_WIDTH
```

We can then outline the pixels in the new representation so they are easier to see. Here we have a blue grid generated by drawGrid().

```
    drawGrid: function(ctx) {
        for (var x = this.PIXEL_WIDTH, y = this.PIXEL_WIDTH;
                x < this.CANVAS_WIDTH; x += this.PIXEL_WIDTH,
                y += this.PIXEL_WIDTH) {
            ctx.strokeStyle = this.BLUE;
            ctx.beginPath();
            ctx.moveTo(x, 0);
            ctx.lineTo(x, this.CANVAS_WIDTH);
            ctx.stroke();

            ctx.beginPath();
            ctx.moveTo(0, y);
            ctx.lineTo(this.CANVAS_WIDTH, y);
            ctx.stroke();
        }
    },
```

We also need to store the data drawn on the grid in a form that can be sent to the server. For simplicity, we can have an array called data which labels an uncoloured, black pixel as 0 and a coloured white pixel as 1. We also need some mouse listeners on the canvas so we know when to call fillSquare() to colour a pixel white while a user is drawing a digit. These listeners should keep track of whether we are in a drawing state and then call fillSquare() to do some simple math and decide which pixels need to be filled in.

```
onMouseMove: function(e, ctx, canvas) {
    if (!canvas.isDrawing) {
        return;
    }
    this.fillSquare(ctx,
        e.clientX - canvas.offsetLeft, e.clientY - canvas.offsetTop);
},

onMouseDown: function(e, ctx, canvas) {
    canvas.isDrawing = true;
    this.fillSquare(ctx,
        e.clientX - canvas.offsetLeft, e.clientY - canvas.offsetTop);
},

onMouseUp: function(e) {
    canvas.isDrawing = false;
},

fillSquare: function(ctx, x, y) {
    var xPixel = Math.floor(x / this.PIXEL_WIDTH);
    var yPixel = Math.floor(y / this.PIXEL_WIDTH);
    this.data[((xPixel - 1)  * this.TRANSLATED_WIDTH + yPixel) - 1] = 1;

    ctx.fillStyle = '#ffffff';
    ctx.fillRect(xPixel * this.PIXEL_WIDTH, yPixel * this.PIXEL_WIDTH,
        this.PIXEL_WIDTH, this.PIXEL_WIDTH);
},
```

Now we're getting closer to the juicy stuff! We need a function that prepares training data to be sent to the server. Here we have a relatively straight forward train() function that does some error checking on the data to be sent, adds it to trainArray and sends it off by calling sendData().

```
train: function() {
    var digitVal = document.getElementById("digit").value;
    if (!digitVal || this.data.indexOf(1) < 0) {
        alert("Please type and draw a digit value in order to train the network");
        return;
    }
    this.trainArray.push({"y0": this.data, "label": parseInt(digitVal)});
    this.trainingRequestCount++;

    // Time to send a training batch to the server.
    if (this.trainingRequestCount == this.BATCH_SIZE) {
        alert("Sending training data to server...");
        var json = {
            trainArray: this.trainArray,
            train: true
        };

        this.sendData(json);
        this.trainingRequestCount = 0;
        this.trainArray = [];
```

```
    }
},
```

An interesting design worth noting here is the use of `trainingRequestCount`, `trainArray`, and `BATCH_SIZE`. What's happening here is that `BATCH_SIZE` is some pre-defined constant for how much training data a client will keep track of before it sends a batched request to the server to be processed by the OCR. The main reason to batch requests is to avoid overwhelming the server with many requests at once. If many clients exist (e.g. many users are on the `ocr.html` page training the system), or if another layer existed in the client that takes scanned drawn digits and translated them to pixels to train the network, a `BATCH_SIZE` of 1 would result in many, unnecessary requests. This approach is good because it gives more flexibility to the client, however, in practice, batching should also take place on the server, when needed. A denial of service (DoS) attack could occur in which a malicious client purposely sends many requests to the server to overwhelm it so that it breaks down.

We will also need a `test()` function. Similar to `train()`, it should do a simple check on the validity of the data and send it off. For `test()`, however, no batching occurs since users should be able to request a prediction and get immediate results.

```
test: function() {
    if (this.data.indexOf(1) < 0) {
        alert("Please draw a digit in order to test the network");
        return;
    }
    var json = {
        image: this.data,
        predict: true
    };
    this.sendData(json);
},
```

Finally, we will need some functions to make an HTTP POST request, receive a response, and handle any potential errors along the way.

```
receiveResponse: function(xmlHttp) {
    if (xmlHttp.status != 200) {
        alert("Server returned status " + xmlHttp.status);
        return;
    }
    var responseJSON = JSON.parse(xmlHttp.responseText);
    if (xmlHttp.responseText && responseJSON.type == "test") {
        alert("The neural network predicts you wrote a \'"
                + responseJSON.result + '\'');
    }
},

onError: function(e) {
    alert("Error occurred while connecting to server: " + e.target.statusText);
},

sendData: function(json) {
    var xmlHttp = new XMLHttpRequest();
    xmlHttp.open('POST', this.HOST + ":" + this.PORT, false);
```

```
xmlHttp.onload = function() { this.receiveResponse(xmlHttp); }.bind(this);
xmlHttp.onerror = function() { this.onError(xmlHttp) }.bind(this);
var msg = JSON.stringify(json);
xmlHttp.setRequestHeader('Content-length', msg.length);
xmlHttp.setRequestHeader("Connection", "close");
xmlHttp.send(msg);
}
```

A Server (`server.py`)

Despite being a small server that simply relays information, we still need to consider how to receive and handle the HTTP requests. First we need to decide what kind of HTTP request to use. In the last section, the client is using POST, but why did we decide on this? Since data is being sent to the server, a PUT or POST request makes the most sense. We only need to send a json body and no URL parameters. So in theory, a GET request could have worked as well but would not make sense semantically. The choice between PUT and POST, however, is a long, on-going debate among programmers; KNPLabs summarizes the issues with humour[5].

Another consideration is whether to send the "train" vs. "predict" requests to different endpoints (e.g. `http://localhost/train` and `http://localhost/predict`) or the same endpoint which then processes the data separately. In this case, we can go with the latter approach since the difference between what is done with the data in each case is minor enough to fit into a short if statement. In practice, it would be better to have these as separate endpoints if the server were to do any more detailed processing for each request type. This decision, in turn impacted what server error codes were used when. For example, a 400 "Bad Request" error is sent when neither "train" or "predict" is specified in the payload. If separate endpoints were used instead, this would not be an issue. The processing done in the background by the OCR system may fail for any reason and if it's not handled correctly within the server, a 500 "Internal Server Error" is sent. Again, if the endpoints were separated, there would have been more room to go into detail to send more appropriate errors. For example, identifying that an internal server error was actually caused by a bad request.

Finally, we need to decide when and where to initialize the OCR system. A good approach would be to initialize it within `server.py` but before the server is started. This is because on first run, the OCR system needs to train the network on some pre-existing data the first time it starts and this may take a few minutes. If the server started before this processing was complete, any requests to train or predict would throw an exception since the OCR object would not yet have been initialized, given the current implementation. Another possible implementation could create some inaccurate initial ANN to be used for the first few queries while the new ANN is asynchronously trained in the background. This alternative approach does allow the ANN to be used immediately, but the implementation is more complex and it would only save on time on server startup if the servers are reset. This type of implementation would be more beneficial for an OCR service that requires high availability.

Here we have the majority of our server code in one short function that handles POST requests.

```
def do_POST(s):
    response_code = 200
    response = ""
    var_len = int(s.headers.get('Content-Length'))
    content = s.rfile.read(var_len);
    payload = json.loads(content);
```

---

[5]`https://knpuniversity.com/screencast/rest/put-versus-post`

```
    if payload.get('train'):
        nn.train(payload['trainArray'])
        nn.save()
    elif payload.get('predict'):
        try:
            response = {
                "type":"test",
                "result":nn.predict(str(payload['image']))
            }
        except:
            response_code = 500
    else:
        response_code = 400

    s.send_response(response_code)
    s.send_header("Content-type", "application/json")
    s.send_header("Access-Control-Allow-Origin", "*")
    s.end_headers()
    if response:
        s.wfile.write(json.dumps(response))
    return
```

Designing a Feedforward ANN (`neural_network_design.py`)

When designing a feedforward ANN, there are a few factors we must consider. The first is what activation function to use. We mentioned activation functions earlier as the decision-maker for a node's output. The type of the decision an activation function makes will help us decide which one to use. In our case, we will be designing an ANN that outputs a value between 0 and 1 for each digit (0-9). Values closer to 1 would mean the ANN predicts this is the drawn digit and values closer to 0 would mean it's predicted to not be the drawn digit. Thus, we want an activation function that would have outputs either close to 0 or close to 1. We also need a function that is differentiable because we will need the derivative for our backpropagation computation. A commonly used function in this case is the sigmoid because it satisfies both these constraints. StatSoft provides a nice list[6] of common activation functions and their properties.

A second factor to consider is whether we want to include biases. We've mentioned biases a couple of times before but haven't really talked about what they are or why we use them. Let's try to understand this by going back to how the output of a node is computed in Figure 15.1. Suppose we had a single input node and a single output node, our output formula would be $y = f(wx)$, where y is the output, $f()$ is the activation function, w is the weight for the link between the nodes, and x is the variable input for the node. The bias is essentially a node whose output is always 1. This would change the output formula to $y = f(wx + b)$ where b is the weight of the connection between the bias node and the next node. If we consider w and b as constants and x as a variable, then adding a bias adds a constant to our linear function input to $f(.)$.

Adding the bias therefore allows for a shift in the y-intercept and in general gives more flexibility for the output of a node. It's often good practice to include biases, especially for ANNs with a small number of inputs and outputs. Biases allow for more flexibility in the output of the ANN and thus

---

[6]http://www.fmi.uni-sofia.bg/fmi/statist/education/textbook/eng/glosa.html

provide the ANN with more room for accuracy. Without biases, we're less likely to make correct predictions with our ANN or would need more hidden nodes to make more accurate predictions.

Other factors to consider are the number of hidden layers and the number of hidden nodes per layer. For larger ANNs with many inputs and outputs, these numbers are decided by trying different values and testing the network's performance. In this case, the performance is measured by training an ANN of a given size and seeing what percentage of the validation set is classified correctly. In most cases, a single hidden layer is sufficient for decent performance, so we only experiment with the number of hidden nodes here.

```
# Try various number of hidden nodes and see what performs best
for i in xrange(5, 50, 5):
    nn = OCRNeuralNetwork(i, data_matrix, data_labels, train_indices, False)
    performance = str(test(data_matrix, data_labels, test_indices, nn))
    print "{i} Hidden Nodes: {val}".format(i=i, val=performance)
```

Here we initialize an ANN with between 5 to 50 hidden nodes in increments of 5. We then call the test() function.

```
def test(data_matrix, data_labels, test_indices, nn):
    avg_sum = 0
    for j in xrange(100):
        correct_guess_count = 0
        for i in test_indices:
            test = data_matrix[i]
            prediction = nn.predict(test)
            if data_labels[i] == prediction:
                correct_guess_count += 1

        avg_sum += (correct_guess_count / float(len(test_indices)))
    return avg_sum / 100
```

The inner loop is counting the number of correct classifications which are then divided by the number of attempted classifications at the end. This gives a ratio or percentage accuracy for the ANN. Since each time an ANN is trained, its weights may be slightly different, we repeat this process 100 times in the outer loop so we can take an average of this particular ANN configuration's accuracy. In our case, a sample run of neural_network_design.py looks like the following:

```
PERFORMANCE
-----------

5 Hidden Nodes: 0.7792
10 Hidden Nodes: 0.8704
15 Hidden Nodes: 0.8808
20 Hidden Nodes: 0.8864
25 Hidden Nodes: 0.8808
30 Hidden Nodes: 0.888
35 Hidden Nodes: 0.8904
40 Hidden Nodes: 0.8896
45 Hidden Nodes: 0.8928
```

From this output we can conclude that 15 hidden nodes would be most optimal. Adding 5 nodes from 10 to 15 gets us ~1% more accuracy, whereas improving the accuracy by another 1% would require adding another 20 nodes. Increasing the hidden node count also increases computational overhead. So it would take networks with more hidden nodes longer to be trained and to make predictions. Thus we choose to use the last hidden node count that resulted in a dramatic increase in accuracy. Of course, it's possible when designing an ANN that computational overhead is no problem and it's top priority to have the most accurate ANN possible. In that case it would be better to choose 45 hidden nodes instead of 15.

Core OCR Functionality

In this section we'll talk about how the actual training occurs via backpropagation, how we can use the network to make predictions, and other key design decisions for core functionality.

Training via Backpropagation (ocr.py)

We use the backpropagation algorithm to train our ANN. It consists of 4 main steps that are repeated for every sample in the training set, updating the ANN weights each time.

First, we initialize the weights to small (between -1 and 1) random values. In our case, we initialize them to values between -0.06 and 0.06 and store them in matrices theta1, theta2, input_layer_bias, and hidden_layer_bias. Since every node in a layer links to every node in the next layer we can create a matrix that has m rows and n columns where n is the number of nodes in one layer and m is the number of nodes in the adjacent layer. This matrix would represent all the weights for the links between these two layers. Here theta1 has 400 columns for our 20x20 pixel inputs and num_hidden_nodes rows. Likewise, theta2 represents the links between the hidden layer and output layer. It has num_hidden_nodes columns and NUM_DIGITS (10) rows. The other two vectors (1 row), input_layer_bias and hidden_layer_bias represent the biases.

```
def _rand_initialize_weights(self, size_in, size_out):
    return [((x * 0.12) - 0.06) for x in np.random.rand(size_out, size_in)]

        self.theta1 = self._rand_initialize_weights(400, num_hidden_nodes)
        self.theta2 = self._rand_initialize_weights(num_hidden_nodes, 10)
        self.input_layer_bias = self._rand_initialize_weights(1,
                                                num_hidden_nodes)
        self.hidden_layer_bias = self._rand_initialize_weights(1, 10)
```

The second step is *forward propagation*, which is essentially computing the node outputs as described in Section 15.3, layer by layer starting from the input nodes. Here, y0 is an array of size 400 with the inputs we wish to use to train the ANN. We multiply theta1 by y0 transposed so that we have two matrices with sizes (num_hidden_nodes x 400) * (400 x 1) and have a resulting vector of outputs for the hidden layer of size num_hidden_nodes. We then add the bias vector and apply the vectorized sigmoid activation function to this output vector, giving us y1. y1 is the output vector of our hidden layer. The same process is repeated again to compute y2 for the output nodes. y2 is now our output layer vector with values representing the likelihood that their index is the drawn number. For example if someone draws an 8, the value of y2 at the 8th index will be the largest if the ANN has made the correct prediction. However, 6 may have a higher likelihood than 1 of being the drawn digit since it looks more similar to 8 and is more likely to use up the same pixels to be drawn as the 8. y2 becomes more accurate with each additional drawn digit the ANN is trained with.

```
# The sigmoid activation function. Operates on scalars.
def _sigmoid_scalar(self, z):
    return 1 / (1 + math.e ** -z)

        y1 = np.dot(np.mat(self.theta1), np.mat(data['y0']).T)
        sum1 =   y1 + np.mat(self.input_layer_bias) # Add the bias
        y1 = self.sigmoid(sum1)

        y2 = np.dot(np.array(self.theta2), y1)
        y2 = np.add(y2, self.hidden_layer_bias) # Add the bias
        y2 = self.sigmoid(y2)
```

The third step is *back propagation*, which involves computing the errors at the output nodes then at every intermediate layer back towards the input. Here we start by creating an expected output vector, actual_vals, with a 1 at the index of the digit that represents the value of the drawn digit and 0s otherwise. The vector of errors at the output nodes, output_errors, is computed by subtracting the actual output vector, y2, from actual_vals. For every hidden layer afterwards, we compute two components. First, we have the next layer's transposed weight matrix multiplied by its output errors. Then we have the derivative of the activation function applied to the previous layer. We then perform an element-wise multiplication on these two components, giving a vector of errors for a hidden layer. Here we call this hidden_errors.

```
        actual_vals = [0] * 10
        actual_vals[data['label']] = 1
        output_errors = np.mat(actual_vals).T - np.mat(y2)
        hidden_errors = np.multiply(np.dot(np.mat(self.theta2).T, output_errors),
                          self.sigmoid_prime(sum1))
```

Weight updates that adjust the ANN weights based on the errors computed earlier. Weights are updated at each layer via matrix multiplication. The error matrix at each layer is multiplied by the output matrix of the previous layer. This product is then multiplied by a scalar called the learning rate and added to the weight matrix. The learning rate is a value between 0 and 1 that influences the speed and accuracy of learning in the ANN. Larger learning rate values will generate an ANN that learns quickly but is less accurate, while smaller values will will generate an ANN that learns slower but is more accurate. In our case, we have a relatively small value for learning rate, 0.1. This works well since we do not need the ANN to be immediately trained in order for a user to continue making train or predict requests. Biases are updated by simply multiplying the learning rate by the layer's error vector.

```
        self.theta1 += self.LEARNING_RATE * np.dot(np.mat(hidden_errors),
                          np.mat(data['y0']))
        self.theta2 += self.LEARNING_RATE * np.dot(np.mat(output_errors),
                          np.mat(y1).T)
        self.hidden_layer_bias += self.LEARNING_RATE * output_errors
        self.input_layer_bias += self.LEARNING_RATE * hidden_errors
```

Testing a Trained Network (ocr.py)

Once an ANN has been trained via backpropagation, it is fairly straightforward to use it for making predictions. As we can see here, we start by computing the output of the ANN, y2, exactly the way we did in step 2 of backpropagation. Then we look for the index in the vector with the maximum value. This index is the digit predicted by the ANN.

```
def predict(self, test):
    y1 = np.dot(np.mat(self.theta1), np.mat(test).T)
    y1 =  y1 + np.mat(self.input_layer_bias) # Add the bias
    y1 = self.sigmoid(y1)

    y2 = np.dot(np.array(self.theta2), y1)
    y2 = np.add(y2, self.hidden_layer_bias) # Add the bias
    y2 = self.sigmoid(y2)

    results = y2.T.tolist()[0]
    return results.index(max(results))
```

Other Design Decisions (ocr.py)

Many resources are available online that go into greater detail on the implementation of backpropagation. One good resource is from a course by the University of Willamette[7]. It goes over the steps of backpropagation and then explains how it can be translated into matrix form. While the amount of computation using matrices is the same as using loops, the benefit is that the code is simpler and easier to read with fewer nested loops. As we can see, the entire training process is written in under 25 lines of code using matrix algebra.

As mentioned in the introduction of Section 15.4, persisting the weights of the ANN means we do not lose the progress made in training it when the server is shut down or abruptly goes down for any reason. We persist the weights by writing them as JSON to a file. On startup, the OCR loads the ANN's saved weights to memory. The save function is not called internally by the OCR but is up to the server to decide when to perform a save. In our case, the server saves the weights after each update. This is a quick and simple solution but it is not optimal since writing to disk is time consuming. This also prevents us from handling multiple concurrent requests since there is no mechanism to prevent simultaneous writes to the same file. In a more sophisticated server, saves could perhaps be done on shutdown or once every few minutes with some form of locking or a timestamp protocol to ensure no data loss.

```
def save(self):
    if not self._use_file:
        return

    json_neural_network = {
        "theta1":[np_mat.tolist()[0] for np_mat in self.theta1],
        "theta2":[np_mat.tolist()[0] for np_mat in self.theta2],
        "b1":self.input_layer_bias[0].tolist()[0],
        "b2":self.hidden_layer_bias[0].tolist()[0]
    };
    with open(OCRNeuralNetwork.NN_FILE_PATH,'w') as nnFile:
        json.dump(json_neural_network, nnFile)

def _load(self):
```

---

[7]http://www.willamette.edu/~gorr/classes/cs449/backprop.html

```
if not self._use_file:
    return

with open(OCRNeuralNetwork.NN_FILE_PATH) as nnFile:
    nn = json.load(nnFile)
self.theta1 = [np.array(li) for li in nn['theta1']]
self.theta2 = [np.array(li) for li in nn['theta2']]
self.input_layer_bias = [np.array(nn['b1'][0])]
self.hidden_layer_bias = [np.array(nn['b2'][0])]
```

15.5 Conclusion

Now that we've learned about AI, ANNs, backpropagation, and building an end-to-end OCR system, let's recap the highlights of this chapter and the big picture.

We started off the chapter by giving background on AI, ANNs, and roughly what we will be implementing. We discussed what AI is and examples of how it's used. We saw that AI is essentially a set of algorithms or problem-solving approaches that can provide an answer to a question in a similar manner as a human would. We then took a look at the structure of a Feedforward ANN. We learned that computing the output at a given node was as simple as summing the products of the outputs of the previous nodes and their connecting weights. We talked about how to use an ANN by first formatting the input and partitioning the data into training and validation sets.

Once we had some background, we started talking about creating a web-based, client-server system that would handle user requests to train or test the OCR. We then discussed how the client would interpret the drawn pixels into an array and perform an HTTP request to the OCR server to perform the training or testing. We discussed how our simple server read requests and how to design an ANN by testing performance of several hidden node counts. We finished off by going through the core training and testing code for backpropagation.

Although we've built a seemingly functional OCR system, this chapter simply scratches the surface of how a real OCR system might work. More sophisticated OCR systems could have pre-processed inputs, use hybrid ML algorithms, have more extensive design phases, or other further optimizations.

## chapter 16

A Pedometer in the Real World

Dessy Daskalov

16.1   A Perfect World

Many software engineers reflecting on their training will remember having the pleasure of living in a very perfect world. We were taught to solve well-defined problems in idealized domains.

Then we were thrown into the real world, with all of its complexities and challenges. It's messy, which makes it all the more exciting. When you can solve a real-life problem, with all of its quirks, you can build software that really helps people.

In this chapter, we'll examine a problem that looks straightforward on the surface, and gets tangled very quickly when the real world, and real people, are thrown into the mix.

We'll work together to build a basic pedometer. We'll start by discussing the theory behind a pedometer and creating a step counting solution outside of code. Then, we'll implement our solution in code. Finally, we'll add a web layer to our code so that we have a friendly interface for a user to work with.

Let's roll up our sleeves, and prepare to untangle a real-world problem.

16.2   Pedometer Theory

The rise of the mobile device brought with it a trend to collect more and more data on our daily lives. One type of data many people collect is the number of steps they've taken over a period of time. This data can be used for health tracking, training for sporting events, or, for those of us obsessed with collecting and analyzing data, just for kicks. Steps can be counted using a pedometer, which often uses data from a hardware accelerometer as input.

What's an Accelerometer?

An accelerometer is a piece of hardware that measures acceleration in the x, y, and z directions. Many people carry an accelerometer with them wherever they go, as it's built into almost all smartphones currently on the market. The x, y, and z directions are relative to the phone.

An accelerometer returns a *signal* in 3-dimensional space. A signal is a set of data points recorded over time. Each component of the signal is a time series representing acceleration in one of the x, y, or z directions. Each point in a time series is the acceleration in that direction at a specific point in time. Acceleration is measured in units of g-force, or g. One g is equal to 9.8 m/s^2, the average acceleration due to gravity on Earth.

Figure 16.1 shows an example signal from an accelerometer with the three time series.

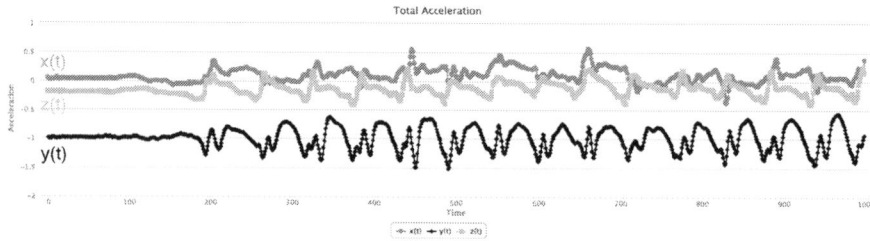

Figure 16.1: Example acceleration signal

The *sampling rate* of the accelerometer, which can often be calibrated, determines the number of measurements per second. For instance, an accelerometer with a sampling rate of 100 returns 100 data points for each x, y, and z time series every second.

Let's Talk About a Walk

When a person walks, they bounce slightly with each step. Just watch the top of a person's head as they walk away from you. Their head, torso, and hips are synchronized in a smooth bouncing motion. While people don't bounce very far, only one or two centimeters, it is one of the clearest, most constant, and most recognizable parts of a person's walking acceleration signal.

A person bounces up and down, in the vertical direction, with each step. If you are walking on Earth (or another big ball of mass floating in space) the bounce is conveniently in the same direction as gravity.

We are going to count steps by using the accelerometer to count bounces up and down. Because the phone can rotate in any direction, we will use gravity to know which direction down is. **A pedometer can count steps by counting the number of bounces in the direction of gravity.**

Let's look at a person walking with an accelerometer-equipped smartphone in his or her shirt pocket (Figure 16.2).

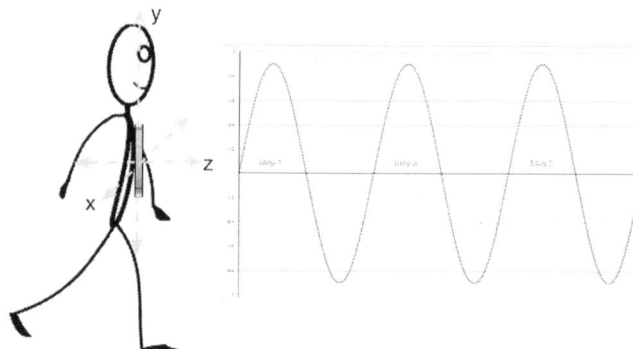

Figure 16.2: Walking

For the sake of simplicity, we'll assume that the person:

- is walking in the z direction;

- bounces with each step in the y direction; and
- maintains the phone in the same orientation throughout the entire walk.

In our perfect world, acceleration from step bounces will form a perfect sine wave in the y direction. Each peak in the sine wave is exactly one step. Step counting becomes a matter of counting these perfect peaks.

Ah, the joys of a perfect world, which we only ever experience in texts like this. Don't fret, things are about to get a little messier, and a lot more exciting. Let's add a little more reality to our world.

Even Perfect Worlds Have Fundamental Forces of Nature

The force of gravity causes an acceleration in the direction of gravity, which we refer to as gravitational acceleration. This acceleration is unique because it is always present and, for the purposes of this chapter, is constant at $9.8\ m/s^2$.

Suppose a smartphone is lying on a table screen-side up. In this orientation, our coordinate system is such that the negative z direction is the one that gravity is acting on. Gravity will pull our phone in the negative z direction, so our accelerometer, *even when perfectly still*, will record an acceleration of $9.8\ m/s^2$ in the negative z direction. Accelerometer data from our phone in this orientation is shown in Figure 16.3.

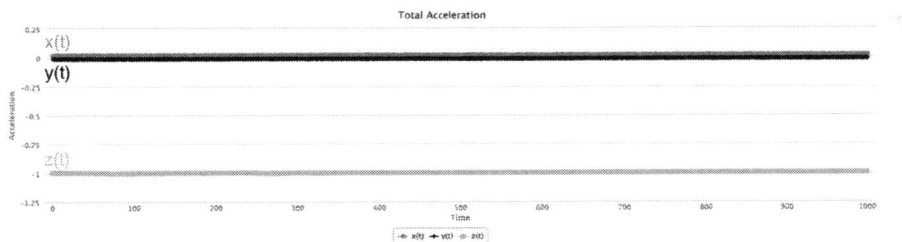

Figure 16.3: Example accelerometer data at rest

Note that $x(t)$ and $y(t)$ remain constant at 0, while $z(t)$ is constant at -1 g. Our accelerometer records all acceleration, including gravitational acceleration.

Each time series measures the *total acceleration* in that direction. Total acceleration is the sum of *user acceleration* and *gravitational acceleration*.

User acceleration is the acceleration of the device due to the movement of the user, and is constant at 0 when the phone is perfectly still. However, when the user is moving with the device, user acceleration is rarely constant, since it's difficult for a person to move with a constant acceleration.

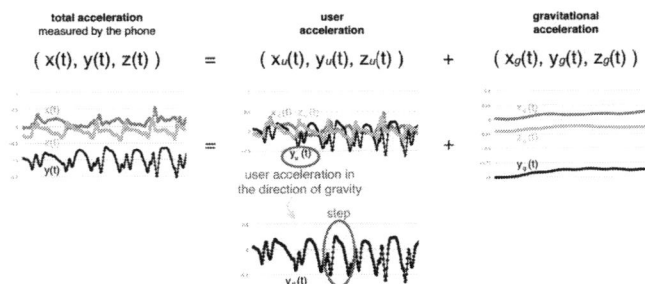

Figure 16.4: Component signals

To count steps, we're interested in the bounces created by the user in the direction of gravity. That means we're interested in isolating the 1-dimensional time series which describes **user acceleration in the direction of gravity** from our 3-dimensional acceleration signal (Figure 16.4).

In our simple example, gravitational acceleration is 0 in $x(t)$ and $z(t)$ and constant at 9.8 m/s^2 in $y(t)$. Therefore, in our total acceleration plot, $x(t)$ and $z(t)$ fluctuate around 0 while $y(t)$ fluctuates around -1 g. In our user acceleration plot, we notice that—because we have removed gravitational acceleration—all three time series fluctuate around 0. Note the obvious peaks in $y_u(t)$. Those are due to step bounces! In our last plot, gravitational acceleration, $y_g(t)$ is constant at -1 g, and $x_g(t)$ and $z_g(t)$ are constant at 0.

So, in our example, the 1-dimensional user acceleration in the direction of gravity time series we're interested in is $y_u(t)$. Although $y_u(t)$ isn't as smooth as our perfect sine wave, we can identify the peaks, and use those peaks to count steps. So far, so good. Now, let's add even more reality to our world.

People Are Complicated Creatures

What if a person carries the phone in a bag on their shoulder, with the phone in a more wonky position? To make matters worse, what if the phone rotates in the bag part way through the walk, as in Figure 16.5?

Figure 16.5: A more complicated walk

Yikes. Now all three of our components have a non-zero gravitational acceleration, so the user acceleration in the direction of gravity is now split amongst all three time series. To determine user acceleration in the direction of gravity, we first have to determine which direction gravity is acting in. To do this, we have to split total acceleration in each of the three time series into a user acceleration time series and a gravitational acceleration time series (Figure 16.6).

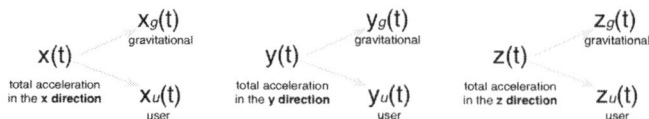

Figure 16.6: More complicated component signals

Then we can isolate the portion of user acceleration in each component that is in the direction of gravity, resulting in just the user acceleration in the direction of gravity time series.

Let's define this as two steps below:

1. Splitting total acceleration into user acceleration and gravitational acceleration.
2. Isolating user acceleration in the direction of gravity.

We'll look at each step separately, and put on our mathematician hats.

1. Splitting Total Acceleration Into User Acceleration and Gravitational Acceleration

We can use a tool called a *filter* to split a total acceleration time series into a user acceleration time series and a gravitational acceleration time series.

Low-Pass and High-Pass Filters

A filter is a tool used in signal processing to remove an unwanted component from a signal.

A *low-pass filter* allows low-frequency signals through, while attenuating signals higher than a set threshold. Conversely, a *high-pass filter* allows high-frequency signals through, while attenuating signals below a set threshold. Using music as an analogy, a low-pass filter can eliminate treble, and a high-pass filter can eliminate bass.

In our situation, the frequency, measured in Hz, indicates how quickly the acceleration is changing. A constant acceleration has a frequency of 0 Hz, while a non-constant acceleration has a non-zero frequency. This means that our constant gravitational acceleration is a 0 Hz signal, while user acceleration is not.

For each component, we can pass total acceleration through a low-pass filter, and we'll be left with just the gravitational acceleration time series. Then we can subtract gravitational acceleration from total acceleration, and we'll have the user acceleration time series (Figure 16.7).

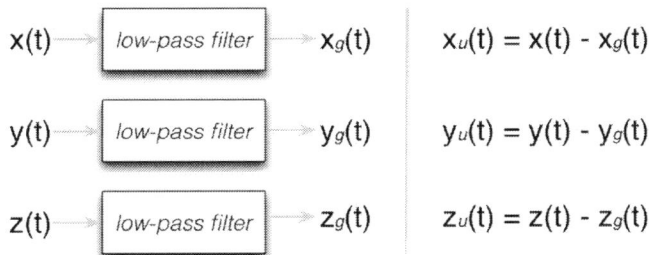

$$x(t) \longrightarrow \boxed{\text{low-pass filter}} \longrightarrow x_g(t) \qquad x_u(t) = x(t) - x_g(t)$$

$$y(t) \longrightarrow \boxed{\text{low-pass filter}} \longrightarrow y_g(t) \qquad y_u(t) = y(t) - y_g(t)$$

$$z(t) \longrightarrow \boxed{\text{low-pass filter}} \longrightarrow z_g(t) \qquad z_u(t) = z(t) - z_g(t)$$

Figure 16.7: A low-pass filter

There are numerous varieties of filters. The one we'll use is called an infinite impulse response (IIR) filter. We've chosen an IIR filter because of its low overhead and ease of implementation. The IIR filter we've chosen is implemented using the formula:

$$output_i = \alpha_0(input_i\beta_0 + input_{i-1}\beta_1 + input_{i-2}\beta_2 - output_{i-1}\alpha_1 - output_{i-2}\alpha_2)$$

The design of digital filters is outside of the scope of this chapter, but a very short teaser discussion is warranted. It's a well-studied, fascinating topic, with numerous practical applications. A digital filter can be designed to cancel any frequency or range of frequencies desired. The α and β values in the formula are coefficients, set based on the cutoff frequency, and the range of frequencies we want to preserve.

We want to cancel all frequencies except for our constant gravitational acceleration, so we've chosen coefficients that attenuate frequencies higher than 0.2 Hz. Notice that we've set our threshold slightly higher than 0 Hz. While gravity does create a true 0 Hz acceleration, our real, imperfect world has real, imperfect accelerometers, so we're allowing for a slight margin of error in measurement.

Implementing a Low-Pass Filter

Let's work through a low-pass filter implementation using our earlier example. We'll split:

- $x(t)$ into $x_g(t)$ and $x_u(t)$,
- $y(t)$ into $y_g(t)$ and $y_u(t)$, and
- $z(t)$ into $z_g(t)$ and $z_u(t)$.

We'll initialize the first two values of gravitational acceleration to 0, so that the formula has initial values to work with.

$$x_g(0) = x_g(1) = y_g(0) = y_g(1) = z_g(0) = z_g(1) = 0$$

Then we'll implement the filter formula for each time series.

$$x_g(t) = \alpha_0(x(t)\beta_0 + x(t-1)\beta_1 + x(t-2)\beta_2 - x_g(t-1)\alpha_1 - x_g(t-2)\alpha_2)$$

$$y_g(t) = \alpha_0(y(t)\beta_0 + y(t-1)\beta_1 + y(t-2)\beta_2 - y_g(t-1)\alpha_1 - y_g(t-2)\alpha_2)$$

$$z_g(t) = \alpha_0(z(t)\beta_0 + z(t-1)\beta_1 + z(t-2)\beta_2 - z_g(t-1)\alpha_1 - z_g(t-2)\alpha_2)$$

The resulting time series after low-pass filtering are in Figure 16.8.

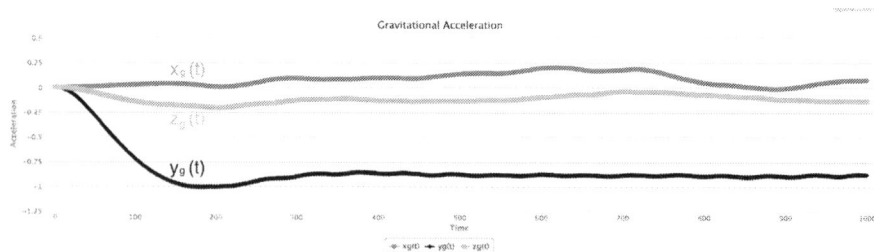

Figure 16.8: Gravitational acceleration

$x_g(t)$ and $z_g(t)$ hover around 0, and $y_g(t)$ very quickly drops to $-1g$. The initial 0 value in $y_g(t)$ is from the initialization of the formula.

Now, to calculate user acceleration, we can subtract gravitational acceleration from our total acceleration:

$$x_u(t) = x(t) - x_g(t)$$
$$y_u(t) = y(t) - y_g(t)$$
$$z_u(t) = z(t) - z_g(t)$$

The result is the time series seen in Figure 16.9. We've successfully split our total acceleration into user acceleration and gravitational acceleration!

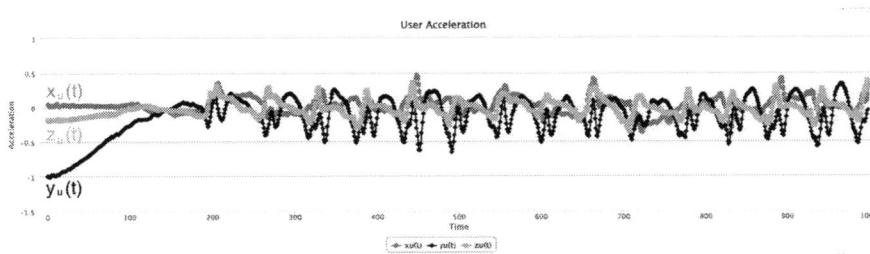

Figure 16.9: Split acceleration

2. Isolating User Acceleration in the Direction of Gravity

$x_u(t)$, $y_u(t)$, and $z_u(t)$ include all movements of the user, not just movements in the direction of gravity. Our goal here is to end up with a 1-dimensional time series representing user acceleration in the direction of gravity. This will include portions of user acceleration in each of the directions.

Let's get to it. First, some linear algebra 101. Don't take that mathematician hat off just yet!

The Dot Product

When working with coordinates, you won't get very far before being introduced to the *dot product*, one of the fundamental tools used in comparing the magnitude and direction of x, y, and z coordinates.

The dot product takes us from 3-dimensional space to 1-dimensional space (Figure 16.10). When we take the dot product of the two time series, user acceleration and gravitational acceleration, both of which are in 3-dimensional space, we'll be left with a single time series in 1-dimensional space representing the portion of user acceleration in the direction of gravity. We'll arbitrarily call this new time series $a(t)$, because, well, every important time series deserves a name.

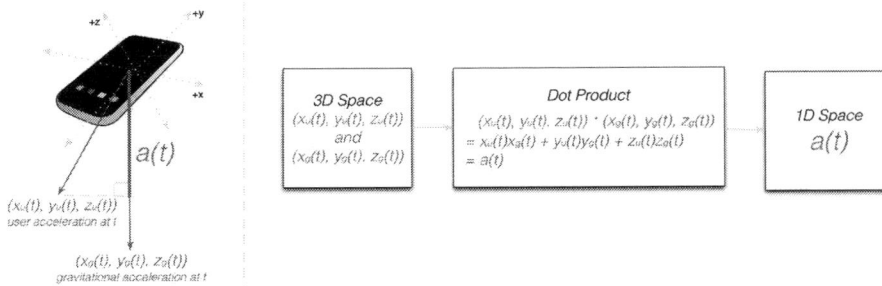

Figure 16.10: The dot product

Implementing the Dot Product

We can implement the dot product for our earlier example using the formula $a(t) = x_u(t)x_g(t) + y_u(t)y_g(t) + z_u(t)z_g(t)$, leaving us with $a(t)$ in 1-dimensional space (Figure 16.11).

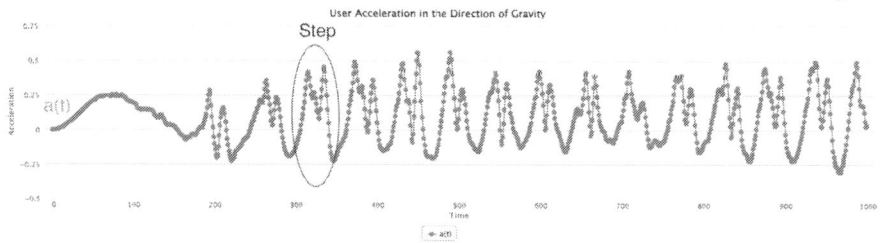

Figure 16.11: Implementing the dot product

We can now visually pick out where the steps are in $a(t)$. The dot product is very powerful, yet beautifully simple.

Solutions in the Real World

We saw how quickly our seemingly simple problem became more complex when we threw in the challenges of the real world and real people. However, we're getting a lot closer to counting steps, and we can see how $a(t)$ is starting to resemble our ideal sine wave. But, only "kinda, sorta" starting to. We still need to make our messy $a(t)$ time series smoother. There are four main issues (Figure 16.12) with $a(t)$ in its current state. Let's examine each one.

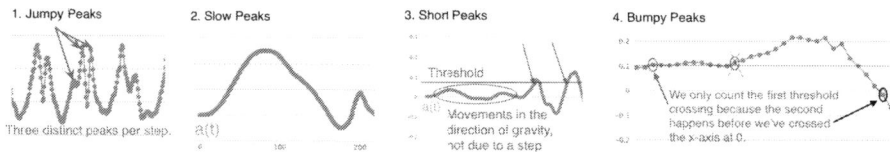

Figure 16.12: Jumpy, slow, short, bumpy

1. Jumpy Peaks

$a(t)$ is very "jumpy", because a phone can jiggle with each step, adding a high-frequency component to our time series. This jumpiness is called noise. By studying numerous data sets, we've determined that a step acceleration is at maximum 5 Hz. We can use a low-pass IIR filter to remove the noise, picking α and β to attenuate all signals above 5 Hz.

2. Slow Peaks

With a sampling rate of 100, the slow peak displayed in $a(t)$ spans 1.5 seconds, which is too slow to be a step. In studying enough samples of data, we've determined that the slowest step we can take is at a 1 Hz frequency. Slower accelerations are due to a low-frequency component, that we can again remove using a high-pass IIR filter, setting α and β to cancel all signals below 1 Hz.

3. Short Peaks

As a person is using an app or making a call, the accelerometer registers small movements in the direction of gravity, presenting themselves as short peaks in our time series. We can eliminate these short peaks by setting a minimum threshold, and counting a step every time $a(t)$ crosses that threshold in the positive direction.

4. Bumpy Peaks

Our pedometer should accommodate many people with different walks, so we've set minimum and maximum step frequencies based on a large sample size of people and walks. This means that we may sometimes filter slightly too much or too little. While we'll often have fairly smooth peaks, we can, once in a while, get a "bumpier" peak. Figure 16.12 zooms in on one such peak.

When bumpiness occurs at our threshold, we can mistakenly count too many steps for one peak. We'll use a method called *hysteresis* to address this. Hysteresis refers to the dependence of an output on past inputs. We can count threshold crossings in the positive direction, as well as 0 crossings in the negative direction. Then, we only count steps where a threshold crossing occurs after a 0 crossing, ensuring we count each step only once.

Peaks That Are Juuuust Right

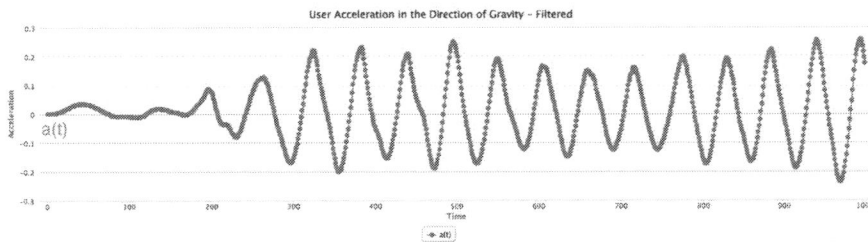

Figure 16.13: Tweaked peaks

In accounting for these four scenarios, we've managed to bring our messy $a(t)$ fairly close to our ideal sine wave (Figure 16.13), allowing us to count steps.

Recap

The problem, at first glance, looked straightforward. However, the real world and real people threw a few curve balls our way. Let's recap how we solved the problem:

1. We started with total acceleration, $(x(t), y(t), z(t))$.
2. We used a low-pass filter to split total acceleration into user acceleration and gravitational acceleration, $(x_u(t), y_u(t), z_u(t))$ and $(x_g(t), y_g(t), z_g(t))$, respectively.
3. We took the dot product of $(x_u(t), y_u(t), z_u(t))$ and $(x_g(t), y_g(t), z_g(t))$ to obtain the user acceleration in the direction of gravity, $a(t)$.
4. We used a low-pass filter again to remove the high-frequency component of $a(t)$, removing noise.
5. We used a high-pass filter to cancel the low-frequency component of $a(t)$, removing slow peaks.
6. We set a threshold to ignore short peaks.
7. We used hysteresis to avoid double-counting steps with bumpy peaks.

As software developers in a training or academic setting, we may have been presented with a perfect signal and asked to write code to count the steps in that signal. While that may have been an interesting coding challenge, it wouldn't have been something we could apply in a live situation. We saw that in reality, with gravity and people thrown into the mix, the problem was a little more complex. We used mathematical tools to address the complexities, and were able to solve a real-world problem. It's time to translate our solution into code.

16.3   Diving Into Code

Our goal for this chapter is to create a web application in Ruby that accepts accelerometer data, parses, processes, and analyzes the data, and returns the number of steps taken, the distance travelled, and the elapsed time.

Preliminary Work

Our solution requires us to filter our time series several times. Rather than peppering filtering code throughout our program, it makes sense to create a class that takes care of the filtering, and if we ever need to enhance or modify it, we'll only ever need to change that one class. This strategy is called *separation of concerns*, a commonly used design principle which promotes splitting a program into distinct pieces, where every piece has one primary concern. It's a beautiful way to write clean, maintainable code that's easily extensible. We'll revisit this idea several times throughout the chapter.

Let's dive into the filtering code, contained in, logically, a `Filter` class.

```
class Filter

  COEFFICIENTS_LOW_0_HZ = {
    alpha: [1, -1.979133761292768, 0.979521463540373],
    beta:  [0.000086384997973502, 0.000172769995947004, 0.000086384997973502]
  }
  COEFFICIENTS_LOW_5_HZ = {
    alpha: [1, -1.80898117793047, 0.827224480562408],
    beta:  [0.095465967120306, -0.172688631608676, 0.095465967120306]
  }
  COEFFICIENTS_HIGH_1_HZ = {
    alpha: [1, -1.905384612118461, 0.910092542787947],
    beta:  [0.953986986993339, -1.907503180919730, 0.953986986993339]
  }

  def self.low_0_hz(data)
    filter(data, COEFFICIENTS_LOW_0_HZ)
  end

  def self.low_5_hz(data)
    filter(data, COEFFICIENTS_LOW_5_HZ)
  end

  def self.high_1_hz(data)
    filter(data, COEFFICIENTS_HIGH_1_HZ)
  end
```

```
private

  def self.filter(data, coefficients)
    filtered_data = [0,0]
    (2..data.length-1).each do |i|
      filtered_data << coefficients[:alpha][0] *
                      (data[i]              * coefficients[:beta][0] +
                       data[i-1]            * coefficients[:beta][1] +
                       data[i-2]            * coefficients[:beta][2] -
                       filtered_data[i-1] * coefficients[:alpha][1] -
                       filtered_data[i-2] * coefficients[:alpha][2])
    end
    filtered_data
  end

end
```

Anytime our program needs to filter a time series, we can call one of the class methods in `Filter` with the data we need filtered:

- `low_0_hz` is used to low-pass filter signals near 0 Hz
- `low_5_hz` is used to low-pass filter signals at or below 5 Hz
- `high_1_hz` is used to high-pass filter signals above 1 Hz

Each class method calls `filter`, which implements the IIR filter and returns the result. If we wish to add more filters in the future, we only need to change this one class. Note is that all magic numbers are defined at the top. This makes our class easier to read and understand.

Input Formats

Our input data is coming from mobile devices such as Android phones and iPhones. Most mobile phones on the market today have accelerometers built in, that are able to record total acceleration. Let's call the input data format that records total acceleration the *combined format*. Many, but not all, devices can also record user acceleration and gravitational acceleration separately. Let's call this format the *separated format*. A device that has the ability to return data in the separated format necessarily has the ability to return data in the combined format. However, the inverse is not always true. Some devices can only record data in the combined format. Input data in the combined format will need to be passed through a low-pass filter to turn it into the separated format.

We want our program to handle all mobile devices on the market with accelerometers, so we'll need to accept data in both formats. Let's look at the two formats we'll be accepting individually.

Combined Format

Data in the combined format is total acceleration in the x, y, and z directions, over time. x, y, and z values will be separated by a comma, and samples per unit time will be separated by a semi-colon.

$$x_1, y_1, z_1; \ldots x_n, y_n, z_n;$$

Separated Format

The separated format returns user acceleration and gravitational acceleration in the x, y, and z directions, over time. User acceleration values will be separated from gravitational acceleration values by a pipe.

$$x_1^u, y_1^u, z_1^u | x_1^g, y_1^g, z_1^g; \ldots x_n^u, y_n^u, z_n^u | x_n^g, y_n^g, z_n^g;$$

I Got Multiple Input Formats But a Standard Ain't One

Dealing with multiple input formats is a common programming problem. If we want our entire program to work with both formats, every single piece of code dealing with the data would need to know how to handle both formats. This can become very messy, very quickly, especially if a third (or a fourth, or a fifth, or a hundredth) input format is added.

Standard Format

The cleanest way for us to deal with this is to take our two input formats and fit them into a standard format as soon as possible, allowing the rest of the program to work with this new standard format. Our solution requires that we work with user acceleration and gravitational acceleration separately, so our standard format will need to be split into the two accelerations (Figure 16.14).

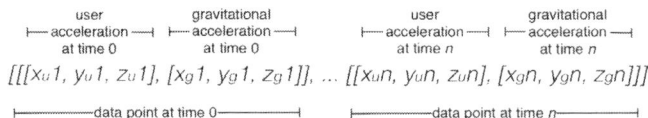

Figure 16.14: Standard format

Our standard format allows us to store a time series, as each element represents acceleration at a point in time. We've defined it as an array of arrays of arrays. Let's peel that onion.

- The first array is just a wrapper to hold the all of the data.
- The second set of arrays contains one array per data sample taken. If our sampling rate is 100 and we sample data for 10 seconds, we'll have $100 * 10$, or 1000, arrays in this second set.
- The third set of arrays is the pair of arrays enclosed within the second set. They both contain acceleration data in the x, y, and z directions; the first representing user acceleration and the second, gravitational acceleration.

The Pipeline

The input into our system will be data from an accelerometer, information on the user taking the walk (gender, stride, etc.), and information on the trial walk itself (sampling rate, actual steps taken, etc.). Our system will apply the signal processing solution, and output the number of steps calculated, the delta between the actual steps and calculated steps, the distance travelled, and the elapsed time. The entire process from input to output can be viewed as a pipeline (Figure 16.15).

In the spirit of separation of concerns, we'll write the code for each distinct component of the pipeline—parsing, processing, and analyzing—individually.

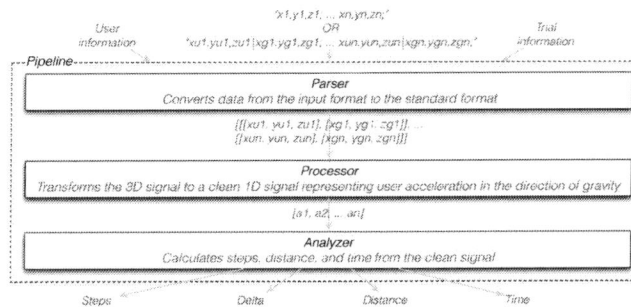
Figure 16.15: The pipeline

Parsing

Given that we want our data in the standard format as early as possible, it makes sense to write a parser that allows us to take our two known input formats and convert them to a standard output format as the first component of our pipeline. Our standard format splits out user acceleration and gravitational acceleration, which means that if our data is in the combined format, our parser will need to first pass it through a low-pass filter to convert it to the standard format.

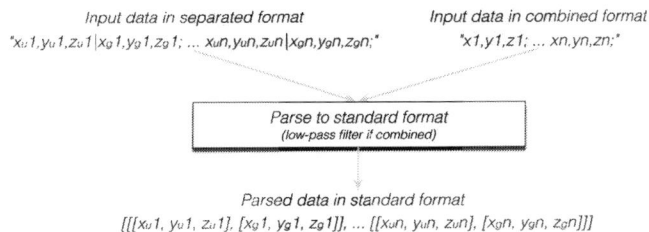
Figure 16.16: Initial workflow

In the future, if we ever have to add another input format, the only code we'll have to touch is this parser. Let's separate concerns once more, and create a Parser class to handle the parsing.

```
class Parser

  attr_reader :parsed_data

  def self.run(data)
    parser = Parser.new(data)
    parser.parse
    parser
  end

  def initialize(data)
    @data = data
  end

  def parse
    @parsed_data = @data.to_s.split(';').map { |x| x.split('|') }
                    .map { |x| x.map { |x| x.split(',').map(&:to_f) } }
```

```ruby
    unless @parsed_data.map { |x| x.map(&:length).uniq }.uniq == [[3]]
      raise 'Bad Input. Ensure data is properly formatted.'
    end

    if @parsed_data.first.count == 1
      filtered_accl = @parsed_data.map(&:flatten).transpose.map do |total_accl|
        grav = Filter.low_0_hz(total_accl)
        user = total_accl.zip(grav).map { |a, b| a - b }
        [user, grav]
      end

      @parsed_data = @parsed_data.length.times.map do |i|
        user = filtered_accl.map(&:first).map { |elem| elem[i] }
        grav = filtered_accl.map(&:last).map { |elem| elem[i] }
        [user, grav]
      end
    end
  end

end
```

Parser has a class-level run method as well as an initializer. This is a pattern we'll use several times, so it's worth a discussion. Initializers should generally be used for setting up an object, and shouldn't do a lot of work. Parser's initializer simply takes data in the combined or separated format and stores it in the instance variable @data. The parse instance method uses @data internally, and does the heavy lifting of parsing and setting the result in the standard format to @parsed_data. In our case, we'll never need to instantiate a Parser instance without having to immediately call parse. Therefore, we add a convenient class-level run method that instantiates an instance of Parser, calls parse on it, and returns the instance of the object. We can now pass our input data to run, knowing we'll receive an instance of Parser with @parsed_data already set.

Let's take a look at our hard-working parse method. The first step in the process is to take string data and convert it to numerical data, giving us an array of arrays of arrays. Sound familiar? The next thing we do is ensure that the format is as expected. Unless we have exactly three elements per the innermost arrays, we throw an exception. Otherwise, we continue on.

Note the differences in @parsed_data between the two formats at this stage. In the *combined format* it contains arrays of exactly *one* array:

$$[[[x_1, y_1, z_1]], \ldots [[x_n, y_n, z_n]]]$$

In the *separated format* it contains arrays of exactly *two* arrays:

$$[[[x_u^1, y_u^1, z_u^1], [x_g^1, y_g^1, z_g^1]], \ldots [[x_u^n, y_u^n, z_u^n], [x_g^n, y_g^n, z_g^n]]]$$

The separated format is already in our desired standard format after this operation. Amazing. However, if the data is combined (or, equivalently, has exactly one array where the separated format would have two), then we proceed with two loops. The first loop splits total acceleration into gravitational and user, using Filter with a :low_0_hz type, and the second loop reorganizes the data into the standard format.

parse leaves us with @parsed_data holding data in the standard format, regardless of whether we started off with combined or separated data. What a relief!

336 A Pedometer in the Real World

As our program becomes more sophisticated, one area for improvement is to make our users' lives easier by throwing exceptions with more specific error messages, allowing them to more quickly track down common input formatting problems.

Processing

Based on the solution we defined, we'll need our code to do a couple of things to our parsed data before we can count steps:

1. Isolate movement in the direction of gravity using the dot product.
2. Remove jumpy (high-frequency) and slow (low-frequency) peaks with a low-pass filter followed by a high-pass filter.

We'll handle short and bumpy peaks by avoiding them during step counting.

Now that we have our data in the standard format, we can process it to get in into a state where we can analyze it to count steps (Figure 16.17).

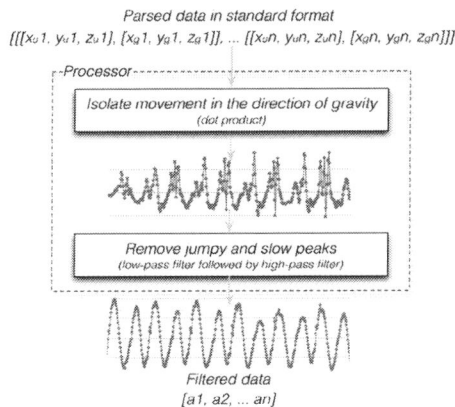

Figure 16.17: Processing

The purpose of processing is to take our data in the standard format and incrementally clean it up to get it to a state as close as possible to our ideal sine wave. Our two processing operations, taking the dot product and filtering, are quite distinct, but both are intended to process our data, so we'll create one class called a Processor.

```
class Processor

  attr_reader :dot_product_data, :filtered_data

  def self.run(data)
    processor = Processor.new(data)
    processor.dot_product
    processor.filter
    processor
  end

  def initialize(data)
    @data = data
  end
```

```
def dot_product
  @dot_product_data = @data.map do |x|
    x[0][0] * x[1][0] + x[0][1] * x[1][1] + x[0][2] * x[1][2]
  end
end

def filter
  @filtered_data = Filter.low_5_hz(@dot_product_data)
  @filtered_data = Filter.high_1_hz(@filtered_data)
end

end
```

Again, we see the `run` and `initialize` methods pattern. `run` calls our two processor methods, `dot_product` and `filter`, directly. Each method accomplishes one of our two processing operations. `dot_product` isolates movement in the direction of gravity, and `filter` applies the low-pass and high-pass filters in sequence to remove jumpy and slow peaks.

Pedometer Functionality

Provided information about the person using the pedometer is available, we can measure more than just steps. Our pedometer will measure **distance travelled** and **elapsed time**, as well as **steps taken**.

Distance Travelled

A mobile pedometer is generally used by one person. Distance travelled during a walk is calculated by multiplying the steps taken by the person's stride length. If the stride length is unknown, we can use optional user information like gender and height to approximate it. Let's create a User class to encapsulate this related information.

```
class User

  GENDER      = ['male', 'female']
  MULTIPLIERS = {'female' => 0.413, 'male' => 0.415}
  AVERAGES    = {'female' => 70.0,  'male' => 78.0}

  attr_reader :gender, :height, :stride

  def initialize(gender = nil, height = nil, stride = nil)
    @gender = gender.to_s.downcase unless gender.to_s.empty?
    @height = Float(height) unless height.to_s.empty?
    @stride = Float(stride) unless stride.to_s.empty?

    raise 'Invalid gender' if @gender && !GENDER.include?(@gender)
    raise 'Invalid height' if @height && (@height <= 0)
    raise 'Invalid stride' if @stride && (@stride <= 0)

    @stride ||= calculate_stride
  end
```

```
private

  def calculate_stride
    if gender && height
      MULTIPLIERS[@gender] * height
    elsif height
      height * (MULTIPLIERS.values.reduce(:+) / MULTIPLIERS.size)
    elsif gender
      AVERAGES[gender]
    else
      AVERAGES.values.reduce(:+) / AVERAGES.size
    end
  end

end
```

At the top of our class, we define constants to avoid hardcoding magic numbers and strings throughout. For the purposes of this discussion, let's assume that the values in MULTIPLIERS and AVERAGES have been determined from a large sample size of diverse people.

Our initializer accepts gender, height, and stride as optional arguments. If the optional parameters are passed in, our initializer sets instance variables of the same names, after some data formatting. We raise an exception for invalid values.

Even when all optional parameters are provided, the input stride takes precedence. If it's not provided, the calculate_stride method determines the most accurate stride length possible for the user. This is done with an if statement:

- The most accurate way to calculate stride length is to use a person's height and a multiplier based on gender, provided we have a valid gender and height.
- A person's height is a better predictor of stride than their gender is. If we have height but not gender, we can multiply the height by the average of the two values in MULTIPLIERS.
- If all we have is a gender, we can use the average stride length from AVERAGES.
- Finally, if we don't have anything, we can take the average of the two values in AVERAGES and use that as our stride.

Note that the further down the if statement we get, the less accurate our stride length becomes. In any case, our User class determines the stride length as best it can.

Elapsed Time

The time spent travelling is measured by dividing the number of data samples in our Processor's @parsed_data by the sampling rate of the device, if we have it. Since the rate has more to do with the trial walk itself than the user, and the User class in fact does not have to be aware of the sampling rate, this is a good time to create a very small Trial class.

```
class Trial

  attr_reader :name, :rate, :steps

  def initialize(name, rate = nil, steps = nil)
    @name  = name.to_s.delete(' ')
```

```
  @rate  = Integer(rate.to_s) unless rate.to_s.empty?
  @steps = Integer(steps.to_s) unless steps.to_s.empty?

  raise 'Invalid name'  if @name.empty?
  raise 'Invalid rate'  if @rate && (@rate <= 0)
  raise 'Invalid steps' if @steps && (@steps < 0)
 end

end
```

All of the attribute readers in `Trial` are set in the initializer based on parameters passed in:

- name is a name for the specific trial, to help differentiate between the different trials.
- rate is the sampling rate of the accelerometer during the trial.
- steps is used to set the actual steps taken, so that we can record the difference between the actual steps the user took and the ones our program counted.

Much like our User class, some information is optional. We're given the opportunity to input details of the trial, if we have it. If we don't have those details, our program bypasses calculating the additional results, such as time spent travelling. Another similarity to our User class is the prevention of invalid values.

Steps Taken

It's time to implement our step counting strategy in code. So far, we have a Processor class that contains `@filtered_data`, which is our clean time series representing user acceleration in the direction of gravity. We also have classes that give us the necessary information about the user and the trial. What we're missing is a way to analyze `@filtered_data` with the information from User and `Trial`, and count steps, measure distance, and measure time.

The analysis portion of our program is different from the data manipulation of the Processor, and different from the information collection and aggregation of the User and Trial classes. Let's create a new class called `Analyzer` to perform this data analysis.

```
class Analyzer

 THRESHOLD = 0.09

 attr_reader :steps, :delta, :distance, :time

 def self.run(data, user, trial)
  analyzer = Analyzer.new(data, user, trial)
  analyzer.measure_steps
  analyzer.measure_delta
  analyzer.measure_distance
  analyzer.measure_time
  analyzer
 end

 def initialize(data, user, trial)
  @data  = data
  @user  = user
```

```ruby
    @trial = trial
  end

  def measure_steps
    @steps = 0
    count_steps = true

    @data.each_with_index do |data, i|
      if (data >= THRESHOLD) && (@data[i-1] < THRESHOLD)
        next unless count_steps

        @steps += 1
        count_steps = false
      end

      count_steps = true if (data < 0) && (@data[i-1] >= 0)
    end
  end

  def measure_delta
    @delta = @steps - @trial.steps if @trial.steps
  end

  def measure_distance
    @distance = @user.stride * @steps
  end

  def measure_time
    @time = @data.count/@trial.rate if @trial.rate
  end

end
```

The first thing we do in `Analyzer` is define a `THRESHOLD` constant, which we'll use to avoid counting short peaks as steps. For the purposes of this discussion, let's assume we've analyzed numerous diverse data sets and determined a threshold value that accommodated the largest number of those data sets. The threshold can eventually become dynamic and vary with different users, based on the calculated versus actual steps they've taken; a learning algorithm, if you will.

Our `Analyzer`'s initializer takes a data parameter and instances of `User` and `Trial`, and sets the instance variables `@data`, `@user`, and `@trial` to the passed-in parameters. The `run` method calls `measure_steps`, `measure_delta`, `measure_distance`, and `measure_time`. Let's take a look at each method.

measure_steps

Finally! The step counting portion of our step counting app. The first thing we do in `measure_steps` is initialize two variables:

- `@steps` is used to count the number of steps.
- `count_steps` is used for hysteresis to determine if we're allowed to count steps at a point in time.

We then iterate through @processor.filtered_data. If the current value is greater than or equal to THRESHOLD, and the previous value was less than THRESHOLD, then we've crossed the threshold in the positive direction, which could indicate a step. The unless statement skips ahead to the next data point if count_steps is false, indicating that we've already counted a step for that peak. If we haven't, we increment @steps by 1, and set count_steps to false to prevent any more steps from being counted for that peak. The next if statement sets count_steps to true once our time series has crossed the x-axis in the negative direction, and we're on to the next peak.

There we have it, the step counting portion of our program! Our Processor class did a lot of work to clean up the time series and remove frequencies that would result in counting false steps, so our actual step counting implementation is not complex.

It's worth noting that we store the entire time series for the walk in memory. Our trials are all short walks, so that's not currently a problem, but eventually we'd like to analyze long walks with large amounts of data. Ideally, we'd want to stream data in, only storing very small portions of the time series in memory. Keeping this in mind, we've put in the work to ensure that we only need the current data point and the data point before it. Additionally, we've implemented hysteresis using a Boolean value, so we don't need to look backward in the time series to ensure we've crossed the x-axis at 0.

There's a fine balance between accounting for likely future iterations of the product, and over-engineering a solution for every conceivable product direction under the sun. In this case, it's reasonable to assume that we'll have to handle longer walks in the near future, and the costs of accounting for that in step counting are fairly low.

measure_delta

If the trial provides actual steps taken during the walk, measure_delta will return the difference between the calculated and actual steps.

measure_distance

The distance is measured by multiplying our user's stride by the number of steps. Since the distance depends on the step count, measure_steps must be called before measure_distance.

measure_time

As long as we have a sampling rate, time is calculated by dividing the total number of samples in filtered_data by the sampling rate. It follows, then, that time is calculated in seconds.

Tying It All Together With the Pipeline

Our Parser, Processor, and Analyzer classes, while useful individually, are definitely better together. Our program will often use them to run through the pipeline we introduced earlier. Since the pipeline will need to be run frequently, we'll create a Pipeline class to run it for us.

```
class Pipeline

  attr_reader :data, :user, :trial, :parser, :processor, :analyzer

  def self.run(data, user, trial)
    pipeline = Pipeline.new(data, user, trial)
    pipeline.feed
    pipeline
  end

  def initialize(data, user, trial)
    @data  = data
    @user  = user
    @trial = trial
  end

  def feed
    @parser    = Parser.run(@data)
    @processor = Processor.run(@parser.parsed_data)
    @analyzer  = Analyzer.run(@processor.filtered_data, @user, @trial)
  end

end
```

We use our now-familiar run pattern and supply Pipeline with accelerometer data, and instances of User and Trial. The feed method implements the pipeline, which entails running Parser with the accelerometer data, then using the parser's parsed data to run Processor, and finally using the processor's filtered data to run Analyzer. The Pipeline keeps @parser, @processor, and @analyzer instance variables, so that the program has access to information from those objects for display purposes through the app.

16.4   Adding A Friendly Interface

We're through the most labour intensive part of our program. Next, we'll build a web app to present the data in a format that is pleasing to a user. A web app naturally separates the data processing from the presentation of the data. Let's look at our app from a user's perspective before the code.

A User Scenario

When a user first enters the app by navigating to /uploads, they see a table of existing data and a form to submit new data by uploading an accelerometer output file and trial and user information (Figure 16.18).

Submitting the form stores the data to the file system, parses, processes, and analyzes it, and redirects back to /uploads with the new entry in the table.

Clicking the **Detail** link for an entry presents the user with the following view in Figure 16.19.

The information presented includes values input by the user through the upload form, values calculated by our program, and graphs of the time series following the dot product operation, and again following filtering. The user can navigate back to /uploads using the *Back to Uploads* link.

Figure 16.18: Upload view

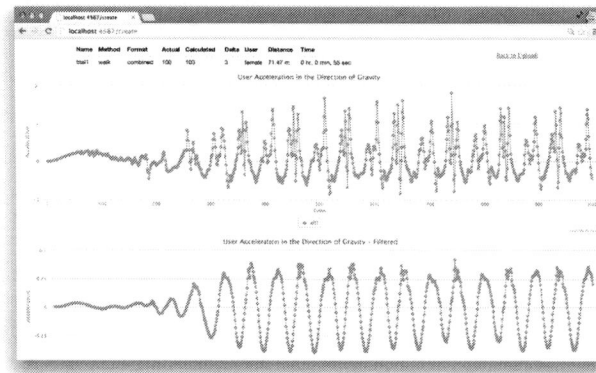

Figure 16.19: Detail view

Let's look at what the outlined functionality above implies for us, technically. We'll need two major components that we don't yet have:

1. A way to store and retrieve user input data.
2. A web application with a basic interface.

Let's examine each of these two requirements.

1. Storing and Retrieving Data

Our app needs to store input data to, and retrieve data from, the file system. We'll create an `Upload` class to do this. Since the class deals only with the file system and doesn't relate directly to the implementation of the pedometer, we've left it out for brevity, but it's worth discussing its basic functionality. Our `Upload` class has three class-level methods for file system access and retrieval, all of which return one or more instances of `Upload`:

- `create` takes a file along with user and trial information. It stores the file to the file system, under a filename it generates to contain the user and trial information. The `@file_path`, `@user`, and `@trial` instance variables allow access to the file path, user object, and trial object, respectively.

- find takes a file path and returns an instance of Upload.
- all returns an array of Upload instances, one for each accelerometer data file in the file system.

Separation of Concerns in Upload

Once again, we've been wise to separate concerns in our program. All code related to storage and retrieval is contained in the Upload class. As our application grows, we'll likely want to use a database rather than saving everything to the file system. When the time comes for that, all we have to do it change the Upload class. This makes our refactoring simple and clean.

In the future, we can save User and Trial objects to the database. The create, find, and all methods in Upload will then be relevant to User and Trial as well. That means we'd likely refactor those out into their own class to deal with data storage and retrieval in general, and each of our User, Trial, and Upload classes would inherit from that class. We might eventually add helper query methods to that class, and continue building it up from there.

2. Building a Web Application

Web apps have been built many times over, so we'll leverage the important work of the open source community and use an existing framework to do the boring plumbing work for us. The Sinatra framework does just that. In the tool's own words, Sinatra is "a DSL for quickly creating web applications in Ruby". Perfect.

Our web app will need to respond to HTTP requests, so we'll need a file that defines a route and associated code block for each combination of HTTP method and URL. Let's call it pedometer.rb.

```
get '/uploads' do
  @error = "A #{params[:error]} error has occurred." if params[:error]
  @pipelines = Upload.all.inject([]) do |a, upload|
    a << Pipeline.run(File.read(upload.file_path), upload.user, upload.trial)
    a
  end

  erb :uploads
end

get '/upload/*' do |file_path|
  upload = Upload.find(file_path)
  @pipeline = Pipeline.run(File.read(file_path), upload.user, upload.trial)

  erb :upload
end

post '/create' do
  begin
    Upload.create(params[:data][:tempfile], params[:user], params[:trial])

    redirect '/uploads'
  rescue Exception => e
    redirect '/uploads?error=creation'
  end
end
```

`pedometer.rb` allows our app to respond to HTTP requests for each of our routes. Each route's code block either retrieves data from, or stores data to, the file system through `Upload`, and then renders a view or redirects. The instance variables instantiated will be used directly in our views. The views simply display the data and aren't the focus of our app, so we we'll leave the code for them out of this chapter.

Let's look at each of the routes in `pedometer.rb` individually.

GET /uploads

Navigating to `http://localhost:4567/uploads` sends an HTTP GET request to our app, triggering our `get '/uploads'` code. The code runs the pipeline for all of the uploads in the file system and renders the `uploads` view, which displays a list of the uploads, and a form to submit new uploads. If an error parameter is included, an error string is created, and the `uploads` view will display the error.

GET /upload/*

Clicking the **Detail** link for each upload sends an HTTP GET to /upload with the file path for that upload. The pipeline runs, and the `upload` view is rendered. The view displays the details of the upload, including the charts, which are created using a JavaScript library called HighCharts.

POST /create

Our final route, an HTTP POST to `create`, is called when a user submits the form in the `uploads` view. The code block creates a new `Upload`, using the `params` hash to grab the values input by the user through the form, and redirects back to /uploads. If an error occurs in the creation process, the redirect to /uploads includes an error parameter to let the user know that something went wrong.

16.5   A Fully Functional App

Voilà! We've built a fully functional app, with true applicability.

The real world presents us with intricate, complex challenges. Software is uniquely capable of addressing these challenges at scale with minimal resources. As software engineers, we have the power to create positive change in our homes, our communities, and our world. Our training, academic or otherwise, likely equipped us with the problem-solving skills to write code that solves isolated, well-defined problems. As we grow and hone our craft, it's up to us to extend that training to address practical problems, tangled up with all of the messy realities of our world. I hope that this chapter gave you a taste of breaking down a real problem into small, addressable parts, and writing beautiful, clean, extensible code to build a solution.

Here's to solving interesting problems in an endlessly exciting world.

## chapter 17

The Same-Origin Policy
Eunsuk Kang, Santiago Perez De Rosso, and Daniel Jackson

17.1   Introduction

The same-origin policy (SOP) is an important part of the security mechanism of every modern browser. It controls when scripts running in a browser can communicate with one another (roughly, when they originate from the same website). First introduced in Netscape Navigator, the SOP now plays a critical role in the security of web applications; without it, it would be far easier for a malicious hacker to peruse your private photos on Facebook, read your email, or empty your bank account.

But the SOP is far from perfect. At times, it is too restrictive; there are cases (such as mashups) in which scripts from different origins should be able to share a resource but cannot. At other times it is not restrictive enough, leaving corner cases that can be exploited using common attacks such as cross-site request forgery. Furthermore, the design of the SOP has evolved organically over the years and puzzles many developers.

The goal of this chapter is to capture the essence of this important—yet often misunderstood—feature. In particular, we will attempt to answer the following questions:

- Why is the SOP necessary? What are the types of security violations that it prevents?
- How is the behavior of a web application affected by the SOP?
- What are different mechanisms for bypassing the SOP?
- How secure are these mechanisms? What are potential security issues that they introduce?

Covering the SOP in its entirety is a daunting task, given the complexity of the parts that are involved—web servers, browsers, HTTP, HTML documents, client-side scripts, and so on. We would likely get bogged down by the gritty details of all these parts (and consume our 500 lines before even reaching SOP). But how can we hope to be precise without representing crucial details?

17.2   Modeling with Alloy

This chapter is somewhat different from others in this book. Instead of building a working implementation, we will construct an executable model that serves as a simple yet precise description of the SOP. Like an implementation, the model can be executed to explore dynamic behaviors of the system, but unlike an implementation, the model omits low-level details that may get in the way of understanding the essential concepts.

The approach we take might be called "agile modeling" because of its similarities to agile programming. We work incrementally, assembling the model bit by bit. Our evolving model is at every point something that can be executed. We formulate and run tests as we go, so that by the end we have not only the model itself but also a collection of *properties* that it satisfies.

To construct this model, we use *Alloy*, a language for modeling and analyzing software design. An Alloy model cannot be executed in the traditional sense of program execution. Instead, a model can be (1) *simulated* to produce an *instance*, which represents a valid scenario or configuration of a system, and (2) *checked* to see whether the model satisfies a desired property.

Despite the above similarities, agile modeling differs from agile programming in one key respect: Although we'll be running tests, we actually won't be writing any. Alloy's analyzer generates test cases automatically, and all that needs to be provided is the property to be checked. Needless to say, this saves a lot of trouble (and text). The analyzer actually executes all possible test cases up to a certain size (called a *scope*); this typically means generating all starting states with at most some number of objects, and then choosing operations and arguments to apply up to some number of steps. Because so many tests (typically billions) are executed, and because all possible configurations that a state can take are covered (albeit within the scope), this analysis tends to expose bugs more effectively than conventional testing (and is sometimes described as "bounded verification").

Simplifications

Because the SOP operates in the context of browsers, servers, HTTP, and so on, a complete description would be overwhelming. So our model (like all models) abstracts away irrelevant aspects, such as how network packets are structured and routed. But it also simplifies some relevant aspects, which means that the model cannot fully account for all possible security vulnerabilities.

For example, we treat HTTP requests like remote procedure calls, ignoring the fact that responses to requests might come out of order. We also assume that DNS (the domain name service) is static, so we cannot consider attacks in which a DNS binding changes during an interaction. In principle, though, it would be possible to extend our model to cover all these aspects, although it's in the very nature of security analysis that no model (even if it represents the entire codebase) can be guaranteed to be complete.

17.3   Roadmap

Here is the order in which we will proceed with our model of the SOP. We will begin by building models of three key components that we need in order for us to talk about the SOP: HTTP, the browser, and client-side scripting. We will build on top of these basic models to define what it means for a web application to be *secure*, and then introduce the SOP as a mechanism that attempts to achieve the required security properties.

We will then see that the SOP can sometimes be too restrictive, getting in the way of a web application's proper functioning. So we will introduce four different techniques that are commonly used to bypass the restrictions that are imposed by the policy.

Feel free to explore the sections in any order you'd like. If you are new to Alloy, we recommend starting with the first three sections (HTTP, Browser, and Script), as they introduce some of the basic concepts of the modeling language. While you are making your way through the chapter, we also encourage you to play with the models in the Alloy Analyzer; run them, explore the generated scenarios, and try making modifications and seeing their effects. It is freely available for download[1].

---

[1]`http://alloy.mit.edu`

17.4   Model of the Web

HTTP

The first step in building an Alloy model is to declare some sets of objects. Let's start with resources:

```
sig Resource {}
```

The keyword `sig` identifies this as an Alloy *signature* declaration. This introduces a set of resource objects; think of these, just like the objects of a class with no instance variables, as blobs that have identity but no content. When the analysis runs, this set will be determined, just as a class in an object-oriented language comes to denote a set of objects when the program executes.

Resources are named by URLs (*uniform resource locators*):

```
sig Url {
  protocol: Protocol,
  host: Domain,
  port: lone Port,
  path: Path
}
sig Protocol, Port, Path {}
sig Domain { subsumes: set Domain }
```

Here we have five signature declarations, introducing a set of URLs and four additional sets for each of the basic kinds of objects they comprise. Within the URL declaration, we have four *fields*. Fields are like instance variables in a class; if u is a URL, for example, then u.protocol would represent the protocol of that URL (just like dot in Java). But in fact, as we'll see later, these fields are relations. You can think of each one as if it were a two-column database table. Thus protocol is a table with the first column containing URLs and the second column containing protocols. And the innocuous looking dot operator is in fact a rather general kind of relational join, so that you could also write protocol.p for all the URLs with a protocol p—but more on that later.

Note that paths, unlike URLs, are treated as if they have no structure—a simplification. The keyword `lone` (which can be read "less than or equal to one") says that each URL has at most one port. The path is the string that follows the host name in the URL, and which (for a simple static server) corresponds to the file path of the resource; we're assuming that it's always present, but can be an empty path.

Let us introduce clients and servers, each of which contains a mapping from paths to resources:

```
abstract sig Endpoint {}
abstract sig Client extends Endpoint {}
abstract sig Server extends Endpoint {
  resources: Path -> lone Resource
}
```

The `extends` keyword introduces a subset, so the set Client of all clients, for example, is a subset of the set Endpoint of all endpoints. Extensions are disjoint, so no endpoint is both a client and a server. The `abstract` keyword says that all extensions of a signature exhaust it, so its occurrence in the declaration of Endpoint, for example, says that every endpoint must belong to one of the subsets (at this point, Client and Server). For a server s, the expression s.resources will denote a map from paths to resources (hence the arrow in the declaration). Recall that each field is actually a relation that includes the owning signature as a first column, so this field represents a three-column relation on `Server`, `Path` and `Resource`.

To map a URL to a server, we introduce a set `Dns` of domain name servers, each with a mapping from domains to servers:

```
one sig Dns {
  map: Domain -> Server
}
```

The keyword `one` in the signature declaration means that (for simplicity) we're going to assume exactly one domain name server, and there will be a single DNS mapping, given by the expression `Dns.map`. Again, as with the serving resources, this could be dynamic (and in fact there are known security attacks that rely on changing DNS bindings during an interaction) but we're simplifying.

In order to model HTTP requests, we also need the concept of *cookies*, so let's declare them:

```
sig Cookie {
  domains: set Domain
}
```

Each cookie is scoped with a set of domains; this captures the fact that a cookie can apply to `*.mit.edu`, which would include all domains with the suffix `mit.edu`.

Finally, we can put this all together to construct a model of HTTP requests:

```
abstract sig HttpRequest extends Call {
  url: Url,
  sentCookies: set Cookie,
  body: lone Resource,
  receivedCookies: set Cookie,
  response: lone Resource,
}{
  from in Client
  to in Dns.map[url.host]
}
```

We're modeling an HTTP request and response in a single object; the `url`, `sentCookies` and `body` are sent by the client, and the `receivedCookies` and `response` are sent back by the server.

When writing the `HttpRequest` signature, we found that it contained generic features of calls, namely that they are from and to particular things. So we actually wrote a little Alloy module that declares the `Call` signature, and to use it here we need to import it:

```
open call[Endpoint]
```

It's a polymorphic module, so it's instantiated with `Endpoint`, the set of things calls are from and to. (The module appears in full in Section 17.10.)

Following the field declarations in `HttpRequest` is a collection of constraints. Each of these constraints applies to all members of the set of HTTP requests. The constraints say that (1) each request comes from a client, and (2) each request is sent to one of the servers specified by the URL host under the DNS mapping.

One of the prominent features of Alloy is that a model, no matter how simple or detailed, can be executed at any time to generate sample system instances. Let's use the `run` command to ask the Alloy Analyzer to execute the HTTP model that we have so far:

```
run {} for 3     -- generate an instance with up to 3 objects of every signature type
```

As soon as the analyzer finds a possible instance of the system, it automatically produces a diagram of the instance, like in Figure 17.1.

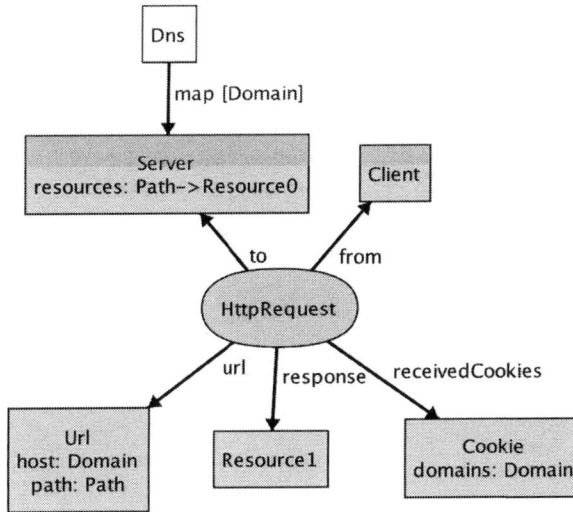

Figure 17.1: A possible instance

This instance shows a client (represented by node `Client`) sending an `HttpRequest` to `Server`, which, in response, returns a resource object and instructs the client to store `Cookie` at `Domain`.

Even though this is a tiny instance with seemingly few details, it signals a flaw in our model. Note that the resource returned from the request (`Resource1`) does not exist in the server. We neglected to specify an obvious fact about the server; namely, that every response to a request is a resource that the server stores. We can go back to our definition of `HttpRequest` and add a constraint:

```
abstract sig HttpRequest extends Call { ... }{
   ...
   response = to.resources[url.path]
}
```

Rerunning now produces instances without the flaw.

Instead of generating sample instances, we can ask the analyzer to *check* whether the model satisfies a property. For example, one property we might want is that when a client sends the same request multiple times, it always receives the same response back:

```
check {
    all r1, r2: HttpRequest | r1.url = r2.url implies r1.response = r2.response
} for 3
```

Given this check command, the analyzer explores every possible behavior of the system (up to the specified bound), and when it finds one that violates the property, displays that instance as a *counterexample*, as shown in Figure 17.2 and Figure 17.3.

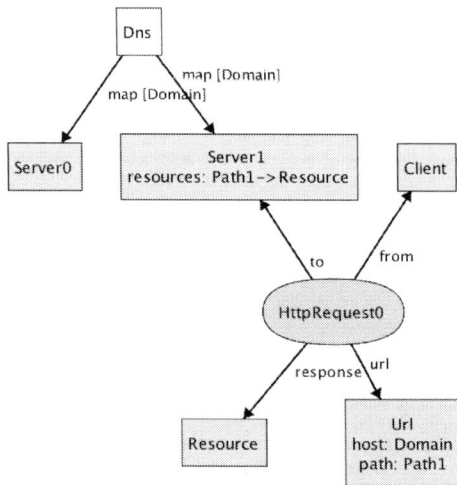

Figure 17.2: Counterexample at time 0

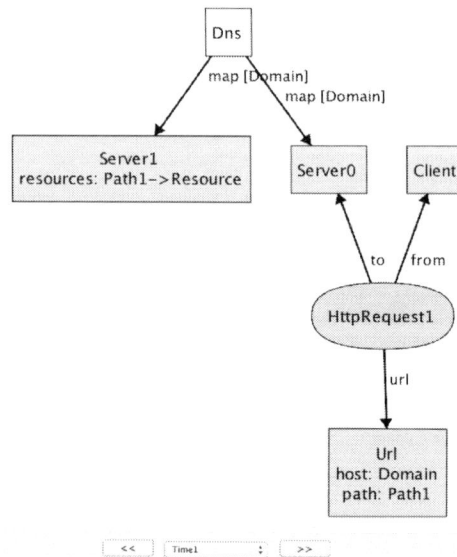

Figure 17.3: Counterexample at time 1

This counterexample again shows an HTTP request being made by a client, but with two different servers. (In the Alloy visualizer, objects of the same type are distinguished by appending numeric suffixes to their names; if there is only one object of a given type, no suffix is added. Every name that appears in a snapshot diagram is the name of an object. So—perhaps confusingly at first sight—the names Domain, Path, Resource, Url all refer to individual objects, not to types.)

Note that while the DNS maps Domain to both Server0 and Server1 (in reality, this is a common practice for load balancing), only Server1 maps Path to a resource object, causing HttpRequest1 to result in an empty response: another error in our model. To fix this, we add an Alloy *fact* recording that any two servers to which DNS maps a single host provide the same set of resources:

```
fact ServerAssumption {
  all s1, s2: Server |
    (some Dns.map.s1 & Dns.map.s2) implies s1.resources = s2.resources
}
```

When we re-run the check command after adding this fact, the analyzer no longer reports any counterexamples for the property. This doesn't mean the property has been proven to be true, since there might be a counterexample in a larger scope. But it is unlikely that the property is false, since the analyzer has tested all possible instances involving 3 objects of each type.

If desired, however, we can re-run the analysis with a larger scope for increased confidence. For example, running the above check with the scope of 10 still does not produce any counterexample, suggesting that the property is likely to be valid. However, keep in mind that given a larger scope, the analyzer needs to test a greater number of instances, and so it will likely take longer to complete.

Browser

Let's now introduce browsers into our model:

```
sig Browser extends Client {
  documents: Document -> Time,
  cookies: Cookie -> Time,
}
```

This is our first example of a signature with *dynamic fields*. Alloy has no built-in notions of time or behavior, which means that a variety of idioms can be used. In this model, we're using a common idiom in which you introduce a notion of Time, and attach it as a final column for every time-varying field. For example, the expression b.cookies.t represents the set of cookies that are stored in browser b at a particular time t. Likewise, the documents field associates a set of documents with each browser at a given time. (For more details about how we model the dynamic behavior, see Section 17.10.)

Documents are created from a response to an HTTP request. They can also be destroyed if, for example, the user closes a tab or the browser, but we leave this out of the model. A document has a URL (the one from which the document was originated), some content (the DOM), and a domain:

```
sig Document {
  src: Url,
  content: Resource -> Time,
  domain: Domain -> Time
}
```

The inclusion of the Time column for the latter two fields tells us that they can vary over time, and its omission for the first (src, representing the source URL of the document) indicates that the source URL is fixed.

To model the effect of an HTTP request on a browser, we introduce a new signature, since not all HTTP requests will originate at the level of the browser; the rest will come from scripts.

```
sig BrowserHttpRequest extends HttpRequest {
  doc: Document
}{
  -- the request comes from a browser
  from in Browser
  -- the cookies being sent exist in the browser at the time of the request
  sentCookies in from.cookies.start
  -- every cookie sent must be scoped to the url of the request
  all c: sentCookies | url.host in c.domains

  -- a new document is created to display the content of the response
  documents.end = documents.start + from -> doc
  -- the new document has the response as its contents
  content.end = content.start ++ doc -> response
  -- the new document has the host of the url as its domain
  domain.end = domain.start ++ doc -> url.host
  -- the document's source field is the url of the request
  doc.src = url

  -- new cookies are stored by the browser
  cookies.end = cookies.start + from -> sentCookies
}
```

This kind of request has one new field, doc, representing the document created in the browser from the resource returned by the request. As with HttpRequest, the behavior is described as a collection of constraints. Some of these say when the call can happen: for example, that the call has to come from a browser. Some constrain the arguments of the call: for example, that the cookies must be scoped appropriately. And some constrain the effect, using a common idiom that relates the value of a relation after the call to its value before.

For example, to understand the constraint documents.end = documents.start + from -> doc remember that documents is a 3-column relation on browsers, documents and times. The fields start and end come from the declaration of Call (which we haven't seen, but is included in the listing at the end), and represent the times at the beginning and end of the call. The expression documents.end gives the mapping from browsers to documents when the call has ended. So this constraint says that after the call, the mapping is the same, except for a new entry in the table mapping from to doc.

Some constraints use the ++ relational *override* operator: e1 ++ e2 contains all tuples of e2, and additionally, any tuples of e1 whose first element is not the first element of a tuple in e2. For example, the constraint content.end = content.start ++ doc -> response says that after the call, the content mapping will be updated to map doc to response (overriding any previous mapping of doc). If we were to use the union operator + instead, then the same document might (incorrectly) be mapped to multiple resources in the after state.

Script

Next, we will build on the HTTP and browser models to introduce *client-side scripts*, which represent pieces of code (typically in JavaScript) executing inside a browser document (context).

```
sig Script extends Client { context: Document }
```

A script is a dynamic entity that can perform two different kinds of action: (1) it can make HTTP requests (i.e., Ajax requests) and (2) it can perform browser operations to manipulate the content and properties of a document. The flexibility of client-side scripts is one of the main catalysts of the rapid development of Web 2.0, but is also the reason why the SOP was created in the first place. Without the SOP, scripts would be able to send arbitrary requests to servers, or freely modify documents inside the browser—which would be bad news if one or more of the scripts turned out to be malicious.

A script can communicate to a server by sending an XmlHttpRequest:

```
sig XmlHttpRequest extends HttpRequest {}{
  from in Script
  noBrowserChange[start, end] and noDocumentChange[start, end]
}
```

An XmlHttpRequest can be used by a script to send/receive resources to/from a server, but unlike BrowserHttpRequest, it does not immediately result in the creation of a new page or other changes to the browser and its documents. To say that a call does not modify these aspects of the system, we define predicates noBrowserChange and noDocumentChange:

```
pred noBrowserChange[start, end: Time] {
  documents.end = documents.start and cookies.end = cookies.start
}
pred noDocumentChange[start, end: Time] {
  content.end = content.start and domain.end = domain.start
}
```

What kind of operations can a script perform on documents? First, we introduce a generic notion of *browser operations* to represent a set of browser API functions that can be invoked by a script:

```
abstract sig BrowserOp extends Call { doc: Document }{
  from in Script and to in Browser
  doc + from.context in to.documents.start
  noBrowserChange[start, end]
}
```

Field doc refers to the document that will be accessed or manipulated by this call. The second constraint in the signature facts says that both doc and the document in which the script executes (from.context) must be documents that currently exist inside the browser. Finally, a BrowserOp may modify the state of a document, but not the set of documents or cookies that are stored in the browser. (Actually, cookies can be associated with a document and modified using a browser API, but we omit this detail for now.)

A script can read from and write to various parts of a document (usually called DOM elements). In a typical browser, there are a large number of API functions for accessing the DOM (e.g., document.getElementById), but enumerating all of them is not important for our purpose. Instead, we will simply group them into two kinds—ReadDom and WriteDom—and model modifications as wholesale replacements of the entire document:

```
sig ReadDom extends BrowserOp { result: Resource }{
  result = doc.content.start
  noDocumentChange[start, end]
}
```

```
sig WriteDom extends BrowserOp { newDom: Resource }{
  content.end = content.start ++ doc -> newDom
  domain.end = domain.start
}
```

ReadDom returns the content of the target document, but does not modify it; WriteDom, on the other hand, sets the new content of the target document to newDom.

In addition, a script can modify various properties of a document, such as its width, height, domain, and title. For our discussion of the SOP, we are only interested in the domain property, which we will introduce in a later section.

17.5   Example Applications

As we've seen earlier, given a run or check command, the Alloy Analyzer generates a scenario (if it exists) that is consistent with the description of the system in the model. By default, the analyzer arbitrarily picks *any* one of the possible system scenarios (up to the specified bound), and assigns numeric identifiers to signature instances (Server0, Browser1, etc.) in the scenario.

Sometimes, we may wish to analyze the behavior of a *particular* web application, instead of exploring scenarios with a random configuration of servers and clients. For example, imagine that we wish to build an email application that runs inside a browser (like Gmail). In addition to providing basic email features, our application might display a banner from a third-party advertisement service, which is controlled by a potentially malicious actor.

In Alloy, the keywords one sig introduce a *singleton* signature containing exactly one object; we saw an example above with Dns. This syntax can be used to specify concrete atoms. For example, to say that there is one inbox page and one ad banner (each of which is a document) we can write:

```
one sig InboxPage, AdBanner extends Document {}
```

With this declaration, every scenario that Alloy generates will contain at least these two Document objects.

Likewise, we can specify particular servers, domains and so on, with a constraint (which we've called Configuration) to specify the relationships between them:

```
one sig EmailServer, EvilServer extends Server {}
one sig EvilScript extends Script {}
one sig EmailDomain, EvilDomain extends Domain {}
fact Configuration {
  EvilScript.context = AdBanner
  InboxPage.domain.first = EmailDomain
  AdBanner.domain.first = EvilDomain
  Dns.map = EmailDomain -> EmailServer + EvilDomain -> EvilServer
}
```

For example, the last constraint in the fact specifies how the DNS is configured to map domain names for the two servers in our system. Without this constraint, the Alloy Analyzer may generate scenarios where EmailDomain is mapped to EvilServer, which are not of interest to us. (In practice, such a mapping may be possible due to an attack called *DNS spoofing*, but we will rule it out from our model since it lies outside the class of attacks that the SOP is designed to prevent.)

Let us introduce two additional applications: an online calendar and a blog site:

```
one sig CalendarServer, BlogServer extends Document {}
one sig CalendarDomain, BlogDomain extends Domain {}
```

We should update the constraint about the DNS mapping above to incorporate the domain names for these two servers:

```
fact Configuration {
  ...
  Dns.map = EmailDomain -> EmailServer + EvilDomain -> EvilServer +
            CalendarDomain -> CalendarServer + BlogDomain -> BlogServer
}
```

In addition, let us say that that the email, blog, and calendar applications are all developed by a single organization, and thus, share the same base domain name. Conceptually, we can think of `EmailServer` and `CalendarServer` having subdomains email and calendar, sharing `example.com` as the common superdomain. In our model, this can be represented by introducing a domain name that *subsumes* others:

```
one sig ExampleDomain extends Domain {}{
   subsumes = EmailDomain + EvilDomain + CalendarDomain + this
}
```

Note that `this` is included as a member of `subsumes`, since every domain name subsumes itself.

There are other details about these applications that we omit here (see `example.als` for the full model). But we will revisit these applications as our running example throughout the remainder of this chapter.

17.6   Security Properties

Before we get to the SOP itself, there is an important question that we have not discussed yet: What exactly do we mean when we say our system is *secure*?

Not surprisingly, this is a tricky question to answer. For our purposes, we will turn to two well-studied concepts in information security—*confidentiality* and *integrity*. Both of these concepts talk about how information should be allowed to pass through the various parts of the system. Roughly, *confidentiality* means that a critical piece of data should only be accessible to parts that are deemed trusted, and *integrity* means that trusted parts only rely on data that have not been maliciously tampered with.

Dataflow Properties

In order to specify these security properties more precisely, we first need to define what it means for a piece of data to *flow* from one part of the system to another. In our model so far, we have described interactions between two endpoints as being carried out through *calls*; e.g., a browser interacts with a server by making HTTP requests, and a script interacts with the browser by invoking browser API operations. Intuitively, during each call, a piece of data may flow from one endpoint to another as an *argument* or *return value* of the call. To represent this, we introduce a notion of `DataflowCall` into the model, and associate each call with a set of `args` and `returns` data fields:

```
sig Data in Resource + Cookie {}

sig DataflowCall in Call {
  args, returns: set Data,  --- arguments and return data of this call
}{
 this in HttpRequest implies
    args = this.sentCookies + this.body and
    returns = this.receivedCookies + this.response
 ...
}
```

For example, during each call of type HttpRequest, the client transfers sentCookies and body to the server, and receives receivedCookies and response as return values.

More generally, arguments flow from the sender of the call to the receiver, and return values flow from the receiver to the sender. This means that the only way for an endpoint to access a new piece of data is by receiving it as an argument of a call that the endpoint accepts, or a return value of a call that the endpoint invokes. We introduce a notion of DataflowModule, and assign field accesses to represent the set of data elements that the module can access at each time step:

```
sig DataflowModule in Endpoint {
  -- Set of data that this component initially owns
  accesses: Data -> Time
}{
  all d: Data, t: Time - first |
    -- This endpoint can only access a piece of data "d" at time "t" only when
   d -> t in accesses implies
      -- (1) It already had access in the previous time step, or
      d -> t.prev in accesses or
      -- there is some call "c" that ended at "t" such that
      some c: Call & end.t |
        -- (2) the endpoint receives "c" that carries "d" as one of its arguments or
        c.to = this and d in c.args or
        -- (3) the endpoint sends "c" that returns "d"
        c.from = this and d in c.returns
}
```

We also need to restrict data elements that a module can provide as arguments or return values of a call. Otherwise, we may get weird scenarios where a module can make a call with an argument that it has no access to.

```
sig DataflowCall in Call { ... } {
  -- (1) Any arguments must be accessible to the sender
  args in from.accesses.start
  -- (2) Any data returned from this call must be accessible to the receiver
  returns in to.accesses.start
}
```

Now that we have means to describe data flow between different parts of the system, we are (almost) ready to state security properties that we care about. But recall that confidentiality and integrity are *context-dependent* notions; these properties make sense only if we can talk about some agents within the system as being trusted (or malicious). Similarly, not all information is equally important: we need to distinguish between data elements that we consider to be critical or malicious (or neither):

```
sig TrustedModule, MaliciousModule in DataflowModule {}
sig CriticalData, MaliciousData in Data {}
```

Then, the confidentiality property can be stated as an *assertion* on the flow of critical data into non-trusted parts of the system:

```
// No malicious module should be able to access critical data
assert Confidentiality {
  no m: Module - TrustedModule, t: Time |
    some CriticalData & m.accesses.t
}
```

The integrity property is the dual of confidentiality:

```
// No malicious data should ever flow into a trusted module
assert Integrity {
  no m: TrustedModule, t: Time |
    some MaliciousData & m.accesses.t
}
```

Threat Model

A threat model describes a set of actions that an attacker may perform in an attempt to compromise a security property of a system. Building a threat model is an important step in any secure system design; it allows us to identify (possibly invalid) assumptions that we have about the system and its environment, and prioritize different types of risks that need to be mitigated.

In our model, we consider an attacker that can act as a server, a script or a client. As a server, the attacker may set up malicious web pages to solicit visits from unsuspecting users, who, in turn, may inadvertently send sensitive information to the attacker as part of a HTTP request. The attacker may create a malicious script that invokes DOM operations to read data from other pages and relays those data to the attacker's server. Finally, as a client, the attacker may impersonate a normal user and send malicious requests to a server in an attempt to access the user's data. We do not consider attackers that eavesdrop on the connection between different network endpoints; although it is a threat in practice, the SOP is not designed to prevent it, and thus it lies outside the scope of our model.

Checking Properties

Now that we have defined the security properties and the attacker's behavior, let us show how the Alloy Analyzer can be used to automatically check that those properties hold even in the presence of the attacker. When prompted with a check command, the analyzer explores *all* possible dataflow traces in the system and produces a counterexample (if one exists) that demonstrates how an assertion might be violated:

```
check Confidentiality for 5
```

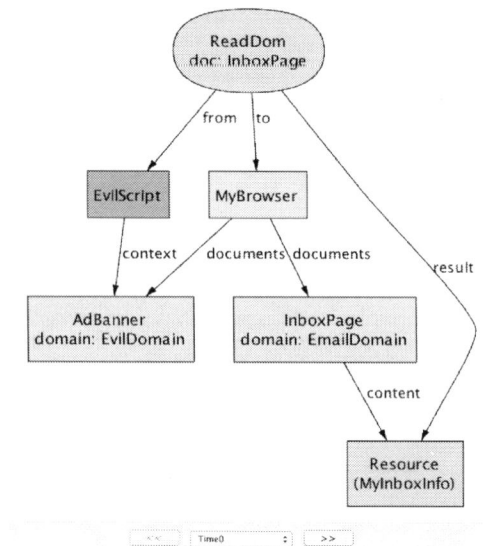

Figure 17.4: Confidentiality counterexample at time 0

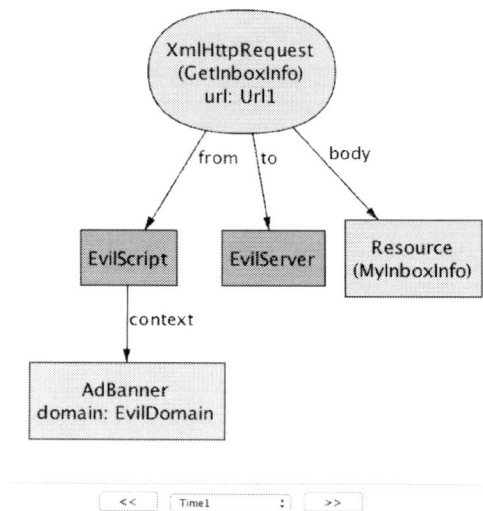

Figure 17.5: Confidentiality counterexample at time 1

For example, when checking the model of our example application against the confidentiality property, the analyzer generates the scenario seen in Figure 17.4 and Figure 17.5, which shows how EvilScript may access a piece of critical data (MyInboxInfo).

This counterexample involves two steps. In the first step (Figure 17.4), EvilScript, executing inside AdBanner from EvilDomain, reads the content of InboxPage, which originates from EmailDomain. In the next step (Figure 17.5), EvilScript sends the same content (MyInboxInfo) to EvilServer by making an XmlHtttpRequest call. The core of the problem here is that a script executing under one domain is able to read the content of a document from another domain; as we will see in the next section, this is exactly one of the scenarios that the SOP is designed to prevent.

There may be multiple counterexamples to a single assertion. Consider Figure 17.6, which shows a different way in which the system may violate the confidentiality property.

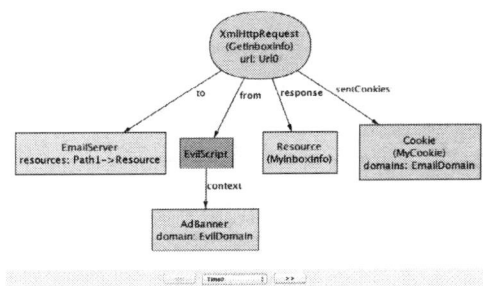

Figure 17.6: Another confidentiality violation

In this scenario, instead of reading the content of the inbox page, `EvilScript` directly makes a `GetInboxInfo` request to `EmailServer`. Note that the request includes a cookie (`MyCookie`), which is scoped to the same domain as the destination server. This is potentially dangerous, because if the cookie is used to represent the user's identity (e.g., a session cookie), `EvilScript` can effectively pretend to be the user and trick the server into responding with the user's private data (`MyInboxInfo`). Here, the problem is again related to the liberal ways in which a script may be used to access information across different domains—namely, that a script executing under one domain is able to make an HTTP request to a server with a different domain.

These two counterexamples tell us that extra measures are needed to restrict the behavior of scripts, especially since some of those scripts could be malicious. This is exactly where the SOP comes in.

17.7 Same-Origin Policy

Before we can state the SOP, the first thing we should do is to introduce the notion of an *origin*, which is composed of a protocol, host, and optional port:

```
sig Origin {
  protocol: Protocol,
  host: Domain,
  port: lone Port
}
```

For convenience, let us define a function that, given a URL, returns the corresponding origin:

```
fun origin[u: Url] : Origin {
    {o: Origin | o.protocol = u.protocol and o.host = u.host and o.port = u.port }
}
```

The SOP itself has two parts, restricting the ability of a script to (1) make DOM API calls and (2) send HTTP requests. The first part of the policy states that a script can only read from and write to a document that comes from the same origin as the script:

```
fact domSop {
  all o: ReadDom + WriteDom |   let target = o.doc, caller = o.from.context |
```

```
    origin[target] = origin[caller]
}
```

An instance such as the first script scenario (from the previous section) is not possible under domSop, since `Script` is not allowed to invoke `ReadDom` on a document from a different origin.

The second part of the policy says that a script cannot send an HTTP request to a server unless its context has the same origin as the target URL—effectively preventing instances such as the second script scenario.

```
fact xmlHttpReqSop {
    all x: XmlHttpRequest | origin[x.url] = origin[x.from.context.src]
}
```

As we can see, the SOP is designed to prevent the two types of vulnerabilities that could arise from actions of a malicious script; without it, the web would be a much more dangerous place than it is today.

It turns out, however, that the SOP can be *too* restrictive. For example, sometimes you *do* want to allow communication between two documents of different origins. By the above definition of an origin, a script from `foo.example.com` would not be able to read the content of `bar.example.com`, or send a HTTP request to `www.example.com`, because these are all considered distinct hosts.

In order to allow some form of cross-origin communication when necessary, browsers implemented a variety of mechanisms for relaxing the SOP. Some of these are more well-thought-out than others, and some have pitfalls that, when badly used, can undermine the security benefits of the SOP. In the following sections, we will describe the most common of these mechanisms, and discuss their potential security pitfalls.

17.8   Techniques for Bypassing the SOP

The SOP is a classic example of the tension between functionality and security; we want to make sure our sites are robust and functional, but the mechanism for securing it can sometimes get in the way. Indeed, when the SOP was initially introduced, developers ran into trouble building sites that made legitimate uses of cross-domain communication (e.g., mashups).

In this section, we will discuss four techniques that have been devised and frequently used by web developers to bypass the restrictions imposed by the SOP: (1) The `document.domain` property relaxation; (2) JSONP; (3) PostMessage; and (4) CORS. These are valuable tools, but if used without caution, may render a web application vulnerable to exactly the kinds of attacks that the SOP was designed to thwart in the first place.

Each of these four techniques is surprisingly complex, and if described in full detail, would merit its own chapter. So here we just give a brief impression of how they work, potential security problems that they introduce, and how to prevent these problems. In particular, we will ask the Alloy Analyzer to check, for each technique, whether it could be abused by an attacker to undermine the two security properties that we defined earlier:

```
check Confidentiality for 5
check Integrity for 5
```

Based on insights from the counterexamples that the analyzer generates, we will discuss guidelines for safely using these techniques without falling into security pitfalls.

Domain Property

As the first technique on our list, we will look at the use of the document.domain property as a way of bypassing the SOP. The idea behind this technique is to allow two documents from different origins to access each other's DOM simply by setting the document.domain property to the same value. So, for example, a script from email.example.com could read or write the DOM of a document from calendar.example.com if the scripts in both documents set the document.domain property to example.com (assuming both source URLs have also the same protocol and port).

We model the behavior of setting the document.domain property as a type of browser operation called SetDomain:

```
// Modify the document.domain property
sig SetDomain extends BrowserOp { newDomain: Domain }{
  doc = from.context
  domain.end = domain.start ++ doc -> newDomain
  -- no change to the content of the document
  content.end = content.start
}
```

The newDomain field represents the value to which the property should be set. There's a caveat, though: scripts can only set the domain property to a right-hand, fully qualified fragment of its hostname. (I.e., email.example.com can set it to example.com but not to google.com.) We use a fact to capture this rule about subdomains:

```
// Scripts can only set the domain property to only one that is a right-hand,
// fully-qualified fragment of its hostname
fact setDomainRule {
  all d: Document | d.src.host in (d.domain.Time).subsumes
}
```

If it weren't for this rule, any site could set the document.domain property to any value, which means that, for example, a malicious site could set the domain property to your bank domain, load your bank account in an iframe, and (assuming the bank page has set its domain property) read the DOM of your bank page.

Let us go back to our original definition of the SOP, and relax its restriction on DOM access in order to take into account the effect of the document.domain property. If two scripts set the property to the same value, and they have the same protocol and port, then these two scripts can interact with each other (that is, read and write each other's DOM).

```
fact domSop {
  -- For every successful read/write DOM operation,
  all o: ReadDom + WriteDom |  let target = o.doc, caller = o.from.context |
    -- (1) target and caller documents are from the same origin, or
    origin[target] = origin[caller] or
    -- (2) domain properties of both documents have been modified
    (target + caller in (o.prevs <: SetDomain).doc and
      -- ...and they have matching origin values.
      currOrigin[target, o.start] = currOrigin[caller, o.start])
}
```

Here, `currOrigin[d, t]` is a function that returns the origin of document d with the property `document.domain` at time t as its hostname.

It is worth pointing out that the `document.domain` properties for *both* documents must be *explictly* set sometime after they are loaded into the browser. Let us say that document A is loaded from `example.com`, and document B from `calendar.example.com` has its domain property modified to `example.com`. Even though the two documents now have the same domain property, they will *not* be able to interact with each other, unless document A also explictly sets its property to `example.com`. At first, this seems like a rather strange behavior. However, without this, various bad things can happen. For example, a site could be subject to a cross-site scripting attack from its subdomains: A malicious script in document B might modify its domain property to `example.com` and manipulate the DOM of document A, even though the latter never intended to interact with document B.

Analysis: Now that we have relaxed the SOP to allow cross-origin communication under certain circumstances, do the security guarantees of the SOP still hold? Let us ask the Alloy Analyzer to tell us whether the `document.domain` property could be abused by an attacker to access or tamper with a user's sensitive data.

Indeed, given the new, relaxed definition of the SOP, the analyzer generates a counterexample scenario to the confidentiality property:

```
check Confidentiality for 5
```

This scenario consists of five steps; the first three steps show a typical use of `document.domain`, where two documents from distinct origins, `CalendarPage` and `InboxPage`, communicate by setting their domain properties to a common value (`ExampleDomain`). The last two steps introduce another document, `BlogPage`, that has been compromised with a malicious script that attempts to access the content of the other two documents.

At the beginning of the scenario (Figure 17.7 and Figure 17.8), `InboxPage` and `CalendarPage` have domain properties with two distinct values (`EmailDomain` and `ExampleDomain`, respectively), so the browser will prevent them from accessing each other's DOM. The scripts running inside the documents (`InboxScript` and `CalendarScript`) each execute the `SetDomain` operation to modify their domain properties to `ExampleDomain` (which is allowed because `ExampleDomain` is a superdomain of the original domain).

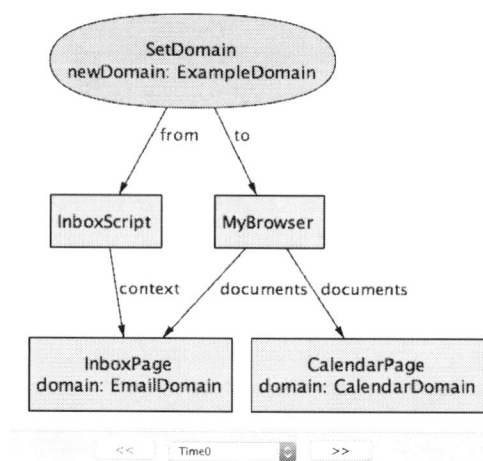

Figure 17.7: Cross-origin counterexample at time 0

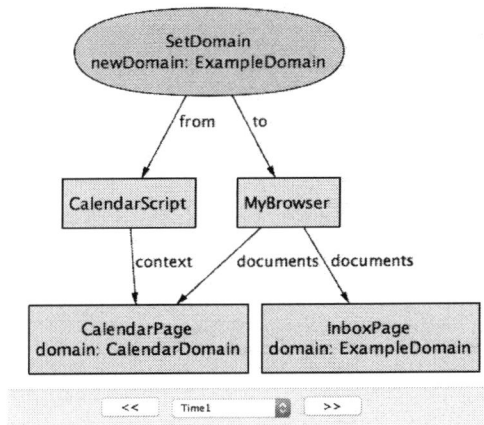

Figure 17.8: Cross-origin counterexample at time 1

Having done this, they can now access each other's DOM by executing ReadDom or WriteDom operations, as in Figure 17.9.

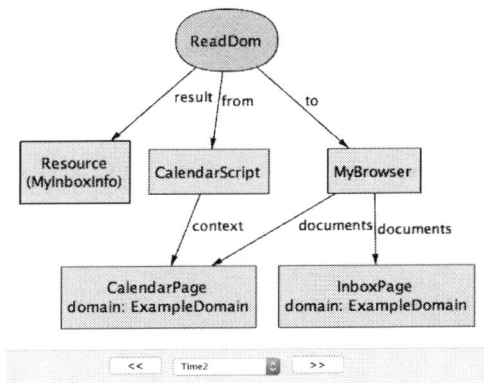

Figure 17.9: Cross-origin counterexample at time 2

Note that when you set the domain of email.example.com and calendar.example.com to example.com, you are allowing not only these two pages to communicate between each other, but also *any* other page that has example.com as a superdomain (e.g., blog.example.com). An attacker also realizes this, and constructs a special script (EvilScript) that runs inside the attacker's blog page (BlogPage). In the next step (Figure 17.10), the script executes the SetDomain operation to modify the domain property of BlogPage to ExampleDomain.

Now that BlogPage has the same domain property as the other two documents, it can successfully execute the ReadDOM operation to access their content (Figure 17.11.)

This attack points out one crucial weakness of the domain property method for cross-origin communication: The security of an application that uses this method is only as strong as the weakest link in all of the pages that share the same base domain. We will shortly discuss another method called PostMessage, which can be used for a more general class of cross-origin communication while also being more secure.

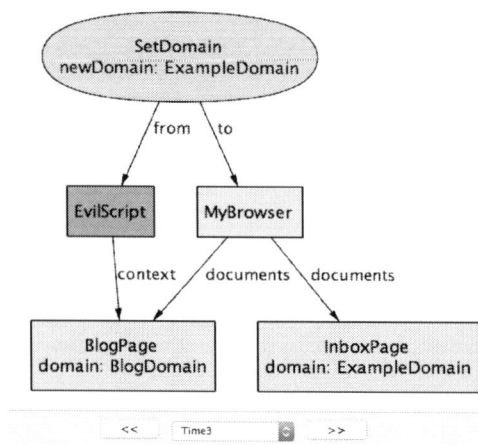

Figure 17.10: Cross-origin counterexample at time 3

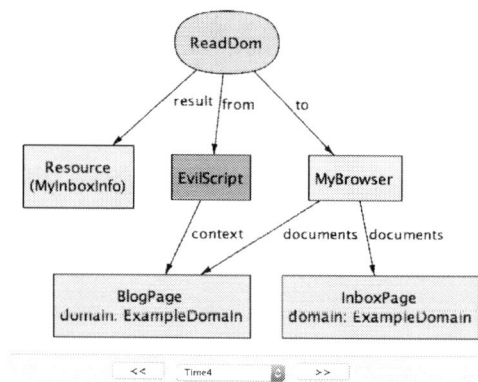

Figure 17.11: Cross-origin counterexample at time 4

JSON with Padding (JSONP)

Before the introduction of CORS (which we will discuss shortly), JSONP was perhaps the most popular technique for bypassing the SOP restriction on XMLHttpRequest, and still remains widely used today. JSONP takes advantage of the fact that script inclusion tags in HTML (i.e., `<script>`) are exempt from the SOP*; that is, you can include a script from *any* URL, and the browser readily executes it in the current document:

(* Without this exemption, it would not be possible to load JavaScript libraries, such as JQuery, from other domains.)

```
<script src="http://www.example.com/myscript.js"></script>
```

A script tag can be used to obtain code, but how do we use it to receive arbitrary *data* (e.g., a JSON object) from a different domain? The problem is that the browser expects the content of `src` to be a piece of JavaScript code, and so simply having it point at a data source (e.g., a JSON or HTML file) results in a syntax error.

One workaround is to wrap the desired data inside a string that the browser recognizes as valid JavaScript code; this string is sometimes called *padding* (hence the name "JSON with padding").

This padding could be any arbitrary JavaScript code, but conventionally, it is the name of a callback function (already defined in the current document) that is to be executed on the response data:

```
<script src="http://www.example.com/mydata?jsonp=processData"></script>
```

The server on `www.example.com` recognizes it as a JSONP request, and wraps the requested data inside the `jsonp` parameter:

```
processData(mydata)
```

which is a valid JavaScript statement (namely, the application of function "processData" on value "mydata"), and is executed by the browser in the current document.

In our model, JSONP is modeled as a kind of HTTP request that includes the identifier of a callback function in the field `padding`. After receiving a JSONP request, the server returns a response that has the requested resource (`payload`) wrapped inside the callback function (cb).

```
sig CallbackID {}  // identifier of a callback function
// Request sent as a result of <script> tag
sig JsonpRequest in BrowserHttpRequest {
  padding: CallbackID
}{
  response in JsonpResponse
}
sig JsonpResponse in Resource {
  cb: CallbackID,
  payload: Resource
}
```

When the browser receives the response, it executes the callback function on the payload:

```
sig JsonpCallback extends EventHandler {
  cb: CallbackID,
  payload: Resource
}{
  causedBy in JsonpRequest
  let resp = causedBy.response |
    cb = resp.@cb and
    -- result of JSONP request is passed on as an argument to the callback
    payload = resp.@payload
}
```

(EventHandler is a special type of call that must take place sometime after another call, which is denoted by causedBy; we will use event handlers to model actions that are performed by scripts in response to browser events.)

Note that the callback function executed is the same as the one that's included in the response (cb = resp.@cb), but *not* necessarily the same as padding in the original JSONP request. In other words, for the JSONP communication to work, the server is responsible for properly constructing a response that includes the original padding as the callback function (i.e., ensure that JsonRequest.padding = JsonpResponse.cb). In principle, the server can choose to include any callback function (or any piece of JavaScript), including one that has nothing to do with padding in the request. This highlights a potential risk of JSONP: the server that accepts the JSONP requests must be trustworthy and secure, because it has the ability to execute any piece of JavaScript code in the client document.

Analysis: Checking the Confidentiality property with the Alloy Analyzer returns a counterexample that shows one potential security risk of JSONP. In this scenario, the calendar application (CalendarServer) makes its resources available to third-party sites using a JSONP endpoint (GetSchedule). To restrict access to the resources, CalendarServer only sends back a response with the schedule for a user if the request contains a cookie that correctly identifies that user.

Note that once a server provides an HTTP endpoint as a JSONP service, anyone can make a JSONP request to it, including malicious sites. In this scenario, the ad banner page from EvilServer includes a *script* tag that causes a GetSchedule request, with a callback function called Leak as padding. Typically, the developer of AdBanner does not have direct access to the victim user's session cookie (MyCookie) for CalendarServer. However, because the JSONP request is being sent to CalendarServer, the browser automatically includes MyCookie as part of the request; CalendarServer, having received a JSONP request with MyCookie, will return the victim's resource (MySchedule) wrapped inside the padding Leak (Figure 17.12.)

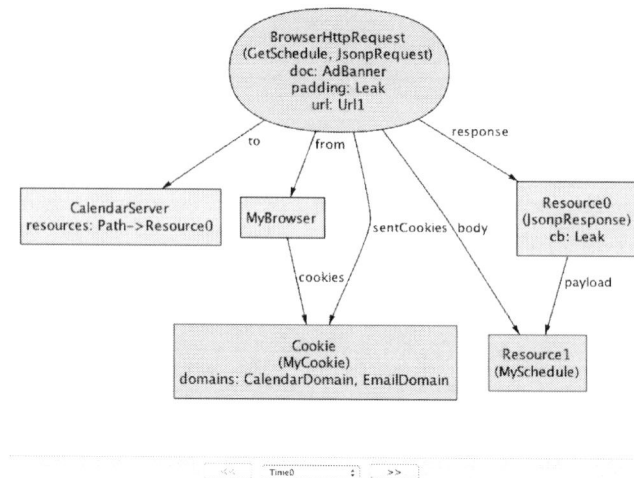

Figure 17.12: JSONP counterexample at time 0

In the next step, the browser interprets the JSONP response as a call to Leak(MySchedule) (Figure 17.13). The rest of the attack is simple; Leak can simply be programmed to forward the input argument to EvilServer, allowing the attacker to access the victim's sensitive information.

This attack, an example of *cross-site request forgery* (CSRF), shows an inherent weakness of JSOPN; *any* site on the web can make a JSONP request simply by including a <script> tag and access the payload inside the padding. The risk can be mitigated in two ways: (1) ensure that a JSONP request never returns sensitive data, or (2) use another mechanism in place of cookies (e.g., secret tokens) to authorize the request.

PostMessage

PostMessage is a new feature in HTML5 that allows scripts from two documents (of possibly different origins) to communicate with each other. It offers a more disciplined alternative to the method of setting the domain property, but brings its own security risks.

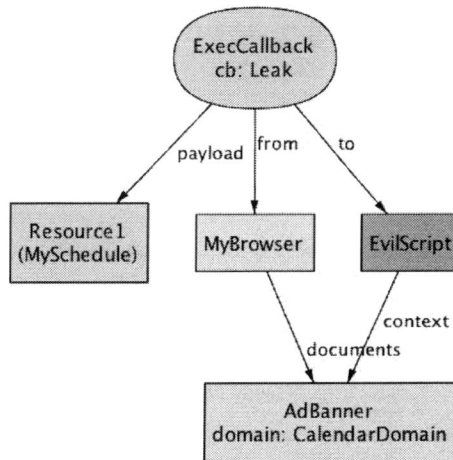

Figure 17.13: JSONP counterexample at time 1

PostMessage is a browser API function that takes two arguments: (1) the data to be sent (message), and (2) the origin of the document receiving the message (targetOrigin):

```
sig PostMessage extends BrowserOp {
  message: Resource,
  targetOrigin: Origin
}
```

To receive a message from another document, the receiving document registers an event handler that is invoked by the browser as a consequence of a PostMessage:

```
sig ReceiveMessage extends EventHandler {
  data: Resource,
  srcOrigin: Origin
}{
  causedBy in PostMessage
  -- "ReceiveMessage" event is sent to the script with the correct context
  origin[to.context.src] = causedBy.targetOrigin
  -- messages match
  data = causedBy.@message
  -- the origin of the sender script is provided as "srcOrigin" param
  srcOrigin = origin[causedBy.@from.context.src]
}
```

The browser passes two parameters to ReceiveMessage: a resource (data) that corresponds to the message being sent, and the origin of the sender document (srcOrigin). The signature fact contains four constraints to ensure that each ReceiveMessage is well-formed with respect to its corresponding PostMessage.

Analysis: Again, let us ask the Alloy Analyzer whether PostMessage is a secure way of performing cross-origin communication. This time, the analyzer returns a counterexample for the Integrity property, meaning the attacker is able to exploit a weakness in `PostMessage` to introduce malicious data into a trusted application.

Note that by default, the PostMessage mechanism does not restrict who is allowed to send PostMessage; in other words, any document can send a message to another document as long as the latter has registered a `ReceiveMessage` handler. For example, in the following instance generated from Alloy, `EvilScript`, running inside `AdBanner`, sends a malicious `PostMessage` to a document with the target origin of `EmailDomain` (Figure 17.14.)

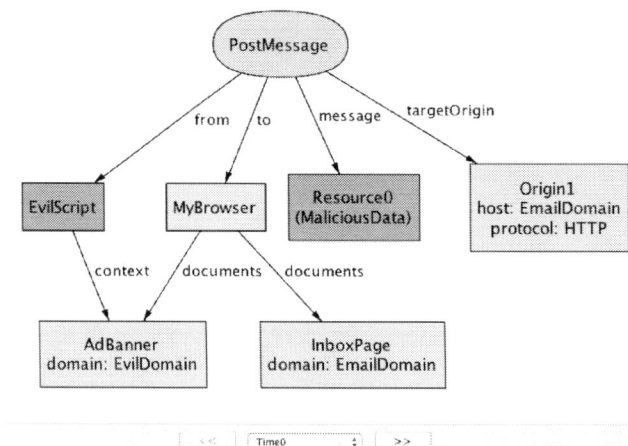

Figure 17.14: PostMessage counterexample at time 0

The browser then forwards this message to the document(s) with the corresponding origin (in this case, InboxPage). Unless InboxScript specifically checks the value of `srcOrigin` to filter out messages from unwanted origins, InboxPage will accept the malicious data, possibly leading to further security attacks. (For example, it may embed a piece of JavaScript to carry out an XSS attack.) This is shown in Figure 17.14.

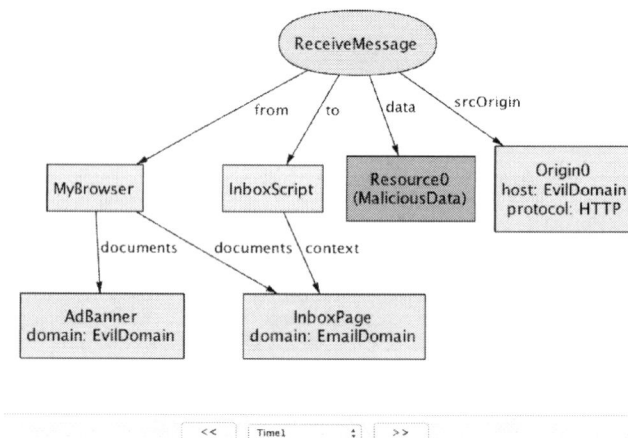

Figure 17.15: PostMessage counterexample at time 1

As this example illustrates, `PostMessage` is not secure by default, and it is the responsibility of the receiving document to *additionally* check the `srcOrigin` parameter to ensure that the message is coming from a trustworthy document. Unfortunately, in practice, many sites omit this check, enabling a malicious document to inject bad content as part of a `PostMessage`[2].

However, the omission of the origin check may not simply be the result of programmer ignorance. Implementing an appropriate check on an incoming PostMessage can be tricky; in some applications, it is hard to determine in advance the list of trusted origins from which messages are expected to be received. (In some apps, this list may even change dynamically.) This, again, highlights the tension between security and functionality: PostMessage can be used for secure cross-origin communication, but only when a whitelist of trusted origins is known.

Cross-Origin Resource Sharing (CORS)

Cross-Origin Resource Sharing (CORS) is a mechanism designed to allow a server to share its resources with sites from different origins. In particular, CORS can be used by a script from one origin to make requests to a server with a different origin, effectively bypassing the restriction of the SOP on cross-origin Ajax requests.

Briefly, a typical CORS process involves two steps: (1) a script wanting to access a resource from a foreign server includes, in its request, an "Origin" header that specifies the origin of the script, and (2) the server includes an "Access-Control-Allow-Origin" header as part of its response, indicating a set of origins that are allowed to access the server's resource. Normally, without CORS, a browser would prevent the script from making a cross-origin request in the first place, conforming to the SOP. However, with CORS enabled, the browser allows the script to send the request and access its response, but *only if* "Origin" is one of the origins specified in "Access-Control-Allow-Origin".

(CORS additionally includes a notion of *preflight* requests, not discussed here, to support complex types of cross-origin requests besides GETs and POSTs.)

In Alloy, we model a CORS request as a special kind of `XmlHttpRequest`, with two extra fields `origin` and `allowedOrigins`:

```
sig CorsRequest in XmlHttpRequest {
  -- "origin" header in request from client
  origin: Origin,
  -- "access-control-allow-origin" header in response from server
  allowedOrigins: set Origin
}{
  from in Script
}
```

We then use an Alloy fact `corsRule` to describe what constitutes a valid CORS request:

```
fact corsRule {
  all r: CorsRequest |
    -- the origin header of a CORS request matches the script context
    r.origin = origin[r.from.context.src] and
    -- the specified origin is one of the allowed origins
    r.origin in r.allowedOrigins
}
```

---

[2]Sooel Son and Vitaly Shmatikov. *The Postman Always Rings Twice: Attacking and Defending postMessage in HTML5 Websites.* Network and Distributed System Security Symposium (NDSS), 2013.

Analysis: Can CORS be misused in a way that would allow the attacker to compromise the security of a trusted site? When prompted, the Alloy Analyzer returns a simple counterexample for the `Confidentiality` property.

Here, the developer of the calendar application decides to share some of its resources with other applications by using the CORS mechanism. Unfortunately, `CalendarServer` is configured to return `Origin` (which represents the set of all origin values) for the `access-control-allow-origin` header in CORS responses. As a result, a script from any origin, including `EvilDomain`, is allowed to make a cross-site request to `CalendarServer` and read its response (Figure 17.16).

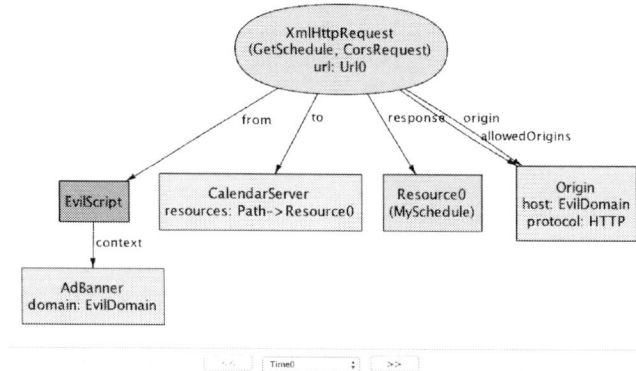

Figure 17.16: CORS counterexample

This example highlights one common mistake that developers make with CORS: Using the wildcard value "*" as the value of "access-control-allow-origin" header, allowing any site to access a resource on the server. This access pattern is appropriate if the resource is considered public and accessible to anyone. However, it turns out that many sites use "*" as the default value even for private resources, inadvertently allowing malicious scripts to access them through CORS requests[3].

Why would a developer ever use the wildcard? It turns out that specifying the allowed origins can be tricky, since it may not be clear at design time which origins should be granted access at runtime (similar to the PostMessage issue discusssed above). A service may, for example, allow third-party applications to subscribe dynamically to its resources.

17.9 Conclusion

In this chapter, we set out to construct a document that provides a clear understanding of the SOP and its related mechanisms by building a *model* of the policy in a language called Alloy. Our model of the SOP is not an implementation in the traditional sense, and can't be deployed for use, unlike artifacts shown in other chapters. Instead, we wanted to demonstrate the key elements behind our approach to "agile modeling": (1) starting out with a small, abstract model of the system and *incrementally* adding details as necessary, (2) specifying *properties* that the system is expected to satisfy, and (3) applying *rigorous analysis* to explore potential flaws in the design of the system. Of course, this chapter was written long after the SOP was first introduced, but we believe that this type of modeling would potentially be even more beneficial if it is done during the early stage of system design.

---

[3]Sebastian Lekies, Martin Johns, and Walter Tighzert. *The State of the Cross-Domain Nation.* Web 2.0 Security and Privacy (W2SP), 2011.

Besides the SOP, Alloy has been used to model and reason about a variety of systems across different domains—ranging from network protocols, semantic web, bytecode security to electronic voting and medical systems. For many of these systems, Alloy's analysis led to discovery of design flaws and bugs that had eluded the developers, in some cases, for years. We invite our readers to visit the Alloy page[4] and try building a model of their favorite system!

17.10 Appendix: Reusing Modules in Alloy

As mentioned earlier in this chapter, Alloy makes no assumptions about the behavior of the system being modeled. The lack of a built-in paradigm allows the user to encode a wide range of modeling idioms using a small core of the basic language constructs. We could, for example, specify a system as a state machine, a data model with complex invariants, a distributed event model with a global clock, or whatever idiom is most suitable for the problem at hand. Commonly used idioms can be captured as a generic module and reused across multiple systems.

In our model of the SOP, we model the system as a set of endpoints that communicate with each other by making one or more *calls*. Since *call* is a fairly generic notion, we encapsulate its description in a separate Alloy module, to be imported from other modules that rely on it – similar to standard libraries in programming languages:

```
module call[T]
```

In this module declaration, T represents a type parameter that can be instantiated to a concrete type that is provided when the module is imported. We will soon see how this type parameter is used.

It is often convenient to describe the system execution as taking place over a global time frame, so that we can talk about calls as occurring before or after each other (or at the same time). To represent the notion of time, we introduce a new signature called Time:

```
open util/ordering[Time] as ord
sig Time {}
```

In Alloy, util/ordering is a built-in module that imposes a total order on the type parameter, and so by importing ordering[Time], we obtain a set of Time objects that behave like other totally ordered sets (e.g., natural numbers).

Note that there is absolutely nothing special about Time; we could have named it any other way (for example, Step or State), and it wouldn't have changed the behavior of the model at all. All we are doing here is using an additional column in a relation as a way of representing the content of a field at different points in a system execution; for example, cookies in the Browser signature. In this sense, Time objects are nothing but helper objects used as a kind of index.

Each call occurs between two points in time—its start and end times, and is associated with a sender (represented by from) and a receiver (to):

```
abstract sig Call { start, end: Time, from, to: T }
```

Recall that in our discussion of HTTP requests, we imported the module call by passing Endpoint as its type parameter. As a result, the parametric type T is instantiated to Endpoint, and we obtain a set of Call objects that are associated with a pair of sender and receiver endpoints. A module can be imported multiple times; for example, we could declare a signature called UnixProcess, and instantiate the module call to obtain a distinct set of Call objects that are sent from one Unix process to another.

## chapter 18

A Rejection Sampler
Jessica B. Hamrick

18.1   Introduction

Frequently, in computer science and engineering, we run into problems that can't be solved using an equation. These problems usually involve complex systems, noisy inputs, or both. Here are just a few examples of real-world problems that do not have exact, analytic solutions:

1. You have built a computer model of an airplane, and want to determine how well the airplane will hold up under different weather conditions.
2. You want to determine whether chemical runoff from a proposed factory will affect the water supply of nearby residents, based on a model of groundwater diffusion.
3. You have a robot which captures noisy images from its camera, and want to recover the three-dimensional structure of the object that those images depict.
4. You want to compute how likely you are to win at chess if you take a particular move.

Even though these types of problems cannot be solved exactly, we can often achieve an approximate solution to them using techniques known as *Monte Carlo sampling* methods. In Monte Carlo methods, the key idea is to take many *samples*, which will then allow you to estimate the solution.[1]

What is Sampling?

The term *sampling* means generating random values from some probability distribution. For example, the value you get from rolling a six-sided die is a sample. The card you draw from the top of the deck after it has been shuffled is a sample. The location where the dart hits the board is also a sample. The only difference between these various samples is that they are generated from different *probability distributions*. In the case of the die, the distribution places equal weight across six values. In the case of the card, the distribution places equal weight across 52 values. In the case of the dart board, the distribution places weight across a circular area (though it might not be uniformly distributed, depending on your skill as a dart player).

There are two ways we usually want to use samples. The first is just to generate a random value to be used later: for example, randomly drawing cards in a computer game of poker. The second way that samples are used is for estimation. For example, if you suspected that your friend was playing with loaded dice, you might want to roll the dice many times to see if some numbers came up more often than you would expect. Or, you might just want to characterize the range of possibilities, as

---

[1]This chapter assumes some familiarity with statistics and probability theory.

in the airplane example above. Weather is a fairly chaotic system, meaning that it is impossible to compute *exactly* whether the airplane will survive a particular weather situation. Instead, you could simulate the behavior of the airplane under many different weather conditions, multiple times, which would allow you to see under which conditions the airplane is most likely to fail.

Programming with Samples and Probabilities

As with most applications in computer science, you can make design decisions when programming with samples and probabilities that will influence the overall cleanliness, coherence, and correctness of your code. In this chapter, we will go through a simple example of how to sample random items in a computer game. In particular, we will focus on the design decisions which are specific to working with probabilities, including functions both for sampling and for evaluating probabilities, working with logarithms, allowing reproducibility, and separating the process of generating samples from the specific application.

A Brief Aside About Notation

We will use mathematical notation like $p(x)$ to indicate that p is the *probability density function* (PDF) or *probability mass function* (PMF) over values x of a random variable. A PDF is a *continuous* function $p(x)$ such that $\int_{-\infty}^{\infty} p(x)\, \mathrm{d}x = 1$, whereas a PMF is a *discrete* function $p(x)$ such that $\sum_{x \in \mathbb{Z}} p(x) = 1$, where $\mathbb{Z}$ is the set of all integers.

The probability distribution in the case of the dart board would be a continuous PDF, while the probability distribution in the case of a die would be a discrete PMF. In both cases, $p(x) \geq 0$ for all x; i.e., the probabilities have to be non-negative.

There are two things that we might want to do with a probability distribution. Given a value (or location) x, we might want to *evaluate* what the probability density (or mass) is at that location. In mathematical notation, we would write this as $p(x)$ (the probability density at the value x).

Given the PDF or PMF, we might also want to *sample* a value x in a manner proportional to the distribution (such that we are more likely to get a sample at places where the probability is higher). In mathematical notation, we write this as $x \sim p$, to indicate that x is sampled proportional to p.

18.2   Sampling Magical Items

As a simple example to demonstrate the various design decisions involved with programming with probabilities, let's imagine we're writing a roleplaying game (RPG). We would like a method of generating bonus stats for the magical items that are randomly dropped by monsters. We might decide that the maximum bonus we want an item to confer is +5, and that higher bonuses are less likely than lower bonuses. If B is a random variable over the values of the bonus, then:

$$p(B = +1) = 0.55 \quad p(B = +2) = 0.25 \quad p(B = +3) = 0.12 \quad p(B = +4) = 0.06 \quad p(B = +5) = 0.02$$

We can also specify that there are six stats (dexterity, constitution, strength, intelligence, wisdom, and charisma) that our bonus should be distributed between. So, an item with a +5 bonus could have those points distributed across different stats (e.g., +2 wisdom and +3 intelligence) or concentrated within a single stat (e.g., +5 charisma).

How would we randomly sample from this distribution? The easiest way is probably to first sample the overall item bonus, then sample the way the bonus is distributed across the stats. Conveniently, the probability distributions of the bonus and the way that it is distributed are both instances of the *multinomial distribution*.

18.3   The Multinomial Distribution

The multinomial distribution is used when you have several possible outcomes, and you want to characterize the probability of each of those outcomes occurring. The classic example used to explain the multinomial distribution is the *ball and urn*. The idea is that you have an urn with different colored balls in it (for example, 30% red, 20% blue, and 50% green). You pull out a ball, record its color, put it back in the urn, and then repeat this multiple times. In this case, an *outcome* corresponds to drawing a ball of a particular color, and the probability of each outcome corresponds to the proportion of balls of that color (e.g., for the outcome of drawing a blue ball, the probability is $p(\text{blue}) = 0.20$). The multinomial distribution is then used to describe the possible combinations of outcomes when multiple balls are drawn (e.g., two green and one blue).

The code in this section is located in the file `multinomial.py`.

The `MultinomialDistribution` Class

In general, there are two use cases for a distribution: we might want to *sample* from that distribution, and we might want to *evaluate the probability* of a sample (or samples) under that distribution's PMF or PDF. While the actual computations needed to perform these two functions are fairly different, they rely on a common piece of information: what the *parameters* of the distribution are. In the case of the multinomial distribution, the parameters are the event probabilities, p (which correspond to the proportions of the different colored balls in the urn example above).

The simplest solution would be to simply create two functions that both take the same parameters, but are otherwise independent. However, I will usually opt to use a class for representing my distributions. There are several advantages to doing so:

1. You only need to pass in the parameters once, when creating the class.
2. There are additional attributes we might want to know about a distribution: the mean, variance, derivative, etc. Once we have even a handful of functions that operate on a common object, it is even more convenient to use a class rather than passing the same parameters to many different functions.
3. It is usually a good idea to check that the parameter values are valid (for example, in the case of the multinomial distribution, the vector p of event probabilities should sum to 1). It is much more efficient to do this check once, in the constructor of the class, rather than every time one of the functions is called.
4. Sometimes computing the PMF or PDF involves computing constant values (given the parameters). With a class, we can pre-compute these constants in the constructor, rather than having to compute them every time the PMF or PDF function is called.

In practice, this is how many statistics packages work, including SciPy's own distributions, which are located in the `scipy.stats` module. While we are using other SciPy functions, however, we are not using their probability distributions, both for the sake of illustration, and because there is currently no multinomial distribution in SciPy.

Here is the constructor code for the class:

```
import numpy as np

class MultinomialDistribution(object):

    def __init__(self, p, rso=np.random):
        """Initialize the multinomial random variable.

        Parameters
        ----------
        p: numpy array of length 'k'
            The event probabilities
        rso: numpy RandomState object (default: None)
            The random number generator

        """

        # Check that the probabilities sum to 1. If they don't, then
        # something is wrong! We use 'np.isclose' rather than checking
        # for exact equality because in many cases, we won't have
        # exact equality due to floating-point error.
        if not np.isclose(np.sum(p), 1.0):
            raise ValueError("event probabilities do not sum to 1")

        # Store the parameters that were passed in
        self.p = p
        self.rso = rso

        # Precompute log probabilities, for use by the log-PMF, for
        # each element of 'self.p' (the function 'np.log' operates
        # elementwise over NumPy arrays, as well as on scalars.)
        self.logp = np.log(self.p)
```

The class takes as arguments the event probabilities, p, and a variable called rso. First, the constructor checks that the parameters are valid; i.e., that p sums to 1. Then it stores the arguments that were passed in, and uses the event probabilities to compute the event *log* probabilities. (We'll go into why this is necessary in a bit). The rso object is what we'll use later to produce random numbers. (We'll talk more about what it is a bit later as well).

Before we get into the rest of the class, let's go over two points related to the constructor.

Descriptive versus Mathematic Variable Names

Usually, programmers are encouraged to use descriptive variable names: for example, it would be considered better practice to use the names independent_variable and dependent_variable rather than x and y. A standard rule of thumb is to never use variable names that are only one or two characters. However, you'll notice that in the constructor to our MultinomialDistribution class, we use the variable name of p, which is in violation of typical naming conventions.

While I agree that such naming conventions should apply in almost every domain, there is one exception: math. The difficulty with coding up mathematical equations is that those equations usually have variable names which are just a single letter: x, y, α, etc. So, if you were translating them directly into code, the easiest variable names would be x, y, and alpha. Obviously, these are not the most informative variable names (the name x does not convey much information), but having more descriptive variable names can also make it harder to switch between the the code and the equation.

I think that when you are writing code that directly implements an equation, the same variable names should be used as those in the equation. This makes it easy to see which parts of the code are implementing which pieces of the equation. This, of course, can make the code harder to understand in isolation, so it is especially important that the comments then do a good job of explaining what the goal of the various computations are. If the equation is listed in an academic paper, the comments should reference the equation number so it can be easily looked up.

Importing NumPy

You may have noticed that we imported the numpy module as np. This is standard practice in the world of numerical computing, because NumPy provides a huge number of useful functions, many of which might be used even in a single file. In the simple examples from this chapter, we only use eleven NumPy functions, but the number can be much higher: it is not uncommon for me to use around forty different NumPy functions throughout a project!

There are a few options for importing NumPy. We could use from numpy import *, but that is generally poor style, because it makes it hard to determine where the functions came from. We could import the functions individually with from numpy import array, log, ..., but that gets clumsy fairly quickly. We could just use import numpy, but this often results in code being much more difficult to read. Both of the following examples are hard to read, but the one using np rather than numpy is significantly clearer:

```
>>> numpy.sqrt(numpy.sum(numpy.dot(numpy.array(a), numpy.array(b))))
>>> np.sqrt(np.sum(np.dot(np.array(a), np.array(b))))
```

Sampling from a Multinomial Distribution

Taking a sample from a multinomial distribution is actually fairly straightforward, because NumPy provides us with a function that does it: np.random.multinomial[2].

Despite the fact that this function already exists, there are a few design decisions surrounding it that we can make.

Seeding the Random Number Generator

Even though we do want to draw a *random* sample, we sometimes want our results to be reproducible: even though the numbers seem random, if we were to run the program again, we might want it to use the *same* sequence of "random" numbers.

In order to allow for the generation of such "reproducibly random" numbers, we need to tell our sampling function *how* to generate the random numbers. We can accomplish this through use of a NumPy RandomState object, which is essentially a random number generator object that can be passed around. It has most of the same functions as np.random; the difference is that we get to control where the random numbers come from. We create it as follows:

```
>>> import numpy as np
>>> rso = np.random.RandomState(230489)
```

---

[2]NumPy includes functions to draw samples from many different types of distributions. For a full list, take a look at the random sampling module, np.random.

where the number passed to the RandomState constructor is the *seed* for the random number generator. As long as we instantiate it with the same seed, a RandomState object will produce the same "random" numbers in the same order, thus ensuring replicability:

```
>>> rso.rand()
0.5356709186237074
>>> rso.rand()
0.6190581888276206
>>> rso.rand()
0.23143573416770336
>>> rso.seed(230489)
>>> rso.rand()
0.5356709186237074
>>> rso.rand()
0.6190581888276206
```

Earlier, we saw that the constructor took an argument called rso. This rso variable is a RandomState object that has already been initialized. I like to make the RandomState object an optional parameter: it is occasionally convenient to not be *forced* to use it, but I do want to have the *option* of using it (which, if I were to just use the np.random module, I would not be able to do).

So, if the rso variable is not given, then the constructor defaults to np.random.multinomial. Otherwise, it uses the multinomial sampler from the RandomState object itself[3].

What's a Parameter?

Once we've decided whether to use np.random.multinomial or rso.multinomial, sampling is just a matter of calling the appropriate function. However, there is one other decision that we might consider: What counts as a parameter?

Earlier, I said that the outcome probabilities, p, were the parameters of the multinomial distribution. However, depending on who you ask, the number of events, n, can *also* be a parameter of the multinomial distribution. So, why didn't we include n as an argument to the constructor?

This question, while relatively specific to the multinomial distribution, actually comes up fairly frequently when dealing with probability distributions, and the answer really depends on the use case. For a multinomial, can you make the assumption that the number of events is always the same? If so, then it might be better to pass in n as an argument to the constructor. If not, then requiring n to be specified at object creation time could be very restrictive, and might even require you to create a new distribution object every time you need to draw a sample!

I usually don't like to be that restricted by my code, and thus choose to have n be an argument to the sample function, rather than having it be an argument to the constructor. An alternate solution could be to have n be an argument to the constructor, but also include methods to allow for the value of n to be changed, without having to create an entirely new object. For our purposes, though, this solution is probably overkill, so we'll stick to just having it be an argument to sample:

---

[3]The functions in np.random actually do rely on a random number generator that we can control: NumPy's global random number generator. You can set the global seed with np.seed. There's a tradeoff to using the global generator vs. a local RandomState object. If you use the global generator, then you don't have to pass around a RandomState object everywhere. However, you also run the risk of depending on some third party code that also uses the global generator without your knowledge. If you use a local object, then it is easier to find out whether there is nondeterminism coming from somewhere other than your own code.

```
def sample(self, n):
    """Samples draws of 'n' events from a multinomial distribution with
    outcome probabilities 'self.p'.

    Parameters
    ----------
    n: integer
        The number of total events

    Returns
    -------
    numpy array of length 'k'
        The sampled number of occurrences for each outcome

    """
    x = self.rso.multinomial(n, self.p)
    return x
```

Evaluating the Multinomial PMF

Although we don't explicitly need to compute the probability of the magical items that we generate, it is almost always a good idea to write a function that can compute the distribution's probability mass function (PMF) or probability density function (PDF). Why?

One reason is that we can use it for testing: if we take many samples with our sampling function, then they should approximate the exact PDF or PMF. If after many samples the approximation is poor or obviously wrong, then we know there is a bug in our code somewhere.

Another reason to implement the PMF or PDF is that frequently, you will actually need it later down the line and simply don't realize it initially. For example, we might want to classify our randomly generated items as *common*, *uncommon*, and *rare*, depending on how likely they are to be generated. To determine this, we need to be able to compute the PMF.

Finally, in many cases, your particular use case will dictate that you implement the PMF or PDF from the beginning, anyway.

The Multinomial PMF Equation

Formally, the multinomial distribution has the following equation:

$$p(\mathbf{x}; \mathbf{p}) = \frac{(\sum_{i=1}^{k} x_i)!}{x_1! \cdots x_k!} p_1^{x_1} \cdots p_k^{x_k}$$

where $\mathbf{x} = [x_1, \ldots, x_k]$ is a vector of length k specifying the number of times each event happened, and $\mathbf{p} = [p_1, \ldots, p_k]$ is a vector specifying the probability of each event occurring. As mentioned above, the event probabilities $\mathbf{p}$ are the *parameters* of the distribution.

The factorials in the equation above can actually be expressed using a special function, Γ, called the *gamma function*. When we get to writing the code, it will be more convenient and efficient to use the gamma function rather than factorial, so we will rewrite the equation using Γ:

$$p(\mathbf{x}; \mathbf{p}) = \frac{\Gamma((\sum_{i=1}^{k} x_i) + 1)}{\Gamma(x_1 + 1) \cdots \Gamma(x_k + 1)} p_1^{x_1} \cdots p_k^{x_k}$$

Working with Log Values

Before getting into the actual code needed to implement the equation above, I want to emphasize one of the the most important design decisions when writing code with probabilities: working with log values. What this means is that rather than working directly with probabilities $p(x)$, we should be working with *log*-probabilities, $\log p(x)$. This is because probabilities can get very small very quickly, resulting in underflow errors.

To motivate this, consider that probabilities must range between 0 and 1 (inclusive). NumPy has a useful function, `finfo`, that will tell us the limits of floating point values for our system. For example, on a 64-bit machine, we see that the smallest usable positive number (given by `tiny`) is:

```
>>> import numpy as np
>>> np.finfo(float).tiny
2.2250738585072014e-308
```

While that may seem very small, it is not unusual to encounter probabilities of this magnitude, or even smaller. Moreover, it is a common operation to multiply probabilities, yet if we try to do this with very small probabilities, we encounter underflow problems:

```
>>> tiny = np.finfo(float).tiny
>>> # if we multiply numbers that are too small, we lose all precision
>>> tiny * tiny
0.0
```

However, taking the log can help alleviate this issue because we can represent a much wider range of numbers with logarithms than we can normally. Officially, log values range from $-\infty$ to zero. In practice, they range from the `min` value returned by `finfo`, which is the smallest number that can be represented, to zero. The `min` value is *much* smaller than the log of the `tiny` value (which would be our lower bound if we did not work in log space):

```
>>> # this is our lower bound normally
>>> np.log(tiny)
-708.39641853226408
>>> # this is our lower bound when using logs
>>> np.finfo(float).min
-1.7976931348623157e+308
```

So, by working with log values, we can greatly expand our range of representable numbers. Moreover, we can perform multiplication with logs by using addition, because $\log(x \cdot y) = \log(x) + \log(y)$. Thus, if we do the multiplication above with logs, we do not have to worry (as much) about loss of precision due to underflow:

```
>>> # the result of multiplying small probabilities
>>> np.log(tiny * tiny)
-inf
>>> # the result of adding small log probabilities
>>> np.log(tiny) + np.log(tiny)
-1416.7928370645282
```

Of course, this solution is not a magic bullet. If we need to derive the number from the logarithm (for example, to add probabilities, rather than multiply them), then we are back to underflow:

```
>>> tiny*tiny
0.0
>>> np.exp(np.log(tiny) + np.log(tiny))
0.0
```

Still, doing all our computations with logs can save a lot of headache. We might be forced to lose that precision if we need to go back to the original numbers, but we at least maintain *some* information about the probabilities—enough to compare them, for example—that would otherwise be lost.

Writing the PMF Code

Now that we have seen the importance of working with logs, we can actually write our function to compute the log-PMF:

```
def log_pmf(self, x):
    """Evaluates the log-probability mass function (log-PMF) of a
    multinomial with outcome probabilities 'self.p' for a draw 'x'.

    Parameters
    ----------
    x: numpy array of length 'k'
        The number of occurrences of each outcome

    Returns
    -------
    The evaluated log-PMF for draw 'x'

    """
    # Get the total number of events
    n = np.sum(x)

    # equivalent to log(n!)
    log_n_factorial = gammaln(n + 1)
    # equivalent to log(x1! * ... * xk!)
    sum_log_xi_factorial = np.sum(gammaln(x + 1))

    # If one of the values of self.p is 0, then the corresponding
    # value of self.logp will be -inf. If the corresponding value
    # of x is 0, then multiplying them together will give nan, but
    # we want it to just be 0.
    log_pi_xi = self.logp * x
    log_pi_xi[x == 0] = 0
    # equivalent to log(p1^x1 * ... * pk^xk)
    sum_log_pi_xi = np.sum(log_pi_xi)

    # Put it all together
    log_pmf = log_n_factorial - sum_log_xi_factorial + sum_log_pi_xi
    return log_pmf
```

For the most part, this is a straightforward implementation of the equation above for the multinomial PMF. The gammaln function is from scipy.special, and computes the log-gamma function,

$\log \Gamma(x)$. As mentioned above, it is more convenient to use the gamma function rather than a factorial function; this is because SciPy gives us a log-gamma function, but not a log-factorial function. We could have computed a log factorial ourselves, using something like:

```
log_n_factorial = np.sum(np.log(np.arange(1, n + 1)))
sum_log_xi_factorial = np.sum([np.sum(np.log(np.arange(1, i + 1))) for i in x])
```

but it is easier to understand, easier to code, and more computationally efficient if we use the gamma function already built in to SciPy.

There is one edge case that we need to tackle: when one of our probabilities is zero. When $p_i = 0$, then $\log p_i = -\infty$. This would be fine, except for the following behavior when infinity is multiplied by zero:

```
>>> # it's fine to multiply infinity by integers...
>>> -np.inf * 2.0
-inf
>>> # ...but things break when we try to multiply by zero
>>> -np.inf * 0.0
nan
```

nan means "not a number", and it is almost always a pain to deal with, because most computations with nan result in another nan. So, if we don't handle the case where $p_i = 0$ and $x_i = 0$, we will end up with a nan. That will get summed with other numbers, producing another nan, which is just not useful. To handle this, we check specifically for the case when $x_i = 0$, and set the resulting $x_i \cdot \log(p_i)$ also to zero.

Let's return for a moment to our discussion of using logs. Even if we really only need the PMF, and not the log-PMF, it is generally better to *first* compute it with logs, and then exponentiate it if we need to:

```
def pmf(self, x):
    """Evaluates the probability mass function (PMF) of a multinomial
    with outcome probabilities 'self.p' for a draw 'x'.

    Parameters
    ----------
    x: numpy array of length 'k'
        The number of occurrences of each outcome

    Returns
    -------
    The evaluated PMF for draw 'x'

    """
    pmf = np.exp(self.log_pmf(x))
    return pmf
```

To further drive home the importance of working with logs, we can look at an example with just the multinomial:

```
>>> dist = MultinomialDistribution(np.array([0.25, 0.25, 0.25, 0.25]))
>>> dist.log_pmf(np.array([1000, 0, 0, 0])
```

```
-1386.2943611198905
>>> dist.log_pmf(np.array([999, 0, 0, 0]))
-1384.9080667587707
```

In this case, we get *extremely* small probabilities (which, you will notice, are much smaller than the tiny value we discussed above). This is because the fraction in the PMF is huge: 1000 factorial can't even be computed due to overflow. But, the *log* of the factorial can be:

```
>>> from scipy.special import gamma, gammaln
>>> gamma(1000 + 1)
inf
>>> gammaln(1000 + 1)
5912.1281784881639
```

If we had tried to compute just the PMF using the gamma function, we would have ended up with gamma(1000 + 1) / gamma(1000 + 1), which results in a nan value (even though we can see that it should be 1). But, because we do the computation with logarithms, it's not an issue and we don't need to worry about it!

18.4   Sampling Magical Items, Revisited

Now that we have written our multinomial functions, we can put them to work to generate our magical items. To do this, we will create a class called MagicItemDistribution, located in the file rpg.py:

```
class MagicItemDistribution(object):

    # these are the names (and order) of the stats that all magical
    # items will have
    stats_names = ("dexterity", "constitution", "strength",
                   "intelligence", "wisdom", "charisma")

    def __init__(self, bonus_probs, stats_probs, rso=np.random):
        """"Initialize a magic item distribution parameterized by `bonus_probs`
        and `stats_probs`.

        Parameters
        ----------
        bonus_probs: numpy array of length m
            The probabilities of the overall bonuses. Each index in
            the array corresponds to the bonus of that amount (e.g.,
            index 0 is +0, index 1 is +1, etc.)

        stats_probs: numpy array of length 6
            The probabilities of how the overall bonus is distributed
            among the different stats. `stats_probs[i]` corresponds to
            the probability of giving a bonus point to the ith stat;
            i.e., the value at `MagicItemDistribution.stats_names[i]`.

        rso: numpy RandomState object (default: np.random)
            The random number generator
```

```
    """
    # Create the multinomial distributions we'll be using
    self.bonus_dist = MultinomialDistribution(bonus_probs, rso=rso)
    self.stats_dist = MultinomialDistribution(stats_probs, rso=rso)
```

The constructor to our `MagicItemDistribution` class takes parameters for the bonus probabilities, the stats probabilities, and the random number generator. Even though we specified above what we wanted the bonus probabilities to be, it is generally a good idea to encode parameters as arguments that are passed in. This leaves open the possibility of sampling items under different distributions. (For example, maybe the bonus probabilities would change as the player's level increases.) We encode the *names* of the stats as a class variable, `stats_names`, though this could just as easily be another parameter to the constructor.

As mentioned previously, there are two steps to sampling a magical item: first sampling the overall bonus, and then sampling the distribution of the bonus across the stats. As such, we code these steps as two methods: `_sample_bonus` and `_sample_stats`:

```
def _sample_bonus(self):
    """Sample a value of the overall bonus.

    Returns
    -------
    integer
        The overall bonus

    """
    # The bonus is essentially just a sample from a multinomial
    # distribution with n=1; i.e., only one event occurs.
    sample = self.bonus_dist.sample(1)

    # 'sample' is an array of zeros and a single one at the
    # location corresponding to the bonus. We want to convert this
    # one into the actual value of the bonus.
    bonus = np.argmax(sample)
    return bonus

def _sample_stats(self):
    """Sample the overall bonus and how it is distributed across the
    different stats.

    Returns
    -------
    numpy array of length 6
        The number of bonus points for each stat

    """
    # First we need to sample the overall bonus
    bonus = self._sample_bonus()

    # Then, we use a different multinomial distribution to sample
    # how that bonus is distributed. The bonus corresponds to the
```

```
# number of events.
stats = self.stats_dist.sample(bonus)
return stats
```

We *could* have made these a single method—especially since `_sample_stats` is the only function that depends on `_sample_bonus`—but I have chosen to keep them separate, both because it makes the sampling routine easier to understand, and because breaking it up into smaller pieces makes the code easier to test.

You'll also notice that these methods are prefixed with an underscore, indicating that they're not really meant to be used outside the class. Instead, we provide the function `sample`:

```
def sample(self):
    """Sample a random magical item.

    Returns
    -------
    dictionary
        The keys are the names of the stats, and the values are
        the bonus conferred to the corresponding stat.

    """
    stats = self._sample_stats()
    item_stats = dict(zip(self.stats_names, stats))
    return item_stats
```

The `sample` function does essentially the same thing as `_sample_stats`, except that it returns a dictionary with the stats' names as keys. This provides a clean and understandable interface for sampling items—it is obvious which stats have how many bonus points—but it also keeps open the option of using just `_sample_stats` if one needs to take many samples and efficiency is required.

We use a similar design for evaluating the probability of items. Again, we expose high-level methods `pmf` and `log_pmf` which take dictionaries of the form produced by `sample`:

```
def log_pmf(self, item):
    """Compute the log probability of the given magical item.

    Parameters
    ----------
    item: dictionary
        The keys are the names of the stats, and the values are
        the bonuses conferred to the corresponding stat.

    Returns
    -------
    float
        The value corresponding to log(p(item))

    """
    # First pull out the bonus points for each stat, in the
    # correct order, then pass that to _stats_log_pmf.
    stats = np.array([item[stat] for stat in self.stats_names])
    log_pmf = self._stats_log_pmf(stats)
```

```
        return log_pmf

def pmf(self, item):
    """Compute the probability the given magical item.

    Parameters
    ----------
    item: dictionary
        The keys are the names of the stats, and the values are
        the bonus conferred to the corresponding stat.

    Returns
    -------
    float
        The value corresponding to p(item)

    """
    return np.exp(self.log_pmf(item))
```

These methods rely on _stats_log_pmf, which computes the probability of the stats (but which takes an array rather than a dictionary):

```
def _stats_log_pmf(self, stats):
    """Evaluate the log-PMF for the given distribution of bonus points
    across the different stats.

    Parameters
    ----------
    stats: numpy array of length 6
        The distribution of bonus points across the stats

    Returns
    -------
    float
        The value corresponding to log(p(stats))

    """
    # There are never any leftover bonus points, so the sum of the
    # stats gives us the total bonus.
    total_bonus = np.sum(stats)

    # First calculate the probability of the total bonus
    logp_bonus = self._bonus_log_pmf(total_bonus)

    # Then calculate the probability of the stats
    logp_stats = self.stats_dist.log_pmf(stats)

    # Then multiply them together (using addition, because we are
    # working with logs)
    log_pmf = logp_bonus + logp_stats
    return log_pmf
```

The method _stats_log_pmf, in turn, relies on _bonus_log_pmf, which computes the probability of the overall bonus:

```
def _bonus_log_pmf(self, bonus):
    """Evaluate the log-PMF for the given bonus.

    Parameters
    ----------
    bonus: integer
        The total bonus.

    Returns
    -------
    float
        The value corresponding to log(p(bonus))

    """
    # Make sure the value that is passed in is within the
    # appropriate bounds
    if bonus < 0 or bonus >= len(self.bonus_dist.p):
        return -np.inf

    # Convert the scalar bonus value into a vector of event
    # occurrences
    x = np.zeros(len(self.bonus_dist.p))
    x[bonus] = 1

    return self.bonus_dist.log_pmf(x)
```

We can now create our distribution as follows:

```
>>> import numpy as np
>>> from rpg import MagicItemDistribution
>>> bonus_probs = np.array([0.0, 0.55, 0.25, 0.12, 0.06, 0.02])
>>> stats_probs = np.ones(6) / 6.0
>>> rso = np.random.RandomState(234892)
>>> item_dist = MagicItemDistribution(bonus_probs, stats_probs, rso=rso)
```

Once created, we can use it to generate a few different items:

```
>>> item_dist.sample()
{'dexterity': 0, 'strength': 0, 'constitution': 0,
 'intelligence': 0, 'wisdom': 0, 'charisma': 1}
>>> item_dist.sample()
{'dexterity': 0, 'strength': 0, 'constitution': 1,
 'intelligence': 0, 'wisdom': 2, 'charisma': 0}
>>> item_dist.sample()
{'dexterity': 1, 'strength': 0, 'constitution': 1,
 'intelligence': 0, 'wisdom': 0, 'charisma': 0}
```

And, if we want, we can evaluate the probability of a sampled item:

```
>>> item = item_dist.sample()
>>> item
{'dexterity': 0, 'strength': 0, 'constitution': 0,
 'intelligence': 0, 'wisdom': 2, 'charisma': 0}
>>> item_dist.log_pmf(item)
-4.9698132995760007
>>> item_dist.pmf(item)
0.0069444444444444441
```

18.5   Estimating Attack Damage

We've seen one application of sampling: generating random items that monsters drop. I mentioned earlier that sampling can also be used when you want to estimate something from the distribution as a whole, and there are certainly cases in which we could use our MagicItemDistribution to do this. For example, let's say that damage in our RPG works by rolling some number of D12s (twelve-sided dice). The player gets to roll one die by default, and then add dice according to their strength bonus. So, for example, if they have a +2 strength bonus, they can roll three dice. The damage dealt is then the sum of the dice.

We might want to know how much damage a player might deal after finding some number of weapons; e.g., as a factor in setting the difficulty of monsters. Let's say that after collecting two items, we want the player to be able to defeat monsters within three hits in about 50% of the battles. How many hit points should the monster have?

One way to answer this question is through sampling. We can use the following scheme:

1. Randomly pick a magic item.
2. Based on the item's bonuses, compute the number of dice that will be rolled when attacking.
3. Based on the number of dice that will be rolled, generate a sample for the damage inflicted over three hits.
4. Repeat steps 1-3 many times. This will result in an approximation to the distribution over damage.

Implementing a Distribution Over Damage

The class DamageDistribution (also in rpg.py) shows an implementation of this scheme:

```
class DamageDistribution(object):

    def __init__(self, num_items, item_dist,
                 num_dice_sides=12, num_hits=1, rso=np.random):
        """Initialize a distribution over attack damage. This object can
        sample possible values for the attack damage dealt over
        'num_hits' hits when the player has 'num_items' items, and
        where attack damage is computed by rolling dice with
        'num_dice_sides' sides.

        Parameters
        ----------
        num_items: int
            The number of items the player has.
```

```
        item_dist: MagicItemDistribution object
            The distribution over magic items.
        num_dice_sides: int (default: 12)
            The number of sides on each die.
        num_hits: int (default: 1)
            The number of hits across which we want to calculate damage.
        rso: numpy RandomState object (default: np.random)
            The random number generator

        """

        # This is an array of integers corresponding to the sides of a
        # single die.
        self.dice_sides = np.arange(1, num_dice_sides + 1)

        # Create a multinomial distribution corresponding to one of
        # these dice.  Each side has equal probabilities.
        self.dice_dist = MultinomialDistribution(
            np.ones(num_dice_sides) / float(num_dice_sides), rso=rso)

        self.num_hits = num_hits
        self.num_items = num_items
        self.item_dist = item_dist

    def sample(self):
        """Sample the attack damage.

        Returns
        -------
        int
            The sampled damage

        """
        # First, we need to randomly generate items (the number of
        # which was passed into the constructor).
        items = [self.item_dist.sample() for i in xrange(self.num_items)]

        # Based on the item stats (in particular, strength), compute
        # the number of dice we get to roll.
        num_dice = 1 + np.sum([item['strength'] for item in items])

        # Roll the dice and compute the resulting damage.
        dice_rolls = self.dice_dist.sample(self.num_hits * num_dice)
        damage = np.sum(self.dice_sides * dice_rolls)
        return damage
```

The constructor takes as arguments the number of sides the dice have, how many hits we want to compute damage over, how many items the player has, a distribution over magic items (of type MagicItemDistribution) and a random state object. By default, we set num_dice_sides to 12 because, while it is technically a parameter, it is unlikely to change. Similarly, we set num_hits to 1 as a default because a more likely use case is that we just want to take one sample of the damage for a single hit.

We then implement the actual sampling logic in `sample`. (Note the structural similarity to `MagicItemDistribution`.) First, we generate a set of possible magic items that the player has. Then, we look at the strength stat of those items, and from that compute the number of dice to roll. Finally, we roll the dice (again relying on our trusty multinomial functions) and compute the damage from that.

What Happened to Evaluating Probabilities?

You may have noticed that we didn't include a `log_pmf` or `pmf` function in our `DamageDistribution`. This is because we actually do not know what the PMF should be! This would be the equation:

$$\sum_{item_1,\ldots,item_m} p(\text{damage}|item_1,\ldots,item_m)p(item_1)\cdots p(item_m)$$

What this equation says is that we would need to compute the probability of every possible damage amount, given every possible set of m items. We actually *could* compute this through brute force, but it wouldn't be pretty. This is actually a perfect example of a case where we want to use sampling to approximate the solution to a problem that we can't compute exactly (or which would be very difficult to compute exactly). So, rather than having a method for the PMF, we'll show in the next section how we can approximate the distribution with many samples.

Approximating the Distribution

Now we have the machinery to answer our question from earlier: If the player has two items, and we want the player to be able to defeat the monster within three hits 50% of the time, how many hit points should the monster have?

First, we create our distribution object, using the same `item_dist` and `rso` that we created earlier:

```
>>> from rpg import DamageDistribution
>>> damage_dist = DamageDistribution(2, item_dist, num_hits=3, rso=rso)
```

Now we can draw a bunch of samples, and compute the 50th percentile (the damage value that is greater than 50% of the samples):

```
>>> samples = np.array([damage_dist.sample() for i in xrange(100000)])
>>> samples.min()
3
>>> samples.max()
154
>>> np.percentile(samples, 50)
27.0
```

If we were to plot a histogram of how many samples we got for each amount of damage, it would look something like Figure 18.1.

There is a pretty wide range of damage that the player could potentially inflict, but it has a long tail: the 50th percentile is at 27 points, meaning that in half the samples, the player inflicted no more than 27 points of damage. Thus, if we wanted to use this criteria for setting monster difficulty, we would give them 27 hit points.

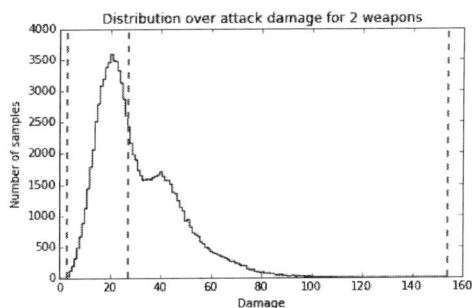

Figure 18.1: Damage Distribution

18.6 Summary

In this chapter, we've seen how to write code for generating samples from a non-standard probability distribution, and how to compute the probabilities for those samples as well. In working through this example, we've covered several design decisions that are applicable in the general case:

1. Representing probability distributions using a class, and including functions both for sampling and for evaluating the PMF (or PDF).
2. Computing the PMF (or PDF) using logarithms.
3. Generating samples from a random number generator object to enable reproducible randomness.
4. Writing functions whose inputs/outputs are clear and understandable (e.g., using dictionaries as the output of `MagicItemDistribution.sample`) while still exposing the less clear but more efficient and purely numeric version of those functions (e.g., `MagicItemDistribution._sample_stats`).

Additionally, we've seen how sampling from a probability distribution can be useful both for producing single random values (e.g., generating a single magical item after defeating a monster) and for computing information about a distribution that we would otherwise not know (e.g., discovering how much damage a player with two items is likely to deal). Almost every type of sampling you might encounter falls under one of these two categories; the differences only have to do with what distributions you are sampling from. The general structure of the code—independent of those distributions—remains the same.

## chapter 19

Web Spreadsheet
Audrey Tang

This chapter introduces a web spreadsheet written in 99 lines of the three languages natively supported by web browsers: HTML, JavaScript, and CSS.

The ES5 version of this project is available as a jsFiddle[1].

19.1   Introduction

When Tim Berners-Lee invented the web in 1990, *web pages* were written in HTML by marking up text with angle-bracketed *tags*, assigning a logical structure to the content. Text marked up within <a>...</a> became *hyperlinks* that would refer the user to other pages on the web.

In the 1990s, browsers added various presentational tags to the HTML vocabulary, including some notoriously nonstandard tags such as <blink>...</blink> from Netscape Navigator and <marquee>...</marquee> from Internet Explorer, causing widespread problems in usability and browser compatibility.

In order to restrict HTML to its original purpose—describing a document's logical structure— browser makers eventually agreed to support two additional languages: CSS to describe presentational styles of a page, and JavaScript (JS) to describe its dynamic interactions.

Since then, the three languages have become more concise and powerful through twenty years of co-evolution. In particular, improvements in JS engines made it practical to deploy large-scale JS frameworks, such as AngularJS[2].

Today, cross-platform *web applications* (such as web spreadsheets) are as ubiquitous and popular as platform-specific applications (such as VisiCalc, Lotus 1-2-3 and Excel) from the previous century.

How many features can a web application offer in 99 lines with AngularJS? Let's see it in action!

19.2   Overview

The spreadsheet[3] directory contains our showcase for late-2014 editions of the three web languages: HTML5[4] for structure, CSS3[5] for presentation, and the JS ES6 "Harmony"[6] standard for interaction.

---

[1] http://jsfiddle.net/audreyt/LtDyP/
[2] http://angularjs.org/
[3] https://github.com/audreyt/500lines/tree/master/spreadsheet/code
[4] http://www.w3.org/TR/html5/
[5] http://www.w3.org/TR/css3-ui/
[6] http://git.io/es6features

It also uses web storage[7] for data persistence and web workers[8] for running JS code in the background. As of this writing, these web standards are supported by Firefox, Chrome, and Internet Explorer 11+, as well as mobile browsers on iOS 5+ and Android 4+.

Now let's open our spreadsheet[9] in a browser (Figure 19.1):

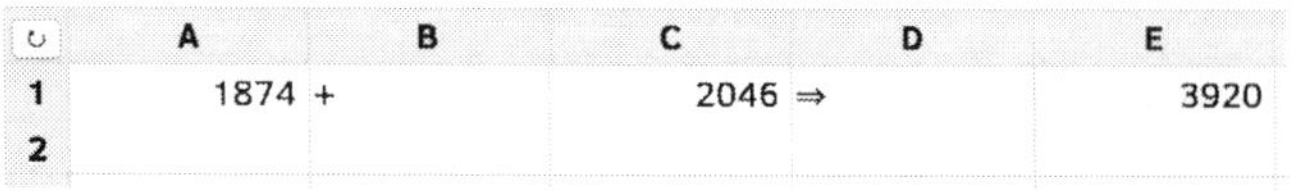

↻	A	B	C	D	E
1	1874 +		2046 ⇒		3920
2					

Figure 19.1: Initial Screen

Basic Concepts

The spreadsheet spans two dimensions, with *columns* starting from **A**, and *rows* starting from **1**. Each *cell* has a unique *coordinate* (such as **A1**) and *content* (such as "1874"), which belongs to one of four *types*:

- Text: "+" in **B1** and "->" in **D1**, aligned to the left.
- Number: "1874" in **A1** and "2046" in **C1**, aligned to the right.
- Formula: =A1+C1 in **E1**, which *calculates* to the *value* "3920", displayed with a light blue background.
- Empty: All cells in row **2** are currently empty.

Click "3920" to set *focus* on **E1**, revealing its formula in an *input box* (Figure 19.2).

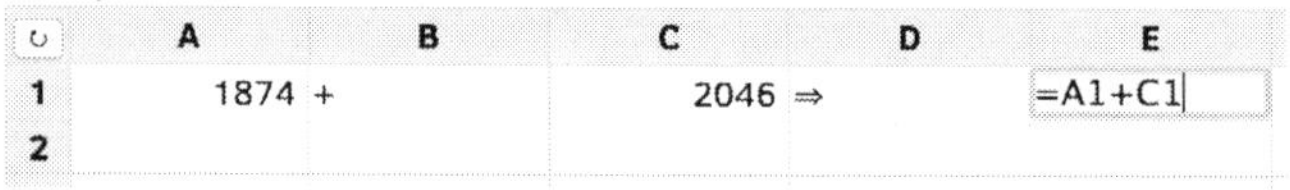

↻	A	B	C	D	E
1	1874 +		2046 ⇒		=A1+C1
2					

Figure 19.2: Input Box

Now let's set focus on **A1** and *change* its content to "1", causing **E1** to *recalculate* its value to "2047" (Figure 19.3).

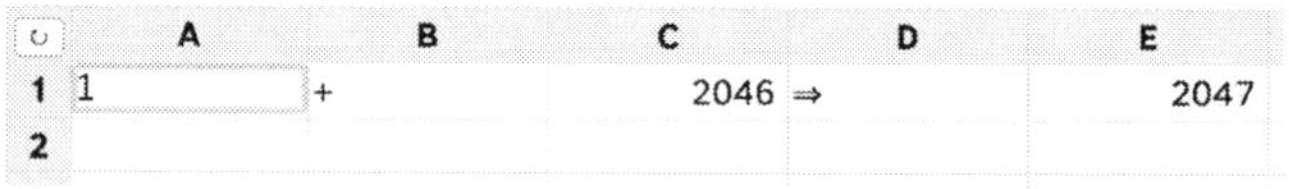

↻	A	B	C	D	E
1	1 +		2046 ⇒		2047
2					

Figure 19.3: Changed Content

Press **ENTER** to set focus to **A2** and change its content to =Date(), then press **TAB**, change the content of **B2** to =alert(), then press **TAB** again to set focus to C2 (Figure 19.4).

This shows that a formula may calculate to a number ("2047" in **E1**), a text (the current time in **A2**, aligned to the left), or an *error* (red letters in **B2**, aligned to the center).

Next, let's try entering =for(;;){}, the JS code for an infinite loop that never terminates. The spreadsheet will prevent this by automatically *restoring* the content of **C2** after an attempted change.

Now reload the page in the browser with **Ctrl-R** or **Cmd-R** to verify that the spreadsheet content is *persistent*, staying the same across browser sessions. To *reset* the spreadsheet to its original contents, press the 'curved arrow' button on the top-left corner.

---

[7] http://www.whatwg.org/specs/web-apps/current-work/multipage/webstorage.html
[8] http://www.whatwg.org/specs/web-apps/current-work/multipage/workers.html
[9] http://audreyt.github.io/500lines/spreadsheet/

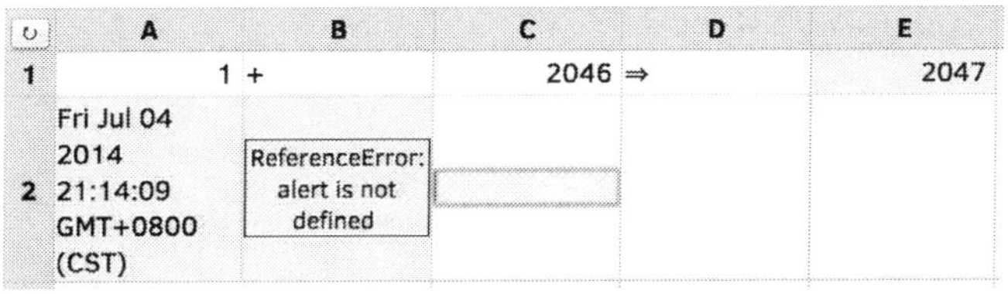

Figure 19.4: Formula Error

Progressive Enhancement

Before we dive into the 99 lines of code, it's worthwhile to disable JS in the browser, reload the page, and note the differences (Figure 19.5).

- Instead of a large grid, only a 2x2 table remains onscreen, with a single content cell.
- Row and column labels are replaced by {{ row }} and {{ col }}.
- Pressing the reset button produces no effect.
- Pressing **TAB** or clicking into the first line of content still reveals an editable input box.

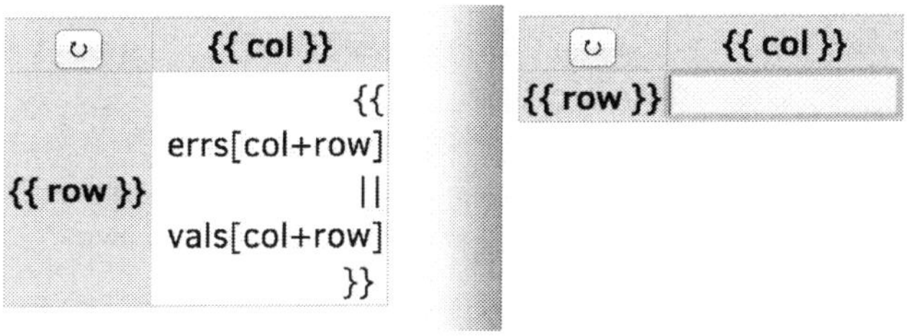

Figure 19.5: With JavaScript Disabled

When we disable the dynamic interactions (JS), the content structure (HTML) and the presentational styles (CSS) remain in effect. If a website is useful with both JS and CSS disabled, we say it adheres to the *progressive enhancement* principle, making its content accessible to the largest audience possible.

Because our spreadsheet is a web application with no server-side code, we must rely on JS to provide the required logic. However, it does work correctly when CSS is not fully supported, such as with screen readers and text-mode browsers.

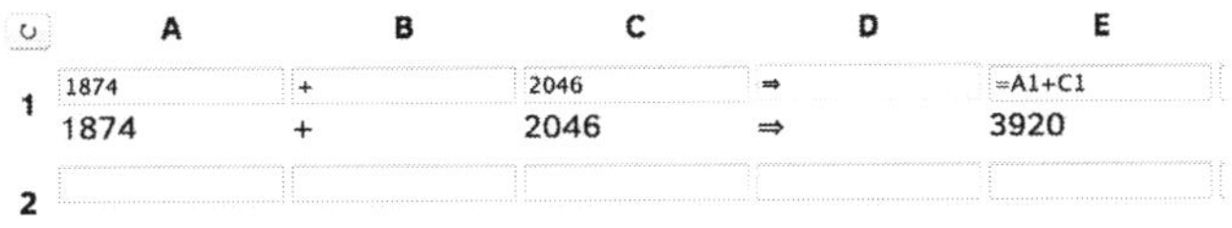

Figure 19.6: With CSS Disabled

As shown in Figure 19.6, if we enable JS in the browser and disable CSS instead, the effects are:

- All background and foreground colors are gone.
- The input box and the cell value are both displayed, instead of just one at a time.
- Otherwise, the application still works the same as the full version.

19.3 Code Walkthrough

Figure 19.7 shows the links between HTML and JS components. In order to make sense of the diagram, let's go through the four source code files, in the same sequence as the browser loads them.

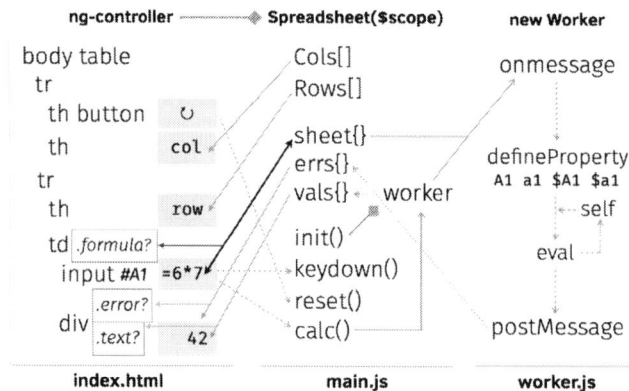

Figure 19.7: Architecture Diagram

- **index.html**: 19 lines
- **main.js**: 38 lines (excluding comments and blank lines)
- **worker.js**: 30 lines (excluding comments and blank lines)
- **styles.css**: 12 lines

HTML

The first line in index.html declares that it's written in HTML5 with the UTF-8 encoding:

```
<!DOCTYPE html><html><head><meta charset="UTF-8">
```

Without the charset declaration, the browser may display the reset button's Unicode symbol as â†», an example of *mojibake*: garbled text caused by decoding issues.

The next three lines are JS declarations, placed within the head section as usual:

```
<script src="lib/angular.js"></script>
<script src="main.js"></script>
<script>
    try { angular.module('500lines') }
    catch(e){ location="es5/index.html" }
</script>
```

The <script src="..."> tags load JS resources from the same path as the HTML page. For example, if the current URL is http://abc.com/x/index.html, then lib/angular.js refers to http://abc.com/x/lib/angular.js.

The try{ angular.module('500lines') } line tests if main.js is loaded correctly; if not, it tells the browser to navigate to es5/index.html instead. This *redirect-based graceful degradation* technique ensures that for pre-2015 browsers with no ES6 support, we can use the translated-to-ES5 versions of JS programs as a fallback.

The next two lines load the CSS resource, close the head section, and begin the body section containing the user-visible part:

```
<link href="styles.css" rel="stylesheet">
</head><body ng-app="500lines" ng-controller="Spreadsheet" ng-cloak>
```

The ng-app and ng-controller attributes above tell AngularJS[10] to call the 500lines module's Spreadsheet function, which would return a *model*: an object that provides *bindings* on the document *view*. (The ng-cloak attribute hides the document from display until the bindings are in place.)

As a concrete example, when the user clicks the <button> defined in the next line, its ng-click attribute will trigger and call reset() and calc(), two named functions provided by the JS model:

```
<table><tr>
 <th><button type="button" ng-click="reset(); calc()"></button></th>
```

The next line uses ng-repeat to display the list of column labels on the top row:

```
<th ng-repeat="col in Cols">{{ col }}</th>
```

For example, if the JS model defines Cols as ["A","B","C"], then there will be three heading cells (th) labeled accordingly. The {{ col }} notation tells AngularJS to *interpolate* the expression, filling the contents in each th with the current value of col.

Similarly, the next two lines go through values in Rows — [1,2,3] and so on — creating a row for each one and labeling the leftmost th cell with its number:

```
</tr><tr ng-repeat="row in Rows">
 <th>{{ row }}</th>
```

Because the <tr ng-repeat> tag is not yet closed by </tr>, the row variable is still available for expressions. The next line creates a data cell (td) in the current row and uses both col and row variables in its ng-class attribute:

```
<td ng-repeat="col in Cols" ng-class="{ formula: ('=' === sheet[col+row][0]) }">
```

A few things are going on here. In HTML, the class attribute describes a *set of class names* that allow CSS to style them differently. The ng-class here evaluates the expression ('=' === sheet[col+row][0]); if it is true, then the <td> gets formula as an additional class, which gives the cell a light-blue background as defined in line 8 of **styles.css** with the .formula *class selector*.

The expression above checks if the current cell is a formula by testing if = is the initial character ([0]) of the string in sheet[col+row], where sheet is a JS model object with coordinates (such as "E1") as properties, and cell contents (such as "=A1+C1") as values. Note that because col is a string and not a number, the + in col+row means concatenation instead of addition.

Inside the <td>, we give the user an input box to edit the cell content stored in sheet[col+row]:

```
<input id="{{ col+row }}" ng-model="sheet[col+row]" ng-change="calc()"
    ng-model-options="{ debounce: 200 }" ng-keydown="keydown( $event, col, row )">
```

---

[10]http://angularjs.org/

Here, the key attribute is ng-model, which enables a *two-way binding* between the JS model and the input box's editable content. In practice, this means that whenever the user makes a change in the input box, the JS model will update sheet[col+row] to match the content, and trigger its calc() function to recalculate values of all formula cells.

To avoid repeated calls to calc() when the user presses and holds a key, ng-model-options limits the update rate to once every 200 milliseconds.

The id attribute here is interpolated with the coordinate col+row. The id attribute of a HTML element must be different from the id of all other elements in the same document. This ensures that the #A1 *ID selector* refers to a single element, instead of a set of elements like the class selector .formula. When the user presses the **UP/DOWN/ENTER** keys, the keyboard-navigation logic in keydown() will use ID selectors to determine which input box to focus on.

After the input box, we place a <div> to display the calculated value of the current cell, represented in the JS model by objects errs and vals:

```
<div ng-class="{ error: errs[col+row], text: vals[col+row][0] }">
    {{ errs[col+row] || vals[col+row] }}</div>
```

If an error occurs when computing a formula, the text interpolation uses the error message contained in errs[col+row], and ng-class applies the error class to the element, allowing CSS to style it differently (with red letters, aligned to the center, etc.).

When there is no error, the vals[col+row] on the right side of || is interpolated instead. If it's a non-empty string, the initial character ([0]) will evaluate to true, applying the text class to the element that left-aligns the text.

Because empty strings and numeric values have no initial character, ng-class will not assign them any classes, so CSS can style them with right alignment as the default case.

Finally, we close the ng-repeat loop in the column level with </td>, close the row-level loop with </tr>, and end the HTML document with:

```
    </td>
  </tr></table>
</body></html>
```

JS: Main Controller

The main.js file defines the 500lines module and its Spreadsheet controller function, as required by the <body> element in index.html.

As the bridge between the HTML view and the background worker, it has four tasks:

- Define the dimensions and labels of columns and rows.
- Provide event handlers for keyboard navigation and the reset button.
- When the user changes the spreadsheet, send its new content to the worker.
- When computed results arrive from the worker, update the view and save the current state.

The flowchart in Figure 19.8 shows the controller-worker interaction in more detail:

Now let's walk through the code. In the first line, we request the AngularJS $scope:

```
angular.module('500lines', []).controller('Spreadsheet', function ($scope, $timeout) {
```

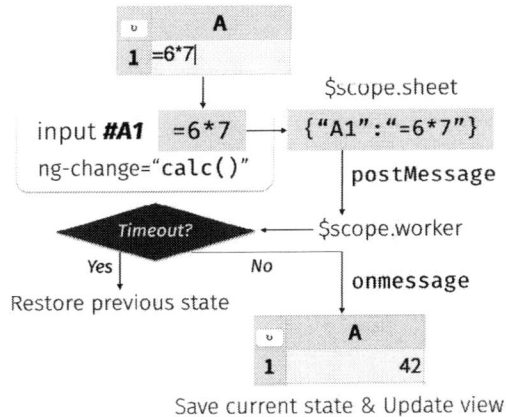

Figure 19.8: Controller-Worker Flowchart

The $ in $scope is part of the variable name. Here we also request the $timeout[11] service function from AngularJS; later on, we will use it to prevent infinite-looping formulas.

To put Cols and Rows into the model, simply define them as properties of $scope:

```
// Begin of $scope properties; start with the column/row labels
$scope.Cols = [], $scope.Rows = [];
for (col of range( 'A', 'H' )) { $scope.Cols.push(col); }
for (row of range( 1, 20 )) { $scope.Rows.push(row); }
```

The ES6 for…of[12] syntax makes it easy to loop through ranges with a start and an end point, with the helper function range defined as a generator[13]:

```
function* range(cur, end) { while (cur <= end) { yield cur;
```

The function* above means that range returns an iterator[14], with a while loop that would yield[15] a single value at a time. Whenever the for loop demands the next value, it will resume execution right after the yield line:

```
// If it's a number, increase it by one; otherwise move to next letter
cur = (isNaN( cur ) ? String.fromCodePoint( cur.codePointAt()+1 ) : cur+1);
} }
```

To generate the next value, we use isNaN to see if cur is meant as a letter (NaN stands for "not a number.") If so, we get the letter's code point value[16], increment it by one, and convert the codepoint[17] back to get its next letter. Otherwise, we simply increase the number by one.

---

[11]https://docs.angularjs.org/api/ng/service/\$timeout
[12]https://developer.mozilla.org/en-US/docs/Web/JavaScript/Reference/Statements/for...of
[13]https://developer.mozilla.org/en-US/docs/Web/JavaScript/Reference/Statements/function*
[14]https://developer.mozilla.org/en-US/docs/Web/JavaScript/Guide/The_Iterator_protocol
[15]https://developer.mozilla.org/en-US/docs/Web/JavaScript/Reference/Operators/yield
[16]https://developer.mozilla.org/en-US/docs/Web/JavaScript/Reference/Global_Objects/String/codePointAt
[17]https://developer.mozilla.org/en-US/docs/Web/JavaScript/Reference/Global_Objects/String/fromCodePoint

Next up, we define the keydown() function that handles keyboard navigation across rows:

```
// UP(38) and DOWN(40)/ENTER(13) move focus to the row above (-1) and below (+1).
$scope.keydown = ({which}, col, row)=>{ switch (which) {
```

The arrow function[18] receives the arguments ($event, col, row) from <input ng-keydown>, using destructuring assignment[19] to assign $event.which into the which parameter, and checks if it's among the three navigational key codes:

```
case 38: case 40: case 13: $timeout( ()=>{
```

If it is, we use $timeout to schedule a focus change after the current ng-keydown and ng-change handler. Because $timeout requires a function as argument, the ()=>{...} syntax constructs a function to represent the focus-change logic, which starts by checking the direction of movement:

```
const direction = (which === 38) ? -1 : +1;
```

The const declarator means direction will not change during the function's execution. The direction to move is either upward (-1, from **A2** to **A1**) if the key code is 38 (**UP**), or downward (+1, from **A2** to **A3**) otherwise.

Next up, we retrieve the target element using the ID selector syntax (e.g. "#A3"), constructed with a template string[20] written in a pair of backticks, concatenating the leading #, the current col and the target row + direction:

```
const cell = document.querySelector( `#${ col }${ row + direction }` );
if (cell) { cell.focus(); }
} );
} };
```

We put an extra check on the result of querySelector because moving upward from **A1** will produce the selector #A0, which has no corresponding element, and so will not trigger a focus change — the same goes for pressing **DOWN** at the bottom row.

Next, we define the reset() function so the reset button can restore the contents of the sheet:

```
// Default sheet content, with some data cells and one formula cell.
$scope.reset = ()=>{
$scope.sheet = { A1: 1874, B1: '+', C1: 2046, D1: '->', E1: '=A1+C1' }; }
```

The init() function tries restoring the sheet content from its previous state from the localStorage[21], and defaults to the initial content if it's our first time running the application:

```
// Define the initializer, and immediately call it
($scope.init = ()=>{
// Restore the previous .sheet; reset to default if it's the first run
$scope.sheet = angular.fromJson( localStorage.getItem( '' ) );
if (!$scope.sheet) { $scope.reset(); }
$scope.worker = new Worker( 'worker.js' );
}).call();
```

---

[18]https://developer.mozilla.org/en-US/docs/Web/JavaScript/Reference/arrow_functions
[19]https://developer.mozilla.org/en-US/docs/Web/JavaScript/New_in_JavaScript/1.7\#Pulling_fields_
from_objects_passed_as_function_parameter
[20]https://developer.mozilla.org/en-US/docs/Web/JavaScript/Reference/template_strings
[21]https://developer.mozilla.org/en-US/docs/Web/Guide/API/DOM/Storage\#localStorage

A few things are worth nothing in the `init()` function above:

- We use the `($scope.init = ()=>{...}).call()` syntax to define the function and immediately call it.
- Because localStorage only stores strings, we *parse* the sheet structure from its JSON[22] representation using `angular.fromJson()`.
- At the last step of `init()`, we create a new web worker[23] thread and assign it to the worker scope property. Although the worker is not directly used in the view, it's customary to use `$scope` to share objects used across model functions, in this case between `init()` here and `calc()` below.

While sheet holds the user-editable cell content, `errs` and `vals` contain the results of calculations — errors and values — that are read-only to the user:

```
// Formula cells may produce errors in .errs; normal cell contents are in .vals
[$scope.errs, $scope.vals] = [ {}, {} ];
```

With these properties in place, we can define the `calc()` function that triggers whenever the user makes a change to sheet:

```
// Define the calculation handler; not calling it yet
$scope.calc = ()=>{
  const json = angular.toJson( $scope.sheet );
```

Here we take a snapshot of the state of sheet and store it in the constant json, a JSON string. Next up, we construct a `promise` from $timeout[24] that cancels the upcoming computation if it takes more than 99 milliseconds:

```
const promise = $timeout( ()=>{
  // If the worker has not returned in 99 milliseconds, terminate it
  $scope.worker.terminate();
  // Back up to the previous state and make a new worker
  $scope.init();
  // Redo the calculation using the last-known state
  $scope.calc();
}, 99 );
```

Since we made sure that `calc()` is called at most once every 200 milliseconds via the `<input ng-model-options>` attribute in HTML, this arrangement leaves 101 milliseconds for `init()` to restore sheet to the last known-good state and make a new worker.

The worker's task is to calculate `errs` and `vals` from the contents of sheet. Because **main.js** and **worker.js** communicate by message-passing, we need an `onmessage` handler to receive the results once they are ready:

```
// When the worker returns, apply its effect on the scope
$scope.worker.onmessage = ({data})=>{
  $timeout.cancel( promise );
  localStorage.setItem( '', json );
  $timeout( ()=>{ [$scope.errs, $scope.vals] = data; } );
};
```

---

[22]https://developer.mozilla.org/en-US/docs/Glossary/JSON
[23]https://developer.mozilla.org/en-US/docs/Web/API/Worker
[24]https://docs.angularjs.org/api/ng/service/\$timeout

If onmessage is called, we know that the sheet snapshot in json is stable (i.e., containing no infinite-looping formulas), so we cancel the 99-millisecond timeout, write the snapshot to local-Storage, and schedule a UI update with a $timeout function that updates errs and vals to the user-visible view.

With the handler in place, we can post the state of sheet to the worker, starting its calculation in the background:

```
    // Post the current sheet content for the worker to process
    $scope.worker.postMessage( $scope.sheet );
  };

  // Start calculation when worker is ready
  $scope.worker.onmessage = $scope.calc;
  $scope.worker.postMessage( null );
});
```

JS: Background Worker

There are three reasons for using a web worker to calculate formulas, instead of using the main JS thread for the task:

- While the worker runs in the background, the user is free to continue interacting with the spreadsheet without getting blocked by computation in the main thread.
- Because we accept any JS expression in a formula, the worker provides a *sandbox* that prevents formulas from interfering with the page that contains them, such as by popping out an alert() dialog box.
- A formula can refer to any coordinates as variables. The other coordinates may contain another formula that might end in a cyclic reference. To solve this problem, we use the worker's *global scope* object self, and define these variables as *getter functions* on self to implement the cycle-prevention logic.

With these in mind, let's take a look at the worker's code.

The worker's sole purpose is defining its onmessage handler. The handler takes sheet, calculates errs and vals, and posts them back to the main JS thread. We begin by re-initializing the three variables when we receive a message:

```
let sheet, errs, vals;
self.onmessage = ({data})=>{
  [sheet, errs, vals] = [ data, {}, {} ];
```

In order to turn coordinates into global variables, we first iterate over each property in sheet, using a for...in loop:

```
  for (const coord in sheet) {
```

ES6 introduces const and let declares *block scoped* constants and variables; const coord above means that functions defined in the loop would capture the value of coord in each iteration.

In contrast, var coord in earlier versions of JS would declare a *function scoped* variable, and functions defined in each loop iteration would end up pointing to the same coord variable.

Customarily, formula variables are case-insensitive and can optionally have a $ prefix. Because JS variables are case-sensitive, we use map to go over the four variable names for the same coordinate:

```
// Four variable names pointing to the same coordinate: A1, a1, $A1, $a1
[ '', '$' ].map( p => [ coord, coord.toLowerCase() ].map(c => {
  const name = p+c;
```

Note the shorthand arrow function syntax above: p => ... is the same as (p) => { ... }.

For each variable name, like A1 and $a1, we define an accessor property[25] on self that calculates vals["A1"] whenever they are evaluated in an expression:

```
// Worker is reused across calculations, so only define each variable once
if ((Object.getOwnPropertyDescriptor( self, name ) || {}).get) { return; }

// Define self['A1'], which is the same thing as the global variable A1
Object.defineProperty( self, name, { get() {
```

The { get() { ... } } syntax above is shorthand for { get: ()=>{ ... } }. Because we define only get and not set, the variables become *read-only* and cannot be modified from user-supplied formulas.

The get accessor starts by checking vals[coord], and simply returns it if it's already calculated:

```
if (coord in vals) { return vals[coord]; }
```

If not, we need to calculate vals[coord] from sheet[coord].

First we set it to NaN, so self-references like setting **A1** to =A1 will end up with NaN instead of an infinite loop:

```
vals[coord] = NaN;
```

Next we check if sheet[coord] is a number by converting it to numeric with prefix +, assigning the number to x, and comparing its string representation with the original string. If they differ, then we set x to the original string:

```
// Turn numeric strings into numbers, so =A1+C1 works when both are numbers
let x = +sheet[coord];
if (sheet[coord] !== x.toString()) { x = sheet[coord]; }
```

If the initial character of x is =, then it's a formula cell. We evaluate the part after = with eval.call(), using the first argument null to tell eval to run in the *global scope*, hiding the *lexical scope* variables like x and sheet from the evaluation:

```
// Evaluate formula cells that begin with =
try { vals[coord] = (('=' === x[0]) ? eval.call( null, x.slice( 1 ) ) : x);
```

If the evaluation succeeds, the result is stored into vals[coord]. For non-formula cells, the value of vals[coord] is simply x, which may be a number or a string.

If eval results in an error, the catch block tests if it's because the formula refers to an empty cell not yet defined in self:

```
} catch (e) {
  const match = /\$?[A-Za-z]+[1-9][0-9]*\b/.exec( e );
  if (match && !( match[0] in self )) {
```

---

[25]https://developer.mozilla.org/en-US/docs/Web/JavaScript/Reference/Global_Objects/Object/
defineProperty

In that case, we set the missing cell's default value to "0", clear `vals[coord]`, and re-run the current computation using `self[coord]`:

```
            // The formula refers to a uninitialized cell; set it to 0 and retry
            self[match[0]] = 0;
            delete vals[coord];
            return self[coord];
        }
```

If the user gives the missing cell a content later on in `sheet[coord]`, then the temporary value would be overridden by `Object.defineProperty`.

Other kinds of errors are stored in `errs[coord]`:

```
            // Otherwise, stringify the caught exception in the errs object
            errs[coord] = e.toString();
        }
```

In case of errors, the value of `vals[coord]` will remain NaN because the assignment did not finish executing.

Finally, the get accessor returns the calculated value stored in `vals[coord]`, which must be a number, a Boolean value, or a string:

```
        // Turn vals[coord] into a string if it's not a number or Boolean
        switch (typeof vals[coord]) {
            case 'function': case 'object': vals[coord]+='';
        }
        return vals[coord];
    } } );
  }));
}
```

With accessors defined for all coordinates, the worker goes through the coordinates again, invoking each accessor with `self[coord]`, then posts the resulting `errs` and `vals` back to the main JS thread:

```
    // For each coordinate in the sheet, call the property getter defined above
    for (const coord in sheet) { self[coord]; }
    return [ errs, vals ];
}
```

CSS

The **styles.css** file contains just a few selectors and their presentational styles. First, we style the table to merge all cell borders together, leaving no spaces between neighboring cells:

```
table { border-collapse: collapse; }
```

Both the heading and data cells share the same border style, but we can tell them apart by their background colors: heading cells are light gray, data cells are white by default, and formula cells get a light blue background:

```
th, td { border: 1px solid #ccc; }
th { background: #ddd; }
td.formula { background: #eef; }
```

The displayed width is fixed for each cell's calculated values. Empty cells receive a minimal height, and long lines are clipped with a trailing ellipsis:

```
td div { text-align: right; width: 120px; min-height: 1.2em;
        overflow: hidden; text-overflow: ellipsis; }
```

The text alignment and decorations are determined by each value's type, as reflected by the text and error class selectors:

```
div.text { text-align: left; }
div.error { text-align: center; color: #800; font-size: 90%; border: solid 1px #800 }
```

As for the user-editable input box, we use *absolute positioning* to overlay it on top of its cell, and make it transparent so the underlying div with the cell's value shows through:

```
input { position: absolute; border: 0; padding: 0;
        width: 120px; height: 1.3em; font-size: 100%;
        color: transparent; background: transparent; }
```

When the user sets focus on the input box, it springs into the foreground:

```
input:focus { color: #111; background: #efe; }
```

Furthermore, the underlying div is collapsed into a single line, so it's completely covered by the input box:

```
input:focus + div { white-space: nowrap; }
```

19.4   Conclusion

Since this book is *500 Lines or Less*, a web spreadsheet in 99 lines is a minimal example—please feel free to experiment and extend it in any direction you'd like.

Here are some ideas, all easily reachable in the remaining space of 401 lines:

- A collaborative online editor using ShareJS[26], AngularFire[27] or GoAngular[28].
- Markdown syntax support for text cells, using angular-marked[29].
- Common formula functions (SUM, TRIM, etc.) from the OpenFormula standard[30].
- Interoperate with popular spreadsheet formats, such as CSV and SpreadsheetML via SheetJS[31].
- Import from and export to online spreadsheet services, such as Google Spreadsheet and EtherCalc[32].

---

[26] http://sharejs.org/
[27] http://angularfire.com
[28] http://goangular.org/
[29] http://ngmodules.org/modules/angular-marked
[30] https://en.wikipedia.org/wiki/OpenFormula
[31] http://sheetjs.com/
[32] http://ethercalc.net/

A Note on JS versions

This chapter aims to demonstrate new concepts in ES6, so we use the Traceur compiler[33] to translate source code to ES5 to run on pre-2015 browsers.

If you prefer to work directly with the 2010 edition of JS, the as-javascript-1.8.5[34] directory has **main.js** and **worker.js** written in the style of ES5; the source code[35] is line-by-line comparable to the ES6 version with the same line count.

For people preferring a cleaner syntax, the as-livescript-1.3.0[36] directory uses LiveScript[37] instead of ES6 to write **main.ls** and **worker.ls**; it is 20 lines shorter[38] than the JS version.

Building on the LiveScript language, the as-react-livescript[39] directory uses the ReactJS[40] framework; it is 10 lines more longer[41] than the AngularJS equivalent, but runs considerably faster.

If you are interested in translating this example to alternate JS languages, send a pull request[42]—I'd love to hear about it!

---

[33]https://github.com/google/traceur-compiler
[34]https://audreyt.github.io/500lines/spreadsheet/as-javascript-1.8.5/
[35]https://github.com/audreyt/500lines/tree/master/spreadsheet/as-javascript-1.8.5
[36]https://audreyt.github.io/500lines/spreadsheet/as-livescript-1.3.0/
[37]http://livescript.net/
[38]https://github.com/audreyt/500lines/tree/master/spreadsheet/as-livescript-1.3.0
[39]https://audreyt.github.io/500lines/spreadsheet/as-react-livescript/
[40]https://facebook.github.io/react/
[41]https://github.com/audreyt/500lines/tree/master/spreadsheet/as-react-livescript
[42]https://github.com/audreyt/500lines/pulls

## chapter 20

Static Analysis

Leah Hanson

20.1   Introduction

You may be familiar with a fancy IDE that draws red underlines under parts of your code that don't compile. You may have run a linter on your code to check for formatting or style problems. You might run your compiler in super-picky mode with all the warnings turned on. All of these tools are applications of static analysis.

Static analysis is a way to check for problems in your code without running it. "Static" means at compile time rather than at run time, and "analysis" means we're analyzing the code. When you've used the tools I mentioned above, it may have felt like magic. But those tools are just programs—they are made of source code that was written by a person, a programmer like you. In this chapter, we're going to talk about how to implement a couple of static analysis checks. In order to do this, we need to know what we want the check to do and how we want to do it.

We can get more specific about what you need to know by describing the process as three stages:

1. Deciding what you want to check for.

You should be able to explain the general problem you'd like to solve, in terms that a user of the programming language would recognize. Examples include:

- Finding misspelled variable names
- Finding race conditions in parallel code
- Finding calls to unimplemented functions

2. Deciding how exactly to check for it.

While we could ask a friend to do one of the tasks listed above, they aren't specific enough to explain to a computer. To tackle "misspelled variable names", for example, we'd need to decide what misspelled means here. One option would be to claim variable names should be composed of English words from the dictionary; another option is to look for variables that are only used once (the one time you mistyped it).

If we know we're looking for variables that are only used once, we can talk about kinds of variable usages (having their value assigned versus read) and what code would or would not trigger a warning.

3. Implementation details.

This covers the actual act of writing the code, the time spent reading the documentation for libraries you use, and figuring out how to get at the information you need to write the analysis. This could involve reading in a file of code, parsing it to understand the structure, and then making your specific check on that structure.

We're going to work through these steps for each of the individual checks implemented in this chapter. Step 1 requires enough understanding of the language we're analyzing to empathize with the problems its users face. All the code in this chapter is Julia code, written to analyze Julia code.

20.2   A Very Brief Introduction to Julia

Julia is a young language aimed at technical computing. It was released at version 0.1 in the spring of 2012; as of the start of 2015, it has reached version 0.3. In general, Julia looks a lot like Python, but with some optional type annotations and without any object-oriented stuff. The feature that most programmers will find novel in Julia is multiple dispatch, which has a pervasive impact on both API design and on other design choices in the language.

Here is a snippet of Julia code:

```
# A comment about increment
function increment(x::Int64)
  return x + 1
end

increment(5)
```

This code defines a method of the function increment that takes one argument, named x, of type Int64. The method returns the value of x + 1. Then, this freshly defined method is called with the value 5; the function call, as you may have guessed, will evaluate to 6.

Int64 is a type whose values are signed integers represented in memory by 64 bits; they are the integers that your hardware understands if your computer has a 64-bit processor. Types in Julia define the representation of data in memory, in addition to influencing method dispatch.

The name increment refers to a generic function, which may have many methods. We have just defined one method of it. In many languages, the terms "function" and "method" are used interchangeably; in Julia, they have distinct meanings. This chapter will make more sense if you are careful to understand "function" as a named collection of methods, where a "method" is a specific implementation for a specific type signature.

Let's define another method of the increment function:

```
# Increment x by y
function increment(x::Int64, y::Number)
  return x + y
end

increment(5) # => 6
increment(5,4) # => 9
```

Now the function increment has two methods. Julia decides which method to run for a given call based on the number and types of the arguments; this is called *dynamic multiple dispatch*:

- **Dynamic** because it's based on the types of the values used at runtime.
- **Multiple** because it looks at the types and order of all the arguments.
- **Dispatch** because this is a way of matching function calls to method definitions.

To put this in the context of languages you may already know, object-oriented languages use single dispatch because they only consider the first argument. (In x.foo(y), the first argument is x.)

Both single and multiple dispatch are based on the types of the arguments. The x::Int64 above is a type annotation purely for dispatch. In Julia's dynamic type system, you could assign a value of any type to x during the function without an error.

We haven't really seen the "multiple" part yet, but if you're curious about Julia, you'll have to look that up on your own. We need to move on to our first check.

20.3   Checking the Types of Variables in Loops

As in most programming languages, writing very fast code in Julia involves an understanding of how the computer works and how Julia works. An important part of helping the compiler create fast code for you is writing type-stable code; this is important in Julia and JavaScript, and is also helpful in other JIT'd languages. When the compiler can see that a variable in a section of code will always contain the same specific type, the compiler can do more optimizations than if it believes (correctly or not) that there are multiple possible types for that variable. You can read more about why type stability (also called "monomorphism") is important for JavaScript online[1].

Why This Is Important

Let's write a function that takes an Int64 and increases it by some amount. If the number is small (less than 10), let's increase it by a big number (50), but if it's big, let's only increase it by 0.5.

```
function increment(x::Int64)
  if x < 10
    x = x + 50
  else
    x = x + 0.5
  end
  return x
end
```

This function looks pretty straightforward, but the type of x is unstable. I selected two numbers: 50, an Int64, and 0.5, a Float64. Depending on the value of x, it might be added to either one of them. If you add an Int64 like 22, to a Float64 like 0.5, you'll get a Float64 (22.5). Because the type of variable in the function (x) could change depending on the value of the arguments to the function (x), this method of increment and specifically the variable x are type-unstable.

Float64 is a type that represents floating-point values stored in 64 bits; in C, it is called a double. This is one of the floating-point types that 64-bit processors understand.

As with most efficiency problems, this issue is more pronounced when it happens during loops. Code inside for loops and while loops is run many, many times, so making it fast is more important than speeding up code that is only run once or twice. Therefore, our first check is to look for variables that have unstable types inside loops.

---

[1] http://mrale.ph/blog/2015/01/11/whats-up-with-monomorphism.html

First, let's look at an example of what we want to catch. We'll be looking at two functions. Each of them sums the numbers 1 to 100, but instead of summing the whole numbers, they divide each one by 2 before summing it. Both functions will get the same answer (2525.0); both will return the same type (Float64). However, the first function, unstable, suffers from type-instability, while the second one, stable, does not.

```
function unstable()
    sum = 0
    for i=1:100
        sum += i/2
    end
    return sum
end
```

```
function stable()
    sum = 0.0
    for i=1:100
        sum += i/2
    end
    return sum
end
```

The only textual difference between the two functions is in the initialization of sum: sum = 0 versus sum = 0.0. In Julia, 0 is an Int64 literal and 0.0 is a Float64 literal. How big of a difference could this tiny change make?

Because Julia is Just-In-Time (JIT) compiled, the first run of a function will take longer than subsequent runs. (The first run includes the time it takes to compile the function for these argument types.) When we benchmark functions, we have to be sure to run them once (or precompile them) before timing them.

```
julia> unstable()
2525.0
```

```
julia> stable()
2525.0
```

```
julia> @time unstable()
elapsed time: 9.517e-6 seconds (3248 bytes allocated)
2525.0
```

```
julia> @time stable()
elapsed time: 2.285e-6 seconds (64 bytes allocated)
2525.0
```

The @time macro prints out how long the function took to run and how many bytes were allocated while it was running. The number of bytes allocated increases every time new memory is needed; it does not decrease when the garbage collector vacuums up memory that's no longer being used. This means that the bytes allocated is related to the amount of time we spend allocating and managing memory, but does not imply that we had all of that memory in use at the same time.

If we wanted to get solid numbers for stable versus unstable we would need to make the loop much longer or run the functions many times. However, it looks like unstable is probably slower.

More interestingly, we can see a large gap in the number of bytes allocated; unstable has allocated around 3 KB of memory, where stable is using 64 bytes.

Since we can see how simple unstable is, we might guess that this allocation is happening in the loop. To test this, we can make the loop longer and see if the allocations increase accordingly. Let's make the loop go from 1 to 10000, which is 100 times more iterations; we'll look for the number of bytes allocated to also increase about 100 times, to around 300 KB.

```
function unstable()
  sum = 0
  for i=1:10000
    sum += i/2
  end
  return sum
end
```

Since we redefined the function, we'll need to run it so it gets compiled before we measure it. We expect to get a different, larger answer from the new function definition, since it's summing more numbers now.

```
julia> unstable()
2.50025e7

julia>@time unstable()
elapsed time: 0.000667613 seconds (320048 bytes allocated)
2.50025e7
```

The new unstable allocated about 320 KB, which is what we would expect if the allocations are happening in the loop. To explain what's going on here, we're going to look at how Julia works under the hood.

This difference between unstable and stable occurs because sum in unstable must be boxed while sum in stable can be unboxed. Boxed values consist of a type tag and the actual bits that represent the value; unboxed values only have their actual bits. But the type tag is small, so that's not why boxing values allocates a lot more memory.

The difference comes from what optimizations the compiler can make. When a variable has a concrete, immutable type, the compiler can unbox it inside the function. If that's not the case, then the variable must be allocated on the heap, and participate in the garbage collector. Immutable types are a concept specific to Julia. A value of an immutable type can't be changed.

Immutable types are usually types that represent values, rather than collections of values. For example, most numeric types, including Int64 and Float64, are immutable. (Numeric types in Julia are normal types, not special primitive types; you could define a new MyInt64 that's the same as the provided one.) Because immutable types cannot be modified, you must make a new copy every time you want change one. For example 4 + 6 must make a new Int64 to hold the result. In contrast, the members of a mutable type can be updated in-place; this means you don't have to make a copy of the whole thing to make a change.

The idea of x = x + 2 allocating memory probably sounds pretty weird; why would you make such a basic operation slow by making Int64 values immutable? This is where those compiler optimizations come in: using immutable types doesn't (usually) slow this down. If x has a stable, concrete type (such as Int64), then the compiler is free to allocate x on the stack and mutate x in place. The problem is only when x has an unstable type (so the compiler doesn't know how big or what type it will be); once x is boxed and on the heap, the compiler isn't completely sure that some other piece of code isn't using the value, and thus can't edit it.

Because sum in stable has a concrete type (Float64), the compiler knows that it can store it unboxed locally in the function and mutate its value; sum will not be allocated on the heap and new copies don't have to be made every time we add i/2.

Because sum in unstable does not have a concrete type, the compiler allocates it on the heap. Every time we modify sum, we allocated a new value on the heap. All this time spent allocating values on the heap (and retrieving them every time we want to read the value of sum) is expensive.

Using 0 versus 0.0 is an easy mistake to make, especially when you're new to Julia. Automatically checking that variables used in loops are type-stable helps programmers get more insight into what the types of their variables are in performance-critical sections of their code.

Implementation Details

We'll need to find out which variables are used inside loops and we'll need to find the types of those variables. We'll then need to decide how to print them in a human-readable format.

- How do we find loops?
- How do we find variables in loops?
- How do we find the types of a variable?
- How do we print the results?
- How do we tell if the type is unstable?

I'm going to tackle the last question first, since this whole endeavour hinges on it. We've looked at an unstable function and seen, as programmers, how to identify an unstable variable, but we need our program to find them. This sounds like it would require simulating the function to look for variables whose values might change—which sounds like it would take some work. Luckily for us, Julia's type inference already traces through the function's execution to determine the types.

The type of sum in unstable is Union(Float64,Int64). This is a UnionType, a special kind of type that indicates that the variable may hold any of a set of types of values. A variable of type Union(Float64,Int64) can hold values of type Int64 or Float64; a value can only have one of those types. A UnionType joins any number of types (e.g., UnionType(Float64, Int64, Int32) joins three types). We're going to look for is UnionTyped variables inside loops.

Parsing code into a representative structure is a complicated business, and gets more complicated as the language grows. In this chapter, we'll be depending on internal data structures used by the compiler. This means that we don't have to worry about reading files or parsing them, but it does mean we have to work with data structures that are not in our control and that sometimes feel clumsy or ugly.

Besides all the work we'll save by not having to parse the code by ourselves, working with the same data structures that the compiler uses means that our checks will be based on an accurate assessment of the compilers understanding—which means our check will be consistent with how the code actually runs.

This process of examining Julia code from Julia code is called introspection. When you or I introspect, we're thinking about how and why we think and feel. When code introspects, it examines the representation or execution properties of code in the same language (possibly its own code). When code's introspection extends to modifying the examined code, it's called metaprogramming (programs that write or modify programs).

Introspection in Julia

Julia makes it easy to introspect. There are four functions built in to let us see what the compiler is thinking: code_lowered, code_typed, code_llvm, and code_native. Those are listed in order of what step in the compilation process their output is from; the first one is closest to the code we'd type in and the last one is the closest to what the CPU runs. For this chapter, we'll focus on code_typed, which gives us the optimized, type-inferred abstract syntax tree (AST).

code_typed takes two arguments: the function of interest, and a tuple of argument types. For example, if we wanted to see the AST for a function foo when called with two Int64s, then we would call code_typed(foo, (Int64,Int64)).

```
function foo(x,y)
  z = x + y
  return 2 * z
end
```

```
code_typed(foo,(Int64,Int64))
```

This is the structure that code_typed would return:

```
1-element Array{Any,1}:
 :($(Expr(:lambda, {:x,:y}, {{:z},{{:x,Int64,0},{:y,Int64,0},{:z,Int64,18}},{}},
  :(begin  # none, line 2:
        z = (top(box))(Int64,(top(add_int))(x::Int64,y::Int64))::Int64 # line 3:
        return (top(box))(Int64,(top(mul_int))(2,z::Int64))::Int64
    end::Int64))))
```

This is an Array; this allows code_typed to return multiple matching methods. Some combinations of functions and argument types may not completely determine which method should be called. For example, you could pass in a type like Any (instead of Int64). Any is the type at the top of the type hierarchy; all types are subtypes of Any (including Any). If we included Any in our tuple of argument types, and had multiple matching methods, then the Array from code_typed would have more than one element in it; it would have one element per matching method.

Let's pull our example Expr out to make it easier to talk about.

```
julia> e = code_typed(foo,(Int64,Int64))[1]
 :($(Expr(:lambda, {:x,:y}, {{:z},{{:x,Int64,0},{:y,Int64,0},{:z,Int64,18}},{}},
  :(begin  # none, line 2:
        z = (top(box))(Int64,(top(add_int))(x::Int64,y::Int64))::Int64 # line 3:
        return (top(box))(Int64,(top(mul_int))(2,z::Int64))::Int64
    end::Int64))))
```

The structure we're interested in is inside the Array: it is an Expr. Julia uses Expr (short for expression) to represent its AST. (An abstract syntax tree is how the compiler thinks about the meaning of your code; it's kind of like when you had to diagram sentences in grade school.) The Expr we get back represents one method. It has some metadata (about the variables that appear in the method) and the expressions that make up the body of the method.

Now we can ask some questions about e.

We can ask what properties an Expr has by using the names function, which works on any Julia value or type. It returns an Array of names defined by that type (or the type of the value).

```
julia> names(e)
3-element Array{Symbol,1}:
 :head
 :args
 :typ
```

We just asked e what names it has, and now we can ask what value each name corresponds to. An Expr has three properties: head, typ and args.

```
julia> e.head
:lambda
```

```
julia> e.typ
Any
```

```
julia> e.args
3-element Array{Any,1}:
 {:x,:y}
 {{:z},{{:x,Int64,0},{:y,Int64,0},{:z,Int64,18}},{}}
 :(begin  # none, line 2:
        z = (top(box))(Int64,(top(add_int))(x::Int64,y::Int64))::Int64 # line 3:
        return (top(box))(Int64,(top(mul_int))(2,z::Int64))::Int64
    end::Int64)
```

We just saw some values printed out, but that doesn't tell us much about what they mean or how they're used.

- head tells us what kind of expression this is; normally, you'd use separate types for this in Julia, but Expr is a type that models the structure used in the parser. The parser is written in a dialect of Scheme, which structures everything as nested lists. head tells us how the rest of the Expr is organized and what kind of expression it represents.
- typ is the inferred return type of the expression; when you evaluate any expression, it results in some value. typ is the type of the value that the expression will evaluate to. For nearly all Exprs, this value will be Any (which is always correct, since every possible type is a subtype of Any). Only the body of type-inferred methods and most expressions inside them will have their typ set to something more specific. (Because type is a keyword, this field can't use that word as its name.)
- args is the most complicated part of Expr; its structure varies based on the value of head. It's always an Array{Any} (an untyped array), but beyond that the structure changes.

In an Expr representing a method, there will be three elements in e.args:

```
julia> e.args[1] # names of arguments as symbols
2-element Array{Any,1}:
 :x
 :y
```

Symbols are a special type for representing the names of variables, constants, functions, and modules. They are a different type from strings because they specifically represent the name of a program construct.

```
julia> e.args[2] # three lists of variable metadata
3-element Array{Any,1}:
 {:z}
 {{:x,Int64,0},{:y,Int64,0},{:z,Int64,18}}
 {}
```

The first list above contains the names of all local variables; we only have one (z) here. The second list contains a tuple for each variable in and argument to the method; each tuple has the variable name, the variable's inferred type, and a number. The number conveys information about how the variable is used, in a machine- (rather than human-) friendly way. The last list is of captured variable names; it's empty in this example.

```
julia> e.args[3] # the body of the method
:(begin  # none, line 2:
        z = (top(box))(Int64,(top(add_int))(x::Int64,y::Int64))::Int64 # line 3:
        return (top(box))(Int64,(top(mul_int))(2,z::Int64))::Int64
    end::Int64)
```

The first two args elements are metadata about the third. While the metadata is very interesting, it isn't necessary right now. The important part is the body of the method, which is the third element. This is another Expr.

```
julia> body = e.args[3]
:(begin  # none, line 2:
        z = (top(box))(Int64,(top(add_int))(x::Int64,y::Int64))::Int64 # line 3:
        return (top(box))(Int64,(top(mul_int))(2,z::Int64))::Int64
    end::Int64)

julia> body.head
:body
```

This Expr has head :body because it's the body of the method.

```
julia> body.typ
Int64
```

The typ is the inferred return type of the method.

```
julia> body.args
4-element Array{Any,1}:
 :( # none, line 2:)
 :(z = (top(box))(Int64,(top(add_int))(x::Int64,y::Int64))::Int64)
 :( # line 3:)
 :(return (top(box))(Int64,(top(mul_int))(2,z::Int64))::Int64)
```

args holds a list of expressions: the list of expressions in the method's body. There are a couple of annotations of line numbers (i.e., :(# line 3:)), but most of the body is setting the value of z (z = x + y) and returning 2 * z. Notice that these operations have been replaced by Int64-specific intrinsic functions. The top(function-name) indicates an intrinsic function; something that is implemented in Julia's code generation, rather than in Julia.

We haven't seen what a loop looks like yet, so let's try that.

```
julia> function lloop(x)
           for x = 1:100
               x *= 2
           end
       end
lloop (generic function with 1 method)

julia> code_typed(lloop, (Int,))[1].args[3]
:(begin  # none, line 2:
        #s120 = $(Expr(:new, UnitRange{Int64}, 1, :(((top(getfield))(Intrinsics,
         :select_value))((top(sle_int))(1,100)::Bool,100,(top(box))(Int64,(top(
         sub_int))(1,1))::Int64)::Int64)))::UnitRange{Int64}
        #s119 = (top(getfield))(#s120::UnitRange{Int64},:start)::Int64        unless
         (top(box))(Bool,(top(not_int))(#s119::Int64 === (top(box))(Int64,(top(
         add_int))((top(getfield))
         (#s120::UnitRange{Int64},:stop)::Int64,1))::Int64::Bool))::Bool goto 1
        2:
        _var0 = #s119::Int64
        _var1 = (top(box))(Int64,(top(add_int))(#s119::Int64,1))::Int64
        x = _var0::Int64
        #s119 = _var1::Int64 # line 3:
        x = (top(box))(Int64,(top(mul_int))(x::Int64,2))::Int64
        3:
        unless (top(box))(Bool,(top(not_int))((top(box))(Bool,(top(not_int))
         (#s119::Int64 === (top(box))(Int64,(top(add_int))((top(getfield))(
         #s120::UnitRange{Int64},:stop)::Int64,1))::Int64::Bool))::Bool))::Bool
         goto 2
        1:       0:
        return
    end::Nothing)
```

You'll notice there's no for or while loop in the body. As the compiler transforms the code from what we wrote to the binary instructions the CPU understands, features that are useful to humans but that are not understood by the CPU (like loops) are removed. The loop has been rewritten as label and goto expressions. The goto has a number in it; each label also has a number. The goto jumps to the the label with the same number.

Detecting and Extracting Loops

We're going to find loops by looking for goto expressions that jump backwards.

We'll need to find the labels and gotos, and figure out which ones match. I'm going to give you the full implementation first. After the wall of code, we'll take it apart and examine the pieces.

```
# This is a function for trying to detect loops in the body of a Method
# Returns lines that are inside one or more loops
function loopcontents(e::Expr)
  b = body(e)
  loops = Int[]
  nesting = 0
  lines = {}
  for i in 1:length(b)
```

```
    if typeof(b[i]) == LabelNode
      l = b[i].label
      jumpback = findnext(x-> (typeof(x) == GotoNode && x.label == l)
                             || (Base.is_expr(x,:gotoifnot) && x.args[end] == l),
                          b, i)
      if jumpback != 0
        push!(loops,jumpback)
        nesting += 1
      end
    end
    if nesting > 0
      push!(lines,(i,b[i]))
    end

    if typeof(b[i]) == GotoNode && in(i,loops)
      splice!(loops,findfirst(loops,i))
      nesting -= 1
    end
  end
  lines
end
```

And now to explain in pieces:

```
b = body(e)
```

We start by getting all the expressions in the body of method, as an Array. body is a function that I've already implemented:

```
# Return the body of a Method.
# Takes an Expr representing a Method,
# returns Vector{Expr}.
function body(e::Expr)
  return e.args[3].args
end
```

And then:

```
loops = Int[]
nesting = 0
lines = {}
```

loops is an Array of label line numbers where gotos that are loops occur. nesting indicates the number of loops we are currently inside. lines is an Array of (index, Expr) tuples.

```
for i in 1:length(b)
  if typeof(b[i]) == LabelNode
    l = b[i].label
    jumpback = findnext(
      x-> (typeof(x) == GotoNode && x.label == l)
          || (Base.is_expr(x,:gotoifnot) && x.args[end] == l),
      b, i)
```

```
    if jumpback != 0
      push!(loops,jumpback)
      nesting += 1
    end
  end
```

We look at each expression in the body of e. If it is a label, we check to see if there is a goto that jumps to this label (and occurs after the current index). If the result of findnext is greater than zero, then such a goto node exists, so we'll add that to loops (the Array of loops we are currently in) and increment our nesting level.

```
  if nesting > 0
    push!(lines,(i,b[i]))
  end
```

If we're currently inside a loop, we push the current line to our array of lines to return.

```
    if typeof(b[i]) == GotoNode && in(i,loops)
      splice!(loops,findfirst(loops,i))
      nesting -= 1
    end
  end
  lines
end
```

If we're at a GotoNode, then we check to see if it's the end of a loop. If so, we remove the entry from loops and reduce our nesting level.

The result of this function is the lines array, an array of (index, value) tuples. This means that each value in the array has an index into the method-body-Expr's body and the value at that index. Each element of lines is an expression that occurred inside a loop.

Finding and Typing Variables

We just finished the function loopcontents which returns the Exprs that are inside loops. Our next function will be loosetypes, which takes a list of Exprs and returns a list of variables that are loosely typed. Later, we'll pass the output of loopcontents into loosetypes.

In each expression that occurred inside a loop, loosetypes searches for occurrences of symbols and their associated types. Variable usages show up as SymbolNodes in the AST; SymbolNodes hold the name and inferred type of the variable.

We can't just check each expression that loopcontents collected to see if it's a SymbolNode. The problem is that each Expr may contain one or more Expr; each Expr may contain one or more SymbolNodes. This means we need to pull out any nested Exprs, so that we can look in each of them for SymbolNodes.

```
# given 'lr', a Vector of expressions (Expr + literals, etc)
# try to find all occurrences of a variables in 'lr'
# and determine their types
function loosetypes(lr::Vector)
  symbols = SymbolNode[]
  for (i,e) in lr
```

```
    if typeof(e) == Expr
      es = copy(e.args)
      while !isempty(es)
        e1 = pop!(es)
        if typeof(e1) == Expr
          append!(es,e1.args)
        elseif typeof(e1) == SymbolNode
          push!(symbols,e1)
        end
      end
    end
  end
  loose_types = SymbolNode[]
  for symnode in symbols
    if !isleaftype(symnode.typ) && typeof(symnode.typ) == UnionType
      push!(loose_types, symnode)
    end
  end
  return loose_types
end

  symbols = SymbolNode[]
  for (i,e) in lr
    if typeof(e) == Expr
      es = copy(e.args)
      while !isempty(es)
        e1 = pop!(es)
        if typeof(e1) == Expr
          append!(es,e1.args)
        elseif typeof(e1) == SymbolNode
          push!(symbols,e1)
        end
      end
    end
  end
```

The while loop goes through the guts of all the Exprs, recursively. Every time the loop finds a SymbolNode, it adds it to the vector symbols.

```
  loose_types = SymbolNode[]
  for symnode in symbols
    if !isleaftype(symnode.typ) && typeof(symnode.typ) == UnionType
      push!(loose_types, symnode)
    end
  end
  return loose_types
end
```

Now we have a list of variables and their types, so it's easy to check if a type is loose. loosetypes does that by looking for a specific kind of non-concrete type, a UnionType. We get a lot more "failing" results when we consider all non-concrete types to be "failing". This is because we're evaluating each method with its annotated argument types, which are likely to be abstract.

Making This Usable

Now that we can do the check on an expression, we should make it easier to call on a user's code. We'll create two ways to call checklooptypes:

1. On a whole function; this will check each method of the given function.
2. On an expression; this will work if the user extracts the results of code_typed themselves.

```
## for a given Function, run checklooptypes on each Method
function checklooptypes(f::Callable;kwargs...)
  lrs = LoopResult[]
  for e in code_typed(f)
    lr = checklooptypes(e)
    if length(lr.lines) > 0 push!(lrs,lr) end
  end
  LoopResults(f.env.name,lrs)
end


# for an Expr representing a Method,
# check that the type of each variable used in a loop
# has a concrete type
checklooptypes(e::Expr;kwargs...) =
 LoopResult(MethodSignature(e),loosetypes(loopcontents(e)))
```

We can see both options work about the same for a function with one method:

```
julia> using TypeCheck

julia> function foo(x::Int)
          s = 0
          for i = 1:x
            s += i/2
          end
          return s
       end
foo (generic function with 1 method)

julia> checklooptypes(foo)
foo(Int64)::Union(Int64,Float64)
    s::Union(Int64,Float64)
    s::Union(Int64,Float64)


julia> checklooptypes(code_typed(foo,(Int,))[1])
(Int64)::Union(Int64,Float64)
    s::Union(Int64,Float64)
    s::Union(Int64,Float64)
```

Pretty Printing

I've skipped an implementation detail here: how did we get the results to print out to the REPL?

First, I made some new types. `LoopResults` is the result of checking a whole function; it has the function name and the results for each method. `LoopResult` is the result of checking one method; it has the argument types and the loosely typed variables.

The `checklooptypes` function returns a `LoopResults`. This type has a function called `show` defined for it. The REPL calls `display` on values it wants to display; `display` will then call our `show` implementation.

This code is important for making this static analysis usable, but it is not doing static analysis. You should use the preferred method for pretty-printing types and output in your implementation language; this is just how it's done in Julia.

```
type LoopResult
  msig::MethodSignature
  lines::Vector{SymbolNode}
  LoopResult(ms::MethodSignature,ls::Vector{SymbolNode}) = new(ms,unique(ls))
end

function Base.show(io::IO, x::LoopResult)
  display(x.msig)
  for snode in x.lines
    println(io,"\t",string(snode.name),"::",string(snode.typ))
  end
end

type LoopResults
  name::Symbol
  methods::Vector{LoopResult}
end

function Base.show(io::IO, x::LoopResults)
  for lr in x.methods
    print(io,string(x.name))
    display(lr)
  end
end
```

20.4   Looking For Unused Variables

Sometimes, as you're typing in your program, you mistype a variable name. The program can't tell that you meant for this to be the same variable that you spelled correctly before; it sees a variable used only one time, where you might see a variable name misspelled. Languages that require variable declarations naturally catch these misspellings, but many dynamic languages don't require declarations and thus need an extra layer of analysis to catch them.

We can find misspelled variable names (and other unused variables) by looking for variables that are only used once—or only used one way.

Here is an example of a little bit of code with one misspelled name.

```
function foo(variable_name::Int)
  sum = 0
  for i=1:variable_name
```

```
        sum += variable_name
    end
    variable_nme = sum
    return variable_name
end
```

This kind of mistake can cause problems in your code that are only discovered when it's run. Let's assume you misspell each variable name only once. We can separate variable usages into writes and reads. If the misspelling is a write (i.e., worng = 5), then no error will be thrown; you'll just be silently putting the value in the wrong variable—and it could be frustrating to find the bug. If the misspelling is a read (i.e., right = worng + 2), then you'll get a runtime error when the code is run; we'd like to have a static warning for this, so that you can find this error sooner, but you will still have to wait until you run the code to see the problem.

As code becomes longer and more complicated, it becomes harder to spot the mistake—unless you have the help of static analysis.

Left-Hand Side and Right-Hand Side

Another way to talk about "read" and "write" usages is to call them "right-hand side" (RHS) and "left-hand side" (LHS) usages. This refers to where the variable is relative to the = sign.

Here are some usages of x:

- Left-hand side:

    - x = 2
    - x = y + 22
    - x = x + y + 2
    - x += 2 (which de-sugars to x = x + 2)

- Right-hand side:

    - y = x + 22
    - x = x + y + 2
    - x += 2 (which de-sugars to x = x + 2)
    - 2 * x
    - x

Notice that expressions like x = x + y + 2 and x += 2 appear in both sections, since x appears on both sides of the = sign.

Looking for Single-Use Variables

There are two cases we need to look for:

1. Variables used once.
2. Variables used only on the LHS or only on the RHS.

We'll look for all variable usages, but we'll look for LHS and RHS usages separately, to cover both cases.

Finding LHS Usages

To be on the LHS, a variable needs to have an = sign to be to the left of. This means we can look for = signs in the AST, and then look to the left of them to find the relevant variable.

In the AST, an = is an Expr with the head : (=). (The parentheses are there to make it clear that this is the symbol for = and not another operator, :=.) The first value in args will be the variable name on its LHS. Because we're looking at an AST that the compiler has already cleaned up, there will (nearly) always be just a single symbol to the left of our = sign.

Let's see what that means in code:

```julia
julia> :(x = 5)
:(x = 5)

julia> :(x = 5).head
:(=)

julia> :(x = 5).args
2-element Array{Any,1}:
  :x
 5

julia> :(x = 5).args[1]
:x
```

Below is the full implementation, followed by an explanation.

```julia
# Return a list of all variables used on the left-hand-side of assignment (=)
#
# Arguments:
#   e: an Expr representing a Method, as from code_typed
#
# Returns:
#   a Set{Symbol}, where each element appears on the LHS of an assignment in e.
#
function find_lhs_variables(e::Expr)
  output = Set{Symbol}()
  for ex in body(e)
    if Base.is_expr(ex,:(=))
      push!(output,ex.args[1])
    end
  end
  return output
end
```

```julia
  output = Set{Symbol}()
```

We have a set of Symbols; those are variables names we've found on the LHS.

```julia
  for ex in body(e)
    if Base.is_expr(ex,:(=))
      push!(output,ex.args[1])
    end
  end
```

We aren't digging deeper into the expressions, because the code_typed AST is pretty flat; loops and ifs have been converted to flat statements with gotos for control flow. There won't be any assignments hiding inside function calls' arguments. This code will fail if anything more than a symbol is on the left of the equal sign. This misses two specific edge cases: array accesses (like a[5], which will be represented as a :ref expression) and properties (like a.head, which will be represented as a :. expression). These will still always have the relevant symbol as the first value in their args, it might just be buried a bit (as in a.property.name.head.other_property). This code doesn't handle those cases, but a couple lines of code inside the if statement could fix that.

```
push!(output,ex.args[1])
```

When we find a LHS variable usage, we push! the variable name into the Set. The Set will make sure that we only have one copy of each name.

Finding RHS usages

To find all the other variable usages, we also need to look at each Expr. This is a bit more involved, because we care about basically all the Exprs, not just the :(=) ones and because we have to dig into nested Exprs (to handle nested function calls).

Here is the full implementation, with explanation following.

```
# Given an Expression, finds variables used in it (on right-hand-side)
#
# Arguments: e: an Expr
#
# Returns: a Set{Symbol}, where each e is used in a rhs expression in e
#
function find_rhs_variables(e::Expr)
  output = Set{Symbol}()

  if e.head == :lambda
    for ex in body(e)
      union!(output,find_rhs_variables(ex))
    end
  elseif e.head == :(=)
    for ex in e.args[2:end]  # skip lhs
      union!(output,find_rhs_variables(ex))
    end
  elseif e.head == :return
    output = find_rhs_variables(e.args[1])
  elseif e.head == :call
    start = 2  # skip function name
    e.args[1] == TopNode(:box) && (start = 3)  # skip type name
    for ex in e.args[start:end]
      union!(output,find_rhs_variables(ex))
    end
  elseif e.head == :if
   for ex in e.args # want to check condition, too
     union!(output,find_rhs_variables(ex))
   end
  elseif e.head == :(::)
```

```
    output = find_rhs_variables(e.args[1])
  end

  return output
end
```

The main structure of this function is a large if-else statement, where each case handles a different head-symbol.

```
output = Set{Symbol}()
```

`output` is the set of variable names, which we will return at the end of the function. Since we only care about the fact that each of these variables has be read at least once, using a `Set` frees us from worrying about the uniqueness of each name.

```
if e.head == :lambda
  for ex in body(e)
    union!(output,find_rhs_variables(ex))
  end
```

This is the first condition in the if-else statement. A `:lambda` represents the body of a function. We recurse on the body of the definition, which should get all the RHS variable usages in the definition.

```
elseif e.head == :(=)
  for ex in e.args[2:end]  # skip lhs
    union!(output,find_rhs_variables(ex))
  end
```

If the head is `:(=)`, then the expression is an assignment. We skip the first element of args because that's the variable being assigned to. For each of the remaining expressions, we recursively find the RHS variables and add them to our set.

```
elseif e.head == :return
  output = find_rhs_variables(e.args[1])
```

If this is a return statement, then the first element of `args` is the expression whose value is returned; we'll add any variables in there into our set.

```
elseif e.head == :call
  # skip function name
  for ex in e.args[2:end]
    union!(output,find_rhs_variables(ex))
  end
```

For function calls, we want to get all variables used in all the arguments to the call. We skip the function name, which is the first element of `args`.

```
elseif e.head == :if
  for ex in e.args # want to check condition, too
    union!(output,find_rhs_variables(ex))
  end
```

An Expr representing an if statement has the head value :if. We want to get variable usages from all the expressions in the body of the if statement, so we recurse on each element of args.

```
elseif e.head == :(::)
  output = find_rhs_variables(e.args[1])
end
```

The :(::) operator is used to add type annotations. The first argument is the expression or variable being annotated; we check for variable usages in the annotated expression.

```
return output
```

At the end of the function, we return the set of RHS variable usages.

There's a little more code that simplifies the method above. Because the version above only handles Exprs, but some of the values that get passed recursively may not be Exprs, we need a few more methods to handle the other possible types appropriately.

```
# Recursive Base Cases, to simplify control flow in the Expr version
find_rhs_variables(a) = Set{Symbol}()  # unhandled, should be immediate val e.g. Int
find_rhs_variables(s::Symbol) = Set{Symbol}([s])
find_rhs_variables(s::SymbolNode) = Set{Symbol}([s.name])
```

Putting It Together

Now that we have the two functions defined above, we can use them together to find variables that are either only read from or only written to. The function that finds them will be called unused_locals.

```
function unused_locals(e::Expr)
  lhs = find_lhs_variables(e)
  rhs = find_rhs_variables(e)
  setdiff(lhs,rhs)
end
```

unused_locals will return a set of variable names. It's easy to write a function that determines whether the output of unused_locals counts as a "pass" or not. If the set is empty, the method passes. If all the methods of a function pass, then the function passes. The function check_locals below implements this logic.

```
check_locals(f::Callable) = all([check_locals(e) for e in code_typed(f)])
check_locals(e::Expr) = isempty(unused_locals(e))
```

20.5   Conclusion

We've done two static analyses of Julia code—one based on types and one based on variable usages.

Statically-typed languages already do the kind of work our type-based analysis did; additional type-based static analysis is mostly useful in dynamically typed languages. There have been (mostly research) projects to build static type inference systems for languages including Python, Ruby, and Lisp. These systems are usually built around optional type annotations; you can have static types when you want them, and fall back to dynamic typing when you don't. This is especially helpful for integrating some static typing into existing code bases.

Non-typed-based checks, like our variable-usage one, are applicable to both dynamically and statically typed languages. However, many statically typed languages, like C++ and Java, require you to declare variables, and already give basic warnings like the ones we created. There are still custom checks that can be written; for example, checks that are specific to your project's style guide or extra safety precautions based on security policies.

While Julia does have great tools for enabling static analysis, it's not alone. Lisp, of course, is famous for having the code be a data structure of nested lists, so it tends to be easy to get at the AST. Java also exposes its AST, although the AST is much more complicated than Lisp's. Some languages or language tool-chains are not designed to allow mere users to poke around at internal representations. For open-source tool chains (especially well-commented ones), one option is to add hooks to the enviroment that let you access the AST.

In cases where that won't work, the final fallback is writing a parser yourself; this is to be avoided when possible. It's a lot of work to cover the full grammar of most programming languages, and you'll have to update it yourself as new features are added to the language (rather than getting the updates automatically from upstream). Depending on the checks you want to do, you may be able to get away with parsing only some lines or a subset of language features, which would greatly decrease the cost of writing your own parser.

Hopefully, your new understanding of how static analysis tools are written will help you understand the tools you use on your code, and maybe inspire you to write one of your own.

## chapter 21

A Template Engine
Ned Batchelder

21.1   Introduction

Most programs contain a lot of logic, and a little bit of literal textual data. Programming languages are designed to be good for this sort of programming. But some programming tasks involve only a little bit of logic, and a great deal of textual data. For these tasks, we'd like to have a tool better suited to these text-heavy problems. A template engine is such a tool. In this chapter, we build a simple template engine.

The most common example of one of these text-heavy tasks is in web applications. An important phase in any web application is generating HTML to be served to the browser. Very few HTML pages are completely static: they involve at least a small amount of dynamic data, such as the user's name. Usually, they contain a great deal of dynamic data: product listings, friends' news updates, and so on.

At the same time, every HTML page contains large swaths of static text. And these pages are large, containing tens of thousands of bytes of text. The web application developer has a problem to solve: how best to generate a large string containing a mix of static and dynamic data? To add to the problem, the static text is actually HTML markup that is authored by another member of the team, the front-end designer, who wants to be able to work with it in familiar ways.

For purposes of illustration, let's imagine we want to produce this toy HTML:

```
<p>Welcome, Charlie!</p>
<p>Products:</p>
<ul>
    <li>Apple: $1.00</li>
    <li>Fig: $1.50</li>
    <li>Pomegranate: $3.25</li>
</ul>
```

Here, the user's name will be dynamic, as will the names and prices of the products. Even the number of products isn't fixed: at another moment, there could be more or fewer products to display.

One way to make this HTML would be to have string constants in our code, and join them together to produce the page. Dynamic data would be inserted with string substitution of some sort. Some of our dynamic data is repetitive, like our lists of products. This means we'll have chunks of HTML that repeat, so those will have to be handled separately and combined with the rest of the page.

Producing our toy page in this way might look like this:

```
# The main HTML for the whole page.
PAGE_HTML = """
<p>Welcome, {name}!</p>
<p>Products:</p>
<ul>
{products}
</ul>
"""

# The HTML for each product displayed.
PRODUCT_HTML = "<li>{prodname}: {price}</li>\n"

def make_page(username, products):
    product_html = ""
    for prodname, price in products:
        product_html += PRODUCT_HTML.format(
            prodname=prodname, price=format_price(price))
    html = PAGE_HTML.format(name=username, products=product_html)
    return html
```

This works, but we have a mess on our hands. The HTML is in multiple string constants embedded in our application code. The logic of the page is hard to see because the static text is broken into separate pieces. The details of how data is formatted is lost in the Python code. In order to modify the HTML page, our front-end designer would need to be able to edit Python code to make HTML changes. Imagine what the code would look like if the page were ten (or one hundred) times more complicated; it would quickly become unworkable.

21.2 Templates

The better way to produce HTML pages is with *templates*. The HTML page is authored as a template, meaning that the file is mostly static HTML, with dynamic pieces embedded in it using special notation. Our toy page above could look like this as a template:

```
<p>Welcome, {{user_name}}!</p>
<p>Products:</p>
<ul>
{% for product in product_list %}
    <li>{{ product.name }}:
        {{ product.price|format_price }}</li>
{% endfor %}
</ul>
```

Here the focus is on the HTML text, with logic embedded in the HTML. Contrast this document-centric approach with our logic-centric code above. Our earlier program was mostly Python code, with HTML embedded in the Python logic. Here our program is mostly static HTML markup.

The mostly-static style used in templates is the opposite of how most programming languages work. For example, with Python, most of the source file is executable code, and if you need literal static text, you embed it in a string literal:

```
def hello():
    print("Hello, world!")

hello()
```

When Python reads this source file, it interprets text like `def hello():` as instructions to be executed. The double quote character in `print("Hello, world!")` indicates that the following text is meant literally, until the closing double quote. This is how most programming languages work: mostly dynamic, with some static pieces embedded in the instructions. The static pieces are indicated by the double-quote notation.

A template language flips this around: the template file is mostly static literal text, with special notation to indicate the executable dynamic parts.

```
<p>Welcome, {{user_name}}!</p>
```

Here the text is meant to appear literally in the resulting HTML page, until the '{{' indicates a switch into dynamic mode, where the `user_name` variable will be substituted into the output.

String formatting functions such as Python's `"foo = {foo}!".format(foo=17)` are examples of mini-languages used to create text from a string literal and the data to be inserted. Templates extend this idea to include constructs like conditionals and loops, but the difference is only of degree.

These files are called templates because they are used to produce many pages with similar structure but differing details.

To use HTML templates in our programs, we need a *template engine*: a function that takes a static template describing the structure and static content of the page, and a dynamic *context* that provides the dynamic data to plug into the template. The template engine combines the template and the context to produce a complete string of HTML. The job of a template engine is to interpret the template, replacing the dynamic pieces with real data.

By the way, there's often nothing particular about HTML in a template engine, it could be used to produce any textual result. For example, they are also used to produce plain-text email messages. But usually they are used for HTML, and occasionally have HTML-specific features, such as escaping, which makes it possible to insert values into the HTML without worrying about which characters are special in HTML.

21.3   Supported Syntax

Template engines vary in the syntax they support. Our template syntax is based on Django, a popular web framework. Since we are implementing our engine in Python, some Python concepts will appear in our syntax. We've already seen some of this syntax in our toy example at the top of the chapter, but this is a quick summary of all of the syntax we'll implement.

Data from the context is inserted using double curly braces:

```
<p>Welcome, {{user_name}}!</p>
```

The data available to the template is provided in the context when the template is rendered. More on that later.

Template engines usually provide access to elements within data using a simplified and relaxed syntax. In Python, these expressions all have different effects:

```
dict["key"]
obj.attr
obj.method()
```

In our template syntax, all of these operations are expressed with a dot:

```
dict.key
obj.attr
obj.method
```

The dot will access object attributes or dictionary values, and if the resulting value is callable, it's automatically called. This is different than the Python code, where you need to use different syntax for those operations. This results in simpler template syntax:

```
<p>The price is: {{product.price}}, with a {{product.discount}}% discount.</p>
```

You can use functions called *filters* to modify values. Filters are invoked with a pipe character:

```
<p>Short name: {{story.subject|slugify|lower}}</p>
```

Building interesting pages usually requires at least a small amount of decision-making, so conditionals are available:

```
{% if user.is_logged_in %}
    <p>Welcome, {{ user.name }}!</p>
{% endif %}
```

Looping lets us include collections of data in our pages:

```
<p>Products:</p>
<ul>
{% for product in product_list %}
    <li>{{ product.name }}: {{ product.price|format_price }}</li>
{% endfor %}
</ul>
```

As with other programming languages, conditionals and loops can be nested to build complex logical structures.

Lastly, so that we can document our templates, comments appear between brace-hashes:

```
{# This is the best template ever! #}
```

21.4   Implementation Approaches

In broad strokes, the template engine will have two main phases: *parsing* the template, and then *rendering* the template.

Rendering the template specifically involves:

- Managing the dynamic context, the source of the data
- Executing the logic elements
- Implementing dot access and filter execution

The question of what to pass from the parsing phase to the rendering phase is key. What does parsing produce that can be rendered? There are two main options; we'll call them *interpretation* and *compilation*, using the terms loosely from other language implementations.

In an interpretation model, parsing produces a data structure representing the structure of the template. The rendering phase walks that data structure, assembling the result text based on the instructions it finds. For a real-world example, the Django template engine uses this approach.

In a compilation model, parsing produces some form of directly executable code. The rendering phase executes that code, producing the result. Jinja2 and Mako are two examples of template engines that use the compilation approach.

Our implementation of the engine uses compilation: we compile the template into Python code. When run, the Python code assembles the result.

The template engine described here was originally written as part of coverage.py, to produce HTML reports. In coverage.py, there are only a few templates, and they are used over and over to produce many files from the same template. Overall, the program ran faster if the templates were compiled to Python code, because even though the compilation process was a bit more complicated, it only had to run once, while the execution of the compiled code ran many times, and was faster than interpreting a data structure many times.

It's a bit more complicated to compile the template to Python, but it's not as bad as you might think. And besides, as any developer can tell you, it's more fun to write a program to write a program than it is to write a program!

Our template compiler is a small example of a general technique called code generation. Code generation underlies many powerful and flexible tools, including programming language compilers. Code generation can get complex, but is a useful technique to have in your toolbox.

Another application of templates might prefer the interpreted approach, if templates will be used only a few times each. Then the effort to compile to Python won't pay off in the long run, and a simpler interpretation process might perform better overall.

21.5 Compiling to Python

Before we get to the code of the template engine, let's look at the code it produces. The parsing phase will convert a template into a Python function. Here is our small template again:

```
<p>Welcome, {{user_name}}!</p>
<p>Products:</p>
<ul>
{% for product in product_list %}
    <li>{{ product.name }}:
        {{ product.price|format_price }}</li>
{% endfor %}
</ul>
```

Our engine will compile this template to Python code. The resulting Python code looks unusual, because we've chosen some shortcuts that produce slightly faster code. Here is the Python (slightly reformatted for readability):

```
def render_function(context, do_dots):
    c_user_name = context['user_name']
    c_product_list = context['product_list']
```

```
    c_format_price = context['format_price']

    result = []
    append_result = result.append
    extend_result = result.extend
    to_str = str

    extend_result([
        '<p>Welcome, ',
        to_str(c_user_name),
        '!</p>\n<p>Products:</p>\n<ul>\n'
    ])
    for c_product in c_product_list:
        extend_result([
            '\n    <li>',
            to_str(do_dots(c_product, 'name')),
            ':\n            ',
            to_str(c_format_price(do_dots(c_product, 'price'))),
            '</li>\n'
        ])
    append_result('\n</ul>\n')
    return ''.join(result)
```

Each template is converted into a `render_function` function that takes a dictionary of data called the context. The body of the function starts by unpacking the data from the context into local names, because they are faster for repeated use. All the context data goes into locals with a `c_` prefix so that we can use other local names without fear of collisions.

The result of the template will be a string. The fastest way to build a string from parts is to create a list of strings, and join them together at the end. `result` will be the list of strings. Because we're going to add strings to this list, we capture its append and `extend` methods in the local names `result_append` and `result_extend`. The last local we create is a `to_str` shorthand for the `str` built-in.

These kinds of shortcuts are unusual. Let's look at them more closely. In Python, a method call on an object like `result.append("hello")` is executed in two steps. First, the append attribute is fetched from the result object: `result.append`. Then the value fetched is invoked as a function, passing it the argument `"hello"`. Although we're used to seeing those steps performed together, they really are separate. If you save the result of the first step, you can perform the second step on the saved value. So these two Python snippets do the same thing:

```
# The way we're used to seeing it:
result.append("hello")

# But this works the same:
append_result = result.append
append_result("hello")
```

In the template engine code, we've split it out this way so that we only do the first step once, no matter how many times we do the second step. This saves us a small amount of time, because we avoid taking the time to look up the append attribute.

This is an example of a micro-optimization: an unusual coding technique that gains us tiny improvements in speed. Micro-optimizations can be less readable, or more confusing, so they are only justified for code that is a proven performance bottleneck. Developers disagree on how much micro-optimization is justified, and some beginners overdo it. The optimizations here were added only after timing experiments showed that they improved performance, even if only a little bit. Micro-optimizations can be instructive, as they make use of some exotic aspects of Python, but don't over-use them in your own code.

The shortcut for `str` is also a micro-optimization. Names in Python can be local to a function, global to a module, or built-in to Python. Looking up a local name is faster than looking up a global or a built-in. We're used to the fact that `str` is a builtin that is always available, but Python still has to look up the name `str` each time it is used. Putting it in a local saves us another small slice of time because locals are faster than builtins.

Once those shortcuts are defined, we're ready for the Python lines created from our particular template. Strings will be added to the result list using the `append_result` or `extend_result` shorthands, depending on whether we have one string to add, or more than one. Literal text in the template becomes a simple string literal.

Having both append and extend adds complexity, but remember we're aiming for the fastest execution of the template, and using extend for one item means making a new list of one item so that we can pass it to extend.

Expressions in `{{ ... }}` are computed, converted to strings, and added to the result. Dots in the expression are handled by the `do_dots` function passed into our function, because the meaning of the dotted expressions depends on the data in the context: it could be attribute access or item access, and it could be a callable.

The logical structures `{% if ... %}` and `{% for ... %}` are converted into Python conditionals and loops. The expression in the `{% if/for ... %}` tag will become the expression in the `if` or `for` statement, and the contents up until the `{% end... %}` tag will become the body of the statement.

21.6   Writing the Engine

Now that we understand what the engine will do, let's walk through the implementation.

The Templite class

The heart of the template engine is the Templite class. (Get it? It's a template, but it's lite!)

The Templite class has a small interface. You construct a Templite object with the text of the template, then later you can use the `render` method on it to render a particular context, the dictionary of data, through the template:

```
# Make a Templite object.
templite = Templite('''
    <h1>Hello {{name|upper}}!</h1>
    {% for topic in topics %}
        <p>You are interested in {{topic}}.</p>
    {% endfor %}
    ''',
    {'upper': str.upper},
)

# Later, use it to render some data.
```

```
text = templite.render({
    'name': "Ned",
    'topics': ['Python', 'Geometry', 'Juggling'],
})
```

We pass the text of the template when the object is created so that we can do the compile step just once, and later call render many times to reuse the compiled results.

The constructor also accepts a dictionary of values, an initial context. These are stored in the Templite object, and will be available when the template is later rendered. These are good for defining functions or constants we want to be available everywhere, like upper in the previous example.

Before we discuss the implementation of Templite, we have a helper to define first: CodeBuilder.

CodeBuilder

The bulk of the work in our engine is parsing the template and producing the necessary Python code. To help with producing the Python, we have the CodeBuilder class, which handles the bookkeeping for us as we construct the Python code. It adds lines of code, manages indentation, and finally gives us values from the compiled Python.

One CodeBuilder object is responsible for a complete chunk of Python code. As used by our template engine, the chunk of Python is always a single complete function definition. But the CodeBuilder class makes no assumption that it will only be one function. This keeps the CodeBuilder code more general, and less coupled to the rest of the template engine code.

As we'll see, we also use nested CodeBuilders to make it possible to put code at the beginning of the function even though we don't know what it will be until we are nearly done.

A CodeBuilder object keeps a list of strings that will together be the final Python code. The only other state it needs is the current indentation level:

```
class CodeBuilder(object):
    """Build source code conveniently."""

    def __init__(self, indent=0):
        self.code = []
        self.indent_level = indent
```

CodeBuilder doesn't do much. add_line adds a new line of code, which automatically indents the text to the current indentation level, and supplies a newline:

```
def add_line(self, line):
    """Add a line of source to the code.

    Indentation and newline will be added for you, don't provide them.

    """
    self.code.extend([" " * self.indent_level, line, "\n"])
```

indent and dedent increase or decrease the indentation level:

```
INDENT_STEP = 4      # PEP8 says so!

def indent(self):
```

438   A Template Engine

```
    """Increase the current indent for following lines."""
    self.indent_level += self.INDENT_STEP

def dedent(self):
    """Decrease the current indent for following lines."""
    self.indent_level -= self.INDENT_STEP
```

add_section is managed by another CodeBuilder object. This lets us keep a reference to a place in the code, and add text to it later. The self.code list is mostly a list of strings, but will also hold references to these sections:

```
def add_section(self):
    """Add a section, a sub-CodeBuilder."""
    section = CodeBuilder(self.indent_level)
    self.code.append(section)
    return section
```

__str__ produces a single string with all the code. This simply joins together all the strings in self.code. Note that because self.code can contain sections, this might call other CodeBuilder objects recursively:

```
def __str__(self):
    return "".join(str(c) for c in self.code)
```

get_globals yields the final values by executing the code. This stringifies the object, executes it to get its definitions, and returns the resulting values:

```
def get_globals(self):
    """Execute the code, and return a dict of globals it defines."""
    # A check that the caller really finished all the blocks they started.
    assert self.indent_level == 0
    # Get the Python source as a single string.
    python_source = str(self)
    # Execute the source, defining globals, and return them.
    global_namespace = {}
    exec(python_source, global_namespace)
    return global_namespace
```

This last method uses some exotic features of Python. The exec function executes a string containing Python code. The second argument to exec is a dictionary that will collect up the globals defined by the code. So for example, if we do this:

```
python_source = """\
SEVENTEEN = 17

def three():
    return 3
"""
global_namespace = {}
exec(python_source, global_namespace)
```

then global_namespace['SEVENTEEN'] is 17, and global_namespace['three'] is an actual function named three.

Although we only use CodeBuilder to produce one function, there's nothing here that limits it to that use. This makes the class simpler to implement, and easier to understand.

CodeBuilder lets us create a chunk of Python source code, and has no specific knowledge about our template engine at all. We could use it in such a way that three different functions would be defined in the Python, and then get_globals would return a dict of three values, the three functions. As it happens, our template engine only needs to define one function. But it's better software design to keep that implementation detail in the template engine code, and out of our CodeBuilder class.

Even as we're actually using it—to define a single function—having get_globals return the dictionary keeps the code more modular because it doesn't need to know the name of the function we've defined. Whatever function name we define in our Python source, we can retrieve that name from the dict returned by get_globals.

Now we can get into the implementation of the Templite class itself, and see how and where CodeBuilder is used.

The Templite class implementation

Most of our code is in the Templite class. As we've discussed, it has both a compilation and a rendering phase.

Compiling

All of the work to compile the template into a Python function happens in the Templite constructor. First the contexts are saved away:

```
def __init__(self, text, *contexts):
    """Construct a Templite with the given `text`.

    `contexts` are dictionaries of values to use for future renderings.
    These are good for filters and global values.

    """
    self.context = {}
    for context in contexts:
        self.context.update(context)
```

Notice we used *contexts as the parameter. The asterisk denotes that any number of positional arguments will be packed into a tuple and passed in as contexts. This is called argument unpacking, and means that the caller can provide a number of different context dictionaries. Now any of these calls are valid:

```
t = Templite(template_text)
t = Templite(template_text, context1)
t = Templite(template_text, context1, context2)
```

The context arguments (if any) are supplied to the constructor as a tuple of contexts. We can then iterate over the contexts tuple, dealing with each of them in turn. We simply create one combined dictionary called self.context which has the contents of all of the supplied contexts. If duplicate names are provided in the contexts, the last one wins.

To make our compiled function as fast as possible, we extract context variables into Python locals. We'll get those names by keeping a set of variable names we encounter, but we also need to track the names of variables defined in the template, the loop variables:

```
self.all_vars = set()
self.loop_vars = set()
```

Later we'll see how these get used to help construct the prologue of our function. First, we'll use the CodeBuilder class we wrote earlier to start to build our compiled function:

```
code = CodeBuilder()

code.add_line("def render_function(context, do_dots):")
code.indent()
vars_code = code.add_section()
code.add_line("result = []")
code.add_line("append_result = result.append")
code.add_line("extend_result = result.extend")
code.add_line("to_str = str")
```

Here we construct our CodeBuilder object, and start writing lines into it. Our Python function will be called render_function, and will take two arguments: context is the data dictionary it should use, and do_dots is a function implementing dot attribute access.

The context here is the combination of the data context passed to the Templite constructor, and the data context passed to the render function. It's the complete set of data available to the template that we made in the Templite constructor.

Notice that CodeBuilder is very simple: it doesn't "know" about function definitions, just lines of code. This keeps CodeBuilder simple, both in its implementation, and in its use. We can read our generated code here without having to mentally interpolate too many specialized CodeBuilder.

We create a section called vars_code. Later we'll write the variable extraction lines into that section. The vars_code object lets us save a place in the function that can be filled in later when we have the information we need.

Then four fixed lines are written, defining a result list, shortcuts for the methods to append to or extend that list, and a shortcut for the str() builtin. As we discussed earlier, this odd step squeezes just a little bit more performance out of our rendering function.

The reason we have both the append and the extend shortcut is so we can use the most effective method, depending on whether we have one line to add to our result, or more than one.

Next we define an inner function to help us with buffering output strings:

```
buffered = []
def flush_output():
    """Force 'buffered' to the code builder."""
    if len(buffered) == 1:
        code.add_line("append_result(%s)" % buffered[0])
    elif len(buffered) > 1:
        code.add_line("extend_result([%s])" % ", ".join(buffered))
    del buffered[:]
```

As we create chunks of output that need to go into our compiled function, we need to turn them into function calls that append to our result. We'd like to combine repeated append calls into one extend call. This is another micro-optimization. To make this possible, we buffer the chunks.

The buffered list holds strings that are yet to be written to our function source code. As our template compilation proceeds, we'll append strings to buffered, and flush them to the function source when we reach control flow points, like if statements, or the beginning or ends of loops.

The flush_output function is a *closure*, which is a fancy word for a function that refers to variables outside of itself. Here flush_output refers to buffered and code. This simplifies our calls to the function: we don't have to tell flush_output what buffer to flush, or where to flush it; it knows all that implicitly.

If only one string has been buffered, then the append_result shortcut is used to append it to the result. If more than one is buffered, then the extend_result shortcut is used, with all of them, to add them to the result. Then the buffered list is cleared so more strings can be buffered.

The rest of the compiling code will add lines to the function by appending them to buffered, and eventually call flush_output to write them to the CodeBuilder.

With this function in place, we can have a line of code in our compiler like this:

```
buffered.append("'hello'")
```

which will mean that our compiled Python function will have this line:

```
append_result('hello')
```

which will add the string hello to the rendered output of the template. We have multiple levels of abstraction here which can be difficult to keep straight. The compiler uses buffered.append("'hello'"), which creates append_result('hello') in the compiled Python function, which when run, appends hello to the template result.

Back to our Templite class. As we parse control structures, we want to check that they are properly nested. The ops_stack list is a stack of strings:

```
ops_stack = []
```

When we encounter an {% if .. %} tag (for example), we'll push 'if' onto the stack. When we find an {% endif %} tag, we can pop the stack and report an error if there was no 'if' at the top of the stack.

Now the real parsing begins. We split the template text into a number of tokens using a regular expression, or *regex*. Regexes can be daunting: they are a very compact notation for complex pattern matching. They are also very efficient, since the complexity of matching the pattern is implemented in C in the regular expression engine, rather than in your own Python code. Here's our regex:

```
tokens = re.split(r"(?s)({{.*?}}|{%.*?%}|{#.*?#})", text)
```

This looks complicated; let's break it down.

The re.split function will split a string using a regex. Our pattern is parenthesized, so the matches will be used to split the string, and will also be returned as pieces in the split list. Our pattern will match our tag syntaxes, but we've parenthesized it so that the string will be split at the tags, and the tags will also be returned.

The (?s) flag in the regex means that a dot should match even a newline. Next we have our parenthesized group of three alternatives: {{.*?}} matches an expression, {%.*?%} matches a tag, and {#.*?#} matches a comment. In all of these, we use .*? to match any number of characters, but the shortest sequence that matches.

The result of re.split is a list of strings. For example, this template text:

```
<p>Topics for {{name}}: {% for t in topics %}{{t}}, {% endfor %}</p>
```

would be split into these pieces:

```
[
    '<p>Topics for ',           # literal
    '{{name}}',                 # expression
    ': ',                       # literal
    '{% for t in topics %}',    # tag
    '',                         # literal (empty)
    '{{t}}',                    # expression
    ', ',                       # literal
    '{% endfor %}',             # tag
    '</p>'                      # literal
]
```

Once the text is split into tokens like this, we can loop over the tokens, and deal with each in turn. By splitting them according to their type, we can handle each type separately.

The compilation code is a loop over these tokens:

```
for token in tokens:
```

Each token is examined to see which of the four cases it is. Just looking at the first two characters is enough. The first case is a comment, which is easy to handle: just ignore it and move on to the next token:

```
if token.startswith('{#'):
    # Comment: ignore it and move on.
    continue
```

For the case of {{...}} expressions, we cut off the two braces at the front and back, strip off the white space, and pass the entire expression to _expr_code:

```
elif token.startswith('{{'):
    # An expression to evaluate.
    expr = self._expr_code(token[2:-2].strip())
    buffered.append("to_str(%s)" % expr)
```

The _expr_code method will compile the template expression into a Python expression. We'll see that function later. We use the to_str function to force the expression's value to be a string, and add that to our result.

The third case is the big one: {% ... %} tags. These are control structures that will become Python control structures. First we have to flush our buffered output lines, then we extract a list of words from the tag:

```
elif token.startswith('{%'):
    # Action tag: split into words and parse further.
    flush_output()
    words = token[2:-2].strip().split()
```

Now we have three sub-cases, based on the first word in the tag: if, for, or end. The if case shows our simple error handling and code generation:

```
if words[0] == 'if':
    # An if statement: evaluate the expression to determine if.
    if len(words) != 2:
        self._syntax_error("Don't understand if", token)
    ops_stack.append('if')
    code.add_line("if %s:" % self._expr_code(words[1]))
    code.indent()
```

The if tag should have a single expression, so the words list should have only two elements in it. If it doesn't, we use the _syntax_error helper method to raise a syntax error exception. We push 'if' onto ops_stack so that we can check the endif tag. The expression part of the if tag is compiled to a Python expression with _expr_code, and is used as the conditional expression in a Python if statement.

The second tag type is for, which will be compiled to a Python for statement:

```
elif words[0] == 'for':
    # A loop: iterate over expression result.
    if len(words) != 4 or words[2] != 'in':
        self._syntax_error("Don't understand for", token)
    ops_stack.append('for')
    self._variable(words[1], self.loop_vars)
    code.add_line(
        "for c_%s in %s:" % (
            words[1],
            self._expr_code(words[3])
        )
    )
    code.indent()
```

We do a check of the syntax and push 'for' onto the stack. The _variable method checks the syntax of the variable, and adds it to the set we provide. This is how we collect up the names of all the variables during compilation. Later we'll need to write the prologue of our function, where we'll unpack all the variable names we get from the context. To do that correctly, we need to know the names of all the variables we encountered, self.all_vars, and the names of all the variables defined by loops, self.loop_vars.

We add one line to our function source, a for statement. All of our template variables are turned into Python variables by prepending c_ to them, so that we know they won't collide with other names we're using in our Python function. We use _expr_code to compile the iteration expression from the template into an iteration expression in Python.

The last kind of tag we handle is an end tag; either {% endif %} or {% endfor %}. The effect on our compiled function source is the same: simply unindent to end the if or for statement that was started earlier:

```
elif words[0].startswith('end'):
    # Endsomething.  Pop the ops stack.
    if len(words) != 1:
        self._syntax_error("Don't understand end", token)
    end_what = words[0][3:]
    if not ops_stack:
        self._syntax_error("Too many ends", token)
```

```
            start_what = ops_stack.pop()
            if start_what != end_what:
                self._syntax_error("Mismatched end tag", end_what)
            code.dedent()
```

Notice here that the actual work needed for the end tag is one line: unindent the function source. The rest of this clause is all error checking to make sure that the template is properly formed. This isn't unusual in program translation code.

Speaking of error handling, if the tag isn't an `if`, a `for`, or an `end`, then we don't know what it is, so raise a syntax error:

```
        else:
            self._syntax_error("Don't understand tag", words[0])
```

We're done with the three different special syntaxes (`{{...}}`, `{#...#}`, and `{%...%}`). What's left is literal content. We'll add the literal string to the buffered output, using the `repr` built-in function to produce a Python string literal for the token:

```
        else:
            # Literal content.  If it isn't empty, output it.
            if token:
                buffered.append(repr(token))
```

If we didn't use `repr`, then we'd end up with lines like this in our compiled function:

```
append_result(abc)       # Error! abc isn't defined
```

We need the value to be quoted like this:

```
append_result('abc')
```

The repr function supplies the quotes around the string for us, and also provides backslashes where needed:

```
append_result('"Don\'t you like my hat?" he asked.')
```

Notice that we first check if the token is an empty string with `if token:`, since there's no point adding an empty string to the output. Because our regex is splitting on tag syntax, adjacent tags will have an empty token between them. The check here is an easy way to avoid putting useless `append_result("")` statements into our compiled function.

That completes the loop over all the tokens in the template. When the loop is done, all of the template has been processed. We have one last check to make: if `ops_stack` isn't empty, then we must be missing an end tag. Then we flush the buffered output to the function source:

```
        if ops_stack:
            self._syntax_error("Unmatched action tag", ops_stack[-1])

        flush_output()
```

We had created a section at the beginning of the function. Its role was to unpack template variables from the context into Python locals. Now that we've processed the entire template, we know the names of all the variables, so we can write the lines in this prologue.

We have to do a little work to know what names we need to define. Looking at our sample template:

```
<p>Welcome, {{user_name}}!</p>
<p>Products:</p>
<ul>
{% for product in product_list %}
    <li>{{ product.name }}:
        {{ product.price|format_price }}</li>
{% endfor %}
</ul>
```

There are two variables used here, user_name and product. The all_vars set will have both of those names, because both are used in {{...}} expressions. But only user_name needs to be extracted from the context in the prologue, because product is defined by the loop.

All the variables used in the template are in the set all_vars, and all the variables defined in the template are in loop_vars. All of the names in loop_vars have already been defined in the code because they are used in loops. So we need to unpack any name in all_vars that isn't in loop_vars:

```
for var_name in self.all_vars - self.loop_vars:
    vars_code.add_line("c_%s = context[%r]" % (var_name, var_name))
```

Each name becomes a line in the function's prologue, unpacking the context variable into a suitably named local variable.

We're almost done compiling the template into a Python function. Our function has been appending strings to result, so the last line of the function is simply to join them all together and return them:

```
code.add_line("return ''.join(result)")
code.dedent()
```

Now that we've finished writing the source for our compiled Python function, we need to get the function itself from our CodeBuilder object. The get_globals method executes the Python code we've been assembling. Remember that our code is a function definition (starting with def render_function(..):), so executing the code will define render_function, but not execute the body of render_function.

The result of get_globals is the dictionary of values defined in the code. We grab the render_function value from it, and save it as an attribute in our Templite object:

```
self._render_function = code.get_globals()['render_function']
```

Now self._render_function is a callable Python function. We'll use it later, during the rendering phase.

Compiling Expressions

We haven't yet seen a significant piece of the compiling process: the _expr_code method that compiles a template expression into a Python expression. Our template expressions can be as simple as a single name:

```
{{user_name}}
```

or can be a complex sequence of attribute accesses and filters:

```
{{user.name.localized|upper|escape}}
```

Our `_expr_code` method will handle all of these possibilities. As with expressions in any language, ours are built recursively: big expressions are composed of smaller expressions. A full expression is pipe-separated, where the first piece is dot-separated, and so on. So our function naturally takes a recursive form:

```
def _expr_code(self, expr):
    """Generate a Python expression for 'expr'."""
```

The first case to consider is that our expression has pipes in it. If it does, then we split it into a list of pipe-pieces. The first pipe-piece is passed recursively to `_expr_code` to convert it into a Python expression.

```
if "|" in expr:
    pipes = expr.split("|")
    code = self._expr_code(pipes[0])
    for func in pipes[1:]:
        self._variable(func, self.all_vars)
        code = "c_%s(%s)" % (func, code)
```

Each of the remaining pipe pieces is the name of a function. The value is passed through the function to produce the final value. Each function name is a variable that gets added to `all_vars` so that we can extract it properly in the prologue.

If there were no pipes, there might be dots. If so, split on the dots. The first part is passed recursively to `_expr_code` to turn it into a Python expression, then each dot name is handled in turn:

```
elif "." in expr:
    dots = expr.split(".")
    code = self._expr_code(dots[0])
    args = ", ".join(repr(d) for d in dots[1:])
    code = "do_dots(%s, %s)" % (code, args)
```

To understand how dots get compiled, remember that `x.y` in the template could mean either `x['y']` or `x.y` in Python, depending on which works; if the result is callable, it's called. This uncertainty means that we have to try those possibilities at run time, not compile time. So we compile `x.y.z` into a function call, `do_dots(x, 'y', 'z')`. The dot function will try the various access methods and return the value that succeeded.

The `do_dots` function is passed into our compiled Python function at run time. We'll see its implementation in just a bit.

The last clause in the `_expr_code` function handles the case that there was no pipe or dot in the input expression. In that case, it's just a name. We record it in `all_vars`, and access the variable using its prefixed Python name:

```
else:
    self._variable(expr, self.all_vars)
    code = "c_%s" % expr
return code
```

Helper Functions

During compilation, we used a few helper functions. The _syntax_error method simply puts together a nice error message and raises the exception:

```python
def _syntax_error(self, msg, thing):
    """Raise a syntax error using 'msg', and showing 'thing'."""
    raise TempliteSyntaxError("%s: %r" % (msg, thing))
```

The _variable method helps us with validating variable names and adding them to the sets of names we collected during compilation. We use a regex to check that the name is a valid Python identifier, then add the name to the set:

```python
def _variable(self, name, vars_set):
    """Track that 'name' is used as a variable.

    Adds the name to 'vars_set', a set of variable names.

    Raises an syntax error if 'name' is not a valid name.

    """
    if not re.match(r"[_a-zA-Z][_a-zA-Z0-9]*$", name):
        self._syntax_error("Not a valid name", name)
    vars_set.add(name)
```

With that, the compilation code is done!

Rendering

All that's left is to write the rendering code. Since we've compiled our template to a Python function, the rendering code doesn't have much to do. It has to get the data context ready, and then call the compiled Python code:

```python
def render(self, context=None):
    """Render this template by applying it to 'context'.

    'context' is a dictionary of values to use in this rendering.

    """
    # Make the complete context we'll use.
    render_context = dict(self.context)
    if context:
        render_context.update(context)
    return self._render_function(render_context, self._do_dots)
```

Remember that when we constructed the Templite object, we started with a data context. Here we copy it, and merge in whatever data has been passed in for this rendering. The copying is so that successive rendering calls won't see each others' data, and the merging is so that we have a single dictionary to use for data lookups. This is how we build one unified data context from the contexts provided when the template was constructed, with the data provided now at render time.

Notice that the data passed to `render` could overwrite data passed to the Templite constructor. That tends not to happen, because the context passed to the constructor has global-ish things like filter definitions and constants, and the context passed to `render` has specific data for that one rendering.

Then we simply call our compiled `render_function`. The first argument is the complete data context, and the second argument is the function that will implement the dot semantics. We use the same implementation every time: our own _do_dots method.

```
def _do_dots(self, value, *dots):
    """Evaluate dotted expressions at runtime."""
    for dot in dots:
        try:
            value = getattr(value, dot)
        except AttributeError:
            value = value[dot]
        if callable(value):
            value = value()
    return value
```

During compilation, a template expression like `x.y.z` gets turned into `do_dots(x, 'y', 'z')`. This function loops over the dot-names, and for each one tries it as an attribute, and if that fails, tries it as a key. This is what gives our single template syntax the flexibility to act as either `x.y` or `x['y']`. At each step, we also check if the new value is callable, and if it is, we call it. Once we're done with all the dot-names, the value in hand is the value we want.

Here we used Python argument unpacking again (`*dots`) so that _do_dots could take any number of dot names. This gives us a flexible function that will work for any dotted expression we encounter in the template.

Note that when calling `self._render_function`, we pass in a function to use for evaluating dot expressions, but we always pass in the same one. We could have made that code part of the compiled template, but it's the same eight lines for every template, and those eight lines are part of the definition of how templates work, not part of the details of a particular template. It feels cleaner to implement it like this than to have that code be part of the compiled template.

21.7 Testing

Provided with the template engine is a suite of tests that cover all of the behavior and edge cases. I'm actually a little bit over my 500-line limit: the template engine is 252 lines, and the tests are 275 lines. This is typical of well-tested code: you have more code in your tests than in your product.

21.8 What's Left Out

Full-featured template engines provide much more than we've implemented here. To keep this code small, we're leaving out interesting ideas like:

- Template inheritance and inclusion
- Custom tags
- Automatic escaping
- Arguments to filters
- Complex conditional logic like else and elif

- Loops with more than one loop variable
- Whitespace control

Even so, our simple template engine is useful. In fact, it is the template engine used in coverage.py to produce its HTML reports.

21.9   Summing up

In 252 lines, we've got a simple yet capable template engine. Real template engines have many more features, but this code lays out the basic ideas of the process: compile the template to a Python function, then execute the function to produce the text result.

## chapter 22

A Simple Web Server

Greg Wilson

22.1   Introduction

The web has changed society in countless ways over the last two decades, but its core has changed very little. Most systems still follow the rules that Tim Berners-Lee laid out a quarter of a century ago. In particular, most web servers still handle the same kinds of messages they did then, in the same way.

This chapter will explore how they do that. At the same time, it will explore how developers can create software systems that don't need to be rewritten in order to add new features.

22.2   Background

Pretty much every program on the web runs on a family of communication standards called Internet Protocol (IP). The member of that family which concerns us is the Transmission Control Protocol (TCP/IP), which makes communication between computers look like reading and writing files.

Programs using IP communicate through sockets. Each socket is one end of a point-to-point communication channel, just like a phone is one end of a phone call. A socket consists of an IP address that identifies a particular machine and a port number on that machine. The IP address consists of four 8-bit numbers, such as 174.136.14.108; the Domain Name System (DNS) matches these numbers to symbolic names like aosabook.org that are easier for human beings to remember.

A port number is a number in the range 0-65535 that uniquely identifies the socket on the host machine. (If an IP address is like a company's phone number, then a port number is like an extension.) Ports 0-1023 are reserved for the operating system's use; anyone else can use the remaining ports.

The Hypertext Transfer Protocol (HTTP) describes one way that programs can exchange data over IP. HTTP is deliberately simple: the client sends a request specifying what it wants over a socket connection, and the server sends some data in response (Figure 22.1.) The data may be copied from a file on disk, generated dynamically by a program, or some mix of the two.

The most important thing about an HTTP request is that it's just text: any program that wants to can create one or parse one. In order to be understood, though, that text must have the parts shown in Figure 22.2.

The HTTP method is almost always either "GET" (to fetch information) or "POST" (to submit form data or upload files). The URL specifies what the client wants; it is often a path to a file on disk, such as /research/experiments.html, but (and this is the crucial part) it's completely up to

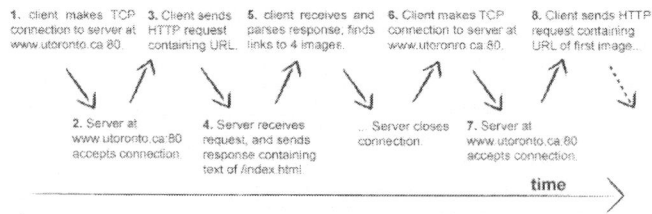

Figure 22.1: The HTTP Cycle

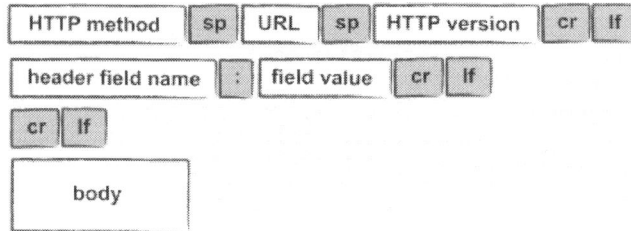

Figure 22.2: An HTTP Request

the server to decide what to do with it. The HTTP version is usually "HTTP/1.0" or "HTTP/1.1"; the differences between the two don't matter to us.

HTTP headers are key/value pairs like the three shown below:

```
Accept: text/html
Accept-Language: en, fr
If-Modified-Since: 16-May-2005
```

Unlike the keys in hash tables, keys may appear any number of times in HTTP headers. This allows a request to do things like specify that it's willing to accept several types of content.

Finally, the body of the request is any extra data associated with the request. This is used when submitting data via web forms, when uploading files, and so on. There must be a blank line between the last header and the start of the body to signal the end of the headers.

One header, called Content-Length, tells the server how many bytes to expect to read in the body of the request.

HTTP responses are formatted like HTTP requests (Figure 22.3):

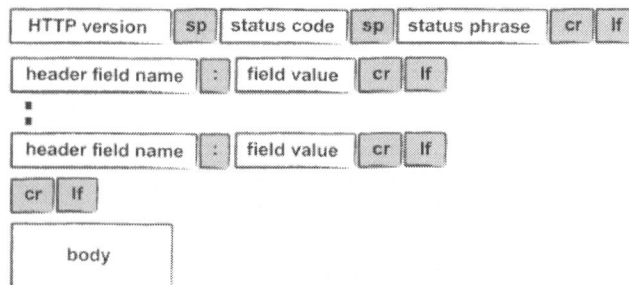

Figure 22.3: An HTTP Response

The version, headers, and body have the same form and meaning. The status code is a number indicating what happened when the request was processed: 200 means "everything worked", 404 means "not found", and other codes have other meanings. The status phrase repeats that information in a human-readable phrase like "OK" or "not found".

For the purposes of this chapter there are only two other things we need to know about HTTP.

The first is that it is *stateless*: each request is handled on its own, and the server doesn't remember anything between one request and the next. If an application wants to keep track of something like a user's identity, it must do so itself.

The usual way to do this is with a cookie, which is a short character string that the server sends to the client, and the client later returns to the server. When a user performs some function that requires state to be saved across several requests, the server creates a new cookie, stores it in a database, and sends it to her browser. Each time her browser sends the cookie back, the server uses it to look up information about what the user is doing.

The second thing we need to know about HTTP is that a URL can be supplemented with parameters to provide even more information. For example, if we're using a search engine, we have to specify what our search terms are. We could add these to the path in the URL, but what we should do is add parameters to the URL. We do this by adding '?' to the URL followed by 'key=value' pairs separated by '&'. For example, the URL `http://www.google.ca?q=Python` asks Google to search for pages related to Python: the key is the letter 'q', and the value is 'Python'. The longer query `http://www.google.ca/search?q=Python&amp;client=Firefox` tells Google that we're using Firefox, and so on. We can pass whatever parameters we want, but again, it's up to the application running on the web site to decide which ones to pay attention to, and how to interpret them.

Of course, if '?' and '&' are special characters, there must be a way to escape them, just as there must be a way to put a double quote character inside a character string delimited by double quotes. The URL encoding standard represents special characters using '%' followed by a 2-digit code, and replaces spaces with the '+' character. Thus, to search Google for "grade = A+" (with the spaces), we would use the URL `http://www.google.ca/search?q=grade+%3D+A%2B`.

Opening sockets, constructing HTTP requests, and parsing responses is tedious, so most people use libraries to do most of the work. Python comes with such a library called `urllib2` (because it's a replacement for an earlier library called `urllib`), but it exposes a lot of plumbing that most people never want to care about. The Requests[1] library is an easier-to-use alternative to `urllib2`. Here's an example that uses it to download a page from the AOSA book site:

```
import requests
response = requests.get('http://aosabook.org/en/500L/web-server/testpage.html')
print 'status code:', response.status_code
print 'content length:', response.headers['content-length']
print response.text

status code: 200
content length: 61
<html>
  <body>
    <p>Test page.</p>
  </body>
</html>
```

`request.get` sends an HTTP GET request to a server and returns an object containing the response. That object's `status_code` member is the response's status code; its `content_length`

---

[1]`https://pypi.python.org/pypi/requests`

member is the number of bytes in the response data, and text is the actual data (in this case, an HTML page).

22.3 Hello, Web

We're now ready to write our first simple web server. The basic idea is simple:
1. Wait for someone to connect to our server and send an HTTP request;
2. parse that request;
3. figure out what it's asking for;
4. fetch that data (or generate it dynamically);
5. format the data as HTML; and
6. send it back.

Steps 1, 2, and 6 are the same from one application to another, so the Python standard library has a module called BaseHTTPServer that does those for us. We just have to take care of steps 3-5, which we do in the little program below:

```
import BaseHTTPServer

class RequestHandler(BaseHTTPServer.BaseHTTPRequestHandler):
    '''Handle HTTP requests by returning a fixed 'page'.'''

    # Page to send back.
    Page = '''\
<html>
<body>
<p>Hello, web!</p>
</body>
</html>
'''

    # Handle a GET request.
    def do_GET(self):
        self.send_response(200)
        self.send_header("Content-Type", "text/html")
        self.send_header("Content-Length", str(len(self.Page)))
        self.end_headers()
        self.wfile.write(self.Page)

#-------------------------------------------------------------------

if __name__ == '__main__':
    serverAddress = ('', 8080)
    server = BaseHTTPServer.HTTPServer(serverAddress, RequestHandler)
    server.serve_forever()
```

The library's BaseHTTPRequestHandler class takes care of parsing the incoming HTTP request and deciding what method it contains. If the method is GET, the class calls a method named do_GET. Our class RequestHandler overrides this method to dynamically generate a simple page: the text is stored in the class-level variable Page, which we send back to the client after sending a 200 response code, a `Content-Type` header telling the client to interpret our data as HTML, and the page's length. (The end_headers method call inserts the blank line that separates our headers from the page itself.)

But RequestHandler isn't the whole story: we still need the last three lines to actually start a server running. The first of these lines defines the server's address as a tuple: the empty string means "run on the current machine", and 8080 is the port. We then create an instance of `BaseHTTPServer.HTTPServer` with that address and the name of our request handler class as parameters, then ask it to run forever (which in practice means until we kill it with Control-C).

If we run this program from the command line, it doesn't display anything:

```
$ python server.py
```

If we then go to `http://localhost:8080` with our browser, though, we get this in our browser:

```
Hello, web!
```

and this in our shell:

```
127.0.0.1 - - [24/Feb/2014 10:26:28] "GET / HTTP/1.1" 200 -
127.0.0.1 - - [24/Feb/2014 10:26:28] "GET /favicon.ico HTTP/1.1" 200 -
```

The first line is straightforward: since we didn't ask for a particular file, our browser has asked for '/' (the root directory of whatever the server is serving). The second line appears because our browser automatically sends a second request for an image file called /favicon.ico, which it will display as an icon in the address bar if it exists.

22.4   Displaying Values

Let's modify our web server to display some of the values included in the HTTP request. (We'll do this pretty frequently when debugging, so we might as well get some practice.) To keep our code clean, we'll separate creating the page from sending it:

```
class RequestHandler(BaseHTTPServer.BaseHTTPRequestHandler):

    # ...page template...

    def do_GET(self):
        page = self.create_page()
        self.send_page(page)

    def create_page(self):
        # ...fill in...

    def send_page(self, page):
        # ...fill in...
```

send_page is pretty much what we had before:

```
    def send_page(self, page):
        self.send_response(200)
        self.send_header("Content-type", "text/html")
        self.send_header("Content-Length", str(len(page)))
        self.end_headers()
        self.wfile.write(page)
```

The template for the page we want to display is just a string containing an HTML table with some formatting placeholders:

```
    Page = '''\
<html>
<body>
<table>
<tr>  <td>Header</td>        <td>Value</td>          </tr>
<tr>  <td>Date and time</td> <td>{date_time}</td>    </tr>
<tr>  <td>Client host</td>   <td>{client_host}</td>  </tr>
<tr>  <td>Client port</td>   <td>{client_port}s</td> </tr>
<tr>  <td>Command</td>       <td>{command}</td>       </tr>
<tr>  <td>Path</td>          <td>{path}</td>          </tr>
</table>
</body>
</html>
'''
```

and the method that fills this in is:

```
    def create_page(self):
        values = {
            'date_time'   : self.date_time_string(),
            'client_host' : self.client_address[0],
            'client_port' : self.client_address[1],
            'command'     : self.command,
            'path'        : self.path
        }
        page = self.Page.format(**values)
        return page
```

The main body of the program is unchanged: as before, it creates an instance of the HTTPServer class with an address and this request handler as parameters, then serves requests forever. If we run it and send a request from a browser for `http://localhost:8080/something.html`, we get:

```
Date and time  Mon, 24 Feb 2014 17:17:12 GMT
Client host    127.0.0.1
Client port    54548
Command        GET
Path           /something.html
```

Notice that we do *not* get a 404 error, even though the page something.html doesn't exist as a file on disk. That's because a web server is just a program, and can do whatever it wants when it gets a request: send back the file named in the previous request, serve up a Wikipedia page chosen at random, or whatever else we program it to.

22.5 Serving Static Pages

The obvious next step is to start serving pages from the disk instead of generating them on the fly. We'll start by rewriting do_GET:

```
def do_GET(self):
    try:

        # Figure out what exactly is being requested.
        full_path = os.getcwd() + self.path

        # It doesn't exist...
        if not os.path.exists(full_path):
            raise ServerException("'{0}' not found".format(self.path))

        # ...it's a file...
        elif os.path.isfile(full_path):
            self.handle_file(full_path)

        # ...it's something we don't handle.
        else:
            raise ServerException("Unknown object '{0}'".format(self.path))

    # Handle errors.
    except Exception as msg:
        self.handle_error(msg)
```

This method assumes that it's allowed to serve any files in or below the directory that the web server is running in (which it gets using os.getcwd). It combines this with the path provided in the URL (which the library automatically puts in self.path, and which always starts with a leading '/') to get the path to the file the user wants.

If that doesn't exist, or if it isn't a file, the method reports an error by raising and catching an exception. If the path matches a file, on the other hand, it calls a helper method named handle_file to read and return the contents. This method just reads the file and uses our existing send_content to send it back to the client:

```
def handle_file(self, full_path):
    try:
        with open(full_path, 'rb') as reader:
            content = reader.read()
        self.send_content(content)
    except IOError as msg:
        msg = "'{0}' cannot be read: {1}".format(self.path, msg)
        self.handle_error(msg)
```

Note that we open the file in binary mode—the 'b' in 'rb'—so that Python won't try to "help" us by altering byte sequences that look like a Windows line ending. Note also that reading the whole file into memory when serving it is a bad idea in real life, where the file might be several gigabytes of video data. Handling that situation is outside the scope of this chapter.

To finish off this class, we need to write the error handling method and the template for the error reporting page:

```
Error_Page = """\
    <html>
    <body>
    <h1>Error accessing {path}</h1>
```

```
            <p>{msg}</p>
        </body>
    </html>
    """

    def handle_error(self, msg):
        content = self.Error_Page.format(path=self.path, msg=msg)
        self.send_content(content)
```

This program works, but only if we don't look too closely. The problem is that it always returns a status code of 200, even when the page being requested doesn't exist. Yes, the page sent back in that case contains an error message, but since our browser can't read English, it doesn't know that the request actually failed. In order to make that clear, we need to modify handle_error and send_content as follows:

```
    # Handle unknown objects.
    def handle_error(self, msg):
        content = self.Error_Page.format(path=self.path, msg=msg)
        self.send_content(content, 404)

    # Send actual content.
    def send_content(self, content, status=200):
        self.send_response(status)
        self.send_header("Content-type", "text/html")
        self.send_header("Content-Length", str(len(content)))
        self.end_headers()
        self.wfile.write(content)
```

Note that we don't raise ServerException when a file can't be found, but generate an error page instead. A ServerException is meant to signal an internal error in the server code, i.e., something that *we* got wrong. The error page created by handle_error, on the other hand, appears when the *user* got something wrong, i.e., sent us the URL of a file that doesn't exist. [2]

22.6   Listing Directories

As our next step, we could teach the web server to display a listing of a directory's contents when the path in the URL is a directory rather than a file. We could even go one step further and have it look in that directory for an index.html file to display, and only show a listing of the directory's contents if that file is not present.

But building these rules into do_GET would be a mistake, since the resulting method would be a long tangle of if statements controlling special behaviors. The right solution is to step back and solve the general problem, which is figuring out what to do with a URL. Here's a rewrite of the do_GET method:

```
    def do_GET(self):
        try:
```

---

[2] We're going to use handle_error several times throughout this chapter, including several cases where the status code 404 isn't appropriate. As you read on, try to think of how you would extend this program so that the status response code can be supplied easily in each case.

```
            # Figure out what exactly is being requested.
            self.full_path = os.getcwd() + self.path

            # Figure out how to handle it.
            for case in self.Cases:
                handler = case()
                if handler.test(self):
                    handler.act(self)
                    break

        # Handle errors.
        except Exception as msg:
            self.handle_error(msg)
```

The first step is the same: figure out the full path to the thing being requested. After that, though, the code looks quite different. Instead of a bunch of inline tests, this version loops over a set of cases stored in a list. Each case is an object with two methods: test, which tells us whether it's able to handle the request, and act, which actually takes some action. As soon as we find the right case, we let it handle the request and break out of the loop.

These three case classes reproduce the behavior of our previous server:

```
class case_no_file(object):
    '''File or directory does not exist.'''

    def test(self, handler):
        return not os.path.exists(handler.full_path)

    def act(self, handler):
        raise ServerException("'{0}' not found".format(handler.path))


class case_existing_file(object):
    '''File exists.'''

    def test(self, handler):
        return os.path.isfile(handler.full_path)

    def act(self, handler):
        handler.handle_file(handler.full_path)


class case_always_fail(object):
    '''Base case if nothing else worked.'''

    def test(self, handler):
        return True

    def act(self, handler):
        raise ServerException("Unknown object '{0}'".format(handler.path))
```

and here's how we construct the list of case handlers at the top of the RequestHandler class:

```
class RequestHandler(BaseHTTPServer.BaseHTTPRequestHandler):
    '''
    If the requested path maps to a file, that file is served.
    If anything goes wrong, an error page is constructed.
    '''

    Cases = [case_no_file(),
             case_existing_file(),
             case_always_fail()]

    ...everything else as before...
```

Now, on the surface this has made our server more complicated, not less: the file has grown from 74 lines to 99, and there's an extra level of indirection without any new functionality. The benefit comes when we go back to the task that started this chapter and try to teach our server to serve up the index.html page for a directory if there is one, and a listing of the directory if there isn't. The handler for the former is:

```
class case_directory_index_file(object):
    '''Serve index.html page for a directory.'''

    def index_path(self, handler):
        return os.path.join(handler.full_path, 'index.html')

    def test(self, handler):
        return os.path.isdir(handler.full_path) and \
               os.path.isfile(self.index_path(handler))

    def act(self, handler):
        handler.handle_file(self.index_path(handler))
```

Here, the helper method index_path constructs the path to the index.html file; putting it in the case handler prevents clutter in the main RequestHandler. test checks whether the path is a directory containing an index.html page, and act asks the main request handler to serve that page.

The only change needed to RequestHandler is to add a case_directory_index_file object to our Cases list:

```
    Cases = [case_no_file(),
             case_existing_file(),
             case_directory_index_file(),
             case_always_fail()]
```

What about directories that don't contain index.html pages? The test is the same as the one above with a not strategically inserted, but what about the act method? What should it do?

```
class case_directory_no_index_file(object):
    '''Serve listing for a directory without an index.html page.'''

    def index_path(self, handler):
        return os.path.join(handler.full_path, 'index.html')
```

```
    def test(self, handler):
        return os.path.isdir(handler.full_path) and \
                not os.path.isfile(self.index_path(handler))

    def act(self, handler):
        ???
```

It seems we've backed ourselves into a corner. Logically, the act method should create and return the directory listing, but our existing code doesn't allow for that: RequestHandler.do_GET calls act, but doesn't expect or handle a return value from it. For now, let's add a method to RequestHandler to generate a directory listing, and call that from the case handler's act:

```
class case_directory_no_index_file(object):
    '''Serve listing for a directory without an index.html page.'''

    # ...index_path and test as above...

    def act(self, handler):
        handler.list_dir(handler.full_path)


class RequestHandler(BaseHTTPServer.BaseHTTPRequestHandler):

    # ...all the other code...

    # How to display a directory listing.
    Listing_Page = '''\
        <html>
        <body>
        <ul>
        {0}
        </ul>
        </body>
        </html>
        '''

    def list_dir(self, full_path):
        try:
            entries = os.listdir(full_path)
            bullets = ['<li>{0}</li>'.format(e)
                for e in entries if not e.startswith('.')]
            page = self.Listing_Page.format('\n'.join(bullets))
            self.send_content(page)
        except OSError as msg:
            msg = "'{0}' cannot be listed: {1}".format(self.path, msg)
            self.handle_error(msg)
```

22.7   The CGI Protocol

Of course, most people won't want to edit the source of their web server in order to add new functionality. To save them from having to do so, servers have always supported a mechanism called the Common Gateway Interface (CGI), which provides a standard way for a web server to run an external program in order to satisfy a request.

For example, suppose we want the server to be able to display the local time in an HTML page. We can do this in a standalone program with just a few lines of code:

```
from datetime import datetime
print '''\
<html>
<body>
<p>Generated {0}</p>
</body>
</html>'''.format(datetime.now())
```

In order to get the web server to run this program for us, we add this case handler:

```
class case_cgi_file(object):
    '''Something runnable.'''

    def test(self, handler):
        return os.path.isfile(handler.full_path) and \
                handler.full_path.endswith('.py')

    def act(self, handler):
        handler.run_cgi(handler.full_path)
```

The test is simple: does the file path end with .py? If so, RequestHandler runs this program.

```
    def run_cgi(self, full_path):
        cmd = "python " + full_path
        child_stdin, child_stdout = os.popen2(cmd)
        child_stdin.close()
        data = child_stdout.read()
        child_stdout.close()
        self.send_content(data)
```

This is horribly insecure: if someone knows the path to a Python file on our server, we're just letting them run it without worrying about what data it has access to, whether it might contain an infinite loop, or anything else.[3]

Sweeping that aside, the core idea is simple:

1. Run the program in a subprocess.
2. Capture whatever that subprocess sends to standard output.
3. Send that back to the client that made the request.

The full CGI protocol is much richer than this—in particular, it allows for parameters in the URL, which the server passes into the program being run—but those details don't affect the overall architecture of the system...

...which is once again becoming rather tangled. RequestHandler initially had one method, handle_file, for dealing with content. We have now added two special cases in the form of

---

[3]Our code also uses the popen2 library function, which has been deprecated in favor of the subprocess module. However, popen2 was the less distracting tool to use in this example.

`list_dir` and `run_cgi`. These three methods don't really belong where they are, since they're primarily used by others.

The fix is straightforward: create a parent class for all our case handlers, and move other methods to that class if (and only if) they are shared by two or more handlers. When we're done, the `RequestHandler` class looks like this:

```
class RequestHandler(BaseHTTPServer.BaseHTTPRequestHandler):

    Cases = [case_no_file(),
             case_cgi_file(),
             case_existing_file(),
             case_directory_index_file(),
             case_directory_no_index_file(),
             case_always_fail()]

    # How to display an error.
    Error_Page = """\
        <html>
        <body>
        <h1>Error accessing {path}</h1>
        <p>{msg}</p>
        </body>
        </html>
        """

    # Classify and handle request.
    def do_GET(self):
        try:

            # Figure out what exactly is being requested.
            self.full_path = os.getcwd() + self.path

            # Figure out how to handle it.
            for case in self.Cases:
                if case.test(self):
                    case.act(self)
                    break

        # Handle errors.
        except Exception as msg:
            self.handle_error(msg)

    # Handle unknown objects.
    def handle_error(self, msg):
        content = self.Error_Page.format(path=self.path, msg=msg)
        self.send_content(content, 404)

    # Send actual content.
    def send_content(self, content, status=200):
        self.send_response(status)
        self.send_header("Content-type", "text/html")
```

```
            self.send_header("Content-Length", str(len(content)))
            self.end_headers()
            self.wfile.write(content)
```

while the parent class for our case handlers is:

```
class base_case(object):
    '''Parent for case handlers.'''

    def handle_file(self, handler, full_path):
        try:
            with open(full_path, 'rb') as reader:
                content = reader.read()
            handler.send_content(content)
        except IOError as msg:
            msg = "'{0}' cannot be read: {1}".format(full_path, msg)
            handler.handle_error(msg)

    def index_path(self, handler):
        return os.path.join(handler.full_path, 'index.html')

    def test(self, handler):
        assert False, 'Not implemented.'

    def act(self, handler):
        assert False, 'Not implemented.'
```

and the handler for an existing file (just to pick an example at random) is:

```
class case_existing_file(base_case):
    '''File exists.'''

    def test(self, handler):
        return os.path.isfile(handler.full_path)

    def act(self, handler):
        self.handle_file(handler, handler.full_path)
```

22.8   Discussion

The differences between our original code and the refactored version reflect two important ideas. The first is to think of a class as a collection of related services. RequestHandler and base_case don't make decisions or take actions; they provide tools that other classes can use to do those things.

The second is extensibility: people can add new functionality to our web server either by writing an external CGI program, or by adding a case handler class. The latter does require a one-line change to RequestHandler (to insert the case handler in the Cases list), but we could get rid of that by having the web server read a configuration file and load handler classes from that. In both cases, they can ignore most lower-level details, just as the authors of the BaseHTTPRequestHandler class have allowed us to ignore the details of handling socket connections and parsing HTTP requests.

These ideas are generally useful; see if you can find ways to use them in your own projects.

Colophon

The cover font is Museo from the exljibris foundry, by Jos Buivenga. The text font is T_EXGyre Termes and the heading font is T_EXGyre Heros, both by Bogusław Jackowski and Janusz M. Nowacki. The code font is Inconsolata by Raph Levien.

The front cover photo is composed of twenty-three separate focus-stacked images of watch gear assemblies. The picture was taken by Kellar Wilson. (`http://kellarwilson.smugmug.com/`)

This book was built with open source software (with the exception of the cover). Programs like LaTeX, Pandoc, and Python were especially helpful.

19195334R00264

Printed in Great Britain
by Amazon